Praise for Implementing CIFS

"I think *Implementing CIFS* is simply the best conceptual overview of SMB I have seen."

—Stanley Hopcroft
Network Specialist

"You've done an incredibly nice job of steering the line between a damn good read and an essential systems manual."

—Danny Smith
Senior Systems Administrator
Cinesite Digital Studios

"You know you totally rule. I am in awe of your RFCness."

—Mark W. "catfood" Schumann
Software Under Flap

"I was just reading your book. It's very funny! :-)"

—Michael B. Allen
jCIFS Team

BRUCE PERENS' OPEN SOURCE SERIES

Implementing CIFS: The Common Internet File System

■ Christopher R. Hertel

PRENTICE HALL
PRENTICE HALL
Professional Technical Reference
Upper Saddle River, NJ 07458
www.phptr.com/perens
www.ubiqx.org/cifs

Library of Congress Cataloging-in-Publication Data

A CIP record of this book can be obtained from the Library of Congress.

Production Supervisor: *Faye Gemmellaro*
Manufacturing Buyer: *Maura Zaldivar*
Cover Design Director: *Jerry Votta*
Executive Editor: *Jill Harry*
Editorial Assistant: *Brenda Mulligan*
Marketing Manager: *Dan DePasquale*

TK
5105.55
.H47
2004

Published by Pearson Education, Inc.
Publishing as Prentice Hall Professional Technical Reference
Upper Saddle River, New Jersey 07458

**Prentice Hall offers excellent discounts on this book when ordered in quantity for bulk purchases or special
sales. For more information, please contact: U.S. Corporate and Government Sales, 1–800–382–3419,
corpsales@pearsontechgroup.com. For sales outside of the United States, please contact: International Sales,
1–317–581–3793, international@pearsontechgroup.com.**

ISBN 0–13–047116-X

Pearson Education LTD.
Pearson Education Australia PTY, Limited
Pearson Education Singapore, Pte. Ltd.
Pearson Education North Asia Ltd.
Pearson Education Canada, Ltd.
Pearson Educación de Mexico, S.A. de C.V.
Pearson Education—Japan
Pearson Education Malaysia, Pte. Ltd.

Queen Victoria, it is said, so enjoyed Alice's Adventures in Wonderland *that she asked for a copy of the author's next work. Carroll obliged with the* Syllabus of Plane Algebraical Geometry. *Her Majesty was not amused.*

In that same spirit, I dedicate this effort to the memory of my mother.

About Prentice Hall Professional Technical Reference

With origins reaching back to the industry's first computer science publishing program in the 1960s, and formally launched as its own imprint in 1986, Prentice Hall Professional Technical Reference (PH PTR) has developed into the leading provider of technical books in the world today. Our editors now publish over 200 books annually, authored by leaders in the fields of computing, engineering, and business.

Our roots are firmly planted in the soil that gave rise to the technical revolution. Our bookshelf contains many of the industry's computing and engineering classics: Kernighan and Ritchie's *C Programming Language*, Nemeth's *UNIX System Adminstration Handbook*, Horstmann's *Core Java*, and Johnson's *High-Speed Digital Design*.

PH PTR acknowledges its auspicious beginnings while it looks to the future for inspiration. We continue to evolve and break new ground in publishing by providing today's professionals with tomorrow's solutions.

PRENTICE
HALL
PTR

About the Cover Art

On June 28, 1778, two years after American Independence had been declared, a young woman made her way through the sweltering heat of a Revolutionary battlefield carrying pitchers of water to heat-weakened men. Mary Ludwig Hays — "Molly Pitcher," as she was called — looked up to see that one of the men who had fallen from heatstroke was her own husband, John. She resolutely made her way to his cannon just as an officer was preparing to order it retired for want of a gunner. Setting down her pitchers, Molly picked up the ramrod and took her husband's place at the muzzle.

The story of the woman gunner was told and retold by the soldiers of the Revolution, and "Molly Pitcher" became a legend around battlefield campfires. She came to symbolize all of the women who took up arms for American Independence.

During the war, General George Washington made Mary Hays a sergeant, and afterward she was pensioned as a lieutenant by the Continental Army. Mary Hays lived into her 70s and is buried in Carlisle, PA.

Amy J. Gavel, Esq.
July, 2003

Contents

Foreword

Writing a book is hard — writing a *good* book is very hard, and describing an area as complex as CIFS is a nightmare. The biggest pleasure of being involved with the production of this reference is in the clarity and depth of the end result — the impossible has been achieved, for the benefit of all involved in this protocol.

CIFS is an important protocol — indeed, in Windows networks it could be considered as important as TCP/IP, as almost all communication between Windows machines can flow over it. It provides file and print services, and, among other things, is a carrier for Remote Procedure Call and NT Domain services. When I came to CIFS in 2001, it was out of an interest in the Samba project — an Open Source implementation that I was running on Linux — where I soon became a specialist in Authentication. At the time, there was little good documentation available, particularly on the murky details of authentication.

For that reason, you will find my name scattered all over the Authentication area of this book. As a developer of a CIFS implementation, there are many things that I now know — and needed to know then — that were never clearly written down. Too often, the only reference on some functionality was the C code that implemented it — and the implicit hope that comments vaguely represented reality. I personally spent many hours inspecting the publicly available sources of Samba and Samba-TNG, in the hope of gleaning some extra understanding, some critical detail.

My role in this book was one of many willing victims — exposing all I knew about CIFS, realising how little we had all actually proved, and how much we just assumed. Chris' role was that of interrogator — asking all the difficult questions, and forcing us all to re-evaluate. The end result was a lot of testing, experimentation, and analysis, but also the solid research foundation behind this massive effort.

My hope is that with this book, future developers will no longer be required to pore over cryptic standards drafts — or badly commented C code — to understand the "big picture" into which their software sits.

More remarkably however, *Implementing CIFS* provides a solid technical reference on the protocol as a whole — between the standardese of the SNIA Technical Reference included as an appendix and the clear English of Chris' own chapters is a wealth of technical information that aids even the most experienced developer.

Beyond that, by creating such readable documentation, Implementing CIFS allows more than blind faith in vendors words — CIFS is now assessable to network administrators and other non-programmers who can understand for themselves how this protocol works (and how it doesn't).

By leading readers though the creation of his own basic CIFS client, Chris Hertel ensures that readers have a solid background in the basics — and can continue on to implementing the rest of the protocol sure of their foundations.

I've very much enjoyed working with Chris Hertel on *Implementing CIFS* — finally, I could see a description of this protocol that mere mortals could not only understand, but also enjoy!

Andrew Bartlett
Samba Team
Canberra, Australia
June 2003

Introduction: CIFS from Eight Miles High

Fillet of a fenny snake,
In the cauldron boil and bake;
Eye of newt, and toe of frog,
Wool of bat, and tongue of dog.

— *Macbeth*, Act IV, Scene i,
William Shakespeare

0.1 First Impressions

First impressions are important. The handshake, the smile, here's our brochure, would you like a cup of tea?

Microsoft's Windows family of operating systems makes good first impressions. There's a pleasant sound at start-up, all of the basics are represented by simple icons, and everything else is available through a neatly categorized menu.

As the relationship progresses, however, it becomes clear that there is a lot going on beneath the candy-coated surface. This is particularly true of the CIFS protocol suite. The Network Neighborhood icon that appears on the Windows desktop hides a great deal of gear-churning and behind-the-scenes fussing.

The large installed base of Microsoft's Windows products has granted *de facto* standard status to CIFS. Unfortunately, implementation documentation and detailed protocol specifications are scarce, incomplete, and inconsistent. This is a problem for network administrators, third-party CIFS implementors, and anyone else who wants to know more about the ingredients than you can read on the bottom of the box.

Despite the dearth of good under-the-hood documentation, there are several non-Windows CIFS products. Some of these are based on older versions of Microsoft's own software, but the majority were created by studying the few available references and reverse-engineering to fill in the gaps.

0.2   What is CIFS?

CIFS is a network filesystem plus a set of auxiliary services supported by a bunch of underlying protocols. Any and all of these various bits have been called CIFS, which leaves us with a somewhat muddy definition. To make things easier, we'll start by saying that CIFS is "Microsoft's way of doing network file sharing," and work out the details as we go on.

The name "CIFS," of course, is an acronym. It stands for **C**ommon **I**nternet **F**ile **S**ystem, a title which deserves a bit of dissection.

Common

The term has a variety of connotations, but we will assume that Microsoft was thinking of *common* in the sense of *commonly available* or *commonly used*. All Microsoft operating systems have had some form of CIFS networking available or built in, and there are implementations of CIFS for most major non-MS operating systems as well.

Unfortunately, there is not yet a specification for CIFS that is complete, correct, authoritative, and freely available. Microsoft defines CIFS by their implementations and, as we shall see, their attempts at documenting the complete suite have been somewhat random. This has an adverse impact on the *commonality* of the system.

Internet

At the time that the "CIFS" name was coined many people felt that Microsoft was late to the table regarding the exploitation of the Internet. As will be described further on, the naming scheme they used back then (based on a piece of older LAN technology known as NetBIOS) doesn't scale to large networks — certainly not the Internet. The idea that CIFS would become an Internet standard probably came out of the work that was being done to redesign Microsoft's networking products for Windows NT5 (now known as Windows 2000 or W2K). Under W2K, CIFS can use the Domain Name System (DNS) for name resolution.

File System

CIFS allows you to share directories, files, printers, and other cool computer stuff across a network. That's the filesystem part. To make use of these shared resources you need to be able to find and identify them, and you also need to control access so that unauthorized folk won't fiddle where they shouldn't. This means that there is a hefty amount of administrivia to be managed, so CIFS file sharing comes surrounded by an entourage. There are separate, but intertwined protocols for service announcement, naming, authentication, and authorization. Some are based on published standards, others are not, and most have changed over the years.

0.2.1 *A Recipe for Protocol Soup*

The filesharing protocol at the heart of CIFS is an updated version of the venerable **S**erver **M**essage **B**lock (SMB) protocol, which dates back to the mid-1980s. The new name first appeared around 1996/97 when Microsoft submitted draft CIFS specifications to the **I**nternet **E**ngineering **T**ask **F**orce (IETF). Those drafts have since expired, and more recent documentation made available by Microsoft comes encumbered with confusing (and pointless) licensing restrictions.

The SMB protocol was originally developed to run over NetBIOS (**Net**work **B**asic **I**nput **O**utput **S**ystem) LANs. This is a nasty little skeleton in the CIFS closet. Until W2K, NetBIOS support was required for SMB transport. The machine and service names visible in the Windows "Network Neighborhood" are, basically, NetBIOS addresses.

With Windows 3.11 (Windows for Workgroups), Microsoft introduced a service announcement and location system called the Browse Service. This service maintains the list of available file and print services that is presented via the Network Neighborhood (named "My Network Places" in newer Windows products). Also with Windows 3.11 Microsoft introduced the "workgroup" concept. Workgroups simplified network management by organizing servers and services into administrative groups. Microsoft expanded upon the workgroup concept under Windows NT to create NT Domains.[1]

---

1. The terms "NT Domain" and "W2K Domain" will be used to distinguish Microsoft's authentication/authorization domains from Domain Name System (DNS) domains.

As if that were not enough, there are also several SMB "dialects." These roughly correspond to major OS product releases or updates from Microsoft, and each adds extensions to the core SMB protocol. In their IETF CIFS draft, Microsoft presented an SMB dialect that was independent of NetBIOS, and W2K does include such a beast. As part of the split with NetBIOS, W2K also offers new name resolution, service announcement, authentication, and authorization mechanisms — all based, more or less, upon Internet standards.

Don't worry. Like most complex problems, this can all be understood by breaking it down into little pieces and studying each one in turn. The whole is not so terrible once you understand the parts.

0.3   The CIFS Community

Microsoft's implementations are the *de facto* CIFS standards. This is no surprise, as the SMB protocol was originally developed by IBM, Microsoft, Intel, and 3Com specifically for MS-DOS and PC-DOS. It is Microsoft's current massive dominance in the desktop world, however, that makes the CIFS marketplace worthwhile. Several companies earn their money by selling CIFS client and server software, or fileserver hardware with CIFS support. Without complete documentation, these third-party vendors might be forced to rely only on their own reverse-engineering or on licensed derivations of Microsoft's own implementations. This would reduce the "commonality" of CIFS and, given Microsoft's dominant market share, could have a negative impact on competitors' ability to compete.

Fortunately, there is a lot of communication within the CIFS community. There is also a renegade band of coders known as the Samba Team. Since 1991, they have been gathering information and implementing their own CIFS server, called Samba. (Note how the letters "s," "m," and "b" appear in sequence in the Samba name. Cool, eh?) Samba is published as Open Source under the terms of the GNU General Public License. Samba Team members typically share what they learn, and have even been known to write a little documentation now and again. Samba is included with most distributions of Linux and several commercial Unix flavors as well.

Samba has generated a few related projects, including SMB client filesystems for Linux, AmigaOS, and other platforms. There is also Richard Sharpe's `libsmbclient`, the Samba-TNG project, the jCIFS project, and this book.

0.3.1 *Visiting the Network Neighborhood*

On most days, members of the CIFS community can be found hanging out on Microsoft's CIFS mailing list, the Samba-Technical mailing list, or the jCIFS mailing list. In addition to these virtual geek cafés there is the mostly-annual CIFS conference. In the past it has been sponsored by such luminary organizations as EMC, Microsoft, Network Appliance, SCO, and the Storage Networking Industry Association. The conference provides an opportunity for CIFS developers to meet each other face-to-face, swap stories, whine, and (best of all) test their products with & against everyone else's. If you are serious about implementing CIFS, we'll see you there.

Service Network GmbH is the primary sponsor of yet another conference of interest. The first Samba eXPerience (aka sambaXP) was held in Göttingen, Germany, in April of 2002. It was very successful, and has become an annual event. While it is specific to Samba and related Open Source implementations (Samba-TNG, jCIFS, etc.), the information exchanged is valuable to anyone interested in CIFS networking.

0.3.2 *Community Collaborations*

It should also be noted that an effort, organized at one of the CIFS conferences and lead by the **S**torage **N**etwork **I**ndustry **A**ssociation (SNIA), has been under-way within the CIFS community to draft an "open" CIFS reference with input from many interested parties. Version 1.0 of the SNIA CIFS Technical Reference has been released and is available on the SNIA web site. For more information, poke around the SNIA CIFS Working Group web pages.

0.4 Audience

This book is aimed at developers who want to add CIFS compatibility to their products. It will also be very helpful to network and system administrators who need to understand the curious things that CIFS does on the wire, in the server, and at the desktop. In addition, there is empirical evidence which suggests that the Internet security community (both the light and the dark sides) is keenly interested in the (mis)behavior of the CIFS suite. This is a technical book, and knowledge of programming and TCP/IP networking is assumed.

The protocol descriptions, however, start with the basics and build up, so very little previous knowledge of CIFS is expected.

For the programmer, there are several code examples. They have all been tested under Debian GNU/Linux, but you may need to do a little work to get them to run elsewhere. The code is intended to be illustrative rather than functional. It works, but it is not production-quality. That's okay, since part of the purpose of this book is to help you write your own code — if that's where your interests lie. If you don't care about source code you can safely skip much of it. Those who do like source can find additional examples at `http://ubiqx.org/libcifs/`.

A certain amount of SMB/CIFS protocol information has been available since the early days, but finding the important bits typically involves digging through detailed technical references, protocol specifications, packet dumps, web pages, whitepapers, source code, and mailing list archives. That's a lot of work, and a nuisance, and annoying. As a result, CIFS development has become an arcane art practiced by an elite few... and that's a darned shame.

This book attempts to solve this problem by selectively digging through the muck and presenting the uncovered gems in a coherent form, thus making the CIFS suite more accessible to more people.

0.5   Scope

Our focus is on the inner workings of CIFS filesharing, particularly the client side. Through necessity (and a macabre sense of fascination) we will also cover NetBIOS LAN emulation over TCP/IP, basic SMB authentication, and browsing. We will delicately dance around the NT Domain system and CIFS for W2K. These are much bigger and hairier, and deserve their own books.[2]

The book is separated into three main parts:

I. NBT: NetBIOS over TCP/IP

This part covers the NBT protocol, which is an implementation of the NetBIOS API on top of TCP/IP. NBT is necessary for communicating with older CIFS servers and clients.

---

2. ...and if we find any such books, we will list them in the References section.

II. SMB: The Server Message Block Protocol

Part II covers SMB, the filesharing protocol at the core of CIFS. This part also covers authentication.

III. Browsing: Advertising Services

The Browser Service is built on top of NBT and SMB and is used to distribute information about the SMB fileservers available on the network.

Following these three parts are appendices, a glossary, bibliography for further reading, and an index — all the good stuff you would expect in such a book.

0.6   Acknowledgements and Thanks

The investigation of CIFS is a forensic art. This book is an attempt to coalesce the knowledge gathered by the CIFS community and present it in a useful form. My thanks go to the Samba Team, particularly Andrew Tridgell who started the Samba project and suggested that I start the jCIFS project. Thanks are also due to the jCIFS Team for raising — and often answering — so many good questions, and particularly to Michael B. Allen for churning out so much working code.

Acknowledgements also go to the folks on the Samba-Technical mailing list, the Samba-TNG mailing list, Microsoft's CIFS mailing list, and the folks at Microsoft who were able to provide insights into the workings of CIFS.

Writing documentation of this sort is a lengthy and annoying process. Special thanks go to the believers: Rachel, Aled, and Amalia; and also to the four-legs: Neko, Marika, Bran, and Maddie.

Additional notes of praise and recognition (in no particular order) to David Hirsch, Jeanne Dzurenko, Judy Diebel, Paul Nelis, Virginia Norton, Dave Farmer, John Ladwig, Susan Levy Haskell, Tim Howling, Olaf Barthel, Amy Gavel, Stephanie Cohen, Andrew Bartlett, Prairie Barnes, Chris Yerkes, James Carey, and Tom Barron.

The majority of the diagrams in this book were produced using the Dia diagram editor. The document was originally created as 100% hand-crafted and W3C-validated HTML using a simple text editor. CVS was used for document source management.

0.6.1 *The Book*

Thanks to Mark Taub for believing that I could turn my online ramblings into an honest-to-goodness book, and to Jill Harry for being "the boss" and gently but firmly guiding me through the process. Thanks also to Bruce Perens for including my book as part of his series, and to all the folks at Prentice Hall who helped to make this dream a reality.

The book was raked over the coals for technical correctness by Andrew Bartlett and Jerry Carter, both of the Samba Team and both nearly as pedantic as I am. They deserve a lot of credit for the good stuff that is contained herein (the bugs are my fault).

The original HTML source was skillfully converted to publisher-ready form by Alina Kirsanova, and then carefully copy-edited by Dmitry Kirsanov. They did excellent work. Any errors in grammar or formatting which remain are probably the result of my being a prima donna and insisting on having my own way.

0.7   About the Author

 Christopher R. Hertel is one of those guys in the bright orange vests who lean up against a shovel in the construction zones along the Information Superhighway. By day, he is a Network Design Engineer at the University of Minnesota. He is also a member of the Samba Team, a founding member of the jCIFS Team, and an inconsistently average foil fencer. Most important of all, he is a full-time dad and husband.

0.7.1 *Quick Story*

A few years back I was interviewing for a job that I really thought I wanted. During the technical interview, I was asked "Is NetBEUI routable?" My head was full of protocol specs and packet headers, and I got a little flustered. I confused NetBEUI with the general idea of encapsulated NetBIOS. Of course I gave the wrong answer, and I did not get the job.

They say success is the sweetest and most honest form of revenge. ☺

0.8   License

Code examples are licensed under the terms of the GNU Lesser General Public License. This allows you to build libraries from the licensed code and use those libraries with your own code, even if your code is proprietary. The library source code, however, must be made available if you distribute your product. See the LGPL for details.

PART I

NBT:
NetBIOS
over TCP/IP

1

A Short Bio of NetBIOS

Groan + Grump = GroanUmp

— Me, speculating on the etymology
of the term "Grown-up" for my children

It all started back in the frontier days of the PC when Microsoft was a lot smaller, IBM seemed a whole lot bigger, and Apple owned personal computer territory as far as the eye could see. Back then, you didn't need no dang standards. If you wanted to sell LANs, you just went out and branded yourself a protocol. Apple had AppleTalk, Digital had DECnet, and, for their longhorn mainframes, IBM had **S**ystems **N**etwork **A**rchitecture (SNA). SNA was a mighty big horse for little PCs, so IBM hired on a company called Sytec and together they rustled up a product they called "PC Network." Not an inspiring name, but it was a simpler time.

PC Network was a Local Area Network (LAN) system designed to support about 80 nodes at best, with no provisions for routing. NetBIOS (**Net**work **B**asic **I**nput **O**utput **S**ystem) was the software interface to the PC Network hardware. It offered a set of commands that could control the hardware, establish and delete sessions, transfer data, etc.

1.1   NetBIOS and DOS: The Early Years

Starting with DOS version 3.1, Microsoft used the NetBIOS API to transport SMB file service messages. They created something called a *redirector*, and its job was to catch disk drive or port references (e.g. "C:" or "LPT3:") and look them up in a table. If the device was *not* in the table, the call was passed along to DOS. If the device *was* in the table, then the call would be *redirected*. For example:

- Using the SUBST command, a user could substitute a drive letter for a local path. This simple aliasing provided convenient shortcuts for long path names:

  ```
  subst S: C:\FILES\DEEP\IN\A\DIRECTORY
  ```

- Using the NET command, a drive letter could be mapped to a remote file service. So, if the redirector found a remote service entry in its table, it would convert the request into an SMB packet and send it out via NetBIOS:

  ```
  net use N: \\SERVER\SERVICE
  ```

  Note the double backslash preceding the server name. This syntax is part of Microsoft's "**U**niversal **N**aming **C**onvention" (UNC) for network services.

  These commands are still available from within the DOS shells of contemporary Windows products. It is worthwhile to fiddle with them a bit. At the DOS prompt, you can type NET HELP for a summary of the NET command and its options.[1]

---

1. ...or, if you type the way I do, you can enter NEWT KELP to generate an error message.

2

Speaking NetBIOS

Genuine Imitation

— Well known oxymoron

The hardware part of IBM's PC Network is no longer in use and the protocol that actually ran on the wire is all but forgotten, yet the NetBIOS API remains. Vast sweeping hoards of programs — including DOS itself — were written to use NetBIOS. Like COBOL, it may never die.

Many vendors, eager for a piece of the Microsoft desktop pie, figured out how to implement the NetBIOS API on top of other protocols. There is NetBIOS over DECnet, NetBIOS over NetWare, NetBIOS over mashed potatoes and gravy with creamed corn, NetBIOS over SNA, NetBIOS over TCP/IP, and more. Of these, the most popular, tasty, and important is NetBIOS over TCP/IP, and that's what this chapter is really all about.

NetBIOS over TCP/IP is sometimes called *NetBT* or *NBT*. Folks from IBM — for reasons unfathomable — sometimes call it *TCPBEUI*. NBT is the simplest and most common name, so we'll stick with that.

On the 7-layer OSI reference model, NetBIOS is a session-layer (layer 5) API. Under DOS and its offspring, applications talk to NetBIOS by filling in a record structure known as a Network Control Block (NCB) and signaling an interrupt. The NCBs are used to pass commands and messages between applications and the underlying protocol stack.

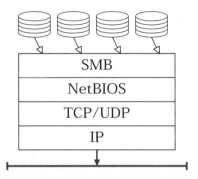

Figure 2.1:   *The NetBIOS layer*

The NetBIOS layer is sandwiched between the Server Message Block (SMB) filesharing protocol and the underlying network transport layer.

Fortunately, the NetBIOS API is specific to DOS and its kin. Unix and other systems do not need to implement the NetBIOS API, as there is no legacy of programs that use it. Instead, these systems participate in NBT networks by directly handling the TCP and UDP packets described in two IETF (Internet Engineering Task Force) *Request for Comments* documents: RFC 1001 and RFC 1002 (known collectively as Internet Standard #19). These RFCs describe a set of services that work together to create virtual NetBIOS LANs over IP.

2.1   Emulating "NetBIOS LANs"

At this point, we hit an interesting twist in the terminology. NetBIOS is a driver that presents an API; it is neither a protocol nor a topology. The API does, however, make a number of assumptions about the workings of the underlying network, and it presents some quirky restrictions. The terms "NetBIOS Network" and "NetBIOS LAN" are commonly used to identify the network architecture that is, essentially, *defined* by the NetBIOS API.

RFCs 1001 and 1002 list three basic services that must be supported in order to implement NetBIOS LAN emulation. These are:

- the Name Service,
- the Datagram Service, and
- the Session Service.

The Name Service is used to map NetBIOS names (addresses) to IP addresses in the underlying IP network. The Datagram Service provides for the delivery of NetBIOS datagrams via UDP. Finally, the Session Service is used to establish and maintain point-to-point, connection-oriented NetBIOS sessions over TCP.

2.1.1 *The NetBIOS Name Service*

The NetBIOS LAN architecture is very simple. No routers, no switches — just a bunch of nodes connected to a (virtual) wire. Unlike IP, there is no need for separate hardware addresses, network addresses, or even port numbers. Instead, the communications endpoints are identified by 16-byte strings known as "NetBIOS names."

NetBIOS addressing is dynamic. Applications may add names as needed and remove those names when they are finished. Each node on the LAN will also have a default name, known as the *Machine Name* or the *Workstation Service Name*, which is typically added when NetBIOS starts. The process of adding a name is called *registration*.

There are two kinds of names that can be registered: *unique* and *group*. Group names may be shared by multiple clients, thus providing a mechanism for multicast. In contrast, unique names may only be used by one client per LAN. Keep in mind, though, that these are virtual LANs which may actually be spread out across different subnets in a routed IP internetwork.

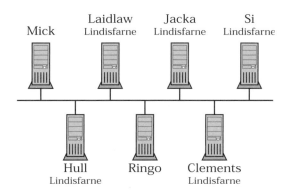

Figure 2.2: *Group names*

In addition to their Machine Names, some of the nodes on this IP LAN have registered the group name Lindisfarne. Nodes Mick and Ringo are not members of the group Lindisfarne.

The Name Service is supposed to keep track of all the NetBIOS names in use within the virtual LAN and ensure that messages sent to a given NetBIOS name are directed to the correct underlying IP address. It does this in two ways:

On an IP LAN

Each node keeps a list of the names it has registered (that is, the names it "owns"). When sending a message, the first step is to send an IP broadcast query, called a NAME QUERY REQUEST. If there is a machine on the IP LAN that owns the queried name, it will reply by sending a NAME QUERY RESPONSE.

So, to send a message to the node which has registered the name EADFRITH, the sender calls out "Yo! Eadfrith!" EADFRITH responds with an "I am here!" message, giving its IP address.

This is known as "B mode" (broadcast) name resolution, and the participants are referred to as "B **n**odes." In B mode, each node keeps track of — and answers queries for — its own names, so the NetBIOS Name Service "database" is a distributed database.

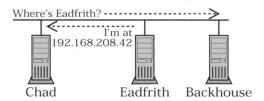

Figure 2.3:   *B mode name resolution*

Node Chad wishes to contact node Eadfrith. Since the underlying transport is IP, Chad must first discover the IP address of Eadfrith.

Chad sends a broadcast name query to all nodes on the local segment, asking Eadfrith to respond. All other nodes should ignore the request.

Over a routed Internet

Broadcasts aren't meant to cross subnet boundaries, so a different mechanism is used when the nodes are separated by routers.

The Network Administrator chooses a machine to be the **NetBIOS Name Server** (NBNS, aka WINS Server[1]). Typically this will be a Unix host running Samba, or a Windows NT or W2K server. In order to use the NBNS, all of the nodes that are participating in the virtual NetBIOS LAN must be given the server's IP address. This can be done by entering the address in the client's NetBIOS configuration or, on Windows systems, via DHCP.

NBT client nodes send NetBIOS name registrations and queries directly to the NBNS, which maintains a central database of all registered names in the virtual LAN. This is known as "P mode" (point-to-point) name resolution, and its participants are referred to as "P nodes."

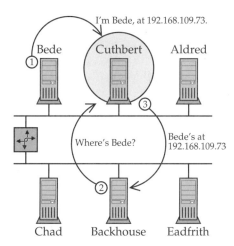

Figure 2.4:   *P mode name resolution*

1.   Node Bede registers its name with Cuthbert, the NBNS (WINS server).

2.   Node Backhouse is looking for Bede and sends a query to Cuthbert.

3.   Cuthbert provides the IP address of Bede to Backhouse.

These are the two basic modes of NetBIOS name resolution over NBT. There are, of course, others. The RFCs describe "M mode" (mixed mode) which combines characteristics of P and B modes. "H mode" (hybrid mode)

---

1. Microsoft calls their NBNS implementation "**W**indows **I**nternet **N**ame **S**ervice" (WINS). The term WINS is now commonly used instead of NBNS, but we will be pedantic and stick with the latter.

was introduced later; it is similar to M mode except for the order in which B and P mode behavior is applied.

The Name Service runs on UDP port 137. According to the RFCs the use of TCP port 137 can be negotiated for some queries, though few (if any) implementations actually support this.

2.1.2   *The NetBIOS Datagram Service*

In the IP world, TCP provides connection-oriented sessions in which packets are acknowledged, put in order, and retransmitted if lost. This creates the illusion of a continuous, sequential data stream from one end to the other. In contrast, UDP datagrams are simply sent. Thus, UDP requires less overhead, but it is less reliable than TCP. NetBIOS also provides connection-oriented (session) and connectionless (datagram) communications. Naturally, NBT maps NetBIOS sessions to TCP and NetBIOS datagrams to UDP.

The Datagram Distribution Service is the NBT service that handles NetBIOS datagram transport. It runs on UDP port 138, and can handle unicast (also known as "specific"), multicast (group), and broadcast NetBIOS datagrams.

Unicast (specific)

The handling of unicast datagrams is fairly straightforward. The Name Service is used to resolve the destination name to an IP address. The NetBIOS packet is then encapsulated in a UDP packet and sent to the specified IP.

Multicast (group) and broadcast

According to the RFCs, a **B** node can simply encapsulate NetBIOS multicast and broadcast datagrams in UDP and send them to the IP broadcast address. The UDP datagram will then be picked up by all local nodes listening on the Datagram Service port (138/UDP). Thus, NetBIOS broadcast datagrams will reach all nodes in the virtual LAN. In the case of multicast datagrams, nodes which are not members of the group (have not registered the group name) will discard the message.

P, **M**, and **H** nodes are a bit more complicated, as you might expect. When the virtual LAN extends beyond the physical LAN, an IP broadcast will not reach all of the nodes in the NetBIOS name space. In order to deliver group and broadcast datagrams, the NBNS database must be consulted. How this is (or isn't) actually done will be explained in strikingly painful detail later on. Chapter 5 on page 115 is dedicated to the workings of datagram distribution.

The Datagram Service is probably the second least well understood aspect of NBT, most likely because its correct implementation isn't critical to filesharing. Many implementations get it wrong, and there is much debate over the value of getting it right.

2.1.3 · *The NetBIOS Session Service*

The Session Service is the traditional transport for SMB, and this is our primary reason for caring about NetBIOS at all. The Session Service runs on TCP port 139.[2] There is no particular mechanism for multicast or broadcast because each session is, by definition, a one-to-one connection. The RFCs do, however, briefly discuss what might happen if a session setup request were sent to a group name (see RFC 1001, Section 16.1.1.2).

We will get to the details of session creation, use, and closure when we discuss Session Service implementation.

Weirdness Alert

TCP/138 has no defined behavior under NBT and Microsoft never implemented support for NBT Name Resolution over TCP/137, yet some versions of Windows seem to listen on these two TCP ports when NBT is active.

```
C:\> netstat -a

Active Connections

   Proto  Local Address      Foreign Address   State
   TCP    paris:137          PARIS:0           LISTENING
   TCP    paris:138          PARIS:0           LISTENING
   TCP    paris:nbsession    PARIS:0           LISTENING
   UDP    paris:nbname       *:*
   UDP    paris:nbdatagram   *:*
```

It turns out that this is due to a known bug in the netstat *utility included with older Windows releases.*

---

2. If the NBT authors had used TCP/138 instead of 139 for the Session Service, they could have saved a couple of ports. Instead, TCP/138 and UDP/139 are wasted.

 **Email**

From: Jean-Baptiste Marchand
  To: Chris Hertel

Hello,

I've noticed that, in Section 2.1, there is a weirdness alert about
the Windows netstat program showing TCP ports 137 and 138 open,
whereas only UDP ports 137 and 138 are actually opened by the NetBT
driver.

In fact, it is a known problem in Windows NT (this is fixed in
Windows 2000 and later) that netstat shows TCP ports opened, whereas
only UDP ports with the same number are opened. This is documented
in an entry of Microsoft's knowledge base (Q194171).

This article states that this is only a display problem. This is
true and can be verified using any TCP port scanner.

2.2   Scope: The Final Frontier

This is a good point at which to get up, stretch, make a nice hot cup of tea for yourself, take a soothing bath, play with your cat, go for a long walk in the park, take dance lessons, volunteer in your community, sort and organize your old photographs, or join a United Nations Peace Keeping Force. The Datagram Service was previously described as "the second least well understood aspect of NBT." Guess which bit wins first prize.

Scope is an oddity of NBT, not because it was a bad idea (though perhaps it was) but because few have ever bothered to really understand it. In practice this feature is rarely used, in part because it is rarely implemented to its full potential.

In the RFCs, the term *scope* is used as a name for:

- the set of NetBIOS nodes that participate in an NBT virtual LAN,
- an identifier used to distinguish one virtual LAN from another, and
- that which is included within the purpose of the RFC document.

...but the last of these is beyond the scope of this discussion, so let's take a closer look at the first two.

Scope is explained in RFC 1001, Section 9, which starts off by saying:

```
A "NetBIOS Scope" is the population of computers across
which a registered NetBIOS name is known. NetBIOS broadcast
and multicast datagram operations must reach the entire extent
of the NetBIOS scope.
```

This basically means *all nodes connected to the virtual LAN*. So, for B nodes the NetBIOS scope consists of all nodes within the local IP broadcast domain that are running NBT. For P nodes, the NetBIOS scope includes all nodes across the routed internetwork that run NBT and share the same NBNS. For an M or H node, the scope is the union of the local broadcast and the NBNS scopes.

This is all quite straightforward when all NBT nodes are of the same node type, but strange things can happen when you mix modes, particularly in a routed environment.

P & B

Two separate scopes are defined. The B nodes will only see other B nodes on the same wire, and the P nodes will only see other P nodes using the same NBNS. If creating separate NetBIOS vLANs is your goal, then mixing P and B nodes on the same wire is perfectly okay.

P & M

This results in a single scope. The M nodes perform all of the functions of a P node, including registering their names with the NBNS. Thus, all P nodes can see all M nodes, though M nodes on the same wire can bypass the NBNS when resolving names.

B & M

On a single, non-routed IP LAN there will be only one scope. The M nodes will register and resolve names via the broadcast mechanism, making their use of the NBNS pointless.

Things start going terribly wrong, though, when the NetBIOS vLAN is distributed across multiple subnets in a routed internetwork. When this happens the result is multiple, intersecting scopes. B nodes on one subnet will not be able to see any node on any other subnet. M nodes will see all other M nodes, but only the B nodes on their local wire. Thus, parts of the NetBIOS vLAN are hidden from other parts, yet all are somewhat connected via the common M node scope.

One result of this mess is the potential for name collisions. A B node could register a name that is already in the NBNS database, and an M node might register a name that one or more B nodes on remote subnets have already claimed. Name resolution then essentially fails because the same name does not resolve to the same IP address across the fractured scope.

The RFCs recognize this potential for disaster and warn against it. See RFC 1001, Section 10.

P, B, & M

From bad to worse. The P nodes can see all of the M nodes which can see some of the B nodes which cannot see any P nodes at all. B nodes and M (or H) nodes don't mix.

We now have a good handle on our first definition of scope: "*the set of NetBIOS nodes that participate in a virtual LAN.*" What about the second: "*an identifier used to distinguish one virtual LAN from another*"? (This is a good point at which to get up, stretch, make a nice hot cup of tea for yourself...)

Every scope has a name, called the Scope Identifier (Scope ID). The most common Scope ID is the empty string: " ". Indeed, this is the default in Windows, Samba, jCIFS, and every other system encountered so far. The only problem with this name is that it becomes too easy to forget that the Scope ID exists.

We have already seen that distinct NetBIOS vLANs can be created by using the behavior of B, P, M, and H nodes to create separate scopes. For example, multiple scopes are defined when multiple independent NBNS's provide service for P nodes. B nodes on separate IP LANs are also in separate scopes, and so on. The Scope ID provides another, more refined mechanism for separating scopes.

Think of an IP LAN with a bunch of B nodes. Some of the B nodes have Scope ID DOG, and others have Scope ID CAT. Only members of scope DOG will listen to messages sent with that ID; the cats will ignore messages sent to the dogs. So, even though all of the B nodes are on the same wire, we have two separate scopes. The same applies to P and M nodes. The Scope IDs identify, and separate, virtual NetBIOS LANs. Note, though, that an NBNS will handle requests from any node regardless of scope. A single NBNS server can, therefore, support multiple scopes.

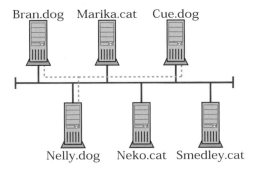

Figure 2.5:   *Multiple named scopes in a broadcast LAN*

Nodes with scope ID DOG are in their own virtual NetBIOS LAN. Nodes with scope ID CAT will ignore broadcasts to the DOG scope.

According to RFC 1001/1002, a node may belong to more than one scope. In practice, however, it is much easier to choose a single scope and stick with it. This is particularly true for DOS and Windows systems because NetBIOS itself has no concept of scope. The Scope ID is a feature of NBT, and programs that call the NetBIOS API have no way of telling NBT which scope to use.

The RFCs suggest that extensions might be added to NetBIOS to manage scope, but using those extensions would require changes to applications. Further, other NetBIOS transports would not support extensions, which would result in compatibility problems.

Confusion Alert

Scope IDs are used by the Name Service and the Datagram Service, but not the Session Service. This seems awkward at first, but it makes sense when you consider that the NetBIOS API itself has no knowledge of scope.

Once again, Scope IDs serve only to identify virtual NetBIOS LANs. They operate at a lower level than the NetBIOS API.

2.3   Thus Endeth the Overview

Now that you have a clear and precise understanding of the workings of Net-BIOS over TCP, go read RFC 1001. That ought to muddy the waters a bit. Clear or not, the next step is to write some code and see what works — and what doesn't. Actual implementation will provide a lot of opportunity to discuss details, bugs, and common errors.

3

The Basics of NBT Implementation

In theory, theory and practice are the same.
In practice, they're not.

— Unknown

Ready?

We have identified the three key parts of NBT: the Name Service, the Datagram Service, and the Session Service. This is enough to get us started. We will begin by coding up a simple Name Service Query, just to see what kind of trouble that gets us into.

Before we start, though, it's probably a good idea to check our tools.

✔ Sniffer

You need one of these. If you have Windows systems available, see if you can get a copy of Microsoft's NetMon (**Net**work **Mon**itor). You will want the latest and most complete version. The advantage of NetMon is that Microsoft have included parsers for many of their protocols.

Another excellent choice is Ethereal, an Open Source protocol analyzer portable to most Unix-ish platforms and to Windows. It can create its own captures or read captures made by several other sniffer packages, including TCPDump and NetMon. Richard Sharpe and Tim Potter of the Samba Team have worked on NetBIOS and SMB packet parsers for Ethereal, which helps a big bunch.

✔ Language

There are a lot of programming languages out there. Samba is written in C, and jCIFS is in Java. The key factors when choosing a language for your implementation are:

- Good network coding capabilities.
- That warm fuzzy feeling you get when you code in a language you truly grok.

Meditate on that for a while. Bad karma in the coding environment will distract you from your purpose.

✔ Test Environment

If you do not have a couple of hubs, a router, various Windows boxes, and some Samba servers in your home, you may need to do your testing at the office. Netiquette and job security would suggest that you test after hours. (Um... actually, you probably shouldn't do any testing on a production network... and check office policy before you sniff.)

✔ Medication

An aromatic black tea, such as a good Earl Grey, is best. Try Lapsang Souchong to get through really difficult coding sessions. Those sweet, mass-produced, over-caffeinated soft drinks will disturb your focus.

Ready!

In this section, we will implement a broadcast NAME QUERY REQUEST. That is, B mode name resolution. This will allow us to introduce some of the basic concepts and establish a frame of reference. In other words, we have to start somewhere and this seems to be as good a place as any.

3.1   You Got the Name, Look Up the Number

The structure of an NBT name query is similar to that of a Domain Name System query. As RFC 1001, Section 11.1.1, explains:

```
The NBNS design attempts to align itself with the
Domain Name System in a number of ways.
```

The goal of this attempted alignment was an eventual merger between the NBNS and the DNS system. The NBT authors even predicted dynamic DNS update. With Windows 2000, Microsoft did move CIFS naming services to Dynamic DNS, though the mechanism is not quite what was envisioned by the authors of the NBT RFCs.

3.1.1 *Encoding NetBIOS Names*

RFCs 1001 and 1002 reference RFC 883 when discussing domain name syntax rules. RFC 883 was later superseded by RFC 1035, but both give the same *preferred*[1] syntax for domain names:

```
<domain>      ::= <subdomain> | " "
<subdomain>   ::= <label> | <subdomain> "." <label>
<label>       ::= <letter> [ [ <ldh-str> ] <let-dig> ]
<ldh-str>     ::= <let-dig-hyp> | <let-dig-hyp> <ldh-str>
<let-dig-hyp> ::= <let-dig> | "-"
<let-dig>     ::= <letter> | <digit>
<letter>      ::= any one of the 52 alphabetic characters A through
                  Z in upper case and a through z in lower case
<digit>       ::= any one of the ten digits 0 through 9
```

This is the syntax that the NBT authors tried to match. Unfortunately, except for the 16-byte length restriction, there are few syntax rules for NetBIOS names. With a few notable exceptions just about any octet value may be used, so the NBT authors came up with a scheme to force NetBIOS names into compliance. Here's how it works:

- Names shorter than 16 bytes are padded on the right with spaces. Longer names are truncated.

- Each byte is divided into two nibbles (4 bits each, unsigned).[2] The result is a string of 32 integer values, each in the range 0..15.

- The ASCII value of the letter 'A' (65, or 0x41) is added to each nibble and the result is taken as a character. This creates a string of 32 characters, each in the range 'A'..'P'.

---

1. Note the use of the term "preferred." A close read of RFCs 883, 1034, 1035, and 2181 shows that the idea of using binary data in DNS records has been around for some time.

2. Some call this a "half-ASCII"-ed encoding scheme.

This is called *First Level Encoding*, and is described in RFC 1001, Section 14.1.

Using First Level Encoding, the name "Neko" would be converted as follows:

char		hex		split		+ 'A'		hex		result
N	=	0x4E		0x04	+	0x41	=	0x45	=	E
				0x0E	+	0x41	=	0x4F	=	O
e	=	0x65		0x06	+	0x41	=	0x47	=	G
				0x05	+	0x41	=	0x46	=	F
k	=	0x6B		0x06	+	0x41	=	0x47	=	G
				0x0B	+	0x41	=	0x4C	=	L
o	=	0x6F		0x06	+	0x41	=	0x47	=	G
				0x0F	+	0x41	=	0x50	=	P
' '	=	0x20		0x02	+	0x41	=	0x43	=	C
				0x00	+	0x41	=	0x41	=	A
' '	=	0x20		0x02	+	0x41	=	0x43	=	C
				0x00	+	0x41	=	0x41	=	A
										:

This results in the string:

EOGFGLGPCACACACACACACACACACACACA

Lovely, isn't it?

...and our first bit of code is in Listing 3.1.

This function reads up to 16 characters from the input string name and converts each to the encoded format, stuffing the result into the target string dst. The space character (0x20) always converts to the two-character value CA so, if the source string is less than 16 bytes, we simply pad the target string with CACA. Note that the target character array must be at least 33 bytes long — one extra byte to account for the nul terminator.[3]

---

3. Such considerations are important when programming in C and its ilk.

Listing 3.1: First Level Encoding

```
#ifndef uchar
#define uchar unsigned char
#endif /* uchar */

uchar *L1_Encode( uchar *dst, const uchar *name )
  {
  int i = 0;
  int j = 0;

  /* Encode the name. */
  while( ('\0' != name[i]) && (i < 16) )
    {
    dst[j++] = 'A' + ((name[i] & 0xF0) >> 4);
    dst[j++] = 'A' + (name[i++] & 0x0F);
    }

  /* Encode the padding bytes. */
  while( j < 32 )
    {
    dst[j++] = 'C';
    dst[j++] = 'A';
    }

  /* Terminate the string. */
  dst[32] = '\0';

  return( dst );
  } /* L1_Encode */
```

Typo Alert

RFC 1001 provides an example of First Level Encoding in Section 14.1. The string "The NetBIOS name" is encoded as:

FEGHGFCAEOGFHEECEJEPFDCAHEGBGNGF

Decoding this string, however, we get "Tge NetBIOS tame." Perhaps it's a secret message.

The correct encoding would be:

FEG̲IGFCAEOGFHEECEJEPFDCAG̲O̲GBGNGF

3.1.2   *Fully Qualified NBT Names*

Now that we've managed to convert the NetBIOS name into a DNS-aligned form, it is time to combine it with the NBT Scope ID. The result will be a fully-qualified NBT address, which we will call the *NBT name*. To be pedantic, when the RFCs talk about First Level Encoding, this fully qualified form is what they really mean.

As expected, the syntax of the Scope ID follows the DNS recommendations given in RFC 883 (and repeated in RFC 1035). That is, a Scope ID looks like a DNS name. So, if the Scope ID is `cat.org`, and the NetBIOS name is `Neko`, the resultant NBT name would be:

```
EOGFGLGPCACACACACACACACACACACACA.CAT.ORG
```

Imagine typing that into your web browser. This is why the RFC 1001/1002 scheme for merging the NBNS with the DNS never took hold.

3.1.3   *Second Level Encoding*

Now that we have an NBT name in a nice familiar format, it is time to convert it into something else.

DNS names (and, therefore, NBT names) are made up of labels separated by dots. Dividing the name above into its component labels gives us:

length	label
32	EOGFGLGPCACACACACACACACACACACACA
3	CAT
3	ORG
0	<nul>

The Second Level Encoded NBT name is a concatenation of the lengths and the labels, as in:

```
'\x20' + "EOGFGLGPCACACACACACACACACACACACA" + '\x03' + "CAT"
+ '\x03' + "ORG" + '\0'
```

The empty label at the end is important. It is a label of zero length, and it represents the root of the DNS (and NBT) namespace. That means that the final nul byte is *part of the encoded NBT name*, and not a mere terminator.

In practice, you can manipulate the encoded NBT name as if it were a
nul-terminated string, but always keep in mind that it is really a series of
length-delimited strings.[4]

Our second bit of code in Listing 3.2 will convert a NetBIOS name and
Scope ID into a Second Level Encoded string.

Listing 3.2: Second Level Encoding

```
int L2_Encode( uchar *dst, const uchar *name, const uchar *scope )
  {
  int lenpos;
  int i;
  int j;

  /* First Level Encode the NetBIOS name.
   * Prefix it with label length.
   * (dec 32 == 0x20)
   */
  if( NULL == L1_Encode( &dst[1], name ) )
    return( -1 );
  dst[0] = 0x20;
  lenpos = 33;

  /* Copy each scope label to dst,
   * adding the length byte as an afterthought.
   */
  if( '\0' != *scope )
    {
    do
      {
      for( i = 0, j = (lenpos + 1);
           ('.' != scope[i]) && ('\0' != scope[i]);
           i++, j++)
        dst[j] = scope[i];

      dst[lenpos] = (uchar)i;
      lenpos      += i + 1;
      scope       += i;
      } while( '.' == *(scope++) );
    dst[lenpos] = '\0';
    }
  return( lenpos + 1 );
  } /* L2_Encode */
```

---

4. "Pedantic" is the politically correct way to say "anal retentive."

Not the prettiest piece of code, but it does the job. We will run through
the function quickly, just to familiarize you with the workings of this particular
programmer's twisted little brain. If the code is fairly obvious to you, feel free
to skip ahead to the next section.

```
if( NULL == L1_Encode( &dst[1], name ) )
  return( -1 );
dst[0] = 0x20;
lenpos = 33;
```

Call `L1_Encode()` to convert the NetBIOS name into its First Level
Encoded form, then prefix the encoded name with a length byte. This gives
us the first label of the encoded NBT name. Note that we check for a NULL
return value. This is paranoia on the programmer's part since this version of
`L1_Encode()` does not return NULL. (An improved version of
`L1_Encode()` might return NULL if it detected an error.)

The variable `lenpos` is set to the offset at which the next length byte
will be written. The `L1_Encode()` function has already placed a nul byte at
this location so, if the scope string is empty, the NBT name is already completely encoded.

```
if( '\0' != *scope )
  {
  do
    {
    :
    } while( '.' == *(scope++) );
  dst[lenpos] = '\0';
  }
```

The processing of scope labels is contained within the do..while loop.
If the scope is empty, we can skip this loop entirely. Note that the root label
is added to the end of the target string, dst, following the scope labels.

```
for( i = 0, j = (lenpos + 1);
     ('.' != scope[i]) && ('\0' != scope[i]);
     i++, j++)
  dst[j] = scope[i];
```

Run through the current label, copying it to the destination string. The
variable i keeps track of the length of the label. A dot or a nul will mark the
end of the current label.

```
dst[lenpos] = (uchar)i;
lenpos      += i + 1;
scope       += i;
```

Write the length byte for the current label, and then move on to the next by advancing `lenpos`. The variable `scope` is advanced by the length of the current label, which should leave it pointing to the dot or nul that terminated the label. It will be advanced one more byte within the `while` clause at the end of the loop.

Hopefully that was a nice, short waste of time. As we progress, it will become necessary to move more quickly and provide less code and less analysis of the code. There is a lot of ground to cover.

3.1.4 *Name Service Packet Headers*

Once again, our attention is drawn to the ancient lore of RFC 883, which was written about four years ahead of RFC 1001/1002 and was eventually replaced by RFC 1035. The comings and goings of the RFCs are a study unto themselves.

NBT Name Service packets are an intentional rip-off of DNS Messages. New flag field values, operation codes, and return codes were added but the design was in keeping with the goal of eventually merging NBNS services into the DNS.

This, conceptually, is what a Name Service packet header looks like:

0	1	2	3	4	5	6	7	8	9	10	11	12	13	14	15
NAME_TRN_ID															
R	OPCODE				NM_FLAGS					RCODE			
QDCOUNT															
ANCOUNT															
NSCOUNT															
ARCOUNT															

Here is a description of the fields:

NAME_TRN_ID

A two-byte transaction identifier. Each time the NBT Name Service starts a new transaction it assigns an ID to it so that it can figure out which responses go with which requests. An obvious way to handle this is to start with zero and increment each time one is used, allowing rollover at 0xFFFF.

For our purposes any number will do. So we will pick something semi-random for ourselves. How 'bout 1964?

R

This one-bit field indicates whether the packet is:

> 0 == a *request*, or
> 1 == a *response*.

Ours is a request. It initiates a transaction, so we will use 0.

OPCODE

Six operations are defined by the RFCs. These are:

> 0x0 == Query
> 0x5 == Name Registration
> 0x6 == Name Release
> 0x7 == WACK (Wait for Acknowledgement)
> 0x8 == Name Refresh
> 0x9 == Name Refresh (Alternate Opcode)

The 0x9 OpCode value is the result of a typo in RFC 1002. In Section 4.2.1.1 a value of 0x8 is listed, but Section 4.2.4 shows a value of 0x9. A sensible implementation will handle either, though 0x8 is the preferred value.

One more OpCode was added after the RFCs were published:

> 0xF == Multi-Homed Name Registration

Our immediate interest, of course, is with the Query operation — OpCode value 0x0.

NM_FLAGS

As the name suggests, this is a set of one-bit flags, as follows:

0	1	2	3	4	5	6
AA	TC	RD	RA	0	0	B

We will go into the details of this later on. For now, note that the B flag means "Broadcast" and that we are attempting to do a broadcast query, so we will want to turn this bit on. We will also set the RD flag. RD stands for "Recursion Desired"; for now, just take it on faith that this bit should be set. All others will be clear (zero).

RCODE

Return codes. This field is always 0x00 in request packets (those with an R value of zero). Each response packet type has its own set of possible RCODE values.

QDCOUNT

The number of names that follow in the query section. We will set this to 1 for our broadcast name query.

ANCOUNT

The number of answers in a POSITIVE NAME QUERY RESPONSE message. This field will be used in the replies we get in response to our broadcast query.

NSCOUNT, ARCOUNT

These are "Name Service Authority Count" and "Additional Record Count," respectively. These can be ignored for now.

So, for a broadcast NAME QUERY REQUEST, our header will look like this:

0	1	2	3	4	5	6	7	8	9	10	11	12	13	14	15
1964															
0	0	0	0	0	0	0	1	0	0	0	1	0	0	0	0
1															
0															
0															
0															

To make it easier to write the code for the above query, we will hand-convert the header into a string of bytes. We could do this in code (in fact, that will be necessary for a real implementation), but dealing with such details at this point would be an unnecessary tangent. So...

```
unsigned char header[] =
  {
  0x07, 0xAC, /* 1964 == 0x07AC.       */
  0x01, 0x10, /* 0 0000 0010001 0000 */
  0x00, 0x01, /* One name query.     */
  0x00, 0x00, /* Zero answers.       */
  0x00, 0x00, /* Zero authorities.   */
  0x00, 0x00  /* Zero additional.    */
  };
```

3.1.5 *The Query Entry*

The query entries follow the header. A query entry consists of a Second Level Encoded NBT name followed by two additional fields: the QUESTION_TYPE and QUESTION_CLASS. Once again, this is taken directly from the DNS query packet.

Under NBT, the QUESTION_TYPE field is limited to two possible values, representing the two types of queries that are defined in the RFCs. These are:

NB == 0x0020

The NAME QUERY REQUEST, which we will use to perform our broadcast query.

NBSTAT == 0x0021

The NODE STATUS REQUEST, also known as an "Adapter Status" query. The latter is a reference to the original NetBIOS API command name.

Only one QUESTION_CLASS is defined for NBT, and that is the Internet Class: 0x0001.

So, our completed NAME QUERY REQUEST packet will consist of:

- the NBT header, as given above,
- the Second Level encoded NBT name,
- the unsigned short values 0x0020 and 0x0001.

3.1.6 *Some Trouble Ahead*

It would seem that it should now be easy to send a broadcast name query. Just put the pieces together and send them to UDP port 137 at the broadcast address. Yes that *should* be easy... except that we are now crossing the line between *theory* and *practice*, and that means trouble. Be brave.

Upper Case/lower case

RFCs 883 and 1035 state that DNS name lookups should be case-insensitive. That is, CAT.ORG is equivalent to cat.org and Cat.Org, etc. Case-insensitive comparison is not difficult, and First Level Encoding always produces a string of upper-case characters in the range 'A'..'P', so we should have no trouble comparing

EOGFGLGPCACACACACACACACACACACACA.CAT.ORG

against

EOGFGLGPCACACACACACACACACACACACA.cat.org

...but what about the original NetBIOS name? The strings "Neko" and "NEKO" translate, respectively, to

EOGFGLGPCACACACACACACACACACACACA

and

EOEFELEPCACACACACACACACACACACACA

These strings do not match, and so we seem to have a problem. Are the two original names considered equivalent? If so, how should we handle them?

RFC 1001 and 1002 do not provide answers to these questions, so we need to look to other sources. Of course, the ultimate source for Truth and Wisdom is empirical information. That is, what actually happens on the wire? A little packet sniffing and a few simple tests will provide the answers we need. Here's the plan:

1. Use lower-case or mixed-case names when configuring your test hosts.
2. Set up your sniffer to capture packets on UDP port 137.
3. Start or restart your test hosts.
4. After a few minutes, stop the capture.

If your sniffer can decode the NetBIOS names (Ethereal and NetMon can) then you will see that the NetBIOS names are all in upper case. This is normal behavior for NBT, even though it is not documented in the RFCs. Scope strings are also converted to upper case before on-the-wire use.

Here is another interesting test that you can perform if you have Windows and Samba systems (and/or others) on your network:

1. Modify the NBT Name Query code (in Listing 3.3 below) so that it converts the NetBIOS name to *lower case* rather than upper case. (That is, change `toupper` to `tolower`.)

2. Recompile.

3. Start your sniffer.

4. Use the code to send some queries. Try group names in particular.

In tests using Samba 2.0 and Windows, Samba servers respond to these lower-case queries while Windows systems do not. This suggests that Windows compares the encoded string, while Samba is decoding the string and performing a case-insensitive comparison on the result. One might argue that Samba's behavior is more robust, but comparing names without decoding them first is certainly faster.[5]

NetBIOS Name Syntax

We have specified a syntax for NBT names. So far, however, we have said little about the syntax for the original NetBIOS name. RFC 1001 says only that the name may not begin with an asterisk ('*'), because the asterisk is used for "wildcard" queries.

At the low level there are few real rules for forming NetBIOS names other than the length limit. Applications, however, often place restrictions on the names that users may choose. Windows, for example, will only allow a specific set of printable characters for workstation names, yet Microsoft's `nbtstat` program is much more accepting.

For the implementor, this is a bit of a problem. You want to be sure that your code can handle any bizarre name that reaches it over the network, yet help the user avoid choosing names that might cause another system to choke.

---

5. Samba's behavior may change if no reason can be found to compare the decoded names. Decoding costs a few cycles, which could be significant in an NBNS implementation.

A good rule of thumb is to warn users against choosing any character that is not legal in a "best practices" DNS label.

Padding Permutations

The space character (0x20) is the designated padding character for NetBIOS names, but there are a few exceptions. One of these is associated with wildcard queries. When sending a wildcard query, the name is padded with nul bytes rather than spaces, giving:

'*'	0	0	0	0	0	0	0	0	0	0	0	0	0	0	0

Which translates to: CKAAAAAAAAAAAAAAAAAAAAAAAAAAAAAA.

Samba will respond to either space- or nul-padded wildcard queries, but Windows will only respond if the name is nul-padded.[6] Once again, this indicates that Samba decodes NBT names before comparison, but Windows does not.

Microsoft has added a few other non-space-padded names as well. These are special case names, used with particular applications. Still, they demonstrate the need for flexibility in our encoding and decoding functions.

Label Length Limits

We did not bother to mention earlier that the label length bytes placed before each label during Second Level Encoding are not 8-bit values. The uppermost two bits are used as flags, leaving only 6 bits for the label length. Normally these flag bits are both zero (unset), so we can ignore them for now and (as with so many other little details) deal with them later on.

With only 6 bits, the length of each label is limited to 63 characters. The overall length of the Second Level Encoded string is further limited to 255 bytes. Our example code does not have any checks to ensure that the Scope ID has the correct syntax, though such tests would be required in any "real" implementation.

---

6. The lab in the basement is rather sparse, and not all versions of Microsoft Windows can be tested. The reported behavior was detected on those variants that were available. We leave it as an exercise for the reader to verify that the behavior is consistent. Please let us know of any contradictory results.

The Fine Print at the End

The RFCs do not say so, but the last byte of the NetBIOS name is reserved.

The practice probably goes back to the early days and IBM. The 16th byte of a NetBIOS name is used to designate the *purpose* of the name. This byte is known as the "suffix" (or sometimes the "type byte"), and it contains a value which indicates the type of the service that registered the name. Some example suffix values include:

    0x00 == Workstation Service (aka Machine Name or Client Service)
    0x03 == Messenger Service
    0x20 == File Server Service
    0x1B == Domain Master Browser

The care and feeding of suffix values is yet another topic to be covered in detail later on. A suffix value of 0x00 is fairly common, so we will use that in our broadcast query. Note that this changes the encoding of the NetBIOS name. Once again, using the name Neko:

    instead of EOEFELEPCACACACACACACACACACACACA,
    you get EOEFELEPCACACACACACACACACACACAAA.

Shorthand Alert

When writing a NetBIOS name, the suffix value is often specified in hex, surrounded by angle brackets. So, the name NEKO with a suffix of 0x1D would be written:

NEKO<1D>

It is also fairly common to use the "#" character to indicate the suffix:

NEKO#1D

We will use the angle bracket notation where appropriate.

3.1.7   *Finally! A Simple Broadcast Name Query*

This next bit of code is full of shortcuts. The packet header is hard-coded, as are the QUESTION_TYPE and QUESTION_CLASS. No syntax checking is done on the scope string. Worst of all, the program sends the query but does not bother to listen for a reply. For that, we will use a sniffer.

Tools such as the nmblookup utility that comes with Samba, or Microsoft's nbtstat program, could also be used to send a name query.

The goal, however, is to implement these tools on our own, and the next bit of code gives us a start.[7]

Listing 3.3: Simple Broadcast Name Query

```
#include <stdio.h>
#include <stdlib.h>
#include <sys/types.h>
#include <sys/socket.h>
#include <netinet/in.h>
#include <arpa/inet.h>
#include <unistd.h>
#include <ctype.h>


#define NBT_BCAST_ADDR "255.255.255.255"

#ifndef uchar
#define uchar unsigned char
#endif /* uchar */

uchar header[] =
  {
  0x07, 0xAC,  /* 1964 == 0x07AC.    */
  0x01, 0x10,  /* Binary 0 0000 0010001 0000 */
  0x00, 0x01,  /* One name query.    */
  0x00, 0x00,  /* Zero answers.      */
  0x00, 0x00,  /* Zero authorities. */
  0x00, 0x00   /* Zero additional.   */
  };

uchar query_tail[] =
  {
  0x00, 0x20,
  0x00, 0x01
  };
```

7. The program in Listing 3.3 has been tested on Debian GNU/Linux and OpenBSD. You may have to fiddle a bit to get it to work on other platforms. Under older versions of NetBSD, OpenBSD, Miami for Amiga, and possibly other BSD-derived TCP stacks, messages sent to the limited broadcast address (255.255.255.255) may not actually be sent as Ethernet broadcasts. On these systems, it will be necessary to change the value of NBT_BCAST_ADDR to the directed broadcast address of the local subnet (the local subnet broadcast address). This bug has been fixed in both NetBSD and in OpenBSD. See the original NetBSD bug report (#7682) for more information.

```
uchar *L1_Encode( uchar        *dst,
                  const uchar *name,
                  const uchar  pad,
                  const uchar  sfx )
  {
  int i = 0;
  int j = 0;
  int k = 0;

  while( ('\0' != name[i]) && (i < 15) )
    {
    k = toupper( name[i++] );
    dst[j++] = 'A' + ((k & 0xF0) >> 4);
    dst[j++] = 'A' +  (k & 0x0F);
    }

  i = 'A' + ((pad & 0xF0) >> 4);
  k = 'A' +  (pad & 0x0F);
  while( j < 30 )
    {
    dst[j++] = i;
    dst[j++] = k;
    }

  dst[30] = 'A' + ((sfx & 0xF0) >> 4);
  dst[31] = 'A' +  (sfx & 0x0F);
  dst[32] = '\0';

  return( dst );
  } /* L1_Encode */

int L2_Encode( uchar        *dst,
               const uchar *name,
               const uchar  pad,
               const uchar  sfx,
               const uchar *scope )
  {
  int lenpos;
  int i;
  int j;

  if( NULL == L1_Encode( &dst[1], name, pad, sfx ) )
    return( -1 );
  dst[0] = 0x20;
  lenpos = 33;
```

```
  if( '\0' != *scope )
    {
    do
      {
      for( i = 0, j = (lenpos + 1);
           ('.' != scope[i]) && ('\0' != scope[i]);
           i++, j++)
        dst[j] = toupper( scope[i] );

      dst[lenpos] = (uchar)i;
      lenpos      += i + 1;
      scope       += i;
      } while( '.' == *(scope++) );
    dst[lenpos] = '\0';
    }

  return( lenpos + 1 );
  } /* L2_Encode */

void Send_Nbtn_Bcast( uchar *msg, int msglen )
  {
  int              s;
  int              true = 1;
  struct sockaddr_in sox;

  s = socket( PF_INET, SOCK_DGRAM, IPPROTO_UDP );
  if( s < 0 )
    {
    perror( "Socket()" );
    exit( 0 );
    }

  if( setsockopt( s, SOL_SOCKET, SO_BROADCAST,
                  &true, sizeof(int) ) < 0 )
    {
    perror( "Setsockopt()" );
    exit( 0 );
    }

  if( 0 == inet_aton( NBT_BCAST_ADDR, &(sox.sin_addr) ) )
    {
    printf( "Invalid IP address.\n" );
    exit( 0 );
    }
  sox.sin_family = AF_INET;
  sox.sin_port   = htons( 137 );
```

```
    if( sendto( s,
                (void *)msg,
                msglen,
                0,
                (struct sockaddr *)&sox,
                sizeof(struct sockaddr_in) ) < 0 )
      {
      perror( "Sendto()" );
      exit( 0 );
      }

    close( s );
    } /* Send_Nbtn_Bcast */

int main( int argc, char *argv[] )
  {
  uchar  bufr[512];
  int    len;
  int    total_len;
  uchar *name;
  uchar *scope;

  if( argc > 1 )
    name = (uchar *)argv[1];
  else
    exit( EXIT_FAILURE );

  if( argc > 2 )
    scope = (uchar *)argv[2];
  else
    scope = "";

  (void)memcpy( bufr, header, (total_len = sizeof(header)) );

  len = L2_Encode( &bufr[total_len], name, ' ', '\0', scope );
  if( len < 0 )
    return( EXIT_FAILURE );
  total_len += len;

  (void)memcpy( &bufr[total_len], query_tail, sizeof( query_tail ));
  total_len += sizeof( query_tail );

  Send_Nbtn_Bcast( bufr, total_len );

  return( EXIT_SUCCESS );
  } /* main */
```

The updated `L1_Encode()` function takes two new parameters: `pad` and `sfx`. These allow us to specify the padding character and the suffix, respectively. The `L2_Encode()` function also takes these additional parameters, so that it can pass them along to `L1_Encode()`, and both functions make use of `toupper()` to ensure that the NetBIOS name and Scope ID are in upper case.

The function `Send_Nbtn_Bcast()` does the job of transmitting a block of data via UDP. The destination is port UDP/137 at the universal broadcast address. The program mainline simply strings together the various pieces of the NBT query, taking the NetBIOS name and Scope ID from the command line.

Compile the code and give the executable the name `namequery`. The program takes one or two arguments. The first is the NetBIOS name, and the second is the Scope ID (the Scope ID is optional). For example, on a Unix system the command line (including the $ prompt) might be:

```
$ namequery neko cat.org
```

Start your sniffer with the filter set to capture only packets sent to/from UDP port 137. If you are using TCPDump or Ethereal, the filter string is: `udp port 137`. Depending on your OS, you may need to have Root or Administrator privileges in order to run the sniffer.

Run `namequery` with the input shown above, and then stop the capture. You should get something like this:

```
+ Frame 1 (100 on wire, 100 captured)
+ Ethernet II
+ Internet Protocol
+ User Datagram Protocol
- NetBIOS Name Service
     Transaction ID: 0x07ac
   + Flags: 0x0110 (Name query)
     Questions: 1
     Answer RRs: 0
     Authority RRs: 0
     Additional RRs: 0
   - Queries
     + NEKO            <00>.CAT.ORG: type NB, class inet
```

This example is copied from Ethereal output.

Compare the parsed output provided by the sniffer against the hard-coded information in the program. They should match up. Next, try a query using a name on your own network and take a look at the response. If you use the name of a Workgroup or NT Domain, you may get responses from several systems.

Another way to get multiple replies is to use a wildcard query. If all NBT nodes on your local LAN use the same Scope ID, and if they are not P nodes, then they will all respond to the wildcard name. To try this, you must first change the call to `L2_Encode()` within `main()` so that it passes `'\0'` as the padding character. That is:

```
total_len += L2_Encode( &bufr[total_len], name, '\0', '\0', scope );
```

Then recompile and give the asterisk as the NetBIOS name:

```
$ namequery "*"
```

Try using other tools such as `nbtstat` in Windows or Samba's `nmblookup` to generate queries, and spend a bit of time looking at the results of these captures. You can also simply let the sniffer run for a while. If your network is active you will see all sorts of NetBIOS packets fly by (particularly if you are on a shared rather than a switched LAN).

3.2   Interlude

We now have method, madness, and a vague sense of the direction. We are ready to head out on the open code. Let us first take a moment to meditate on what we have covered so far. Start by considering this mental image...

Imagine a cold, rainy autumn day. Still thinking of summer, you have forgotten to wear a jacket. The chill of the rain runs through your entire body as you hurry along the street. You try to keep your neck dry by pulling up your thin sweater and hunching your shoulders. Down the road you spot a café. It looks warm and bright inside. You quicken your pace, then dash through the door as the drizzly rain becomes more enthusiastic and thunder rumbles in the distance.

The shop is cozy, but not too small. There are potted plants scattered about. Light jazz plays over well-hidden speakers. The clientele are trendy urban business types having quiet, serious discussions in pairs at small tables. Paintings by a local artist hang on the walls.

You step up to the counter. A young woman with a dozen earrings and short-cut hair smiles and asks you what you would like. A nice, hot cup of tea.

She reaches down behind the counter and grabs a large white mug. Then she opens a box and pulls out a tea bag that is at least three years old, drops it into the mug, and pours in hot water from the sink. "Three dollars" she says, still smiling.

If you are a coffee drinker, you probably don't understand. Replace *"opens a box and pulls out a tea bag"* with *"opens a jar and scoops out one spoonful of freeze-dried instant"* and you will get the point. The point is that details matter. Certainly, an old tea bag in warm water will make a cup of tea... but not one worth drinking.[8]

Just so, our examples provide some working code but are far from satisfying. If we are going to write something truly enjoyable we need to dig into the details.

Let's get to it.

---

8. With a few notable exceptions, this is the way tea is prepared in American cafés. Ick.

4

The Name Service
in Detail

This is gonna hurt me
more than it does you.

— Common lie

Think of the Name Service as a database system. The data may be stored in
an NBNS server (P mode), distributed across all of the participating nodes in
an IP subnet (B mode), or a combination of the two (M or H mode).

Name Service messages are the transactions that maintain and utilize the
NBT name-to-IP-address mapping database. These transactions fall into three
basic categories:

Name Registration/Refresh

The process by which an application adds and maintains a NetBIOS name
to IP address mapping within an NBT scope.

Name Query

The process of resolving a NetBIOS name to an IP address.

Name Release

The process by which a NetBIOS name to IP address mapping is removed
from within an NBT scope.

These three represent the lifecycle of an NBT name.

The RFCs also specify support for the NetBIOS API **Adapter Status
Query** function. Implementation of the Adapter Status Query is quite similar

to that of the Name Query, so it gets lumped in with the Name Service. This is fairly reasonable, since the query packets are almost identical and the most important result of the status query is a list of names owned by the target node.

4.1   NBT Names: Once More with Feeling

Let's review what we've learned so far:

- Though the RFCs do not say so, NetBIOS names should be converted to upper case *before* they are encoded. The practice probably goes back to early IBM implementations. Converting NetBIOS names to upper case allows for comparison of the encoded string, rather than requiring that NBT names be decoded and compared using a case-insensitive function. Some existing implementations use this shortcut, and will not recognize names with encoded lower-case characters.

- The RFCs list NetBIOS names as being 16 bytes in length. It is common practice, however, to implement NetBIOS names as two subfields: a 15-byte name and a one-byte suffix. (That's what Microsoft does so every-one else has to do it too.) The suffix byte actually winds up being quite useful. The suffix byte is read as an integer in the range 0..255, so it is *not* converted to upper-case.

- If the NetBIOS name is less than 15 bytes, it must be padded. The space character ($0x20$) is the designated padding character (though there are some rare, special-case exceptions).

- Other than length and padding, the only restriction the RFCs place on the syntax of a NetBIOS name is that it may not begin with an asterisk ('*').

4.1.1   *Valid NetBIOS Name Characters*

Any octet value can be encoded using the first-level mechanism. In theory, then, any eight-bit value can be part of a NetBIOS name. Keep this in mind and be prepared. There are some very strange names in use in the wild.

In practice, implementations do place some restrictions on the characters that may be used in NetBIOS names. These restrictions are implemented at the application layer, and should be considered artificial. Under Windows 9x, for example, the "Network Identity" control panel allows only the following characters in a machine name:

Valid Windows 9x machine name characters

`' '`	`==`	`0x20`	`'-'`	`==`	`0x2D`
`'!'`	`==`	`0x21`	`'.'`	`==`	`0x2E`
`'#'`	`==`	`0x23`	`'@'`	`==`	`0x40`
`'$'`	`==`	`0x24`	`'^'`	`==`	`0x5E`
`'%'`	`==`	`0x25`	`'_'`	`==`	`0x5F`
`'&'`	`==`	`0x26`	`'{'`	`==`	`0x7B`
`'\''`	`==`	`0x27` (single quote)	`'}'`	`==`	`0x7D`
`'('`	`==`	`0x28`	`'~'`	`==`	`0x7E`
`')'`	`==`	`0x29`	alphanumeric characters		

Yet the same Windows 9x system may also register the special-purpose name "`\x01\x02__MSBROWSE__\x02\x01`", which contains control characters as shown.

Note that the set of alphanumeric characters may include extended characters, such as 'Å' or 'Ü'. Unfortunately, these are often represented by different octet values under different operating systems, or even under different configurations of the same operating system.

Some examples:

Character	ISO Latin-I	DOS Code Page 437
'Ä'	0xC4	0x8E
'Ç'	0xC7	0x80
'É'	0xC9	0x90
'Î'	0xCE	—
'Ö'	0xD6	0x99
'Ñ'	0xD1	0xA5
'Ù'	0xD9	—

As you can see, the mapping between character sets can be a bit of a challenge — particularly since there is no standard character set for use in NBT and no mechanism for negotiating a common character set.[1]

One more thing to consider when dealing with NetBIOS name characters: Windows NT will generate a warning — and W2K an error — if the Machine Name is not also a valid DNS name. You may need to do some testing to determine which characters Windows considers valid DNS label characters.

4.1.2   *NetBIOS Names within Scope*

Under NBT, NetBIOS names exist within a *scope*. The scope is the set of all machines which can "see" the name. For B nodes, the scope is limited to the IP broadcast domain. For P nodes, the scope is limited to the set of nodes that share the same NBNS. For M and H nodes, the scope is the union of the broadcast domain and the shared NBNS.

Scope can be further refined using a *Scope ID*. The Scope ID effectively sub-divides a virtual NetBIOS LAN into separate, named vLANs. Unfortunately, few (if any) implementations actually support multiple Scope IDs so this feature is of limited practical use.

The syntax of the Scope ID matches the best-practices recommendations for DNS domain names. (Some Windows flavors allow almost any character value in a Scope ID string. Sigh.) Scope IDs should be converted to upper case before use on the wire.

 Annoyance Alert

In versions of Windows 95 and '98 that we tested, the Scope ID field in the network setup control panel is greyed out if no WINS server IP address is specified. That is, you cannot enter a Scope ID if your machine is running in B mode.

You can work around this by entering the Scope ID in the right place in the registry, or by entering a (bogus) WINS server IP, entering the Scope ID, saving your changes, rebooting, reopening the network control panel, removing the WINS IP entry, saving your changes, and rebooting again.

---

1. To further complicate matters Microsoft has registered its own character sets, such as the Windows-1252 character set. Windows-1252 is a superset of ISO Latin-1. It uses octets in the range $0x80..0x9F$ (normally reserved for control characters) to represent some additional display characters, such as the trademark symbol (™). This is why non-Microsoft web browsers on non-Microsoft platforms often display question marks all over the screen when they load web pages generated by Microsoft products.

The system does not seem to clear the Scope ID once it has been entered. To clear the Scope ID you must either edit the registry, or enter a (bogus) WINS server IP, clear out the Scope ID in the control panel, save your changes, reboot, reopen the network control panel, remove the WINS IP entry, save your changes, and reboot.

Windows NT behaves correctly, and does allow the entry of a Scope ID in B mode.

4.1.3 *Encoding and Decoding NBT Names*

First Level Encoding converts a 16-byte NetBIOS name into a 32-byte encoded name, and then combines it with the Scope ID. For example:

```
"EOGFGLGPCACACACACACACACACACACAAA.CAT.ORG"
```

We have chosen to call this format the *NBT Name*. Second Level Encoding is applied to the NBT name to create the on-the-wire format, which we will refer to as the *Encoded NBT Name*:

```
"\x20EOGFGLGPCACACACACACACACACACACAAA\x03CAT\x03ORG\0"
```

As previously described, the maximum length of a label in an NBT name is 63 bytes. This is because the label length field is divided into two sub-fields, the first of which is a two-bit flag field with four possible values:

00 == 0: Label Length
01 == 1: Reserved (unused)
10 == 2: Reserved (unused)
11 == 3: Label String Pointer

With both bits clear (zero), the next 6 bits are the label LENGTH. The LENGTH field is an unsigned integer with a value in the range 0..63.

0	1	2	3	4	5	6	7
0	0	LENGTH					

If both flag bits are set, however, then the next *fourteen* bits are a "Label String Pointer"; the offset at which the real label can be found.

0	1	2	3	4	5	6	7	8	9	10	11	12	13	14	15
1	1	LABEL STRING POINTER													

Label String Pointers are used to reduce the size of Name Service messages that might otherwise contain two copies of the same NBT name. For example, a NAME REGISTRATION REQUEST message includes both a QUESTION_RECORD and an ADDITIONAL_RECORD, each of which would otherwise contain the same NBT name. Instead of duplicating the name, however, the ADDITIONAL_RECORD.RR_NAME field contains a label string pointer to the QUESTION_RECORD.QUESTION_NAME field.

Label String Pointers are a prime example of the NBT theory/practice dichotomy, and another throwback to the DNS system. As it turns out, the only Label String Pointer value ever used in NBT is 0xC00C. The reason for this is quite simple. The NBT header is a fixed size (12 bytes), and is always followed by a block that starts with an encoded NBT Name. Thus, the offset of the first name in the packet is always 12 (0x0C). Any further name field in the packet will point back to the first.

So, the rule of thumb is that the encoded NBT name will always be found at byte offset 0x000C. As a shortcut, some implementations work directly with the encoded name and only bother to decode the name when interacting with a user. Decoding, however, is fairly straightforward:

Listing 4.1: Level 2 and Level 1 decoding

```
int L2_Decode( uchar *dst,     /* Decoded name target buffer.  */
               uchar *src,     /* Encoded name source buffer.  */
               int    srcpos,  /* Start position of name.      */
               int    srcmax ) /* Size of source buffer.       */
  {
  int len;
  int pos;
  int next;

  /* Be safe. */
  dst[0] = '\0';

  /* Get encoded string length (doesn't include root label). */
  len = strlen( (char *)&(src[srcpos]) );

  /* If length is zero, return the empty string. */
  if( 0 == len )
    return( 0 );
```

```
  /* Make sure name does not exceed source buffer length. */
  if( len >= (srcmax - srcpos) )
    return( -1 );

  /* Copy source to destination skipping the first label length byte
   * (but including the terminating nul label length).
   */
  (void)memcpy( dst, &(src[srcpos+1]), len );

  /* Now find remaining label length bytes
   * and convert them to dots.
   */
  for( pos = src[srcpos];              /* Read the first label length. */
       '\0' != (next = dst[pos]);  /* While label length is > 0... */
       pos += next + 1 )             /* Move one byte beyond label.  */
    {
    dst[pos] = '.';
    }

  return( --len );  /* Return string length. */
  } /* L2_Decode */

int L1_Decode( uchar *name,     /* Target.  Minimum 16 bytes. */
               uchar *src,      /* Message buffer.            */
               int    srcpos,   /* Start position of name.    */
               int    srcmax ) /* Size of source buffer.      */
  {
  int    i;
  int    suffix;
  uchar *p = &src[srcpos];

  /* Make sure we have 32 bytes worth of message to read.    */
  if( (srcmax - srcpos) < 32 )
    {
    name[0] = '\0';
    return( -1 );
    }

  /* Convert each source pair to their original octet value. */
  for( i = 0; i < 32; i++ )
    name[i/2] = ( (( (int)(p[i]) - 'A' ) << 4)
                + ( (int)(p[++i]) - 'A' ) );
```

```
      /* Copy out suffix byte and replace with nul terminator.  */
      suffix = name[15];
      name[15] = '\0';

      /* Trim off trailing spaces, if any. */
      for( i = 14; (i >= 0) && (' ' == name[i]); i-- )
        name[i] = '\0';

      return( suffix );    /* Return the suffix value as an int.  */
    } /* L1_Decode */
```

The `L2_Decode()` function copies the encoded NBT name to the destination buffer, skipping the first label length byte and replacing internal label length bytes with the dot character. That is, given the input string:

`"\x20EOGFGLGPCACACACACACACACACACACAAA\x03CAT\x03ORG\0"`

it will produce the string:

`"EOGFGLGPCACACACACACACACACACACAAA.CAT.ORG"`

The `L1_Decode()` function decodes the First Level Encoded NetBIOS name, and hands back the suffix byte as its return value.

4.2   NBT Name Service Packets

RFC 1002 lists 17 different Name Service packet types, constructed from three basic building blocks:

- header,
- query records, and
- resource records.

These pieces are described in more detail below.

4.2.1   *Name Service Headers*

The header is an array of six 16-bit values, as follows:

0	1	2	3	4	5	6	7	8	9	10	11	12	13	14	15
NAME_TRN_ID															
FLAGS															
QDCOUNT															
ANCOUNT															
NSCOUNT															
ARCOUNT															

Managing Name Service headers is fairly straightforward. With the exception of the FLAGS field, all of the fields are simple unsigned integers. The entire thing can be represented in memory as an array of unsigned short int, or whatever is appropriate in your programming language of choice.

The FLAGS field is further broken down thus:

0	1	2	3	4	5	6	7	8	9	10	11	12	13	14	15
R	OPCODE				NM_FLAGS							RCODE			

Handling the bits in the FLAGS field is fairly trivial for any seasoned programmer. One simple solution is to shift the values given in RFC 1002, Section 4.2.1.1 into their absolute positions. For example, an OPCODE value of 0x7 (WACK) would be left-shifted 11 bits to align it properly in the OPCODE subfield:

(0x0007 << 11) = 0x3800 = 0011100000000000(bin)

...which puts it where it's supposed to be:

0	1	2	3	4	5	6	7	8	9	10	11	12	13	14	15
R	OPCODE				NM_FLAGS							RCODE			
0	0	1	1	1	0	0	0	0	0	0	0	0	0	0	0

Listing 4.2 presents NS_Header.h, a header file that will be referenced as we move forward. It provides a set of re-aligned FLAGS subfield values plus a few extra constants. These values will be covered below, when we explain how to use each of the Name Service message types.

Listing 4.2: Name Service packet header `FLAGS` subfield values: `NS_Header.h`

```
#define NBTNS_R_BIT         0x8000  /* The 'R'esponse bit   */

/* OPCODE values */
#define OPCODE_QUERY        0x0000  /* Query         (0<<11) */
#define OPCODE_REGISTER     0x2800  /* Registration  (5<<11) */
#define OPCODE_RELEASE      0x3000  /* Release       (6<<11) */
#define OPCODE_WACK         0x3800  /* WACK          (7<<11) */
#define OPCODE_REFRESH      0x4000  /* Refresh       (8<<11) */
#define OPCODE_ALTREFRESH   0x4800  /* Alt Refresh   (9<<11) */
#define OPCODE_MULTIHOMED   0x7800  /* Multi-homed   (f<<11) */
#define OPCODE_MASK         0x7800  /* Mask                 */

/* NM_FLAGS subfield bits */
#define NM_AA_BIT           0x0400  /* Authoritative Answer */
#define NM_TR_BIT           0x0200  /* TRuncation flag      */
#define NM_RD_BIT           0x0100  /* Recursion Desired    */
#define NM_RA_BIT           0x0080  /* Recursion Available  */
#define NM_B_BIT            0x0010  /* Broadcast flag       */

/* Return Codes */
#define RCODE_POS_RSP       0x0000  /* Positive Response    */
#define RCODE_FMT_ERR       0x0001  /* Format Error         */
#define RCODE_SRV_ERR       0x0002  /* Server failure       */
#define RCODE_NAM_ERR       0x0003  /* Name Not Found       */
#define RCODE_IMP_ERR       0x0004  /* Unsupported request  */
#define RCODE_RFS_ERR       0x0005  /* Refused              */
#define RCODE_ACT_ERR       0x0006  /* Active error         */
#define RCODE_CFT_ERR       0x0007  /* Name in conflict     */
#define RCODE_MASK          0x0007  /* Mask                 */

/* Used to set the record count fields. */
#define QUERYREC            0x1000  /* Query Record         */
#define ANSREC              0x0100  /* Answer Record        */
#define NSREC               0x0010  /* NS Rec (never used)  */
#define ADDREC              0x0001  /* Additional Record    */
```

The `NAME_TRN_ID` field is the transaction ID, which should probably be handled by the bit of code that sends and receives the NBT messages. Many implementations use a simple counter to generate new transaction IDs (Samba uses a random number generator), but these should always be checked to ensure that they are not, by chance, the same as the transaction ID of a conversation initiated by some other node. Better yet, the originating node's IP address should be used as an additional key for segregating transactions.

The four COUNT fields indicate the number of Question and Resource Records which follow. In theory, each of these fields can contain a value in the range 0..65535. In practice, however, the count fields will contain either 0 or 1 as shown in the record layouts in RFC 1002, Section 4.2. It appears as though some implementations either ignore these fields or read them as simple booleans.

One final consideration is the byte order of NBT messages. True to its DNS roots, NBT uses network byte order (big-endian). Some microprocessors — including Alpha, MIPS, and Intel i386 family — use or can use little-endian byte order.[2] If your target system is little-endian, or if you want your code to be portable, you will need to ensure that your integers are properly converted to and from network byte order. Many systems provide the htonl(), htons(), ntohl(), and ntohs() functions for exactly this purpose.

Bizarre Twist Alert

The SMB protocol was originally built to run on DOS. DOS was originally built to run on Intel chips, so SMB is little-endian... the opposite of the NBT transport!

This next bit of code is nbt_nsHeader.c. It shows how to create and parse NBT Name Service headers. As with all of the code presented in this book, it is designed to be illustrative, not efficient. (We know you can do better.)

Listing 4.3: Read and write Name Service headers: NS_Header.c

```
#include <netinet/in.h>      /* htons(), ntohs(), etc. */

#include "NS_Header.h"      /* From Listing 4.2.      */

void Put_NS_TID( ushort hdr[], ushort TrnID )
  /* --------------------------------------------------- **
   * Store the transaction ID in the Name Service header.
   * --------------------------------------------------- **
   */
  {
  hdr[0] = htons( TrnID );
  } /* Put_NS_TID */
```

---

2. Big-endian byte order is also known as "normal," "intuitive," or "obvious" byte order. Little-endian is sometimes referred to as "annoying," "dysfunctional," or "stupid." These designations do not, of course, reflect any bias or preference.

```
void Put_NS_Hdr_Flags( ushort hdr[], ushort flags )
  /* ---------------------------------------------------- **
   * Store the flags in the NBT Name Service header.
   * ---------------------------------------------------- **
   */
  {
  hdr[1] = htons( flags );
  } /* Put_NS_Hdr_Flags */

void Put_NS_Hdr_Rec_Counts( ushort hdr[], int reccount )
  /* ---------------------------------------------------- **
   * Place (ushort)1 into each record count field for
   * which the matching flag bit is set in reccount.
   * ---------------------------------------------------- **
   */
  {
  ushort one;

  one = htons( 1 );

  hdr[2] = ( QUERYREC & reccount ) ? one : 0;
  hdr[3] = ( ANSREC   & reccount ) ? one : 0;
  hdr[4] = ( NSREC    & reccount ) ? one : 0;
  hdr[5] = ( ADDREC   & reccount ) ? one : 0;
  } /* Put_NS_Hdr_Rec_Counts */

ushort Get_NS_Hdr_TID( ushort hdr[] )
  /* ---------------------------------------------------- **
   * Read and return the transaction ID.
   * ---------------------------------------------------- **
   */
  {
  return( ntohs( hdr[0] ) );
  } /* Get_NS_Hdr_TID */

ushort Get_NS_Hdr_Flags( ushort hdr[] )
  /* ---------------------------------------------------- **
   * Read and return the flags field.
   * ---------------------------------------------------- **
   */
  {
  return( ntohs( hdr[1] ) );
  } /* Get_NS_Hdr_Flags */
```

```
int Get_NS_Hdr_Rec_Counts( ushort hdr[] )
  /* --------------------------------------------------- **
   * Convert the four record count fields into a single
   * flagset.
   * --------------------------------------------------- **
   */
  {
  int tmp = 0;

  if( hdr[2] )
    tmp |= QUERYREC;

  if( hdr[3] )
    tmp |= ANSREC;
  if( hdr[4] )
    tmp |= NSREC;
  if( hdr[5] )
    tmp |= ADDREC;

  return( tmp );
  } /* Get_NS_Hdr_Rec_Counts */
```

4.2.2   *Name Service Question Records*

The question record is also simple. It consists of an encoded NBT name (in the QUESTION_NAME field) followed by two unsigned 16-bit integer fields: the QUESTION_TYPE and QUESTION_CLASS.

The length of an encoded NBT name is at least 34 bytes, but it will be longer if a Scope ID is used, so the QUESTION_NAME field has no fixed length. There is also no padding done to align the integer fields. The QUESTION_TYPE and QUESTION_CLASS follow immediately after the QUESTION_NAME.

>= 34 bytes	2 bytes	2 bytes
QUESTION_NAME ...	QUESTION_TYPE	QUESTION_CLASS

There are only two valid values for the QUESTION_TYPE field. These are:

NB == 0x0020 indicates a standard Name Query,
NBSTAT == 0x0021 indicates a Node Status Query.

The QUESTION_CLASS field always has a value of:

IN == 0x0001 indicates the "Internet Class."

Go back and take a look at the broadcast name query example presented earlier. In that example, we hard-coded both the NBT Name Service header and the tail-end of the question record. Now that you have a clearer understanding of the fields involved, you should be able to design much more flexible code. Here's a start:

Listing 4.4a: Reading/writing question records: NS_Qrec.h

```
/* Query Type */
#define QTYPE_NB      0x0020  /* Name Query    */
#define QTYPE_NBSTAT  0x0021  /* Adapter Status */

/* Query Class */
#define QCLASS_IN     0x0001  /* Internet Class */
```

Listing 4.4b: Reading/writing question records: NS_Qrec.c

```
#include <string.h>     /* For memcpy() */
#include <netinet/in.h> /* htons(), ntohs(), etc. */

#include "NS_Qrec.h"

int Put_Qrec( uchar       *dst,
              const uchar *name,
              const uchar  pad,
              const uchar  sfx,
              const uchar *scope,
              const ushort qtype )
  /* ---------------------------------------------------- **
   * Store the fully encoded NBT name in the destination
   * buffer.  Also write the QUERY_TYPE and QUERY_CLASS
   * values.
   * ---------------------------------------------------- **
   */
  {
  int    len;
  ushort tmp;
  ushort qclass_in;

  qclass_in = htons( QCLASS_IN );
```

```
  /* Validate the qtype. */
  if( (QTYPE_NB != qtype)
   && (QTYPE_NBSTAT != qtype ) )
    return( -1 );

  len = L2_Encode( dst, name, pad, sfx, scope );
  if( len < 0 )
    return( len );

  tmp = htons( qtype );
  (void)memcpy( &(dst[len]), &tmp, 2 );
  len += 2;

  (void)memcpy( &(dst[len]), &qclass_in, 2 );
  return( len + 2 );
  } /* Put_Qrec */

ushort Get_Qtype( const uchar *qrec, int offset )
  /* ------------------------------------------------- **
   * Read the QUERY_TYPE field from a query record.
   * Note that the offset parameter can be derived using
   * L2_Decode() function in Listing 4.1.  Either that,
   * or use 1+strlen( qrec ).
   * ------------------------------------------------- **
   */
  {
  ushort tmp;

  /* Read the two bytes from the packet.
   */
  tmp  = (ushort)(qrec[offset]) * 256;
  tmp |= qrec[1+offset];

  /* Convert to host byte order and return. */
  return( ntohs( tmp ) );
  } /* Get_Qtype */
```

4.2.3 *Name Service Resource Records*

For convenience, we will break the Resource Record into three sub-parts:

- the Name section,
- the TTL field, and
- the Resource Data section.

The Name section has the same structure as a Query Entry record, except that the RR_NAME field may contain a 16-bit Label String Pointer instead of a complete NBT name.

2 bytes or >= 34 bytes	2 bytes	2 bytes
RR_NAME ...	RR_TYPE	RR_CLASS

The RR_TYPE field is used to indicate the type of the resource record, which has an effect on the structure of the resource data section. The available values for this field are:

```
     A == 0x0001 (not used in practice)
    NS == 0x0002 (not used in practice)
  NULL == 0x000A (not used in practice)
    NB == 0x0020
NBSTAT == 0x0021
```

The values marked as "not used in practice" are described in the RFCs, and indicated as valid values, but are never really used in modern implementations. The value of RR_TYPE will be NB except in a NODE STATUS REPLY, in which case NBSTAT is used.

As with the question record, the RR_CLASS field always has a value of:

```
IN == 0x0001
```

The TTL field follows the name section. It indicates the "Time To Live" value associated with a resource record. Each NBT name-to-IP-address mapping in the NBNS database has a TTL value. This allows records to "fade out" if they are not renewed or properly released. The TTL field is an unsigned long integer, measured in seconds. A value of zero indicates infinite TTL.

0	1	2	3	4	5	6	7	8	9	1 0	1 1	1 2	1 3	1 4	1 5	1 6	1 7	1 8	1 9	2 0	2 1	2 2	2 3	2 4	2 5	2 6	2 7	2 8	2 9	3 0	3 1
TTL																															

The last sub-part of the resource record is the resource data section, which is made up of two fields:

2 bytes	RDLENGTH bytes
RDLENGTH	RDATA ...

The RDLENGTH field is an unsigned 16-bit integer value indicating the length, in bytes, of the RDATA field. The structure of the contents of the RDATA field will vary from one message type to another.

The Resource Record structure, as described in Section 4.2.1.3 of RFC 1002, looks just like this:

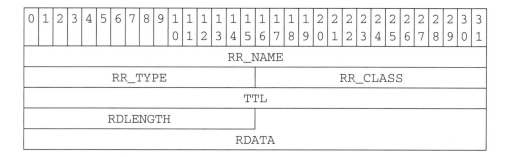

It is always good to have some code to play with. This next set of functions can be used to manipulate Resource Records.

Listing 4.5a: Name Service Resource Records: NS_Rrec.h

```
/* Label String Pointer. */
#define LSP          0xC00C  /* Pointer to offset 12 */

/* Resource Record Type. */
#define RRTYPE_A      0x0001  /* IP Addr RR (unused)   */
#define RRTYPE_NS     0x0002  /* Name Server (unused)  */
#define RRTYPE_NULL   0x000A  /* NULL RR (unused)      */
#define RRTYPE_NB     0x0020  /* NetBIOS               */
#define RRTYPE_NBSTAT 0x0021  /* NB Status Response    */

/* Resource Record Class. */
#define RRCLASS_IN    0x0001  /* Internet Class        */
```

Listing 4.5b: Name Service Resource Records: `NS_Rrec.c`

```c
#include <string.h>       /* For memcpy() */
#include <netinet/in.h> /* htons(), ntohs(), etc. */

#include "NS_Rrec.h"

int Put_RRec_Name( uchar        *rrec,
                   const uchar *name,
                   const uchar  pad,
                   const uchar  sfx,
                   const uchar *scope,
                   const ushort rrtype )

  /* -------------------------------------------------- **
   * Create and store the fully qualified NBT name in the
   * destination buffer.  Also store the RR_TYPE and
   * RR_CLASS values.
   * Return the number of bytes written.
   * -------------------------------------------------- **
   */
  {
  int    len;
  ushort tmp;
  ushort rrclass_in;

  /* Validate the rrtype.
   * Note that we exclude the A, NS, and NULL RRTYPEs
   * as these are never used.
   */
  if( (RRTYPE_NB != rrtype)
   && (RRTYPE_NBSTAT != rrtype ) )
    return( -1 );

  len = L2_Encode( rrec, name, pad, sfx, scope );
  if( len < 0 )
    return( len );

  tmp = htons( rrtype );
  (void)memcpy( &(rrec[len]), &tmp, 2 );
  len += 2;

  rrclass_in = htons( RRCLASS_IN );
  (void)memcpy( &(rrec[len]), &rrclass_in, 2 );
  return( len + 2 );
  } /* Put_RRec_Name */
```

```
int Put_RRec_LSP( uchar *rrec, const ushort rrtype )
  /* ---------------------------------------------------- **
   * Write a Label String Pointer (LSP) instead of an NBT
   * name.  RR_TYPE and RR_CLASS are also written.
   * Return the number of bytes written (always 6).
   * ---------------------------------------------------- **
   */
  {
  ushort tmp;
  ushort lsp;
  ushort rrclass_in;

  lsp = htons( 0xC00C );
  (void)memcpy( rrec, &lsp, 2 );

  tmp = htons( rrtype );
  (void)memcpy( &(rrec[2]), &tmp, 2 );

  rrclass_in = htons( RRCLASS_IN );
  (void)memcpy( &(rrec[4]), &rrclass_in, 2 );
  return( 6 );
  } /* Put_RRec_LSP */

int Put_RRec_TTL( uchar *rrec, int offset, ulong ttl )
  /* ---------------------------------------------------- **
   * Write the TTL value at rrec[offset].
   * By this point it should be obvious that functions or
   * macros for transferring long and short integers to
   * and from packet buffers would be a good idea.
   * ---------------------------------------------------- **
   */
  {
  ttl = htonl( ttl );

  (void)memcpy( &(rrec[offset]), &ttl, 4 );
  return( 4 );
  } /* Put_RRec_TTL */

int Is_RRec_LSP( const uchar *rrec )
  /* ---------------------------------------------------- **
   * Check the Resource Record to see if the name field
   * is actually a Label String Pointer.
   *
   * If the name is not an LSP, the function returns 0.
   * If the name is a valid LSP, the function returns 12
   * (which is the offset into the received packet at
   * which the QUERY_NAME can be found).
```

```
 * If the name contains an invalid label length, or
 * an invalid LSP, the function will return -1.
 * ---------------------------------------------------- **
 */
  {
  if( 0 == (0xC0 & rrec[0]) )
    return( 0 );   /* Not an LSP */

  if( (0xC0 == rrec[0]) && (0x0C == rrec[1]) )
    return( 12 ); /* Valid LSP */

  return( -1 );    /* Bogon */
  } /* Is_RRec_LSP */

ushort Get_RR_type( const uchar *rrec, int offset )
  /* ---------------------------------------------------- **
   * Read the RR_TYPE value.  The offset can be
   * determined by decoding the NBT name using the
   * L2_Decode() function from Listing 4.1.
   * ---------------------------------------------------- **
   */
  {
  ushort tmp;

  /* Read the two bytes from the packet.
   */
  (void)memcpy( &tmp, &(rrec[offset]), 2 );

  /* Convert to host byte order and return. */
  return( ntohs( tmp ) );
  } /* Get_RR_type */

ulong Get_RRec_TTL( const uchar *rrec, int offset )
  /* ---------------------------------------------------- **
   * Read the TTL value.
   * ---------------------------------------------------- **
   */
  {
  ulong tmp;

  (void)memcpy( &tmp, &(rrec[offset]), 4 );
  return( ntohl( tmp ) );
  } /* Get_RRec_TTL */
```

4.3   Conversations with the Name Service

We will now introduce a simple syntax for describing how to fill network packets. This syntax is neither standard nor rigorous, just something the author whipped up to help explain what goes into a message. If it looks like someone else's syntax (one which perhaps took long hours of study, concentration, and thought to develop) then apologies are probably in order.

Disclaimer Alert

Any resemblance to an actual syntax, living or dead, real or imaginary, is entirely coincidental.

A broadcast name query, described using our little syntax, would look like this:

```
NAME QUERY REQUEST (Broadcast)
  {
  HEADER
    {
    NAME_TRN_ID = <Set when packet is transmitted>
    FLAGS
      {
      OPCODE = 0x0
      RD     = TRUE
      B      = TRUE
      }
    QDCOUNT = 1
    }
  QUESTION_RECORD
    {
    QUESTION_NAME  = <Encoded NBT Name>
    QUESTION_TYPE  = NB (0x0020)
    QUESTION_CLASS = IN (0x0001)
    }
  }
```

Basically, the rules are these:

- If a record (a header, question record, or resource record) is not specified, it is not included in the packet. In the example above there are no resource records specified. We know from the example code that there are no resource records in a NAME QUERY REQUEST.

- If a field is not specified, it is zeroed. In the example above the RCODE field of the FLAGS sub-record has a value of 0x0, and the NSCOUNT field (among others) also has a value of 0.

- Comments in angle brackets are short explanations, describing what should go into the field. More complete explanations, if needed, will be found in the accompanying text.

- Comments in parentheses provide additional information, such as the value of a specified constant.

- ...and yes, each squirrelly bracket gets its own line.

It's not a particularly formal syntax, but it will serve the purpose.

4.3.1 *Name Registration*

Nodes send NAME REGISTRATION REQUEST messages when they wish to claim ownership of a name. The messages may be broadcast on the local LAN (B mode), or sent directly to an NBNS (P mode). (M and H mode are combinations of B and P modes with their own special quirks. We will get to those further on.)

A NAME REGISTRATION REQUEST message looks like this:

```
NAME REGISTRATION REQUEST
  {
  HEADER
    {
    NAME_TRN_ID = <Set when packet is transmitted>
    FLAGS
      {
      OPCODE = 0x5 (Registration)
      RD     = TRUE (1)
      B      = <TRUE for broadcast registration, else FALSE>
      }
    QDCOUNT = 1
    ARCOUNT = 1
    }
  QUESTION_RECORD
    {
    QUESTION_NAME  = <Encoded NBT name to be registered>
    QUESTION_TYPE  = NB (0x0020)
    QUESTION_CLASS = IN (0x0001)
    }
```

```
ADDITIONAL_RECORD
  {
  RR_NAME   = 0xC00C (Label String Pointer to QUESTION_NAME)
  RR_TYPE   = NB (0x0020)
  RR_CLASS  = IN (0x0001)
  TTL       = <Zero for broadcast, about three days for unicast>
  RDLENGTH = 6
  RDATA
    {
    NB_FLAGS
      {
      G   = <TRUE for a group name, FALSE for a unique name>
      ONT = <Owner type>
      }
    NB_ADDRESS = <Requesting node's IP address>
    }
  }
}
```

The NAME REGISTRATION REQUEST includes both a QUES-
TION_RECORD and an ADDITIONAL_RECORD. In a sense, it is two messages
in one. It says "Does anyone own this name?" and "I want to own this name!",
both in the same packet.

The NAME REGISTRATION REQUEST gives us our first look at a Label
String Pointer in its native habitat. In the packet above the QUESTION_NAME
and the RR_NAME are the same name, so the latter field contains a pointer
back to the former. The size of the header is constant; if there is a
QUESTION_NAME in a packet it will always be found at offset 0x000C (12).
The field value is 0xC00C because (as is always the case with Label String
Pointers) the first two bits are set in order to indicate that the remainder is a
pointer rather than a 6-bit label length. So, Label String Pointers in NBT
messages always have the value 0xC00C.

The TTL field in the ADDITIONAL_RECORD provides a Time-To-Live
value, in seconds, for the name. In B mode, the TTL value is not significant
and is generally set to zero. In P mode, the TTL is used by the NBNS to determine when to purge old entries from the database, and is typically set to
something on the order of three days in the NAME REGISTRATION
REQUEST. The NBNS may override the client's request and reply with a different TTL value, which the client must accept.

The ADDITIONAL_RECORD.RDATA field is 6 bytes long (as shown in
ADDITIONAL_RECORD.RDLENGTH) and contains two subfields. The first

is the NB_FLAGS field, which provides information about the name and its
owner. It looks something like this:

0	1	2	3	4	5	6	7	8	9	10	11	12	13	14	15
G	ONT		UNUSED												

The NB_FLAGS.G bit indicates whether the name is a group name or a
unique name, and NB_FLAGS.ONT identifies the owner node type. ONT is a
two-bit field with the following possible values:

00 == B node
01 == P node
10 == M node
11 == H node (added by Microsoft)

The ADDITIONAL_RECORD.RDATA.NB_ADDRESS holds the 4-byte
IPV4 address that will be mapped to the name. This should, of course, match
the address of the node registering the name.

Take a good look at the structure of the RDATA subrecord in the NAME
REGISTRATION REQUEST. This is the most common RDATA format, which
gives us an excuse for writing a little more code...

Listing 4.6a: RDATA Address Records: NS_RDaddr.h

```
/* RDATA NB_FLAGS. */
#define GROUP_BIT      0x8000  /* Group indicator      */
#define ONT_B          0x0000  /* Broadcast node       */
#define ONT_P          0x2000  /* Point-to-point node  */
#define ONT_M          0x4000  /* Mixed mode node      */
#define ONT_H          0x6000  /* MS Hybrid mode node  */
#define ONT_MASK       0x6000  /* Mask                 */

/* RDATA NAME_FLAGS. */
#define DRG            0x0100  /* Deregister.          */
#define CNF            0x0800  /* Conflict.            */
#define ACT            0x0400  /* Active.              */
#define PRM            0x0200  /* Permanent.           */
```

Listing 4.6b: RDATA Address Records: `NS_RDaddr.c`

```c
#include <string.h>     /* For memcpy() */
#include <netinet/in.h> /* htons(), ntohs(), etc. */

#include "NS_RDaddr.h"

int Put_RDLength( uchar *rrec,
                  int    offset,
                  ushort rdlen )
  /* ---------------------------------------------------- **
   * Set the value of the RDLENGTH field.
   * ---------------------------------------------------- **
   */
  {
  rdlen = htons( rdlen );

  (void)memcpy( &(rrec[offset]), &rdlen, 2 );
  return( 2 );
  } /* Put_RDLength */

int Put_RD_Addr( uchar           *rrec,
                 int              offset,
                 ushort           nb_flags,
                 struct in_addr nb_addr )
  /* ---------------------------------------------------- **
   * Write IP NB_FLAGS and NB_ADDRESS fields to the
   * packet buffer.
   *
   * See inet(3) on any Linux/Unix/BSD system for more
   * information on 'struct in_addr'.
   * ---------------------------------------------------- **
   */
  {
  nb_flags = htons( nb_flags );
  (void)memcpy( &(rrec[offset]), &nb_flags, 2 );
  (void)memcpy( &(rrec[offset+2]), &nb_addr.s_addr, 4 );
  return( 6 );
  } /* Put_RD_Addr */

ushort Get_RDLength( const uchar *rrec, int offset )
  /* ---------------------------------------------------- **
   * Read the RDLENGTH field to find out how big the
   * RDATA field is.
   * ---------------------------------------------------- **
   */
```

```
    {
    ushort tmp;

    (void)memcpy( &tmp, &(rrec[offset]), 2 );
    return( ntohs( tmp ) );
    } /* Get_RDLength */

ushort Get_RD_NB_Flags( const uchar *rrec, int offset )
    /* ---------------------------------------------------- **
     * Read the NB_FLAGS field from an RDATA record.
     * ---------------------------------------------------- **
     */
    {
    ushort tmp;

    (void)memcpy( &tmp, &(rrec[offset]), 2 );
    return( ntohs( tmp ) );
    } /* Get_RD_NB_Flags */

struct in_addr Get_RD_NB_Addr( const uchar *rrec, int offset )
    /* ---------------------------------------------------- **
     * Read the NB_ADDRESS field from an RDATA record.
     * ---------------------------------------------------- **
     */
    {
    ulong          tmp;
    struct in_addr tmp_addr;

    (void)memcpy( &tmp, &(rrec[offset]), 4 );
    tmp_addr.s_addr = ntohl( tmp );
    return( tmp_addr );
    } /* Get_RD_NB_Addr */
```

4.3.1.1   Broadcast Name Registration

You've seen the basic form of NAME REGISTRATION REQUEST packet. When sending a broadcast registration, the following rules apply.

- The B bit is set.
- The TTL is zero.
- The RDATA.NB_FLAGS.ONT should never be ONT_P, since P nodes never register their names via broadcast.

A node sending a broadcast NAME REGISTRATION REQUEST (the *requester*) may receive a unicast NEGATIVE NAME REGISTRATION RESPONSE from another node that already claims ownership of the name (the *owner*). That is the only valid message in response to a broadcast registration.

```
NAME REGISTRATION RESPONSE (Negative)
  {
  HEADER
    {
    NAME_TRN_ID = <Must match REQUEST transaction ID>
    FLAGS
      {
      R       = TRUE (1; This is a response packet)
      OPCODE = 0x5 (Registration)
      AA      = TRUE (1)
      RD      = TRUE (1)
      RA      = TRUE (1)
      RCODE  = ACT_ERR (0x6)
      B       = FALSE (0; Message is unicast back to requester)
      }
    ANCOUNT = 1
    }
  ANSWER_RECORD
    {
    RR_NAME  = <The Encoded NBT Name>
    RR_TYPE  = NB (0x0020)
    RR_CLASS = IN (0x0001)
    TTL      = 0 (TTL has no meaning in this context)
    RDLENGTH = 6
    RDATA
      {
      NB_FLAGS
        {
        G   = <TRUE for a group name, FALSE for a unique name>
        ONT = <Owner type>
        }
      NB_ADDRESS = <Owner's IP address>
      }
    }
  }
```

When a requester receives a NEGATIVE NAME REGISTRATION RESPONSE, it is obliged to give up. Registration has failed because another node has prior — and conflicting — claim to the name. That is, the name already has an owner.

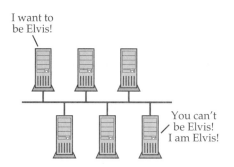

Figure 4.1a: *Broadcast unique/unique name conflict*

A unique name may not be registered if another node already owns that unique name.

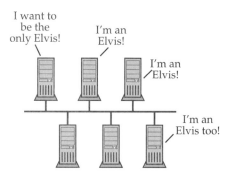

Figure 4.1b: *Broadcast unique/group name conflict*

A unique name may not be registered if the same name is registered as a group name.

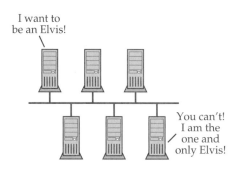

Figure 4.1c: *Broadcast group/unique name conflict*

A group name may not be registered if another node already owns the name as a unique name.

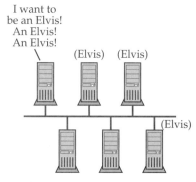

Figure 4.1d: *No conflict when joining a group*

Any node may join a group. Existing group members will not respond to the registration request.

The RCODE field of the response will be ACT_ERR (0x6), indicating that the name is in use. The RDATA field should contain the real owner's name information:

- ▪ NB_FLAGS.G indicates whether the name in use is a group or unique name,

- NB_FLAGS.ONT is the owner's node type,
- NB_ADDRESS is the owner's IP address.

Recall that the NAME REGISTRATION REQUEST contains a name query, so the ANSWER_RECORD in the reply should be constructed as it would be in a POSITIVE NAME QUERY RESPONSE. It is wrong to simply parrot back the information in the request.[3]

NEGATIVE NAME REGISTRATION RESPONSE messages are only sent if a unique name is involved.[4] Owners of a group name will not complain if a requester tries to join the group. If, however, a requester tries to register a unique name that matches an already registered group name, the members of the group will send negative responses. In a broadcast environment, a single unique name registration request can generate a large number of negative replies.

If there are no conflicts the requesting node will hear no complaints, in which case it must retry the request two more times... just to be sure. The RFCs specify a minimum timeout of 250 milliseconds between broadcast retries (Windows uses 750 ms). After the third query has timed out, the requesting node should broadcast a NAME OVERWRITE DEMAND declaring itself the victor and owner of the name. The NAME OVERWRITE DEMAND message is identical to the NAME REGISTRATION REQUEST, except that the RD bit is clear (Recursion Desired is 0).

This next program will allow you to play around with broadcast name registration. It uses functions and constants from previous listings to format a NAME REGISTRATION REQUEST and broadcast it on the local IP subnet, then it listens for and reports any replies it receives.

---

3. It is easy, but wrong, to simply copy back the information from the ADDITIONAL_RECORD of the NAME REGISTRATION REQUEST. The NEGATIVE NAME REGISTRATION RESPONSE should identify the node that currently owns the name. (...And yes, some day I may fix this in Samba.)

4. Elvis is the name of a popular clone of the venerable "vi" text editor.

Listing 4.7: A broadcast name registration

```c
#include <stdio.h>
#include <stdlib.h>
#include <sys/poll.h>
#include <sys/types.h>
#include <sys/socket.h>
#include <netinet/in.h>

#include "NS_Header.h"
#include "NS_Qrec.h"
#include "NS_Rrec.h"
#include "NS_RDaddr.h"

#define NBT_BCAST_ADDR "255.255.255.255"

#define uchar  unsigned char
#define ushort unsigned short

int BuildRegMsg( uchar          *msg,
                 const uchar    *name,
                 struct in_addr addr )
  /* -------------------------------------------------- **
   * Create a Bcast Name Registration Message.
   *
   * This function hard-codes several values.
   * Obviously, a "real" implementation would need
   * to be much more flexible.
   * -------------------------------------------------- **
   */
  {
  ushort *hdr = (ushort *)msg;
  uchar  *rrec;
  ushort flags;
  int    len;
  int    rr_len;

  flags = OPCODE_REGISTER | NM_RD_BIT | NM_B_BIT;

  Put_NS_TID( hdr, 1964 );
  Put_NS_Hdr_Flags( hdr, flags );
  Put_NS_Hdr_Rec_Counts( hdr, (QUERYREC | ADDREC) );
  len = 12;     /* Fixed size of header. */
```

```
len += Put_Qrec( &msg[len],   /* Query Rec Pointer  */
                 name,        /* NetBIOS name       */
                 ' ',         /* Padding char       */
                 '\0',        /* Suffix             */
                 "",          /* Scope ID           */
                 QTYPE_NB );  /* Qtype: Name        */

rrec = &msg[len];
rr_len  = Put_RRec_LSP( rrec, RRTYPE_NB );
rr_len += Put_RRec_TTL( rrec, rr_len, 0 );
rr_len += Put_RDLength( rrec, rr_len, 6 );
rr_len += Put_RD_Addr(  rrec, rr_len, ONT_B, addr );

return( len + rr_len );
} /* BuildRegMsg */

void ReadRegReply( int sock )
  /* ------------------------------------------------- **
   * Read a reply packet, and verify that it contains the
   * expected RCODE value.
   * ------------------------------------------------- **
   */
  {
  uchar  bufr[512];
  int    msglen;
  ushort flags;

  msglen = recv( sock, bufr, 512, 0 );
  if( msglen < 0 )
    {
    perror( "recv()" );
    exit( EXIT_FAILURE );
    }

  if( msglen < 12 )
    {
    printf( "Truncated reply received.\n" );
    exit( EXIT_FAILURE );
    }

  flags = Get_NS_Hdr_Flags( (ushort *)bufr );
```

```
    switch( RCODE_MASK & flags )
      {
      case RCODE_ACT_ERR:
        /* This is the only valid Rcode in response to
         * a broadcast name registration request.
         */
        printf( "RCODE_ACT_ERR: Name is in use.\n" );
        break;
      default:
        printf( "Unexpected return code: 0x%.2x.\n",
                (RCODE_MASK & flags) );
        break;
      }
    } /* ReadRegReply */

int OpenSocket()
  /* ---------------------------------------------------- **
   * Open the UDP socket, enable broadcast, and bind the
   * socket to a high-numbered UDP port so that we can
   * listen for replies.
   * ---------------------------------------------------- **
   */
  {
  int               s;
  int               test = 1;
  struct sockaddr_in sox;

  s = socket( PF_INET, SOCK_DGRAM, IPPROTO_UDP );
  if( s < 0 )
    {
    perror( "socket()" );
    exit( EXIT_FAILURE );
    }

  if( setsockopt( s, SOL_SOCKET, SO_BROADCAST,
                  &test, sizeof(int) ) < 0 )
    {
    perror( "setsockopt()" );
    exit( EXIT_FAILURE );
    }

  sox.sin_addr.s_addr = INADDR_ANY;
  sox.sin_family      = AF_INET;
  sox.sin_port        = 0;  /* 0 == any port */
  test = bind( s, (struct sockaddr *)&sox,
               sizeof(struct sockaddr_in) );
```

```
  if( test < 0 )
    {
    perror( "bind()" );
    exit( EXIT_FAILURE );
    }

  return( s );
  } /* OpenSocket */

void SendBcastMsg( int sock, uchar *msg, int msglen )
  /* -------------------------------------------------- **
   * Nice front-end to the sendto(2) function.
   * -------------------------------------------------- **
   */
  {
  int              result;
  struct sockaddr_in to;

  if( 0 == inet_aton( NBT_BCAST_ADDR, &(to.sin_addr) ) )
    {
    printf( "Invalid destination IP address.\n" );
    exit( EXIT_FAILURE );
    }
  to.sin_family = AF_INET;
  to.sin_port   = htons( 137 );
  result = sendto( sock, (void *)msg, msglen, 0,
                   (struct sockaddr *)&to,
                   sizeof(struct sockaddr_in) );
  if( result < 0 )
    {
    perror( "sendto()" );
    exit( EXIT_FAILURE );
    }
  } /* SendBcastMsg */

int AwaitResponse( int sock, int milliseconds )
  /* -------------------------------------------------- **
   * Wait for an incoming message.
   * One ms == 1/1000 second.
   * -------------------------------------------------- **
   */
  {
  int            result;
  struct pollfd pfd[1];
```

```c
  pfd->fd     = sock;
  pfd->events = POLLIN;
  result = poll( pfd, 1, milliseconds );
  if( result < 0 )
    {
    perror( "poll()" );
    exit( EXIT_FAILURE );
    }

  return( result );
  } /* AwaitResponse */

int main( int argc, char *argv[] )
  /* ------------------------------------------------- **
   * This program demonstrates a Broadcast NBT Name
   * Registration.
   * ------------------------------------------------- **
   */
  {
  int          i;
  int          result;
  int          ns_sock;
  int          msg_len;
  uchar        bufr[512];
  uchar        *name;
  struct in_addr address;

  if( argc != 3 )
    {
    printf( "Usage:  %s <name> <IP>\n", argv[0] );
    exit( EXIT_FAILURE );
    }

  name = (uchar *)argv[1];
  if( 0 == inet_aton( argv[2], &address ) )
    {
    printf( "Invalid IP.\n" );
    printf( "Usage:  %s <name> <IP>\n", argv[0] );
    exit( EXIT_FAILURE );
    }

  ns_sock = OpenSocket();

  msg_len = BuildRegMsg( bufr, name, address );
```

```
for( i = 0; i < 3; i++ )
  {
  printf( "Trying...\n" );
  SendBcastMsg( ns_sock, bufr, msg_len );
  result = AwaitResponse( ns_sock, 750 );
  if( result )
    {
    ReadRegReply( ns_sock );
    exit( EXIT_FAILURE );
    }
  }
printf( "Success: No negative replies received.\n" );

/* Turn off RD bit for NAME OVERWRITE DEMAND. */
Put_NS_Hdr_Flags( (ushort *)bufr,
                  OPCODE_REGISTER | NM_B_BIT );
SendBcastMsg( ns_sock, bufr, msg_len );

close( ns_sock );
return( EXIT_SUCCESS );
} /* main */
```

The transaction ID in the NAME_TRN_ID field should be the same for all three registration attempts, for the final NAME OVERWRITE DEMAND, and for any negative response packets a remote node may care to send. All of these are part of the same transaction.

Blue Screen of Death Alert

Some OEM versions of Windows 95 had a bug that would cause the system to go into "Blue Screen of Death" mode (that is, system crash) if the NetBIOS Machine Name was in conflict. The problem was made worse by PC vendors who would ship systems with NBT turned on, all preconfigured with the same name. Customers who purchased several computers for local networks would turn them on for the first time and all but one would crash.

4.3.1.2 Unicast (NBNS) Name Registration

Unicast name registrations are subtly different from the broadcast variety.

- The B bit is cleared (zero) and the destination IP is the unicast address of the NBNS.

The message is sent "point-to-point" directly to the NBNS, rather than being broadcast on the local LAN. This is the fundamental difference between B and P modes.

- The TTL field has real meaning when you are talking to an NBNS.

  The RFCs do not specify a default TTL value. Windows systems use 300,000 seconds, which is three days, eleven hours and twenty minutes. Samba uses 259,200 seconds, which is three days even. Both of these values are ugly in hex.[5]

- The timeout between retries is longer.

  The longer timeout between retries is based on the assumption that routed links may have higher latency than the local LAN. RFC 1002 specifies a timeout value of five seconds, which is excessive on today's Internet. A client will try to register a name three times, so the total (worst case) timeout would be fifteen seconds. Samba uses a two second per-packet timeout instead, for a total of six seconds. The timeout under Windows is only 1.5 seconds per packet.

The NBNS should respond with a NAME REGISTRATION RESPONSE, which will include one of the following RCODE values:

0x0: Success

POSITIVE NAME REGISTRATION RESPONSE: You win! The NBNS has accepted the registration. Do not forget to send a refresh before the TTL expires (see Section 4.3.3 on page 98).

FMT_ERR (0x1): Format Error

The NBNS did not like your message. Something was wrong with the packet format (perhaps it was mangled on the wire).

SRV_ERR (0x2): Server failure

The NBNS is sick and cannot handle requests just now.

---

5. 3 days 00:00:00 == 259,200 seconds == 0x0003F480 (Samba),
   3 days 11:20:00 == 300,000 seconds == 0x000493E0 (Windows),
   3 days 19:01:20 == 327,680 seconds == 0x00050000.

IMP_ERR (0x4): Unsupported request error

This one is a bit of a mystery. It basically means that the NBNS does not know how to handle a request. The only clue we have to its intended usage is a poorly worded note in RFC 1002, which says:

```
Allowable only for challenging NBNS when gets an Update
type registration request.
```

Huh?

This error occurs only under odd circumstances, which will be explained in more detail later on in this section. Basically, though, an IMP_ERR should only be returned by an NBNS if it receives an unsolicited NAME UPDATE REQUEST from a client. (Be patient, we'll get there.)

RFS_ERR (0x5): Refused error

This indicates that the NBNS has made a policy decision not to register the name.

ACT_ERR (0x6): Active error

The NBNS has verified that the name is in use by another node. You can't have it.

Note that the difference between a positive and negative NAME REGISTRATION RESPONSE is simply the RCODE value.

If you get no response then it is correct to assume that the NBNS is "down." If the name cannot be registered then your node does not own it, and your application should recover as gracefully as possible. In P mode, handle a non-responsive NBNS as you would a NEGATIVE NAME REGISTRATION RESPONSE. (If the client is running in H or M mode, then it may — with caution — revert to B mode operation until the NBNS is available again.)

There are two other packet types that you may receive when registering a name with an NBNS. These are WACK and END-NODE CHALLENGE NAME REGISTRATION RESPONSE. The WACK message tells the client to wait while the NBNS figures things out. This is typically done so that the NBNS has time to send queries to another node that has claimed ownership of the requested name. A WACK looks like this:

```
WAIT FOR ACKNOWLEDGEMENT (WACK) RESPONSE
  {
  HEADER
    {
    NAME_TRN_ID = <Must match REQUEST transaction ID>
    FLAGS
      {
      R      = TRUE (1; This is a response packet)
      OPCODE = 0x7 (WACK)
      AA     = TRUE (1)
      }
    ANCOUNT = 1
    }
  ANSWER_RECORD
    {
    RR_NAME  = <The Encoded NBT Name from the request>
    RR_TYPE  = NB (0x0020; note the typo in RFC 1002, 4.2.16)
    RR_CLASS = IN (0x0001)
    TTL      = <Number of seconds to wait; 0 == Infinite>
    RDLENGTH = 2
    RDATA    = <Copy of the two-byte HEADER.FLAGS field
               of the original request>
    }
  }
```

The key field in the WACK is the TTL field, which tells the client how long to wait for a response. This is used to extend the timeout period on the client, and give the NBNS a chance to do a reality check.

Samba uses a TTL value of 60 seconds, which provides ample time to generate a proper reply. Unless it is shut down after sending the WACK message, Samba's NBNS service will always send a NAME REGISTRATION RESPONSE (positive or negative) well before the 60 seconds has elapsed. Microsoft's WINS takes a different approach, using a value of only 2 seconds. If the 2 seconds expire, however, the requesting client will simply send another NAME REGISTRATION REQUEST, and then another for a total of three tries. WINS should be able to respond within that total timeframe.

WACK messages are sent by honest, hard-working servers that take good care of their clients. In contrast, a lazy and careless NBNS server will send an END-NODE CHALLENGE NAME REGISTRATION RESPONSE. This latter response tells the client that the requested name has a registered owner, but the NBNS is not going to bother to do the work to check that the owner is still up and running and using the name.

Once again, the format of this message is so familiar that there is no need to list all of the fields. The END-NODE CHALLENGE NAME REGISTRATION RESPONSE packet is just a NAME REGISTRATION RESPONSE with:

```
            RCODE = 0x0
               RA = 0 (Recursion Available clear)
ANSWER_RECORD.RDATA = <Information retrieved from the NBNS database>
```

The annoying thing about this packet is that the RCODE value indicates success, making it look almost exactly like a POSITIVE NAME REGISTRATION RESPONSE. *The* RA *bit must be checked to distinguish between the two message types.*

When a client receives an END-NODE CHALLENGE, its duty is to query the owner (the owner's IP address will be in the ANSWER_RECORD. RDATA.NB_ADDRESS field) to see if the owner still wants the name. If the owner does not respond, or if it replies with a NEGATIVE NAME QUERY RESPONSE, then the name is available and the requester may send a NAME UPDATE REQUEST to the NBNS. The NBNS will blindly trust the requester, change the entry, and reply with a POSITIVE NAME REGISTRATION RESPONSE. The NAME UPDATE REQUEST is the same as the unicast NAME REGISTRATION REQUEST except that the RD bit is clear (Recursion Desired is 0).

There is nothing to stop a client from skipping the name query and sending the update message to the NBNS, effectively stealing the name. This is why the RFCs use the term *non-secured* when describing this mechanism.

Terminology Turmoil Alert

*In the RFCs, the terms "*NAME UPDATE REQUEST*" and "*NAME OVERWRITE REQUEST & DEMAND*" are both used to refer to the same packet structure. These terms are interchanged somewhat randomly in the text without any explanation regarding their relationship to one another (all probably due to an editing oversight). This is confusing.*

*In this book we make a semantic distinction between the two message types, and shorten "*NAME OVERWRITE REQUEST & DEMAND*" to simply "*NAME OVERWRITE DEMAND*."*

Here's why:

The RFCs specify that a REQUEST *is a message to which a* RESPONSE *is expected. So, for example, once a* NAME REGISTRATION REQUEST *has been sent the requester must wait a reasonable period of time for a reply, and retry the request twice before giving up. A* DEMAND*, however, never generates a* RESPONSE*. It is simply sent and forgotten so there is no need to wait. Thus, the term "*NAME

OVERWRITE REQUEST & DEMAND" *is contradictory. The message is either a* REQUEST *or a* DEMAND, *but not both.*

To clear things up, we use NAME UPDATE REQUEST *to indicate the packet sent to a non-secured NBNS following a name challenge. The requester expects to receive a* POSITIVE NAME REGISTRATION RESPONSE *in reply to the* NAME UPDATE REQUEST. *In contrast, the* NAME OVERWRITE DEMAND *is sent as the last step in a successful broadcast registration, and no reply is expected.*

Again, these packets all share the same structure as the NAME REGISTRATION REQUEST. *Only the* RD *and* B *flag bits distinguish them syntactically.*

Oh... one more thing. Remember the IMP_ERR return code? It is used to indicate that an NBNS which did *not* send an END-NODE CHALLENGE is annoyed at having received a NAME UPDATE REQUEST from a client. An NBNS server should never receive unsolicited NAME UPDATE REQUESTs from clients.

4.3.1.3 M and H Node Name Registration

Mixed mode (M mode) and Hybrid mode (H mode) are both speed hacks, which combine aspects of Broadcast (B) and Point-to-Point (P) modes to short-cut Name Service operations.

M mode was designed in the days when local LAN traffic was likely to be faster than internetwork links, which were typically carried over leased lines, dial-up connections, tin cans with string, or pigeon (see RFC 1149). Since local broadcasts were both faster and more reliable than traffic to a remote NBNS, M nodes attempt B mode behavior first and try P mode behavior second.

When an M node registers a name, for example, it starts by sending a broadcast NAME REGISTRATION REQUEST. If it receives a negative response it tries no further (thus saving some time). If, however, it receives no complaints after three retries, it will attempt to register with the NBNS as a P node would. If and only if the P mode registration succeeds, the M mode will broadcast a NAME OVERWRITE DEMAND. If the unicast registration fails, the NAME OVERWRITE will not be sent and the node will not assume ownership of the name.

Hybrid mode (H mode) was introduced (probably by Microsoft) after the RFCs were published. H mode assumes that internetwork links are fast and reliable, in which case it makes sense to try P mode behavior first and revert to B mode behavior only if the NBNS does not respond. Compared with M mode, H mode generates less broadcast traffic on local LANs.

H mode is a little trickier than M mode. A node running in H mode will attempt a unicast name registration and, if the NBNS accepts the registration, the H node will assume ownership without generating any broadcast (B mode) traffic at all. If the NetBIOS vLAN is configured properly all of the nodes within the scope will also be registering with the NBNS, thus preventing accidental name conflicts.

If the NBNS is down or unreachable, however, an H node will revert to B mode behavior and hope that no conflicts will arise when the NBNS comes back.

4.3.1.4 Registering Multi-Homed Hosts

A multi-homed host is a machine that has multiple network interfaces (physical or virtual), each with its own IP address assigned. RFCs 1001 and 1002 do not discuss handling of multi-homed hosts.

The annoying thing about multi-homed hosts in an NBT environment is that they try to register their NetBIOS names on each interface, which means multiple IP addresses per name. This is not a problem for group names because group names map to several IP addresses anyway — that's what NBT group names are all about. Unique names *are* a problem because, from the network's point of view, there is no difference between a multi-homed host and multiple machines. To an NBNS, or to B nodes on a local LAN, multiple registrations for the same name will look like a name conflict.

There are three scenarios to consider when working with multi-homed hosts.

B nodes with interfaces on separate subnets

If each IP address is on a separate IP subnet *and* the node is running in B mode then springtime returns to the cities, birds sing, and little children dance for joy. Each name-to-IP-address mapping is unique *within its NBT scope*, which is the broadcast space within the subnet, so there are no name conflicts.

The only multi-homed-specific problem that can occur in this scenario starts with a regular old-fashioned run-of-the-mill name conflict. If there is a name conflict with another node on one or more, but not all, subnets then we have a quandary because the name is valid on some subnets, but not others. Two solutions are possible here: the multi-homed host may decide to disable the name on all interfaces (probably the best option), or just on the interfaces on which the conflict exists.

Another thing to keep in mind is that replies to name queries must return the correct IP address for the subnet, so it is important to know on which interface the query was received. This can be done by checking both the source and destination IP addresses of the original query packet. If the query is a broadcast query, then it is best to send only the IP address of the interface. Unicast queries, however, should contain a full list of the IPs registered to the name. This quirk will be examined further when we tackle P mode multi-homed registration.

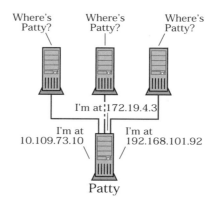

Figure 4.2:   *A multi-homed B node*

Node PATTY has three interfaces, each with an IP address on a differnt subnet. PATTY replies to each broadcast query with the correct IP address for the subnet.

B nodes with interfaces on the same subnet

Problems occur if two or more interfaces have IP addresses on the same subnet. This is equivalent to having two or more separate nodes on the same subnet, all trying to claim the same unique name. There is no standard fix for this situation. Fortunately this configuration is rare, though it *does* occur in the wild — typically when someone tries to build a fault-tolerant or load-balanced server system. The only known work-around is to write additional code to control which of the multi-homed interfaces "owns" a name at any given time.

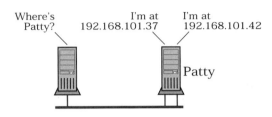

Figure 4.3: *A multi-homed B node with a shared subnet*

In this case, node PATTY has two interfaces, both connected to the same subnet. PATTY sends two correct replies to a broadcast query which looks, on the wire, exactly like a name conflict.

Multi-homed hosts and the NBNS

P mode multi-homed name registration is a circus. In P mode, a multi-homed host will send multiple registrations — one per interface — to the NBNS. Normally the NBNS would reject all but the first such registration, viewing the others as name conflicts. To get around this problem, we use a new OpCode:

0xF == multi-homed name registration.

Instead of sending normal registration requests, the host concurrently sends individual MULTI-HOMED NAME REGISTRATION REQUEST packets from each interface it wishes to register. Other than the OpCode, these are identical to normal NAME REGISTRATION REQUEST packets, though each request has its own NAME_TRN_ID (transaction ID).

The NBNS will respond to the first of these messages by sending a POSITIVE NAME REGISTRATION RESPONSE. It then sends 2-second WACK messages in reply to all the other MULTI-HOMED NAME REGISTRATION REQUEST packets it receives (all that are trying to register the same unique name). The WACK gives the NBNS extra time to process the registration.

Next, the NBNS will send a unicast NAME QUERY REQUEST to the source address of the first message it received (the one that got the POSITIVE NAME REGISTRATION RESPONSE). This is a unicast query (the B bit is clear), so *the query response should contain the complete list of IP addresses that are allowed to share the name.*

The NBNS will then send POSITIVE NAME REGISTRATION RESPONSE messages to all of the WACKed IPs in the list, and a NEGATIVE NAME REGISTRATION RESPONSE, with an RCODE value of ACT_ERR (0x6), to any others. The NBNS finishes with a double back-flip in pike position through flaming hoops into a piece of unbuttered toast and the crowd cheers wildly.

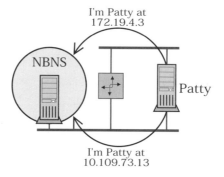

Figure 4.4:   *A multi-homed P node*

Node PATTY has two interfaces, each on a separate subnet. PATTY sends separate registrations to the NBNS. Under normal circumstances, this would be handled as a name conflict.

One problem still remains, however. Consider node LANE (operating in P mode), which is trying to talk to node PATTY. The first thing LANE will do is send a NAME QUERY REQUEST to the NBNS. The NBNS has no way of knowing which IP address represents the best route between LANE and PATTY, so it must send the complete list of PATTY's IPs. LANE has to guess which IP is the best. Typically, the client will choose a destination IP by sending some sort of message (e.g., a unicast name query) to all of the listed IPs to see which one answers first. Note that in order to make this work the NBNS must keep track of all IPs associated with the NBT name registered by the multi-homed host.[6]

---

6. Many thanks to Monyo for providing packet captures.

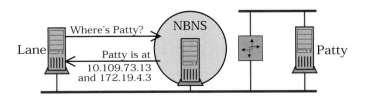

Figure 4.5: *Locating a multi-homed P node*
Node LANE gets two IPs when it asks for PATTY's address.

As you might expect, the handling of M and H mode multi-homed hosts is a fairly straightforward combination of B and P mode behavior. M and H mode name registration for single-homed hosts has already been covered.

4.3.2 *Name Query*

Each NBT node has its own local name table, which holds the list of the Net-BIOS names that the node thinks it owns. NBT nodes may also register their names with a NetBIOS nameserver. Both the local name table and the NBNS database can be used to answer queries.

Name queries look like this:

```
NAME QUERY REQUEST
  {
  HEADER
    {
    NAME_TRN_ID = <Set when packet is transmitted>
    FLAGS
      {
      OPCODE = 0x0 (Query)
      RD     = <Typically TRUE (1); see discussion below>
      B      = <TRUE for broadcast queries, else FALSE (0)>
      }
    QDCOUNT = 1
    }
  QUESTION_RECORD
    {
    QUESTION_NAME  = <Encoded NBT name to be queried>
    QUESTION_TYPE  = NB (0x0020)
    QUESTION_CLASS = IN (0x0001)
    }
  }
```

As you can see from the packet description, name queries are really very simple (just as the eye of a hurricane is calm). The only fiddly bits are the B and RD flags.

- The B bit is used to distinguish between broadcast and unicast queries.

  Broadcast queries are used for name resolution within the broadcast scope, as shown by the example code presented earlier. Since P nodes are excluded from B mode scope, P nodes and the NBNS will both ignore broadcast name queries. Only local B, M, and H nodes (with the same Scope ID as the sender) will respond.

  The only valid reply to a broadcast name query is a POSITIVE NAME QUERY RESPONSE from a node that actually owns the name in question. Queries for group names may generate multiple responses, one per group member on the local LAN.

  In P mode, names are resolved to IP addresses by sending a unicast query to the NBNS, which checks the list of registered names (the NBNS database). If the name is found, the NBNS will reply with a POSITIVE NAME QUERY RESPONSE, otherwise it will send a NEGATIVE NAME QUERY RESPONSE. If the requester gets no response at all, then the NBNS is assumed to be down or unreachable.

  Unicast queries can also be used to determine whether an NBT end node owns a given NetBIOS name. All NBT node types (B, P, M, and H) will respond to unicast queries. As with queries sent to the NBNS, NBT end nodes may reply with either a positive or negative NAME QUERY RESPONSE.

  A unicast query for the wildcard name is the NBT equivalent of a ping.

- The RD bit is used to distinguish between two different types of unicast queries.

  In discussing the use of the B bit, above, we made a subtle distinction between resolution and verification queries. A *name resolution query* is the most familiar. It is used to convert a name to an IP address. Unicast queries sent to the NBNS are always resolution queries. A *verification query* is a unicast query sent to an NBT end node to ask whether the node is using the name in question. In order to send a verification query, the sender must already have the IP of the target NBT end node so name resolution is pointless.

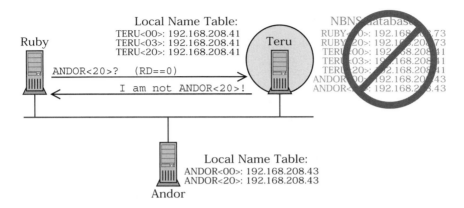

Figure 4.6a: *Verification query (RD == FALSE)*

RUBY sends a unicast query to node TERU asking about ANDOR. The RD bit is *clear*, so TERU does not check the NBNS database. It checks only the local name table and, finding no reference to the name ANDOR<20>, sends a NEGATIVE NAME QUERY RESPONSE.

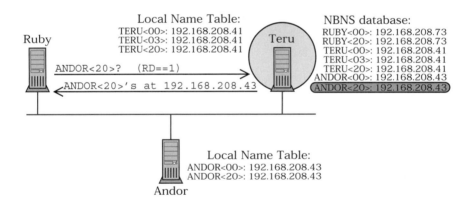

Figure 4.6b: *Verification query (RD == TRUE)*

RUBY sends a unicast query to node TERU asking about ANDOR. The RD bit is *set*, so TERU checks the NBNS database, where it finds an entry for ANDOR<20>. TERU sends a POSITIVE NAME QUERY RESPONSE.

Note that:

■ Broadcast *name resolution queries* are always answered from data in the receiving node's local name table.

- Unicast *name resolution queries* are supposed to be answered from data in the NBNS database.
- Unicast *name verification queries* must be answered from the node's local name table — *not* the NBNS database.

So... what happens if you send a unicast query to a node that is both an NBT participant *and* the NBNS? Which kind of query is it, and which name list should be consulted?

That's where the RD bit comes in. If RD is FALSE then only the local name table is consulted, forcing a verification query. If RD is TRUE and the NBNS service is running on the receiving node, then the NBNS database may also be used to answer the query — that makes it a resolution query.

This particular problem, and its solution, are not covered in the RFCs. The diagram in RFC 1002, Section 4.2.12 shows the RD bit as always set, and this is common practice.[7] The state of the RD bit in a query message is typically ignored, and is only significant in the one case we have described: a unicast query sent to a node that is both an NBT participant and the NBNS.

In summary:

```
/* Pseudocode */
if( the B bit is TRUE )
  { /* It's a broadcast query. */
  if( the receiver is a B, M, or H node )
    {
    entry = lookup name in local name table;
    if( entry was found )
      send( POSITIVE NAME QUERY RESPONSE );
    }
  }
```

---

7. For example, when an NBNS is processing a multi-homed registration it *should* send name queries with the RD bit clear, yet all Windows systems that were tested set the RD bit. It may not matter, however, unless the multi-homed host is also the node running the NBNS, in which case the problem would likely be solved using internal mechanisms (because the NBNS would be sending the query to itself). The right thing to do is to send verification queries with the RD flag turned OFF.

```
else
{ /* It's a unicast query. */
entry = lookup name in local name table;
if( entry was not found & RD is TRUE & receiver is the NBNS )
  {
  entry = lookup name in NBNS database;
  }
if( entry was found )
  send( POSITIVE NAME QUERY RESPONSE );
else
  send( NEGATIVE NAME QUERY RESPONSE );
}
```

Got it? Good. Let's move on...

As with other NBT Name Service requests, if there is no response to a name query within a reasonable timeout period, the query is sent again. This happens twice for a maximum of two retries (that is, three query messages). Timeouts vary from system to system and depend upon the type of query being sent. Query timeouts should be matched to those used for name registration where possible.

Broadcast queries

Between 250 ms and 750 ms is typical. RFC 1002 specifies 250 ms.

Unicast Resolution queries

A range of 1.5 to 2 seconds is common. These queries go to the NBNS, and the expectation is that the NBNS will be able to answer quickly. RFC 1002 specifies 5 seconds.

Verification queries

Intervals of 1.5 to 5 seconds have been spotted. Once again, RFC 1002 specifies 5 seconds.

Timeout values are a balance between reliability and user annoyance. Too short, and replies will be missed. Too long, and the user goes off to make another pot of tea.

4.3.2.1   Negative Query Response

A negative response looks like this:

```
NEGATIVE NAME QUERY RESPONSE
  {
  HEADER
    {
    NAME_TRN_ID = <Same as QUERY REQUEST>
    FLAGS
      {
      R       = TRUE (1; This is a response packet)
      OPCODE  = 0x0 (Query)
      AA      = TRUE (1)
      RD      = <Copy RD bit from QUERY REQUEST>
      RA      = <TRUE if the reply is from the NBNS>
      B       = FALSE (0)
      RCODE   = <Error code>
      }
    ANCOUNT = 1
    }
  ANSWER_RECORD
    {
    RR_NAME  = <The Encoded NBT Name from the request>
    RR_TYPE  = <NB (0x0020), or possibly NULL (0x000A)>
    RR_CLASS = IN (0x0001)
    TTL      = 0
    RDLENGTH = 0
    }
  }
```

RFC 1002 is inconsistent in its descriptions of the RD and RA bits as used in NAME QUERY RESPONSE messages. There is also a small issue regarding the RR_TYPE field. Let's clear things up:

- The diagram in RFC 1002, Section 4.2.14, shows RD always set in the reply. Most implementations do, in fact, set the RD bit in all NAME QUERY RESPONSE messages. To be painfully correct, however, the right thing to do is to copy the RD value from the NAME QUERY REQUEST as described in RFC 1002, Section 4.2.1.1. It really doesn't matter, though, because the RD bit is probably ignored by the node receiving the query response.

- Regarding the RA bit: There is a weird little note in RFC 1002, Section 4.2.15, which states:

```
An end node responding to a NAME QUERY REQUEST always responds
with the AA and RA bits set for both the NEGATIVE and POSITIVE
NAME QUERY RESPONSE packets.
```

That's poop. The RA bit should not be set by an end-node. Only the NBNS should set the RA bit, as explained in 4.2.1.1:

```
RA    3    Recursion Available Flag.

           Only valid in responses from a NetBIOS Name
           Server - must be zero in all other
           responses.
```

In modern usage, the RA bit *should* mean that the responding node is running the NBNS service.

- The diagram in RFC 1002, Section 4.2.14, specifies that RR_TYPE should have a value of 0x000A (NULL). In practice, the value 0x0020 (NB) is used instead (no exceptions were found in testing).

The NEGATIVE NAME QUERY RESPONSE will include an RCODE value, indicating the reason for the negative reply. RFC 1002 lists several possible RCODE values, but at least two of them — IMP_ERR and RFS_ERR — are incorrect as they are never generated in response to a query. The valid values or a NEGATIVE NAME QUERY RESPONSE are:

FMT_ERR (0x1): Format Error
The NBNS did not like your message. Something was wrong with the packet format (perhaps it was mangled on the wire).

SRV_ERR (0x2): Server failure
The NBNS is sick and cannot handle requests just now.

NAM_ERR (0x3): Name Error
The requested name does not exist in the selected name table(s).

4.3.2.2   Positive Query Response

The POSITIVE NAME QUERY RESPONSE is similar to the negative response, with the following differences:

- The RCODE is 0x0 (success),
- the RR_TYPE field always has a value of 0x0020 (NB),
- the TTL field is non-zero, and
- the RDATA field contains an array of IP address information, like so:

```
POSITIVE NAME QUERY RESPONSE
  {
  HEADER
    {
    NAME_TRN_ID = <Same as QUERY REQUEST>
    FLAGS
      {
      R       = TRUE (1; This is a response packet)
      OPCODE = 0x0 (Query)
      AA      = TRUE (1)
      RD      = <Copy RD bit from QUERY REQUEST>
      RA      = <TRUE if the reply is from the NBNS>
      B       = FALSE (0)
      RCODE  = 0x0
      }
    ANCOUNT = 1
    }
  ANSWER_RECORD
    {
    RR_NAME  = <The Encoded NBT Name from the request>
    RR_TYPE  = NB (0x0020)
    RR_CLASS = IN (0x0001)
    TTL       = <Time To Live>
    RDLENGTH = <6   number of entries>
    RDATA
      {
      ADDR_ENTRY[]
        {
        NB_FLAGS
          {
          G   = <TRUE for a group name, FALSE for a unique name>
          ONT = <Owner type>
          }
        NB_ADDRESS = <Owner's IP address>
        }
      }
    }
  }
```

If the packet is sent by the NBNS, the TTL field will contain the number of seconds until the entry's Time-To-Live expires (the remaining TTL). End nodes responding to verification queries will typically use the default TTL value which, as we described earlier, is something around 3 days.

4.3.2.3   The Redirect Name Query Response

The RFCs provide a mechanism whereby one NBNS can redirect a client to another NBNS. That is, the NBNS can return a message saying "I don't know, ask someone else."

No living examples of this mechanism have been seen in the wild. It is probably extinct. Fossil remains may be found in RFC 1001, Section 15.1.5.3, and RFC 1002, Section 4.2.15.

4.3.2.4   A Simple Name Query Revisited

Remember Listing 3.3? In that example we provided code for generating a simple broadcast name query. Listing 4.8 provides an updated version which is a bit more flexible. In particular, the `BuildQuery()` function takes several parameters, allowing you to customize the query you want to send. The program mainline, as given, sends only broadcast queries. It can, however, be easily hacked to create a more versitile command-line tool. This new version also listens for replies.

Listing 4.8: Broadcast name query revisited

```
#include <stdio.h>
#include <stdlib.h>
#include <sys/poll.h>
#include <sys/types.h>
#include <sys/socket.h>
#include <netinet/in.h>

#include "NS_Header.h"
#include "NS_Qrec.h"

#define uchar  unsigned char
#define ushort unsigned short

int BuildQuery( uchar         *msg,
                const int      bcast,
                const int      rdbit,
                const uchar   *name,
                const uchar    pad,
                const uchar    suffix,
                const uchar   *scope,
                const ushort   qtype )
```

```
    /* --------------------------------------------------- **
     * Create a name query.
     *
     * This is much more flexible than the registration
     * example in Listing 4.7.  There are also a lot more
     * parameters.  :-)
     * --------------------------------------------------- **
     */
    {
    ushort *hdr = (ushort *)msg;
    ushort  flags;
    int     len;

    /* RD always set if B is set. */
    if( bcast )
      flags = NM_RD_BIT | NM_B_BIT;
    else
      flags = rdbit ? NM_RD_BIT : 0;

    Put_NS_TID( hdr, 1964 );
    Put_NS_Hdr_Flags( hdr, flags );
    Put_NS_Hdr_Rec_Counts( hdr, QUERYREC );
    len = 12;     /* Fixed size of header. */

    len += Put_Qrec( &msg[len], /* Query Rec Pointer */
                    name,       /* NetBIOS name      */
                    pad,        /* Padding char      */
                    suffix,     /* Suffix            */
                    scope,      /* Scope ID          */
                    qtype );    /* Query type        */

    return( len );
    } /* BuildQuery */

void ReadQueryReply( int sock )
    /* --------------------------------------------------- **
     * Read the query reply message(s).
     * --------------------------------------------------- **
     */
    {
    uchar  bufr[512];
    int    msglen;
    ushort flags;

    msglen = recv( sock, bufr, 512, 0 );
```

```
  if( msglen < 0 )
    {
    perror( "recv()" );
    exit( EXIT_FAILURE );
    }

  if( msglen < 12 )
    {
    printf( "Truncated reply received.\n" );
    exit( EXIT_FAILURE );
    }

  flags = Get_NS_Hdr_Flags( (ushort *)bufr );
  switch( RCODE_MASK & flags )
    {
    case RCODE_POS_RSP:
      printf( "Positive Name Query Response.\n" );
      break;
    case RCODE_FMT_ERR:
      printf( "RCODE_FMT_ERR: Format Error.\n" );
      break;
    case RCODE_SRV_ERR:
      printf( "RCODE_SRV_ERR: Server Error.\n" );
      break;
    case RCODE_NAM_ERR:
      printf( "RCODE_NAM_ERR: Name Not Found.\n" );
      break;
    default:
      printf( "Unexpected return code: 0x%.2x.\n",
              (RCODE_MASK & flags) );
      break;
    }

  } /* ReadQueryReply */

int main( int argc, char *argv[] )
  /* -------------------------------------------------- **
   * This program demonstrates a Broadcast NBT Name Query.
   * -------------------------------------------------- **
   */
  {
  int               i;
  int               result;
  int               ns_sock;
  int               msg_len;
  uchar             bufr[512];
  uchar             *name;
```

```
if( argc != 2 )
  {
  printf( "Usage:  %s <name>\n", argv[0] );
  exit( EXIT_FAILURE );
  }

name = (uchar *)argv[1];

ns_sock = OpenSocket();

msg_len = BuildQuery( bufr,   /* Target buffer.   */
                      1,      /* Broadcast true.  */
                      1,      /* RD bit true.     */
                      name,   /* NetBIOS name.    */
                      ' ',    /* Padding (space). */
                      '\0',   /* Suffix (0x00).   */
                      "",     /* Scope ("").      */
                      QTYPE_NB ); /* Query type. */

for( i = 0; i < 3; i++ )
  {
  printf( "Trying...\n" );
  SendBcastMsg( ns_sock, bufr, msg_len );
  result = AwaitResponse( ns_sock, 750 );
  if( result )
    {
    do
      {
      /* We may get multiple replies. */
      ReadQueryReply( ns_sock );
      } while( AwaitResponse( ns_sock, 750 ) );
    exit( EXIT_SUCCESS );
    }
  }
printf( "No replies received.\n" );

close( ns_sock );
return( EXIT_FAILURE );
} /* main */
```

The sweet and chewey center of a POSITIVE NAME QUERY RESPONSE is the RDATA section, which contains an array of address entries. In most cases there will be only one entry, but a group name or a multi-homed host name may have several associated IP addresses. The contents of the ADDR_ENTRY records should be fairly familiar by now, so we won't dwell on

them. Here are some quick functions which can be used to display the IP
addresses and NB_FLAGS of an ADDR_ENTRY array:

Listing 4.9: Listing ADDR_ENTRY records

```
#include "NS_RDaddr.h"

int Find_RDLength( uchar *msg )
  /* -------------------------------------------------- **
   * Calculate the offset of the RDLENGTH field within a
   * POSITIVE NAME QUERY RESPONSE.
   * -------------------------------------------------- **
   */
  {
  int len;

  len = 12                        /* Length of the header */
      + strlen( &msg[12] ) + 1    /* NBT Name length       */
      + 2 + 2 + 4;                /* Type, Class, & TTL    */
  return( len );
  } /* Find_RDLength */

void List_Addr_Entry( uchar *msg )
  /* -------------------------------------------------- **
   * This function nicely prints the contents of an
   * RDATA.ADDR_ENTRY[] array.
   * -------------------------------------------------- **
   */
  {
  ushort numIPs;
  ushort flags;
  int    offset;
  int    i;

  offset = Find_RDLength( msg );
  numIPs = Get_RDLength( msg, offset ) / 6;
  offset += 2;   /* Move past the RDLENGTH field. */

  for( i = 0; i < numIPs ; i++, offset += 6 )
    {
    /* Read the NB_FLAGS field. */
    flags = Get_RD_NB_Flags( msg, offset );

    /* If there are more than one, number the entries. */
    if( numIPs > 1 )
      printf( "ADDR_ENTRY[%d]: ", i );
```

```
/* Print the IP address. */
printf( "%d.%d.%d.%d\t",
        msg[offset+2], msg[offset+3],
        msg[offset+4], msg[offset+5] );

/* Group or Unique. */
if( GROUP_BIT & flags )
  printf( "<Group>\t" );
else
  printf( "<Unique>\t" );

/* Finally, the owner node type. */
switch( ONT_MASK & flags )
  {
  case ONT_B: printf( "<B-node>\n" ); break;
  case ONT_P: printf( "<P-node>\n" ); break;
  case ONT_M: printf( "<M-node>\n" ); break;
  case ONT_H: printf( "<H-node>\n" ); break;
  }
}
} /* List_Addr_Entry */
```

4.3.3 *Name Refresh*

Name refresh has two purposes. The first is to remind the NBNS that the client exists, thus ensuring that the name entry in the NBNS database does not expire. The second is to rebuild the NBNS database in the event of an NBNS crash. NAME REFRESH REQUEST messages are not needed in B mode since each node keeps track of its own names.

```
NAME REFRESH REQUEST
  {
  HEADER
    {
    NAME_TRN_ID = <Set when packet is transmitted>
    FLAGS
      {
      OPCODE = <0x8 or 0x9> (Refresh)
      RD     = FALSE (0)
      B      = FALSE (0)
      }
    QDCOUNT = 1
    ARCOUNT = 1
    }
```

```
QUESTION_RECORD
  {
  QUESTION_NAME  = <Encoded NBT name to be refreshed>
  QUESTION_TYPE  = NB (0x0020)
  QUESTION_CLASS = IN (0x0001)
  }
ADDITIONAL_RECORD
  {
  RR_NAME  = 0xC00C (Label String Pointer to QUESTION_NAME)
  RR_TYPE  = NB (0x0020)
  RR_CLASS = IN (0x0001)
  TTL      = <Client's default TTL value (3 days)>
  RDLENGTH = 6
  RDATA
    {
    NB_FLAGS
      {
      G   = <TRUE for a group name, FALSE for a unique name>
      ONT = <Owner type>
      }
    NB_ADDRESS = <Requesting node's IP address>
    }
  }
}
```

This message is almost identical to the unicast NAME REGISTRATION REQUEST, with a few small exceptions. Note, in particular, the following:

OPCODE

The NAME REFRESH REQUEST packet uses the Refresh OpCode. Due to a typo in RFC 1002, the OPCODE values 0x8 and 0x9 are considered equivalent and both mean NAME REFRESH REQUEST. 0x8 is more commonly used.

RD

The RD field is set to FALSE, which is a little strange since the NAME REFRESH REQUEST deals directly with the NBNS.

TTL

The TTL field typically contains the client's default TTL value — the same value used in the NAME REGISTRATION REQUEST. Once again, the NBNS has the right to override the client's TTL value in the TTL field of the response.

RDATA

The RDATA should match the data stored by the NBNS. If not, the NBNS will treat the request as if it were a registration request. If the refresh RDATA conflicts with the existing data, the NBNS may need to send a query to validate the older information in its database.

From watching packets on the wire,[8] it seems that Windows systems use the following formula to determine how frequently a refresh message should be sent:

```
Refresh_Time = minimum( 40 minutes, (TTL/2) )
```

Based on the above formula, and considering that the default TTL value used by most clients is about three days, Windows NBNS clients typically send NAME REFRESH REQUEST messages every 40 minutes. This is a fairly high frequency, and it suggests a general lack of faith in the stability of the NBNS.[9]

The NBNS handles a NAME REFRESH REQUEST in exactly the same manner as it handles a NAME REGISTRATION REQUEST. There is little reason to distinguish between the two message types. Indeed, there is no multi-homed variant of the refresh message so multi-homed hosts perform the refresh operation by sending MULTI-HOMED NAME REGISTRATION REQUEST messages.

4.3.4   *Name Release*

Both B and P nodes (and their hybrid offspring, the M and H nodes) send NAME RELEASE messages to announce that they are giving up ownership of a name.

---

8. Many thanks to Jean François for all of his work on WINS behavior and TTL gymnastics.

9. Microsoft may be assuming that the NBNS service is being provided by their own WINS implementation. Samba's NBNS, which is part of the nmbd daemon, periodically writes the contents of its database to a file called wins.dat. The wins.dat file is re-read at startup, and any non-expired names are placed back into the database. This prevents data loss due to a system restart. Samba sends refreshes every TTL/2 seconds, and there have been reports of Samba server names "disappearing" from WINS databases following a Windows system crash. It is likely that newer versions of Samba (V3.0 and beyond) will use Microsoft's formula for calculating name refresh time.

A NAME RELEASE sent in B mode is a NAME RELEASE DEMAND, as no response is expected. Any node receiving the release message will flush the released name from its local cache (if it has one[10]). In P mode, the release message sent by a node is a NAME RELEASE REQUEST, and it is always unicast to the NBNS. The message structure is the same in both cases:

```
NAME RELEASE REQUEST or NAME RELEASE DEMAND
  {
  HEADER
    {
    NAME_TRN_ID = <Set when packet is transmitted>
    FLAGS
      {
      OPCODE = 0x6 (Release)
      B      = <FALSE (0) for REQUEST, TRUE (1) for DEMAND>
      }
    QDCOUNT = 1
    ARCOUNT = 1
    }
  QUESTION_RECORD
    {
    QUESTION_NAME  = <Encoded NBT name to be released>
    QUESTION_TYPE  = NB (0x0020)
    QUESTION_CLASS = IN (0x0001)
    }
  ADDITIONAL_RECORD
    {
    RR_NAME  = 0xC00C (Label String Pointer to QUESTION_NAME)
    RR_TYPE  = NB (0x0020)
    RR_CLASS = IN (0x0001)
    TTL      = 0 (zero)
    RDLENGTH = 6
    RDATA
      {
      NB_FLAGS
        {
        G   = <TRUE for a group name, FALSE for a unique name>
        ONT = <Owner type>
        }
      NB_ADDRESS = <Releasing node's IP address>
      }
    }
  }
```

---

10. Windows systems typically cache resolved names for about seven minutes. Use the nbtstat -c command from the DOS prompt to see the cache contents.

4.3.4.1   Name Release Response

The NBNS will always respond to a NAME RELEASE REQUEST. The response packet looks like this:

```
NAME RELEASE RESPONSE
  {
  HEADER
    {
    NAME_TRN_ID = <Must match REQUEST transaction ID>
    FLAGS
      {
      R       = TRUE (1; This is a response packet)
      OPCODE  = 0x6 (Release)
      AA      = TRUE (1)
      RCODE   = <See discussion>
      B       = FALSE (0)
      }
    ANCOUNT = 1
    }
  ANSWER_RECORD
    {
    RR_NAME  = <The Released Name, encoded as usual>
    RR_TYPE  = NB (0x0020)
    RR_CLASS = IN (0x0001)
    TTL      = 0 (TTL has no meaning in this context)
    RDLENGTH = 6
    RDATA    = <Same as request packet>
    }
  }
```

Possible values for RCODE are:

0x0: Success

POSITIVE NAME RELEASE RESPONSE. The name entry has been removed from the NBNS database.

FMT_ERR (0x1): Format error

Something got messed up, and the NBNS couldn't understand the request.

SRV_ERR (0x2): Server failure

The NBNS is sick and cannot handle requests just now.

NAM_ERR (0x3): Name error

The name does not exist in the NBNS database or, if the name exists, the NB_FLAGS did not match (so it's not really the same name).

RFS_ERR (0x5): Refused error

The NBNS has made a policy decision not to release the name. For some reason, the end node that sent the request does not have authority to remove it.

ACT_ERR (0x6): Active error

The name was found in the database, but the NB_ADDRESS field did not match. Another node owns the name, so your node may not release it.

4.3.5 *Node Status*

The Node Status Request operation goes by many names: "Node Status Query," "Adapter Status Query," "NBSTAT," etc. This NBT message is used to implement the old NetBIOS Adapter Status command, which was used to retrieve information from LAN Adapter cards (LANAs, in PC Network terms).

```
NODE STATUS REQUEST
  {
  HEADER
    {
    NAME_TRN_ID = <Set when packet is transmitted>
    FLAGS
      {
      OPCODE = 0x0 (Query)
      B      = FALSE (0)
      }
    QDCOUNT = 1
    }
  QUESTION_RECORD
    {
    QUESTION_NAME  = <Encoded NBT name to be queried>
    QUESTION_TYPE  = NBSTAT (0x0021)
    QUESTION_CLASS = IN (0x0001)
    }
  }
```

Note that these queries are sent from one end node to another. The NBNS is never involved. This is because the NBNS itself is not connected to an NBT virtual LAN Adapter. The NBNS is part of the infrastructure that *creates* the NetBIOS virtual LAN. Only the end nodes are actually *members of* the LAN.

4.3.5.1 Node Status Response

The response is not as simple as the query. The format of the reply depends upon the type of card and/or virtual adapter used to build the network. In the old days, different implementations of NetBIOS were built on top of different LANAs, or emulated on top of a variety of underlying transport protocols. Each implementation kept track of its own set of status information, so the reply to the Adapter Status command was vendor-specific.

The RFC authors developed their own reply structure, probably based in part on existing samples. The NODE STATUS RESPONSE looks like this:

```
NODE STATUS RESPONSE
  {
  HEADER
    {
    NAME_TRN_ID = <Same as request ID.>
    FLAGS
      {
      R     = TRUE (1)
      OPCODE = 0x0 (Query)
      AA    = TRUE (1)
      }
    ANCOUNT = 1
    }
  ANSWER_RECORD
    {
    RR_NAME  = <The queried name, copied from the request>
    RR_TYPE  = NBSTAT (0x0021)
    RR_CLASS = IN (0x0001)
    TTL      = 0 (TTL has no meaning in this context)
    RDLENGTH = <Total length of following fields>
    RDATA
      {
      NUM_NAMES = <Number of NODE_NAME[] entries>
      NODE_NAME[]
        {
        NETBIOS_NAME = <16-octet NetBIOS name, unencoded>
        NAME_FLAGS   = <See discussion below>
        }
      STATISTICS = <See discussion below>
      }
    }
  }
```

This packet will need some tearing apart.

The RDATA.NUM_NAMES field is one octet in length. The RDA-TA.NODE_NAME array represents the responding node's local name table: the list of names the end node believes it owns. Each entry in the array contains a NETBIOS_NAME field and a NAME_FLAGS field.

The NETBIOS_NAME field is 16 bytes in length. The 16-byte name includes the suffix byte and any required padding, and is *not* encoded. The wildcard name (an asterisk followed by 15 nul bytes) is never included in the name list, which contains only registered names.

The listed NetBIOS names all exist within the same NBT scope. The Scope ID will have been sent as part of the original query, and will be stored as part of the RR_NAME field in the reply. Recall that the empty string, " ", is a valid Scope ID.

Along with each NETBIOS_NAME there is a NAME_FLAGS field, which provides name status information. It looks like this:

0	1	2	3	4	5	6	7	8	9	10	11	12	13	14	15
G	ONT		DRG	CNF	ACT	PRM					UNUSED				

The above is the same as an NB_FLAGS field with four extra bits defined.

DRG: Deregister

When an end node starts the process of releasing a name, it sets this flag. The name will continue to exist in the node's local name table until the name is released.

CNF: Conflict

We have not fully described the Name Conflict condition yet. To put it simply, if two nodes believe they both own the same name (and at least one node claims that the name is unique) then the two nodes are in conflict. One of them has to lose. The loser sets the CNF bit in its local name table and gives up using the disputed name.

ACT: Active

This bit should always be set in the NODE STATUS RESPONSE packets. If, for some strange reason, the end node stores inactive names in its local name table, these are not reported.

PRM: Permanent

According to the RFCs, every NBT end node should register a permanent name. This flag identifies that name. In practice, however, most implementations do not bother with a permanent name and this flag is not used.

These flag values are displayed by Samba's `nmblookup` program. For example:

```
shell

$ nmblookup -S zathras#20
querying zathras on 192.168.101.255
192.168.101.15 zathras<20>
Looking up status of 192.168.101.15
    ZATHRAS         <00> -          B <CONFLICT> <ACTIVE>
    UBIQX           <00> - <GROUP>  B <ACTIVE>
    ZATHRAS         <03> -          B <ACTIVE>
    ZATHRAS         <20> -          B <ACTIVE>
    UBIQX           <1e> - <GROUP>  B <ACTIVE>
```

The above shows that all of the names are ACTIVE, as they should be. The name ZATHRAS<00>, however, has been disabled due to a name conflict. From the column of B's, it is apparent that Zathras is operating in B mode.

Now let's take a look at the RDATA.STATISTICS field.

This is where things really fall apart. Microsoft's STATISTICS blob is quite different from what is specified in the RFCs, and most likely for good reason. At the time the RFCs were published, Microsoft already had at least one NetBIOS implementation. Over time they built a few others, and they had software written to use those implementations. It probably made more sense to stick with familiar layouts than adopt the new one specified in the RFCs.

Fortunately, the data in the STATISTICS record is not particularly interesting, and current systems often fill most of it with zeros anyway. Only the first six bytes are commonly used now. Windows systems will attempt to place an Ethernet MAC address into this space. Samba leaves it zero filled.

Buglet Alert

The NBT Name Service listens on port 137, but queries may originate from any UDP port number. Such is the nature of UDP. Programs like Samba's nmblookup *utility will open a high-numbered UDP port (something above 1023) in order to send a query. The reply should be sent back to that same port.*

In early versions of Windows 95, however, the source port in NODE STATUS REQUEST *messages was ignored. The* NODE STATUS RESPONSE *message was sent to UDP port 137 — the wrong port. As a result, the node that sent the query might never hear the reply.*

Time for another chunk of code. Listing 4.10 sends a NODE STATUS REQUEST message and then parses and displays the reply. As usual, it uses and builds upon functions presented in previous listings.

Listing 4.10: Node Status Request

```
void Hex_Print( uchar *src, int len )
  /* ------------------------------------------------ **
   * Print len bytes of src.  Escape any non-printing
   * characters.
   * ------------------------------------------------ **
   */
  {
  int i;

  for( i = 0; i < len; i++ )
    {
    if( isprint( src[i] ) )
      putchar( src[i] );
    else
      printf( "\\x%.2x", src[i] );
    }
  } /* Hex_Print */

void SendMsg( int             sock,
              uchar           *msg,
              int             msglen,
              struct in_addr  address )
  /* ------------------------------------------------ **
   * Send a message to port UDP/137 at the
   * specified IP address.
   * ------------------------------------------------ **
   */
```

```
    {
    int                 result;
    struct sockaddr_in to;

    to.sin_addr    = address;
    to.sin_family = AF_INET;
    to.sin_port    = htons( 137 );
    result = sendto( sock, (void *)msg, msglen, 0,
                     (struct sockaddr *)&to,
                     sizeof(struct sockaddr_in) );
    if( result < 0 )
      {
      perror( "sendto()" );
      exit( EXIT_FAILURE );
      }
    } /* SendMsg */

void ReadStatusReply( int sock )
  /* --------------------------------------------------- **
   * Read the Node Status Response message, parse the
   * NODE_NAME[] entries, and print everything in a
   * readable format.
   * --------------------------------------------------- **
   */
  {
  uchar  bufr[1024];
  ushort flags;
  int    msglen;
  int    offset;
  int    num_names;
  int    i;

  /* Read the message. */
  msglen = recv( sock, bufr, 1024, 0 );
  if( msglen < 0 )
    {
    perror( "recv()" );
    exit( EXIT_FAILURE );
    }

  /* Find start of RDATA (two bytes beyond RDLENGTH). */
  offset = 2 + Find_RDLength( bufr );

  /* The NUM_NAMES field is one byte long. */
  num_names = bufr[offset++];

  /* Now go through and print each name entry. */
```

```
  for( i = 0; i < num_names; i++, offset += 18 )
    {
    flags = (bufr[offset+16] << 8) | bufr[offset+17];

    printf( "NODE_NAME[%d]: ", i );
    Hex_Print( &bufr[offset], 15 );
    printf( "<%.2x>\t", bufr[offset+15] );

    /* Group or Unique. */
    printf( "[%c", ( GROUP_BIT & flags ) ? 'G' : 'U' );

    /* The owner node type. */
    switch( ONT_MASK & flags )
      {
      case ONT_B: printf( ",B" ); break;
      case ONT_P: printf( ",P" ); break;
      case ONT_M: printf( ",M" ); break;
      case ONT_H: printf( ",H" ); break;
      }

    /* Additional flags */
    if( DRG & flags )
      printf( ",DRG" );
    if( CNF & flags )
      printf( ",CNF" );
    if( ACT & flags )
      printf( ",ACT" );
    if( PRM & flags )
      printf( ",PRM" );

    printf( "]\n" );
    }

  /* Windows systems will also send the MAC address. */
  printf( "MAC: %.2x:%.2x:%.2x:%.2x:%.2x:%.2x\n",
          bufr[offset], bufr[offset+1], bufr[offset+2],
          bufr[offset+3], bufr[offset+4], bufr[offset+5] );
  } /* ReadStatusReply */

int main( int argc, char *argv[] )
  /* ------------------------------------------------ **
   * NBT Node Status Request.
   * ------------------------------------------------ **
   */
```

```
  {
  int           i;
  int           result;
  int           ns_sock;
  int           msg_len;
  uchar         bufr[512];
  struct in_addr address;

  if( argc != 2 )
    {
    printf( "Usage:  %s <IP>\n", argv[0] );
    exit( EXIT_FAILURE );
    }

  if( 0 == inet_aton( argv[1], &address ) )
    {
    printf( "Invalid IP.\n" );
    printf( "Usage:  %s <IP>\n", argv[0] );
    exit( EXIT_FAILURE );
    }

  ns_sock = OpenSocket();

  msg_len = BuildQuery( bufr,   /* Target buffer.    */
                        0,      /* Broadcast false. */
                        0,      /* RD bit false.    */
                        "*",    /* NetBIOS name.    */
                        '\0',   /* Padding (space). */
                        '\0',   /* Suffix (0x00).   */
                        "",     /* Scope ("").      */
                        QTYPE_NBSTAT );

  for( i = 0; i < 3; i++ )
    {
    printf( "Sending NODE STATUS query to %s...\n", argv[1] );
    SendMsg( ns_sock, bufr, msg_len, address );
    result = AwaitResponse( ns_sock, 750 );
    if( result )
      {
      ReadStatusReply( ns_sock );
      exit( EXIT_SUCCESS );
      }
    }
  printf( "No replies received.\n" );
  close( ns_sock );
  return( EXIT_FAILURE );
  } /* main */
```

4.3.6 *Name Conflict Demand*

The name conflict demand is a simple message. It looks exactly like the
NEGATIVE NAME REGISTRATION RESPONSE that we covered earlier,
except that the RCODE field contains CFT_ERR (0x7).

To review:

```
NAME CONFLICT DEMAND
  {
  HEADER
    {
    NAME_TRN_ID = <Whatever you like>
    FLAGS
      {
      R       = TRUE (1)
      OPCODE = 0x5 (Registration)
      AA      = TRUE (1)
      RD      = TRUE (1)
      RA      = TRUE (1)
      RCODE   = CFT_ERR (0x7)
      B       = FALSE (0)
      }
    ANCOUNT = 1
    }
  ANSWER_RECORD
    {
    RR_NAME  = <An NBT name owned by the target node>
    RR_TYPE  = NB (0x0020)
    RR_CLASS = IN (0x0001)
    TTL      = 0
    RDLENGTH = 6
    RDATA
      {
      NB_FLAGS
        {
        G   = <TRUE for a group name, FALSE for a unique name>
        ONT = <Owner type>
        }
      NB_ADDRESS = <Owner's IP address>
      }
    }
  }
```

Once you've got NAME REGISTRATION RESPONSE packets coded
up this one will be easy. The question is, what does it do?

The NAME CONFLICT DEMAND is sent whenever the NBNS or an end node discovers a name conflict somewhere on the NBT network. The goal is to make the offending node aware of the fact that it has stolen another node's name. An NBNS might send one of these if it finds an inconsistency in its database, possibly as a result of synchronizing with another NBNS.[11] An end node will send a NAME CONFLICT DEMAND if it gets conflicting replies to a NAME QUERY REQUEST, working under the assumption that the first response is the correct one.

When a node receives a NAME CONFLICT DEMAND it is supposed to disable the offending name. Any existing connections that were made using that name are unaffected, but the node will no longer respond to name queries for the disabled name, nor will it allow the disabled name to be used for new connections. It's as if the name no longer exists.

There is an obvious security problem with this behavior. An evildoer can easily disable a name on, say, a file server or other important node. That alone could cause a Denial of Service condition but the evildoer can go further by registering the same name itself, thus assuming the identity of the disabled node. For this reason, Samba and most (but not all) Windows systems ignore NAME CONFLICT DEMAND messages.

4.3.6.1   Name Release Demand Revisited

There are actually two messages that can be used to force a node to give up a name. In addition to the NAME CONFLICT DEMAND, there is the NAME RELEASE DEMAND. You may recall that a node operating in B (or M or H) mode will broadcast a release announcement when it wants to release one of its own names. The same message can be unicast to another node to force the node to give up a name it holds.

---

11. Microsoft's WINS servers can be configured to replicate with one another, simultaneously distributing the database for greater reliability and increasing the risk of conflicts and other corruption. WINS replication takes place over TCP port 42, should you care to observe. The replication protocol is fairly straightforward and has been untangled. There are plans to add WINS replication support to Samba sometime after version 3.0 is released.

```
NAME RELEASE DEMAND (unicast)
  {
  HEADER
    {
    NAME_TRN_ID = <Set when packet is transmitted>
    FLAGS
      {
      OPCODE = 0x6 (Release)
      B      = FALSE (0)
      }
    QDCOUNT = 1
    ARCOUNT = 1
    }
  QUESTION_RECORD
    {
    QUESTION_NAME  = <Encoded NBT name to be released>
    QUESTION_TYPE  = NB (0x0020)
    QUESTION_CLASS = IN (0x0001)
    }
  ADDITIONAL_RECORD
    {
    RR_NAME  = 0xC00C (Label String Pointer to QUESTION_NAME)
    RR_TYPE  = NB (0x0020)
    RR_CLASS = IN (0x0001)
    TTL      = 0 (zero)
    RDLENGTH = 6
    RDATA
      {
      NB_FLAGS
        {
        G   = <TRUE for a group name, FALSE for a unique name>
        ONT = <Target node's owner type>
        }
      NB_ADDRESS = <Target node's IP address>
      }
    }
  }
```

As with the NAME CONFLICT DEMAND, most (but not all) systems ignore this message. Play around... see what you find.

4.4   Enough Already

We could dig deeper. We could provide finer detail. We could, for instance, discuss the design, implementation, care, and feeding of a full-scale NBNS...

but not now. It's getting late and we still have a lot of NBT ground to cover. Go ahead and take a quick break. Hug the spouse, make a fresh pot of tea, visit the facilities, scratch the dog, and then we'll move on to the Datagram Service.

When you get back, we will start by overstating one of the key points of this section: that the purpose of the Name Service is to create a virtual NetBIOS LAN on top of a TCP/IP (inter)network.

5

The Datagram Service in Detail

If a tree falls in the forest,
and no one is there to hear it...

Let's drill home this key concept one more time:

> NBT provides a set of services which combine to create a virtual NetBIOS LAN over TCP/UPD/IP transport.

This would be a senseless thing to do *except* for the fact that lots of software uses (or used to use) the NetBIOS API. The whole point is to maintain the form and function of the API while completely replacing the guts and machinery which lie beneath. This point gets lost, however, when we deal with systems that are not derived from MS-DOS and have no use for NetBIOS itself. On these systems we work directly with the guts of NBT and, therefore, are easily confused by the odd behavior of the machinery.

So, to provide a little context, here are the four NetBIOS API functions which the Datagram Service was designed to support:

- `Send Specific Datagram`
- `Receive Specific Datagram`
- `Send Broadcast Datagram`
- `Receive Broadcast Datagram`

Let's start by looking at the two `Send Datagram` functions. These two API calls provide us with three transmission options: unicast, multicast, and broadcast. Here's how they work:

Send Specific Datagram

This function requires a NetBIOS name as a parameter.

- If the name is unique, the datagram is *unicast*.
- If the name is a group name, then the datagram is *multicast*.

Send Broadcast Datagram

This function does not accept a NetBIOS name. Broadcast datagrams are sent the length and breadth of the NetBIOS LAN, and picked up by any node that is listening.

That was easy. Now let's look at what happens when we map those functions onto UDP/IP at the NBT layer...

Send Specific Datagram

A `NAME QUERY REQUEST` is issued to discover whether the destination name is a unique or group name.

- If it is a unique name, then the message can be encapsulated in a UDP packet and sent to the IP address given in the `NAME QUERY RESPONSE`. In NBT terminology, this is a `DIRECT UNIQUE DATAGRAM`.
- If it is a group name...
  - If the sender is operating in B mode, it will broadcast the packet on the local IP subnet so that all group members can receive it.
  - If the sender is *not* operating in B mode, then the datagram is forwarded to the **NetBIOS Datagram Distribution** Server (NBDD).

  In NBT terminology, a multicast datagram is known as a `DIRECT GROUP DATAGRAM`.

Send Broadcast Datagram

The wildcard name (with the sender's Scope ID appended) is used as the destination name.

- If the sender is operating in B mode, it will broadcast the packet on the local IP subnet. All NBT nodes within the same scope will be able to receive the message.

- If the sender is *not* operating in B mode, then the datagram is forwarded to the NBDD.

As you can see from the description, unicast datagrams are easy, B mode is easy, but handling multicast or broadcast in P, or M, or H mode is a bit more complicated. We'll give that topic a section heading all its own, just to show that it is a fairly hefty chunk of tofu.

5.1   Datagram Distribution over Routed IP Internetworks

The **N**et**B**IOS **D**atagram **D**istribution Server (NBDD) compliments the NBNS. It assists in extending the virtual NetBIOS LAN across a routed IP internetwork by relaying multicast and broadcast NetBIOS datagrams to nodes on remote subnets. The NBDD's job is to make sure that the datagrams get to where they're supposed to go. It works something like a lawn sprinkler — one input leads to a spray of outputs. Here's what happens:

- A P (or M or H) node sends a datagram to the NBDD.
- The NBDD consults the NBNS database and gathers the IP addresses of all intended recipients.
- The NBDD then sends a copy of the message, via unicast UDP datagrams, to each of the IP addresses in the list.

That seems simple enough, but we claimed earlier that the Datagram Service is the second least well understood aspect of NBT. What are we missing?

A closer inspection reveals an obvious problem. If the number of destination nodes is large, a whole bigbunch of traffic will be generated — possibly enough to bring the NBT virtual LAN to its knees (which might really, really annoy people). The NBDD design will work well enough for small, trusted networks but it simply does not scale.

Another problem is that RFC 1001 offers a loophole for implementors: the NBDD is permitted to silently ignore requests to relay datagrams. If, for any reason (including laziness on the implementor's part) the NBDD will not

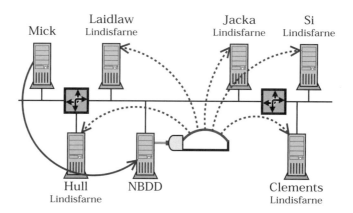

Figure 5.1:   *The Datagram Distribution Server*

Node MICK wants to send a message to all members of group LINDISFARNE, but the NetBIOS LAN is distributed across a routed IP internetwork. MICK sends the datagram to the NBDD which relays the message to all group members.

or can not relay a datagram, it simply discards the message without sending any sort of error message back to the originating node.

This loophole might make the NBDD so unreliable as to be useless, except that the Datagram Service also supports a query operation that allows the client to ask the NBDD whether or not it will relay a message. If the NBDD answers the query with a "yes," then the client can send the datagram with the assurance that it will be relayed to all intended recipients. A negative reply means that the NBDD will not relay the message.

 Reminder Alert

Datagrams are not considered reliable. As with the UDP service in an IP network, it is expected that some NetBIOS datagrams may be lost.

By allowing the NBDD to silently discard datagrams, however, the lack of reliability is amplified well beyond what would be expected from simple network packet loss.

One more monkey-wrench to throw into the works... Given a multicast (not broadcast) datagram, if the NBDD will not relay the message, the client can give it another shot. The client has already performed a Name Service NAME QUERY REQUEST operation, and received a NAME QUERY RESPONSE from the NBNS. It did this to determine that the destination name was, in fact, a group name rather than a unique name. If the NBNS is RFC-compliant, then the NAME QUERY RESPONSE will contain a list of all the IP addresses of the group members. If the NBDD won't relay the message, then the client can unicast the datagram to each entry in the list.

To summarize:

- Unicast datagrams are simply sent to the intended recipient.
- In B mode, multicast/broadcast datagrams are broadcast on the local LAN.
- For multicast/broadcast datagrams in P, H, and M modes the NBDD should be queried to see if will relay the datagram.
  - If a positive response is received, then send the datagram to the NBDD for distribution.
  - Else:
    - If the datagram is multicast and the Name Server returned a complete IP list, then send the message via unicast datagrams to each IP in the list.
    - Else, broadcast the datagram on the local subnet and hope that some nodes will receive it.

Confused? Don't be surprised if you are. It isn't a pretty system... and it gets worse. Because of the potential network problems and the awkwardness of the design, very few implementations even try to match the RFC specification. Unfortunately, no one has come up with a better solution... which means that what actually exists in the wild is worse than what was just described.

5.2   The NBDD and the Damage Done

To be blunt, Microsoft messed up the Datagram Service. Their NBNS implementation (WINS) does not report all of the IP addresses associated with a group name. Instead, group names are mapped to a single IP address — the limited broadcast address: 255.255.255.255. This is contrary to the RFCs, and it causes a few problems.

Without a list of IPs for each group name, the NBDD cannot be implemented at all. With no NBDD and no IP list, there is no way to ensure that multicast and broadcast datagrams will be sent to all group members. This breaks the continuity of the NetBIOS virtual LAN. On a "real" NetBIOS LAN, a message sent to a group name would actually reach all members of that group. That is what should happen under NBT as well, but it doesn't. The best that can be done is to broadcast on the local subnet, in which case *some* members of the group *may* get the message.

Microsoft must have realized their mistake, because they later created what they call "Internet Group" names (also called "Special Group" names). For names in this category, WINS comes close to behaving like a proper NBNS; it will store up to 25 IP addresses per name, deleting the oldest entry to make room if necessary. For these names, a POSITIVE NAME QUERY RESPONSE from a WINS server will list up to 25 valid IP addresses.

Internet Group names are identified by their suffix. Originally only group names with the 0x1C suffix were given special treatment, but more recently (with W2K?) group names with a suffix value of 0x20 can be defined as having Internet Group status. Note that unique names may also have these suffixes but, since they are not group names, no special handling is required.

Sadly, most non-Microsoft implementations (including Samba) follow Microsoft's example. They map group names to the 255.255.255.255 IP address, store only 25 IPs for Special Group names, and fail to implement the NBDD.[1] This can cause trouble for some clients (OS/2, for example) which expect RFC behavior.

Sigh.

5.3   Implementing a Workable Datagram Service

That last section was a bit of a rant. Sorry. Time to pick up the pieces and move on. Let's talk about how the parts that work actually work.

As with the Name Service, each Datagram Service packet has a header. The datagram header is 10 bytes long, arranged as follows:

---

1. Network Telesystems, which has since been acquired by Efficient Networks, used to have an NBNS implementation that handled group names correctly and worked quite well with IBM's OS/2. Brian Landy has also written a set of patches for Samba's nmbd daemon which provide more complete NBDD support. See http://www.landy.cx/.

0	1	2	3	4	5	6	7	8	9	10	11	12	13	14	15
MSG_TYPE								FLAGS							
DGM_ID															
SOURCE_IP															
SOURCE_PORT															

Here is a quick rundown of the fields:

MSG_TYPE (1 byte)

This field is something like the OPCODE field in the Name Service header. It indicates which type of Datagram Service message is being sent. It has the following possible values:

```
0x10 == DIRECT_UNIQUE DATAGRAM
0x11 == DIRECT_GROUP DATAGRAM
0x12 == BROADCAST DATAGRAM
0x13 == DATAGRAM ERROR
0x14 == DATAGRAM QUERY REQUEST
0x15 == DATAGRAM POSITIVE QUERY RESPONSE
0x16 == DATAGRAM NEGATIVE QUERY RESPONSE
```

The first three of these represent unicast, multicast, and broadcast datagrams, respectively. The DATAGRAM ERROR packet is used to report errors within the Datagram Service. (There are only three errors defined in the RFCs.) The final three types are used in the query mechanism described earlier.

FLAGS (1 byte)

This field breaks down into a set of bitwise subfields:

0	1	2	3	4	5	6	7
UNUSED				SNT		F	M

SNT: *Sending Node Type*

This subfield has the following set of possible values (in binary):

```
00 == B node
01 == P node
10 == M node
11 == NBDD
```

Microsoft did not implement the NBDD. They did, however, introduce H mode. In practice the value `11` is used to indicate that the sending node is an H node.

F: FIRST flag

Indicates that this is the first (and possibly only) packet in a fragmented series.

M: MORE flag

Indicates that the message is fragmented, and that the next fragment should follow.

The `F` and `M` flags are used to manage fragmented messages, which will be described in more detail real soon now.

DGM_ID (2 bytes)

The Datagram ID is similar in purpose to the `NAME_TRN_ID` field in Name Service headers. There should be a unique `DGM_ID` for each (conceptual) call to the NetBIOS `Send Specific Datagram` or `Send Broadcast Datagram` functions. More about this when we discuss fragmented messages.

SOURCE_IP (4 bytes)

The IP address of the *originating* node. If the datagram is being relayed via the NBDD, then the IP header (at the IP layer of the stack, rather than the NBT layer) will contain the IP address of the NBDD. The `SOURCE_IP` field keeps track of the IP address of the node that actually composed the datagram.

SOURCE_PORT (2 bytes)

As with the `SOURCE_IP` field, this field indicates the UDP port used by the originating node.

The above fields are common to all Datagram Service messages. RFC 1002 includes two more fields in its header layout: the `DGM_LENGTH` and

PACKET_OFFSET fields. It is kind of silly to have those fields in the header, as they are specific to the messages which actually carry a data payload: the DIRECT_UNIQUE, DIRECT_GROUP, and BROADCAST DATAGRAM message types.

Since the DGM_LENGTH and PACKET_OFFSET fields are associated with the datagram transport messages, we will break with tradition and put those fields together with the message structure. Here is a record layout:

0	1	2	3	4	5	6	7	8	9	10	11	12	13	14	15
DGM_LENGTH															
PACKET_OFFSET															
SOURCE_NAME															
DESTINATION_NAME															
USER_DATA															

DGM_LENGTH (2 bytes)

The formula given for calculating the value of the DGM_LENGTH field is:

```
DGM_LENGTH = length( SOURCE_NAME )
           + length( DESTINATION_NAME )
           + length( USER_DATA )
```

That is, the number of bytes following the PACKET_OFFSET field.[2]

PACKET_OFFSET (2 bytes)

Used in conjunction with the F and M flags in the header to allow reconstruction of fragmented NetBIOS datagrams.

SOURCE_NAME (34..255 bytes)

The encoded NBT name of the sending application. Recall that NBT names are communication endpoints in much the same way that a UDP or TCP port is an endpoint. The correct SOURCE_NAME must be supplied to identify the service or application that sent the datagram.

---

2. This field is probably not even used by most implementations. For a long time, Samba miscalculated the DGM_LENGTH field by including the length of the 14-byte RFC header. This bug (fixed as of 2.2.4) did not seem to cause any trouble.

DESTINATION_NAME (34..255 bytes)

The encoded NBT name of the destination application or service. For broadcast datagrams, the DESTINATION_NAME will be the wildcard name — an asterisk ('*') followed by fifteen nul bytes. The NBT name must include the Scope ID (even if it is the default empty scope, " ").

USER_DATA (0..512 bytes)

The actual data to be transmitted.

That's basically all there is to it, with the exception of fragmentation. The example packet below describes an unfragmented message.

```
DATAGRAM_HEADER (unfragmented)
  {
  MSG_TYPE = <10 = unicast, 11 = multicast, 12 = broadcast>
  FLAGS
    {
    SNT = <Node type, as shown above>
    F   = TRUE   (This is the first in the series)
    M   = FALSE  (No additional fragments follow)
    }
  DGM_ID      = <Datagram identifier>
  SOURCE_IP   = <IP address of the originating node>
  SOURCE_PORT = <Originating UDP port>
  }
DATAGRAM_DATA
  {
  DGM_LENGTH       = <Name lengths plus USER_DATA length>
  PACKET_OFFSET    = 0
  SOURCE_NAME      = <Fully encoded NBT name of the sender>
  DESTINATION_NAME = <Fully encoded NBT name of the receiver>
  USER_DATA        = <Datagram payload>
  }
```

Some quick notes:

- The DGM_ID should be unique with respect to other active datagrams originating from the same source. With 64K values from which to choose, this should not be difficult.
- Once again, the SOURCE_IP, SOURCE_PORT, and SOURCE_NAME are all relative to the originator of the datagram. An NBDD does not alter these fields when it relays a message.

■ NBT datagrams are sent *within* scope. The Scope ID must be present in the SOURCE_NAME and DESTINATION_NAME fields, even if it is the empty scope (" ").

5.3.1   *Fragmenting Datagrams*

A little way back, we mentioned the NetBIOS API Send Specific Datagram and Send Broadcast Datagram functions. These functions each accept up to 512 bytes of data on input. Given that number, the maximum on-the-wire size of an NBT datagram is:

```
   10 bytes (Header)
+   2 bytes (DGM_LENGTH)
+   2 bytes (PACKET_OFFSET)
+ 255 bytes (maximum size of SOURCE_NAME)
+ 255 bytes (maximum size of DESTINATION_NAME)
+ 512 bytes (maximum size of USER_DATA)
-----
 1036 bytes
```

and that, of course, does not include the UDP and IP headers. The whole thing is fairly chunky — easily more than double the size of the data actually being sent.

The RFC authors were concerned that the UDP transport might not carry datagrams that big, so they provided a mechanism for breaking the USER_DATA into smaller fragments, like so:

first fragment
```
FLAGS.F       = TRUE (This is the first fragment)
FLAGS.M       = TRUE (Additional fragments follow)
PACKET_OFFSET = 0
```

middle fragments
```
FLAGS.F       = FALSE (This is the not the first fragment)
FLAGS.M       = TRUE  (Additional fragments follow)
PACKET_OFFSET = <Data offset of fragment>
```

final fragment
```
FLAGS.F       = FALSE (This is not the first fragment)
FLAGS.M       = FALSE (No more fragments follow)
PACKET_OFFSET = <Data offset of fragment>
```

The value of the PACKET_OFFSET field is the sum of the lengths of all previous fragments. This value is included in the message so that the receiver can keep the fragments in sync as it rebuilds the original USER_DATA. This is necessary, because datagrams do not always arrive in the order in which they were sent.

Now that you have learned all of that, you can forget most of it. As is typical for the Datagram Service, the fragmentation feature is rarely — if ever — used. The IP layer has its own mechanism for handling large packets so NBT datagram fragmentation is redundant.

It is possible that someone, somewhere, has implemented fragmentation, so an NBT implementation should be prepared to deal with it. One simple option is to discard fragments. This can be considered valid because the Datagram Service is considered "unreliable."

Something else to keep in mind: The 512-byte maximum size for the USER_DATA field is required at the NetBIOS layer, but not the NBT layer. Since the NetBIOS API is not required for implementing NBT, you mustn't expect that the datagrams you receive will fit within the limit. Code defensively.

5.3.2   *Receiving Datagrams*

NBT receives datagram messages on UDP port 138, so clients must listen on that port at the UDP level. When a message datagram is received (MSG_TYPE is one of 0x10, 0x11, or 0x12) the DESTINATION_NAME is checked against the local name table. If the name is not found, the client should reply with a DATAGRAM ERROR MESSAGE. The available error codes are:

```
0x82 == DESTINATION NAME NOT PRESENT
0x83 == INVALID SOURCE NAME FORMAT
0x84 == INVALID DESTINATION NAME FORMAT
```

The first value is used whenever the DESTINATION_NAME is not in the local name table at the receiving end. The other two codes are sent whenever the source or destination NBT names, respectively, cannot be parsed.

If the name is found in the local table, then the datagram may be passed to any application or service that is listening for the given DESTINA-TION_NAME. The NetBIOS API provides the Receive Specific Datagram and Receive Broadcast Datagram calls for this purpose.

If there are no `Receive Datagram` requests waiting, the datagram is quietly discarded.

NBDD processing (for those bold enough to want to implement an NBDD) is similar. When the NBDD receives a datagram it will search the NBNS database instead of the local name table. Error messages are returned as above for missing or malformed names.

One more note: As a safety precaution, the receiving node should probably verify that the `SOURCE_IP` field in the datagram header matches either the source address in the IP header, or the NBDD address (if there is one).

5.3.3 *Querying the NBDD*

The NBDD query message is simply an NBT Datagram Service header with the `DESTINATION_NAME` appended:

```
DATAGRAM_HEADER
  {
  MSG_TYPE = 0x14 (DATAGRAM QUERY REQUEST)
  FLAGS
    {
    SNT = <Node type>
    F   = TRUE
    M   = FALSE
    }
  DGM_ID       = <Datagram identifier>
  SOURCE_IP    = <IP address of the originating node>
  SOURCE_PORT = <Originating UDP port>
  }
DATAGRAM_DATA
  {
  DESTINATION_NAME = <Encoded NBT name of the intended receiver>
  }
```

If there is an NBDD, and if it can relay the request, it will change the `MSG_TYPE` field to `0x15` (`POSITIVE QUERY RESPONSE`) and echo the packet back to the sender. If the NBDD is unwilling or unable to relay the message it will set `MSG_TYPE` to `0x16` (`NEGATIVE QUERY RESPONSE`) before sending the reply.

5.3.4 *The Second Least Well Understood Aspect of NBT*

It really should have been much simpler, but given the design flaws and implementation errors it is no wonder people have trouble with the Datagram Service. Our hope is that this section has cleared things up a bit, and explained the problems well enough to make them easier to solve.

Just to finish up, here are a few tips:

- The NBDD should never relay datagrams to itself. If the NBDD host is also an NBT end node, then it must deliver datagrams to itself *and then pass them along to the NBDD*. There is no way to know if a received datagram is intended for the end node or the NBDD.

- Likewise, if a host is acting as both end node and NBDD, the end node processing should *not* generate DESTINATION NAME NOT PRESENT (0x82) errors. The datagram should be passed along to the NBDD instead.

- The NBNS should store all IP addresses associated with a group name. If necessary, it can return the local broadcast IP address (255.255.255.255) in response to name queries, thus maintaining compatibly with Microsoft's WINS. Storing all group name IP addresses is necessary for NBDD implementation.

- Set a limit on the size of the IP list to which an NBDD will relay messages.

- Don't worry about it. If you get the basics right, your system will work well enough. Very few systems expect a complete and proper NBT Datagram Service implementation.

6

The Session Service in Detail

> The best way to eliminate the problem is to remove Scopes completely.
>
> — John Terpstra, Samba Team, in a message to the Samba-Technical mailing list

This is the last big chunk of NBT. It is also the easiest, which should bring a great sigh of relief. We have already covered all of the background material we need to cover, so there is no need to waste any time with preliminaries. Let's dive right in...

6.1   Session Service Header

The Session Service header, as presented in RFC 1002, is as follows:

0	1	2	3	4	5	6	7	8	9	10	11	12	13	14	15
TYPE								FLAGS							
LENGTH															

The FLAGS field breaks down further into:

0	1	2	3	4	5	6	7
reserved							E

The reserved bits are always supposed to be zero, and the E bit is an additional high-order bit which is prepended to the LENGTH field. Another way to look at the layout is like this:

0	1	2	3	4	5	6	7	8	9	1 0	1 1	1 2	1 3	1 4	1 5	1 6	1 7	1 8	1 9	2 0	2 1	2 2	2 3	2 4	2 5	2 6	2 7	2 8	2 9	3 0	3 1
		TYPE								reserved						LENGTH (17 bits)															

We will stick with the latter, simpler format and ignore the FLAGS field, which is never really used.

The LENGTH field contains the number of bytes of payload, and the TYPE field is used to distinguish between the six different Session Service message types, which are:

0x00 == Session Message
0x81 == Session Request
0x82 == Positive Session Response
0x83 == Negative Session Response
0x84 == Retarget Session Response
0x85 == Session Keepalive

Each of these message types is explained below.

6.2   Creating an NBT Session

The first step in setting up an NBT session is to discover the IP address of the remote node. The IP address is, of course, required in order to create the TCP session that will carry the NBT session. The NBT Name Service is generally used to find the remote host's IP address, though several implementations support kludges which bypass the Name Service. Once the TCP session is established (something we assume you know how to do) the NBT session is initiated using a SESSION REQUEST message, which looks like this:

```
SESSION REQUEST
  {
  HEADER
    {
    TYPE   = 0x81 (Session Request)
    LENGTH = 68   (See discussion below)
    }
  CALLED_NAME  = <Destination Level 2 Encoded NetBIOS name>
  CALLING_NAME = <Source Level 2 Encoded NetBIOS name>
  }
```

One oddity of the Session Service is that the Scope ID is dropped from the name fields in the SESSION REQUEST message. That results in a fixed length of 34 bytes per name. That's one byte for the leading label (always 0x20), 32 bytes for the First Level Encoded NetBIOS name, and one more byte for the trailing label (always 0x00). The payload of a SESSION REQUEST message is, therefore, fixed at 2 × 34 = 68 bytes.

 Caveat Alert
The RFCs do not specify whether the Scope ID should or should not be included in the CALLED or CALLING NAME. It would make sense to assume that the Scope ID should be included, since both the Name Service and Datagram Service require the Scope ID, but that's not how things actually work on the wire.

As it is, the behavior of the Session Service is inconsistent with the rest of the NBT system. Fortunately, Scope is enforced by the Name Service, so it is not critical that it be enforced by the Session Service.

There are three possible replies to the SESSION REQUEST message:

0x82: POSITIVE SESSION RESPONSE

The remote node has accepted the session request, and the session is established. Kewl!

```
POSITIVE SESSION RESPONSE
  {
  HEADER
    {
    TYPE   = 0x82
    LENGTH = 0
    }
  }
```

0x83: NEGATIVE SESSION RESPONSE

Something went wrong, and the remote node has rejected the session request.

```
NEGATIVE SESSION RESPONSE
  {
  HEADER
    {
    TYPE   = 0x83
    LENGTH = 1
    }
  ERROR_CODE = <A Session Service Error Code>
  }
```

The one-byte ERROR_CODE field is supposed to indicate the cause of the trouble. Possible values are:

0x80: Not Listening On Called Name

The remote node has registered the CALLED NAME, but no application or service is listening for session connection requests on that name.

0x81: Not Listening For Calling Name

The remote node has registered the CALLED NAME and is listening for connections, but it doesn't want to talk to you. It is expecting a call from some other CALLING NAME.

There are some interesting implications to this. It means that a server could, potentially, be selective about which nodes may connect. On the other hand, it would be trivial to spoof the CALLING NAME.

0x82: Called Name Not Present

The remote node has not even registered the CALLED NAME. Better re-try your name resolution.

0x83: Insufficient Resources

The remote node is busy and cannot take your call at this time.

0x8F: Unspecified Error

Something is wrong on the far end, but we are not quite sure what the problem is.

It is annoying that the error code values overlap the Session Service message type values.

0x84: RETARGET SESSION RESPONSE

This Session Service message tells the calling node to try a different IP address and/or port number, something like a `Redirect` directive on a web page. When a client receives a RETARGET SESSION RESPONSE message in response to a SESSION REQUEST, it is supposed to close the existing TCP connection and open a new one using the IP address and port number provided.

```
RETARGET SESSION RESPONSE
  {
  HEADER
    {
    TYPE   = 0x84
    LENGTH = 6
    }
  RETARGET_IP_ADDRESS = <New IP address>
  PORT                = <New TCP port number>
  }
```

This feature opens up some interesting possibilities. Retargeting could be used for load balancing, fault tolerance, or to allow unprivileged users to run their own SMB servers on high-numbered ports.

Of course, client support for this feature is inconsistent. Based on some simple tests, it seems that Samba's `smbclient` handles retargeting just fine, as do Windows 95 and Windows 98. In contrast, Windows 2000 deals with the RETARGET SESSION RESPONSE as if it were an error message of some sort. W2K will retry the original IP address and port number, and then give up.

Listing 6.1: Session retargeting

```
#include <ctype.h>
#include <stdlib.h>
#include <string.h>
#include <stdarg.h>
#include <stdio.h>
#include <errno.h>
#include <unistd.h>
```

```c
#include <sys/types.h>
#include <sys/socket.h>
#include <netinet/in.h>
#include <arpa/inet.h>

void PrintL1Name( uchar *src, int max )
  /* -------------------------------------------------- **
   * Decode and pretty-print an L1-encoded NetBIOS name.
   * -------------------------------------------------- **
   */
  {
  int        suffix;
  static char namestr[16];

  suffix = L1_Decode( namestr, src, 1, max );
  Hex_Print( namestr, strlen( namestr ) );
  printf( "<%.2x>", suffix );
  }/* PrintL1Name */

int Get_SS_Length( uchar *hdr )
  /* -------------------------------------------------- **
   * Read the length field from an SMB Session Service
   * header.
   * -------------------------------------------------- **
   */
  {
  int tmp;

  tmp  = (hdr[1] & 1) << 16;
  tmp |= hdr[2] << 8;
  tmp |= hdr[3];
  return( tmp );
  } /* Get_SS_Length */

int OpenPort139( void )
  /* -------------------------------------------------- **
   * Open port 139 for listening.
   * Note: this requires root privilege, and Samba's
   *       SMBD daemon must not be running on its
   *       default port.
   * -------------------------------------------------- **
   */
  {
  int                result;
  int                sock;
  struct sockaddr_in sox;
```

```
/* Create the socket. */
sock = socket( PF_INET, SOCK_STREAM, IPPROTO_TCP );
if( sock < 0 )
  {
  printf( "Failed to create socket(); %s.\n",
          strerror( errno ) );
  exit( EXIT_FAILURE );
  }

/* Bind the socket to any interface, port TCP/139. */
sox.sin_addr.s_addr = INADDR_ANY;
sox.sin_family      = AF_INET;
sox.sin_port        = htons( 139 );
result = bind( sock,
               (struct sockaddr *)&sox,
               sizeof(struct sockaddr_in) );
if( result < 0 )
  {
  printf( "Failed to bind() socket; %s.\n",
          strerror( errno ) );
  exit( EXIT_FAILURE );
  }

/* Post the listen request. */
result = listen( sock, 5 );
if( result < 0 )
  {
  printf( "Failed to listen() on socket; %s.\n",
          strerror( errno ) );
  exit( EXIT_FAILURE );
  }

/* Ready... */
return( sock );
} /* OpenPort139 */

void Listen( struct in_addr trg_addr, int trg_port )
  /* ------------------------------------------------- **
   * Accepts incoming connections, sends a retarget
   * message, and then disconnects.
   * ------------------------------------------------- **
   */
  {
  int               listen_sock;
  int               reply_sock;
  int               result;
  struct sockaddr_in remote_addr;
```

```
socklen_t            addr_len;
uchar                recvbufr[1536];
uchar                replymsg[10];

listen_sock = OpenPort139();

/* Fill in the redirect message. */
replymsg[0] = 0x84;    /* Retarget code. */
replymsg[1] = 0;
replymsg[2] = 0;
replymsg[3] = 6;       /* Remaining length. */
(void)memcpy( &(replymsg[4]), &trg_addr.s_addr, 4 );
trg_port = htons( trg_port );
(void)memcpy( &(replymsg[8]), &trg_port, 2 );

printf( "Waiting for connections...\n" );
for(;;)  /* Until killed. */
  {
  /* Wait for a connection. */
  addr_len = sizeof( struct sockaddr_in );
  reply_sock = accept( listen_sock,
                       (struct sockaddr *)&remote_addr,
                       &addr_len );

  /* If the accept() failed exit with an error message. */
  if( reply_sock < 0 )
    {
    printf( "Error accept()ing a connection: %s\n",
            strerror(errno) );
    exit( EXIT_FAILURE );
    }

  result = recv( reply_sock, recvbufr, 1536, 0 );
  if( result < 0 )
    {
    printf( "Error receiving packet: %s\n",
            strerror(errno) );
    }
  else
    {
    printf( "SESSION MESSAGE\n  {\n" );
    printf( "  TYPE   = 0x%.2x\n", recvbufr[0] );
    printf( "  LENGTH = %d\n", Get_SS_Length( recvbufr ) );
```

```
      if( 0x81 == recvbufr[0] )
        {
        int offset;

        printf( "  CALLED_NAME  = " );
        PrintL1Name( &recvbufr[4], result );
        offset = 5 + strlen( &(recvbufr[4]) );
        printf( "\n  CALLING_NAME = " );
        PrintL1Name( &recvbufr[offset], result );
        printf( "\n  }\nSending Retarget message.\n" );
        (void)send( reply_sock, (void *)replymsg, 10, 0 );
        }
      else
        printf( "  }\nPacket Dropped.\n" );
      }
    close( reply_sock );
    }
  } /* Listen */

int main( int argc, char *argv[] )
  /* -------------------------------------------------- **
   * Simple daemon that listens on port TCP/139 and
   * redirects incoming traffic to another IP and port.
   * -------------------------------------------------- **
   */
  {
  int              target_port;
  struct in_addr target_address;

  if( argc != 3 )
    {
    printf( "Usage:  %s <IP> <PORT>\n", argv[0] );
    exit( EXIT_FAILURE );
    }

  if( 0 == inet_aton( argv[1], &target_address ) )
    {
    printf( "Invalid IP.\n" );
    printf( "Usage:  %s <IP> <PORT>\n", argv[0] );
    exit( EXIT_FAILURE );
    }

  target_port = atoi( argv[2] );
```

```
if( 0 == target_port )
  {
  printf( "Invalid Port number.\n" );
  printf( "Usage:  %s <IP> <PORT>\n", argv[0] );
  exit( EXIT_FAILURE );
  }

Listen( target_address, target_port );
return( EXIT_SUCCESS );
} /* main */
```

One more note regarding the Retarget message: there are NetBIOS name issues to consider. The CALLED NAME must be in the name table of the node that sends the RETARGET SESSION RESPONSE message, but it must also be accepted by the node to which the session is retargeted. That may take some juggling to get right.

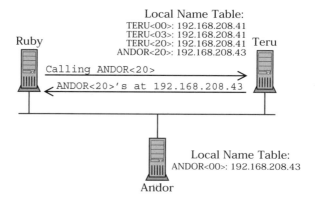

Figure 6.1:   *Naming and session retargeting*

Node Ruby is trying to open a connection to a service named ANDOR<20>. Node Teru has the name ANDOR<20> in its local name table, so Ruby tries to connect to node Teru. Teru retargets Ruby to IP address 192.168.208.43 which (we hope) will accept the connection from Ruby.

The RETARGET SESSION RESPONSE message does not work well with normal NetBIOS name management.

For those interested in playing with retargeting, it is fairly easily done. Samba's smbd daemon can be told to listed on a non-standard port and, as a bonus, it ignores the CALLED NAME in the session request. You can run the retarget daemon listed above in combination with the Samba nmbd Name Service daemon, and retarget connections to smbd running on a high port on the same machine, or running on a remote machine.

6.3   Maintaining an NBT Session

There are two more Session Service message types to cover:

0x00: SESSION MESSAGE

Once you have established a session (by sending a SESSION REQUEST and receiving a POSITIVE SESSION RESPONSE) you are ready to send messages. Each message is prefixed with a SESSION MESSAGE header, which looks like this:

```
HEADER
  {
  TYPE   = 0x00
  LENGTH = <Length of data to follow>
  }
```

Since the TYPE byte has a value of 0x00, and the next seven bits are always supposed to be zero as well, the Session Message header may be viewed simply as a long integer length value.

```
length  = ntohl( *(ulong *)packet );
```

It might be wise to mask out the unused FLAGS bits, just in case.

0x85: SESSION KEEPALIVE

The Keepalive is used to detect a lost connection. Basically, if one node hasn't sent anything to the other node for a while (typically five to six minutes), it will send a SESSION KEEPALIVE, just to make sure the remote end is still listening. The receiver simply discards the message.

```
HEADER
  {
  TYPE   = 0x85
  LENGTH = 0
  }
```

TCP is a connection-oriented protocol, so the Keepalive should generate an ACKnowledgement, or possibly a series of retries if the TCP

ACK doesn't show up right away. The Keepalive message forces TCP to verify that the connection is still working, and to report back if there is a problem. If a problem *is* detected, the client or server can gracefully shut down its end of the connection.

RFC 1001 makes it clear that sending the NBT Session Service Keepalive message is optional. TCP itself also has a keepalive mechanism, which should be used instead, if possible.

6.4   Closing an NBT Session

Nothing to it. Once all activity across the session has stopped, simply shut down the TCP connection. At the NBT level, there are no special messages to send when closing the session.

7

Where It All Went Wrong

It was a dark and stormy night.

— Paul Clifford,
Edward George Bulwer-Lytton

Implementation is the journey from Theory to Practice. The two extremes, as we have shown, are divided by a vast chasm wherein dwell all the evil monsters from all the cheesy sci-fi TV shows ever produced. For NBT implementors the journey can be perilous, and those who have gone before have blazed a somewhat twisted trail. Here are some of the dangers you will encounter along the way...

7.1 The `0x1D` Dirty Little Secret

Master Browser Servers (which are described later in the book) register unique names with the suffix `0x1D`. The WINS server will happily acknowledge such registrations — and then drop them into a black hole and forget about them. When queried, the WINS server denies the existence of any `0x1D` unique names. Nodes from one subnet can never know about the Master Browsers on other subnets, and there may be multiple nodes using the same unique `0x1D` name.

B nodes are immune to this behavior, since they do not make use of NBNS services. If the NBT vLAN is operating in M or H mode, however, the

Master Browser names will be unique *within the local IP subnet only*. The same name may be registered by another Master Browser on a separate subnet. Since the WINS server does not keep any record of 0x1D names, Master Browsers can only be located using a broadcast query, which means that P nodes can never find 0x1D names.

The strange handling of 0x1D names may be related to the lack of NBDD functionality. As you can see, an implementation that strays from the path will quickly find itself lost in a jungle of exceptions, special cases, and other yucky stuff from an old episode of "Outer Limits."

7.2   Twenty-five IPs or Less

An NBNS is supposed to keep a complete list of all IPs associated with each NBT name (group or multi-homed). If the list is too large to fit in a single UDP Name Query Reply datagram then, according to the RFCs, the NBNS is supposed to send a partial list with the TRuncation bit set. The client may then repeat the query using TCP port 137.

...but that never happens. If anyone ever did provide support for NBT Name Service over TCP, the code is now lost in space. As explained earlier, when WINS sends a NAME QUERY RESPONSE it will contain a maximum of 25 IPs per name.

7.3   Special Handling Required for 0x1B Names

A Domain Master Browser (a special kind of Master Browser, which is described later on in the book) will register unique names with a suffix of 0x1B. These names get special treatment in WINS. Whenever a 0x1B name is registed in WINS, the WINS server will look for a matching 0x1C group name and modify the entry.

As you may recall from our diatribe in the Datagram section, 0x1C group names are "Internet Group" or "Special Group" names, and WINS will keep track of 25 IP addresses per 0x1C group name. The weird thing is that WINS also sorts this IP list so that the IP address associated with the 0x1B name is at the top of the list.

Why?

Well, see, the `0x1C` names represent the set of Domain Controllers for a given NT Domain. Only the Primary Domain Controller is allowed to run the Domain Master Browser service and register the `0x1B` name. So, by sorting the IP list, WINS ensures that the IP address of the Primary Domain Controller is always the first IP address in the `0x1C` list of Domain Controllers.

7.4   Alternate Name Resolution

There are several ways to bypass the NBT Name Service. The simplest is the use of an `LMHOSTS` file, which provides NetBIOS name to IP address mappings. `LMHOSTS` is similar in concept to the `/etc/hosts` file commonly used by Unix-y systems to provide TCP/IP name mappings.

Another Name Service bypass trick involves using DNS names or IP addresses instead of NetBIOS names to find remote services. This trick is generally used when connecting to an SMB server via the NBT Session Service. The obvious problem here is that the Session Service expects that the `CALLED NAME` in the `SESSION MESSAGE` be correct.

There are several work-arounds to the naming problem.

- One may *guess* that the service name matches the first label of the DNS name. This often works, but it is not guaranteed.

- Another option is to send a `NODE STATUS REQUEST` and look through the reply for a unique name with a suffix of `0x20`, which is likely to be the correct service name. (The SMB Server Service always uses the suffix `0x20`.)

- The ugliest (and also the most common) solution is to place the NetBIOS name "`*SMBSERVER`" into the `CALLED NAME` field (encoded, of course). This special name was introduced with Windows NT 4.0, and is now supported by Samba and several commercial implementations. It is accepted for Session Service connections to the SMB Server Service, no matter what NetBIOS name is actually registered. Note that "`*SMBSERVER`" starts with an asterisk, which makes it an illegal NetBIOS name. The "`*SMBSERVER`" name is never registered, and name queries for this name should always fail.

7.5   The Awful Truth

The awful truth is that an NBT implementation must accommodate — and often comply with — the errors, kludges, omissions, and fumbles of the past. The installed base is simply too big to try and get it right. Not to worry. You now have enough information to build a working NBT implementation. Writing an NBNS and NBDD server should also be within reach, and you can pull code from some of the many Open Source projects that are out there (as long as you respect the licenses). We have covered all of the major pitfalls, and NBT is a resilient little system. Making it work is a lot easier than getting it right.

PART **II**

SMB:
The Server
Message Block
Protocol

8

A Little Background on SMB

Your mileage may vary.

— Advertiser's disclaimer

 **Email**

From: Steven French, Senior Software Engineer, IBM
  To: Chris Hertel

Chris,

Hope things are going well in the cold north...

I thought the following info would be interesting to you. I met the
original "inventor" of SMB a few years ago - Dr. Barry Feigenbaum -
who back in the early 80's was working on network software
architecture for the infant IBM PCs, working for IBM in the Boca
Raton plant in Florida. He mentioned that it was first called the
"BAF" protocol (after his initials) but he later changed it to SMB.
In the early DOS years IBM and Microsoft (with some input from Intel
and 3Com) contributed to it but by the time of the first OS/2 server
version (LANMAN1.0 dialect and later) Microsoft did much of the work
(for "LAN Manager" and its relatives).

Like NetBIOS, the Server Message Block protocol originated a long time ago at IBM. Microsoft embraced it, extended it, and in 1996 gave it a marketing upgrade by renaming it "CIFS."

Over the years there have been several attempts to document and standardize the SMB/CIFS protocol:

- Microsoft keeps an archive of documentation covering older versions of SMB/CIFS. The collection spans a period of roughly ten years, starting at about 1988 with the SMB Core Protocol. The collection is housed, it seems, on a dusty FTP server in a forgotten corner of a machine room somewhere in the Pacific Northwest. The URL for the CIFS archive is `ftp://ftp.microsoft.com/developr/drg/CIFS/`.

- In 1992, X/Open (now known as The Open Group) published an SMB specification titled *Protocols for X/Open PC Interworking: SMB, Version 2*. The book is now many years out of date and SMB has evolved a bit since its publication, yet it is still considered one of the best references available.[1] The Open Group is a standards body so the outdated version of SMB described in the X/Open book is, after all, a standard protocol.

- A few years later, Microsoft submitted a set of CIFS Internet Drafts to the IETF (**I**nternet **E**ngineering **T**ask **F**orce), but those drafts were somewhat incomplete and inaccurate; they were allowed to expire. Microsoft's more recent attempts at documenting CIFS (starting in March, 2002) have been rendered useless by awkward licensing restrictions, and from all accounts contain no new information.[2] The expired IETF Internet Drafts (by Paul Leach and Dilip Naik) are still available from the Microsoft FTP server described above and other sources around the web.

- The CIFS Working Group of the **S**torage **N**etwork **I**ndustry **A**ssociation (SNIA) has published a *CIFS Technical Reference* based on the earlier IETF drafts. The SNIA document is neither a specification nor a standard, but it is freely available from the SNIA website.

---

1. The X/Open SMB documentation is out of print, but electronic copies are now available online (free registration required). See `http://www.opengroup.org/products/publications/catalog/`, and look for documents #C195 and #C209.

2. I must rely on anecdotal evidence to support this claim. Due to the licensing restrictions, I have not read these documents, which were released in March of 2002.

Without a current and authoritative protocol specification, there is no external reference against which to measure the "correctness" of an implementation, and no way to hold anyone accountable. Since Microsoft is the market leader, with a proven monopoly on the desktop, the behavior of their clients and servers is the standard against which all other implementations are measured.

Jeremy Allison, the Samba Team's First Officer,[3] has stated that "The level of detail required to interoperate successfully is simply not documentable." One reason that this is true is that Microsoft can "enhance" SMB behavior at will. Combined with the dearth of authoritative references, this means that the only criteria for a well-behaved SMB implementation is that it works with Microsoft products. As a result, subtle inconsistencies and variations have crept into the protocol. They are discovered in much the same way that a dog-owner discovers poop in the yard in springtime when the snow melts.[4]

Many people dread spring chores, but spring also brings the flowers. The children play, the dog chases a butterfly, the birds sing... and it all seems suddenly worthwhile. It's the same with the work we have ahead. Things are not really too bad, once you've gotten started.

8.1 Getting Started

This part of the book will cover the basics of SMB, enumerate and describe some of the SMB message types (commands), discuss protocol dialects, give some details on authentication, and provide a few examples. That should be enough to help you develop a working knowledge of the protocol, a working SMB client, and possibly a simple server.

Bear in mind, though, that SMB is more complex and less well defined than NBT. In the NBT section it was possible to describe every message type and provide a comprehensive review of the entire NBT protocol. It is not practical to cover all of SMB in the same way. Instead, the goal here is to explain

---

3. ...and Tactical Officer. He's the one with the prosthetic forehead.

4. I live in Minnesota, where it most definitely snows in winter. I share my home with a Pembrokeshire Welsh Corgi and a Golden Retriever, so the springtime scenario described above is vividly real and meaningful to me. Some of my Australian Samba Team friends have suggested that people in other parts of the world may find it less familiar. Use your imagination.

the basics of SMB, provide details that are missing from other sources, and describe how to go about exploring SMB on your own. In other words, the goal is to develop understanding rather than simply providing knowledge.

The textbook for this class is the latest version of the SNIA *CIFS Technical Reference*. Additional sources are listed in the References section near the end of this book. The most important tool, however, is probably the protocol analyzer. Warm up your copy of Ethereal or NetMon, and get ready to do some packet shoveling.

8.2   NBT or Not NBT

Before we actually start, there is one more thing to mention: The SMB protocol is supposed to be "transport independent." That is, SMB *should* work over any reliable transport that meets a few basic criteria. NBT is one such transport, but SMB does not really require the NetBIOS API. It can, for instance, be run directly over TCP/IP.

Just for fun, we will refer to SMB over TCP/IP without NBT as "naked" or "raw." When running naked, SMB defaults to using TCP port 445 instead of the NBT Session Service port (TCP/139). Windows 2000, Windows XP, and Samba all support raw transport, but the large number of "legacy" Windows clients still in use suggest that NBT will not go away any time soon.

Other than the new port number, there are only two notable differences between NBT and naked transport. The first is that naked transport does not make use of the NBT SESSION REQUEST and POSITIVE SESSION RESPONSE messages. The second is that the two transports interpret the SESSION MESSAGE header a bit differently.

Recall (from Chapter 6 on page 129) that the NBT Session Service prepends a four-byte header to each SESSION MESSAGE, like so:

0	1	2	3	4	5	6	7	8	9	1 0	1 1	1 2	1 3	1 4	1 5	1 6	1 7	1 8	1 9	2 0	2 1	2 2	2 3	2 4	2 5	2 6	2 7	2 8	2 9	3 0	3 1
0 (zero)								<reserved>								LENGTH (17 bits)															

The LENGTH field, as shown, is 17 bits wide.[5] Raw TCP transport also prepends a four-byte header, but there are no reserved bits so the LENGTH may use three full bytes:

0	1	2	3	4	5	6	7	8	9	1 0	1 1	1 2	1 3	1 4	1 5	1 6	1 7	1 8	1 9	2 0	2 1	2 2	2 3	2 4	2 5	2 6	2 7	2 8	2 9	3 0	3 1
0 (zero)								LENGTH (24 bits)																							

Appendix B of the SNIA *CIFS Technical Reference* is the only source that was found which clearly shows the naked transport LENGTH field as being 24 bits wide. This 24-bit field translates to 16 megabytes, though, and that's a bigbunch — more than is typically practical. Fortunately, the actual maximum message size is something that is negotiated when the client and server establish the session.

When we discuss the SMB messages themselves we will ignore the SESSION MESSAGE headers, since they are part of the transport, not the SMB protocol.

---

5. There are some old archived conversations on Microsoft's CIFS mailing list which suggest that some implementors were — and possibly still are — only allowing for a 16 bit LENGTH field in the NBT SESSION MESSAGE.

9

An Introductory Tour
of SMB

> The devil is in the details.
>
> — Popular saying

We will start with a quick museum tour of SMB. Our guide will be the venerable **U**niversal **N**aming **C**onvention (UNC). You may remember UNC from the brief introduction way back in Chapter 1 on page 3. UNC will provide directions and point out highlights along the tour.

Please stay together, everyone.

The UNC directions are presented in terms of a path, much like the **U**niform **R**esource **I**dentifier (URI) paths that are used on the World Wide Web. To explain UNC, let us first consider something more modern and familiar:

```
http://ubiqx.org/cifs/index.html
```

That string is in *URI* syntax, as used by web browsers, and it breaks down to provide these landmarks:

```
      http == The protocol to use.
 ubiqx.org == The name of the server.
      cifs == The directory path.
  SMB.html == The file name.
```

The landmarks guide us along a path which eventually leads us to the file we wanted to access.

The SMB protocol pre-dates the use of URIs and was originally designed for use on LANs, not internetworks, so it naturally has a different (though surprisingly similar) way of specifying paths. A **U**niversal **N**aming **C**onvention (UNC) path comparable to the URI path above might look something like this:

```
\\ubiqx\cifs\SMB.html
```

...and would parse out like this:

```
  ubiqx == The name of the server.
   cifs == The directory path.
SMB.html == The file name.
```

Very similar indeed.

One obvious difference between the two formats is that UNC doesn't provide a protocol specification. That's *not* because it always assumes SMB. The UNC format can support all sorts of filesharing protocols, but it is up to the underlying operating system or application to try to figure out which one to use. Protocol and transport discovery are handled by trial-and-error, with each possibility tested until something works. As you might imagine, a system with AppleTalk, NetWare, and SMB all enabled may have a lot of work to do.

The UNC format is handled natively by Microsoft & IBM's extended family of operating systems: DOS, OS/2, and Windows.[1] Samba's `smbclient` utility can also parse UNC names, but it does so at the application level rather than within the OS, and it only ever tries to deal with SMB. Even so, `smbclient` must handle both NBT and naked transport, which can be tricky.

9.1   The Server Identifier

The first stop on our UNC tour of SMB is the server name field, which is really a server *identifier* field because it will accept addresses in addition to names. This book concerns itself with only two transports — NBT and naked TCP transport — so the only identifiers we care about are:

---

1. Steve French says that OS/2 may have been the first OS to fully support the UNC scheme.

- NetBIOS names,
- DNS names, and
- IP addresses.

NetBIOS and DNS names both resolve to IP addresses, so all three are equivalent.

Sort of...

Recall that the NBT SESSION REQUEST packet requires a CALLED NAME in order to set up an NBT session with the server. Without a correct CALLED NAME, the NBT SESSION REQUEST *may* be rejected (different implementations behave differently). So...

- if the transport is NBT (not raw),
- and the server is identified using a DNS name or IP address...

...then we're in a bit of a pickle. How do we find the correct NetBIOS name to put into the CALLED NAME field? There really is no "right" way to reverse-map an IP address to a particular NetBIOS service name. The solution to this problem involves some guessing, and it's not pretty. We will go into detail when we discuss the interface between SMB and the transport layer.

Of course, if SMB is running over raw transport then there is no NBT SESSION REQUEST message and, therefore, no CALLED NAME. In that case, the NetBIOS name isn't needed at all, which saves a lot of fuss and bother.

9.2   The Directory Path

The directory path looks just like a directory path, but there is one small thing that makes it different. That thing is called the "share name."

Whenever a resource is made available (shared) via SMB it is given a share name. The share name doesn't need to be the same as the actual name of the object being shared as it exists on the server. For example, consider the directory path below:

```
/dogs/corgi/stories/jolyon/
```

Suppose we just want to share the /stories subdirectory. If we simply call it "stories" no one will know what kind of stories it contains, so we should give it a more descriptive name. We might, for example, call it "dogbytes".

The share name takes the place of the actual directory name when the share is accessed via SMB. If the server is named "petserver", then the UNC path to the same directory would be:

```
\\petserver\dogbytes\jolyon\
```

As shown in Figure 9.1, there can be more than one share name pointing to the same directory and access rules may be applied on a per-share basis. The idea is similar, in some ways, to that of symbolic links (symlinks) in Unix, or shortcuts in Windows. The share is a named pointer — with its own set of attributes — to the object being made available by the server.

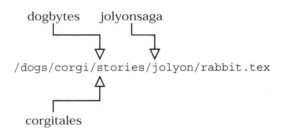

Figure 9.1:   *SMB shares*

Share names are similar to Unix `symlinks`. Multiple share names may point to the same directory on the server or to different directories. Each share may have its own set of permissions.

9.3   The File

This is the last stop on our quick UNC tour of SMB.

Files, like directories, should be fairly familiar and fairly straightforward. As has been continually demonstrated, however, things in the CIFS world are not always as simple as they ought to be. Our point of interest on this part of the tour is the distinction between server filesystem syntax and semantics — and client expectations... a very gnarled knot for CIFS implementors.

Consider, for example, a bunch of Windows clients connecting to an SMB server running on Linux. On the Linux system the filenames `Corgi`,

`corgi`, and `CORGI` would all be distinct because Linux filesystems are typically case-sensitive. Windows, however, expects filenames to be case-insensitive, so all three names are the same from the Windows point of view. Thus, we have a conflict. How does a Linux server make all three files available to the Windows client?

Other difficult issues include:

- filename lengths,
- valid characters,
- file access permissions, and
- the end-of-line delimiter in text files.

These are complex problems, not easily solved. The CIFS protocol suite is *not* designed to be agnostic with regard to such things. In fact, CIFS goes out of its way at times to support features that are specific to DOS, OS/2, and Windows.

...and that concludes our tour. It's time to visit the gift shoppe.

9.4   The SMB URL

The UNC format is specific to one family of operating systems. Earlier on, though, we compared UNC with the more portable and modern URI format. That's called foreshadowing. It's a literary trick used to build suspense and anticipation.

There is, in fact, such a thing as an SMB URL. It fits into the general URI syntax[2] and can be used to specify files, directories, and other SMB-shared stuff. It is intended as a more portable and more complete way to specify SMB paths at the application level.

As of this writing, the SMB URL is only documented in an IETF Internet Draft, and is not yet any kind of standard. That hasn't stopped folks from implementing it, though. The SMB URL is supported in a wide variety of products including the KDE and GNOME desktop GUI environments, web browsers such as Galeon and Konqueror, and Open Source CIFS projects like

---

2. The distinction between a URL and a URI is subtle, and confuses me to no end. Fortunately, it is not something we need to worry about.

jCIFS and `libsmbclient` (the latter is included with Samba). Thursby Software and Apple Computer also make use of the SMB URL in their commercial CIFS implementations.

That's good news for CIFS implementors because it means that there is an accepted, cross-platform way to identify SMB-shared resources, both within LANs and across the Internet.

9.5   Was That Trip Really Necessary?

Our quick UNC tour provided an introduction to some of the basic concepts — and annoyances — of SMB. We will expand upon those ideas as we dig more deeply into the protocol. The UNC format itself is also important for a variety of reasons, both historical and practical. Not least among these is that UNC strings are used within some of the SMB messages that cross the wire.

The SMB URL format is equally significant. It is portable, flexible, and gaining in popularity. It will also form the basis for examples given later in the text. If you are implementing an SMB client, you will most likely want to have some convention for identifying resources. You could invent your own, or use UNC, but the SMB URL is probably your best option.

10

First Contact: Reaching the Server

Getting there is half the fun.

— Unknown

We are approaching this thing in layers. A little history, a quick introductory tour... and now this. It may seem like a bit of a diversion, but the goal in this section is to figure out how a client finds the server and initiates a connection. No, we're not dealing with SMB protocol yet, but we can't send SMB messages until we can talk to a server.

Think of a telephone call. If you want to call your cousin in New York, the first thing you need to know is the telephone number. You could ask your uncle for the number or look it up in the telephone book, or perhaps you have it written on a scrap of paper somewhere in the kitchen with your favorite tofu recipes. If you dial the wrong number you will annoy some guy in a gas station in Brooklyn. When you dial the correct number, the underlying system will go through a complex process to set up the connection so that you can start talking to your cousin (or, more likely, to the answering machine).

Similarly, if you want to connect to an SMB server you might need to resolve a NetBIOS or DNS name to an IP address. Once you have the address, you can attempt to open a session with the server.

Consider this simple SMB URL:

```
smb://server/
```

From the user's perspective, that should be enough to build an initial connection to an SMB server named "`server`".

From an implementation point of view, the first thing to do with this example is to parse out the "`server`" substring. In URI parlance, the field we are looking for is called the "host non-terminal,"[1] and it contains the name or address of the server to which we are trying to connect. Our term for the parsed-out string is "Server Identifier." Once we have extracted it, the next thing we need to know how to do is interpret it so that we can use the information to create the session.

10.1   Interpreting the Server Identifier

The SMB URL format supports the use of three different identifier types in the host field. We went over them briefly before. They are the IP address, DNS name, or NetBIOS name of the destination. Our next task is to figure out which is which.

Presentation is everything, and it turns out that the code for interpreting the Server Identifier is verbose and tedious. Most of the busywork for handling NetBIOS names was covered in Part I, and there are plenty of tools for dealing with IP addresses and DNS names, so to save time we will *describe* how to interpret and resolve the address (and let you write the code yourself).[2]

It could be an IP address.

Check the syntax of the input to determine whether it is a valid representation of an IP address. Do this test first. It is quick, and does not involve sending any queries out over the network. The `inet_aton()` function, common on Unix-like operating systems, does the job nicely for the four-byte IPv4 addresses used today.

IP version 6 (IPv6) addresses are different. They are longer, harder for a human to read, and potentially more complicated to parse out.

---

1. The "host" field is not really a field, but the name of a non-terminal in the BNF grammar presented in RFC 2396. That grammar has been amended to support IP version 6 (IPv6) addressing in RFC 2732. The SMB URL format adds support for the use of NetBIOS names and Scope IDs, so it is a further extension of the syntax.

2. Additional source code is available at `http://ubiqx.org/libcifs/`.

Fortunately, when used in URLs they are always contained within square brackets, as in the following example:

```
smb://[fe80::240:f4ff:fe1f:8243]/
```

The square brackets are reserved characters, used specifically for this purpose.[3] They make it easy to identify an IPv6 IP address. Once identified, the IPv6 address can be converted into its internal format by the `inet_pton()` function, which is now supported by many systems.

Note that it is, in theory, possible to register a NetBIOS name that looks exactly like an IP address. What's worse is that it might not be the same as the IP address of the node that registered it. That's nasty. Anyone who would do such a thing should have their keyboard taken away. It is probably not important to handle such situations. Defensive programming practices would suggest being prepared, but in this case the perpetrators deserve the troubles they cause for themselves.

It could be a NetBIOS Name.

If the Server Identifier isn't an IP address, it could be a NetBIOS name. To see if this is the case, the first step is to look for a dot ('.'). The SMB URL format does not allow unescaped dots to appear in the NetBIOS name itself, so if there is a dot character in the raw string then consider the rest of the string to be a Scope ID. For example:

```
smb://my%2Enode.scope/
```

is made up of the NetBIOS name "MY.NODE" and the Scope ID "SCOPE". (The URL escape sequence for encoding a dot is %2E.)

Once the string has been parsed into its NetBIOS Name and Scope ID components, the next thing to do is to send an NBT Name Query. Always use a suffix value of 0x20, which is the prescribed suffix for SMB services. The handling of the query depends, of course, on whether the client is a B, P, M, or H node. For anything other than a B node, the IP address of the NBNS is required. Most client implementations keep such information in some form of configuration file or database.

---

3. See RFC 2732 for information on the use of IPv6 addresses in URLs.

If a positive response is received, keep track of the NetBIOS name and returned IP address. You will need them in order to connect to the server.

It could be a DNS name.

If the Server Identifier is neither an IP address nor a NetBIOS name, try DNS name resolution. The gethostbyname() function is commonly used to resolve DNS names to IP addresses, but be warned that this is a blocking function. It may take quite a while for it to do its job, and your program will do nothing in the meantime.[4] That is one reason why it is typically the last thing to try.

That is how to go about determining which *kind* of Server Identifier you've been given. Isn't overloading fun? Now you see why the code for handling all of this is tedious and verbose. It really is not very difficult, though, it's just that it takes a bit of work to get it all coded up.

10.2 The Destination Port

Port 139 is for NBT, and port 445 is for raw TCP — good rules of thumb. Recall, though, that the NBT Session Service provides a mechanism for redirection. In addition, some security protocols use high-numbered ports to tunnel SMB connections through firewalls. That means that the use of non-standard ports should be supported on the client side.

The SMB URL allows the specification of a destination port number, like so:

```
smb://server:1928/
```

Once again, that fits into standard URI syntax. If you spend any time using a web browser, the port field should be familiar.

What this all means, however, is that the port number does not always indicate which transport should be used. Rather the opposite; if the port number is *not* specified, the default port depends upon the transport. Knowing

---

4. Samba's nmbd daemon spawns a separate process to handle DNS queries, just to get around this very problem.

which transport to choose is, once again, something that requires some figuring out.

10.3   Transport Discovery

As has been stated previously, we are only considering the NBT and naked TCP transports. Both of these are IP-based and the behavior of SMB over these two is nearly identical, so it does not seem as though separating them would be very important... but this is CIFS we're talking about.

The crux of the problem is whether or not the NBT SESSION REQUEST message is required. If the server is expecting correct NBT semantics, then we will need to find a valid NetBIOS name to place into the CALLED NAME field. This is a complicated process, involving a lot of trial-and-error. The recipe presented below is only one way to go about it. A good chef knows how to adjust the ingredients and choose seasonings to get the desired result. This is as much an art as it is a science.

10.3.1 *Run Naked*

Running naked is probably the easiest transport test to try first. The procedure is tasteful and dignified: simply assume that the server is expecting raw TCP transport. Open a TCP connection to port 445 on the server, but *do not* send an NBT SESSION REQUEST — just start sending SMB messages and see if that works. There are four possible results from this test:

1. If nothing is listening on port 445 at the server, the TCP connection will fail. If that happens, the client can fall back to using NBT on port 139.

2. If a non-SMB service is running on the destination port, one end or the other will (hopefully) figure out that the messages being exchanged are incomprehensible, and the connection will be dropped. Again, the fall-back is to try NBT on port 139.

3. The remote end may be expecting NBT transport. This *should* never happen when talking to port 445, but defensive programming practices suggest being prepared. If the server requires NBT transport then it will probably reply to the initial SMB message by sending an NBT NEGATIVE SESSION RESPONSE.

4. The connection might, after all, succeed.

All of the above applies if the user did not specify a non-standard port number. If the input looks more like this:

```
smb://server:2891/
```

then the option of falling back to NBT on port 139 is excluded. In addition, there is no way to guess which transport type should be used if a port number other than 139 or 445 is specified. (In theory, it is also possible to run NBT transport on port 445 and naked transport on port 139. If you catch anyone doing such a twisted thing you should probably notify the authorities.)

Fortunately, Windows systems (Windows 95, 98, and 2000 were tested) return an NBT NEGATIVE SESSION RESPONSE if they get naked semantics on an NBT service port. This makes sense, because it lets the client know that NBT semantics are required. Samba's smbd goes one better and simply ignores the lack of a SESSION REQUEST message. Samba's behavior effectively merges the two transport types and makes the distinction between them irrelevant, which simplifies things on the server side and makes life easier for the client.

The transport discovery process is illustrated using the anachronistic flowchart presented in Figure 10.1.

10.3.2 *Using the NetBIOS Name*

If running naked didn't work, then you will probably need to try NBT transport. Also, back in Section 10.1 we talked about the different types of Server Identifiers that most implementations support. One of those is the NetBIOS name, and it seems logical to assume that if the Server Identifier is a NetBIOS name then the transport will be NBT.

That's two good reasons to give NBT transport a whirl.

As stated earlier, the critical difference between the raw TCP and NBT transports is that NBT requires the SESSION REQUEST/POSITIVE SESSION RESPONSE exchange before the SMB messages can start flowing. The SESSION REQUEST, in turn, must contain a valid CALLED NAME. If the CALLED NAME is not correct, then some server implementations will reject the connection. (Windows seems to be quite picky, but Samba ignores the CALLED NAME field.)

Finding a valid CALLED NAME is easy if the Server Identifier is a NetBIOS name because, well... because there you are. The NetBIOS name *is*

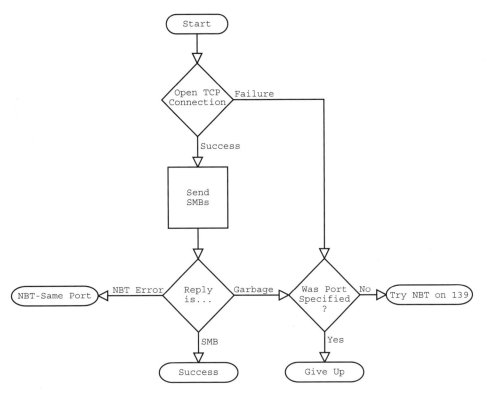

Figure 10.1:   *Transport discovery*

the correct CALLED NAME. Also, since the Server Identifier was resolved via an NBT Name Query, the server's IP address is known. That's everything you need.

There is one small problem with this scenario that could cause a little trouble: some NBNS servers can be configured to pass NetBIOS name queries through to the DNS system, which means that the DNS — not the NBNS — may have resolved the name to an IP address. That would mean that we have a false positive and the Server Identifier is not, in fact, a NetBIOS name. If that happens, you could wind up trying to make an NBT connection to a system that isn't running NBT services. (The opposite of the "run naked" test described above.)

Detecting an SMB service that wants naked transport is not as clean and easy as detecting one that wants NBT. In testing, a Windows 2000 system running naked TCP transport did not respond at all to an NBT SESSION REQUEST, and the client timed out waiting for the reply. This problem is neatly avoided if naked transport is attempted before NBT transport. Since Samba considers the SESSION REQUEST optional, this kind of transport confusion is not an issue when talking to a Samba server.

10.3.3 *Reverse Mapping a NetBIOS Name*

Reverse mapping is the last, desperate means for finding a workable NetBIOS CALLED NAME so that a valid SESSION REQUEST can be sent. Reverse mapping is also quite common. Your code will need to try this technique if naked transport didn't work and the Server Identifier was a DNS name or IP address — a situation which is not unusual.

As stated before, there is no *right* way to do reverse mapping. Fortunately, there are a few almost-right ways to go about it. Here they are:

Try a Node Status query.

Send an NBT NODE STATUS QUERY to the server. If it responds, run through the list of returned names looking for a unique name with a suffix byte value of 0x20. Try using that name as the CALLED NAME when setting up the session. If there are multiple names with a suffix value of 0x20, try them in series until you get a POSITIVE SESSION RESPONSE (or until they all fail).

Stop laughing. It gets better.

Try using the generic CALLED NAME.

This kludge was introduced in Windows NT 4.0 and has been adopted by many other implementations. It is fairly common, but not universal.

The generic CALLED NAME is *SMBSERVER<20> (that is, "*SMBSERVER" with a suffix byte value of 0x20). Think of it as an alias, allowing you to connect to the SMB server without knowing its "real," registered NetBIOS name. The *SMBSERVER<20> name starts with an asterisk, which is against the rules, so it is never registered with the NBT Name Service. If you send a unicast Name Query for this name, the destination node should always send a NEGATIVE NAME QUERY RESPONSE in reply (assuming that it is actually running NBT).

A bit awkward but it does work... sometimes. Now for the *coup de gras*.

Try using the DNS name.

Try using the first label of the DNS name (the hostname of the server) as the CALLED NAME. If you were given an IP address you will need to do a reverse DNS lookup to get a name to play with (we suggested earlier that the DNS name might come in handy). As always, use a suffix byte value of 0x20.

If the first label doesn't work, try the first two labels (retaining the dot) and so on until you have a string that is longer than 15 bytes, at which point you give up.

Yes, there are implementations which actually do this.

If none of those options worked, then it is finally time to send an error message back to the user explaining that the Server Identifier is no good.

Ignorance is Bliss Omission Alert
We have not fully discussed IPv6.
    As it currently stands, NBT doesn't work with IPv6. All of the IP address fields in the NBT messages are four-byte fields, but IPv6 addresses are longer. There has been talk of NetBIOS emulation over IPv6, but if such a thing ever happens (unlikely) it will take a while before the proposal is worked out and accepted.
    Unfortunately, when it comes to SMB over IPv6 the author is clueless. It is probably just like SMB over naked transport, except that the addresses are IPv6 addresses.

10.4   Connecting to the Server

We are still dealing with the transport layer and haven't actually seen any SMBs yet. It is, however, finally time for some code. Listing 10.1 handles the basics of opening the connection with an SMB server. It is example code so, of course, it takes a few shortcuts. For instance, it completely sidesteps Server Identifier interpretation and transport discovery (that is, everything we just covered).

Listing 10.1: Opening a session with an SMB server

```c
#include <stdio.h>
#include <errno.h>
#include <stdarg.h>
#include <stdlib.h>

#include <sys/poll.h>
#include <sys/types.h>
#include <sys/socket.h>
#include <netinet/in.h>
#include <arpa/inet.h>

/* NBT Session Service Packet Type Codes
 */
#define SESS_MSG          0x00
#define SESS_REQ          0x81
#define SESS_POS_RESP     0x82
#define SESS_NEG_RESP     0x83
#define SESS_RETARGET     0x84
#define SESS_KEEPALIVE    0x85

/* NBT Session Service Error Codes
 */
#define ErrNLCalled       0x80
#define ErrNLCalling      0x81
#define ErrCalledNotPrsnt 0x82
#define ErrInsResources   0x83
#define ErrUnspecified    0x8F

ushort nbt_GetShort( uchar *src, int offset )
  /* --------------------------------------------------- **
   * Read two bytes from an NBT message and convert them
   * to an unsigned short int.
   * Note that we read the bytes in NBT byte order, which
   * is the opposite of SMB byte order.
   * --------------------------------------------------- **
   */
  {
  ushort tmp;

  tmp = src[offset];
  tmp = (tmp << 8) | src[offset+1];

  return( tmp );
  } /* nbt_GetShort */
```

```
void Fail( char *fmt, ... )
  /* -------------------------------------------------- **
   * This function formats and prints an error to stdout,
   * then exits the program.
   * A nice quick way to abandon ship.
   * -------------------------------------------------- **
   */
  {
  va_list ap;

  va_start( ap, fmt );
  (void)fprintf( stdout, "Error: " );
  (void)vfprintf( stdout, fmt, ap );
  exit( EXIT_FAILURE );
  } /* Fail */


void NegResponse( uchar *bufr, int len )
  /* -------------------------------------------------- **
   * Negative Session Response error reporting.
   *
   * The Negative Session Response message should always
   * be five bytes in length.  The final byte (bufr[4])
   * contains the error code.
   * -------------------------------------------------- **
   */
  {
  if( len < 5 )
    Fail( "Truncated Negative Session Response.\n" );

  printf( "Negative Session Response: " );

  switch( bufr[4] )
    {
    case ErrNLCalled:
      printf( "Not listening on Called Name.\n" );
      break;
    case ErrNLCalling:
      printf( "Not listening *for* Calling Name.\n" );
      break;
    case ErrCalledNotPrsnt:
      printf( "Called Name not present.\n" );
      break;
    case ErrInsResources:
      printf( "Insufficient resources on server.\n" );
      break;
```

```
      case ErrUnspecified:
        printf( "Unspecified error.\n" );
        break;
      default:
        printf( "Unknown error.\n" );
        break;
      }
    } /* NegResponse */

void Retarget( uchar *bufr, int result )
  /* -------------------------------------------------- **
   * This function is called if we receive a RETARGET
   * SESSION RESPONSE from the server.  The correct thing
   * to do would be to retry the connection, using the
   * returned information.  This function simply reports
   * the retarget response so that the user can manually
   * retry.
   * -------------------------------------------------- **
   */
  {
  if( result < 10 )
    Fail( "Truncated Retarget Session Response.\n" );

  printf( "Retarget Session Response: " );
  printf( "IP = %d.%d.%d.%d, ",
          bufr[4], bufr[5], bufr[6], bufr[7] );
  printf( "Port = %d\n", nbt_GetShort( bufr, 8 ) );
  } /* Retarget */

int MakeSessReq( uchar *bufr,
                 uchar *Called,
                 uchar *Calling )
  /* -------------------------------------------------- **
   * Create an NBT SESSION REQUEST message.
   * -------------------------------------------------- **
   */
  {
  /* Write the header.
   */
  bufr[0] = SESS_REQ;
  bufr[1] = 0;
  bufr[2] = 0;
  bufr[3] = 68;            /* 2x34 bytes in length. */
```

```
/* Copy the Called and Calling names into the buffer.
 */
(void)memcpy( &bufr[4],  Called,  34 );
(void)memcpy( &bufr[38], Calling, 34 );

/* Return the total message length.
 */
return( 72 );
} /* MakeSessReq */

int RecvTimeout( int    sock,
                 uchar *bufr,
                 int    bsize,
                 int    timeout )
/* ---------------------------------------------------- **
 * Attempt to receive a TCP packet within a specified
 * period of time.
 * ---------------------------------------------------- **
 */
{
int           result;
struct pollfd pollfd[1];

/* Wait timeout/1000 seconds for a message to arrive.
 */
pollfd->fd     = sock;
pollfd->events = POLLIN;
pollfd->revents = 0;
result = poll( pollfd, 1, timeout );

/* A result less than zero is an error.
 */
if( result < 0 )
  Fail( "Poll() error: %s\n", strerror( errno ) );

/* A result of zero is a timeout.
 */
if( result == 0 )
  return( 0 );

/* A result greater than zero means a message arrived,
 * so we attempt to read the message.
 */
result = recv( sock, bufr, bsize, 0 );
if( result < 0 )
  Fail( "Recv() error: %s\n", strerror( errno ) );
```

```
/* Return the number of bytes received.
 * (Zero or more.)
 */
return( result );
} /* RecvTimeout */


void RequestNBTSession( int sock,
                        uchar *Called,
                        uchar *Calling )
/* ------------------------------------------------------ **
 * Send an NBT SESSION REQUEST over the TCP connection,
 * then wait for a reply.
 * ------------------------------------------------------ **
 */
{
uchar bufr[128];
int   result;

/* Create the NBT Session Request message.
 */
result = MakeSessReq( bufr, Called, Calling );

/* Send the NBT Session Request message.
 */
result = send( sock, bufr, result, 0 );
if( result < 0 )
  Fail( "Error sending Session Request message: %s\n",
        strerror( errno ) );

/* Now wait for and handle the reply (2 seconds).
 */
result = RecvTimeout( sock, bufr, 128, 2000 );
if( result == 0 )
  {
  printf( "Timeout waiting for NBT Session Response.\n" );
  return;
  }

switch( *bufr )
  {
  case SESS_POS_RESP:
    /* We got what we wanted. */
    printf( "Positive Session Response.\n" );
    return;
```

```
      case SESS_NEG_RESP:
        /* Report an error. */
        NegResponse( bufr, result );
        exit( EXIT_FAILURE );
      case SESS_RETARGET:
        /* We've been retargeted. */
        Retarget( bufr, result );
        exit( EXIT_FAILURE );
      default:
        /* Not a response we expected. */
        Fail( "Unexpected response from server.\n" );
        break;
      }
  } /* RequestNBTSession */

int OpenTCPSession( struct in_addr dst_IP, ushort dst_port )
  /* ------------------------------------------------- **
   * Open a TCP session with the specified server.
   * Return the connected socket.
   * ------------------------------------------------- **
   */
  {
  int               sock;
  int               result;
  struct sockaddr_in sock_addr;

  /* Create the socket.
   */
  sock = socket( PF_INET, SOCK_STREAM, IPPROTO_TCP );
  if( sock < 0 )
    Fail( "Failed to create socket(); %s.\n",
          strerror( errno ) );

  /* Connect the socket to the server at the other end.
   */
  sock_addr.sin_addr   = dst_IP;
  sock_addr.sin_family = AF_INET;
  sock_addr.sin_port   = htons( dst_port );
  result = connect( sock,
                    (struct sockaddr *)&sock_addr,
                    sizeof(struct sockaddr_in) );
  if( result < 0 )
    Fail( "Failed to create socket(); %s.\n",
          strerror( errno ) );

  return( sock );
  } /* OpenTCPSession */
```

```
int main( int argc, char *argv[] )
  /* ------------------------------------------------- **
   * Program mainline.
   * Parse the command-line input and open the connection
   * to the server.
   * ------------------------------------------------- **
   */
  {
  uchar           Called[34];
  uchar           Calling[34];
  struct in_addr  dst_addr;
  int             dst_port = 139;
  int             sock;

  /* Check for the correct number of arguments.
   */
  if( argc < 3 || argc > 4 )
    {
    printf( "Usage:  %s <NAME> <IP> [<PORT>]\n",
            argv[0] );
    exit( EXIT_FAILURE );
    }

  /* Encode the destination name.
   */
  if( '*' == *(argv[1]) )
    (void)L2_Encode( Called, "*SMBSERVER", 0x20, 0x20, "" );
  else
    (void)L2_Encode( Called, argv[1], 0x20, 0x20, "" );

  /* Create a (bogus) Calling Name.
   */
  (void)L2_Encode( Calling, "SMBCLIENT", 0x20, 0x00, "" );

  /* Read the destination IP address.
   * We could do a little more work and resolve
   * the Called Name, but that would add a lot
   * of code to the example.
   */
  if( 0 == inet_aton( argv[2], &dst_addr ) )
    {
    printf( "Invalid IP.\n" );
    printf( "Usage:  %s <NAME> <IP> [<PORT>]\n",
            argv[0] );
    exit( EXIT_FAILURE );
    }
```

```
/* Read the (optional) port number.
 */
if( argc == 4 )
  {
  dst_port = atoi( argv[3] );
  if( 0 == dst_port )
    {
    printf( "Invalid Port number.\n" );
    printf( "Usage:  %s <NAME> <IP> [<PORT>]\n",
            argv[0] );
    exit( EXIT_FAILURE );
    }
  }

/* Open the session.
 */
sock = OpenTCPSession( dst_addr, dst_port );

/* Comment out the next call for raw TCP.
 */
RequestNBTSession( sock, Called, Calling );

/* ** Do real work here. ** */

return( EXIT_SUCCESS );
} /* main */
```

The code in Listing 10.1 provides an outline for setting up the session via NBT or raw TCP. With that step behind us, we won't have to deal with the details of the transport layer any longer. Let's run through some code highlights quickly and put all that transport stuff behind us.

Transport

The program does not attempt to discover which transport to use. As written, it assumes NBT transport. To try naked transport, simply comment out the call to RequestNBTSession() in main().

The command line

Because we are shamelessly avoiding presenting code that interprets Server Identifiers, the example program makes the user do all of the work. The user must enter the NetBIOS name and IP address of the server. Entering a destination port number is optional.

The name entered on the command line will be used as the CALLED NAME. If the input string begins with an asterisk, the generic *SMBSERVER<20> name will be used instead.

The CALLING NAME (NBT source address)

The program inserts SMBCLIENT<00> as the CALLING NAME.

In a correct implementation, the name should be the client's Net-BIOS Machine Name (which is typically the same as the client's DNS hostname) with a suffix byte value if 0x00.

The contents of the CALLING NAME field are not particularly significant. According to the expired Leach/Naik CIFS Internet Draft, the same name from the same IP address is supposed to represent the same client... but you knew that. Samba can make use of the CALLING NAME via a macro in the smb.conf configuration file. The macro is used for all sorts of things, including generating per-client log files.

Transporting SMBs

A key feature of this program is the line within main() which reads:

```
/* ** Do real work here. ** */
```

That's where the SMB stuff is supposed to happen. At that point in the code, the session has been established on top of the transport layer and it is time to start moving those Server Message Blocks.

Use the program above as a starting point for building your own SMB client utility. Add a parser capable of dissecting the UNC or SMB URL format, and then code up Server Identifier resolution and transport discovery, as described above. When you have all of that put together, you will have completed the foundation of your SMB client.

11

SMB in Its Natural Habitat

I never metaphor I couldn't mix.

— Common pun

We have spent a lot of time and effort preparing for this expedition, and we are finally ready to venture into SMB territory. It can be a treacherous journey, though, so before we push ahead we should re-check our equipment.

✔ Test Server

If you are going to start testing, you have to have something at which to fling packets. When choosing a test server, keep in mind that SMB has grown and changed and evolved and adapted and mutated over the years. You want a server that can be configured to meet your testing needs. Samba, of course, is highly configurable. If you know your way around the Windows Registry, you may have luck with those systems as well. In particular, you probably want to avoid strong password encryption during the initial stages. Handling authentication is a big chunk of work, and it is best to try and reduce the number of simultaneous problems to a manageable few.

 Repetitive Terminology Redundancy Notification Alert
The SMB server software running on a file server node is known as the "File Server Service," or just "Server Service."

177

When running on top of NBT, the Server Service always registers a NetBIOS name composed of the Machine Name and, of course, a suffix value of 0x20. *The Machine Name is typically — but not necessarily — the same as the DNS host name.*

✔ Test Client

The next thing you will want is a packet flinger — that is, a working client. You need this for testing and to compare behavior when debugging your own client. Samba offers the smbclient utility, and jCIFS comes with a variety of example programs. Windows systems all have SMB support built-in. That's quite a selection from which to choose.

✔ Sniffer

Always your best friend. A good packet analyzer — one with a lot of built-in knowledge of SMB — will be your trusted guide through the SMB jungle.

✔ Documentation

When exploring NBT we relied upon RFC 1001 and RFC 1002 as if they were ancient maps, drawn on cracked and drying parchment, handed down to us by those who had gone before. In the wilds of SMB territory, we will count on the *SNIA CIFS Technical Reference* as our primary resource. The old X/Open SMB specification and the SMB/CIFS documentation available from Microsoft's FTP server will also come in handy. For the sake of efficiency, from here on out we will be a bit less formal and refer to the SNIA doc as "the SNIA doc," and the X/Open doc as "the X/Open doc."

Yet Another Tasty Terminology Treat Alert

*As we have explained, "SMB" is the **S**erver **M**essage **B**lock protocol. It is also true that "an SMB" is a message. In order to implement SMB, one must learn to send and receive SMBs.*
Got that?

Keep in mind that the goal of our first trip into the wilds of SMB-land is to become familiar with the terrain and to study SMBs in their natural habitat, so we can learn about their anatomy and behavior. We are not ready yet for a detailed study of SMB innards. That will come later.

11.1 Our Very First Live SMBs

We need to capture a few SMBs to see what they look like up close. That means it's time to take a look at the wire and see what's there to be seen. Fire up your protocol analyzer, and then your SMB client. If you can configure your test server to allow anonymous connections (no username, no password) it will simplify things at this stage. If you can't, then things won't run quite as they are shown below. Don't worry, it will be close enough.

For this example, we will use the `Exists.java` program that comes with jCIFS. It is a very simple utility that does nothing more than verify the existence of the object specified by the given SMB URL string, like so:

```
shell
$ java Exists smb://smedley/home
smb://smedley/home exists
$
```

The above shows that we were able to access the HOME share on node SMEDLEY. A similar test can be performed using Samba's `smbclient`, or with the NET USE command under Windows:[1]

```
DOS prompt
C:\> net use \\smedley\home
The command was completed successfully.

C:\> net use /d \\smedley\home
The command was completed successfully.

C:\>
```

These simple commands will generate the packets we want to capture and study. Stop your sniffer and take a look at the trace. You should see a chain of events similar to the following:

---

1. When working with the NET USE command, it is important to remember to close the connection to the server using the /d command-line option. Type NET HELP at the DOS prompt for more information.

```
No. Source   Destination      Protocol Info
--- -------  ---------------  -------- ----------------------------
  1 Marika   255.255.255.255  NBNS     Name query
  2 Smedley  Marika           NBNS     Name query response
  3 Marika   Smedley          TCP      34102 > netbios-ssn [SYN]
  4 Smedley  Marika           TCP      netbios-ssn > 34102 [SYN, ACK]
  5 Marika   Smedley          TCP      34102 > netbios-ssn [ACK]
  6 Marika   Smedley          NBSS     Session request
  7 Smedley  Marika           NBSS     Positive session response
  8 Marika   Smedley          TCP      34102 > netbios-ssn [ACK]
  9 Marika   Smedley          SMB      Negotiate Protocol Request
 10 Smedley  Marika           SMB      Negotiate Protocol Response
 11 Marika   Smedley          SMB      Session Setup AndX Request
 12 Smedley  Marika           SMB      Session Setup AndX Response
 13 Marika   Smedley          TCP      34102 > netbios-ssn [FIN, ACK]
 14 Smedley  Marika           TCP      netbios-ssn > 34102 [FIN, ACK]
 15 Marika   Smedley          TCP      34102 > netbios-ssn [ACK]
```

The above is edited output from an Ethereal capture.[2] The packets were generated using the jCIFS Exists utility, as described above. In this case jCIFS was talking to an old Windows 95 system, but any SMB server should produce the same or similar results.

The trace is reasonably simple. The first thing that node MARIKA does is send a broadcast NBT Name query to find node SMEDLEY, and SMEDLEY responds. Packets 3, 4, and 5 show the TCP session being created. (Note that netbios-ssn is the descriptive name given to port 139.) Packets 6 and 7 are the NBT SESSION REQUEST/SESSION RESPONSE exchange, and packet 8 is an ACK message, which is just TCP taking care of its business.

Packets 9 and 10 are what we want. These are our first SMBs.

11.2   SMB Message Structure

Figure 11.1 provides an overview of SMB gross anatomy. It shows that SMBs are composed of three basic parts:

- the Header,
- the Parameter Block, and

---

2. The original was much more detailed and interesting. It had to be edited so that it would fit on the page, and because all those details can be distracting.

■ the Data Block.

Either or both of the latter two segments may be vestigial (size == 0) in some specimens.

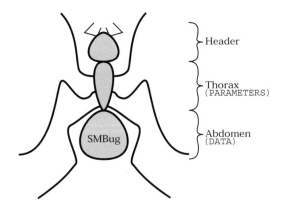

Figure 11.1:   *SMB gross anatomy*

SMB messages are composed of three basic parts: the header, the parameters, and the data.

11.2.1 *SMB Message Header*

Starting at the top, the SMB header is arranged like so:

0	1	2	3	4	5	6	7	8	9	1 0	1 1	1 2	1 3	1 4	1 5	1 6	1 7	1 8	1 9	2 0	2 1	2 2	2 3	2 4	2 5	2 6	2 7	2 8	2 9	3 0	3 1
0xff								'S'								'M'								'B'							
COMMAND								STATUS...																							
...STATUS								FLAGS								FLAGS2															
EXTRA																															
. . .																															
. . .																															
TID																PID															
UID																MID															

We can also dissect the header using the simple syntax presented previously:

```
SMB_HEADER
  {
  PROTOCOL   = "\xffSMB"
  COMMAND    = <SMB Command code (one byte)>
  STATUS     = <Status code>
  FLAGS      = <Old flags>
  FLAGS2     = <New flags>
  EXTRA      = <Sometimes used for additional data>
  TID        = <Tree ID>
  PID        = <Process ID>
  UID        = <User ID>
  MID        = <Multiplex ID>
  }
```

We now have a pair of perspectives on the header structure. Time for some good, old-fashioned descriptive text.

The PROTOCOL and COMMAND fields

The SMB header starts off easily enough. The first four bytes are the protocol identifier string, which always has the same value, "\xffSMB". It's not particularly clear[3] why this is included in the SMBs but there it is, and it's in all of them.

The next byte is the COMMAND field, which tells us what kind of SMB we are looking at. In the NEGOTIATE PROTOCOL messages captured above, the COMMAND field has a value of 0x72 (aka SMB_COM_NEGOTIATE). The SNIA doc has a list of the available command codes. That list is probably complete, but this is SMB we are talking about, so you never know...

The STATUS field

Now things start to get surreally interesting.

DOS and OS/2 use 16-bit error codes, grouped into classes. To accommodate these codes, the STATUS field is subdivided like so:

0	1	2	3	4	5	6	7	8	9	1 0	1 1	1 2	1 3	1 4	1 5	1 6	1 7	1 8	1 9	2 0	2 1	2 2	2 3	2 4	2 5	2 6	2 7	2 8	2 9	3 0	3 1
ErrorClass								<reserved>								ErrorCode															

---

3. ...to me.

Windows NT introduced a new set of 32-bit error codes, known as NT_STATUS codes. These use the entire status field to hold the NT_Status value:

0	1	2	3	4	5	6	7	8	9	1 0	1 1	1 2	1 3	1 4	1 5	1 6	1 7	1 8	1 9	2 0	2 1	2 2	2 3	2 4	2 5	2 6	2 7	2 8	2 9	3 0	3 1
NT_Status																																

With two error code formats from which to choose, the client and server must confer to decide which set will be used. How that is done will be explained later on. Error code handling is a large-sized topic with extra sauce.

FLAGS and FLAGS2

Look around the Web for a copy of a document called COREP.TXT.[4] This is probably the earliest SMB documentation that is also easy to find. In COREP.TXT, you can see that the original SMB header layout reserved fifteen bytes following the error code field. Those 15 bytes have, over time, been carved up for a variety of uses.

The first formerly-reserved byte is now known as the FLAGS field. The bits of the FLAGS field are used to modify the interpretation of the SMB. For example, the highest-order bit is used to indicate whether the SMB is a request (0) or a response (1).

Following the FLAGS field is the two-byte FLAGS2 field. This set of bits is used to indicate the use of newer features, such as the 32-bit NT_STATUS error codes.

The EXTRA field

The EXTRA field takes up most of the remaining formerly-reserved bytes. It contains two subfields, as shown below:

---

4. The first place to look is Microsoft's CIFS FTP site: ftp://ftp.microsoft.com/developr/drg/CIFS/. The COREP.TXT file is formatted for printing on an old-style dot-matrix printer, which makes it look a little goofy in places (e.g. bold font is accomplished by typing a character, then backspacing, then re-typing the same character). The same content is available in an alternate format in the file SMB-CORE.PS. See the References section.

0	1	2	3	4	5	6	7	8	9	1 0	1 1	1 2	1 3	1 4	1 5	1 6	1 7	1 8	1 9	2 0	2 1	2 2	2 3	2 4	2 5	2 6	2 7	2 8	2 9	3 0	3 1
PidHigh																Signature...															
...Signature...																															
...Signature																<unused>															

The `PidHigh` subfield is used to accommodate systems that have 32-bit Process IDs. The original SMB header format only had room for 16-bit PIDs (in the `PID` field, described further on).

The 8-byte `Signature` subfield is for SMB message signing, which uses cryptography to protect against a variety of attacks that might be tried by badguys hoping to gain unauthorized access to SMB shares.

When not in use, these fields must be filled with zeros.

TID, PID, UID, and MID

TID

The "Tree ID." In SMB, a share name typically represents a directory or subdirectory tree on the server. The SMB used to open a share is called a "Tree Connect" because it allows the client to connect to the shared [sub]directory tree. That's where the name comes from. The `TID` field is used to identify connections to shares once they have been established.

PID

The "Process ID." This value is set by the client, and is intended as an identifier for the process sending the SMB request. The most important thing to note regarding the `PID` is that file locking and access modes are maintained relative to the value in this field.

The `PID` is 16 bits wide, but it can be extended to 32 bits using the `EXTRA.PidHigh` field described earlier.

UID

The "User ID." This is also known as a `VUID` (**V**irtual **U**ser **ID**). It is assigned by the server after the user has authenticated and is valid until the user logs off. It does not need to be the user's actual User ID on the server system. Think of it as a session token assigned to a successful logon.

MID

>   The "Multiplex ID." This is used by the client to keep track of multiple outstanding requests. The server must echo back the MID and the PID provided in the client request. The client can use those values to make sure that the reply is matched up to the correct request.

The TID and [V]UID are assigned and managed by the server, while the PID and MID are assigned by the client. It is important to note that the values in these fields do not necessarily have any meaning outside of the SMB connection. The PID, for example, does not need to be the actual ID of the client process. The client and server assign values to these fields in order to keep track of context, and that's all.

11.2.2 *SMB Message Parameters*

In the middle of the SMB message are two fields labeled WordCount and Words[]. For our purposes, we will identify these two fields as being the SMB_PARAMETERS block, which looks like this:

0	1	2	3	4	5	6	7	8	9	1 0	1 1	1 2	1 3	1 4	1 5	1 6	1 7	1 8	1 9	2 0	.	.	.
WordCount							Words...																

```
SMB_PARAMETERS
  {
  WordCount            = <Number of words in the Words array>
  Words[WordCount]     = <SMB parameters; varies with SMB command>
  }
```

The Words field is simply a block of data that is 2 × WordCount bytes in length. Perhaps at one time the intention was that it would contain only two-byte values (a quick look at COREP.TXT suggests that this is the case). In practice, all sorts of stuff is thrown in there.

Each SMB message type (species?) has a different record structure that is carried in the Words block. Think of that structure as representing the parameters passed to a function (the function identified by the SMB command code listed in the header).

11.2.3 *SMB Message Data*

Following the SMB_PARAMETERS is another block of data, the content of which also varies in structure on a per-SMB basis:

0	1	2	3	4	5	6	7	8	9	1 0	1 1	1 2	1 3	1 4	1 5	1 6	1 7	1 8	1 9	2 0	.	.	.
ByteCount																	Bytes...						

```
SMB_DATA
  {
  ByteCount       = <Number of bytes in the Bytes field>
  Bytes[ByteCount] = <Contents varies with SMB command>
  }
```

The Bytes field holds the data to be manipulated. For example, it may contain the data retrieved in response to a READ operation, or the data to be written by a WRITE operation. In many cases, though, the SMB_DATA block is just another record structure with several subfields. Through time, SMB has evolved lazily and any functional distinction that may have separated the Parameter and Data blocks has been blurred.

Note that the SMB_DATA.ByteCount field is an unsigned short, while the SMB_PARAMETERS.WordCount field is an unsigned byte. That means that the SMB_PARAMETERS.Words block is limited in length to 510 bytes (2 × 255), while SMB_DATA.Bytes may be as much as 65535 bytes in length. If you add all that up, and then add in the SMB_PARAMETERS.WordCount field, the SMB_DATA.ByteCount field, and the size of the header, you will find that the whole thing fits easily into the $2^{17} - 1$ bytes made available in the NBT SESSION MESSAGE header.

11.3 Case in Point: NEGOTIATE PROTOCOL

Now that we have an overview of the structure of SMB messages, we can take a closer look at our live specimen. Remember packets 9 and 10 from the capture we made earlier? They show a NEGOTIATE PROTOCOL exchange. Let's get out the tweezers, the pocket knife, and dad's hammer and see what's inside.

```
NEGOTIATE_PROTOCOL_REQUEST
  {
  SMB_HEADER
    {
    PROTOCOL    = "\xffSMB"
    COMMAND     = SMB_COM_NEGOTIATE (0x72)
    STATUS
      {
      ErrorClass = 0x00    (Success)
      ErrorCode  = 0x0000 (No Error)
      }
    FLAGS       = 0x18 (Pathnames are case-insensitive)
    FLAGS2      = 0x8001 (Unicode and long filename support)
    EXTRA
      {
      PidHigh     = 0x0000
      Signature   = 0 (all bytes zero filled)
      }
    TID         = 0 (Not yet known)
    PID         = <Client Process ID>
    UID         = 0 (Not yet known)
    MID         = 2 (often 0 or 1, but varies per OS)
    }
  SMB_PARAMETERS
    {
    WordCount = 0
    Words     = <empty>
    }
  SMB_DATA
    {
    ByteCount = 12
    Bytes
      {
      BufferFormat = 0x02 (Dialect)
      Name         = "NT LM 0.12" (nul terminated)
      }
    }
  }
```

The breakdown of packet 9 shows the SMB NEGOTIATE PROTOCOL REQUEST as sent by the jCIFS Exists utility. Other clients will use slightly different values, but they are all variations on the same theme. Some features worth noting:

■ The COMMAND field has a value of 0x72 (SMB_COM_NEGOTIATE). That's how we know that this is a NEGOTIATE PROTOCOL message.

We also know that it is a REQUEST rather than a RESPONSE because the highest-order bit in the FLAGS field has a value of zero (0).

- The STATUS field is all zeros at this point because we haven't yet done anything to cause an error. Also, the error messages are presented in the older DOS format. This is because jCIFS is indicating, via a bit in the FLAGS2 field, that it is using the DOS format. We'll dig into those bits later on.

- Several fields (the EXTRA.Signature, the TID, and the UID, to name a few) contain zeros. The content of these fields has not yet been determined, and they may or may not be filled in later on. It all depends upon the types of SMB requests that are issued. Stay tuned.

- In this particular SMB the Parameter block is empty and all of the useful information is being carried in the Data block. In contrast, the response packet from the server (packet 10) makes use of both the Parameter and Data blocks (assuming that there are no errors). See for yourself by looking at the NEGOTIATE PROTOCOL RESPONSE in your capture.

  The Data block in the request contains the list of protocols that the client is able to speak. jCIFS only knows one dialect, so only one name is listed in the message above. As you can see, jCIFS implements the "NT LM 0.12" dialect (the most recent and widely supported as of this writing). Other clients, such as Samba's smbclient, support a longer list of dialects.

11.4 The AndX Mutation

In the trace given above, Ethereal has identified packets 11 and 12 as being a SESSION SETUP ANDX exchange.[5] The term "ANDX" at the end of the names indicates that these messages belong to a curious class of creatures known as "AndX messages." SMB AndX messages are actually several SMBs combined into a single symbiotic packet as shown in Figure 11.2. It is an efficient mutation.

---

5. Ethereal version 0.9.3 will report the name of the last AndX Command in the chain, rather than the first. This was fixed somewhere between 0.9.3 and 0.9.6. The trick with Ethereal is to update early and often.

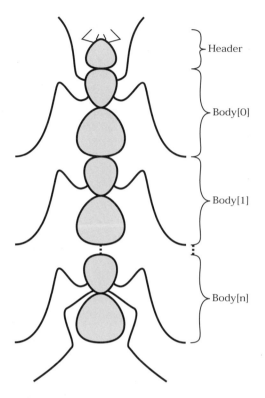

Figure 11.2:   *AndX SMBs*

AndX SMBs combine several SMB messages into one. Only one header is used, but each parameter block contains information identifying the next AndX body segment.

AndX messages work something like a linked list. Each Parameter block in an AndX message begins with the following structure:

0	1	2	3	4	5	6	7	8	9	1 0	1 1	1 2	1 3	1 4	1 5	1 6	1 7	1 8	1 9	2 0	2 1	2 2	2 3	2 4	2 5	2 6	2 7	2 8	2 9	3 0	3 1
AndXCommand								<reserved>								AndXOffset															

The `AndXCommand` field provides the SMB command code for the *next* AndX block in the list (*not* the current one). The `AndXOffset` contains the byte index, relative to the start of the SMB header, of that next AndX block — think of it as a pointer. Since the `AndXOffset` value is independent of the `SMB_PARAMETERS.WordCount` and `SMB_DATA.ByteCount` values, it is possible to provide padding between the AndX blocks as shown in Figure 11.3.

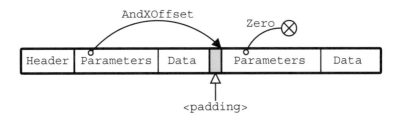

Figure 11.3:   *AndX SMB chaining*

The `AndXOffset` value in each AndX parameter block gives the offset (relative to the start of the SMB) of the next AndX block. The `AndXOffset` of the last AndX block has a value of zero (0).

Now that we have a general idea of what an SMB AndX message looks like we are ready to dissect packet 11. It looks like this:

```
SESSION_SETUP_ANDX_REQUEST
  {
  SMB_HEADER
    {
    PROTOCOL  = "\xffSMB"
    COMMAND   = SMB_COM_SESSION_SETUP_ANDX (0x73)
    STATUS
      {
      ErrorClass = 0x00    (Success)
      ErrorCode  = 0x0000 (No Error)
      }
    FLAGS     = 0x18 (Pathnames are case-insensitive)
    FLAGS2    = 0x0001 (Long filename support)
    EXTRA
      {
      PidHigh    = 0x0000
      Signature  = 0 (all bytes zero filled)
      }
    TID       = 0 (Not yet known)
    PID       = <Client Process ID>
    UID       = 0 (Not yet known)
    MID       = 2 (often 0 or 1, but varies per OS)
    }
  ANDX_BLOCK[0] (Session Setup AndX Request)
    {
    SMB_PARAMETERS
```

```
      {
      WordCount       = 13
      AndXCommand     = SMB_COM_TREE_CONNECT_ANDX (0x75)
      AndXOffset      = 79
      MaxBufferSize   = 1300
      MaxMpxCount     = 2
      VcNumber        = 1
      SessionKey      = 0
      CaseInsensitivePasswordLength = 0
      CaseSensitivePasswordLength   = 0
      Capabilities    = 0x00000014
      }
    SMB_DATA
      {
      ByteCount       = 20
      AccountName     = "GUEST"
      PrimaryDomain   = "?"
      NativeOS        = "Linux"
      NativeLanMan    = "jCIFS"
      }
    }
  ANDX_BLOCK[1] (Tree Connect AndX Request)
    {
    SMB_PARAMETERS
      {
      WordCount       = 4
      AndXCommand     = SMB_COM_NONE (0xFF)
      AndXOffset      = 0
      Flags           = 0x0000
      PasswordLength  = 1
      }
    SMB_DATA
      {
      ByteCount       = 22
      Password        = ""
      Path            = "\\SMEDLEY\HOME"
      Service         = "?????"  (yes, really)
      }
    }
  }
```

There is a lot of information in that message, but we are not yet ready to dig into the details. There is just too much to cover all of it at once. Our goals right now are simply to highlight the workings of the AndX blocks, and to provide a glimpse inside the SESSION SETUP ANDX and TREE CONNECT ANDX sub-messages so that we will have something to talk about later on.

The block labeled ANDX_BLOCK[0] is the body of the SESSION SETUP REQUEST, and ANDX_BLOCK[1] contains the TREE CONNECT REQUEST. Note that the AndXCommand field in the final AndX block is given a value of 0xFF. This, in addition to the zero offset in the AndXOffset field, indicates the end of the AndX list.

11.5   The Flow of Conversation

SMB conversations start after the session has been established via the transport layer. As a rule, the client always speaks first. Clients send requests, servers respond, and that's the way SMB is supposed to work. This is a hard-and-fast rule which means, of course, that there is an exception. Fortunately, we can (and will) put off talking about that exception until we talk about Opportunistic Locks (OpLocks).

The NEGOTIATE PROTOCOL REQUEST/RESPONSE is always the first SMB exchange in the conversation. The client and server need to know what language to speak before they can say anything else. This is also a hard-and-fast rule, but there are no exceptions (which is an exception to the rule that all hard-and-fast rules have exceptions).

Once the dialect has been selected, the next formality is to establish an SMB session using the SMB SESSION SETUP REQUEST message. We keep running into terminology twists, and here we have yet another. The SMB SESSION SETUP exchange sets up an SMB session within the NBT or naked TCP session.

Huh?

Well, yes, that's confusing. The problem is that we are talking about two different kinds of sessions here.

- There is the network session built at layer 5 of the OSI model, on top of the transport layer.
- There is the user logon session.

Ah, there's a clue! The SESSION SETUP is used to perform authentication and establish a *user* session with the server.[6] A quick look at the SESSION

---

6. We are dealing with a vague definition here. According to the SNIA doc, the SESSION SETUP is meant to "set up" the session created by the NEGOTIATE PROTOCOL, which also

SETUP ANDX REQUEST block in the packet above shows that the Exists utility did in fact send a username — the name "GUEST", passed via the AccountName field — to the server.

Once the user session is established, the client may try to connect to a share using a TREE CONNECT SMB. It is a hard-and-fast rule that TREE CONNECT SMBs must follow the SESSION SETUP. There is an exception to this as well, which we will cover when we get to share-mode vs. user-mode authentication.

Figure 11.4 shows the right way to start an SMB conversation. Combining the SESSION SETUP ANDX and TREE CONNECT ANDX SMBs into a single AndX message is optional (jCIFS' Exists does, but Samba's smbclient doesn't). Once the conversation has been initiated using the above sequence, the client is free to improvise.

11.6 A Little More Code

There is another small detail you may have noticed while studying the captured SMB packets — or perhaps you remember this from one of the *Alert* boxes in the NBT section: SMBs are written using little-endian byte order. If your target platform is big-endian, or if you want your code to be portable to big-endian systems, you will need to be able to handle the conversion between host and SMB byte order.

The htonl(), htons(), ntohl(), and ntohs() functions won't help us here. They convert between host and network byte order. We need to be able to convert between host and SMB order (and SMB order is definitely not the same as network order).

So, to solve the problem, we need a little bit of code, which is presented here mostly to get it out of the way so that we won't have to bother with it when we are dealing with more complex issues. The functions in Listing 11.1 read short and long integer values directly from incoming message buffers and write them directly to outgoing message buffers.

---

makes some sort of sense. Thing is, there may be multiple SESSION SETUP exchanges following the NEGOTIATE PROTOCOL, meaning multiple SMB user sessions per NBT or naked TCP transport session. The waters are muddy.

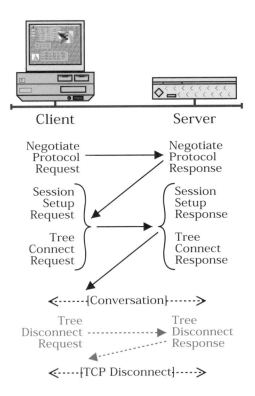

Client   Server

Negotiate   Negotiate
Protocol   Protocol
Request   Response

Session   Session
Setup   Setup
Request   Response

Tree   Tree
Connect   Connect
Request   Response

<------{Conversation}------>

Tree   Tree
Disconnect -------------> Disconnect
Request   Response

<------{TCP Disconnect}------>

Figure 11.4: *A simple SMB conversation*

The client makes requests (some of which may be batched in AndX messages) and the server responds. The jCIFS `Exists` utility sends a `NEGOTIATE PROTOCOL REQUEST` followed by batched `SESSION SETUP` plus `TREE CONNECT` AndX requests. The `TREE DISCONNECT` exchange at the end is optional. When the client closes the session at the transport layer, all resources are released.

Listing 11.1: Reading and writing integer values

```
ushort smb_GetShort( uchar *src, int offset )
  /* ------------------------------------------------- **
   * Read a short integer converting it to host byte
   * order from a byte array in SMB byte order.
   * ------------------------------------------------- **
   */
  {
  ushort tmp;

  /* Low order byte is first in the buffer. */
  tmp  = (ushort)(src[offset]);
```

```
  /* High order byte is next in the buffer. */
  tmp |= ( (ushort)(src[offset+1]) << 8 );

  return( tmp );
  } /* smb_GetShort */

void smb_SetShort( uchar *dst, int offset, ushort val )
  /* -------------------------------------------------- **
   * Write a short integer in host byte order to the
   * buffer in SMB byte order.
   * -------------------------------------------------- **
   */
  {
  /* Low order byte first. */
  dst[offset]   = (uchar)(val & 0xFF);

  /* High order byte next. */
  dst[offset+1] = (uchar)((val >> 8) & 0xFF);
  } /* smb_SetShort */

ulong smb_GetLong( uchar *src, int offset )
  /* -------------------------------------------------- **
   * Read a long integer converting it to host byte order
   * from a byte array in SMB byte order.
   * -------------------------------------------------- **
   */
  {
  ulong tmp;

  tmp  = (ulong)(src[offset]);
  tmp |= ( (ulong)(src[offset+1]) << 8 );
  tmp |= ( (ulong)(src[offset+2]) << 16 );
  tmp |= ( (ulong)(src[offset+3]) << 24 );
  return( tmp );
  } /* smb_GetLong */

void smb_SetLong( uchar *dst, int offset, ulong val )
  /* -------------------------------------------------- **
   * Write a long integer in host byte order to the
   * buffer in SMB byte order.
   * -------------------------------------------------- **
   */
  {
  dst[offset]   = (uchar)(val & 0xFF);
  dst[offset+1] = (uchar)((val >> 8) & 0xFF);
  dst[offset+2] = (uchar)((val >> 16) & 0xFF);
  dst[offset+3] = (uchar)((val >> 24) & 0xFF);
  } /* smb_SetLong */
```

11.7 Take a Break

Our field trip into SMB territory is now over. We have covered a lot of ground, collected samples, and taken a look at SMBs in the wild. Our next step will be doing the lab work — studying our specimens under a microscope. It is time to take a break, relax, and reflect on what we have learned so far.

Time for a cup of tea.

In the next section we will go back over the SMB header in a lot more detail with the goal of explaining some of the key concepts that we have only touched on so far. You will probably want to be well rested and in a good mood for that.

12

The SMB Header
in Detail

1st rule of Oriental Cuisine:
Never look inside the eggroll.

During that first expedition into SMB territory we continually deferred, among other things, studying the finer details of the SMB header. We were trying to cover the general concepts, but now we need to dig into the guts of SMB to see how things really work. Latex gloves and lab coats required.

Let's start by revisiting the header layout. Just for review, here's what it looks like:

0	1	2	3	4	5	6	7	8	9	1 0	1 1	1 2	1 3	1 4	1 5	1 6	1 7	1 8	1 9	2 0	2 1	2 2	2 3	2 4	2 5	2 6	2 7	2 8	2 9	3 0	3 1
0xff								'S'								'M'								'B'							
COMMAND								STATUS...																							
..STATUS								FLAGS								FLAGS2															
EXTRA																															
...																															
...																															
TID																PID															
UID																MID															

197

The first four bytes are constant, so we won't worry about those. The COMMAND field is fairly straightforward too; it's just a one byte field containing an SMB command code. The list of available codes is given in Section 5.1 of the SNIA doc. The rest of the header is where the fun lies...

12.1 The SMB_HEADER.STATUS Field Exposed

Things get interesting starting at the STATUS field. It wouldn't be so bad except for the fact that there are two possible error code formats to consider. There is the DOS and OS/2 format, and then there is the NT_STATUS format. In C language terms, the STATUS field looks something like this:

```
typedef union
  {
  ulong NT_Status;
  struct
    {
    uchar  ErrorClass;
    uchar  reserved;
    ushort ErrorCode;
    } DosError;
  } Status;
```

From the client side, one way to deal with the split personality problem is to use the DOS codes exclusively.[1] These are fairly well documented (by SMB standards), and *should* be supported by all SMB servers. Using DOS codes is probably a good choice, but there is a catch... there are some advanced features which simply don't work unless the client negotiates NT_STATUS codes.

 Strange Behavior Alert

If the client negotiates Extended Security with a Windows 2000 server and also nego-tiates DOS error codes, then the SESSION SETUP ANDX will fail, and return a DOS hardware error. (!?)

---

1. This is exactly what jCIFS does (up through release 0.6.6 and the 0.7.0beta series). There has been a small amount of discussion about supporting the NT_STATUS codes, but it's not clear whether there is any need to change.

```
STATUS
  {
  ErrorClass = 0x03    (Hardware Error)
  ErrorCode  = 0x001F (General Error)
  }
```

> *Perhaps W2K doesn't know which DOS error to return, and is guessing. The bigger question is, why does this fail at all?*
> *The same SMB conversation with the NT_STATUS capability enabled works just fine. Perhaps, when the coders were coding that piece of code, they assumed that only clients capable of using NT_STATUS codes would also use the Extended Security feature. Perhaps that assumption came from the knowledge that all **Windows** systems that could handle Extended Security would negotiate NT_STATUS. We can only guess...*
> *This is one of the oddities of SMB, and another fine bit of forensic SMB research by Andrew Bartlett of the Samba Team.*

Another reason to support NT_STATUS codes is that they provide finer-grained diagnostics, simply because there are more of them defined than there are DOS codes. Samba has a fairly complete list of the known NT_STATUS codes, which can be found in the `samba/source/include/nterr.h` file in the Samba distribution. The list of DOS codes is in `doserr.h` in the same directory.

We have already described the structure of the DOS error codes. NT_STATUS codes also have a structure, and it looks like this:

0	1	2	3	4	5	6	7	8	9	1 0	1 1	1 2	1 3	1 4	1 5	1 6	1 7	1 8	1 9	2 0	2 1	2 2	2 3	2 4	2 5	2 6	2 7	2 8	2 9	3 0	3 1
Level	<reserved>		Facility									ErrorCode																			

In testing, it appears as though the `Facility` field is always set to zero (`FACILITY_NULL`) for SMB errors. That leaves us with the `Level` and `ErrorCode` fields to provide variety... and, as we have suggested, there is quite a bit of variety. Samba's `nterr.h` file lists over 500 NT_STATUS codes, while `doserr.h` lists only 99 (and some of those are repeats).

`Level` is one of the following:

00 == Success
01 == Information
10 == Warning
11 == Error

Since the next two bits (the <reserved> bits) are always zero, the highest-order nibble will have one of the following values: 0x0, 0x4, 0x8, or 0xC. At the other end of the longword, the ErrorCode is read as an unsigned short (just like the DOS ErrorCode field).

The availability of Samba's list of NT_STATUS codes makes things easy. It took a bit of effort to generate that list, however, as most of the codes are not documented in an accessible form. Andrew Tridgell described the method below, which he used to generate a list of valid NT_STATUS codes. His results were used to create the nterr.h file used in Samba.

Tridge's Trick

1. *Modify the source of Samba's* smbd *daemon so that whenever you try to delete a file that matches a specific pattern it will return an NT_STATUS error code. (Do this on a testing copy, of course. This hack is not meant for production.) For example, return an error whenever the filename to be deleted matches* "STATUS_CODE_HACK_FILENAME.*". *Another thing to do is to include the specific error number as the filename extension, so that the name*

   ```
   STATUS_CODE_HACK_FILENAME.0xC000001D
   ```

   will cause Samba to return an NT_STATUS code of 0xC000001D.

2. *Create the files on the server side first so you have something to delete. That is easily done with a shell script, such as this:*

   ```
   #!/bin/bash
   #
   i=0;j=256
   while [ $i -lt $j ]
   do
     touch `printf "STATUS_CODE_HACK_FILENAME.0xC000%.4x" $i`
     i=`expr $i + 1`
   done
   ```

   Change the values of i *and* j *to generate different ranges.*

3. *On a Windows NT or Windows 2000 system, mount the Samba share containing the generated* STATUS_CODE_HACK* *files. Next, open a DOS command shell and, one by one, delete the files. For each file, Samba should return the specified NT_STATUS code... and Windows will interpret the code and tell you what it means. If the code is not defined, Windows will tell you that as well.*

4. *If you capture the delete transactions using Microsoft's NetMon tool, it will show you the symbolic names that Microsoft uses for the NT_STATUS codes.*

Okay, now for the next conundrum...

Servers have it tougher than clients. Consider a server that needs to respond to one client using DOS error codes, and to another client using NT_STATUS codes. That's bad enough, but consider what happens when that server needs to query yet another server in order to complete some operation. For example, a file server might need to contact a Domain Controller in order to authenticate the user.

The problem is that, no matter which STATUS format the Domain Controller uses when responding to the file server, it will be the wrong format for one of the clients. To solve this problem the server needs to provide a consistent mapping between DOS and NT_STATUS codes.

Windows NT and Windows 2000 both have such mappings built-in but, of course, the details are not published (a partial list is given in Section 6 of the SNIA doc). Andrew Bartlett used a trick similar to Tridge's in order to generate the required mappings. His setup uses a Samba server running as a Primary Domain Controller (PDC), and a Windows 2000 system providing SMB file services. A third system, running Samba's smbtorture testing utility, acts as the client. When the client system tries to log on to the Windows server, Windows passes the login request to the Samba PDC.

The test works like this:

 Andrew Bartlett's Trick

1. *Modify Samba's authentication code to reject login attempts for any username beginning with "0x". Translate the login name (e.g. "0xC000001D") into an NT_STATUS code, and return that in the* STATUS *field.*

2. *Configure* smbtorture *to negotiate DOS error codes. Aim* smbtorture *at the W2K SMB server and try logging in as user* 0xC0000001, 0xC0000002... *etc.*

3. *For each login attempt from the client, the Windows SMB server will receive a login failure message from the Samba PDC. Since* smbtorture *has requested DOS error codes, the W2K pickle-in-the-middle is forced to translate the NT_STATUS values into DOS error codes... and that's how you discover Microsoft's mapping of NT_STATUS codes to DOS error codes.*

   The test configuration is shown in Figure 12.1.

Andrew's test must be rerun periodically. The mappings have been known to change when Windows service packs are installed. See the file

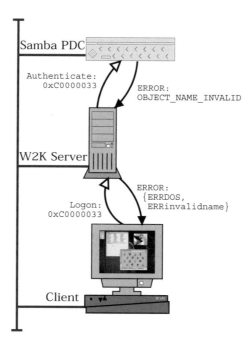

Figure 12.1:   *Andrew Bartlett's test configuration*

The polite way to ask Windows for its NT_STATUS-to-DOS error code mappings.

The client sends a logon request to the W2K server, which forwards it to the Samba PDC. The PDC rejects the login, using the Username as the NT_STATUS code. The client requested DOS error codes, so the W2K system must translate.

`samba/source/libsmb/errormap.c` in the Samba distribution for more fun and adventure.[2]

12.2   The FLAGS and FLAGS2 Fields Tell All

Most (but not all) of the bits in the older FLAGS field are of interest only to older servers. They represent features that have been superseded by newer features in newer servers. It would be nice if all of the old stuff would just go away

---

2. After all that work... Sometime around August of 2002, Microsoft posted a bit of documentation listing the DOS error codes that they have defined. Not all are used in CIFS, but it's a nice list to have. In addition, they have documented an NTDLL.DLL function that converts DOS error codes into NT_STATUS codes. (Thanks to Jeremy for finding these.)

so that we wouldn't have to worry about it. It does seem, in fact, as though this is slowly happening. (Maybe it would be better if the old stuff stayed and the new stuff had never happened. Hmmm...)

In any case, this next table presents the FLAGS bits in order of descending significance — the opposite of the order used in the SNIA doc. English speaking people tend to read from left to right and from top to bottom, so it seems logical (as this book is, more or less, written in English)[3] to transpose the left-to-right order into a top-to-bottom table.

SMB_HEADER.FLAGS

Bit	Name / Bitmask / Values	Description
7	SMB_FLAGS_SERVER_TO_REDIR 0x80 0: request 1: reply	What an awful name! On DOS, OS/2, and Windows systems, the client is built into the operating system and is called a "redirector," which is where the "SERVER_TO_REDIR" part of the name comes from. Basically, though, this is simply the reply flag.
6	SMB_FLAGS_REQUEST_BATCH_OPLOCK 0x40 0: Exclusive 1: Batch	**Obsolete.** If bit 5 is set, then bit 6 is the "batch OpLock" (aka OPBATCH) bit. Bit 6 should be clear if bit 5 is clear. In a request from the client, this bit is used to indicate whether the client wants an exclusive OpLock (0) or a batch OpLock (1). In a response, this bit indicates that the server has granted the batch OpLock. OpLocks (opportunistic locks) will be covered later. This bit is only used in the deprecated SMB_COM_OPEN, SMB_COM_CREATE, and SMB_COM_CREATE_NEW SMBs. It should be zero in all other SMBs.

3. The English language is Copyright © 1597 by William Shakespeare & Co., used by permission. All rights deserved.

SMB_HEADER.FLAGS

Bit	Name / Bitmask / Values	Description
		The SMB_COM_OPEN_ANDX SMB has a separate set of flags that handle OpLock requests, as does the SMB_COM_NT_CREATE_ANDX SMB.

5	SMB_FLAGS_REQUEST_OPLOCK
	0x20
	0: no OpLock
	1: OpLock
		Obsolete.
		    This is the "OpLock" bit. If this bit is set in a request, it indicates that the client wants to obtain an OpLock. If set in the reply, it indicates that the server has granted the OpLock.
		    OpLocks (opportunistic locks) will be covered later.
		    This bit is only used in the deprecated SMB_COM_OPEN, SMB_COM_CREATE, and SMB_COM_CREATE_NEW SMBs. It should be zero in all other SMBs. The SMB_COM_OPEN_ANDX SMB has a separate set of flags that handle OpLock requests, as does the SMB_COM_NT_CREATE_ANDX SMB. (Sigh.)

4	SMB_FLAGS_CANONICAL_PATHNAMES 0x10 0: Host format 1: Canonical	**Obsolete.** This was supposed to be used to indicate whether or not pathnames in SMB messages were mapped to their "canonical" form. Thing is, it doesn't do much good to write a client or server that doesn't map names to the canonical form (which is basically DOS, OS/2, or Windows compatible). This bit should always be set (1).

`SMB_HEADER.FLAGS`

Bit	Name / Bitmask / Values	Description

3	`SMB_FLAGS_CASELESS_PATHNAMES`
	`0x08`
	0: case-sensitive
	1: caseless
		When this bit is clear (0), pathnames should be treated as case-sensitive. When the bit is set, pathnames are considered caseless.
		
		All good in theory. The trouble is that some systems assume caseless pathnames no matter what the state of this bit. Best practice on the client side is to leave this bit set (1) and always assume caseless pathnames.

2	`0x04`	**\<Reserved\> (must be zero).** ...well, sort of. This bit is clearly listed as "Reserved (must be zero)" in both the SNIA and the X/Open docs, yet the latter contains some odd references to optionally using this bit in conjunction with OpLocks. It's probably a typo. Best bet is to clear it (0) and leave it alone.

1	`SMB_FLAGS_CLIENT_BUF_AVAIL`
	`0x02`
	0: Not posted
	1: Buffer posted
		Obsolete.
		This was probably useful with other transports, such as NetBEUI. If the client sets this bit, it is telling the server that it has already posted a buffer to receive the server's response. The expired Leach/Naik Internet Draft says that this allows a "send without acknowledgment" from the server.
		This bit should be clear (0) for use with NBT and naked TCP transports.

0	`SMB_FLAGS_SUPPORT_LOCKREAD`
	`0x01`
	0: Not supported
	1: Supported
		Obsolete.
		If this bit is set in the SMB NEGOTIATE PROTOCOL RESPONSE, then the server supports the deprecated `SMB_COM_LOCK_AND_READ` and `SMB_COM_WRITE_AND_UNLOCK` SMBs. Unless you are implementing outdated dialects, this bit should be clear (0).

The NEGOTIATE PROTOCOL REQUEST that we dissected back in Section 11.3 on page 186 shows only the SMB_FLAGS_CANONICAL_PATH-NAMES and SMB_FLAGS_CASELESS_PATHNAMES bits set, which is probably the best thing for new implementations to do. Testing with other clients may reveal other workable combinations.

Now let's take a look at the newer flags in the FLAGS2 field.

SMB_HEADER.FLAGS2

Bit	Name / Bitmask / Values	Description
15	SMB_FLAGS2_UNICODE_STRINGS 0x8000 0: ASCII 1: Unicode	If set (1), this bit indicates that string fields within the SMB message are encoded using a two-byte, little endian Unicode format. The SNIA doc says that the format is UTF-16LE but some folks on the Samba Team say it's really UCS-2LE. The latter is probably correct, but it may not matter as both formats are probably the same for the Basic Multilingual Plane. Doesn't Unicode sound like fun?[4] If clear (0), all strings are in 8-bit ASCII format (by which we actually mean 8-bit OEM character set format).
14	SMB_FLAGS2_32BIT_STATUS 0x4000 0: DOS error code 1: NT_STATUS code	Indicates whether the STATUS field is in DOS or NT_STATUS format. This may also be used to help the server guess which format the client prefers before it has actually been negotiated.
13	SMB_FLAGS2_READ_IF_EXECUTE 0x2000 0: Execute != Read 1: Execute confers Read	A quirky little bit this. If set (1), it indicates that execute permission on a file also grants read permission. It is only useful in read operations.

---

4. One of the reasons that the jCIFS project was started is that Java has built-in Unicode support, which solves a lot of problems. That, plus the native threading model and a few other features, made an SMB implementation in Java very tempting. Support for Unicode in a CIFS implementation is not really optional any more except, perhaps, in the simplest of client systems. Unfortunately, Unicode is way beyond the scope of this book. See the References section for some web links to get you started with Unicode.

SMB_HEADER.FLAGS2

Bit	Name / Bitmask / Values	Description
12	SMB_FLAGS2_DFS_PATHNAME 0x1000 0: Normal pathname 1: DFS pathname	This is used with the **D**istributed **F**ile **S**ystem (DFS), which we haven't covered yet. If this bit is set (1), it indicates that the client knows about DFS, and that the server should resolve any UNC names in the SMB message by looking in the DFS namespace. If this bit is clear (0), the server should not check the DFS namespace.
11	SMB_FLAGS2_EXTENDED_SECURITY 0x0800 0: Normal security 1: Extended security	If set (1), this bit indicates that the sending node understands Extended Security. We'll touch on this again when we discuss authentication.
10	0x0400	**<Reserved> (must be zero)**
9	0x0200	**<Reserved> (must be zero)**
8	0x0100	**<Reserved> (must be zero)**
7	0x0080	**<Reserved> (must be zero)**
6	SMB_FLAGS2_IS_LONG_NAME 0x0040 0: 8.3 format 1: Long names	If set (1), then any pathnames that the SMB contains are long pathnames, else the pathnames are in 8.3 format. Any new CIFS implementation really should support long names.
5	0x0020	**<Reserved> (must be zero)**
4	0x0010	**<Reserved> (must be zero)**
3	0x0008	**<Reserved> (must be zero)**
2	SMB_FLAGS2_SECURITY_SIGNATURE 0x0004 0: No signature 1: Message Authentication Code	If set, the SMB contains a **M**essage **A**uthentication **C**ode (MAC). The MAC is used to authenticate each packet in a session, to prevent various attacks.

SMB_HEADER.FLAGS2

Bit	Name / Bitmask / Values	Description
1	SMB_FLAGS2_EAS 0x0002 0: No EAs 1: Extended Attributes	Indicates that the client understands Extended Attributes. Note that the SNIA doc talks about "Extended Attributes" *and* about "Extended File Attributes." These are two completely different concepts. Extended Attributes are a feature of OS/2. They are mentioned in Section 1.1.6 (page 2) of the SNIA doc and explained in better detail on page 87. Extended File Attributes are described in Section 3.13 (page 30) of the SNIA doc. The SMB_FLAGS2_EAS bit deals with Extended Attribute support.
0	SMB_FLAGS2_KNOWS_LONG_NAMES 0x0001 0: Client wants 8.3 1: Long pathnames okay	Set by the client to let the server know that long names are acceptable in the response.

Some of the flags are used to modify the interpretation of the SMB message, while others are used to negotiate features. Some do both. It may take some experimentation to find the safest way to handle these bits. Implementations are not consistent, so new code must be fine-tuned.

You may need to refer back to these tables as we dig further into the details. Note that the constant names listed above may not match those in the SNIA doc, or those in other docs or available source code. There doesn't seem to be a lot of agreement on the names.

12.3 EXTRA! EXTRA! Read All About It!

Um, actually we are going to delay covering the EXTRA field yet again. EXTRA.PidHigh will be thrown in with the PID field, and EXTRA.Signature will be handled as part of authentication.

12.4 `TID` and `UID`: Separated at Birth?

It would seem logical that the [V]`UID` and `TID` fields would be somehow related. Both are assigned and managed by the server, and we said before that the
`SESSION SETUP` (where the logon occurs) is supposed to happen *before* the
`TREE CONNECT`.

Well, put all that aside and pay attention to this little story...

Storytime

*Once upon a time there were many, many magic kingdoms taking up office space in
cities and towns around the world. In each of these magic kingdoms there were lots of
overpaid advisors called VeePees. The VeePees were all jealous of one another, but they
were more jealous of the underpaid wizards in the IT department who had power over
the data and could work spells and make the numbers come out all right.*

*Then, one day, evil marketing magicians appeared and convinced the VeePees
that they could steal all of the power away from the wizards of IT and have it for
themselves. To do this, the only thing the VeePees would need was a magic box called
a PeeCee (the name appealed to the VeePees). PeeCees, of course, were not cheap
but the lure of power was great and the marketing magicians knew that the VeePees
had control of the budget.*

*Soon, the wizards of IT discovered that their supplies of mag-tapes and 8-inch
floppies were dwindling, and that no one had bothered to update the service contracts
on their VAXes. Worse, the VeePees started taunting them, saying "We don't need you
any more. We have spreadsheets." The wise wizards of IT smiled quietly, went back
to their darkened cubicles, and entertained themselves by implementing EMACS in
TECO macro language. They did not seem at all surprised when the VeePees showed
up asking questions like "What happens if I format C-colon?" and "Should I Abort,
Retry, or — um — Fail?" The wizards understood what the VeePees did not: With
power there must be equal measures of knowledge and understanding, otherwise the
power will consume the data — and the user.*

*The marketing magicians, seeing that their golden goose was molting, came up
with a bold plan. They conjured up a LAN system and connected it to a shiny new fileserver, which they gave to the IT wizards. At first, the wizards were delighted by the
wonderful new server and the beautiful strands of network cable running all over the
kingdom. They quickly realized, however, that they had been tricked. The client/server
architecture had effectively separated authority from responsibility, and the wizards
were left with only the latter.*

*...and so it is unto this very day. The VeePees and their minions have their PeeCees
and hold the power of the data, but they remain under the influence of the sinister
marketing magicians. The wizards of IT are still underpaid, have little or no say when
decisions are made, and are held responsible and told to clean up the mess whenever
anything goes wrong. A wholly dysfunctional arrangement.*

So what the purplebananafish does this have to do with TIDs and UIDs? Well, see, it's like this...

Early corporate LANs, such as those in our story, were small and self-contained. The driving goal was to make sure that the data was available to everyone in the office who could legitimately claim to need access. Security was not considered a top priority, so PC OSes (e.g. DOS) did not support complicated minicomputer features like user-based authentication. Given the environment, it is not surprising that the authentication system originally built into SMB was (by today's standards) quite primitive. Passwords, if they were used at all, were assigned to shares — not users — and everyone who wanted to access the same share would use the same password.

This early form of SMB authentication is now known as "Share Level" security. It does not include the concept of user accounts, so the UID field is always zero. The password is included in the TREE CONNECT message, and a valid TID indicates a successfully authenticated connection. In fact, though the UID field is listed in the SMB message format layout described in the ancient COREP.TXT scrolls, *it is not mentioned again anywhere else in that document.* There is no mention of a SESSION SETUP message either.

There are some interesting tricks that add a bit of flexibility to Share Level security. For example, a single share may have multiple passwords assigned, each granting different access rights. It is fairly common, for instance, to assign separate passwords for read-only vs. read/write access to a share.

Another interesting fudge is often used to provide access to user home directories. The server (which, in this case, understands user-based authentication even if the protocol and/or client do not) simply offers usernames as share names. When a user connects to the share matching their username, they give their own login password. The server then checks the username/password pair using its normal account validation routines. Thus, user-based authentication can be mapped to Share Level security (see Figure 12.2).

Figure 12.2:   *User-based authentication via Share Level security*

Each share name maps to a username (Chico, Groucho, etc.). The server will accept the user's logon password as the TREE CONNECT password.

Share Level security, though still used, is considered deprecated. It has been replaced with "User Level" security which, of course, makes use of username/password instead of sharename/password pairs.

Under User Level security, the SESSION SETUP is performed as the authentication step *before* any TREE CONNECT requests may be sent. If the logon succeeds, the server will assign a valid (non-zero) UID. Subsequent TREE CONNECT attempts can use the UID as an authentication token when requesting access to a share. If User Level security is in use, the password field in the TREE CONNECT message will be blank.

So, with User Level security, the client must authenticate to get a valid UID, and then present the UID to gain access to shares. Thing is, more than one UID may be generated within a single connection, and the UID used to connect to the share does not need to be the same as the one used to access files within the share.

12.5 PID and MID **Revealed**

Simply put:

- a PID identifies a client process,
- a [PID, MID] pair identifies a thread within a process.

That's the idea, anyway. The client provides values for these fields when it sends a request to the server, and the server is supposed to echo the values back in the response. That way, the client can match the reply to the original request.

Some systems (such as Windows and OS/2) multiplex all of the SMB traffic between a client and a server over a single TCP connection. If the client OS is multi-tasking there may be several active SMB sessions running concurrently, so there may be several requests outstanding at any given time. The SMB conversations are all intertwined, so the client needs a way to sort out the replies and hand them off to the correct thread within the correct process (see Figure 12.3).

The PID field is also used to maintain the semantics of local file I/O. Think about a simple program, like the one in Listing 12.1 which opens a file in read-only mode and dumps the contents. Consider, in particular, the call to the open() function, which returns a file descriptor. File descriptors are

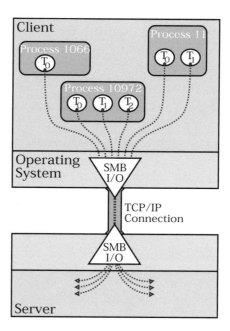

Figure 12.3:   *Multiplexing SMB over a single TCP connection*

Instead of opening individual TCP connections, one per process, some systems multiplex all SMB traffic to a given server over a single connection. (T_0, T_1, etc. are threads within a process.)

maintained on a per-process basis — that is, each process has its own private set. The descriptor is an integer used by the operating system to identify an internal record that keeps track of lots of information about the open file, such as:

- Is the file open for reading, writing, or both?
- What is the current file pointer offset within the file?
- Do we have any locks on the file?

Listing 12.1: Quick dump

```
#include <stdio.h>
#include <stdlib.h>
#include <unistd.h>
#include <sys/types.h>
#include <sys/stat.h>
#include <fcntl.h>
```

```c
#define bSIZE 1024

int main( int argc, char *argv[] )
  /* --------------------------------------------------- **
   * Copy file contents to stdout.
   * --------------------------------------------------- **
   */
  {
  int     fd_in;
  int     fd_out;
  ssize_t count;
  char    bufr[bSIZE];

  if( argc != 2 )
    {
    (void)fprintf( stderr,
                   "Usage: %s <filename>\n", argv[0] );
    exit( EXIT_FAILURE );
    }

  fd_in = open( argv[1], O_RDONLY );
  if( fd_in < 0 )
    {
    perror( "open()" );
    exit( EXIT_FAILURE );
    }
  fd_out = fileno( stdout );

  do
    {
    count = read( fd_in, bufr, bSIZE );
    if( count > 0 )
      count = write( fd_out, bufr, (size_t)count );
    } while( bSIZE == count );

  if( count < 0 )
    {
    perror( "read()/write()" );
    exit( EXIT_FAILURE );
    }

  (void)close( fd_in );
  exit( EXIT_SUCCESS );
  } /* main */
```

Now take all of that and stretch it out across a network. The files physically reside on the server and information about locks, offsets, etc. must be kept on the server side. The process that has opened the files, however, resides on the client and all of the file status information is relevant within the context of that process. That brings us back to what we said before: The PID identifies a client process. It lets the server keep track of client context, and associate it correctly with the right customer when the requests come rolling in.

Further complicating things, some clients support multiple threads running within a process. Threads share context (memory, file descriptors, etc.) with their sister threads within the same process, but each thread may generate SMB traffic all on its own. The MID field is used to make sure that server replies get back to the thread that sent the request. The server really doesn't do much with the MID. It just echoes it back to the client so, in fact, the client could make whatever use it wanted of the MID field. Using it as a thread identifier is probably the most practical thing to do.

There is an important rule which the client should obey with regard to the MID and PID fields: only one SMB request should ever be outstanding per [PID, MID] pair per connection. The reason for this rule is that the client will generally need to know the result of a request before sending the next request, especially if an error occurred. The problems which might result should this rule be broken probably depend upon the server, but defensive programming practices would suggest avoiding trouble.

12.5.1 EXTRA.PidHigh *Dark Secrets Uncovered*

Earlier on we promised to cover the EXTRA.PidHigh field. Well, a promise is a promise...

The PidHigh field is supposed to be a PID extension, allowing the use of 32-bit rather than 16-bit values as process identifiers. As with all extensions, however, there is the basic problem of backward compatibility.

In this case, trouble shows up if (and only if) the client supports 32-bit process IDs but the server does not. In that situation, the client must have a mechanism for mapping 32-bit process IDs to 16-bit values that can fit into the PID field. It doesn't need to be an elaborate mapping scheme, and it is unlikely that there will be 64K client processes talking to the same server at the same time, so it should be a simple problem to solve.

Since that mapping mechanism needs to be in place in order for the client to work with servers that don't support the `PidHigh` field, there's no reason to use 32-bit process IDs at all. In testing, it appears as though the `PidHigh` field is, in fact, always zero (except in some obscure security negotiations that are still not completely understood). Best bet, leave it zero.

12.6 SMB Header Final Report

Code...

The next Listing 12.2 provides support for reading and writing SMB message headers. Most of the header fields are simple integer values, so we can use the `smb_Set*()` and `smb_Get*()` functions from Listing 11.1 to move the data in and out of the header buffer. To make subsequent code easier to read, we provide a set of macros with nice clear names to front-end the function calls and assignments that are actually used.

Listing 12.2a: SMB Header [De]Construction: `MB_Header.h`

```
/* SMB Headers are always 32 bytes long.
 */
#define SMB_HDR_SIZE 32

/* FLAGS field bitmasks.
 */
#define SMB_FLAGS_SERVER_TO_REDIR        0x80
#define SMB_FLAGS_REQUEST_BATCH_OPLOCK   0x40
#define SMB_FLAGS_REQUEST_OPLOCK         0x20
#define SMB_FLAGS_CANONICAL_PATHNAMES    0x10
#define SMB_FLAGS_CASELESS_PATHNAMES     0x08
#define SMB_FLAGS_RESERVED               0x04
#define SMB_FLAGS_CLIENT_BUF_AVAIL       0x02
#define SMB_FLAGS_SUPPORT_LOCKREAD       0x01
#define SMB_FLAGS_MASK                   0xFB

/* FLAGS2 field bitmasks.
 */
#define SMB_FLAGS2_UNICODE_STRINGS       0x8000
#define SMB_FLAGS2_32BIT_STATUS          0x4000
#define SMB_FLAGS2_READ_IF_EXECUTE       0x2000
#define SMB_FLAGS2_DFS_PATHNAME          0x1000
#define SMB_FLAGS2_EXTENDED_SECURITY     0x0800
```

```
#define SMB_FLAGS2_RESERVED_01          0x0400
#define SMB_FLAGS2_RESERVED_02          0x0200
#define SMB_FLAGS2_RESERVED_03          0x0100
#define SMB_FLAGS2_RESERVED_04          0x0080
#define SMB_FLAGS2_IS_LONG_NAME         0x0040
#define SMB_FLAGS2_RESERVED_05          0x0020
#define SMB_FLAGS2_RESERVED_06          0x0010
#define SMB_FLAGS2_RESERVED_07          0x0008
#define SMB_FLAGS2_SECURITY_SIGNATURE   0x0004
#define SMB_FLAGS2_EAS                  0x0002
#define SMB_FLAGS2_KNOWS_LONG_NAMES     0x0001
#define SMB_FLAGS2_MASK                 0xF847

/* Field offsets.
 */
#define SMB_OFFSET_CMD      4
#define SMB_OFFSET_NTSTATUS 5
#define SMB_OFFSET_ECLASS   5
#define SMB_OFFSET_ECODE    7
#define SMB_OFFSET_FLAGS    9
#define SMB_OFFSET_FLAGS2   10
#define SMB_OFFSET_EXTRA    12
#define SMB_OFFSET_TID      24
#define SMB_OFFSET_PID      26
#define SMB_OFFSET_UID      28
#define SMB_OFFSET_MID      30

/* SMB command codes are given in the
 * SNIA doc.
 */

/* Write a command byte to the header buffer.
 */
#define smb_hdrSetCmd( bufr, cmd ) \
        (bufr)[SMB_OFFSET_CMD] = (cmd)

/* Read a command byte; returns uchar.
 */
#define smb_hdrGetCmd( bufr ) \
        (uchar)((bufr)[SMB_OFFSET_CMD])

/* Write a DOS Error Class to the header buffer.
 */
#define smb_hdrSetEclassDOS( bufr, Eclass ) \
        (bufr)[SMB_OFFSET_ECLASS] = (Eclass)
```

```
/* Read a DOS Error Class; returns uchar.
 */
#define smb_hdrGetEclassDOS( bufr ) \
        (uchar)((bufr)[SMB_OFFSET_ECLASS])

/* Write a DOS Error Code to the header buffer.
 */
#define smb_hdrSetEcodeDOS( bufr, Ecode ) \
        smb_SetShort( bufr, SMB_OFFSET_ECODE, Ecode )

/* Read a DOS Error Code; returns ushort.
 */
#define smb_hdrGetEcodeDOS( bufr ) \
        smb_GetShort( bufr, SMB_OFFSET_ECODE )

/* Write an NT_STATUS code.
 */
#define smb_hdrSetNTStatus( bufr, nt_status ) \
     smb_PutLong( bufr, SMB_OFFSET_NTSTATUS, nt_status )

/* Read an NT_STATUS code; returns ulong.
 */
#define smb_hdrGetNTStatus( bufr ) \
        smb_GetLong( bufr, SMB_OFFSET_NTSTATUS )

/* Write FLAGS to the header buffer.
 */
#define smb_hdrSetFlags( bufr, flags ) \
  (bufr)[SMB_OFFSET_FLAGS] = (flags)

/* Read FLAGS; returns uchar.
 */
#define smb_hdrGetFlags( bufr ) \
        (uchar)((bufr)[SMB_OFFSET_FLAGS])

/* Write FLAGS2 to the header buffer.
 */
#define smb_hdrSetFlags2( bufr, flags2 ) \
        smb_SetShort( bufr, SMB_OFFSET_FLAGS2, flags2 )

/* Read FLAGS2; returns ushort.
 */
#define smb_hdrGetFlags2( bufr ) \
        smb_GetShort( bufr, SMB_OFFSET_FLAGS2 )
```

```
/* Write the TID.
 */
#define smb_hdrSetTID( bufr, TID ) \
        smb_SetShort( bufr, SMB_OFFSET_TID, TID )

/* Read the TID; returns ushort.
 */
#define smb_hdrGetTID( bufr ) \
        smb_GetShort( bufr, SMB_OFFSET_TID )

/* Write the PID.
 */
#define smb_hdrSetPID( bufr, PID ) \
        smb_SetShort( bufr, SMB_OFFSET_PID, PID )

/* Read the PID; returns ushort.
 */
#define smb_hdrGetPID( bufr ) \
        smb_GetShort( bufr, SMB_OFFSET_PID )

/* Write the [V]UID.
 */
#define smb_hdrSetUID( bufr, UID ) \
        smb_SetShort( bufr, SMB_OFFSET_UID, UID )

/* Read the [V]UID; returns ushort.
 */
#define smb_hdrGetUID( bufr ) \
        smb_GetShort( bufr, SMB_OFFSET_UID )

/* Write the MID.
 */
#define smb_hdrSetMID( bufr, MID ) \
        smb_SetShort( bufr, SMB_OFFSET_MID, MID )

/* Read the MID; returns ushort.
 */
#define smb_hdrGetMID( bufr ) \
        smb_GetShort( bufr, SMB_OFFSET_MID )

/* Function prototypes.
 */
```

```c
int smb_hdrInit( uchar *bufr, int bsize );
  /* --------------------------------------------------- **
   * Initialize an empty header structure.
   * Returns -1 on error, the SMB header size on success.
   * --------------------------------------------------- **
   */

int smb_hdrCheck( uchar *bufr, int bsize );
  /* --------------------------------------------------- **
   * Perform some quick checks on a received buffer to
   * make sure it's safe to read.  This function returns
   * a negative value if the SMB header is invalid.
   * --------------------------------------------------- **
   */
```

Listing 12.2b: SMB Header [De]Construction: `MB_Header.c`

```c
#include "smb_header.h"

const char *smb_hdrSMBString = "\xffSMB";

int smb_hdrInit( uchar *bufr, int bsize )
  /* --------------------------------------------------- **
   * Initialize an empty header structure.
   * Returns -1 on error, the SMB header size on success.
   * --------------------------------------------------- **
   */
  {
  int i;

  if( bsize < SMB_HDR_SIZE )
    return( -1 );

  for( i = 0; i < 4; i++ )
    bufr[i] = smb_hdrSMBString[i];
  for( i = 4; i < SMB_HDR_SIZE; i++ )
    bufr[i] = '\0';

  return( SMB_HDR_SIZE );
  } /* smb_hdrInit */
```

```
int smb_hdrCheck( uchar *bufr, int bsize )
  /* -------------------------------------------------- **
   * Perform some quick checks on a received buffer to
   * make sure it's safe to read.  This function returns
   * a negative value if the SMB header is invalid.
   * -------------------------------------------------- **
   */
  {
  int i;

  if( NULL == bufr )
    return( -1 );

  if( bsize < SMB_HDR_SIZE )
    return( -2 );

  for( i = 0; i < 4; i++ )
    if( bufr[i] != smb_hdrSMBString[i] )
      return( -3 );

  return( SMB_HDR_SIZE );
  } /* smb_hdrCheck */
```

The smb_hdrInit() and smb_hdrCheck() functions are there
primarily to ensure that the SMB headers are reasonably sane. They check for
things like the buffer size, and ensure that the "\xffSMB" string is included
correctly in the header buffer.

Note that none of these functions or macros handle the reading and
writing of the four-byte session header, though that would be trivial. The
SESSION MESSAGE header is part of the transport layer, not SMB. It is
handled as a simple network-byte-order longword; something from the NBT
Session Service that has been carried over into naked transport. (We covered
all this back in Chapter 6 on page 129 and Section 8.2 on page 150.)

13

Protocol Negotiation

I don't have an accent.
—Oh yes you do.

CIFS is a very rich and varied protocol suite, a fact that is evident in the number of SMB dialects that exist. Five are listed in the X/Open SMB protocol specification, and the SNIA doc — published ten years later — lists eleven. That's a bigbunch, and they probably missed a few. Each new dialect may add new SMBs, deprecate old ones, or extend existing ones. As if that were not enough, implementations introduce subtle variations within dialects.

All that in mind, our goal in this section will be to provide an overview of the available dialects, cover the workings of the NEGOTIATE PROTOCOL SMB exchange, and take a preliminary peek at some of the concepts that we have yet to consider (things like virtual circuits and authentication). For the most part, the examples and discussion will be based on the "NT LM 0.12" dialect. The majority of the servers currently available support some variation of NT LM 0.12, and at least one client implementation (jCIFS) has managed to get by without supporting any others. Server writers should be warned, however, that there really are a lot of clients still around that use older calls. Even new clients will use older calls, simply because of the difficulty of acquiring reliable documentation on the newer stuff.

13.1   A Smattering of SMB Dialects

In keeping with tradition, the list of dialects is presented as a table with the dialect name in the left-hand column and a short description in the right, ordered from oldest to newest. Most of the references to these dialects seem to do it this way. Our list is not quite as complete as you might find elsewhere. The aim here is to highlight some of the better-known examples in order to provide a bit of context for the examination of the SMB_COM_NEGOTIATE message.

Where relevant, important differences between dialects will be noted. It would be very difficult, however, to try to document all of the features of each dialect and all of the changes between them. If you really, really need to know more (which is likely, if you are working on server code) see the SNIA doc, the X/Open doc, the expired IETF drafts, and the other old Microsoft documentation that is still freely available from their FTP server.[1]

SMB dialects

Dialect Identifier	Notes
PC NETWORK PROGRAM 1.0	Also known as the **Core Protocol**. This is the original stuff, as documented in COREP.TXT. According to ancient lore, this dialect is sometimes also identified by the string "PCLAN1.0".
MICROSOFT NETWORKS 1.03	This is the **Core Plus Protocol**. It extends a few Core Protocol SMB commands, and adds a few new ones.
MICROSOFT NETWORKS 3.0	Known as the **Extended 1.0 Protocol** or **LAN Manager 1.0**. This dialect was created when IBM and Microsoft were working together on OS/2. This particular variant was designed for DOS clients, which understood a narrower set of error codes than OS/2.
LANMAN1.0	Identical to the MICROSOFT NETWORKS 3.0 dialect except that it was intended for use with OS/2 clients, so a larger set of error codes was available. OS/2 and DOS both expect that the STATUS field will be in the DOS-style ErrorClass / ErrorCode format. Again, this dialect is also known as **LAN Manager 1.0** or as the **Extended 1.0 Protocol**.

---

1. ...or was, last time I checked. Once again, that URL is: ftp://ftp.microsoft.com/ developr/drg/CIFS/. See the References section for links to specific documents.

SMB dialects

Dialect Identifier	Notes
`LM1.2X002`	Called the **Extended 2.0 Protocol**; also known as **LAN Manager 2.0**. This dialect represents OS/2 LANMAN version 2.0, and it introduces a few new SMBs. The identifier for the DOS version of this dialect is "`DOS LM1.2X002`". As before, the key difference between the DOS and OS/2 dialects is simply that the OS/2 version provides a larger set of error codes.
`LANMAN2.1`	Called the **LAN Manager 2.1** dialect (no surprise there), this version is documented in a paper titled *Microsoft Networks SMB File Sharing Protocol Extensions, Document Version 3.4*. You can find it by searching the web for a file named "`SMB-LM21.DOC`". You will likely need a conversion tool of some sort in order to read the file, as it is encoded in an outdated form of a proprietary Microsoft format (it's a word-processing file). The cool thing about the `SMB-LM21.DOC` document is that instead of explaining how LANMAN2.1 works it describes how LANMAN2.1 differs from its predecessor, LANMAN2.0. That's useful for people who want to know how the protocol has evolved.
`Samba`	You may see this dialect listed in the protocol negotiation request coming from a Samba-based client such as `smbclient`, KDE Konqueror (which uses Samba's `libsmbclient` library), or the Linux `SMBFS` implementation. No one from the Samba Team seems to remember when, or why, this was added. It doesn't appear to be used any more (if, indeed, it ever was).
`NT LM 0.12`	This dialect, sometimes called NT LANMAN, was developed for use with Windows NT. All of the Windows 9x clients also claim to speak it, as do Windows 2000 and XP. As mentioned above, this is currently the most widely supported dialect. It is, quite possibly, also the sloppiest with all sorts of variations and differing implementations.
`CIFS`	Following the release of the IETF CIFS protocol drafts, many people thought that Microsoft would produce a "CIFS" dialect, and many documents refer to it. No such beast has actually materialized, however. Maybe that's a good thing.

Section 3.16 of the SNIA *CIFS Technical Reference, V1.0* provides a list of of SMB message types categorized by the dialect in which they were introduced. There is also a slightly more complete list of dialects in Section 5.4 of the SNIA doc.

13.2 Greetings: The NEGOTIATE PROTOCOL REQUEST

We have already provided a detailed breakdown of a NEGOTIATE PROTOCOL REQUEST SMB (back in Section 11.3 on page 186), so we don't need to go to the trouble of fully dissecting it again. The interesting part of the request is the data section (the parameter section is empty). If we were to write a client that supported all of the dialects in our chart, the NEGOTIATE_PROTOCOL_REQUEST.SMB_DATA field would break out something like this:

```
SMB_DATA
  {
  ByteCount = 131
  Bytes
    {
    Dialect[0] = "\x02PC NETWORK PROGRAM 1.0"
    Dialect[1] = "\x02MICROSOFT NETWORKS 1.03"
    Dialect[2] = "\x02MICROSOFT NETWORKS 3.0"
    Dialect[3] = "\x02LANMAN1.0"
    Dialect[4] = "\x02LM1.2X002"
    Dialect[5] = "\x02LANMAN2.1"
    Dialect[6] = "\x02Samba"
    Dialect[7] = "\x02NT LM 0.12"
    Dialect[8] = "\x02CIFS"
    }
  }
```

Each dialect string is preceded by a byte containing the value 0x02. This, perhaps, was originally intended to make it easier to parse the buffer. In addition to the 0x02 prefix the dialect strings are nul-terminated, so if you go to the trouble of counting up the bytes to see if the ByteCount value is correct in this example don't forget to add 1 to each string length.

Listing 13.1 provides code for creating a NEGOTIATE PROTOCOL REQUEST message. It also takes care of writing an NBT Session Message header for us — something we must not forget to do.

Listing 13.1: Negotiate Protocol Request

```
/* Define the SMB message command code.
 */
#define SMB_COM_NEGOTIATE 0x72

int nbt_SessionHeader( uchar *bufr, ulong size )
  /* ---------------------------------------------------- **
   * This function writes the NBT Session Service header.
   * Note that we use NBT byte order, not SMB.
   * ---------------------------------------------------- **
   */
  {
  if( size > 0x0001FFFF )  /* That's the NBT maximum. */
    return( -1 );
  bufr[0] = 0;
  bufr[1] = (size >> 16) & 0xFF;
  bufr[2] = (size >>  8) & 0xFF;
  bufr[3] = size & 0xFF;
  return( (int)size );
  } /* nbt_SessionHeader */

int smb_NegProtRequest( uchar  *bufr,
                        int     bsize,
                        int     namec,
                        uchar **namev )
  /* ---------------------------------------------------- **
   * Build a Negotiate Protocol Request message.
   * ---------------------------------------------------- **
   */
  {
  uchar *smb_bufr;
  int    i;
  int    length;
  int    offset;
  ushort bytecount;
  uchar  flags;
  ushort flags2;

  /* Set aside four bytes for the session header. */
  bsize    = bsize - 4;
  smb_bufr = bufr + 4;
```

```
/* Make sure we have enough room for the header,
 * the WORDCOUNT field, and the BYTECOUNT field.
 * That's the absolute minimum (with no dialects).
 */
if( bsize < (SMB_HDR_SIZE + 3) )
  return( -1 );

/* Initialize the SMB header.
 * This zero-fills all header fields except for
 * the Protocol field ("\ffSMB").
 * We have already tested the buffer size so
 * we can void the return value.
 */
(void)smb_hdrInit( smb_bufr, bsize );

/* Hard-coded flags values...
 */
flags  = SMB_FLAGS_CANONICAL_PATHNAMES;
flags |= SMB_FLAGS_CASELESS_PATHNAMES;
flags2 = SMB_FLAGS2_KNOWS_LONG_NAMES;

/* Fill in the header.
 */
smb_hdrSetCmd(    smb_bufr, SMB_COM_NEGOTIATE );
smb_hdrSetFlags(  smb_bufr, flags );
smb_hdrSetFlags2( smb_bufr, flags2 );

/* Fill in the (empty) parameter block.
 */
smb_bufr[SMB_HDR_SIZE] = 0;

/* Copy the dialect names into the message.
 * Set offset to indicate the start of the
 * BYTES field, skipping BYTECOUNT.  We will
 * fill in BYTECOUNT later.
 */
offset = SMB_HDR_SIZE + 3;
for( bytecount = i = 0; i < namec; i++ )
  {
  length = strlen(namev[i]) + 1;        /* includes nul  */
  if( bsize < (offset + 1 + length) )   /* includes 0x02 */
    return( -1 );
  smb_bufr[offset++] = '\x02';
  (void)memcpy( &smb_bufr[offset], namev[i], length );
  offset += length;
  bytecount += length + 1;
  }
```

```
/* The offset is now the total size of the SMB message.
 */
if( nbt_SessionHeader( bufr, (ulong)offset ) < offset )
  return( -1 );

/* The BYTECOUNT field starts one byte beyond the end
 * of the header (one byte for the WORDCOUNT field).
 */
smb_SetShort( smb_bufr, (SMB_HDR_SIZE + 1), bytecount );

/* Return the total size of the packet.
 */
return( offset + 4 );
} /* smb_NegProtRequest */
```

13.3   Gesundheit: The NEGOTIATE PROTOCOL RESPONSE

The NEGOTIATE PROTOCOL RESPONSE SMB is more complex than the request. In addition to the dialect selection, it also contains a variety of other parameters that let the client know the capabilities, limitations, and expectations of the server. Most of these values are stuffed into the SMB_PARAMETERS block, but there are a few fields defined in the SMB_DATA block as well.

13.3.1   *NegProt Response Parameters*

The NEGOTIATE_PROTOCOL_RESPONSE.SMB_PARAMETERS.Words block for the NT LM 0.12 dialect is 17 words (34 bytes) in size, and is structured as shown below. Earlier dialects use a different structure and, of course, the server should always match the reply to the dialect it selects.

```
typedef struct
  {
  uchar WordCount;                    /* Always 17 for this struct */
  struct
    {
    ushort DialectIndex;              /* Selected dialect index    */
    uchar  SecurityMode;              /* Server security flags     */
    ushort MaxMpxCount;               /* Maximum Multiplex Count    */
    ushort MaxNumberVCs;              /* Maximum Virtual Circuits   */
    ulong  MaxBufferSize;             /* Maximum SMB message size   */
    ulong  MaxRawSize;                /* Obsolete                   */
    ulong  SessionKey;                /* Unique session ID          */
    ulong  Capabilities;              /* Server capabilities flags  */
    ulong  SystemTimeLow;             /* Server time; low bytes     */
    ulong  SystemTimeHigh;            /* Server time; high bytes    */
    short  ServerTimeZone;            /* Minutes from UTC; signed   */
    uchar  EncryptionKeyLength; /* 0 or 8                          */
    } Words;
  } smb_NegProt_Rsp_Params;
```

That requires a lot of discussion. Let's tear it up and take a close look at the tiny pieces.

DialectIndex

Things start off fairly simply. The `DialectIndex` field contains the index of the dialect string that the server has selected, which will be the highest-level dialect that the server understands. The dialect strings are numbered starting with zero, so to choose "NT LM 0.12" from the list in the example request the server would return 7 in the `DialectIndex` field.

SecurityMode

`SecurityMode` is a bitfield that provides some information about the authentication sub-protocol that the server is expecting. Four flag bits are defined; they are described below. Challenge/Response and **M**essage **A**uthentication **C**ode (MAC) message signing will be explained later (this is becoming our mantra), when we cover authentication. It will take a little while to get there, but keep your eyes open for additional clues along the way.

`SecurityMode`

Bit	Name / Bitmask / Values	Description
7–4	0xF0	**<Reserved> (must be zero)**
3	NEGOTIATE_SECURITY_SIGNATURES_REQUIRED 0x08 0: Message signing is optional 1: Message signing is required	If set, this bit indicates that the server is requiring the use of a **M**essage **A**uthentication **C**ode (MAC) in each packet. If the bit is clear then message signing is optional. This bit should be zero if the next bit (mask 0x04) is zero.
2	NEGOTIATE_SECURITY_SIGNATURES_ENABLED 0x04 0: Message signing not supported 1: Server can perform message signing	If set, the server is indicating that it is capable of performing **M**essage **A**uthentication **C**ode (MAC) message signing. This bit should be zero if the next bit (mask 0x02) is zero.
1	NEGOTIATE_SECURITY_CHALLENGE_RESPONSE 0x02 0: Plaintext Passwords 1: Challenge/Response	This bit indicates whether or not the server supports Challenge/Response authentication (which will be covered further on). If the bit is clear, then plaintext passwords must be used. If set, the server may (optionally) reject plaintext authentication. If this bit is clear and the client rejects the use of plaintext, then there is no way to perform the logon and the client will be unable to connect to the server.

`SecurityMode`

Bit	Name / Bitmask / Values	Description

0	`NEGOTIATE_SECURITY_USER_LEVEL`
	`0x01`
	0: Share Level
	1: User Level
		Ah! Finally something we've already covered!
		     This bit indicates whether the server, as a whole, is operating under Share Level or User Level security. Share and User Level security were explained along with the `TID` and `UID` header fields, back in Section 12.4 on page 209.

MaxMpxCount

Remember the `PID` and `MID` fields in the header? They could be used to multiplex several sessions over a single TCP/IP connection. The thing is, the server might not be able to handle more than a fixed number of total outstanding requests.

The `MaxMpxCount` field lets the server tell the client how many requests, in total, it can handle concurrently. It is the client's responsibility to ensure that there are no more than `MaxMpxCount` outstanding requests in the pipe at any time. That may mean that client processes will block, waiting for their turn to send an SMB.

MaxNumberVCs

The `MaxNumberVCs` field specifies the maximum number of **V**irtual **C**ircuits (VCs) that the server is able to accommodate. VCs are yet another mechanism by which multiple SMB sessions could, in theory, be multiplexed over a single transport-layer session. Note the use of the phrase "in theory." The dichotomy between theory and practice is a recurring theme in the study of CIFS.

MaxBufferSize

`MaxBufferSize` is the size (in bytes) of the largest message that the server can receive.

Keep in mind that the transport layer will fragment and defragment packets as necessary. It is, therefore, possible to send very large SMBs and let the lower layers worry about ensuring safe, fast, reliable delivery.

How big can an SMB message be?

In the NT LM 0.12 dialect, the `MaxBufferSize` field is an unsigned longword. As described much earlier on, however, the `Length` field in the NBT SESSION MESSAGE is 17 bits wide and the naked transport header has a 24-bit `Length` field. So the session headers place slightly more reasonable limits on the maximum size of a single SMB message.

MaxRawSize

This is the maximum size of a raw data buffer.

The X/Open doc describes the READ RAW and WRITE RAW SMBs, which were introduced with the Extended 1.0 version of SMB (the `MICROSOFT NETWORKS 3.0` and `LANMAN1.0` dialects). These were a speed hack. For a large read or write operation, the first message would be a proper SMB, but subsequent messages would be sent in "raw" mode, with no SMB or session header. The raw blocks could be as large as `MaxRawSize` bytes in length. Once again, the transport layer was expected to take care of fragmentation/defragmentation as well as resending of any lost packets.

Raw mode is not used much any more. Among other things, it conflicts with message signing because the raw messages have no header in which to put the MAC Signature. Thus, the `MaxRawSize` field is considered obsolete.[2]

SessionKey

The `SessionKey` is supposed to be used to identify the session in which a VC has been opened. Documentation on the use of this field is very

---

2. There may be a further problem with raw mode. Microsoft has made some obtuse references to obscure patents which may or may not be related to READ RAW and WRITE RAW. The patents in question have been around for quite some time, and were not mentioned in any of the SMB/CIFS documentation that Microsoft released up until March of 2002. Still, the best bet is to avoid READ RAW and WRITE RAW (since they are not particularly useful anyway) and/or check with a patent lawyer. The Samba Team released a statement regarding this issue, see http://us1.samba.org/samba/ms_license.html.

poor, however, and the commentary in various mailing list archives shows that there is not much agreement about what to do with it.

In theory, the `SessionKey` value should be echoed back to the server whenever the client sends a `SESSION SETUP` request. Samba's `smbclient` does this, but some versions of jCIFS always reply with zero, and they don't seem to have any trouble with it. In testing, it also appears that Windows 2000 servers do not generate a session key. They send zero in `NEGOTIATE PROTOCOL RESPONSE` messages. Hmmm...

It would seem that the use of this field was never clearly defined — anywhere by anyone — and that most servers really don't care what goes there. It is probably safest if the client echoes back the value sent by the server.

Capabilities

This is a grab-bag bitfield, similar in style to the `FLAGS` and `FLAGS2` fields in the header except, of course, that it is not included in every message. The bits of the `Capabilities` field indicate specific server features of which the client may choose to take advantage.

We are already building up a backlog of unexplained features. We will also postpone the discussion of the `Capabilities` field until we get some of the other stuff out of the way.

SystemTimeLow and SystemTimeHigh

The `SystemTime` fields are shown as two unsigned longs in the SNIA doc. We might write it as:

```
typedef struct
  {
  ulong timeLow;
  ulong timeHigh;
  } smb_Time;
```

Keeping byte order in mind, the completed time value should be read as two little-endian 32-bit integers. The result, however, should be handled as a 64-bit *signed* value representing the number of tenths of a microsecond since January 1, 1601, 00:00:00.0 UTC.

WHAT?!?!

Yes, you read that right folks. The time value is based on that unwieldy little formula. Read it again five times and see if you don't get a headache. Looks as though we need to get out the protractor, the astrolabe, and the didgeridoo and try a little calculating. Let's start with some complex scientific equations:

- 1 microsecond = 10^{-6} seconds,
- 1/10 microsecond = 10^{-7} seconds.

In other words, the server time is given in units of 10^{-7} seconds.[3] Many CIFS implementations handle these units by converting them into Unix-style measurements. Unix, of course, bases its time measurements on an equally obscure date: January 1, 1970, 00:00:00.0 UTC.[4] Converting between the two schemes requires knowing the difference (in seconds) between the two base times.

 Email

```
        From: Andrew Narver
In-Reply-To: A message from Mike Allen sent to Microsoft's CIFS
             mailing list and the Samba-Technical mailing list.

> (what's the number of seconds between 1601 and 1970 again?)

Between Jan 1, 1601 and Jan 1, 1970, you have 369 complete
years, of which 89 are leap years (1700, 1800, and 1900 were
not leap years). That gives you a total of 134774 days or
11644473600 seconds.
```

So, if you want to convert the SystemTime to a Unix time_t value, you need to do something like this:

```
unix_time = (time_t)(((smb_time)/10000000) - 11644473600);
```

which gives you the server's system time in seconds since January 1, 1970, 00:00:00.0 UTC.

---

3. There is no name for 10^{-7} seconds. Other fractions of seconds have names with prefixes like deci, centi, milli, micro, nano, pico, even zepto, but there is no prefix that applies to 10^{-7}. In honor of the fact that this rare measure of time is used in the CIFS protocol suite, I propose that it be called a **bozo**second.

4. January 1, 1970, 00:00:00.0 UTC, known as "the Epoch," is sometimes excused as being the approximate birthdate of Unix.

ServerTimeZone

ServerTimeZone, of course, is the timezone in which the server believes it resides. It is represented as an offset relative to UTC, in minutes. Minutes, that is. Multiply by 60 in order to get seconds, or 600,000,000 to get tenths of a microsecond.

The available documentation (the SNIA doc and the Leach/Naik IETF draft) states that this field is an *un*signed short integer. They're wrong. The field is a signed value which is subtracted from the SystemTime to give local time.

If, for example, your server is located in the beautiful city of Saint Paul, Minnesota, it would be in the US Central timezone[5] which is six hours west of UTC. The value in the ServerTimeZone field would, therefore be 360 minutes. (Except, of course, during the summer when Daylight Savings Time is in effect, in which case it would be 300 minutes.) On the other hand, if your server is in Moscow in the winter, the ServerTimeZone value would be −180.

The basic rule of thumb:

```
LocalTime = SystemTime - ( ServerTimeZone × 600000000 )
```

...which returns local time in units of 10^{-7} seconds, based on January 1601 as described above.

If you found all of that to be complicated, you will be relieved to know that this is only one of many different time formats used in SMB. Time And Date Encoding is covered in Section 3.7 of the SNIA doc.

EncryptionKeyLength

This is the last field in the NEGOTIATE_PROTOCOL_RESPONSE. SMB_PARAMETERS block. It provides the length, in bytes, of the Challenge used in Challenge/Response authentication. SMB Challenges, if present, are always 8 bytes long, so the EncryptionKeyLength will have a value of either 8 or 0 — the latter if Challenge/Response authentication is not in use.

---

5. This is probably because Saint Paul is at the center of the universe. The biomagnetic center of the universe used to be located across the river in Minneapolis until they closed it down. It was a little out of whack in the same way that the magnetic poles are not quite where they should be. The magnetic north pole, for instance, is on or near an island in northern Canada instead of at the center of the Arctic Ocean where it belongs.

The name of this field is probably a hold-over from some previous enhancement to the protocol — still in use for "historical reasons."

Wow... a lot of stuff there. No time to sit and chat about it right now, though. We still need to finish out the examination of the `NEGOTIATE_PROTOCOL_RESPONSE.SMB_DATA` block.

13.3.2 *NegProt Response Data*

`SMB_DATA`, of course, is handed to us as an array of bytes with the length provided in the `ByteCount` field. The parsing of those bytes depends upon the values in the `SMB_PARAMETER` block that we just examined. The structure is completely different depending upon whether Extended Security has been negotiated.

Here is what it looks like, more or less, in the NT LM 0.12 dialect:

```
typedef struct
  {
  ushort ByteCount;          /* Number of bytes to follow  */
  union
    {
    struct
      {
      uchar GUID[16];        /* 16-byte Globally Unique ID */
      uchar SecurityBlob[];  /* Auth-system dependent      */
      } ext_sec;             /* Extended Security          */
    struct
      {
      uchar EncryptionKey[]; /* 0 or 8 bytes long          */
      uchar DomainName[];    /* nul-terminated string      */
      } non_ext_sec;         /* Non-Extended Security      */
    } Bytes;
  } smb_NegProt_Rsp_Data;
```

The first thing to note is that this `SMB_DATA.Bytes` block structure is the union of two smaller structures:

- `ext_sec` is used if Extended Security has been negotiated,
- `non_ext_sec` is used otherwise.

The second thing to note is that this is pseudo-code, not valid C code. Some of the array lengths are unspecified because we don't know the byte-length of the fields ahead of time. In real code, you will probably need to use pointers or some other mechanism to extract the variable-length data from the buffer.

Okay, let's chop that structure into little bits...

GUID

GUID stands for **G**lobally **U**nique **ID**entifier. The GUID field is always 16 bytes long.

As of this writing, research by Samba Team members shows that this value is probably the same as the GUID identifier used by Active Directory to keep track of servers in the database. Standalone servers (which are not listed in any Active Directory) also generate and use a GUID. Go figure.

Though this field is only present when Extended Security is enabled, it is not, strictly speaking, a security field. The value is well known and easily forged. It is not clear (yet) why this field is even sent to the client. In testing, a Samba server was configured to fill the GUID field with its own 16-byte Server Service NetBIOS name... and that worked just fine.

SecurityBlob

The SecurityBlob is — as the name says — a blob of security information. In other words, it is a block of data that contains authentication information particular to the Extended Security mechanism being used. Obviously, this field will need to be covered in the Authentication section.

The SecurityBlob is variable in length. Fortunately, the GUID field is always 16 bytes, so the length of the SecurityBlob is (ByteCount - 16) bytes.

EncryptionKey

This field should be called Challenge because that's what it actually contains — the Challenge used in Challenge/Response authentication. The SMB Challenge, if present, is always eight bytes long. If plaintext passwords are in use then there is no Challenge, the EncryptionKey will be empty, and the SMB_PARAMETERS.EncryptionKeyLength field will contain 0.

DomainName

This field sometimes contains the NetBIOS name of the Workgroup or NT Domain to which the server belongs. (We have talked a bit, in previous sections, about Workgroups and NT Domains so the terms should be somewhat familiar.) In testing, Samba servers always provided a name in the `DomainName` field; Windows systems less reliably so. Windows 98, for example, would sometimes provide a value and sometimes not.[6]

The SNIA doc calls this field the `OEMDomainName` and claims that the characters will be eight-bit values using the OEM character set of the server (that's the 7-bit ASCII character set augmented by an extended DOS code page which defines characters for the upper 128 octet values). In fact, this field may contain either a string of 8-bit OEM characters or a Unicode string with 16-bit characters. The value of `SMB_HEADER.FLAGS2.SMB_FLAGS2_UNICODE_STRINGS` will let you know how to read the `DomainName` field.

13.4 Are We There Yet?

Okay, let's be honest... Ripping apart that `NEGOTIATE PROTOCOL RESPONSE` SMB was about as exciting as the epic saga of undercooked toast. It doesn't get any better than that, though, and there's a lot more of it. Implementing SMB is a game of patience and persistence. It also helps if you get a cheap thrill from fiddly little details. (Just don't go parsing your packets in public or people will look at you funny.)

It seems, too, that our overview of the SMB Header and the `NEGOTIATE PROTOCOL` exchange has left a bit of a mess on the floor. We have pulled a lot of concepts off of the shelves and out of the closets, and we will need to do some sorting and organizing before we can put them back. Let's see what we've got:

- Opportunistic Locks (OpLocks), which were taking up space in the `SMB_HEADER.FLAGS` field,
- Virtual Circuits (we found these in the box labeled `MaxNumberVCs`),

---

6. A lot of time was wasted trying to figure out which configuration options would change the behavior. The results were inconclusive. At first it seemed as though the DomainName was included if the Windows 98 system was running in User Level security mode and passing logins through to an NT Domain Controller. Further testing, however, showed that this was not a hard-and-fast rule. It should also be mentioned that if the systems are running naked transport there may not be an NT Domain or Workgroup name. SMB can be mightily inconsistent — but not all the time.

- The `Capabilities` bits (and pieces),
- Distributed File System (DFS), which spilled out when `FLAGS2` fell open,
- Character Encoding — which seems to get into everything, sort of like cat hair and dust,
- Extended vs. DOS Attributes,
- Long vs. short names, and...
- Authentication, including plaintext passwords, Challenge/Response, Extended Security, and Packet Signing.

The only way to approach all of these topics is one-at-a-time. ...but first, take another break. Every now and then, it is a good idea to stop and think about what has been covered so far. This is one of those times. We have finished tearing apart SMB headers and the body of a `NEGOTIATE PROTOCOL` message. That should provide some familiarity with the overall structure of SMBs. Try doing some packet captures, or skim through the SNIA *CIFS Technical Reference*. It should all begin to make a little more sense now than it did when we started.

14

Session Setup

...it is a tale
Told by an idiot, full of sound
and fury, signifying nothing.

— *Macbeth*, Act V, Scene v,
William Shakespeare

Originally, the SESSION SETUP was not required by — or even defined as part of — the SMB protocol. It was introduced in the LANMAN days in order to handle User Level authentication and could be skipped if the server was in Share Level security mode. These days, however, the SESSION SETUP takes care of a lot of unfinished business, like cleaning up some of the debris left by the NEGOTIATE PROTOCOL RESPONSE. In the NT LM 0.12 dialect there *must* be a SESSION SETUP exchange before a TREE CONNECT may be sent, even if the server is operating in Share Level security mode.

14.1 SESSION SETUP ANDX REQUEST Parameters

The SESSION SETUP SMB is actually a SESSION SETUP ANDX, which simply means that there's an AndX block in the parameter section. In the NT LM 0.12 dialect, the Parameter block is formatted as shown below:

```
typedef struct
  {
  uchar WordCount;  /* 12 or 13 words */
  struct
    {
    struct
      {
      uchar  Command;
      uchar  Reserved;
      ushort Offset;
      } AndX;
    ushort MaxBufferSize;
    ushort MaxMpxCount;
    ushort VcNumber;
    ulong  SessionKey;
    ushort Lengths[];  /* 1 or 2 elements */
    ulong  Reserved;
    ulong  Capabilities;
    } Words;
  } smb_SessSetupAndX_Req_Params;
```

When looking at these C-like structures, keep in mind that they are intended as descriptions rather than specifications. On the wire, the parameters are packed tightly into the SMB messages, and they are not aligned. Though the structures show the type and on-the-wire ordering of the fields, the C programming language does not guarantee that the layout will be retained in memory. That's why our example code includes all those functions and macros for packing and unpacking the packets.[1]

Many of the fields in the SESSION_SETUP_ANDX.SMB_PARAMETERS block should be familiar from the NEGOTIATE PROTOCOL RESPONSE SMB. This time, though, it's the client's turn to set the limits.

MaxBufferSize

MaxBufferSize is the size (in bytes) of the largest message that the *client* can receive. It is typically less than or equal to the server's MaxBufferSize, but it doesn't need to be.

---

1. To be pedantic, the correct terms are "marshaling" and "unmarshaling." "Marshaling" means collecting data in system-internal format and re-organizing it into a linear format for transport to another system (virtual, physical, or otherwise). "Unmarshaling," of course, is the reverse process. These terms are commonly associated with Remote Procedure Call (RPC) protocols, but some have argued (not unreasonably) that SMB is a simple form of RPC.

MaxMpxCount

This must always be less than or equal to the server-specified MaxMpxCount. This is the client's way of letting the server know how many outstanding requests it will allow. The server might use this value to pre-allocate resources.

VcNumber

This field is used to establish a Virtual Circuit (VC) with the server. Keep reading, we're almost there...

SessionKey

Just echo back whatever you got in the NEGOTIATE PROTOCOL RESPONSE.

Lengths

For efficiency's sake the structure above provides the Lengths field, defined as an array of unsigned short integers and described as having one or two elements. The SNIA doc and other references go to a lot more trouble and provide two separate and complete versions of the entire SESSION SETUP REQUEST structure.

Basically, though, if Extended Security has been negotiated then the Lengths field is a single ushort, known as SecurityBlobLength in the SNIA doc. (We touched on the concept of security blobs briefly back in Section 13.3.2.) If Extended Security is *not* in use then there will be two ushort fields identified by the excessively long names:

- CaseInsensitivePasswordLength and
- CaseSensitivePasswordLength.

Obviously, all of this stuff falls into the general category of authentication, and will be covered in more detail when we finally focus on that topic.

Reserved

Four bytes of must-be-zero.

Capabilities

This field contains the client capabilities flag bits.

You might notice, upon careful examination, that the client does not send back a `MaxRawSize` value. That's because it can specify raw read/write sizes in the `SMB_COM_RAW_READ` and `SMB_COM_RAW_WRITE` requests, if it sends them. These SMBs are considered obsolete, so newer clients really shouldn't be using them.

There are a couple of fields in the `SESSION SETUP REQUEST` which touch on esoteric concepts that we have been promising to explain for quite a while now — specifically virtual circuits and capabilities — so let's get it over with...

14.1.1 *Virtual Circuits*

It does seem as though there's a good deal of cruft in the SMB protocol. The `SessionKey`, for example, appears to be a vestigial organ, the purpose of which has been mostly forgotten. Originally, such fields may have been intended to compensate for a limitation in a specific transport or an older implementation, or to solve some other problem that isn't a problem any more.

Consider virtual circuits...

The LAN Manager documentation available from Microsoft's ftp site provides the best clues regarding virtual circuits (see `SMB-LM1X.PS`, for instance). According to those docs a virtual circuit (VC) represents a single transport layer connection, and the `VcNumber` is a tag used to identify a specific transport link between a specific client/server pair.

That concept probably needs to be considered in context.

The LANMAN dialects were developed in conjunction with OS/2 (an honest-to-goodness, really-truly, multitasking OS). OS/2 clients pass SMB traffic through a redirector — just like DOS and Windows — and it seems as though there was some concern that multiplexing the SMB traffic from several processes across a single connection might cause a bit of a bottleneck. So, to avoid congestion, the redirector could create additional connections to facilitate faster transfers for individual processes.[2] Under this scheme, all of the transport level connections from a client to a server were considered part of a single logical

---

2. If you enjoy digging into odd details, this is a great one. See the `SMB-LM1X.PS` file, also known as Microsoft Networks/SMB File Sharing Protocol Extensions, Version 2.0, Document Version 3.3. In particular, see the definition of a VC on page 2, and the description of the "Virtual Circuit Environment" in Section 4.a on page 10.

"session" (we now, officially, have way too many meanings for that term). Within that logical session there could, conversely, be multiple transport level connections — aka virtual circuits — up to the limit set in the NEGOTIATE PROTOCOL RESPONSE.

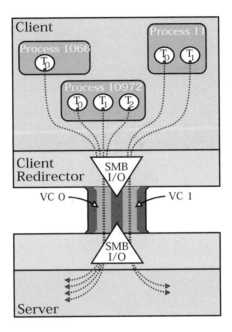

Figure 14.1: *Virtual circuits*

Process 11 has the use of virtual circuit number 1 (VC 1). VC 0 and VC 1 are separate TCP/IP connections, yet both VCs are part of the same logical client/server "session" (and the term "session" is clearly overused).

Figure 14.1 illustrates the point, and here's how it's supposed to work:

- Logical Session Creation
  - The client makes an initial connection to the SMB server, performs the NEGOTIATE PROTOCOL exchange, and establishes the session by sending a SESSION SETUP ANDX REQUEST.
  - The VcNumber in the initial SESSION SETUP ANDX REQUEST is zero (0).
- Additional VC Creation
  - An additional transport level connection is created.

- The client sends a new SESSION SETUP ANDX REQUEST with a VcNumber greater than zero, but less than the MaxNumberVCs sent by the server.

- The SessionKey field in the SESSION SETUP ANDX REQUEST must match the SessionKey returned in the initial NEGOTIATE PROTOCOL RESPONSE. That's how the new VC is bound to the existing logical session.

Ah-hahhh! The mystery of the SessionKey field is finally revealed. Kind of a let-down, isn't it?

Whenever a new transport-layer connection is created, the client is supposed to assign a new VC number. Note that the VcNumber on the initial connection is expected to be zero to indicate that the client is starting from scratch and is creating a new logical session. If an additional VC is given a VcNumber of zero, the server *may* assume that any existing connections with that same client are now bogus, and shut them down.

Why do such a thing?

The explanation given in the LANMAN documentation, the Leach/Naik IETF draft, and the SNIA doc is that clients may crash and reboot without first closing their connections. The zero VcNumber is the client's signal to the server to clean up old connections. Reasonable or not, that's the logic behind it. Unfortunately, it turns out that there are some annoying side-effects that result from this behavior. It is possible, for example, for one rogue application to completely disrupt SMB filesharing on a system simply by sending Session Setup requests with a zero VcNumber. Connecting to a server through a NAT (**N**etwork **A**ddress **T**ranslation) gateway is also problematic, since the NAT makes multiple clients appear to be a single client by placing them all behind the same IP address.[3]

The biggest problem with virtual circuits, however, is that they are not really needed any more (if, in fact, they ever were). As a result, they are handled inconsistently by various implementations and are not entirely to be trusted. On the client-side, the best thing to do is to ignore the concept and view each transport connection as a separate logical session, one VC per session. Oh! ...and contrary to the specs the client should always use a VcNumber of one, never zero.

---

3. See *Microsoft Knowledge Base Article #301673* for more information.

On the server side, it is important to keep in mind that the TID, UID, PID, and MID are all supposed to be relative to the VC. In particular, TID and UID values negotiated on one VC have no meaning (and no authority) on another VC, even if both VCs appear to be from the same client. Another important note is that the server should *not* disconnect existing VCs upon receipt of a new VC with a zero VcNumber. As described above, doing so is impractical and may break things. The server should let the transport layer detect and report session disconnects. At most, a zero VcNumber might be a good excuse to send a keep-alive packet.

The whole VC thing probably seemed like a good idea at the time.

14.1.2 Capabilities *Bits*

Remember a little while back when we said that there were subtle variations within SMB dialects? Well, some of them are not all that subtle once you get to know them. The Capabilities bits formalize several such variations by letting the client and server negotiate which special features will be supported. The server sends its Capabilities field in the NEGOTIATE PROTOCOL RESPONSE, and the client returns its own set of capabilities in the SESSION SETUP ANDX REQUEST.

The table below provides a listing of the capabilities defined for servers. The client set is smaller.

Server capabilities

Bit	Name / Bitmask	Description
31	CAP_EXTENDED_SECURITY 0x80000000	Set to indicate that Extended Security exchanges are supported.
30	CAP_COMPRESSED_DATA 0x40000000	If set, this bit indicates that the server can compress Data blocks before sending them.[4] This might be useful to improve throughput of large file transfers over low-bandwidth links. This capability requires

---

4. There are a few small notes scattered about the SNIA doc that suggest that the prescribed compression algorithm is something called LZNT. I haven't been able to find a definitive reference that explains what LZNT is, but it appears from the name that it is a form of Lempel-Ziv compression.

Server capabilities

Bit	Name / Bitmask	Description
		that the CAP_BULK_TRANSFER capability also be set. Currently, however, there are no known implementations that support bulk transfer.
29	CAP_BULK_TRANSFER 0x20000000	If set, the server supports the SMB_COM_READ_BULK and SMB_COM_WRITE_BULK SMBs. There are no known implementations which support CAP_BULK_TRANSFER and/or CAP_COMPRESSED_DATA. Samba does not even bother to define constants for these capabilities.
23	CAP_UNIX 0x00800000	Microsoft reserved this bit based on a proposal (by Byron Deadwiler at Hewlett-Packard) for a small set of Unix extensions. The SNIA doc describes these extensions in an appendix. Note, however, that the proposal was made and the appendix written before the extensions were widely implemented. Samba supports the SMB Unix extensions, but probably not exactly as specified in the SNIA doc.
15	CAP_LARGE_WRITEX 0x00008000	If set, the server supports a special mode of the SMB_COM_WRITE_ANDX SMB which allows the client to send more data than would normally fit into the server's receive buffers, up to a maximum of 64 Kbytes.
14	CAP_LARGE_READX 0x00004000	Similar to the CAP_LARGE_WRITEX, this bit indicates whether the server can handle SMB_COM_READ_ANDX requests for blocks of data larger than the reported maximum buffer size. The theoretical maximum is 64 Kbytes, but the client should never request more data than it can receive.
13	CAP_INFOLEVEL_PASSTHROUGH 0x00002000	Samba calls this the CAP_W2K_SMBS bit. In testing, NT 4.0 systems did not set this bit, but W2K systems did. Basically, it indicates support for some advanced requests.
12	CAP_DFS 0x00001000	If set, this bit indicates that the server supports Microsoft's Distributed File System.

Server capabilities

Bit	Name / Bitmask	Description
9	CAP_NT_FIND 0x00000200	This is a mystery bit. There is very little documentation about it and what does exist is not particularly helpful. The SNIA doc simply says that this bit is "Reserved," but the notes regarding the CAP_NT_SMBS bit state that the latter implies the former. (Counter-examples have been found in some references, but not on the wire during testing. Your mileage may vary.) Basically, though, if this bit is set it indicates that the server supports an extended set of function calls belonging to a class of calls known as "transactions."
8	CAP_LOCK_AND_READ 0x00000100	If set, the server is reporting that it supports the obsolete SMB_COM_LOCK_AND_READ SMB. ...but go back and look at the SMB_HEADER.FLAGS bits described earlier. The lowest order FLAGS bit is SMB_FLAGS_SUPPORT_LOCKREAD, and it is also supposed to indicate whether or not the server supports SMB_COM_LOCK_AND_READ (as well as the complimentary SMB_COM_WRITE_AND_UNLOCK). The thing is, traces from Windows NT and Windows 2000 systems show the CAP_LOCK_AND_READ bit set while the SMB_FLAGS_SUPPORT_LOCKREAD is clear. That doesn't make a lot of sense. Well... it *may* be that the server is indicating that it supports the SMB_COM_LOCK_AND_READ SMB but *not* the SMB_COM_WRITE_AND_UNLOCK SMB, or it may be that the server may be using the Capabilities field in preference to the FLAGS field. Avoid the use of the SMB_COM_LOCK_AND_READ and SMB_COM_WRITE_AND_UNLOCK SMBs and everything should turn out alright.

Server capabilities

Bit	Name / Bitmask	Description
7	CAP_LEVEL_II_OPLOCKS 0x00000080	If set, Level II OpLocks are supported in addition to Exclusive and Batch OpLocks.
6	CAP_STATUS32 0x00000040	If set, this bit indicates that the server supports the 32-bit NT_STATUS error codes.
5	CAP_RPC_REMOTE_APIS 0x00000020	If set, this bit indicates that the server permits remote management via Remote Procedure Call (RPC) requests. RPC is way beyond the scope of this book.
4	CAP_NT_SMBS 0x00000010	If set, this bit indicates that the server supports some advanced SMBs that were designed for use with Windows NT and above. These are, essentially, an extension to the NT LM 0.12 dialect. According to the SNIA doc, the CAP_NT_SMBS implies CAP_NT_FIND.
3	CAP_LARGE_FILES 0x00000008	If set, this bit indicates that the server can handle 64-bit file sizes. With 32-bit file sizes, files are limited to 4 GB in size.
2	CAP_UNICODE 0x00000004	Set to indicate that the server supports Unicode.
1	CAP_MPX_MODE 0x00000002	If set, the server supports the (obsolete) SMB_COM_READ_MPX and SMB_COM_WRITE_MPX SMBs.
0	CAP_RAW_MODE 0x00000001	If set, the server supports the (obsolete) SMB_COM_READ_RAW and SMB_COM_WRITE_RAW SMBs.

On the server side, the implementor's rule of thumb regarding capabilities is to start by supporting as few as possible and add new ones one at a time. Each bit is a cornucopia — or Pandora's box — of new features and requirements, and most represent a very large development effort. As usual, if there is documentation it is generally either scarce or encumbered.

Things are not quite so bad if you are implementing a client, though the client also has a list of capabilities that it can declare. The client list is as follows:

Client capabilities

Bit	Name / Bitmask	Description
31	CAP_EXTENDED_SECURITY 0x80000000	Set to indicate that Extended Security exchanges are supported.
		The SNIA doc and the older IETF Draft do not list this as a capability set by the client. On the wire, however, it is clearly used as such by Windows, Samba, and by Steve French's CIFS VFS for Linux. If the server indicates Extended Security support in its Capabilities field, then the client may set this bit to indicate that it also supports Extended Security.
9	CAP_NT_FIND 0x00000200	If set, this bit indicates that the client is capable of utilizing the CAP_NT_FIND capability of the server.
7	CAP_LEVEL_II_OPLOCKS 0x00000080	If set, this bit indicates that the client understands Level II OpLocks.
6	CAP_STATUS32 0x00000040	Indicates that the client understands 32-bit NT_STATUS error codes.
4	CAP_NT_SMBS 0x00000010	Likewise, I'm sure.
		As with the CAP_NT_FIND bit, the client will set this to let the server know that it, too, understands the extended set of SMBs and function calls that are available if the server has set the CAP_NT_SMBS bit.
3	CAP_LARGE_FILES 0x00000008	The client sets this to let the server know that it can handle 64-bit file sizes and offsets.
2	CAP_UNICODE 0x00000004	Set to indicate that the client understands Unicode.

The client should not set any bits that were not also set by the server. That is, the Capabilities bits sent *to* the server should be the intersection (bitwise AND) of the client's actual capabilities and the set sent *by* the server.

The Capabilities bits are like the razor-sharp barbs on a government fence. Attempting to hurdle any one of them can shred your implementation.

Consider adding Unicode support to a system that doesn't already have it. Ooof! That's going to be a lot of work.[5]

Some `Capabilities` bits indicate support for sets of function calls that can be made via SMB. These function calls, which are sometimes referred to as "sub-protocols," fall into two separate (but similar) categories:

- **R**emote **A**dministration **P**rotocol (RAP),
- **R**emote **P**rocedure **C**all (RPC).

Of the two, the RAP sub-protocol is older and (relatively speaking) simpler. Depending upon the SMB dialect, server support for some RAP calls is assumed rather than negotiated. Fortunately, much of RAP is documented... if you know where to look.[6]

Microsoft's RPC system — known as MS-RPC — is newer, and has a lot in common with the better-known DCE/RPC system. MS-RPC over SMB allows the client to make calls to certain Windows DLL library functions on the server side which, in turn, allows the client to do all sorts of interesting things. Of course, if you are building a server and you want to support the MS-RPC calls you have to implement all of the required functions in addition to SMB itself. Unfortunately, much of MS-RPC is undocumented.[7]

The MS-RPC function call APIs are defined using a language called **M**icrosoft **I**nterface **D**efinition **L**anguage (MIDL). There is a fair amount of information about MIDL available on the web and *some* of the function interface definitions have been published. CIFS implementors have repeatedly asked Microsoft for open access to all of the CIFS-relevant MIDL source files. Unencumbered access to the MIDL source would go a long way towards opening up the CIFS protocol suite. Since MIDL provides only the interface

---

5. It was, in fact, a lot of work for the Samba Team. Those involved did a tremendous job, and they deserve several rounds of applause. Things were much easier for jCIFS because Java natively supports Unicode.

6. Information on RAP calls is scattered among several sources, including the archives of Microsoft's CIFS mailing list. The SNIA doc has enough to get you started with the basics of RAP, but see also the file `cifsrap2.txt` which can be found on Microsoft's aforementioned FTP site.

7. Luke Kenneth Casson Leighton's book *DCE/RPC over SMB: Samba and Windows NT Domain Internals* is an essential reference for CIFS developers who need to know more about MS-RPC.

specifications and not the function internals, Microsoft could release them without exposing their proprietary DLL source code.

Both the RAP and MS-RPC sub-protocols provide access to a large set of features, and both are too big to be covered in detail here. Complete documentation of all of the nooks and crannies of CIFS would probably require a set of books large enough to cause an encyclopedia to cringe in awe, so it would seem that our attempt to clean up the mess we made with the NEGOTIATE PROTOCOL exchange has instead created an even bigger mess and left some permanent stains on the carpet. Ah, well. Such is the nature of CIFS.

14.2   SESSION SETUP ANDX REQUEST Data

The dissection of the SMB_PARAMETERS portion of the SESSION SETUP ANDX REQUEST cleared up a few issues and exposed a few others. Now we get to look at the SMB_DATA block and see what further mysteries may lie uncovered.

Fortunately, the Data block is much less daunting. It contains a few fields used for authentication and the rest is just useful bits of information about the client's operating environment. The structure looks like this:

```
typedef struct
  {
  ushort ByteCount;
  struct
    {
    union
      {
      uchar SecurityBlob[];
      struct
        {
        uchar CaseInsensitivePassword[];
        uchar CaseSensitivePassword[];
        uchar Pad[];
        uchar AccountName[];
        uchar PrimaryDomain[];
        } non_ext_sec;
      } auth_stuff;
    uchar NativeOS[];
    uchar NativeLanMan[];
    uchar Pad2[];
    } Bytes;
  } smb_SessSetupAndx_Req_Data;
```

auth_stuff

As you may by now have come to expect, the structure of the `auth_stuff` field depends upon whether or not Extended Security has been negotiated. We have shown it as a union type just to emphasize the point. Under Extended Security, the blob will contain a structure specific to the type of Extended Security being used. The `Security-BlobLength` value in the Parameter block indicates the size (in bytes) of the `SecurityBlob`.

If Extended Security has not been negotiated, the structure will contain the following fields:

CaseInsensitivePassword and CaseSensitivePassword

If these names seem familiar it's because the associated length fields were in the Parameter block, described above. These fields are, of course, used in authentication. Chapter 15 on page 257 covers authentication in detail.

Pad

If Unicode is in use, then the `Pad` field will contain a single nul byte (`0x00`) to force two-byte alignment of the following fields (which are Unicode strings).

As you know, the Parameter block is made up of a single byte followed by an array of zero or more words. It starts on a word boundary, but the `WordCount` byte knocks it off balance, so it never ends on a word boundary. That means that the Data block always starts misaligned.[8] Typically, that's not considered a problem for data in SMB messages. It is not clear why, but it seems that when Unicode support was added to SMB it was decided that Unicode strings should be word-aligned within the SMB message (even though they are likely to be copied out of the message before they're fiddled). That's why the `Pad` byte is there.

---

8. I vaguely remember a conversation with Tridge in which he indicated that there was an obscure exception to the misalignment of the Data block. I'm not sure which SMB, or which dialect, but if I recall correctly there's one SMB that has an extra byte just before the `ByteCount` field. Keep your eyes open.

Note that if Unicode support is enabled the password fields will always contain an even number of bytes. Strange but true. Here's why:

- On Windows server systems, plaintext passwords and Unicode are mutually exclusive. The password hashes used for authentication are always an even number of bytes.

- Unlike Windows, Samba *can* be configured to use plaintext passwords and Unicode. In that configuration, the `CaseInsensitivePassword` field will be empty and the `CaseSensitivePassword` field will contain the password in Unicode format — two bytes per character.

Note the subtle glitch here. If Samba is configured to send Unicode plaintext passwords, the `CaseSensitivePassword` field will *not* be word-aligned because the `Pad` byte comes afterward. It seems that the designers of the NT LM 0.12 dialect did not consider the possibility of plaintext Unicode passwords.

`AccountName`

This is the username field. If Unicode has been negotiated, then the username is presented in Unicode. Otherwise, the string is converted to uppercase and sent using the 8-bit OEM character set.

`PrimaryDomain`

As with the `AccountName`, this value is converted to uppercase unless it is being sent in Unicode format.

Whenever possible, this field should contain the NetBIOS name of the NT Domain to which the user belongs. Basically, it allows the client to specify the NT Domain in which the username and password are valid — the Authentication Domain. A correct value is not always needed, however. If the server is not a member of an NT Domain, then it will have its own authentication database, and no Domain Controller need be consulted.

Some testing was done with Windows NT 4.0 and Windows 2000 systems that were not members of an NT Domain. As clients, these systems sent their own NetBIOS machine names in the `PrimaryDomain` field. The `smbclient` utility sent the workgroup name, as specified in the `smb.conf` file. jCIFS just sent a question mark. All of these variations seem to work, as long as the server maintains its own authentication database. The PrimaryDomain field is really only useful when authenticating against a Domain Controller.

...and that's the end of the auth_stuff block. On to the rest of it.

NativeOS

This string identifies the host operating system. Windows systems, of course, will fill this field with their OS name and some revision information. This field will be expressed in Unicode if that format has been negotiated.

NativeLanMan

Similar to the NativeOS field, this one contains a short description of the client SMB software. Smbclient fills this field with the name "Samba." jCIFS used to just say "foo" here, but starting with release 0.7.0beta10 it says "jCIFS." The successful use of "foo" demonstrates, however, that the field is not used for anything critical on the server side. Just error reporting, most likely.

 Email

```
    From: Gerald (Jerry) Carter
      To: Chris Hertel
 Subject: NativeLanMan

Note that NT4 misaligns the NativeLanMan string by one byte
(see Ethereal for details). Also note that Samba uses this
string to distinguish between W2K/XP/2K3 for the %a smb.conf
variable. So it is used by the server in some cases.
```

Pad2

Some systems add one or two extra nul bytes at the end of the SESSION SETUP. Not all clients do this; it appears to be more common if Unicode has been negotiated. The extra bytes pad the end of the SESSION SETUP to the next word boundary. If these bytes are present, they are generally included in the total count given in the ByteCount field.

We have done a lot of work ripping apart packet structures and studying the internal organs. Don't worry, that's the last of it. You should be familiar enough with this stuff by now, so from here on out we will rely on the SNIA doc and packet traces to provide the gory details.

Don't Know When to Quit Alert

Some of the Windows systems that were tested did not place the correct number of nul bytes at the ends of some Unicode strings. Consider, for example, this snippet from an Ethereal capture:

```
0000029F                      57 00 69 00 6e 00 64 00       W.i.n.d.
000002AF 6f 00 77 00 73 00 20 00 4e 00 54 00 20 00 31 00   o.w.s. .N.T. .1.
000002BF 33 00 38 00 31 00 00 00 00 00 57 00 69 00 6e 00   3.8.1... ..W.i.n.
000002CF 64 00 6f 00 77 00 73 00 20 00 4e 00 54 00 20 00   d.o.w.s.  .N.T. .
000002DF 34 00 2e 00 30 00 00 00 00 00 4...o... ..
```

Look closely, and you will see that there are two extra nul bytes following each of the two Unicode strings in the hex dump. Under UCS-2LE encoding, the nul string terminator would be encoded as two nul bytes (00 00). In the sample above, however, there are four null bytes (00 00 00 00) following the last Unicode character of each string.

In this next excerpt, taken from a SESSION SETUP ANDX RESPONSE *SMB, it appears as though one of the terminating nul bytes at the end of the* PrimaryDomain *field has been lost:*

```
0000008F                                     57 00            W.
0000009F 69 00 6e 00 64 00 6f 00 77 00 73 00 20 00 35 00   i.n.d.o. w.s. .5.
000000AF 2e 00 30 00 00 00 57 00 69 00 6e 00 64 00 6f 00   ..0...W. i.n.d.o.
000000BF 77 00 73 00 20 00 32 00 30 00 30 00 30 00 20 00   w.s. .2. 0.0.0. .
000000CF 4c 00 41 00 4e 00 20 00 4d 00 61 00 6e 00 61 00   L.A.N. . M.a.n.a.
000000DF 67 00 65 00 72 00 00 00 55 00 42 00 49 00 51 00   g.e.r... U.B.I.Q.
000000EF 58 00 00                                          X..
```

The first two bytes of the last line (58 00) are the letter 'X' in UCS-2LE encoding. They should be followed by two nul bytes... but there's only one.

14.3 The SESSION SETUP ANDX RESPONSE SMB

The SESSION SETUP ANDX RESPONSE SMB structure is described in Section 4.1.2 of the SNIA doc.

In the NT LM 0.12 dialect, there are two versions of the SESSION SETUP ANDX RESPONSE message. They differ, of course, based on whether or not Extended Security is in use. In the Extended Security version the

Parameter block has a `SecurityBlobLength` field, and there is an associated `SecurityBlob` within the Data block. These two fields are missing from the non-Extended Security version. Other than that, the two are the same.

The `SESSION SETUP ANDX RESPONSE` message also has an interesting little bitfield called `SMB_PARAMETERS.Action`. Only the low-order bit (bit 0) of this field is defined. If set, it indicates that the username was not recognized by the server (that is, authentication failed — no such user) but the logon is being allowed to succeed anyway.

That's rather odd, eh?

What it means is this: If the username (in the `AccountName` field) is not recognized, the server *may* choose to grant *anonymous* or *guest* authorization instead. Anonymous access typically provides only very limited access to the server. For example, it may allow the use of a limited set of RAP function calls such as those used for querying the Browse Service.

So, the `Action` bit is used to indicate that the logon attempt failed, but anonymous access was granted instead. No error code will be returned in this case, so the `Action` bit is the only indication to the client that the rules have changed. Server-side support for this behavior is optional.

15

Authentication

Car locks are there
to keep the honest people honest.

— Something my brother Robert
once told me. (He sells cars.)

Now for the big one...

If you are familiar with authentication schemes, then this section should be comfortable for you. If not, then perhaps it's time for a fresh pot of tea. Some people find their first experience with the innards of password security to be a bit intimidating, possibly because the encryption formulae are sometimes made to look a lot like mathematics. Authentication itself isn't really that complex, though. The basic idea is that the would-be users need to prove that they are who they say they are in order to get what they want. The proof is usually in the form of something private or secret — something that only the user has or knows.

Consider, for example, the key to an automobile (something you have). With the key in hand, you are able to unlock the door, turn the ignition switch, and start the engine. As far as the car is concerned, you have proven that you have the right to drive. Likewise with the password you use to access your computer (something you know). If you enter a valid username/password pair at the login prompt, then you can access the system. Unfortunately passwords, like keys, can be stolen or forged or copied. Just as locks can be picked, so passwords can be cracked.[1]

In the early days of SMB, when the LANs were small and sheltered, there was very little concern for the safety of the password itself. It was sent in plaintext (unencrypted) over the wire from the client to the server. Eventually, though, corporate networks got bigger, modems were installed to provide access from home and on the road, the "disgruntled employee" boogeyman learned how to use a keyboard, and everything got connected to the Internet. These were hard times for plaintext passwords, so a series of schemes was developed to keep the passwords safe — each more complex than its predecessor.

For SMB, the initial attempt was called LAN Manager Challenge/Response authentication, often simply abbreviated "LM." The LM scheme turned out to be too simple and too easy to crack, and was replaced with something stronger called Windows NT Challenge/Response (known as "NTLM"). NTLM was superseded by NTLMv2 which has, in turn, been replaced with a modified version of MIT's Kerberos system.

Got that?

We'll go through them all in various degrees of detail. The LM algorithm is fairly simple, so we can provide a thorough description. At the other extreme, Kerberos is an entire system unto itself and anything more than an overview would be overkill.

15.1 Anonymous and Guest Login

Gather and study piles of SMB packet captures and you will notice that some SESSION SETUP requests contain no username and password at all. These are *anonymous* logins, and they are used to access special-purpose SMB shares such as the hidden "IPC$" share (the **I**nter-**P**rocess **C**ommunications share).

---

1. In addition to "something you have" and "something you know" there is another class of access tokens sometimes described as "something you are." This latter class, also known as "biometrics," includes such things as your fingerprints, your DNA pattern, your brainwaves, and your karmic aura. Some folks have argued that these features are simply "something you have" that is a little harder (or more painful) to steal. There was great hope that biometrics would offer improvements over the other authentication tokens, but it seems that they may be just as easy to crack. For example, a group of researchers in Japan was able to fool fingerprint scanners using fake fingertips created from gelatin and other common ingredients.

You can learn more about IPC$ in Part III on page 335. Put simply, though, this share allows one system to query another using RAP function calls.

Anonymous login may be a design artifact; something created in the days of Share Level security when it seemed safe to leave a share unprotected, and still with us today because it cannot easily be removed. Maybe not. One guess is as good as another.

"GUEST" account logons are also often sent sans password. The guest login is sometimes used in the same way as the anonymous login, but there are additional permissions which a guest account may have. Guest accounts are maintained like other "normal" accounts, so they can be a security problem and are commonly disabled. When SMB is doing its housekeeping, the anonymous login is generally preferred over the guest login.

15.2 Plaintext Passwords

This is the easiest SMB authentication mechanism to implement — and the least secure. It's roughly equivalent to leaving your keys in the door lock after you've parked the car. Sure, the car is locked, but...

Plaintext passwords may still be sufficient for use in small, isolated networks, such as home networks or small office environments (assuming no disgruntled employees and a well-configured firewall on the uplink — or no Internet connection at all). Plaintext passwords also provide us with a nice opportunity to get our feet wet in the mired pool of authentication. We can look at the packets and clearly see what is happening on the wire. Note, however, that many newer clients are configured to prevent the use of plaintext. Windows clients have registry entries that must be twiddled in order to permit plaintext passwords, and jCIFS did not support them at all until version 0.7.

In order to set up a workable test environment you will need a server that does not expect encrypted passwords, and a client that doesn't mind sending the passwords in the clear. That is *not* an easy combination to come by. Most contemporary SMB clients and servers disable plaintext by default. It is easy, however, to configure Samba so that it requests unencrypted passwords. Just change the encrypt passwords parameter to no in the smb.conf file, like so:

```
; Disable encrypted passwords.
encrypt passwords = no
```

Don't forget to signal `smbd` to reload the configuration file after making this change.

On the client side we will, once again, use the jCIFS `Exists` utility in our examples. If you would rather use a Windows client for your own tests, you can find a collection of helpful registry settings in the `docs/Registry/` subdirectory of the Samba distribution. You will probably need to change the registry settings to permit the Windows client to send plaintext passwords. Another option as a testing tool is Samba's `smbclient` utility, which does not seem to argue if the server tells it not to encrypt the passwords.

This is what our updated `Exists` test looks like:

```shell
$ java -DdisablePlainTextPasswords=false Exists \
> smb://pat:p%40ssw0rd@smedley/home
smb://pat:p%40ssw0rd@smedley/home exists
$
```

A few things to note:

- The `-DdisablePlainTextPasswords=false` command-line option tells jCIFS that it should permit the use of plaintext.

- The username and password are passed to jCIFS via the SMB URL. The syntax is fairly common for URLs.[2] Basically, it looks like this:

  `smb://[[user[:password]@]host[:port]]`

  The username in our example is `pat`.

- The password in our example is `p@ssw0rd`, but the '@' in the password conflicts with the '@' used to separate the `userinfo` field from the `hostport` field.[3] To resolve the conflict we encode the '@' in `p@ssw0rd` using the URL escape sequence "%40", which gives us `p%40ssw0rd`.

---

2. ...sort of. Support for inclusion of a password within a URL is considered very dangerous. The recommendation from the authors of RFC 2396 is that new applications should not recognize the password field and that the application should instead prompt for both the username and password.

3. Yet again we seek the wisdom of the RFCs. See Appendix A of RFC 2396 for the full generic syntax of URLs, and RFC 2732 for the IPv6 update.

■ If at all possible, applications should be written to request the password in a more secure fashion, and to hide it once it has been given. The [:password] syntax is not part of the general URL syntax definition, and its use is highly discouraged. Having the password display on the screen is as naughty as sending it across the wire in plaintext.

15.2.1 *User Level Security with Plaintext Passwords*

User and Share Level security were described back in Section 12.4 on page 209, along with the TID and [V]UID header fields. The SecurityMode field of the NEGOTIATE PROTOCOL RESPONSE SMB will indicate the authentication expectations of the server. For User Level plaintext passwords, the value of the SecurityMode field will be 0x01.

Below is an example SESSION_SETUP_ANDX.SMB_DATA block such as would be generated by the jCIFS Exists tool. Note, once again, that the discussion is focused on the NT LM 0.12 dialect.

```
SMB_DATA
  {
  ByteCount = 27
  Bytes
    {
    CaseInsensitivePassword = "p@ssw0rd"
    CaseSensitivePassword   = <NULL>
    Pad                     = <NULL>
    AccountName             = "PAT"
    PrimaryDomain           = "?"
    NativeOS                = "Linux"
    NativeLanMan            = "jCIFS"
    }
  }
```

There are always fiddly little details to consider when working with SMB. In this case, we need to talk about upper- and lowercase. (bLeCH.) The example above shows that the AccountName field has been converted to uppercase. This is common practice, but it is not really necessary and some implementations don't bother. It is a holdover from the early days of SMB when lots of things (filenames, passwords, share names, NetBIOS names, bagels, and pop singers) were converted to uppercase as a matter of course. Some older servers (pre-NT LM 0.12) may require uppercase usernames, but newer servers shouldn't care. Converting to uppercase is probably the safest option, just in case...

Although the `AccountName` in the example is uppercase, the `CaseInsensitivePassword` is not. Hmmm... Odd, eh? The situation here is that some server operating systems (e.g. most Unixy OSes) use case-sensitive password verification algorithms. If the password is sent all uppercase it probably won't match what the OS expects, resulting in a login failure even though the user entered the correct password. The field may be labeled case-insensitive (and that really is what it is *intended* to be) but some server OSes prefer to have the original password, case preserved, just as the user entered it.

This is a sticky problem, though, because some clients *insist* on converting passwords to uppercase before sending them to the server. Windows 95 and '98 may do this, for example. As you might have come to expect by now, the reason for this odd behavior is backward compatibility. There are older (pre-NT LM 0.12) servers still running that will reject passwords that are not all uppercase. Windows 9x systems solve the problem by forcing all passwords to uppercase even when the NT LM 0.12 dialect has been selected. Samba's `smbd` server, which generally runs on case-sensitive platforms, must go through a variety of contortions to get uppercase plaintext passwords to be accepted.[4]

Another annoyance is that Windows 98 will pad the plaintext password string to 24 bytes, filling the empty space with semi-random garbage. This behavior was noted in testing, but there wasn't time to investigate the problem in-depth so it may or may not be wide-spread. Still, it's the odd case that will break things. Server implementors should be careful to both check the field length *and* look for the first terminating nul byte when reading the plaintext password.

In short, client-side handling of the plaintext `CaseInsensitive-Password` is inconsistent and problematic — and the server has to compensate. That's why you need piles of SMB packet captures and lots of different clients to test against when writing a server implementation. It *can* be done, but it takes a bit of perseverance. When writing a new client, ensure that the client sends the password as the user intended. If that fails, and the dialect is pre-NT LM 0.12, then convert to uppercase and try again. Believe it or not, the use of challenge/response authentication bypasses much of this trouble.

---

4. See the discussion of the `password level` parameter in Samba's `smb.conf(5)` documentation for more information about these problems.

...but that's only half the story. In addition to the `CaseInsensitivePassword` field there is also a `CaseSensitivePassword` field in the data block, and we haven't even touched on that yet. This latter field is only used if Unicode has been negotiated, and it is rare that both Unicode and plaintext will be used simultaneously. It can happen, though. As mentioned earlier, Samba can be easily configured to provide support for Unicode plaintext passwords.[5] In theory, this should be a simple switch from ASCII to Unicode. In practice, no client really supports it yet — and weird things have been seen on the wire. For example:

- Clients disagree on the length of the Unicode password string in `CaseSensitivePassword`. Some count the pair of nul bytes that terminate the string, others do not. (For comparison, the length of the ASCII `CaseInsensitivePassword` string does include the terminating nul, so it seems there is precedent.)

- In testing, more than one client stored the length of the Unicode password in the `CaseInsensitivePasswordLength` field... but that's where the ASCII password length is supposed to go. The Unicode password length should be in the `CaseSensitivePasswordLength` field. How should the server interpret the password in this situation — as ASCII or Unicode?

- One client added a nul byte at the beginning of the Unicode password string, probably intended as a padding byte to force word alignment. The extra nul byte was being read as the first byte of the `CaseSensitivePassword`, thus misaligning the Unicode string. Another client went further and counted the extra byte in the total length of the Unicode password string. As a result, the password length was given as an odd number of bytes (which should never happen).

Empirically, it would seem that Unicode plaintext passwords were never meant to be.

---

5. I don't know whether a Windows server can be configured to support Unicode plaintext passwords. To test against Samba, however, you need to use Samba version 3.0 or above. On the client side, Microsoft has a Knowledge Base article — and a patch — that addresses some of the message formatting problems in Windows 2000 (see *Microsoft Knowledge Base Article #257292*). Thanks to Nir Soffer for finding this article.

An interesting fact-ette that can be gleaned from this discussion is that there is a linkage between the password fields and the negotiation of Unicode. Simply put:

ASCII (OEM character set) <==> `CaseInsensitivePassword`
Unicode <==> `CaseSensitivePassword`

That is, ASCII plaintext passwords are stored in the `CaseInsensitivePassword` field, and Unicode plaintext passwords should be placed into the `CaseSensitivePassword` field. Indeed, Ethereal names these two fields, respectively, "ANSI Password" and "Unicode Password" instead of using the longer names shown above. This relationship carries over to the challenge/response passwords as well, as we shall soon see.

15.2.2 *Share Level Security with Plaintext Passwords*

We won't spend too much time on this. It is easy to see by looking at packet captures. Basically, in Share Level security mode the plaintext password is passed to the server in the TREE CONNECT ANDX request instead of the SESSION SETUP ANDX. In the NT LM 0.12 dialect, however, a valid username should also be placed into the SESSION SETUP AccountName field if at all possible. Doing so allows the server to map Share Level security to its own user-based authentication system.

Interesting Implementation Alert

Samba does not completely implement Share Level security. Though all of the required SMBs are supported, Samba does not provide any way to assign a password to a share.
Many SMB clients will provide a username (if one is available) in the SESSION SETUP ANDX *SMB even though it is not (technically) required at Share Level. If there is no username available, however, Samba will attempt (through various methods — some of which might be considered kludgey) to guess an appropriate username for the connection. Read through the* smb.conf(5) *manual page if you are interested in the details.*

15.3 LM Challenge/Response

In plaintext mode, the client proves that it knows the password by sending the password itself to the server. In challenge/response mode, the goal is to prove that the password is known without risking any exposure. It's a bit of a magic trick. Here's how it's done:

1. The server generates a random string of bytes — random enough that it is not likely to come up again in a very, very long time (thus preventing replay attacks). This string is called the *challenge*.

2. The challenge is sent to the client.

3. Both the client and server encrypt the challenge using a key that is derived from the user's password. The client sends its result back to the server. This is the *response*.

4. If the client's response matches the server's result, then the server knows (beyond a reasonable doubt) that the client knows the correct key. If they don't match, authentication fails.

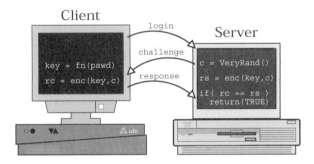

Figure 15.1: *Challenge/response*

The server generates a random challenge, which it sends to the client. Both systems encrypt the challenge using the secret encryption key. The client sends its result (`rc`) to the server. If the client's result matches the server's result (`rs`), then the two nodes have matching keys.

That's a rough, general overview of challenge/response. The details of its use in LAN Manager authentication are a bit more involved, but are fairly easy to explain. As we dig deeper, keep in mind that the goal is to protect the password while still allowing authentication to occur. Also remember that LM challenge/response was the first attempt to add encrypted password support to SMB.

15.3.1 *DES*

The formula used to generate the LM response makes use of the U.S. Department of Commerce **D**ata **E**ncryption **S**tandard (DES) function, in block mode. DES has been around a long time. There are a lot of references which describe it and a good number of implementations available, so we will not spend a whole lot of time studying DES itself.[6] For our purposes, the important thing to know is that the DES function — as used with SMB — takes two input parameters and returns a result, like so:

```
result = DES( key, source );
```

The `source` and `result` are both eight-byte blocks of data, the `result` being the DES encryption of the `source`. In the SNIA doc, as in the Leach/Naik draft, the `key` is described as being seven bytes (56 bits) long. Documentation on DES itself gives the length of the `key` as eight bytes (64 bits), but each byte contains a parity bit so there really are only 56 bits worth of "key" in the 64-bit key. As shown in Figure 15.2, there is a simple formula for mapping 56 bits into the required 64-bit format. The seven byte string is simply copied, seven *bits* at a time, into an eight byte array. A parity bit (odd parity) is inserted following each set of seven bits (but some existing DES implementations use zero and ignore the parity bit).

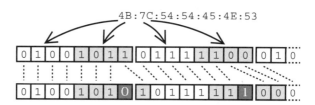

Figure 15.2:   *DES key manglement*

Converting a seven byte key (56 bits) into an eight byte key with odd parity for use with DES. Some DES implementations perform this step internally.

The `key` is used by the DES algorithm to encrypt the `source`. Given the same `key` and `source`, DES will always return the same `result`.

---

6. If you are interested in the workings of DES, Bruce Schneier's *Applied Cryptography, Second Edition* provides a very complete discussion. See the References section.

15.3.2 *Creating the Challenge*

The challenge needs to be very random, otherwise the logon process could be made vulnerable to "replay" attacks.

A replay attack is fairly straightforward. The attacker captures the exchange between the server and the client and keeps track of the challenge, the response, and the username. The attacker then tries to log on, hoping that the challenge will be repeated (this step is easier if the challenge is at all predictable). If the server sends a challenge that is in the stored list, the attacker can use the recorded username and response to fake a logon. No password cracking required.

Given that the challenge is eight bytes (64 bits) long, and that random number generators are pretty good these days, it is probably best to create the challenge using a random number function. The better the random number generator, the lower the likelihood (approaching 1 in 2^{64}) that a particular challenge will be repeated.

The X/Open doc (which was written a long time ago) briefly describes a different approach to creating the challenge. According to that document, a seven-byte pseudo-random number is generated using an internal counter and the system time. That value is then used as the key in a call to DES(), like so:

```
Ckey = fn( time( NULL ), counter++ );
challenge = DES( Ckey, "????????" );
```

(The source string is honest-to-goodnessly given as eight question marks.)

That formula actually makes a bit of sense, though it's probably overkill. The pseudo-random Ckey is non-repeating (because it's based on the time), so the resulting challenge is likely to be non-repeating as well. Also note that the pseudo-random value is passed as the key, not the source, in the call to DES(). That makes it much more difficult to reverse and, since it changes all the time, reversing it is probably not useful anyway.

As Andrew Bartlett[7] points out, however, the time and counter inputs are easily guessed so the challenge is predictable, which is a potential weakness. Adding a byte or two of truly random "salt" to the Ckey in the recipe above would prevent such predictability.

---

7. ...without whom the Authentication section would never have been written.

 **Email**

```
From: Andrew Bartlett
  To: Chris Hertel
Subject: SMB Challenge...
```

Actually, given comments I've read on some SMB cracking sites, it would not surprise me if MS still does (or at least did) use exactly this for the challenges.

I still think you should address the X/Open function not as 'overkill' but as 'flawed'.

Using a plain random number generator is probably faster, easier, and safer.

15.3.3 *Creating the LM Hash*

LM challenge/response authentication prevents password theft by ensuring that the plaintext password is never transmitted across a network or stored on disk. Instead, a separate value known as the "LM Hash" is generated. It is the LM Hash that is stored on the server side for use in authentication, and used on the client side to create the response from the challenge.

The LM Hash is a sixteen byte string, created as follows:

1. The password, as entered by the user, is either padded with nuls (0x00) or trimmed to fourteen (14) bytes.[8]

   - Note that the 14-byte password string is not handled as a nul-terminated string. If the user enters 14 or more bytes, the last byte in the modified string will *not* be nul.

   - Also note that the password is given in the 8-bit OEM character set (extended ASCII), not Unicode.

2. The 14-byte password string is converted to all uppercase.

3. The uppercase 14-byte password string is chopped into two 7-byte keys.

---

8. Both the the X/Open doc and the expired Leach/Naik draft state that the padding character is a space, not a nul. They are incorrect. It really is a nul.

4. The seven-byte keys are each used to DES-encrypt the string constant "KGS!@#$%", which is known as the "magic" string.[9]

5. The two 8-byte results are then concatenated together to form the 16-byte LM Hash.

That outline would make a lot more sense as code, wouldn't it? Well, you're in luck. Listing 15.1 shows how the steps given above might be implemented.

Listing 15.1: LM Hash function

```
static const uchar SMB_LMHash_Magic[8] =
  { 'K', 'G', 'S', '!', '@', '#', '$', '%' };

uchar *smb_LMHash( const uchar *password, uchar *result )
  /* ------------------------------------------------- **
   * Generate an LM Hash.
   * password - pointer to the raw password string.
   * result   - pointer to at least 16 bytes of memory
   *            into which the LM Hash will be written.
   * Returns a pointer to the LM Hash (== result).
   * ------------------------------------------------- **
   */
  {
  uchar  tmp_pass[14] = { 0,0,0,0,0,0,0,0,0,0,0,0,0,0 };
  uchar *hash;
  uchar  K1[7];
  uchar  K2[7];
  int    i;

  /* Copy at most 14 bytes of password to tmp_pass.
   * If the string is shorter, the unused bytes will
   * be nul-filled.
   */
  (void)strncpy( tmp_pass, password, 14 );

  /* Convert to uppercase.
   */
  for( i = 0; i < 14; i++ )
    tmp_pass[i] = toupper( tmp_pass[i] );
```

---

9. The magic string was considered secret, and was not listed in the Leach/Naik draft. The story of Tridge and Jeremy's (pre-DMCA) successful effort to reverse-engineer this value is quite entertaining.

```
/* Split tmp_pass into two 7-byte keys.
 */
(void)memcpy( K1, tmp_pass, 7 );
(void)memcpy( K2, (tmp_pass + 7), 7 );

/* Use the keys to encrypt the 'magic' string.
 * Place each encrypted half into the result
 * buffer.
 */
hash = DES( K1, SMB_LMHash_Magic );
(void)memcpy( result, hash, 8 );
hash = DES( K2, SMB_LMHash_Magic );
(void)memcpy( (result + 8), hash, 8 );

/* Return a pointer to the result.
 */
return( result );
} /* smb_LMHash */
```

15.3.4 *Creating the LM Response*

Now we get to the actual logon. When a NEGOTIATE PROTOCOL REQUEST arrives from the client, the server generates a new challenge on the fly and hands it back in the NEGOTIATE PROTOCOL RESPONSE.

On the client side, the user is prompted for the password. The client generates the LM Hash from the password, and then uses the hash to DES-encrypt the challenge. Of course, it's not a straightforward DES operation. As you may have noticed, the LM Hash is 16 bytes but the DES() function requires 7-byte keys. Ah, well... Looks as though there's a bit more padding and chopping to do.

1. The password entered by the user is converted to a 16-byte LM Hash as described above.

2. The LM Hash is padded with five nul bytes, resulting in a string that is 21 bytes long.

3. The 21 byte string is split into three 7-byte keys.

4. The challenge is encrypted three times, once with each of the three keys derived from the LM Hash.

5. The results are concatenated together, forming a 24-byte string which is returned to the server. This, of course, is the response.

Once again, we provide demonstrative code. Listing 15.2 shows how the LM Response would be generated.

Listing 15.2: LM Response function

```
uchar *smb_LMResponse( const uchar *LMHash,
                             uchar *chal,
                             uchar *resp )
  /* ------------------------------------------------ **
   * Generate an LM Response
   * LMHash - pointer to the LM Hash of the password.
   * chal   - Pointer to the challenge.
   * resp   - pointer to at least 24 bytes of memory
   *          into which the LM response will be written.
   * Returns a pointer to the LM response (== resp).
   * ------------------------------------------------ **
   */
  {
  uchar  P21[21];
  uchar  K[7];
  uchar  *result;
  int    i;

  /* Copy the LM Hash to P21 and pad with nuls to 21 bytes.
   */
  (void)memcpy( P21, LMHash, 16 );
  (void)memset( (P21 + 16), 0, 5 );

  /* A compact method of splitting P21 into three keys,
   * generating a DES encryption of the challenge for
   * each key, and combining the results.
   * (i * 7) will give 0, 7, 14 and
   * (i * 8) will give 0, 8, 16.
   */
  for( i = 0; i < 3; i++ )
    {
    (void)memcpy( K, (P21 + (i * 7)) , 7 );
    result = DES( K, chal );
    (void)memcpy( (resp + (i * 8)), result, 8 );
    }

  /* Return the response.
   */
  return( resp );
  } /* smb_LMResponse */
```

The server, which has the username and associated LM Hash tucked away safely in its authentication database, also generates the 24-byte response string. When the client's response arrives, the server compares its own value against the client's. If they match, then the client has authenticated.

Under User Level security, the client sends its LM Response in the `SESSION_SETUP_ANDX.CaseInsensitivePassword` field of the `SESSION SETUP` request (yes, the LM *response* is in the `SESSION SETUP REQUEST`). With Share Level security, the LM Response is placed in the `TREE_CONNECT_ANDX.Password` field.

15.3.5 *LM Challenge/Response: Once More with Feeling*

The details sometimes obfuscate the concepts, and vice versa. We have presented a general overview of the challenge/response mechanism, as well as the particular formulae of the LAN Manager scheme. Let's go through it once again, quickly, just to put the pieces together and cover anything that we may have missed.

The LM Hash

The LM Hash is derived from the password. It is used instead of the password so that the latter won't be exposed. A copy of the LM Hash is stored on the server (or Domain Controller) in the authentication database.

On the down side, the LM Hash is *password equivalent*. Because of the design in the LM challenge/response mechanism, a cracker[10] can use the LM Hash to break into a system. The password itself is not, in fact, needed. Thus, the LM Hash must be protected as if it were the password.

The Challenge

If challenge/response is required by the server, the `SecurityMode` field of the `NEGOTIATE PROTOCOL RESPONSE` will have bit `0x02` set, and the challenge will be found in the `EncryptionKey` field.

---

10. A "cracker," not a "hacker." The former is someone who cracks passwords or authentication schemes with the goal of cracking into a system (naughty). The latter is one who studies and fiddles with software and systems to see how they work and, possibly, to make them work better (nice). The popular media has mangled the distinction. Don't make the same mistake. If you are reading this book, you most likely are a hacker (and that's good).

Challenge/response may be used with either User Level or Share Level security.

The Logon

On the client side, the user will — at some point — be prompted for a password. The password is converted into the LM Hash. Meanwhile, the server (or NT Domain Controller) has its own copy of the LM Hash, stored in the authentication database. Both systems use the LM Hash to generate the LM Response from the challenge.

The LM Response

The client sends the LM Response to the server in either the `SESSION_SETUP_ANDX.CaseInsensitivePassword` field or the `TREE_CONNECT_ANDX.Password` field, depending upon the security level of the server. The server compares the client's response against its own to see if they match.

The `SESSION SETUP ANDX RESPONSE`

To finish up, the server will send back a `SESSION SETUP ANDX RESPONSE`. The `STATUS` field will indicate whether the logon was successful or not.

Well, that's a lot of work and it certainly goes a long way towards looking complicated. Unfortunately, looking complicated isn't enough to truly protect a password. LM challenge/response is an improvement over plaintext, but there are some problems with the formula and it turns out that it is not, in fact, a very *big* improvement.

Let's consider what an attacker might do to try and break into a system. We've already explained the replay attack. Other common garden varieties include the "dictionary" and the "brute force" attack, both of which simply try pushing possible passwords through the algorithm until one of them returns the same response as seen on the wire. The dictionary attack is typically faster because it uses a database of likely passwords, so tools tend to try this first. The brute force method tries all (remaining) possible combinations of bytes, which is usually a longer process. Unfortunately, all of the upper-casing, nul-padding, chopping, and concatenating used in the LM algorithm makes LM challenge/response very susceptible to these attacks. Here's why:

The LM Hash formula pads the original password with nul bytes. If the password is short enough (seven or fewer characters) then, when the 14-byte padded password is split into two seven-byte DES keys, the second key will always be a string of seven nuls. Given the same input, DES produces the same output:

```
0xAAD3B435B51404EE = DES( "\0\0\0\0\0\0\0", "KGS!@#$%" )
```

which results in an LM Hash in which the second set of eight bytes are known:

0	1	2	3	4	5	6	7	8	9	10	11	12	13	14	15
result 0								result 1							
??	??	??	??	??	??	??	??	AA	D3	B4	35	B5	14	04	EE

To create the LM Response, the LM Hash is padded with nuls to 21 bytes, and then split again into three DES keys:

0	1	2	3	4	5	6	7	8	9	10	11	12	13	14	15	16	17	18	19	20
key 0							key 1							key 2						
??	??	??	??	??	??	??	??	AA	D3	B4	35	B5	14	04	EE	00	00	00	00	00

Now the problem is obvious. If the original password was seven bytes or less, then almost two-thirds of the encryption key used to generate the LM Response will be a known, constant value. The password cracking tools leverage this information to reduce the size of the *keyspace* (the set of possible passwords) that needs to be tested to find the password. Less obvious, but clear enough if you study the LM Response algorithm closely, is that short passwords are only part of the problem. Because the hash is created in pieces, it is possible to attack the password in 7-byte chunks even if it is longer than 7 bytes.

Converting to uppercase also diminishes the keyspace, because lowercase characters do not need to be tested at all. The smaller the keyspace, the faster a dictionary or brute-force attack can run through the possible options and discover the original password.[11]

---

11. Jeremy Allison proved it could be done with a little tool called PWdump. Mudge and other folks at the L0pht then expanded on the idea and built the now semi-infamous L0phtCrack tool. In July of 1997, Mudge posted a long and detailed description of the decomposition of LM challenge/response, a copy of which can be found at: http://www.insecure.org/sploits/l0phtcrack.lanman.problems.html. For a curious counterpoint, see *Microsoft Knowledge Base Article #147706.*

15.4 NTLM Challenge/Response

At some point in the evolution of Windows NT a new, improved challenge/response formula was introduced. It was similar to the LAN Manager version, with the following changes:

1. Instead of using the uppercase ASCII (OEM character set) password, NTLM challenge/response generates the hash from the mixed-case Unicode (UCS-2LE) representation of the password. This change alone makes the password much more difficult to crack.

2. Instead of the DES() function, NTLM uses the MD4() message digest function described in RFC 1320. This function produces a 16-byte hash (the NTLM Hash)[12] but requires no padding or trimming of the input (though the resulting 16-byte NTLM Hash is still padded with nuls to 21 bytes for use in generating the NTLM Response.)

3. The NTLM Response is sent to the server in the SESSION_SETUP_ANDX.CaseSensitivePassword field.

...and that's basically it. The rest of the formula is the same.

So what does it buy us?

The first advantage of NTLM is that the passwords are more complex. They're mixed case and in Unicode, which means that the keyspace is much larger. The second advantage over LM is that the MD4() function doesn't require fixed length input. That means no padding bytes and no chopping to over-simplify the keys. The NTLM Hash itself is more robust than the LM Hash, so the NTLM Response is much more difficult to reverse.

Unfortunately, the NTLM Response is still created using the same algorithm as is used with LM, which provides only 56-bit encryption. Worse, clients often include *both* the NTLM Response *and* the LM Response (derived from the weaker LM Hash) in the SESSION SETUP ANDX REQUEST. They do this to maintain backward compatibility with older servers. Even if the server refuses to accept the LM Response, the client has sent it. Ouch.

---

12. Andrew Bartlett prefers to call this the "NT Hash," stating that the NT Hash is passed through the LM response algorithm to produce the NTLM (NT+LM) response.

Brain Overflow Alert

The next section describes the NTLMv2 algorithm. It's not really that difficult, but it can get tedious — especially if your head is still swimming from the LM and NTLM algorithms. Jerry Carter of the Samba Team warns that your brain may explode if you try to understand it all the first time through. (Most veteran CIFS engineers have had this happen at least twice.)

*You may want to skim through Section 15.5 and possibly Section 15.9, which describes **M**essage **A**uthentication **C**odes (MACs). You can always come back and read them again after you've iced your cranium.*

15.5 NTLM Version 2

NTLMv2, as it's called, has some additional safeguards thrown into the recipe that make it more complex — and hopefully more secure — than its predecessors. There are, however, two small problems with NTLMv2:

- Good documentation on the inner workings of NTLMv2 is rare.
- Although it is widely available, NTLMv2 does not seem to be widely used.

Regarding the first point, Appendix B of Luke K. C. Leighton's book *DCE/RPC over SMB: Samba and Windows NT Domain Internals* provides a recipe for NTLMv2 authentication. We'll do our best to expand on Luke's description. The other option, of course, is to look at available Open Source code.

The second point is really a conjecture, based in part on the fact that it took a very long time to get NTLMv2 implemented in Samba and few seemed to care. Indeed, NTLMv2 support had already been added to Samba-TNG by Luke and crew, and needed only to be copied over. It seems that the delay in adding it to Samba was not a question of know-how, but of priorities.

Another factor is that NTLMv2 is not required by default on most Windows systems. When challenge/response is negotiated, even newer Windows versions will default to using the LM/NTLM combination unless they are specifically configured not to.

15.5.1 *The NTLMv2 Toolbox*

We have already fussed with the DES algorithm and toyed with the MD4 algorithm. Now we get to use the HMAC-MD5 Message Authentication Code hash. This one's a power tool with razor-sharp keys and swivel-action hashing. The kind of thing your Dad would never let you play with when you were a kid. Like all good tools, though, it's neither complex nor dangerous once you learn how it works.

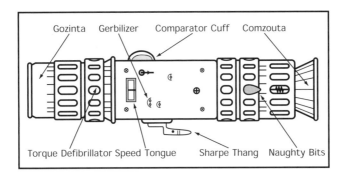

Gozinta   Gerbilizer   Comparator Cuff   Comzouta

Torque Defibrillator Speed Tongue   Sharpe Thang   Naughty Bits

Figure 15.3:   *HMAC-MD5*

The HMAC-MD5 is a popular tool for use in message authentication. It is lightweight, powerful, efficient, and ergonomic.

HMAC-MD5 is actually a combination of two different algorithms: HMAC and MD5. HMAC is a **M**essage **A**uthentication **C**ode (MAC) algorithm that takes a hashing function (such as MD5) and adds a secret key to the works so that the resulting hash can be used to verify the *authenticity* of the data. The MD5 algorithm is basically an industrial-strength version of MD4. Put them together and you get HMAC-MD5.

HMAC-MD5 is quite well documented,[13] and there are a lot of implementations available. It's also much less complicated than it appears in Figure 15.3, so we won't need to go into any of the details. For our purposes, what you need to know is that the HMAC_MD5() function takes a key and some source data as inputs, and returns a 16-byte (128-bit) output.

---

13. MD4 is explained in RFC 1320 and MD5 is in RFC 1321; HMAC in general, and HMAC-MD5 in particular, is written up in RFC 2104 — an embarrassment of riches! As usual with this sort of thing, a deeper understanding can be gained by reading about it in Bruce Schneier's *Applied Cryptography, Second Edition* (see the References section).

Hmmm... Well, it's not actually quite that simple. See, MD4, MD5, and HMAC-MD5 all work with variable-length input, so they also need to know how big their input parameters are. The function call winds up looking something like this:

```
hash16 = HMAC_MD5( Key, KeySize, Data, DataSize );
```

There is, as it turns out, more than one way to skin an HMAC-MD5. Some implementations use a whole set of functions to compute the result:

- the first function accepts the key and creates an initial *context*,
- the second function may be called repeatedly, each time passing the context and the next block of data,
- and the final function is used to close the context and return the resulting hash.

Conceptually, though, the multi-function approach is the same as the simpler example shown above. That is: Key and Data in, 16-byte hash out.

 Not Quite Entirely Unlike Standard Alert

The HMAC-MD5 function can handle very large Key inputs. Internally, though, there is a maximum keysize of 64 bytes. If the key is too long, the function uses the MD5 hash of the key instead. In other words, inside the HMAC_MD5() function there is some code that does this:

```
if( KeySize > 64 )
  {
  Key = MD5( Key, KeySize );
  KeySize = 16;
  }
```

In his book, Luke explains that the function used by Windows systems is actually a variation on HMAC-MD5 known as HMACT64, which can be quickly defined as follows:

```
#define HMACT64( K, Ks, D, Ds ) \
        HMAC_MD5( K, ((Ks > 64)?64:Ks), D, Ds )
```

In other words, the HMACT64() function is the same as HMAC_MD5() except that it truncates the input Key to 64 bytes rather than hashing it down to 16 bytes using the MD5() function as prescribed in the specification.

As you read on, you will probably notice that the keys used by the NTLMv2 challenge/response algorithm are never more that 16 bytes, so the distinction is moot for our purposes. We bother to explain it only because HMACT64() may be used elsewhere in CIFS (in some dark corner that we have not visited) and it might be a useful tidbit of information for you to have.

Another important tool is the older NTLM hash algorithm. It was described earlier but it is simple enough that we can present it again, this time in pseudo-code:

```
uchar *NTLMhash( uchar *password )
  {
  UniPasswd = UCS2LE( password );
  KeySize   = 2 * strlen( password );
  return( MD4( UniPasswd, KeySize ) );
  }
```

The ASCII password is converted to Unicode UCS-2LE format, which requires two bytes per character. The `KeySize` is simply the length of that (Unicode) password string, which we calculate here by doubling the ASCII string length (which is probably cheating). Finally, we generate the MD4 hash (that's MD4, not MD5) of the password, and that's all there is to it.

Note that the string terminator is not counted in the `KeySize`. That is common behavior for NTLM and NTLMv2 challenge/response when working with Unicode strings.

The NTLM Hash is of interest because the SMB/CIFS designers at Microsoft (if indeed such people truly exist any more, except in legend) used it to cleverly avoid upgrade problems. With LM and NTLM, the hash is created from the password. Under NTLMv2, however, the older NTLM (v1) Hash is used *instead of the password* to generate the new hash. A server or Domain Controller being upgraded to use NTLMv2 may already have the older NTLM hash values in its authentication database. The stored values can be used to generate the new hashes — no password required. That avoids the nasty chicken-and-egg problem of trying to upgrade to NTLMv2 Hashes on a system that only allows NTLMv2 authentication.

15.5.2 *The NTLMv2 Password Hash*

The NTLMv2 Hash is created from:

- the NTLM Hash (which, of course, is derived from the password),
- the user's username, and
- the name of the logon destination.

The process works as shown in the following pseudo-code example:

```
v1hash  = NTLMhash( password );
UniUser = UCS2LE( upcase( user ) );
UniDest = UCS2LE( upcase( destination ) );
data    = uni_strcat( UniUser, UniDest );
datalen = 2 * (strlen( user ) + strlen( destination ));
v2hash  = HMAC_MD5( v1hash, 16, data, datalen );
```

Let's clarify that, shall we?

v1hash

The NTLM Hash, calculated as described previously.

UniUser

The username, converted to uppercase UCS-2LE Unicode.

UniDest

The NetBIOS name of either the SMB server or NT Domain against which the user is trying to authenticate.

data

The two Unicode strings are concatenated and passed as the Data parameter to the HMAC_MD5() function.

datalen

The length of the concatenated Unicode strings, excluding the nul termination. Once again, doubling the ASCII string lengths is probably cheating.

v2hash

The NTLM Version 2 Hash.

A bit more explanation is required regarding the destination value (which gets converted to UniDest).

In theory, the client can use NTLMv2 challenge/response to log into a standalone server *or* to log into an NT Domain. In the former case, the server will have an authentication database of its very own, but an NT Domain logon requires authentication against the central database maintained by the Domain Controllers.

So, in theory, the destination name could be either the NetBIOS name of the standalone server *or* the NetBIOS name of the NT Domain (no NetBIOS suffix byte in either case). In practice, however, the server logon doesn't seem to work reliably. The Windows systems used in testing were unable to use NTLMv2 authentication with one another when they were in standalone mode, but once they joined the NT Domain NTLMv2 logons worked just fine.[14]

15.5.3 *The NTLMv2 Response*

The NTLMv2 Response is calculated using the NTLMv2 Hash as the `Key`. The `Data` parameter is composed of the challenge plus a blob of data which we will refer to as "the blob." The blob will be explained shortly. For now, just think of it as a mostly-random bunch of garblement. The formula is shown in this pseudo-code example:

```
blob = RandomBytes( blobsize );
data = concat( ServerChallenge, 8, blob, blobsize );
hmac = HMAC_MD5( v2hash, 16, data, (8 + blobsize) );
v2resp = concat( hmac, 16, blob, blobsize );
```

Okay, let's take a closer look at that and see if we can force it to make some sense.

1. The first step is blob generation. The blob is normally around 64 bytes in size, give or take a few bytes. The pseudo-code above suggests that the bytes are entirely random, but in practice there is a formula (explained below) for creating the blob.

2. The next step is to append the blob to the end of the challenge. This, of course, is the same challenge sent by the server and used by all of the other challenge/response mechanisms.

0	1	2	3	4	5	6	7	8	9	10	11	12	.	.	.
challenge								blob...							

3. The challenge and blob are HMAC'd using the NTLMv2 Hash as the key.

---

14. The lab in the basement is somewhat limited which, in turn, limits my ability to do rigorous testing of esoteric CIFS nuances. You should probably verify these results yourself. Andrew Bartlett (him again!) turned up an interesting quirk regarding the NTLMv2 Response calculation when authenticating against a standalone server. It seems that the NT Domain name is left blank in the v2hash calculation. That is: `destination = ""`;

4. The NTLMv2 Response is created by appending the blob to the tail of the `HMAC_MD5()` result. That's 16 bytes of HMAC followed by `blobsize` bytes of blob.

0	1	2	3	4	5	6	7	8	9	1 0	1 1	1 2	1 3	1 4	1 5	1 6	1 7	1 8	1 9	2 0	.	.	.
hmac																blob...							

If the client sends the NTLMv2 Response, it will take the place of the NTLM Response in the `SESSION_SETUP_ANDX.CaseSensitive-Password` field. Note that, unlike the older NTLM Response, the NTLMv2 Response algorithm uses 128-bit encryption all the way through.

15.5.4 *Creating the Blob*

If you have ever taken a college-level Invertebrate Zoology course, you may find the dissection of the blob to be nauseatingly familiar. The rest of you... try not to be squeamish. One more warning before we cut into this: The blob's structure may not matter at all. We'll explain why a little later on.

Okay, now that the disclaimers are out of the way, we can get back to work. The blob does have a structure, which is more or less as follows:

4 bytes

The value seen in testing is consistently `0x01010000`. (Note that those are nibbles, not bits.) The field is broken out as follows:

1 byte

Response type identification number. The only known value is `0x01`.

1 byte

The identification number of the maximum response type that the client understands. Again, the only known value is `0x01`.

2 bytes

Reserved. Must be zero (`0x0000`).

4 bytes

> The value seen in testing is always 0x00000000. This field may, however, be reserved for some purpose.

8 bytes

> A timestamp, in the same 64-bit format as described back in Section 13.3.1 on page 227.

8 bytes

> The "blip": An eight-byte random value, sometimes referred to as the "Client Challenge." More on this later, when we talk about LMv2 challenge/response.

4 bytes

> Unknown.
>
> Comments in the Samba-TNG code and other sources suggest that this is meant to be either a 4-byte field or a pair of 2-byte fields. These fields should contain offsets to other data. That interpretation is probably based on empirical observation, but in the testing done for this book there was no pattern to the data in these fields. It may be that some implementations provide offsets and others just fill this space with left-over buffer garbage. Variety is the spice of life.

variable length

> A list of structures containing NetBIOS names in Unicode.

4 bytes

> Unknown. (Appears to be more buffer garbage.)

The list of names near the end of the blob may contain the NT Domain and/or the server name. As with the names used to generate the NTLMv2 Hash, these are NetBIOS names in uppercase UCS-2LE Unicode with no string termination and no suffix byte. The name list also has a structure:

2 bytes

> Name type.

> **0x0000**
>
> > Indicates the end of the list.

0x0001

The name is a NetBIOS machine name (e.g. a server name).

0x0002

The name is an NT Domain NetBIOS name.

0x0003

The name is the server's DNS hostname.

0x0004

The name is a W2K Domain name (a DNS name).

2 bytes

The length, in bytes, of the name. If the name type is 0x0000, then this field will also be 0x0000.

variable length

The name, in uppercase UCS-2LE Unicode format.

The blob structure is probably related to (the same as?) data formats used in the more advanced security systems available under Extended Security.[15]

15.5.5 *Improved Security Through Confusion*

Now that we have the formula worked out, let's take a closer look at the NTLMv2 challenge/response algorithm and see how much better it is than NTLM.

With the exception of the password itself, all of the inputs to NTLMv2 are known or knowable from a packet capture. Even the blob can be read off the wire, since it is sent as part of the response. That means that the problem is still a not-so-simple case of solving for a single variable: the password.

---

15. Luke Kenneth Casson Leighton's book *DCE/RPC over SMB: Samba and Windows NT Domain Internals* gives an outline of the structure of the data blob used in NTLMv2 Response creation. Using Luke's book as a starting point, the details presented above were worked out during a late-night IRC session. My thanks to Andrew Bartlett, Richard Sharpe, and Vance Lankhaar for their patience, commitment, and sudden flashes of insight. Thanks also to Luke Howard for later clarifying some of the finer points.

The NTLMv2 Hash is derived directly from the NTLM (v1) Hash. Since there is no change to the initial input (the password), the keyspace is exactly the same. The only change is that the increased complexity of the algorithm means that there are more encryption hoops through which to jump compared to the simpler NTLM process. It takes more computer time to generate a v2 response, which doesn't impact a normal login but will slow down dictionary and brute force attacks against NTLMv2 (though Moore's Law may compensate). Weak passwords (those that are near the beginning of the password dictionary) are still vulnerable.

Another thing to consider is the blob. If the blob were zero length (empty), the NTLMv2 Response formula would reduce to:

```
v2resp = HMAC_MD5( v2hash, ServerChallenge );
```

which would still be pretty darn secure. So the question is this: Does the inclusion of the blob improve the NTLMv2 algorithm and, if so, how?

Well, see, it's like this... Instead of being produced by the key and challenge alone, the NTLMv2 Response involves the hash of a chunk of semi-random data. As a result, the same challenge will *not* always generate the same response. That's good, because it prevents replay attacks... in theory.

In practice, the randomness of the challenge should be enough to prevent replay attacks. Even if that were not the case, the only way that the blob could help would be if it, too, were non-repeating *and* if the server could somehow verify that the blob was not a repeat. That, quite possibly, is why the timestamp is included.

The timestamp could be used to let the server know that the blob is "fresh" — that is, that it was created a reasonably short amount of time before it was received. Fresh packets can't easily be forged because the response is HMAC-signed using the v2hash as the key (and that's based on the password which is the very thing the cracker doesn't know). Of course, the timestamp test won't work unless the client and server clocks are synchronized, which is not always the case.

In all likelihood the contents of the blob are never tested at all. There is code and commentary in the Samba-TNG source showing that they have done some testing, and that their results indicate that a completely random blob of bytes works just fine. If that's true, then the blob does little to improve the security of the algorithm except perhaps by adding a few more CPU cycles to the processing time.

Bottom line: NTLMv2 challenge/response provides only a minimal improvement over its predecessor.

This isn't the first time that we have put a lot of effort into figuring out some complex piece of the protocol only to discover that it's almost pointless, and it probably won't be the last time either.

 **Email**

From: Ronald Tschalär
  To: Chris Hertel
Subject: The point of client nonces

In section 15.5.5 you talk about the "client challenge" a bit, but miss the point of it: the client nonce (as it should really more correctly be called) is there to prevent precomputed dictionary attacks by the server, and has nothing to do with replay attacks against the server (which, as you correctly state, is what the server-challenge is for).

If there's no client nonce, then a rogue server can pick a fixed server-nonce (server-challenge), take dictionary, and precompute all the responses. Then any time a client connects to it it sends the fixed challenge, and upon receipt of the client's response it can do a simple database lookup to find the password (assuming the password was in the dictionary). However, if the client adds its own bit of random stuff to the response computation, then this attack (by the server) is not possible. Hence the client-nonce.

Even with client nonces a rogue server can still try to use a dictionary to figure out your password, but the server has to run the complete dictionary on each response, instead of being able to precompute and use the results for all responses.

15.5.6 *Insult to Injury: LMv2*

There is yet one more small problem with the NTLMv2 Response, and that problem is known as *pass-through* authentication. Simply put, a server can *pass* the authentication process *through* to an NT Domain Controller. The trouble is that some servers that use pass-through assume that the response string is only 24 bytes long.

You may recall that both the LM and NTLM responses are, in fact, 24 bytes long. Because of the blob, however, the NTLMv2 response is much longer. If a server truncates the response to 24 bytes before forwarding it to the NT Domain Controller almost all of the blob will be lost. Without the blob, the Domain Controller will have no way to verify the response so authentication will fail.

To compensate, a simpler response — known as the LMv2 response — is also calculated and returned alongside the NTLMv2 response. The formula is identical to that of NTLMv2, except that the blob is really small.

```
blip = RandomBytes( 8 );
data = concat( ServerChallenge, 8, blip, 8 );
hmac = HMAC_MD5( v2hash, 16, data, 16 );
LMv2resp = concat( hmac, 16, blip, 8 );
```

The "blip," as we've chosen to call it, is sometimes referred to as the "Client Challenge." If you go back and look, you'll find that the blip value is also included in the blob, just after the timestamp. It is fairly easy to spot in packet captures. The blip is 8 bytes long so that the resulting LMv2 Response will be 24 bytes, exactly the size needed for pass-through authentication.

If it is true that the contents of the blob are not checked, then the LMv2 Response isn't really any less secure than the NTLMv2 Response — even though the latter is bigger.

The LMv2 Response takes the place of the LM Response in the `SESSION_SETUP_ANDX.CaseInsensitivePassword` field.

15.5.7 *Choosing NTLMv2*

The use of NTLMv2 is *not* negotiated between the client and the server. There is nothing in the protocol to determine which challenge/response algorithms should be used.

So, um... how does the client know what to send, and how does the server know what to expect?

The default behavior for Windows clients is to send the LM and NTLM responses, and the default for Windows servers is to accept them. Changing these defaults requires fiddling in the Windows registry. Fortunately, the fiddles are well known and documented so we can go through them quickly and get them out of the way.[16]

---

16. A quick web search for "LMCompatibility" will turn up a lot of references, *Microsoft Knowledge Base Article #147706* among them.

The registry path to look at is:

```
HKEY_LOCAL_MACHINE\System\CurrentControlSet\Control\LSA
```

On Windows 9x the variable is called `LMCompatibility`, but on Windows NT and 2000 it is `LMCompatibilityLevel`. That variable may not be present in the registry, so you might have to add it. In general, it's best to follow Microsoft's instructions when editing the registry.[17]

The settings for `LMCompatibilityLevel` are as follows:

Level	Description	Client Implications	Server Implications
0	The Default	LM and NTLM responses are sent by the client.	The server or Domain Controller will compare the client's responses against the LM, NTLM, LMv2, and NTLMv2 responses. Any valid response is acceptable.
1	NTLMv2 Session Security	This level does nothing to change the algorithm used to generate the response. Instead, at this level and higher a feature called NTLMv2 Session Security is supported. Session Security is only used with Extended Security, and must be negotiated between the client and the server. Session Security is an advanced topic, and won't be covered here.	
2	NTLM Authentication	The LM Response is not sent by the client. Instead, the NTLM Response is sent in both password fields. Replacing the LM Response with the NTLM Response facilitates pass-through authentication. Servers need only hand the 24-byte contents of the `SESSION_SETUP_ANDX.Case-InsensitivePassword` field along to the Domain Controller.	The server or Domain Controller will accept a valid LM, NTLM, LMv2, or NTLMv2 response.

---

17. ...so that if something goes wrong you can blame them, and not me.

Level	Description	Client Implications	Server Implications
3	NTLMv2 Authentication	The client sends the LMv2 and NTLMv2 responses in place of the older LM and NTLM values.	The server or Domain Controller will accept a valid LM, NTLM, LMv2, or NTLMv2 response.
4	NTLM Required	The client sends the LMv2 and NTLMv2 responses.	At this level, the server or Domain Controller will not check LM Responses. It will compare responses using the NTLM, LMv2, and/or NTLMv2 algorithms.
5	NTLMv2 Required	The client sends the LMv2 and NTLMv2 responses.	The server or Domain Controller will compare the client's responses using the LMv2 and NTLMv2 algorithms only.

That's just a quick overview of the settings and their meanings. The important points are these:

- The password hash type is *not* negotiated on the wire, but determined by client and/or server configuration. If the client and server configurations are incompatible, authentication will fail.
- The SMB server or Domain Controller may try several comparisons in order to determine whether or not a given response is valid.

15.6   Extended Security: That Light at the End of the Tunnel

Our discussion of SMB authentication mechanisms is winding down now. There are a few more topics to be covered and a few others that will be carefully, but purposefully, avoided. Extended Security falls somewhere in between. We will dip our toes into its troubled waters, but we won't wade in too deep (or the monsters might get us).

One reason for trepidation is that — as of this writing — Extended Security is still an area of active research and development for the Samba Team and others. Though much has been learned, and much has been implemented, the dark pools are still being explored and the fine points are still being examined. Another deterrent is that Extended Security represents a full set of sub-protocols — a whole, vast world of possibilities to be explored... some other day. As with MS-RPC (which we touched on just long enough to get our fingers burned), the topic is simply too large to cover here.

As suggested in Figure 15.4, Extended Security makes use of nested protocols. Go back to Section 13.3.2 on page 235 and take a look at the `NEGOTIATE_PROTOCOL_RESPONSE.SMB_DATA` structure. Note that the `ext_sec.SecurityBlob` field is nothing more than a block of bytes — and it's what's inside that block that matters. If the client and server agree to use Extended Security, then the whole `NEGOTIATE PROTOCOL RESPONSE / SESSION SETUP REQUEST` business becomes a transport for the authentication protocol.

Figure 15.4:   *Protocols nested like Russian dolls*

CIFS sub-protocols may be nested several layers deep. Extended Security, for example, is carried within SMB within NBT within TCP within IP.

In some cases the security exchange may require several packets and a few round trips to complete. When that happens, a single `NEGOTIATE PROTOCOL RESPONSE / SESSION SETUP REQUEST` pair will not be sufficient to handle it all. The solution to this dilemma is fairly simple: The server sends an error message to force the client to send another `SESSION SETUP REQUEST` containing the next chunk of data.

The process is briefly (and incompletely) described in Section 4.1.2 of the SNIA doc as part of the discussion of the `SESSION SETUP RESPONSE`. Simply put, as long as there are more Extended Security packets required, the server will reply to the `SESSION SETUP REQUEST` by sending a `NEGATIVE`

SESSION SETUP RESPONSE with an NT_STATUS value of 0xC0000016 (which is known as STATUS_MORE_PROCESSING_REQUIRED). The client then sends another SESSION SETUP REQUEST containing the additional data. This continues until the authentication protocol has completed.

There is no DOS error code equivalent for STATUS_MORE_PROCESS-ING_REQUIRED, something we have already whined about in the *Strange Behavior Alert* back in Section 12.1 on page 198. It seems that Extended Security expects that the client can handle NT_STATUS codes, which may be a significant issue for anyone trying to implement an SMB client.[18]

15.6.1 *The Extended Security Authentication Toolkit*

There are several different authentication protocols which may be carried within the SecurityBlob. Those protocols, in turn, are built on top of a whole pile of different languages and APIs and data transfer formats. The result is an alphabet soup of acronyms. Here's a taste:

ASN.1: Abstract Syntax Notation One

ASN.1 is a language used to define the structure and content of objects such as data records and protocol messages. If you are not familiar with ASN.1, you might think of it as a super-duper-hyper version of the typedef in C — only a lot more powerful. ASN.1 was developed as part of the Open Systems Interconnection (OSI) environment, and was originally used for writing specifications. More recently, though, tools have been developed that will generate software from ASN.1.

The development and promotion of the ASN.1 language is managed by the ASN.1 Consortium.

DER: Distinguished Encoding Rules of ASN.1

DER is a set of rules for encoding and decoding ASN.1 data. It provides a standard format for transport of data over a network so that the receiving end can convert the data back into its correct ASN.1 format. DER is a specialized form of a more general encoding known as BER (**B**asic

---

18. It might be worth doing some testing if you really want to use DOS codes in your implementation, but also want Extended Security. It may be possible to use the NT_STATUS codes for this exchange only, or you might try interpreting any unrecognized DOS error code as if it were STATUS_MORE_PROCESSING_REQUIRED.

Encoding **R**ules). DER is designed to work well with security protocols, and is used for encoding Kerberos and LDAP exchanges.

GSS-API: Generic Security Service Application Program Interface

As the name suggests, GSS-API is a generic interface to a set of security services. It makes it possible to write software that does not care what the underlying security mechanisms actually are. GSS-API is documented in RFC 2078.

Kerberos

("Kerberos" is a name, not an acronym.)

Kerberos is *the* preferred authentication system for SMB over naked TCP/IP transport. The use of Kerberos with CIFS is also tied in with GSS-API and SPNEGO.

LDAP: Lightweight Directory Access Protocol

Some folks at the University of Michigan realized that the DAP protocol (which was designed as part of the the Open Systems Interconnection (OSI) environment for use with the X.500 directory system) was just too big and hairy for general-purpose use, so they came up with a "lightweight" version, known as LDAP. LDAP was popularized in the mid-1990's, and support was included with directory service implementations such as Novell's NDS (**N**ovell **D**irectory **S**ervice). When Microsoft created their Active Directory system they followed Novell's lead and added LDAP support as well.

MIDL: Microsoft Interface Definition Language

MIDL is Microsoft's version of the **I**nterface **D**efinition **L**anguage (IDL). It is used to specify the parameters to function calls, particularly function calls made across a network — things like Remote Procedure Call (RPC). MIDL is also used to define the interfaces to Microsoft DLL library functions.

MS-RPC: Microsoft Remote Procedure Call

Paul Leach was one of the founders of Apollo Computer. At Apollo, he worked on a system for distributed computing that eventually became the DCE/RPC system. When Hewlett-Packard purchased Apollo, Leach went to Microsoft. That's probably why the MS-RPC system is so remarkably similar to the DCE/RPC system.

NDR: Network Data Representation

NDR is to DCE/RPC as DER (or BER) is to ASN.1. That is, NDR is an on-the-wire encoding for parameters passed via RPC. When an MS-RPC call is made on the client side, the parameters are converted into NDR format (*marshaled*) for transmission over the network. On the server side, the NDR formatted data is *unmarshaled* and passed into the called function. The process is then reversed to return the results.

NTLMSSP: NTLM Security Support Provider

It seems there are a few variations on the interpretation of the acronym. A quick web search for "NTLMSSP" turns up *NTLM Security Service Provider* and *NTLM Secure Service Provider* in addition to *NTLM Security Support Provider*. No matter. They all amount to the same thing.

NTLMSSP is a Windows authentication service that is accessed in much the same way as MS-RPC services. NTLMSSP authentication requests are formatted into a record structure and converted to NDR format for transport to the NTLMSSP authentication service provider. In addition to Extended Security, NTLMSSP authentication shows up in lots of odd places. It is even used by Microsoft Internet Explorer to authenticate HTTP (web) connections.

SPNEGO: Simple, Protected Negotiation

Also known as "The Simple and Protected GSS-API Negotiation Mechanism," SPNEGO is a protocol that underlies GSS-API. It is used to negotiate the security mechanism to be used between two systems. SPNEGO is documented in RFC 2478.

Quite a list, eh?

As you can see, there is a lot going on below the surface of Extended Security. We could try diving into a few of the above topics, but the waters are deep and the currents are strong and we would quickly be swept away. Out of necessity, we will spend a little time talking about Kerberos, but we won't swim out too far and we will be wearing a PFD (**P**ersonal **F**loatation **D**evice — don'cha just love acronyms?).

15.7 Kerberos

As already stated, we won't be going into depth about Kerberos. There is a lot of documentation available on the Internet and in print, so the wiser course is to suggest some starting points for research. There are, of course, several starting points presented in the References section of this very book. A good place to get your feet wet is Bruce Schneier's *Applied Cryptography, Second Edition*.

Kerberos version 5 is specified in RFC 1510, but this is CIFS we're talking about. Microsoft has made a few "enhancements" to the standard. The best known is probably the inclusion of a proprietary **P**rivilege **A**ccess **C**ertificate (PAC) which carries Windows-specific authorization information. Microsoft heard a lot of grumbling about the PAC, and in the end they did publish the information required by third-party implementors. They even did so under acceptable licensing terms (and the CIFS community sighed a collective sigh of relief). The PAC information is available in a **M**icrosoft **D**eveloper **N**etwork (MSDN) document entitled *Windows 2000 Authorization Data in Kerberos Tickets*.

There are a lot of Kerberos-related RFCs. The interesting ones for our purposes are:

- RFC 1964, which provides information about the use of Kerberos with GSS-API,
- RFC 3244, which covers Microsoft's Kerberos password-set and password-change protocols.

There is also (as of this writing) a set of Internet Drafts that cover Microsoft Kerberos features, including a draft for Kerberos authentication over HTTP.

Finally, a web search for "Microsoft" and "Kerberos" will toss up an abundant salad of opinions and references, both historical and contemporary. Where CIFS is concerned, it seems that there is always either too little or too much information. Microsoft-compatible Kerberos falls under the latter curse. There is a lot of stuff out there, and it is easy to get overwhelmed. If you plan to dive in, find a buddy. Don't swim alone.

15.8 Random Notes on W2K and NT Domain Authentication

We have been delicately dancing around the role of the Domain Controller in authentication. It's time to face the music.

The concept is fairly simple: Take the password database that is normally kept locally by a standalone server and move it to a central authority so that it can be shared by multiple servers, then call the whole thing a "Domain." The central authority that stores the shared database is, of course, the Domain Controller. As shown in Figure 15.5, the result is that the SMB fileserver must now consult the Domain Controller when a user tries to access SMB services.

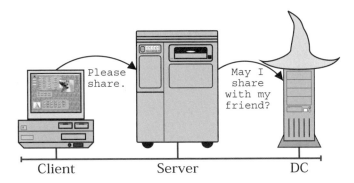

Figure 15.5:   *Centralized authentication*

The **D**omain **C**ontroller (DC) wears a special hat. It keeps track of the common authentication database that is shared by the SMB servers in the Domain. The SMB servers query the DC when a client requests access to SMB services.

That general description applies to both NT and W2K Domains, even though the two are implemented in very different ways. Windows 2000 Domains are based on Active Directory and Kerberos, while Windows NT Domains make use of a **S**ecurity **A**ccounts **M**anager (SAM) Database and MS-RPC.

Let's see what bits of wisdom we can pull out of the hat regarding these two Domain systems...

15.8.1 *A Quick Look at W2K Domains*

As with Microsoft's Kerberos implementation, there is probably too much information available on this topic. A full description would also be very much beyond the stated scope of this book. So, as briefly as possible, here are some notes about W2K Domains and Domain Controllers:

- Windows 2000 Domains are based on the real thing: The Internet Domain Name Service (DNS). The DNS provides a hierarchical namespace, and W2K can take advantage of the DNS hierarchy to form collections of related W2K domains called "trees." Groups of separate W2K Domain trees are known as "forests."

- W2K Domain Controllers run the Active Directory service. **A**ctive **D**irectory (AD) is a database system that can be used to store all sorts of information, including user account data. The design of AD owes a lot to Novell's NDS architecture which, in turn, is based on OSI X.500.

- Data stored in the Active Directory may be accessed using the LDAP protocol.

- Microsoft's Kerberos implementation relies upon the data stored in the Active Directory. The two services are closely linked.

...and that barely begins to scratch the surface. CIFS client and server participation in a W2K Domain requires Kerberos support, but does not require a detailed understanding of Active Directory architecture. The above points are given here primarily for comparison with the NT Domain system notes, presented below.

15.8.2 *A Few Notes about NT Domains*

In contrast to W2K Domains, NT Domains have the following features:

- Windows NT Domains are built upon NetBIOS. The NetBIOS namespace is flat, not hierarchical, so there is no natural way to build relationships among NT Domains. Conceptually, NT Domains are standalone.

- NT authentication information is stored in the **S**ecurity **A**ccounts **M**anager (SAM) Database. The SAM is an extension of the Windows NT Registry database, and it is accessed using a Windows DLL.

- In an NT Domain, the shared SAM database is stored on the Domain Controller and may be accessed using RPC function calls. (Windows 2000, of course, stores the SAM data in the Active Directory, but it can also respond to the RPC calls for compatibility with the NT Domain system.)

There are two mechanisms that an SMB Server can use to ask a Domain Controller to validate a client logon attempt. These are known as *pass-through* and *NetLogon* authentication. The NetLogon mechanism uses MS-RPC, so we won't cover it here except to say that it provides a more intimate relationship between the SMB server and the Domain Controller than does the pass-through mechanism. There are several good sources for further reading listed in the References section. In particular:

- Start with the whitepaper *More Than You Ever Wanted to Know about NT Login Authentication*, by Philip Cox and Paul Hill. It provides a clear and succinct introduction to the Windows NT authentication system.

- Another good overview from a different perspective is provided in the whitepaper *CIFS Authentication and Security* by Bridget Allison (now Bridget Warwick).

- ...and once you're read that you'll be ready for the more in-depth NetLogon coverage in Luke's Leighton's book.

Pass-through, in contrast to NetLogon, is really quite simple. It is also documented in (yet) an(other) expired Leach/Naik IETF draft, titled *CIFS Domain Logon and Pass Through Authentication*, which can be found on Microsoft's CIFS FTP site (under the name `cifslog.txt`).

Basically, pass-through authentication is a man-in-the-middle mechanism. It goes like this:

- The client attempts to log on to the server, but the server has no SAM database so it, in turn, attempts to create an SMB session with the Domain Controller.

- The server sends a NEGOTIATE PROTOCOL REQUEST to the DC. The DC returns a challenge which the server passes back to the client.

- The client does the hard work and generates the various responses (LM, NTLM, etc.), which are sent to the server. The server simply passes them through to the DC in its own SESSION SETUP REQUEST.

■ If the DC returns a POSITIVE SESSION SETUP RESPONSE to the server, then the server will return a POSITIVE SESSION SETUP RESPONSE to the client. Likewise with a negative response.

It should be easy to capture an example of pass-through authentication using your network sniffer. Windows 9x systems (and possibly other Windows varieties) do not support NetLogon so they always use the pass-through method if they are part of an NT Domain. Samba can be configured to use either method.

Radical Rodent Alert

There is an obscure Windows SMB file transfer mode implemented by Windows 98, Windows Me, and possibly other Windows flavors. This mode is known in the community as "rabbit-pellet" mode, and it is triggered by various subtle combinations of conditions. In testing, it appears as though delays in pass-through authentication may be a factor.

In rabbit-pellet mode the client will send a file to the server in very small chunks, somewhere between 512 and 1536 bytes each (give or take). The client will wait for a reply to each write, and will also send a flush request after every one or two writes. This slows down file transfers considerably.

The condition is rare, which is good because it's really annoying when it happens. It's also bad because it has been a very difficult problem to track down.

15.8.3 *It's Good to Have a Backup*

In the NT Domain system, there is a single Domain Controller that is *primarily* responsible for the maintenance of the domain's SAM database. This Domain Controller is known as the (surprise) **P**rimary **D**omain **C**ontroller (PDC).

The domain may also have zero or more **B**ackup **D**omain **C**ontrollers (BDCs). The BDCs keep read-only replicas of the PDC's SAM database. BDCs can be used for authentication just as the PDC can, and if the PDC is accidentally thrown out of a twelfth-story window into an active volcano, a BDC can be "promoted" to fill the role of the dearly departed PDC.

Windows 2000 Domains do things differently. They do not distinguish between Primary and Backup DCs. Instead, Active Directory makes use of something called "multimaster replication." Updates to any replica are propagated to all of the other replicas, so there is no need any longer to specify one copy of the database as the primary.

15.8.4 *Trust Me on This*

This is one of those concepts that we have to cover because — unless you're already familiar with it — you'll read about it somewhere else and think to yourself "What the heck is that all about?"

Somewhere back a few paragraphs it was stated that NT Domains are, conceptually, standalone entities... and so they are, but it is possible to introduce them to one another and get them to cooperate. The agreements forged between the domains are known as "Inter-Domain Trust Relationships."

Let's use an example to explain what this is all about.

Consider a large corporate organization with several divisions, departments, committees, consultants, and such-like. In this corporation, the Business Units Reassignment Planning Division runs the `BURP_DIV` domain, and the Displacement Entry Department calls theirs the `DISENTRY` domain.

Now, let's say that the `BURP_DIV` folks need access to files stored on `DISENTRY` servers (so they can move the files around a bit). One way to handle this would be to create accounts for the `BURP_DIV` users in the `DISENTRY` domain. That would cause a bit of a problem, however, because the `BURP_DIV` users would need two accounts, one per domain. That is likely to result in things like passwords, preferences, and web browser bookmarks getting a bit out of sync. Also, the Benefits Reduction Committee will want to know why all of the `BURP_DIV` employees are moonlighting in the `DISENTRY` department and how they could possibly be doing two jobs at once. It could become quite a mess, resulting in the hiring of dozens of consultants to ensure that the problem is properly ignored.

The better way to handle this situation is to create a *trust relationship* between the `DISENTRY` and `BURP_DIV` domains. With inter-domain trust established, the `BURP_DIV` folks can log on to `DISENTRY` servers using their `BURP_DIV` credentials. As shown in Figure 15.6, the `DISENTRY` Domain Controller will ask the `BURP_DIV` Domain Controllers to validate the logon.

Note that, in the non-extended-security version of the `SESSION SETUP REQUEST` message, there is a field called `PrimaryDomain`. This field identifies the NT domain against which the client wishes to authenticate. That is, the `PrimaryDomain` field should contain the name of the NT Domain to which the user belongs.

Windows 2000 domains also support trust relationships. This is useful for creating trust between two separate W2K Domain trees, or between W2K Domains and NT Domains.

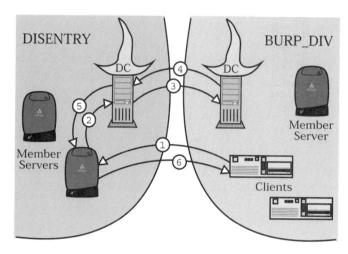

Figure 15.6:   *Inter-domain trust*

1. A client in the BURP_DIV domain tries to access services on a DISENTRY server.
2. The server requests authentication services from a DISENTRY Domain Controller.
3. The DISENTRY Domain Controller trusts the BURP_DIV domain, so it requests authentication services from a BURP_DIV Domain Controller.
4. The BURP_DIV Domain Controller replies to the DISENTRY Domain Controller...
5. ...which replies to the server...
6. ...which replies to the client.

The mechanisms used to support inter-domain trust are very advanced topics, and won't be covered here.

15.9 Random Notes on Message Authentication Codes

Message **A**uthentication **C**odes (MACs) are used to prevent "pickle-in-the-middle" attacks (more commonly known as "<u>man</u>-in-the-middle" attacks).[19] This form of attack is simple to describe, but it can be difficult to pull off in practice (though wireless LAN technology has the potential to make it much easier). Figure 15.7 provides some visuals.

---

19. The latter name — though decidedly less Freudian — is somewhat gender-biased.

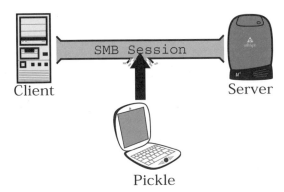

Figure 15.7a: *Attempting a man-in-the-middle attack*
The evil interloper attempts to interpose itself between the legitimate client and server.

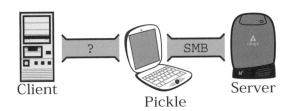

Figure 15.7b: *A successful man-in-the-middle attack*
If the evil interloper succeeds, the server will not notice that the "real" client is gone. The evil interloper may also try to impersonate the server to the client.

Generally speaking, in the pickle-in-the-middle attack an evil interloper allows the "real" client to authenticate with the server and then assumes ownership of the TCP/IP connection, thus bypassing the whole problem of needing to know the password.

There are a number of ways to hijack the TCP session, but with SMB that step isn't necessary. Instead, the evil interloper can simply impersonate the server to fool the client. For instance, if the evil interloper is on the same IP subnet as both the client and server (a B-mode network) then it can usurp the server's name by responding to broadcast name queries sent by the client faster than the server does. Server identity theft can also be accomplished by "poisoning" the NBNS database (or, possibly, the DNS) — that is, by somehow forcing it to swallow false information. A simple way to do that is to register the server's name — with the interloper's IP address — in the NBNS before the server does (perhaps by registering the name while the server is down for maintenance or something).

In any case, when the client tries to open an SMB session with the server it may wind up talking to the evil interloper instead. The evil interloper will pass the authentication request through to the real server, then pass the challenge back to the client, and then pass the client's response to the server... and that... um... um... um... *that looks exactly like pass-through authentication.* In fact, the basic difference between pass-through authentication and this type of attack is the ownership of the box that is relaying the authentication. If the crackers control the box, consider it an attack.

This authentication stuff is fun, isn't it?

So, given a situation in which you are concerned about evil interlopers gaining access to your network, you need a mechanism that allows the client and server to prove to one another *on an ongoing basis* that they are the *real* client and server. That's what the MACs are supposed to do.

Caveat Emptor Alert

As of this writing, SMB MAC signing is an active area of research for the Samba Team. The available documentation regarding **M**essage **A**uthentication **C**odes (MACs) disagrees to some extent with empirical results. The information presented in this section is the best currently available, derived from both the documentation and the testing being done by the Samba Team. As such, it is probably (but not necessarily) very close to reality. Doveryay, no proveryay.

15.9.1 *Generating the Session Key*

The server and client each generate a special key, known as the *Session Key*. There are several potential uses for the Session Key, but we will only be looking at its use in MAC signing.

The Session Key is derived from the password hash — something that only the client and server should know. There are several hash types available: LM, NTLM, LMv2, and NTLMv2. The hash chosen is probably the most advanced hash that the two systems know they share. So, if the client sent an LM Response — but did *not* send an NTLM Response — then the Session Key will be based on the LM Hash. The LM Session Key is calculated as follows:

```
char eightnuls[8] = { 0, 0, 0, 0, 0, 0, 0, 0 };
LM_Session_Key = concat( LM_Hash, 8, eightnuls, 8 );
```

That is, take the first eight bytes of the LM Hash and add eight nul bytes to the end for a total of 16 bytes. Note that the resulting Session Key is not the same as the LM Hash itself. As stated earlier, the password hashes can be used to perform all of the authentication functions we have covered so far, so they must be protected as if they were the actual password. Overwriting the last eight bytes of the hash with zeros serves to obfuscate the hash (though this method is rather weak).

A different formula is used if the client *did* send an NTLM Response. The NTLM Session Key is calculated like so:

```
NTLM_Session_Key = MD4( NTLM_Hash );
```

which means that the NTLM Session Key is the MD4 of the MD4 of the Unicode password. The SNIA doc says there's only one MD4, but that would make the NTLM Session Key the same as the NTLM Hash. Andrew Bartlett of the Samba Team says there are two MD4s; the second does a fine job of protecting the password-equivalent NTLM Hash from exposure.

Moving along to LMv2 and NTLMv2, we find that the Session Key recipe is slightly more complex, but it's all stuff we have seen before. We need the following ingredients:

v2hash

The NTLM Version 2 Hash, which we calculated back in Section 15.5.2 on page 279.

hmac

The result of the HMAC_MD5() function using the v2hash as the key and the server challenge plus the blob (or blip) as the input data. The NTLMv2 hmac was calculated in Section 15.5.3 and sent as the first 16 bytes of the response. The LMv2 hmac was calculated in Section 15.5.6.

The LMv2 and NTLMv2 session keys are computed as follows:

```
LMv2_Session_Key   = HMAC_MD5( v2hash, 16,    lmv2_hmac, 16 );
NTLMv2_Session_Key = HMAC_MD5( v2hash, 16, ntlmv2_hmac, 16 );
```

The client is able to generate the Session Key because it knows the password and other required information (because the user entered the required information at the logon prompt). If the server is standalone, it will have the password hash and other required information in its local SAM database, and can generate the Session Key as well. On the other hand, if the server relies upon a Domain Controller for authentication then it won't have the password hash and won't be able to generate the Session Key.

What's a server to do?

As we have already pointed out, the MAC protocol is designed to prevent a situation that looks exactly like pass-through authentication, so a pass-through server simply cannot do MAC signing. A NetLogon-capable server, however, has a special relationship with the Domain Controller. The NetLogon protocol is secured, so the Domain Controller can generate the Session Key and send it to the server. That's how an NT Domain member server gets hold of the Session Key without ever knowing the user's password or password hash.

15.9.2 *Sequence Numbers*

The client and server each maintain an integer counter which they initialize to zero. Both counters are incremented for every SMB message — that's once for a request and once for a reply. As a result, requests always have an even sequence number and replies always have an odd.

The zero-eth message is always a SESSION SETUP ANDX message, but it may not be the *first* SESSION SETUP ANDX of the session. Recall, from near the beginning of the Authentication section, that the client sometimes uses an anonymous or guest logon to access server information. Watch enough packet captures and you will see that MAC signing doesn't really start until after a real user logon occurs.

Also, it appears from testing that the MAC Signature in the zero-eth message is never checked (and that existing clients send a bogus MAC Signature in the zero-eth packet). That's okay, since the authenticity of the zero-eth message can be verified by the fact that it contains a valid response to the server challenge.

Once the MAC signing has been initialized within a session, all messages are numbered using the same counters and signed using the same Session Key. This is true even if additional SESSION SETUP ANDX exchanges occur.

15.9.3 *Calculating the MAC*

The MAC itself is calculated using the MD5 function. That's the plain MD5, not HMAC-MD5 and not MD4. The input to the MD5 function consists of three concatenated blocks of data:

- the Session Key,
- the response, and
- the SMB message.

We start by combining the Session Key and the response into a single value known as the MAC Key. For LM, NTLM, and LMv2 the MAC Key is created like so:

```
MAC_Key = concat( Session_Key, 16, Response, 24 );
```

The thing to note here is that all of the responses, with the exception of the NTLMv2 Response, are 24 bytes long. So, except for NTLMv2, all auth mechanisms produce a MAC Key that is 40 bytes long. (16 + 24 = 40). Unfortunately, the formula for creating the NTLMv2 MAC Key is not yet known. It is probably similar to the above, however. Possibly identical to the calculation of the LMv2 MAC Key, or possibly the concatenation of the Session Key with the first 28 bytes of the blob.

Okay, now you need to pay careful attention. The last few steps of MAC Signature calculation are a bit fiddly.

1. Start by re-acquainting yourself with the structure of the `SMB_HEADER.EXTRA` field, as described in Section 11.2.1 on page 181. We are particularly interested in the eight bytes labeled `Signature`.

2. The sequence number is written as a longword into the first four bytes of the `SMB_HEADER.EXTRA.Signature` field. The remaining four bytes are zeroed.

3. The MAC Signature is calculated as follows:

```
data = concat( MAC_Key, MAC_Key_Len, SMB_Msg, SMB_Msg_Len );
hash = MD5( data );
MAC  = head( hash, 8 );
```

In words: the MAC Signature is the first eight bytes of the MD5 of the MAC_Key plus the entire SMB message.

4. The eight bytes worth of MAC Signature are copied into the `SMB_HEADER.EXTRA.Signature` field, overwriting the sequence number.

...and that, to the best of our knowledge, is how it's done.

15.9.4 *Enabling and Requiring MAC Signing*

Windows NT systems offer four registry keys to control the use of SMB MAC signing. The first two manage server behavior, and the others represent client settings.

Server: `HKEY_LOCAL_MACHINE\System\CurrentControlSet`
   `\Services\LanManServer\Parameters`
   `EnableSecuritySignature`

> The valid values are zero (0) and one (1). If zero, then MAC signing is disabled on the server side. If one, then the server will support MAC signing.

   `RequireSecuritySignature`

> The valid values are zero (0) and one (1). This parameter is ignored unless MAC signing is enabled via the `EnableSecurity-Signature` parameter. If zero, then MAC signing is optional and will only be used if the client also supports it. If one, then MAC signing is required. If the client does not support MAC signing then authentication will fail.

Client: `HKEY_LOCAL_MACHINE\System\CurrentControlSet`
   `\Services\Rdr\Parameters`
   `EnableSecuritySignature`

> The valid values are zero (0) and one (1). If zero, then MAC signing is disabled on the client side. If one, then the client will support MAC signing.

   `RequireSecuritySignature`

> The valid values are zero (0) and one (1). This parameter is ignored unless MAC signing is enabled via the `EnableSecurity Signature` parameter. If zero, then MAC signing is optional and will only be used if the server also supports it. If one, then MAC signing is required. If the server does not support MAC signing then authentication will fail.

Study those closely and you may detect some small amount of similarity between the client and server parameter settings. (Well, okay, they are mirror images of one another.) Keep in mind that the client and server must have compatible settings or the SESSION SETUP will fail.

These options are also available under Windows 2000, but are managed using security policy settings.[20]

15.10 Non Sequitur Time

A mathematician, a physicist, and an engineer were sitting together in a teashop, sharing a pot of Lapsang Souchong and discussing the relationship between theory and practice. The mathematician said, "One of my students asked me today whether all odd numbers greater than one were prime numbers, so I provided this simple proof:

Stated: All odd numbers greater than one are prime.
3 is prime,
5 is prime,
7 is prime,
9 is divisible by three, so it is odd but not prime.
Contradiction; the statement is false."

"Interesting," replied the physicist. "Perhaps I have the same student. I was asked the same question today. I solved the problem using a thought-experiment, as Galileo might have done. Our experiment was as follows:

By observation we can see that:
3 is prime,
5 is prime,
7 is prime,
9 is experimental error,
11 is prime,
13 is prime..."

---

20. Jean-Baptiste Marchand has done some digging and reports that starting with Windows 2000 the SMB redirector (rdr) has been redesigned, which may impact which registry keys are fiddled. The preferred way to configure SMB MAC signing in Windows 2000 is to use the Local Security Settings/Group Policy Management Console (whatever that is). Basically, this means that Windows 2000 and Windows XP have MAC signing settings comparable to those in Windows NT, but they are handled in a different way.

The engineer interrupted before the physicist could draw a conclusion, and said, "Out in the field we don't have time to mess with theory. We just define all odd numbers as prime and work from there. It's simpler that way."

Consider this as you contemplate what you have learned about SMB authentication.

15.11 Further Study

You should now have all you need to create an SMB session with an SMB server. As you become more comfortable with the system, you will likely become curious about the vast uncharted jungle of Extended Security. Don't be afraid to go exploring. With the background provided here, and the guidebooks listed in the References section, you are well prepared. If you get it all mapped out, do us all a favor: write it up so that everyone can share what you've learned.

A few more bits of advice before we move along...

1. **Know what you've got to work with.** This is one of Andrew Bartlett's rules of thumb. If you are trying to figure out how an encrypted token or key or somesuch is derived, consider the available functions and inputs. Existing tools and values are often reused. Just look through the calculation of the NTLMv2 Response and you'll see what we mean.

2. **Trust but verify.** Read the available documentation and make notes, but don't assume that the documentation is always right. The truth is on the wire. In some cases implementations stray from the specifications, and in other cases (e.g. this book) the documentation is a best-effort attempt at presenting what has been learned. There are few truly definitive sources. Another factor, as you are by now aware, is that there is a tremendous amount of variation in the CIFS world. Something may work correctly in one instance only to surprise you in another.

3. **Don't be surprised.** Don't go looking for weirdness in CIFS, but don't be surprised when you find it. If you expect bad behavior, you may miss the sane and obvious. A lot of CIFS does, in fact, make some sort of sense when you think about it. There are gotchas, though, so be prepared.

These guidelines are quite general, but they apply particularly well to the study of SMB security and authentication.

16

Building Your SMB Vocabulary

...they have weapons
of mass confusion
and aren't afraid to use them.

— iomud on Slashdot

Looking back over our shoulders, we see that we have performed only two SMB exchanges so far: the NEGOTIATE PROTOCOL and the SESSION SETUP. There may be a TREE CONNECT shoved into the packet with the SESSION SETUP as an AndX, but we haven't really described the TREE CONNECT in detail.

So, although we have covered a tremendous amount of material, our progress seems rather pathetic doesn't it? What if the rest of SMB is just as tedious, verbose, and difficult?

Relax. It's not.

Certainly there are other difficulties lying in wait, but the biggest ones have already been identified and we are carefully avoiding them. If you pursue your dream of creating a complete and competitive CIFS implementation then you may, some day, need to know how things like MS-RPC and Extended Security really work inside. Fortunately, you can do without them for now.

Let's just be clear on this before we move along:

There is a lot you can do with CIFS without implementing any of the extended sub-protocols that SMB supports, but if you want to build a complete and competitive CIFS client/server implementation you will need to go well beyond the SMB protocol itself.

That's why it has taken the Samba Team (with help from hundreds if not thousands of people across the Internet) more than ten years to make Samba the industrial-strength server system it is today. Tridge worked out the basics of NBT and SMB in a couple of weeks back in 1991, but new things keep getting tacked on to the system.

When implementing CIFS, the rule of thumb is this: *Implement as little as possible to do the job you need to do.*

The minute you cross the border into uncharted territory, you open up a whole new world to explore and discover. Sometimes, you just don't want to go there. Other times, you must.

Anyway, in the spirit of keeping things simple we will cover only a few more SMB messages, and those in much less depth than we have done so far. There really is no need to study every message, longword, bit, and string. If you've come this far, you should know how to read packet captures and interpret the message definitions in the SNIA doc. It is time to take the training wheels off and learn to *ride*.

16.1   That TREE CONNECT Thingy

We have talked a lot about the TREE CONNECT ANDX REQUEST SMB. There was even an example way back in Section 11.4 on page 188. The example looked like this:

```
SMB_PARAMETERS
  {
  WordCount        = 4
  AndXCommand      = SMB_COM_NONE (0xFF)
  AndXOffset       = 0
  Flags            = 0x0000
  PasswordLength   = 1
  }
SMB_DATA
  {
  ByteCount        = 22
  Password         = ""
  Path             = "\\SMEDLEY\HOME"
  Service          = "?????"  (yes, really)
  }
```

Notice that the TREE CONNECT includes a Password field, but that in this example the Password field is *almost* empty (it contains a nul byte).

If the server negotiates Share Level security, then the password that would otherwise be in the `SESSION_SETUP_ANDX.CaseInsensitive-Password` field will show up in the `TREE_CONNECT_ANDX.Password` field instead. The password may be plaintext, or it may be one of the response values we calculated earlier.

The `TREE_CONNECT_ANDX.Path` field is also worth mentioning. It contains the UNC pathname of the share to which the client is trying to connect. In this example, the client is attempting to access the HOME share on node SMEDLEY. Note that the `Path` will be in Unicode if negotiated.

Finally there is that weird quintuple question mark string in the `TREE_CONNECT_ANDX.Service` field. There are, as it turns out, five possible values for that field:

String	Meaning
`A:`	A filesystem share
`LPT1:`	A shared printer
`IPC`	An interprocess communications named pipe
`COMM`	A serial or other communications device
`?????`	Wildcard

It's annoying for the client to need to know the kind of share to which it is connecting, which is probably why the wildcard option is available. The server will return the service type in the `Service` field of the Response. Note that the `Service` strings are always in 8-bit ASCII characters — never Unicode.

The response (for LANMAN2.1 and above) looks like this:

```
SMB_PARAMETERS
  {
  WordCount       = 3
  AndXCommand     = <Next ANDX command>
  AndXOffset      = <Next ANDX block offset>
  OptionalSupport = <A bitfield>
  }
```

```
SMB_DATA
  {
  ByteCount        = <variable>
  Service          = <"A:" | "LPT1:" | "IPC" | "COMM">
  NativeFileSystem = <"" | "FAT" | "NTFS">
  }
```

The example above shows the empty string, "FAT", or "NTFS" as the valid values for the NativeFileSystem field. Other values are possible. (Samba, for instance, has a configuration option that allows you to put in anything you like.) The empty string is used for the hidden IPC$ share.

There are two bits defined in the OptionalSupport bitfield:

Bit	Meaning
SMB_SUPPORT_SEARCH_BITS 0x0001	The meaning of this bit is explained in the LANMAN2.1 documentation. Basically, it indicates that the server knows how to perform directory searches that filter out some entries based on specific file attributes — for example, the DOS archive bit, the directory attribute, etc. This is old stuff and all current implementations should support it.
SMB_SHARE_IS_IN_DFS 0x0002	This bit, if set, indicates that the UNC name is in the **D**istributed **F**ile **S**ystem (DFS) namespace. DFS is yet to be covered.

There is a note in the SNIA doc that states that some servers will leave out the OptionalSupport field even if the LANMAN2.1 or later dialect is negotiated. It does not say whether SMB_SUPPORT_SEARCH_BITS should be assumed in such cases.

16.2 SMB Echo

Here's a toy we can play with.

ECHO is really as simple as it sounds. It's sort of the SMB equivalent of ping. The client sends a packet with a data block full of bytes, and the server echoes the block back. Simple.

...but this is CIFS we're talking about.

Although the ECHO itself is simple, there are many quirks to be found in existing implementations. We will dig into this just a tiny bit to give you a taste of the kinds of problems you are likely to encounter. Let's start with a quick look at the ECHO REQUEST structure:

```
SMB_PARAMETERS
  {
  WordCount  = 1
  EchoCount  = <In theory, anything from 0 to 65535>
  }
SMB_DATA
  {
  ByteCount  = <Number of data bytes to follow>
  Bytes      = <Your favorite soup recipe?>
  }
```

The EchoCount field is a multiplier. It tells the server to respond EchoCount times. If EchoCount is zero, you shouldn't get any reply at all. If EchoCount is 9,999, then you are likely to get nine thousand, nine hundred, and ninety-nine replies. We say *likely* because of the wide variety of weirdity that can be seen in testing.

One bit of weirdation is that all of the systems that were tested would respond to an ECHO REQUEST even if no SESSION SETUP had been sent and no authentication performed. This behavior is, in fact, per design, but it means that any client that can talk to your server from anywhere can ask for EchoCount replies to a single request. (It would probably be safer for the server to send a ERRSRV/ERRnosupport error message in response to an un-authenticated ECHO REQUEST.)

Other strangisms of note:

- In testing, **Windows 9x** systems returned an "Invalid TID" error unless the TID was set to 0xFFFF. Also, these systems sent back at most a single reply, handling EchoCount as if it were a boolean.

- **Windows NT 4.0** and **Windows 2000** would try to send as many replies as specified in EchoCount. If the data block (SMB_DATA.Bytes) was very large (4K was tested) and the EchoCount very high (e.g., 20,000), the server would eventually give up and reset the connection.

- **Samba** has an upper limit of 100 repetitions. Also, Samba sends the replies fast enough that multiple replies will be batched together in a single TCP packet. (That's normal behavior for a TCP stream.)

■ The **Windows NT 4.0 (Service Pack 6)** system used in testing failed to respond if the payload was greater than 4323 bytes. **Windows 2000** seems to have an upper limit of 16611 bytes, above which it resets the TCP connection.

 Email

```
From: Conrad Minshall, Apple Computer
  To: Chris Hertel
  Cc: Samba Technical Mailing List
Subject: Re: Bizarre limit alert.
```

```
I saw the same "packet drop" with an overlong WRITE_ANDX.  The
maximum buffer size an NT SP6 claims on the NEGOTIATE response
is 0x1104 (4356). This limit is not on the data, the limit
includes the SMB header (32 bytes) and the SMB command. Based
upon the size of an ECHO command I'd expect you could send
4319 bytes, not 4323, so on this topic you'll have to have the
last word... sorry.
```

No apologies. This is CIFS we're talking about.

The ECHO SMB may be one of those things that get coded up just because they're in the documentation and they seem easy. It also appears as though ECHO hasn't been tested much. Certainly, the more it is stressed, the more variation can be seen. There is, however, something to note in the last example in the above list and in the message from Conrad: Once you know what you're looking at, you will find common themes that appear and reappear across a given implementation. These common themes are derived from common internals, and they can provide many clues about the inner workings of the implementation.

Another fine point highlighted by our quick look at the ECHO SMB is that TCP is designed to carry *streams* of data — not discrete packets. This can be seen in the results of the tests against Samba, in which multiple replies were contained in a single TCP packet. At the other extreme, several TCP packets are needed to transfer a single ECHO if it has a very large data payload. As a result, a single read operation may or may not return one and only one complete SMB message.

Oversimplification Alert

The `RecvTimeout()` *function (provided way back in Listing 10.1) makes the assumption that one complete SMB message will be returned per call to the* `recv()` *function. That's a weak assumption. It works well enough for the simple testing we have done so far, but it is not sufficient for a real SMB implementation.*

A better version of `RecvTimeout()` *would verify the received data length against the NBT* `SESSION_MESSAGE.LENGTH` *field value to ensure that only one message is read at a time, and that the complete message is read before it is returned.*

16.3   Readin', Writin', and 'Rithmatic

Here is a quick run-down on some of the basic essentials of SMB.

OPEN_ANDX

This SMB is discussed in examples given throughout the SNIA doc, but there is no actual writeup given there. That's because it was labeled as "obsolescent" in the Leach/Naik CIFS draft. The `NT_CREATE_ANDX` SMB is now considered the more fashionable choice. Servers must still support the `OPEN_ANDX` SMB, however, and there are certainly clients that still send it (even under the NT LM 0.12 dialect).

It's times like these that the earlier documentation comes in really handy.

The `OPEN_ANDX` SMB is used to gain access to a file for further processing (reading, writing, that sort of thing). The open file is identified by a `FID` (**File ID**). The `FID`, of course, is returned by a successful `OPEN_ANDX` call.

READ_ANDX

It seems fairly obvious. This one lets you read blocks of data from a file (or device) on the server. The `READ_ANDX` request supports 64-bit file offsets if the `OffsetHigh` field is present (if it is present, the `WordCount` will be 12).

An oddity of the `READ_ANDX` is the `MaxCountHigh` field, which is only used if the `CAP_LARGE_READX` capability has been set. `MaxCountHigh` is an unsigned long (four bytes) that is supposed to hold the upper 16 bits (two bytes) of the unsigned short (two byte) MaxCount field. Two problems with this:

1. Why use a 32-bit field to hold 16 bits worth of data?

2. Even with CAP_LARGE_READX set, the maximum SMB large read is 64K. That should fit into the MaxCount field with no need for MaxCountHigh.

Play with it and see what happens. Should be interesting.

WRITE_ANDX

Allows writing to a file or device. This SMB can also be extended by two words to include an OffsetHigh field, thus providing 64-bit offsets. There is also a DataLengthHigh field that is comparable to the MaxCountHigh from the READ_ANDX. In this case, though, the DataLengthHigh field is given as an unsigned short. That's only two bytes, which makes more sense.

SEEK_ANDX

This one may be considered deprecated. Newer clients probably don't need to send the SEEK_ANDX, but servers may need to support it just in case.

 **Email**

```
From: Charles Caldarale
  To: jCIFS Mailing List

SMB_COM_SEEK is a useless SMB, since all of the read and write
functions require a file relative address. It's not surprising
it wasn't used; it would have been a waste of network bandwidth
if it had been sent.

- Chuck
```

See also the SNIA doc's comments regarding this SMB.

FLUSH

The SMB_COM_FLUSH has nothing to do with plumbing. It is sent by the client to ask the server to write all data and metadata for an open file (specified by its `FID`) to disk. If a `FID` value of `0xFFFF` is given, the server is being asked to flush all open files relative to the `TID`.

NT_CREATE_ANDX

This SMB is used to open, create, or overwrite a file or directory. It offers a myriad of options for file attributes, file sharing, security, etc. As the "NT" in the name implies, the `NT_CREATE_ANDX` SMB is closely tied to the feature set offered by Windows NT filesystem calls. Here's where you start needing to know more about Windows itself.

One problem with complex calls such as this is that the number of permutations gets to be very high, and it quickly becomes very difficult to test them all.[1] There are various reports describing combinations of values that can cause a Windows NT client or server to go BSOD (**B**lue **S**creen **O**f **D**eath). Have fun with your testing.

There is yet another version of this SMB known as the `NT_TRANSACT_CREATE`, which is implemented as a sub-command of the `SMB_COM_NT_TRANSACTION` SMB. It is used to apply Extended Attributes (EAs) or Security Descriptors (SDs) to a file or directory.

CLOSE

All good things must come to an end. Close the file, say goodnight, sing one more song, and get some rest.

Remember earlier when we talked about SMB messages as if we were dissecting some strange, new species of multi-legged critter? Well, we've moved beyond Entomology, Invertebrate Zoology, Taxonomy, and such. We're now studying really complex stuff like Sociology, Psychology, and Numismatics, and we get to put the little critters into Skinner boxes and see how they react to various stimuli. It's important research, and there are all sorts of interesting things to discover.

Consider, for example, the `SMB_COM_COPY` command. It's supposed to allow you to copy a file from one location on the server to another location.

---

1. I vaguely remember a presentation given by David Korn, author of the Korn Shell (ksh), regarding AT&T's UWIN project. At the end of the presentation there was some discussion regarding the differences between standard Posix APIs and Win32 APIs. It was pointed out that there were hundreds or possibly thousands of permutations of parameter values that could be passed to the Posix `open()` function. The permutations for the equivalent Win32 function, it was reported, was on the order of millions. How the heck do you test all those possibilities?

That saves the client from having to read the data over the wire and write it back again. A good idea, eh? Unfortunately, no one seems to be able to get it to work — at least, not against Windows servers. There has been some limited success in the laboratory...

 Email

```
    From: Greg McCain
      To: Chris Hertel
 Subject: CIFS and SMB_COPY

Chris,

I found that smb_copy will in fact copy a file iff:
 - the src file is in the root of the share
 - you do not specify the full path to the file src and dest files
in the smb_copy command. Instead, just specify the names of the
files (this is out of spec.).

The resulting destination file will be named like the source
file, minus the first character. It will NOT be named as specified
in the dest parameter. Hence "smb_copy wanda -> fred" results in
a second file "anda" in the root of the share.

This works on the .NET server RC1 and Windows 2000 servers
that I've tried. Hope it helps.
```

SMB is an old protocol, and it has gotten sloppy over the years. As you work your way through the SMB messages, implementing first the easy ones and then the more difficult ones, keep this thought in mind: *It's not your fault.*

Say it to yourself now: "It's not my fault."

Very good.

That will prevent you from getting frustrated and doubting your own skill. It's really not your fault.

16.4 Transaction SMBs

We are going to blast through this, so you'd better get your running shoes on.

The purpose of the Transaction SMBs is to carry specialized sub-protocols. Examples include the **R**emote **A**dministration **P**rotocol (RAP) and Microsoft's implementation of DCE/RPC (MS-RPC). There are other, more esoteric sets of calls as well. We will play with some of them when we get to the Browse Service.

Think of these sub-protocols as sets of function calls that are stretched across the network. As suggested in Figure 16.1, a function call is made on the client side and the parameters and data are packed up and shoved across the network. The call is then completed at the remote end and the results (if any) are packed up and shoved back. In CIFS jargon, that's called a *transaction*.

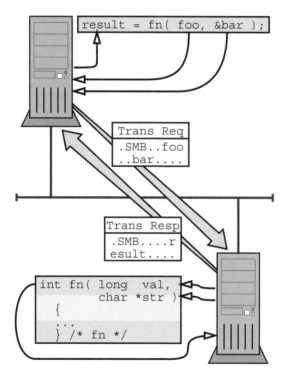

Figure 16.1: *Remote Procedure Call via transaction*

- Software on the client calls the function fn().
- The parameters and pass-by-reference data are packed into an SMB Transaction and sent to the server.
- The server processes the function call.
- If results are expected, the server packs the return value(s) and any pass-by-reference data into a reply transaction.

Transactions are designed to be able to transfer more data than the limit imposed by the negotiated buffer size. They do so by fragmenting the payload. The protocol for sending large **P**rotocol **D**ata **U**nits (PDUs) is described in a variety of documents, but here is a quick run-down:

1. A *primary* Transaction SMB is sent. It includes the total expected size of the transaction (so that the server can prepare to receive the data). It also contains as much of the data as will fit in a single SMB message. If everything fits, skip to step 4.

2. The server sends back an interim response. If the interim response contains an error code then the transaction will be aborted. Otherwise, it is a signal telling the client to continue. The WORDCOUNT and BYTECOUNT fields are both zero in this message (it's a disembodied header).

3. The client sends as many *secondary* Transaction SMBs as necessary to complete the transaction request.

4. The server executes the called function.

5. The server sends as many response messages as necessary to return the results. In some cases the request does not generate results, and no response is required.

There are three primary Transaction SMBs:

```
SMB_COM_TRANSACTION   == 0x25
SMB_COM_TRANSACTION2  == 0x32
SMB_COM_NT_TRANSACT   == 0xA0
```

Those are really long names, so folks on the various mailing lists tend to shorten them to "SMBtrans," "Trans2," and "NTtrans," respectively. Each of these also has a matching secondary:

```
SMB_COM_TRANSACTION_SECONDARY   == 0x26
SMB_COM_TRANSACTION2_SECONDARY  == 0x33
SMB_COM_NT_TRANSACT_SECONDARY   == 0xA1
```

There is very little difference between these three transaction types, except that the NTtrans SMB has 32-bit fields where the other two have 16-bit fields. That means that NTtrans can handle a lot more data (that is, much larger transactions). Besides that, the real difference between these three is the set of functions that are traditionally carried over each.

The SNIA doc and the Leach/Naik CIFS draft provide examples of transactions that use Trans2 and NTtrans. Calls that use SMBtrans are documented elsewhere. Places to look include Luke's book (*DCE/RPC over SMB*), the Leach/Naik Browser and RAP Internet Drafts, and the X/Open documentation (particularly *IPC Mechanisms for SMB*). These (as you already know) are listed in the References section.

16.4.1 *Mailslots and Named Pipes*

Just to simplify things even further, SMBtrans supports yet another layer of abstraction.

Mailslots and Named Pipes are used to access specific sets of remote functions. For example, the "LANMAN" pipe (which is identified as \PIPE\LANMAN) is always used for RAP calls.

Named Pipes are two-way inter-process communications channels. Once opened, they can be read from or written to as if they were files. In contrast, Mailslots are used for one-way, connectionless communications.

...and this is where something unexpected happens. Mailslot messages are sent using SMBs transported via the *NBT Datagram Service*. You'll have to see it to believe it, but that is easily arranged. All you need to do is grab a packet capture of port 138 on an active LAN, one with a few local servers that announce themselves to the working Network Neighborhood. If you don't like to wait, reboot something. A Windows 9x system that offers shares will do nicely.

This topic will be revisited in Part III on page 335. If you want to do some extra-curricular reading, the X/Open *IPC Mechanisms for SMB* document is recommended.

17

The Remaining Oddities

> The first 90% of the job
> takes 90% of the time.
> The remaining 10%
> of the job requires
> another 90% of the time.
>
> — Unknown (but oh so true)

Promises were made, and promises should be kept.

Remember that closet full of concepts that burst open and spilled out all over the floor? Well, we have managed to clean up a good deal of the mess, but there are still a few things that we said we would put away — and we will. We can provide a brief explanation of each of these as we shove them back into the closet, just so you are not surprised when you stumble across them in the literature.

17.1 Opportunistic Locks (OpLocks)

OpLocks are a caching mechanism.

A client may request an OpLock from an SMB server when it opens a file. If the server grants the request, then the client knows that it can safely cache large chunks of the file and not tell the server what it is doing with those cached chunks until it is finished. That saves a lot of network I/O round-trip time and is a very big boost to performance.

The problem, of course, is that other clients may want to access the same file at the same time. As long as everyone is just reading the file things are okay, but if even one client makes a change then all of the cached copies held by the other clients will be out of sync. That's why OpLock handling is a bit tricky.

There are two types of OpLocks that a client may request:

- Exclusive, or
- Batch.

We came across these two when digging into the SMB_HEADER.FLAGS field way back in Section 12.2 on page 202. In olden times, the client would request an OpLock by setting the SMB_FLAGS_REQUEST_OPLOCK bit and, optionally, the SMB_FLAGS_REQUEST_BATCH_OPLOCK bit in the FLAGS field when opening a file. Now-a-days the FLAGS bits are (supposedly) ignored and fields within newer-style SMBs are used instead.

Anyway, an Exclusive OpLock can be granted if no other client or application is accessing the file at all. The client may then read, write, lock, and unlock the cached portions of the file without informing the server. As long as the client holds the Exclusive OpLock, it knows that it won't cause any conflicts. It's sort of like a kid sitting in a corner of the kitchen with a spoon and a big ol' carton of ice cream. As long as no one else is looking, that kid's world is just the spoon and the ice cream.

Batch OpLocks are similar to Exclusive OpLocks except that they cause the client to delay sending a CLOSE SMB to the server. This is done specifically to bypass a weirdity in the way DOS handles batch files (batch files are the DOS equivalent of shell scripts). The problem is that DOS executes these scripts in the following way:

1. Set offset to zero (0).
2. Open the batch file.
3. Seek to the stored offset.
4. If EOF, then exit.
5. Read one line.
6. Store the current offset.
7. Close the batch file.
8. Execute the line.
9. Go back to step 2.

Yes, you've read that correctly. The batch file is opened and closed for every line. It's ugly, but that's what DOS reportedly does and that's why there are Batch OpLocks.

To make Batch OpLocks effective, the client's SMB layer simply delays sending the CLOSE message. If the file is opened again, the CLOSE and OPEN simply cancel each other out and nothing needs to be sent over the wire at all. That also means that the client can keep hold of the cached copy of the batch file so that it doesn't have to re-read it for every line of the script.

There is also a third type of OpLock, known as a Level II OpLock, which the client cannot request but the server may grant. Level II OpLocks are, essentially, "read-only" OpLocks. They permit the client to cache data for reading only. All operations which would change the file or meta-data must still be sent to the server.

Level II OpLocks may be granted when the server cannot grant an Exclusive or Batch OpLock. They allow multiple clients to cache the same file at the same time so, unlike the other two, Level II OpLocks are not exclusive. As long as all of the clients are just reading their cached copies there is no chance of conflict. If one client makes a change, however, then all of the other clients need to be notified that their cached copies are no longer valid. That's called an OpLock Break.

17.1.1 *OpLock Breaks*

It's called an "OpLock Break" because it involves breaking an existing OpLock. The more formal term is "revocation," but no one actually says that when they get together after hours to sit around, drink tea, and whine about CIFS.

OpLock Breaks are sent from the server to the client. This is unusual, because SMB request/response pairs are *always* initiated by the client. The OpLock Break is sent out-of-band by the server, which is against the rules... but this is CIFS we're talking about. Who needs rules?

The OpLock Break is sent in the form of a SMB_COM_LOCKING_ANDX message. The server may send this to reduce an Exclusive or Batch OpLock to a Level II OpLock, or to revoke an existing OpLock entirely. In either case, the client's immediate responsibility is to flush its cache to comply with the new OpLock status. If the client held an Exclusive or Batch OpLock, it must send all writes to the server and request any byte-range locks that it needs in order to continue processing. If the OpLock has been reduced to a Level II OpLock, the client may keep its local cache for read-only purposes.

Note that there is a big difference between OpLocks and the more traditional types of locks. With a traditional file or byte-range lock, the client is in charge once it has obtained a lock. It can maintain it as long as needed, relinquishing it only when it is finished using it. In contrast, an OpLock is like borrowing your neighbor's lawnmower. You have to give it back when your neighbor asks for it.

Support for OpLocks is optional on both the client and the server side, but implementing them provides a hefty performance boost. More information on OpLocks may be found in the Paul Leach/Dan Perry article *CIFS: A Common Internet File System* (listed in the References), as well as the usual sources.

17.2 Distributed File System (DFS)

The CIFS **D**istributed **F**ile **S**ystem (DFS) is not nearly as fancy as it sounds. It is simply a way to collect separate shares into a single, virtual tree structure. It also has some limited ability to provide fileserver redundancy and load balancing.

The key feature of DFS is that it can create links from within a shared tree on one server to shares and directories on another, thus providing a single point of entry to a *virtual* SMB tree. From the user's perspective, the whole thing looks like a single share, even though the resources are scattered across separate SMB servers.

Clear as mud? Perhaps an illustration will help...

In Figure 17.1, the client is shown attempting to access a file on server PETSERVER. Well, that's where the client *thinks* the file resides. On the server side, the name CORGIS in the DOGS directory is actually a link to another UNC pathname, \\DATADOG\CORGIS. Following that link leads us to a different share on a different server.

The server offering the DFS share (PETSERVER, in our example) does not act as a proxy for the client. That is, it won't follow the DFS links itself. Instead, the server sends an error code to the client indicating that there is some additional work to be done. The error code is either a DOS code of ERRSRV/ERRbadtype (0x02/0x0003), or an NT_STATUS code of STATUS_DFS_PATH_NOT_COVERED (0xC0000257).

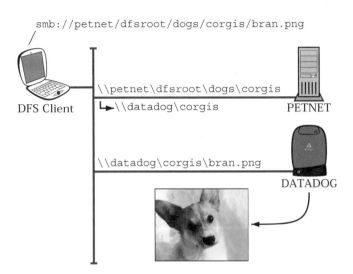

Figure 17.1: *Distributed File System*

The client is using an SMB URL to access an image of a Pembrokeshire Welsh Corgi playing in the snow. The URL is translated into UNC format for use with the SMB protocol. The server traverses the UNC path until it reaches `corgis`, which is a link to a share on a different server.

```
CORGIS ==> \\DATADOG\CORGIS
```

The client is redirected to the new server, where it finally finds the file it wanted.

The client's task, at this point, is to query the server to resolve the link. The client sends a `TRANS2_GET_DFS_REFERRAL` which is passed to the server via the Trans2 transaction mechanism, briefly described earlier. The client will use the information provided in the query response to create a new UNC path. It must then establish an SMB session with the new server. This whole mess is known as a "DFS referral."

It was mentioned above that DFS can provide a certain amount of redundancy. This is possible because the links in the DFS tree may contain multiple references. If the client fails to connect to the first server listed in the referral it can try the second, and so on. DFS can also provide a simple form of load balancing by reshuffling the order in which the list of links is presented each time it is queried. Of course, load balancing and redundancy are only workable if all of the linked copies are in sync.

A quick search on the web will turn up a lot of articles and papers that do a better job of describing the behavior of DFS that the blurb provided here.

If you are planning on implementing DFS, it is worthwhile to read up on the subject a bit, just to get a complete sense of how it is supposed to work from the user or network administrator's perspective. The SNIA doc provides enough information to get you started building a working client implementation. The server side is more complex because doing it right involves implementing a set of management functions as well.

17.3   DOS Attributes, Extended File Attributes, Long Filenames, and Suchlike

These all present the same problem.

The CIFS protocol suite is designed, in its heart and soul, to work with DOS, OS/2, and Windows systems. As a result, the protocols that make up the CIFS suite have a tendency to reflect the behavior of those operating systems.

DOS, of course, is the oldest and simplest of the IBM/Microsoft family of PC OSes. The filesystem used with DOS is the venerable **F**ile **A**llocation **T**able (FAT) filesystem which, according to legend, was originally coded up by Bill Gates himself. The characteristics of the FAT filesystem should be familiar to anyone who has spent any time working with DOS. Consider, for example, the following FAT features:

Case-insensitive filenames

Case is ignored, though file and directory names are stored in uppercase.

8.3 filename format

A name is a maximum of eight bytes in length, optionally followed by a dot ('.') and an extension of at most three bytes. For example: FILENAME.EXT.

No users or groups

FAT does not understand ownership of files.

Six attribute bits

FAT supports six attribute bits, stored in a single byte. The best known are the Archive, Hidden, Read-only, and System bits but there are two more: Volume Label and Directory. These are used to identify the type and handling of a FAT table entry.

It's a fairly spartan system.

There are improvements and extensions that have appeared over the years. The FAT32 filesystem, for example, is a modified version of FAT that uses disk space more efficiently and also supports much larger disk sizes than the original FAT. There is also VFAT, which keeps track of both 8.3 format filenames and longer secondary filenames that may contain a wider variety of characters than the 8.3 format allows. VFAT long filenames are case-preserving (but not case sensitive) so, overall, VFAT allows a lot more creativity with file and directory names.[1]

Even with these extensions, the semantics of the FAT filesystem are not sufficient to meet the needs of more powerful OSes such as OS/2 and Windows NT. These OSes have newer, more complex filesystems which they support in addition to FAT. Specifically, OS/2 has HPFS (**H**igh **P**erformance **F**ile **S**ystem), and Windows NT and W2K can make use of NTFS (**N**ew **T**echnology **F**ile **S**ystem). These newer filesystems have lots and lots of features which, in turn, have to be supported by CIFS.

Problems arise when the server semantics (made available via CIFS) do not match those expected by the client. Consider, for instance, Samba running on a Unix system. Unix filesystems typically have these general characteristics:

Case-sensitive filenames

Case is significant in most Unix filesystems. File and directory names are stored with case preserved.

Longer, more complex filenames

Unix filesystems allow for a great deal of creativity in naming files and directories.

Users and groups

Unix filesystems assign user and group ownership to each directory entry.

---

1. Digging through the documentation, it appears that the FAT family consists of FAT12, FAT16, FAT32, and VFAT. There is documentation on the web that provides implementation details, if you are so inclined.

More, and different, attribute bits

There are three sets of three bits each used for basic file access (read, write, and execute permissions for user, group, and world). There are additional bits defined for more esoteric purposes.

Now consider a Windows application that requires the old 8.3 name format. (Such applications do exist. They make calls to older, 16-bit OS functions that assume 8.3 format.) Unlike VFAT, Unix filesystems do not normally keep track of both long and short names. That causes a problem, and Samba has to compensate by generating 8.3 format names on the fly. The process is called "Name Mangling."

There are other gotchas too. Indeed, name mangling is just the tip of the proverbial iceberg.

One solution that some CIFS vendors have been able to implement is to develop a whole new filesystem for their server platform, one that maintains all of the required attributes and maps between them as necessary. This is a pain, but it works in situations in which the server vendor has control over the deployment of their product. One such filesystem is Microsoft's NTFS, which can handle a very wide variety of attributes and map them to the semantics required by Apple Macintosh clients, Unix clients, DOS clients, OS/2 clients...

You've got the basic idea. Let's run through some of the trouble spots to give you a sense of what you're up against.

Long filenames

Long filenames can be much more descriptive than the old 8.3 names. The problem, of course, is that CIFS must support both long and short (8.3) names to be fully compatible with all of the potential clients out there. Even if a server supports only the NT LM 0.12 dialect, there will still be instances when the 8.3 format is required. Sigh.

DOS attributes

These are the six attribute bits that are supported by the FAT filesystem. These do not map well to the file protections offered by other filesystems. Compare these, for example, against the attribute bits offered by Unix systems.

The timestamps stored in the FAT filesystem may also be different from those used by other systems.

Extended File Attributes

These are an extended set of attribute bits and flags available on systems using the NTFS filesystem. They are a 32-bit superset of the set offered by the FAT system. Extended File Attributes are described in Section 3.13 of the SNIA doc.

The term "Extended File Attributes" is also sometimes misused when discussing NTFS permissions. Permissions are different; they are associated with **A**ccess **C**ontrol **E**ntries (ACEs), and ACEs are gathered together into **A**ccess **C**ontrol **L**ists. There's a whole bigbunch of stuff there that could be explored — and would be, if this were a book about implementing NTFS.

Extended Attributes

These should get special mention because, it seems, CIFS is sufficiently complex that terminology has to be recycled. **E**xtended **A**ttributes (EAs) are not the same as Extended File Attributes.

EAs are a feature of HPFS and, therefore, are supported by NTFS. Basically, they are a separate data space associated with a file into which applications may store additional data or metadata specific to the application (things like author name or a file comment).[2]

CIFS offers facilities to support all of these features and more. That's good news if you are writing client code, because you can pick and choose the sets of attributes you want to support. It's bad for server systems, which may need to offer various levels of compatibility in order to contend with client expectations.

---

2. NTFS is a complex filesystem based on some simple concepts. One such concept is that each "file" is actually a set of "attributes" (records). Many of these attributes are predefined to contain such things as the short name, the long name, file creation and access times, etc. The actual content of the file is stored in a specific, predefined "stream," where a stream is a particular kind of attribute. NTFS supports OS/2-style Extended Attributes in another type of NTFS attribute... and it just gets more confusing from there. There is a lot of documentation on the web about the workings of NTFS, and there is a project aimed at implementing NTFS for Linux.

18

That Just about Wraps Things Up for SMB

Let's just get rid of these horrible protocols.

— Andrew Tridgell,
Samba Team Leader

If the Internet has proven anything, it's that a very large number of primates banging randomly on keyboards over a long enough period of time can and will produce some amazingly useful software. On the other hand, if you gather some of those primates together, place them into cubicles, and train them to perform like circus animals...

...well, we've just put a lot of effort into cleaning up the mess that was made in those cubicles. A shame, really. It was a nice little protocol when it started out.

Although the SNIA gave it their best shot, there are currently no industry committees or standards groups writing *bona fide* specifications to be reviewed and voted on, and no standard test suites to verify conformity. That's not to say that specifications and test suites don't exist — quite the contrary. The problem is that they have no teeth. With no real standards and no real enforcement, the only measure of correctness for an SMB implementation is whether or not it works *most* of the time. Since *most* of the clients out there are Windows clients, the formula simplifies down to whether or not an implementation works with Windows. An additional problem is that SMB itself is not enough for true interoperability with Windows systems — particularly if you want to write a workable server.

In San Jose, California, there is a mansion known as the Winchester Mystery House. It started out as a simple farmhouse, but it was expanded over a period of thirty-eight years by a millionaire widow with an obsessive compulsion to keep on adding new rooms. It has stairways that rise directly into the ceiling, windows in the floor, doors that open to solid walls... and that's just for starters. The building covers four and a half acres and has an estimated 160 rooms.

CIFS is like that.

The original SMB protocol was simple and well suited to its environment. Over the years, however, it has been greatly expanded. Several sub-protocols have been added on as well. These subprotocols (which include the Extended Security protocols, RAP, MS-RPC, etc.) are implemented by Windows — so, if you want to build something truly compatible, SMB alone just isn't enough.

...but don't go away feeling that it is all just a hopeless mess. It is really a question of how much effort you are willing to put into solving the problems you will encounter. Take it one step at a time, because the individual pieces are much less daunting than the whole.

PART III

The Browse Service

19

A Beautiful Day in the Network Neighborhood

Keep off the grass!

— Suburban yard sign

The houses are painted in cheerful colors, there are flowers in the window boxes, people greet you as you walk down the street, and the dogs never bark after sunset. It seems a lovely place in which to open a small teashop and perhaps, someday, retire. Before you decide to move in, though, there are a few things you probably need to know about the Network Neighborhood.

Behind the picture-postcard facade there lies a complex political and social structure, collectively known as the *Browse Service*. Many people consider the Browse Service to be mysterious and secretive, perhaps because most of its business is handled discreetly, out of the view of the casual tourists. The Browse Service lurks in the background, gathering, maintaining, and distributing the *Browse List* — the list of available servers and workgroups.

You can sneak a peek at the Browse List by clicking the Network Neighborhood icon on a Microsoft Windows desktop. If all is working as it should, you will be presented with a neatly organized graphical view of the available SMB filesharing environment. It will look something like the image in Figure 19.1. By selecting icons you can traverse the SMB hierarchy and view workgroups, servers, print queues, shares, directories, and files. In CIFS terms, this is called "browsing" the network.[1]

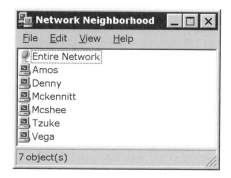

Figure 19.1:   *The Network Neighborhood*
A user's-eye-view of an SMB filesharing network.

19.1   History: From Frontier Town to Bustling Metropolis

The original Browse Service staked its claim alongside the LANMAN1.0 dialect, back in the frontier days of OS/2. Its descendants stayed on and prospered through the LM1.2X002 and LANMAN2.1 days, and then quietly faded into legend. There aren't many systems around today that still earn their keep by running LAN Manager style browsing, as it is known, yet the legacy lives on. Windows systems generally have a server configuration check-box to enable LAN Manager browser announcements, and Samba has an LM ANNOUNCE parameter for the same purpose.

When Windows NT rode into town, it brought along a newfangled Browse Service. Like its predecessor, the new system was built upon the Net-BIOS API. It was an improvement over the older version in that it could exchange and combine Browse Lists with remote Browsers on distant LANs, thus bringing the world a little closer together. That version of the Browse Service

---

1. IBM and Microsoft should not be blamed for any confusion between Network Neighborhood browsing and Web browsing. They started using the term "browse" well before the advent of the web.

is the same one most folks still use today, and it is the one we will be studying in detail.

Then came the Information Superhighway, and Windows 2000 arrived in a bright blue limousine with a fancy new Browse Service hanging on its arm. The W2K browsing system is designed to run on naked TCP transport, and it is built on top of Active Directory and the LDAP protocol. As you may have come to expect by now, covering Directory Services is more than this book is trying to achieve so we won't spend a lot of time on W2K browsing. Besides, Windows 2000 and Windows XP are both backward compatible with previous Windows versions, and can still support the older NetBIOS-based Windows Browse Service.

Another thing that has changed since Windows 2000 arrived is the name of the Network Neighborhood. These days, it is called "My Network Places." A discussion of the implications of the shift in metaphor from one relating the network environment to a cohesive and open community to one of self-centered virtual oligarchy is also way the heck beyond the scope of this book.

19.2   Sociology

The Browse Service, as was stated earlier, has a social structure. SMB servers and clients are expected to be members of cliques known as "workgroups" or "domains." The basic difference between a workgroup and a domain is that the latter provides central authentication services via Domain Controllers.

Just to make life more interesting, there are two types of domain to consider:

Windows 2000 Domains

As explained above, Windows 2000 provides a browse system that is based on Directory Services (Active Directory, etc.). W2K Domains are not NBT-based, so they do not use NetBIOS names. Instead, W2K Domains are closely aligned with the Domain Name System (DNS) and rely on Kerberos for authentication. This is Microsoft's way of grafting their domain architecture onto the Internet Domain Name System.

Windows NT Domains

NT Domains are glorified workgroups, but that's not a particularly helpful description since we haven't really explained what a workgroup is yet.

A workgroup, quite simply, is defined by its NetBIOS name. The workgroup name is typically assigned in the node's configuration, although utilities like `smbclient` and toolkits like jCIFS allow the workgroup name to be specified at run-time. As with the node's machine name, the workgroup name is used as the basis for NetBIOS names that are actually registered — just add the appropriate suffix byte. Systems do not *need* to register any name based on the workgroup unless they are offering services to the workgroup as a whole. Some example workgroup names:

Name & Suffix	Group/Unique	Service/Description
workgroup<00>	group	This name is a remnant of the original LAN Manager browse service.
workgroup<1D>	unique	This name identifies the Local Master Browser (LMB, sometimes called simply "Master Browser") for a subnet.
workgroup<1E>	group	Every node that is capable of acting as a "Browser" registers this group name so that it can listen for election announcements. We'll explain what a "Browser" is in a moment.

That just scratches the surface, and doesn't really tell us anything about NT Domains. Fully explaining what workgroups and NT Domains are all about and how the names listed above are used is something of a recursive problem because the sociology of the Browse Service is intertwined with the politics.

19.3 Politics

On the local level, the Windows Browse Service is a volunteer organization. Nodes that are willing and able to donate some memory and CPU cycles make themselves available to the community by registering a special NetBIOS group name with a suffix byte value of `0x1E`, as shown in the table above. That name is then used to hold an election and choose a workgroup leader.[2] The election winner is given the title of "Master Browser," and it registers a unique NetBIOS name with a suffix byte value of `0x1D`. It also registers the strangely-formatted group name "`\x01\x02__MSBROWSE__\x02\x01`" (that last '`\x01`' is actually the suffix byte).

As you may recall from the rant in Chapter 7 on page 141, Microsoft's WINS server provides special handling for unique names with the `0x1D` suffix. Though the Master Browser may register this name with the WINS server, WINS will deny knowledge of the name when queried. WINS also returns 255.255.255.255 in response to name queries for group names. Most third-party NBNS implementations behave the same way in order to be WINS-compatible.

Two key things happen as a result:

- The NBNS provides no useful information when queried for either the *workgroup*`<1D>` name or the `MSBROWSE<01>`[3] name, so Master Browsers can only be found using NBT Broadcast Name Queries.
- Each separate IP subnet may have a Master Browser with the same unique `0x1D` name. Even if there is an NBNS, there will be no name conflict.T

This is highly unusual behavior for NetBIOS names but, on the plus side, each subnet in the Network Neighborhood gets to have its own elected leader. On the minus side, the Master Browsers cannot exchange information because they cannot talk to one another.

Figure 19.2 shows three separate workgroups, all with the same base name: "WORKGROUP". They are distinct because they cannot exchange and combine Browse Lists. In order to bring these three together, we need yet another special node: the "Domain Master Browser."

---

2. Mnemonic: `0x1Election`.

3. From here on out, we use "`MSBROWSE<01>`" as a shorthand for "`\x01\x02__MS-BROWSE__\x02\x01`" because it's really annoying to have to type all of those hex escapes and underscores every time.

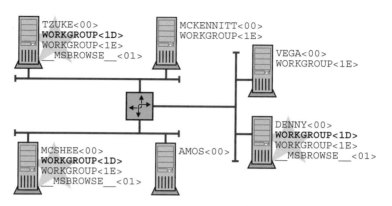

Figure 19.2:   *Isolated Master Browsers*

Because they cannot "see" one another, Master Browsers on separate IP subnets register the same unique NBT name without conflict.

  Pedantic Phrasing Alert

*Just to make it absolutely clear that the elected Master Browser is LAN-locked, and to distinguish it from the Domain Master Browser, from this point forward we will use the term **Local Master Browser (LMB)**.*

The **D**omain **M**aster **B**rowser (DMB) is the workgroup president. Unlike the democratically elected LMB, the DMB is appointed. The Network Manager (that's a human being) must select and configure a node to serve as DMB. The DMB will register the unique NetBIOS name *workgroup*<1B> to identify itself. Since the goal here is to bring together Browse Lists from separate subnets, there must also be an NBNS available so that all of the LMBs on all of the subnets can find the DMB.

Figure 19.3 (which is, admittedly, a bit complex) shows a single, unified workgroup. Node AMOS has been designated to act as the NBNS, and node DENNY has been given the job of Domain Master Browser. Nodes TZUKE and MCSHEE are Local Master Browsers for their own subnets. They will query the NBNS for the name WORKGROUP<1B>, and then contact the DMB in order to exchange Browse Lists. Note that the DMB takes on the role of LMB on its own subnet.

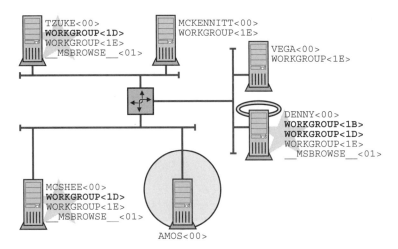

```
TZUKE<00>
WORKGROUP<1D>
WORKGROUP<1E>
__MSBROWSE__<01>

MCKENNITT<00>
WORKGROUP<1E>

VEGA<00>
WORKGROUP<1E>

DENNY<00>
WORKGROUP<1B>
WORKGROUP<1D>
WORKGROUP<1E>
__MSBROWSE__<01>

MCSHEE<00>
WORKGROUP<1D>
WORKGROUP<1E>
__MSBROWSE__<01>

AMOS<00>
```

Figure 19.3:   *A unified workgroup*

The existence of a Domain Master Browser *and* an NBNS allows the Local Master Browsers on each subnet to exchange Browse Lists.

19.3.1   *When Is a Workgroup not a Workgroup?*

A workgroup is not a workgroup when it is an NT Domain.

The difference between a workgroup and an NT Domain is that the latter has a Domain Controller, which is an authentication server. The Domain Controller keeps track of usernames and passwords, and all of the SMB file servers within the NT Domain are expected to consult with the Domain Controller whenever a client sends a `SESSION SETUP REQUEST` SMB.

In the Windows world, the DMB service is always offered by a **P**rimary **D**omain **C**ontroller (PDC). The two are considered inseparable, so if you are using Windows, you must set up a PDC in order to offer DMB services, and vice versa. This is probably why the DMB is called a *Domain* Master Browser.

Samba, on the other hand, lets you set up a DMB without the requirement that you also set up a PDC. Since DMB services do not, in fact, rely upon any NT Domain functionality, the DMB can operate independently. On the other hand, if you *do* wish to set up a PDC, then the PDC node *must* also be the DMB — even with Samba. This latter restriction is a bit goofy. The reason for the requirement is that Microsoft's WINS (and, therefore, any WINS-compatible NBNS) provides special handling for a group name registered by the Domain Controllers. Consider the following table:

Name & Suffix	Group/Unique	Service/Description
nt_domain<1B>	unique	This name is registered by the Domain Master Browser. It must be registered with the NBNS in order to be of any real use.
nt_domain<1C>	Internet group	Registered by all Domain Controllers in the given NT Domain.

The goofy bit, which has been described elsewhere in this book, is that the WINS server keeps track of up to 25 IPs for the <1C> group name. WINS also ensures that the IP address of the node registering the <1B> name is always the first in the <1C> name's IP list. That last quirk is the only real linkage between the DMB and PDC names:

> Within the NBT namespace, the *Primary* Domain Controller is distinguished from the Backup Domain Controllers by the fact that it also runs the DMB service and, therefore, registers the <1B> name.

This all brings up a small nomenclature problem: If there is a DMB running without a PDC (as Samba allows), is the result a workgroup or a domain? That situation was not anticipated by Microsoft, so the terminology doesn't quite work. (Can you call it a *Domain* Master Browser if there's no NT Domain?)

 Careful Clarification Alert

For our purposes, we will use the term workgroup *to specify the scope of the browsing environment even if the workgroup is also an NT Domain. We will use the term* NT Domain *when discussing an authentication domain.*

19.3.2 *Delegating Responsibility*

So far, we have described Local Master Browsers and Domain Master Browsers. There are two additional types of browsers to consider.

Potential Browsers

These are nodes which are willing and able to provide browse services. They have the *workgroup*<1E> name registered and they participate as candidates in browser elections.

Backup Browsers

These are nodes that are selected by the Local Master Browser to assist in handing out the Browse List. Following the election, if there are other Potential Browsers available, the LMB *may* choose one or more of them to be Backup Browsers.

Now we can explain that a "Browser" is any node that participates in the creation and maintenance of the Browse Service. As we have shown, browsers are categorized as *Potential*, *Backup*, *Local Master*, or *Domain Master*. Browser roles are cumulative, and the Domain Master is at the top of the heap.

If the socio-political system seems overly complex, keep in mind that:

- The Windows Browse Service was developed in the days when 386- and 486-class processors were the top of the line.
- The Browse Service is run behind-the-scenes by systems that volunteer CPU time and a bit of memory.
- The more nodes there are on the subnet, the more work that must be done by the Local Master Browser.
- There may be several nodes on the network that are capable of acting as a Browser.
- If the nodes are unstable (frequently rebooted, shut down at the end of the day, etc.) a single copy of the Browse List may be lost.

All of this plays into the design of the Windows Browse Service.

The key thing to remember is that the Local Master Browser (unless it is also the DMB) is a volunteer, and being a Browser is not its primary function. The LMB node is, most likely, running as an SMB server or desktop system, or doing some other work. Allowing the Browse Service to interfere with someone's word processing or spreadsheet recalculations would be a bad thing.

So, on subnets with a lot of nodes, the LMB may select some of the Potential Browsers to act as Backup Browsers. When a client wants a copy of the Browse List, the LMB may direct the client to one or more Backup Browsers instead. The client will cache the IP addresses of the Backup Browsers, and from that point forward send all Browse List queries to one of those nodes. The Backup Browsers are also the most likely nodes to replace the current LMB if it goes down, and the backup copies of the Browse List that they maintain will ensure stability in the Network Neighborhood.

20

Meet the Neighbors

She is a caricature of herself.

— Something my mother used to say
  when she thought her victim
  wasn't listening

We started off with a brief overview of the history and socio-political structure of the Browse Service. Basic guidebook stuff. Now we will meet some of the local citizens, learn about their roles in society, and find out how they interact with one another on a personal level. We will introduce them to you one at a time so you can get to know them before you see them in action. Hopefully, that will help you feel more comfortable as you explore the backstreets of the Network Neighborhood.

A quick note before we go visiting... The Browse Service is built on top of other CIFS services and protocols. Layered protocols have a habit of causing terminology confusion, particularly when the talk turns to "clients" and "servers." The thing to keep in mind is that everything is relative. In this case, everything is relative to the service being offered and the client making use of it. An SMB filesharing client may also be a Browse Service server, and a Browse Service server may also be a Browse Service client, and a Browse Service client... the permutations and combinations are practically (though not actually) endless.

Don't let yourself get confused.

To help abate the ensuing chaos a few new, context-specific terms will need to be defined as we go along. You may want to take notes.

20.1   Browse Service Clientele

The Browse Service has two types of clients:

- systems that wish to announce services, and
- systems that wish to find services on the network.

Think of it in terms of the classified advertising section in your local newspaper. Classifieds are available to people who have something to sell as well as to people who are looking to buy. Both of these are clients of the newspaper.

In some of the available documentation, systems that wish to announce services via the Browse List are referred to as "Non-Browser Servers." That's really icky terminology, since those systems *could* be [Potential | Backup | Local Master] Browsers as well. We will refer to nodes that announce services as "Providers," without trying to straighten out what kind of Browser nodes or SMB servers they may or may not be. To add a sense of symmetry, we will use the term "Consumers" to identify the other kind of Browse Service clients — those that want to *find* services on the network.

So, for our purposes:

- A *Provider* is any node that wishes to announce (via the Browse List) that it has services available.
- A *Consumer* is any node that wishes to get hold of a copy of the Browse List so that it can find services.

We promised to introduce the neighbors one at a time. Let's start with the Providers.

20.1.1 *Providers*

Providers announce themselves to the Local Master Browser by periodically broadcasting a message called a `HostAnnouncement Browser Frame`. The message is sent as an IP broadcast so any NBT node could listen in, but the NBT destination given in the message header is the *workgroup*<1D> name, so the LMB is obviously the intended recipient.

When a node first starts up, it generally announces itself once per minute. After it has been running for a while it will slow down, typically sending an announcement once every 12 minutes. Different implementations behave differently, of course, but the suggestion is that the Provider start with a delay of one minute and double the delay until it exceeds 12 minutes, at which point it should settle on 12 minute intervals.

If a Provider stops announcing itself, its entry in the Browse List will (eventually) time out. The time out formula generally given in the documentation is three times the last known announcement period. In testing, however, some systems reported the `Periodicity` value incorrectly so it is probably safer to assume an announcement period of 12 minutes and use a fixed timeout value of $3 \times 12 = 36$ minutes.

Providers can also remove themselves from the Browse List by sending a `HostAnnouncement` message with an empty list of services. This indicates to the LMB that the host is no longer providing any services. If possible, a Provider should send an empty `HostAnnouncement Browser Frame` when it shuts down.

> **Some Technologies Shouldn't Mix Alert**
> *When cable television companies first decided to get into the **I**nternet **S**ervice **P**rovider (ISP) business they ran into an unexpected problem. A lot of PC vendors were installing Windows preconfigured with SMB filesharing turned on and no passwords by default. When these PCs were connected to the cable Internet service, they would start announcing themselves to one another. People up and down the block found that they could both see and access each other's systems, view files, copy software...*
> *Now that's a Network Neighborhood.*

20.1.2 *Consumers*

It is important to be polite when dealing with your local government. The LMB is your neighbor, after all, and the time it spends handling the Browse List is volunteer time (unless it is also the appointed DMB). It may have other responsibilities as well — spouse, kids, day job as a word processor or fileserver... If everyone in the neighborhood is constantly asking for help, the LMB may wish that it had never been elected.

The *polite* thing for a Browse Service Consumer to do is to ask the LMB for a list of Backup Browsers. We will call this the "BB List" (short for **B**ackup **B**rowser **L**ist) to distinguish it from the Browse List. The Consumer should keep track of the BB List so that any time it needs an updated copy of the Browse List it can query one of the Browsers on that list. That's how the workload is distributed in the Network Neighborhood.

Keeping in mind that Browse Service duties are cumulative, the LMB will probably include itself in the BB List. On small LANs there may not be any Backup Browsers hanging around, so the LMB may be the *only* Browser listed in the BB List.

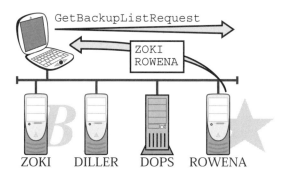

GetBackupListRequest

ZOKI
ROWENA

ZOKI   DILLER   DOPS   ROWENA

Figure 20.1:   *Requesting the Backup Browser list*

Node ZOKI is a Backup Browser, and node ROWENA is the LMB. A Browse Service client broadcasts a request for the Backup Browser List (BB List), and the LMB responds (unicast) with a list of active browsers.

The request for the BB List is sent as a broadcast NBT datagram. The request message, as indicated in Figure 20.1, is known as a GetBackup-ListRequest Browser Frame. If the Consumer does not receive a response to the initial request, it should try again a couple of times. If no reply is received at all, the client *may* call for a new election — once only — and then try again to get a BB list. It may be the case that there are no Potential Browsers on the LAN at all, resulting in no LMB and no local Browse List. Continually calling for new elections in this situation would be futile (and rude).

Let's hope, however, that there is an LMB and that it does respond. The reply from an LMB is known as a GetBackupList<u>Response</u> Browser Frame. It is *not* sent as a broadcast. Instead, the response is sent back to the requester in a unicast datagram (in NBT terminology, a DIRECT UNIQUE DATAGRAM).

...and that's what it takes to find out where copies of the Browse List are kept.

At this point in the proceedings the Consumer has obtained the NBT name of a Browser (either a Backup Browser or the LMB) and is ready to send a query to obtain the Browse List (see Figure 20.2).

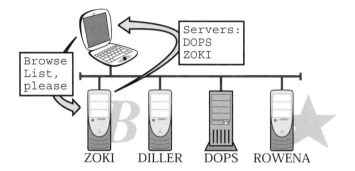

Figure 20.2: *Requesting the Browse List*

Earlier, the Consumer node learned that ZOKI had a copy of the Browse List. The Consumer uses the **R**emote **A**dministration **P**rotocol to request a copy of the Browse List.

In this example, nodes ZOKI and DOPS are Providers, advertising services via the Browse List.

This step is a little more complex than the previous ones. The Browse List might be very large, in which case (recalling the limitations of the NBT Datagram Service) an NBT datagram might not be big enough to hold it all. So instead of using the Datagram Service the Browse List query is sent using the **R**emote **A**dministration **P**rotocol (RAP) which rides on top of the SMB_COM_TRANSACTION message (aka SMBtrans). SMBtrans, in turn, allows for data transfers of up to 64K.

20.2 The Local Master Browser

It's time to meet your elected officials.

All Browser nodes register the *workgroup*<1E> NetBIOS name. The Local Master Browser, as you already know, identifies itself by registering two additional NetBIOS names: *workgroup*<1D> and MSBROWSE<01>. NetBIOS names represent communications end-points — services or applications that are using the NetBIOS API to listen for connections or messages. On the other side of these particular names there is software waiting to hear the chatter of the Browse Service.

The LMB has the following duties.

Maintaining the master copy of the workgroup Browse List for the local IP subnet

The LMB listens on the *workgroup*<1D> name for HostAnnouncement messages from members of its own workgroup. It also listens on the MSBROWSE<01> name so that it can hear DomainAnnouncement Browser Frame messages from other LMBs serving other workgroups on the same LAN (see Figure 20.3). The information collected from these announcements is used to build the Browse List.

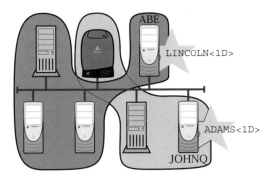

Figure 20.3:   *Multiple workgroups on the same LAN*

Two workgroups, each with their own Local Master Browser, share the same IP subnet. Node ABE will collect the local Browse List for the LINCOLN workgroup, and will also listen for DomainAnnouncement messages from node JOHNQ.

Announcing its workgroup to other LMBs representing other workgroups

The LMB broadcasts DomainAnnouncement messages to the MSBROWSE<01> name to announce itself (and its workgroup) to the LMBs of other workgroups.

Announcing itself to its own workgroup

The LMB periodically sends a LocalMasterAnnouncement Browser Frame to the *workgroup*<1E> name. The Backup Browsers use this announcement to keep track of the LMB so that they can update their copies of the Browse List.

Delegating responsibility to Backup Browsers

The LMB is expected to promote Potential Browsers to Backup Browsers as the need arises. This is done by sending a `BecomeBackup Browser Frame` to the selected Browser node. The LMB should also provide the BB List in response to a `GetBackupListRequest`.

Coordinating with the Domain Master Browser

The LMB should query the NBNS for the *workgroup*`<1B>` name (which is registered by the DMB). There are two exceptions to this rule:

- B-mode nodes will not query the NBNS because remote LANs are outside of their scope and B nodes shouldn't talk to strangers.
- If the LMB is also the workgroup DMB then it doesn't need to query the NBNS to find itself.

Otherwise, the LMB will periodically announce its existence to the DMB by sending a `MasterAnnouncement Browser Frame`. Once the LMB and the DMB know about one another, they will periodically request a copy of each other's Browse Lists. That's how the lists get merged across subnets.

The LMB should also remember which Browse List entries were received from nodes on the local LAN, and which came from the DMB. The LMB is *authoritative* with regard to local nodes, but it must rely upon the DMB for everything else. If there are ever any conflicts, the LMB will favor its own local constituents.

Responding to requests for a copy of the Browse List

The LMB may receive queries for a copy of the Browse List from local Backup Browsers, the Domain Master Browser, or from everyday Consumers who simply want to display the Network Neighborhood.

Participating in Local Elections

Like all Browser nodes, the LMB listens on the *workgroup*`<1E>` name so that it can participate in local Browser Elections.

Quite the busy civil servant.

20.3 Becoming a Backup Browser

A Potential Browser becomes a Backup Browser in one of three ways.

1. If the number of Providers on the local LAN exceeds a predefined limit, the Local Master Browser will select an available Potential Browser and promote it to Backup Browser.

    In theory, the LMB will appoint new Backup Browsers as needed to prevent itself from getting overloaded. Some documentation says that there should be one Backup Browser for every 32 Providers on the local LAN. Other documentation says other things. In any case, the LMB can promote a Potential Browser by sending a `BecomeBackup Browser` Frame.

    The `BecomeBackup Browser` Frame is another NBT broadcast datagram. In this case, it is sent to the group name *workgroup*<1E>, which means that all of the Potential Browsers will receive the message. The NetBIOS machine name of the node to be promoted is carried within the message.

2. A Potential Browser may decide on its own to become a Backup Browser. It simply announces its new status to the LMB by sending out a `HostAnnouncement Browser Frame` with a specific flag set. (The flags will be described when we go into detail about the `NetServerEnum2` RAP call.)

    Note that the Backup Browser uses a `HostAnnouncement` to make itself known. That's the same thing a Provider does to announce services. In fact, the Backup Browser *is* announcing itself as a Provider: it provides access to the Browse List. This stuff gets mighty recursive at times.

    According to the Leach/Naik Browser Internet Draft, an LMB that loses a new election should demote itself to Backup Browser status instead of dropping all the way down to a Potential Browser. The theory is that it is the most likely to be promoted should something bad happen to the new LMB, so it should maintain a fairly up-to-date copy of the Browse List to ensure a smooth transition.

3. Browser roles are cumulative so, to be pedantic, the LMB is also a Backup Browser.

At the time that the Browse Service was created it may have been reasonable to be concerned about one computer bearing the brunt of all of the client requests, particularly on a LAN with a very large number of nodes. Today's computers are capable of handling the load *and* their own work without breaking a sweat. It would take an effort (a purposeful Denial of Service attack, for instance) to cause the LMB any real trouble.

20.4   Crossing the Street with the DMB

Browser roles are cumulative, as we keep saying, so the Domain Master Browser is also the Local Master Browser for its subnet and it must handle all of the duties of an LMB. One such duty is participation in local Browser Elections. Of course, since the DMB is the *appointed* workgroup president it is expected to win the election — which it will do because the election is rigged. More on that when we go into detail regarding the election process.

The DMB listens on the *workgroup*`<1B>` name for (unicast) `Master-Announcement` messages from Local Master Browsers on remote subnets. It keeps track of these announcements and, periodically, contacts the LMBs and asks for a new copy of their local Browse List. The DMB merges the local Browse Lists collected from the various LMBs (including its own) into a master Browse List for the entire workgroup. The LMBs, in turn, will periodically query the DMB and add the remote entries collected in the workgroup master list to their own local Browse Lists. That's how local LANs get a complete copy of the combined workgroup Browse List.

The key to making this all work is the NBT Name Service, the **N**et**B**IOS **N**ame **S**erver (NBNS) in particular. The scattered LMBs use the NBNS (aka WINS server) to find the *workgroup*`<1B>` name, which is registered by the DMB. Without that, cross-subnet browsing would not work because the LMBs would be unable to announce themselves to the DMB, and would also be unable to request copies of the DMB's master list.

Note that B mode NBT nodes do not talk to the NBNS and, therefore, cannot find a remote Domain Master Browser. That's okay, though, because the scope of a B mode NBT LAN is limited to the local IP subnet anyway. Even if a B node could do cross-subnet browsing, it wouldn't (shouldn't) be able to connect to a server on a remote subnet.

In contrast, P nodes *must* transact *all* of their Browse Service business directly with the Domain Master Browser. The NBT Scope available to a P node is the set of names it can resolve via the NBNS. It doesn't do broadcasts, so the only Browser node that it can find is the DMB because the DMB is the only Browser node with a name that can be properly resolved via the NBNS. M and H nodes have the best of both worlds. They can send broadcasts *and* use the NBNS to resolve names.

Now that you have a basic idea of how this stuff works, think about what might have happened if Microsoft had correctly implemented group name handling in their WINS implementation and had also provided a working **N**etBIOS **D**atagram **D**istribution Server (NBDD). If they had done that, the broadcast datagrams used by the Browse Service — the announcements and election requests and such — would have reached the entire extent of the virtual NetBIOS LAN even if it spanned multiple subnets, even across WAN links and such. For better or worse, that would have changed the design and workings of the Browse Service entirely.

20.5 Elections

Browser elections are fun to watch. They have more in common with the noise and chaos of a party convention than with an actual election. The process is something of a shouting match, and the winner is the last one left shouting at the end.

Starting an election is a lot like picking a fight. Some punk computer somewhere on the LAN sends out a challenge, called a `RequestElection Browser Frame`. The message lets all of the Potential Browsers on the LAN know how tough the sender thinks it is (see Figure 20.4). The Potential Browsers respond by broadcasting their own `RequestElection` messages, also declaring how tough they think they are. The Potential Browsers don't really want to fight about it, though, so when they hear a `RequestElection` message from a node that is tougher than they are, they shut up. The specifics of the election criteria will be covered when the we study the browser frames in detail.

Just to complete the fighting analogy, each transmission of a `RequestElection` message during a browser election is called a "round." There are typically four rounds because the eventual winner of the election will repeat

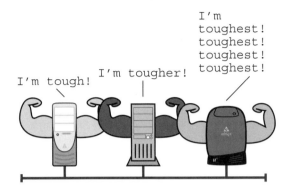

Figure 20.4:   *Browser elections*

The Potential Browsers announce their strengths by sending a `RequestElection` message. The strongest candidate must repeat its announcement several times (typically four) to ensure that all challengers have acquiesced.

its `RequestElection` message four times to ensure that all of its challengers have given up. Once the winner is confident in its victory it sends a `LocalMasterAnnouncement Browser Frame`, which has two purposes. First, it lets all of the Backup Browsers know where to find the LMB. Second, the `LocalMasterAnnouncement` message announces the end of the election. Any further `RequestElection` messages heard on the wire will signal a new Browser Election.

Elections can be forced by sending an empty `RequestElection Browser Frame` — that is, one that announces the sender as being a complete wimp. All of the Potential Browsers on the LAN will have better credentials, so they will try to respond. Elections may be called when a Consumer can no longer find the LMB, or when a new node joins the workgroup and thinks that it has what it takes to be the LMB. When a Domain Master Browser starts up, for instance, it will always call for elections (since it *must* take over the role of LMB).

The `RequestElection` message is another NBT broadcast datagram. It is meant to be sent to the *workgroup*`<1E>` name but it turns out that many clients will accept this message if it is sent to the `MSBROWSE<01>` name as well, so you can actually cause all of the workgroups on a single subnet to hold elections at the same time.

21

Infrastructure: The Mailslot and Named Pipe Abstractions

Nothing lasts longer than
a provisional arrangement.

— Unknown (thanks to Olaf Barthel)

We touched on the Mailslots and Named Pipes back in Section 16.4.1 on page 321, and then we pulled our collective hand away really fast as if those subjects were much too hot to handle. We will need to be brave and give them another go, though, because the Browse Service relies on them. Sorry 'bout that, folks.

Mailslots and Named Pipes are like the wiring and plumbing in an old house.[1] It probably all made sense when it was installed, but over the years new construction has built upon the old. Some parts have been reused, some replaced, and other bits and pieces recycled in ways that make it seem as though no one remembers their original purpose. As long as it looks good on the surface (and isn't a fire hazard), it's okay.

And it really is okay. The old stuff has held up remarkably well. So well, in fact, that it is sometimes forgotten — which is exactly why we need to take a closer look at it.

---

1. "Old" is a relative term. In Minnesota, a 100-year-old house is considered old. In cities like Charleston, SC, the houses go back 300 years or so... and that's nothing compared to what they've got in places like Japan, Europe, the Middle East, etc.

The goal here is to provide a basic understanding of the Named Pipe and Mailslot concepts. We won't be going in too deep. If you want, you can find more detail in the X/Open book *IPC Mechanisms for SMB*. Named Pipes and Mailslots are nifty constructs, and are worthy of further study when you have the time.

21.1   Meet the Plumbing: Named Pipes

As you are by now well aware, SMB is a protocol that implements a network filesystem and, of course, a network filesystem is the result of extrapolating the general concepts that lie behind a disk-based filesystem. The difference is that the network variety uses higher level protocols to stretch things out across a network.

Some disk-based filesystems (such as those used in Unix and its kin) can handle the inclusion of objects that aren't really files at all, but which — through the use of some clever abstraction layers — can be made to look and work like files. For those familiar with such things, common examples include device nodes, the contents of /proc, and Named Pipes.

We are interested in the latter.

A Named Pipe is, at its heart, an interprocess communications channel. It allows two programs running independently to exchange messages. The SMB protocol, as you have already guessed, provides support for Named Pipes, but it can stretch them out over the network so that programs on different machines can talk to one another.

Figure 21.1:   *Named Pipes*

An SMB named pipe is an abstraction that provides two-way communication between processes on remote nodes. The pipe is given a name ("\PIPE\DREAM", in this example) so that it can be easily identified by programs that wish to use it.

A Named Pipe is "named" so that it can be identified by the programs that want to use it. It is a "pipe" because data is shoved in at one end and then falls gracefully out the other. CIFS Named Pipes have some additional qualities:

They are transported over TCP.

The use of SMB (over NBT) over TCP means that Named Pipe transactions are reliable.

They are built on SMBtrans transactions.

SMBtrans allows for data transfers up to 64K in size, per transaction.

They are bi-directional.

As with other protocols that we have studied, data may be sent and received over the same connection.

They are filesystem abstractions.

CIFS Named Pipes can be opened, closed, read from, and written to.

These features make CIFS Named Pipes ideal for transporting network function calls, which is one of the key ways (but not the only way) they are used. The **R**emote **A**dministration **P**rotocol (RAP) and Microsoft's **R**emote **P**rocedure **C**all implementation (MS-RPC) are both built on top of Named Pipes.

Although they are filesystem abstractions, CIFS Named Pipes are kept separate from the real files and directories made available by the SMB Server Service. They are placed in a special share — the IPC$ share — which is "hidden." You won't be able to browse to it using the Windows Network Neighborhood tool. If you know it's there, however, you can access it just as you would any other SMB share — specifically, by sending a SESSION SETUP followed by a TREE CONNECT.

Hidden Expense Alert

Share names that end with a dollar sign ('$') are considered "hidden" shares. It is expected that client software will not display hidden share names unless specifically asked to do so. Note that it is the client, not the server, that takes care of hiding the hidden shares. Samba's smbclient *tool and the jCIFS* List.java *utility will both happily display hidden share names for you.*

Named Pipes within the `IPC$` share have names that match the following format:

`\PIPE\`**`pipename`**

where *pipename* is determined by the service that created the pipe. Since they are filesystem abstractions, it would be logical to assume that the full name of a Named Pipe (in UNC format) would look something like this:

`\\`**`server`**`\IPC$\PIPE\`**`pipename`**

As it turns out, however, the DOS, OS/2, and Windows functions that manipulate Named Pipes abbreviate the name by removing "`\IPC$`" from the string, which gives:

`\\`**`server`**`\PIPE\`**`pipename`**

Named Pipes are created on the SMB server side by applications and tools that are willing to provide specialized services. The architecture is quite analogous to services that register NetBIOS names to make themselves available, it's just that there are more intervening protocol layers which provide additional features. For example, Named Pipes can take advantage of the SMB authentication and MAC signing mechanisms.

Microsoft has created several services that use Named Pipes, but the set of services that are actually available will vary depending upon the host OS and/or the CIFS implementation. Luke K. C. Leighton's book *DCE/RPC over SMB: Samba and Windows NT Domain Internals* (which we have referenced often) lists several known pipes that offer services based on MS-RPC.

Our particular interest, however, is with the specific Named Pipe that will connect us to the **R**emote **A**dministration **P**rotocol service. That pipe is:

`\PIPE\LANMAN`

We will be using it a little later on, when we dig into the one RAP function that is commonly used by the Browser Service: the `NetServerEnum2` function.

...and that is really all we have to say about CIFS Named Pipes.

There is, of course, a lot more that *could* be said. Named Pipes can be used in a variety of ways to support a variety of different kinds of operations. Our goal, however, is to explore the Browse Service, so the scope of this discussion is purposfully limited.

21.2 The Mailslot Metaphor

CIFS supports two kinds of Mailslots :

Class 1: Reliable

Class 1 Mailslots are a whole heck of a lot like Named Pipes. Class 1 messages are packed into an SMBtrans SMB, and then sent across the network using TCP. The only real difference is that Class 1 Mailslot calls indicate only success or failure. They do not return any other results.

We won't be paying any attention to Class 1 Mailslots, because they are not used by the Browse Service.

Class 2: Unreliable and Broadcast

Class 2 Mailslots are a whole 'nother kettle of bananafish. On the surface, they look like Named Pipes and Class 1 Mailslots, but that's just because the interface was designed to be somewhat consistent.

Below the surface, Class 2 Mailslot messages are sent using the NBT Datagram Service. That means that the underlying transport is UDP, not TCP. It also means that Class 2 Mailslot messages can be broadcast or multicast to the local LAN. Another difference is that Class 2 Mailslot messages are simply sent. No result (success, failure, or otherwise) is returned.

Mailslots, like Named Pipes, exist within the `IPC$` share. Mailslot names have a familiar format, as shown below.

`\MAILSLOT\`*mailslotname*

The general form of a Mailslot name. Similar to the convention used for Named Pipes.

`\MAILSLOT\BROWSE`

The Mailslot name used by the Windows NT Browse Service.

`\MAILSLOT\LANMAN`

The Mailslot name used by the older LAN Manager Browse Service.

The Browse Service uses Class 2 Mailslots extensively. With the exception of the `NetServerEnum2` RAP call, all Browse Service announcements and requests are sent using Class 2 Mailslots.

In general, if the destination is local, a Browse Service Mailslot message will be sent as a broadcast at the IP level. Unicast UDP datagrams are used if the destination is on a remote subnet (e.g., a remote DMB). Broadcast messages that contain an NBT group name in the DESTINATION_NAME field are considered Multicast at the NBT level. If the DESTINATION_NAME is unique, the message may still be broadcast to avoid the need to resolve the name using the NBT Name Service. As suggested in Figure 21.2, the receiver of a broadcast datagram should discard the message if it is not listening on the DESTINATION_NAME or the given Mailslot name.

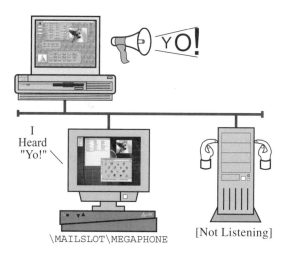

Figure 21.2:   *Class 2 Mailslots*

Class 2 Mailslot messages may be broadcast, multicast (NBT group), or unicast. If a message is sent as a broadcast or multicast datagram, all of the NBT nodes on the LAN will receive it. Those that are not listening on the specified Mailslot (\MAILSLOT\MEGAPHONE, in this case) or on the specified NBT name should discard it.

Class 2 Mailslot messages are kind of quirky. Even though they use the NBT Datagram Service, they are formatted as SMB_COM_TRANSACTION (that is, SMBtrans) messages. That's right: SMB over UDP. Go figure. This may be the result of someone being overly enthusiastic about reusing existing code. In any case, it means that we will be learning how to format an SMBtrans message.

It's Not a Bug It's a Feature Alert

The one-way nature of Mailslot messages has an interesting side-effect, which is this: All Browse Service Mailslot messages are sent to UDP port 138.

The reason for this seemingly incorrect behavior is that the receiver's response to a Mailslot message is not really a reply. It is a "response" in the sense of "stimulus-response." When a browser node receives one of the Browse Service Mailslot Messages, it may react by sending messages of its own. In many cases, those messages must be multicast to a NetBIOS group name, so sending them to the source port of the original "stimulus" datagram would simply not work.

(You're getting to love this stuff, aren't you...)

The upshot is that the only way to properly implement the Browse Service (and Class 2 Mailslots in general) is to run a daemon that listens on UDP/138.

22

The Talk on the Street

> You are a cornflakes-vert.
>
> — Something my friend Kathy
> said to me in High School
> (and I still don't get it)

Enough descriptive hyperbole. Let's get to work.

SMBtrans is an SMB message with the SMB_COM_TRANSACTION command byte specified in the header. It is also the transport for all Browse Service messages. The on-the-wire layout of the body of the SMBtrans, in C-style notation, is as follows:

```
typedef struct
  {
  uchar WordCount;              /* SetupCount + 14            */
  struct                        /* SMB-layer parameters       */
    {
    ushort TotalParamCount;     /* Total param bytes to send  */
    ushort TotalDataCount;      /* Total data bytes to send   */
    ushort MaxParameterCount;   /* Max param bytes to return  */
    ushort MaxDataCount;        /* Max data bytes to return   */
    ushort MaxSetupCount;       /* Max setup words to return  */
    ushort Flags;               /* Explained below            */
    ulong  Timeout;             /* Operation timeout          */
    ushort Reserved;            /* Unused word                */
    ushort ParameterCount;      /* Param bytes in this msg    */
    ushort ParameterOffset;     /* Param offset within SMB    */
    ushort DataCount;           /* Data bytes in this msg     */
    ushort DataOffset;          /* Data offset within SMB     */
```

```
    ushort SetupCount;                /* Setup word count        */
    ushort Setup[];                   /* Setup words             */
    } Words;
  ushort ByteCount;                   /* Number of SMB data bytes */
  struct                              /* SMB-layer data          */
    {
    uchar Name[];                     /* Transaction service name */
    uchar Pad[];                      /* Pad to word boundary    */
    uchar Parameters[];               /* Parameter bytes         */
    uchar Pad1[];                     /* Pad to word boundary    */
    uchar Data[];                     /* Data bytes              */
    } Bytes;
  } smb_Trans_Req;
```

We can, in fact, make some sense of all that... really we can.

22.1   Making Sense of SMBtrans

As has already been pointed out, we are dealing with layered protocols and
layered protocols can cause some terminology confusion. For example, earlier
in the book SMB messages were described as having a header, a parameter
section, and a data section (and there was a cute picture of an insect to highlight
the anatomy). SMB transactions — half a protocol layer up — also have parameters and data. The terms get recycled, as demonstrated by the structure
presented above in which the `Parameters[]` and `Data[]` fields are both
carried within the `SMB_DATA` block (the `Bytes`) of the SMB message.

SMB transaction messages generally represent some sort of network
function call. In an SMB transaction:

- The *Parameters* represent the values passed directly to the function that
  was called.

- The *Data* represents any indirect values, such as objects indicated by
  pointers passed as parameters (i.e. objects passed by reference).

That's a very general description, and it may be slightly inaccurate in
practice. It works well enough in theory, though, and it provides a conceptual
foothold. If you want, you can go one step further and think of the
`SetupCount` and `Setup[]` fields as the transaction header.

Okay, now that we have that out of the way, here's what the SMBtrans
fields are all about:

SMB Parameters

TotalParamCount

You may recall from earlier discussions that the SMBtrans transaction has the ability to carry a total payload of 64 Kbytes — potentially much more than the SMB buffer size will allow. It does this by sending zero or more secondary transaction messages which contain the additional parameters and/or data.

The `TotalParamCount` field indicates the *total* number of parameter bytes that the server should expect to receive over the course of the transaction. It may take multiple messages to get them all there.

TotalDataCount

Similar to the previous field, this indicates the total number of data bytes the server should expect to receive.

If you think about it, you will see that the theoretical SMBtrans data transfer limit is actually $2 \times (216 - 1)$. Both the `Parameter` and `Data` lengths are 16-bit values so, in theory, SMBtrans can send 128 Kbytes (minus two bytes), which is double the 64K we've been claiming.

MaxParameterCount, MaxDataCount, and MaxSetupCount

These fields let the client inform the server of the maximum number of `Parameter[]`, `Data[]`, and `Setup[]` bytes, respectively, that the client is willing to receive in the server's reply. These are total bytes for the transaction, not per-message bytes.

A note regarding the `MaxSetupCount` field: The X/Open documentation lists this as a 16-bit field, but in the Leach/Naik CIFS draft it is given as a single byte followed by a one-byte nul pad. Because the value is given in SMB byte order (and because it will not exceed 255), either way works.

Flags

There are two flags defined in this field, but they don't appear to be used much in Browser Protocol messages.

SMBtrans flags

Bit	Bitmask	Description
15–2	0xFFFC	**<Reserved>** (must be zero)
1	0x0002	If set, this is a one-way transaction and the server should not send a response. In theory, this bit should be set in all Class 2 Mailslot messages, but in packet captures this bit always seems to be clear.
0	0x0001	If set, it indicates that the client wishes to disconnect from the share indicated by the TID field in the SMB header when the transaction completes.
		Mailslot messages will have a zero TID value, so this bit should not be set. RAP calls always use the IPC$ share, which will have been opened using an earlier TREE CONNECT message. So, in theory, this bit *could* be set in RAP calls... but it was clear in all of the packets captured during testing.

Timeout

The documentation is scattered. The X/Open docs provide only a few words regarding this particular field. The SNIA doc has a small section (Section 3.2.9) that covers timeouts in general, and some additional information can be found in various places throughout each of those references.

The field indicates the number of milliseconds (1/1000ths of a second) that the *server* should wait for a transaction to complete. A value of zero indicates that the server should return immediately, sending an error code if it could not obtain required resources right away. A value of –1 indicates that the client is willing to have the server wait forever. The documentation doesn't make it clear, but the correct DOS error code in the case of a timeout is probably ERRSRV/ERRtimeout (0x02/0x0058).

ParameterCount

The number of bytes in the Parameter[] block of this message. Keep in mind that this may be lower than the TotalParamCount value. If it is, then the rest of the parameters will follow in secondary transaction messages.

ParameterOffset

The offset from the beginning of the SMB message at which the parameter block starts.

DataCount

The number of bytes in the `Data[]` block of this message. Once again, this may be lower than the `TotalDataCount` value. If so, the rest of the data will follow in additional messages.

DataOffset

The offset from the beginning of the SMB message at which the data block starts.

SetupCount

The number of setup *words*. As with the `MaxSetupCount` field, `SetupCount` is presented as an unsigned short in the X/Open document but is given as an unsigned byte followed by a one-byte pad in the Leach/Naik draft.

Setup[]

An array of 16-byte values used to "set up" the transaction (the transaction, not the function call). This might be considered the header portion of the transaction.

SMB Data

Name[]

The name of the Named Pipe or Mailslot to which the transaction is being sent (for example, "`\PIPE\LANMAN`").

Parameters[]

The marshalled parameters.

Data[]

The marshalled data. A little later on, we will carefully avoid explaining how the parameters and data get packaged.

Pad and Pad1

Some (but not all) clients and servers will add padding bytes (typically, but not necessarily, nul) to force word or longword alignment of the `Parameters[]` and `Data[]` sections. That really messes things up. You must:

- Be sure to use `ByteCount` to figure out how large the `SMB_DATA` section really is.

- Use `ParameterOffset` and `ParameterCount` to figure out where the transaction parameters begin and how many bytes there are.

- Use `DataOffset` and `DataCount` to figure out where the transaction data begins and how many bytes there are.

  Gotta love this stuff...

There is a lot more information in both the X/Open documentation and the Leach/Naik CIFS drafts. For some reason, specific details regarding SMBtrans were left out of the SNIA doc, although there is a discussion of Mailslots and Named Pipes (and the other transaction types are covered). All of the listed docs do explain how secondary transaction messages may be used to transfer `Setup[]`, `Parameter[]`, and/or `Data[]` blocks that are larger than the allowed SMB buffer size.

There are also some warnings given in the SNIA doc regarding variations in implementation. It seems you need to be careful with CIFS (no surprise there). See the last paragraph of Section 3.15.3 in the SNIA doc if'n your curious.

...but now it's time for some code.

Listing 22.1 is a bit dense, but it does a decent job of putting together an SMBtrans message from parts. It doesn't fill in the NBT or SMB headers, but there are code examples and descriptions elsewhere in the book that cover those issues. What it does do is provide a starting point for managing SMBtrans transactions, particularly those that might exceed the server's SMB buffer limit and need to be fragmented.

Listing 22.1: SMBtrans messages

```
typedef struct
  {
  ushort  SetupCount;          /* Setup word count           */
  ushort  *Setup;              /* Setup words                */
  ushort  Flags;               /* 0x1=Disconnect;0x2=oneway  */
  ulong   Timeout;             /* Server timeout in ms        */
  ushort  MaxParameterCount;   /* Max param bytes to return  */
  ushort  MaxDataCount;        /* Max data bytes to return   */
  ushort  MaxSetupCount;       /* Max setup words to return  */
  ushort  TotalParamCount;     /* Total param bytes to send  */
  ushort  TotalDataCount;      /* Total data bytes to send   */
  ushort  ParamsSent;          /* Parameters already sent    */
  ushort  DataSent;            /* Data already sent          */
  uchar   *Name;               /* Transaction service name   */
  uchar   *Parameters;         /* Parameter bytes            */
  uchar   *Data;               /* Data bytes                 */
  } smb_Transaction_Request;

int SetStr( uchar *dst, int offset, char *src )
  /* ------------------------------------------------- **
   * Quick function to copy a string into a buffer and
   * return the *total* length, including the terminating
   * nul byte.  Does *no* limit checking (bad).
   * Input: dst    - Destination buffer.
   *        offset - Starting point within destination.
   *        src    - Source string.
   * Output: Number of bytes transferred.
   * ------------------------------------------------- **
   */
  {
  int i;

  for( i = 0; '\0' != src[i]; i++ )
    dst[offset+i] = src[i];
  dst[offset+i] = '\0';

  return( i+1 );
  } /* SetStr */

int smb_TransRequest( uchar                    *bufr,
                      int                      bSize,
                      smb_Transaction_Request *Request )
  /* ------------------------------------------------- **
   * Format an SMBtrans request message.
   * ------------------------------------------------- **
   */
```

```
    {
    int    offset = 0;
    int    keep_offset;
    int    bcc_offset;
    int    result;
    int    i;

    /* See that we have enough room for the SMB-level params:
     * Setup + 14 bytes of SMB params + 2 bytes for Bytecount.
     */
    if( bSize < (Request->SetupCount + 14 + 2) )
      Fail( "Transaction buffer too small.\n" );

    /* Fill the SMB-level parameter block.
     */
    bufr[offset++] = (uchar)(Request->SetupCount + 14);
    smb_SetShort( bufr, offset, Request->TotalParamCount );
    offset += 2;
    smb_SetShort( bufr, offset, Request->TotalDataCount );
    offset += 2;
    smb_SetShort( bufr, offset, Request->MaxParameterCount);
    offset += 2;
    smb_SetShort( bufr, offset, Request->MaxDataCount );
    offset += 2;
    smb_SetShort( bufr, offset, Request->MaxSetupCount );
    offset += 2;
    smb_SetShort( bufr, offset, (Request->Flags & 0x0003) );
    offset += 2;
    smb_SetLong(  bufr, offset, Request->Timeout );
    offset += 4;
    smb_SetShort( bufr, offset, 0 );         /* Reserved word */
    offset += 2;
    keep_offset = offset;   /* Remember ParamCount location */
    offset += 8;                 /* Skip ahead to SetupCount. */
    smb_SetShort( bufr, offset, Request->SetupCount );
    offset += 2;
    for( i = 0; i < Request->SetupCount; i++ )
      {
      smb_SetShort( bufr, offset, Request->Setup[i] );
      offset += 2;
      }

    /* Fill the SMB-level data block...
     * We skip the ByteCount field until the end.
     */
    bcc_offset = offset;   /* Keep the Bytecount offset. */
    offset += 2;
```

```
/* We need to have enough room to specify the
 * pipe or mailslot.
 */
if( strlen( Request->Name ) >= (bSize - offset) )
  Fail( "No room for Transaction Name: %s\n",
        Request->Name );

/* Start with the pipe or mailslot name.
 */
offset += SetStr( bufr, offset, Request->Name );

/* Now figure out how many SMBtrans parameter bytes
 * we can copy, and copy them.
 */
result = bSize - offset;
if( result > Request->TotalParamCount )
  result = Request->TotalParamCount;
Request->ParamsSent = result;
if( result > 0 )
  (void)memcpy( &bufr[offset],
                Request->Parameters,
                result );
/* Go back and fill in Param Count and Param Offset.
 */
smb_SetShort( bufr, keep_offset, result );
keep_offset += 2;
smb_SetShort( bufr, keep_offset, SMB_HDR_SIZE + offset );
keep_offset += 2;
offset += result;

/* Now figure out how many SMBtrans data bytes we
 * can copy, and copy them.
 */
result = bSize - offset;
if( result > Request->TotalDataCount )
  result = Request->TotalDataCount;
Request->DataSent = result;
if( result > 0 )
  (void)memcpy( &bufr[offset],
                Request->Data,
                result );
/* Go back and fill in Data Count and Data Offset.
 */
smb_SetShort( bufr, keep_offset, result );
keep_offset += 2;
smb_SetShort( bufr, keep_offset, SMB_HDR_SIZE + offset );
```

```
    keep_offset += 2;           /* not really needed any more */
    offset += result;

    /* Go back and fill in the byte count.
     */
    smb_SetShort( bufr, bcc_offset, offset - (bcc_offset+2) );

    /* Done.
     */
    return( offset );
    } /* smb_TransRequest */
```

The smb_Transaction_Request structure in the listing differs from the wire-format version. The former is designed to keep track of a transaction while it is being built and until it has been completely transmitted. With a little more code, it should be able to compose secondary transaction messages too. Fortunately, all of the Browse Service requests are small enough to fit into a typical SMB buffer, so you shouldn't have to worry about sending secondary SMB transaction messages. At least not right away. On the other hand, a Browse Server's reply to a NetServerEnum2 call can easily exceed the SMB buffer size so you may need to know how to rebuild a fragmented response. With that in mind, we will explain how multi-part messages work when we cover NetServerEnum2.

It is probably worth noting, at this point, just how many layers of abstraction we're dealing with. If you look at a packet capture of an NetServerEnum2 request, you'll find that it is way the heck down at the bottom of a large pile:

```
Ethernet II
+ IP
  + TCP
    + NBT Session Service
      + SMB (SMB_COM_TRANSACTION)
        + SMB Pipe Protocol
          + Microsoft Windows Remote Administration Protocol
            + NetServerEnum2
```

It sure is getting deep around here...

All those layers make things seem more complicated than they really are, but if we chip away at it one small workable piece at a time it will all be easier to understand.

22.2 Browse Service Mailslot Messages

The vast bulk of the Browser Protocol consists of Mailslot messages. These are also relatively simple, which is why we are starting with them instead of RAP. Still, there are a lot of layers to go through in order to get a Mailslot message out onto the wire. Let's get chipping...

The NBT layer

Browser Mailslot messages are transported by the NBT Datagram Service, which was covered in Chapter 5 on page 115. We will ignore most of the fields at the NBT layer, since their values are host specific (things like source IP address and **S**ending **N**ode **T**ype). The important fields, from our persective, are:

```
NBT_Datagram
  {
  MsgType         = <unicast, multicast, broadcast, etc.>
  SourceName      = <NBT Source Name>
  DestinationName = <NBT Destination Name>
  UserData        = <The SMBTrans Message>
  }
```

The values assigned to the `SourceName` and `DestinationName` fields may be written as *machine*<xx> or *workgroup*<yy>, where *machine* and *workgroup* are variable and dependent upon the environment.

The `SourceName` field will contain the name registered by the service sending the request. In practice, this is either the Mailslot Service name (*machine*<00>) or the Server Service name (*machine*<20>). Both have been seen in testing. In most cases it does not matter.

`UserData` will be indicated indirectly by detailing the SMBtrans and Mailslot layers.

The SMB layer

The NBT Datagram Service is connectionless, and Class 2 Mailslots don't send replies. At the SMB level, however, the header fields are used to maintain state or return some sort of error code or security token. Such values have no meaning in a Mailslot message, so almost all of the SMB header fields are pointless in this context. Only the first five bytes are actually used. That would be the `"\xffSMB"` string and the one byte command code, which is always `SMB_COM_TRANSACTION` (0x25).

The rest are all zero. We will not bother to specify the contents of the SMB header in our discussion.

The SMBtrans layer

The SMBtrans transaction fields will be filled in via the `smb_Transaction_Request` structure from Listing 22.1. That way you can map the discussions directly to the code.

For example, if the `Data` block contains ten bytes, the `TotalDataCount` would be filled in like so:

```
smb_Transaction_Request
  {
  TotalDataCount = 10
  }
```

The `SetupCount` and `Setup` fields are constant across all Browser Mailslot messages. The values are specified here so that they don't have to be specified for every message:

```
SetupCount = 3
Setup[]
  {
  0x0001, (Mailslot Opcode   = Mailslot Write)
  0x0001, (Transact Priority = Normal)
  0x0002, (Mailslot Class    = Unreliable/Bcast)
  }
```

Finally, any remaining fields (the values of which have not been otherwise specified or explicitly ignored) should be assumed zero (NULL, nul, nada, non, nerp, nyet, etc.). For example, the `MaxParameterCount`, `MaxDataCount`, and `MaxSetupCount` fields will not be listed because they are always zero in Class 2 Mailslot messages.

The Mailslot Layer

Browser Mailslot messages are carried in the `Data[]` block of the SMBtrans message. They each have their own structure, which will be described using C-style notation.

A few more general notes about Mailslot messages before we forge ahead...

■ Browser Mailslots don't use the SMBtrans `Parameters[]` block, so the `TotalParamCount` is always zero.

- The `Mailslot OpCode` in the `Setup[]` field is set to `0x0001`, which indicates a `Mailslot Write` operation. There are no other operations defined for Mailslots, which kinda makes it pointless. This field has nothing to do with the `OpCode` contained within the Mailslot message itself (described below), which identifies the Browse Service function being performed.

- The `Transact Priority` in the `Setup[]` is supposed to contain a value in the range 0..9, where 9 is the highest. The X/Open docs say that if two messages arrive (practically) simultaniously, the higher priority message should be processed first. The SNIA doc says that this field is ignored. The latter is probably correct, but it doesn't matter much. Most of the captures taken in testing show a priority value of 0 or 1.

- The `Mailslot Class`, also in the `Setup[]`, should always contain `0x0002`, indicating a Class 2 Mailslot. The SNIA doc says that this field is ignored too.[1]

Yet one more additional general note regarding Mailslot messages: the first byte of the `Data` block is always an `OpCode` indicating which of the `\MAILSLOT\BROWSE` (or `\MAILSLOT\LANMAN`) functions is being called. Here's a list of the available functions:

OpCode	Function
1	HostAnnouncement
2	AnnouncementRequest
8	RequestElection
9	GetBackupListRequest
10	GetBackupListResponse
11	BecomeBackupRequest
12	DomainAnnouncement
13	MasterAnnouncement
14	ResetBrowserState
15	LocalMasterAnnouncement

---

1. It is possible that Class 1 Mailslots are not used. At all.

The next step is to describe each of those functions.
Let's get to it...

22.2.1 *Announcement Request*

The AnnouncementRequest frame is fairly simple, so it's a good place to
start. The message structure (carried in the smb_Trans_Req.Bytes.Data
section) looks like this:

```
struct
  {
  uchar  OpCode;
  uchar  Unused;
  uchar *ResponseName;
  } AnnouncementRequest;
```

which means that the AnnouncementRequest frame is made up of an
OpCode, an unused byte, and a character string. (The unused byte may have
been reserved for use as a flags field at one time.)
    The following values are assigned:

```
NBT_Datagram
  {
  MsgType        = 0x11 (DIRECT_GROUP DATAGRAM)
  SourceName     = machine<00>
  DestinationName = workgroup<00>
  }
smb_Transaction_Request
  {
  TotalDataCount = 3 + strlen( ResponseName )
  Name           = "\MAILSLOT\BROWSE"
  Data
    {
    OpCode       = 0x02 (AnnouncementRequest)
    ResponseName = <NetBIOS machine name, no suffix>
    }
  }
```

This frame may also be sent to the MSBROWSE<01> name to request
responses from LMBs for foreign workgroups.
    The TotalDataCount is calculated by adding:

- one byte for the `OpCode`,
- one for the `Unused` byte,
- the string length of the `ResponseName` field, and
- one byte for the `ResponseName` nul terminator.

Don't forget those string terminators.

There is no direct reply to this request, so the `SourceName` and `ResponseName` fields in the packet are ignored. Providers that receive this message are expected to broadcast a `HostAnnouncement` frame (described next) to re-announce their services. They are supposed to wait a random amount of time between 0 and 30 seconds before sending the announcement, to avoid network traffic congestion. In testing, however, many systems ignored this message.

Under the older LAN Manager style browsing, a similar message was sent to the `\MAILSLOT\LANMAN` Mailslot. The LAN Manager `Announce-Request` and `Announce` frame formats are described in Section 5.3.3 of the X/Open doc *IPC Mechanisms for SMB*.

22.2.2 *Host Announcement*

The `HostAnnouncement` is a bit more complicated than the `Announce-mentRequest`. Here's its structure:

```
struct
  {
  uchar  Opcode;
  uchar  UpdateCount;
  ulong  Periodicity;
  uchar *ServerName;
  uchar  OSMajorVers;
  uchar  OSMinorVers;
  ulong  ServerType;
  uchar  BroMajorVers;
  uchar  BroMinorVers;
  ushort Signature;
  uchar *Comment;
  } HostAnnouncement;
```

...and here's how it all pans out:

```
NBT_Datagram
  {
  MsgType          = 0x11 (DIRECT_GROUP DATAGRAM)
  SourceName       = machine<00>
  DestinationName  = workgroup<1D>
  }
smb_Transaction_Request
  {
  TotalDataCount   = 18 + strlen( ServerName + Comment )
  Name             = "\MAILSLOT\BROWSE"
  Data
    {
    OpCode         = 0x01 (HostAnnouncement)
    UpdateCount    = <Incremented after each announcement>
    Periodicity    = <Time until next announcement, in ms>
    ServerName     = <NetBIOS machine name, no suffix>
    OSMajorVers    = 4 <Windows OS version to mimic>
    OSMinorVers    = 5 <Windows OS point version to mimic>
    ServerType     = <Discussion below>
    BroMajorVers   = 15
    BroMinorVers   = 1
    Signature      = 0xaa55
    Comment        = <Server description, max 43 bytes>
    }
  }
```

That needs a once-over.

The announcement is broadcast at the IP level, but the Destination-Name is the local LMB name so the message should only be picked up by the Local Master. Other nodes could, in theory, listen in and keep their own local Browse List copies up-to-date.

The Leach/Naik Browser Draft says that the UpdateCount should be zero and should be ignored by recipients. In practice, it appears that many systems increment that counter for each HostAnnouncement frame that they send. No harm done.

The Periodicity field announces the amount of time, in milliseconds, that the sender plans to wait until it sends another HostAnnouncement frame. As described earlier, the initial period is one minute, but it doubles for each announcement until it would exceed 12 minutes, at which point it is pegged at 12 minutes. In theory, the LMB should remove a host from the Browse List if it has not heard an update from that host after 3 periods have elapsed. In practice, some systems get this value wrong so the LMB should wait 36 minutes.

The `ServerType` field is a complex bitmap. We will dissect it later, as it is also used by the `NetServerEnum2` RAP call.

The Browser version number (15.1) and the `Signature` field are specified in the Leach/Naik Browser draft. Some Windows systems (particularly the Windows 9x family) use a Browser version number of 21.4. No one, it seems, knows why and it doesn't appear that there are any protocol differences between the two versions.

22.2.3 *Election Request*

The `RequestElection` frame is used to start or participate in a Browser Election. It looks like this:

```
struct
  {
  uchar  Opcode;
  uchar  Version;
  ulong  Criteria;
  ulong  UpTime;
  ulong  Reserved;
  uchar *ServerName;
  } RequestElection;
```

In its simplest form, the `RequestElection` can be filled in with zeros. This gives it the lowest possible election criteria. All Potential Browsers in the same workgroup on the same LAN will be able to out-bid the zero-filled request, so a full-scale election will ensue as all Potential Browsers are eligible to participate.

```
NBT_Datagram
  {
  MsgType          = 0x11 (DIRECT_GROUP DATAGRAM)
  SourceName       = machine<00>
  DestinationName = workgroup<1E>
  }
smb_Transaction_Request
  {
  TotalDataCount   = 15
  Name             = "\MAILSLOT\BROWSE"
  Data
    {
    OpCode         = 0x08 (RequestElection)
    }
  }
```

In testing, it was discovered that some Potential Browsers are willing to receive `RequestElection` frames on just about any registered NetBIOS name, including the `MSBROWSE<01>` name.

Once the election gets going, the particpants will all try to out-vote their competition. The details of the election process are convoluted, so they will be set aside for just a little while longer. In the meantime, here is a complete election message, with election criteria filled in.

```
NBT_Datagram
  {
  MsgType          = 0x11 (DIRECT_GROUP DATAGRAM)
  SourceName       = machine<00>
  DestinationName  = workgroup<1E>
  }
smb_Transaction_Request
  {
  TotalDataCount   = 15 + strlen( ServerName )
  Name             = "\MAILSLOT\BROWSE"
  Data
    {
    OpCode         = 0x08 (RequestElection)
    Version        = 1
    Criteria       = <Another complex bitmap>
    UpTime         = <Time since last reboot, in milliseconds>
    ServerName     = <NetBIOS machine name, no suffix>
    }
  }
```

The `Criteria` bitmap will be covered along with the election details. Basically, though, it is read as an unsigned long integer and higher values "win."

22.2.4 *Get Backup List Request*

Another simple one. The message looks like this:

```
struct
  {
  uchar OpCode;
  uchar ReqCount;
  ulong Token;
  } GetBackupListRequest;
```

The Ethereal Network Protocol Analyzer and its many authors should be given a good heaping helping of appreciation just about now. The primary reference for the Browse Service data structures is the expired Leach/Naik Browser Internet Draft, but that document was a draft and is now expired. It cannot be expected that it will be completely accurate. It doesn't include the ReqCount field in its description, and it lists the Token as an unsigned short. That doesn't match what's on the wire. Thankfully, Ethereal knows better.

```
NBT_Datagram
  {
  MsgType           = 0x11 (DIRECT_GROUP DATAGRAM)
  SourceName        = machine<00>
  DestinationName = workgroup<1D>
  }
smb_Transaction_Request
  {
  TotalDataCount  = 6
  Name            = "\MAILSLOT\BROWSE"
  Data
    {
    OpCode          = 0x09 (GetBackupListRequest)
    ReqCount        = <Number of browsers requested>
    Token           = <Whatever>
    }
  }
```

The ReqCount field lets the LMB know how large a list of Backup Browsers the client (the Consumer) would like to receive.

The Token field is echoed back by the LMB when it sends the Get-BackupListResponse. Echoing back the Token is supposed to let the Consumer match the response to the request. This is necessary because the SourceName in the GetBackupListResponse is generally the LMB's machine name, so there is nothing in the response that indicates the workgroup. If the Consumer is trying to query multiple workgroups it could easily lose track.

22.2.5 *Get Backup List Response*

This message is sent in response (but not as a reply) to a GetBackupList-Request. The structure is fairly straightforward:

```
struct
  {
  uchar  OpCode;
  uchar  BackupCount;
  ulong  Token;
  uchar *BackupList;
  } GetBackupListResponse;

NBT_Datagram
  {
  MsgType         = 0x10 (DIRECT_UNIQUE DATAGRAM)
  SourceName      = machine<00>
  DestinationName = <Source name from the request>
  }
smb_Transaction_Request
  {
  TotalDataCount  = 7 + <length of BackupList>
  Name            = "\MAILSLOT\BROWSE"
  Data
    {
    OpCode        = 0x0A (GetBackupListResponse)
    BackupCount   = <Number of browser names returned>
    Token         = <Echo of the request Token>
    BackupList    = <List of Backup Browsers, nul-delimited>
    }
  }
```

At the IP level this message is unicast, and at the NBT level it is sent as a DIRECT_UNIQUE DATAGRAM. This is the closest thing to a Mailslot "reply" that you'll see.

The Token is a copy of the Token that was sent in the GetBackup-List Request that triggered the response. The BackupCount value represents the number of names listed in the BackupList field, which may be less than the number requested.

The BackupList will contain a string of nul-*delimited* substrings. For example, you might get something like this:

```
Data
  {
  OpCode        = 0x0A (GetBackupListResponse)
  BackupCount   = 2
  Token         = 0x61706C65
  BackupList    = "STEFFOND\0CONRAD"
  }
```

which indicates that nodes STEFFOND and CONRAD are both Backup Browsers (and one of them may also be the LMB) for the workgroup. Oh... that string is, of course, nul-terminated as well. Note that you can't use a normal strlen() call to calculate the length of the BackupList. It would just return the length of the first name.

22.2.6 *Local Master Announcement*

The LocalMasterAnnouncement is broadcast by the Local Master Browser. Other nodes, particularly Backup Browsers, can listen for this message and use it to keep track of the whereabouts of the LMB service. If the Local Master Browser for a workgroup hears another node announce itself as the LMB for the same workgroup, then it can call for a new election.

This message is also used to end a Browser Election. The winner declares itself by sending a LocalMasterAnnouncement frame.

The LocalMasterAnnouncement is identical in structure to the HostAnnouncement frame except for its OpCode:

```
smb_Transaction_Request
  {
  Data
    {
    OpCode = 0x0F (LocalMasterAnnouncement)
    }
  }
```

The Leach/Naik draft says that LMBs do not need to send HostAnnouncement frames because the LocalMasterAnnouncement accomplishes the same thing. The real reason that the LMB doesn't need to send HostAnnouncement frames is that HostAnnouncement frames are sent *to the LMB*, and there's no reason for an LMB to announce itself to itself.

22.2.7 *Master Announcement*

The MasterAnnouncement is sent by the LMB to the DMB to let the DMB know that the LMB exists. The message contains the OpCode field and the SMB Server Service name of the LMB. The Server Service name will be registered with the NBNS, so the DMB will be able to look it up as needed.

```
struct
  {
  uchar  OpCode;
  uchar *ServerName;
  } MasterAnnouncement;


NBT_Datagram
  {
  MsgType         = 0x10 (DIRECT_UNIQUE DATAGRAM)
  SourceName      = machine<00>
  DestinationName = workgroup<1B>
  }
smb_Transaction_Request
  {
  TotalDataCount  = 2 + strlen( ServerName )
  Name            = "\MAILSLOT\BROWSE"
  Data
    {
    OpCode        = 0x0D (MasterAnnouncement)
    ServerName    = <NetBIOS machine name, no suffix>
    }
  }
```

When the DMB receives a `MasterAnnouncement`, it should perform a `NetServerEnum2` synchronization with the LMB. It should also keep track of remote LMBs in its workgroup and periodically (every 15 minutes) synchronize Browse Lists with them. Likewise, an LMB will periodically query the DMB. This is how the Browse List is propagated across multiple subnets.

Note that this message is unicast. A broadcast datagram would not reach a remote DMB.

22.2.8 *Domain Announcement*

The `DomainAnnouncement` has the same structure as the `HostAnnouncement` and `LocalMasterAnnouncement` frames. The difference is in the content.

The `DomainAnnouncement` is sent to the `MSBROWSE<01>` name, so that all of the foreign LMBs on the subnet will receive it. Instead of the NetBIOS machine name, the `ServerName` field contains the workgroup name. The NetBIOS machine name is also reported, but it is placed into the `Comment` field.

```
NBT_Datagram
  {
  MsgType          = 0x11 (DIRECT_GROUP DATAGRAM)
  SourceName       = machine<00>
  DestinationName  = "\01\02__MSBROWSE__\02<01>"
  }
smb_Transaction_Request
  {
  TotalDataCount  = 18 + strlen( ServerName + Comment )
  Name            = "\MAILSLOT\BROWSE"
  Data
    {
    OpCode        = 0x0C (DomainAnnouncement)
    UpdateCount   = <Incremented after each announcement>
    Periodicity   = <Time until next announcement, in ms>
    ServerName    = <NetBIOS workgroup name, no suffix>
    OSMajorVers   = 4 <Windows OS version to mimic>
    OSMinorVers   = 5 <Windows OS point version to mimic>
    ServerType    = <Discussion below>
    BroMajorVers  = 15
    BroMinorVers  = 1
    Signature     = 0xaa55
    Comment       = <LMB NetBIOS machine name, no suffix>
    }
  }
```

A note of caution on this one. Some Windows systems send what appears to be garblage in the `BroMajorVers`, `BroMinorVers`, and `Signature` fields. Ethereal compensates by combining these three into a single longword which it calls "Mysterious Field."

22.2.9 *Become Backup Request*

This message is sent by the LMB when it wants to promote a Potential Browser to Backup Browser status.

```
struct
  {
  uchar  OpCode;
  uchar *BrowserName;
  } BecomeBackupRequest;
```

```
NBT_Datagram
  {
  MsgType          = 0x11 (DIRECT_GROUP DATAGRAM)
  SourceName       = machine<00>
  DestinationName  = workgroup<1E>
  }
smb_Transaction_Request
  {
  TotalDataCount  = 2 + strlen( BrowserName )
  Name            = "\MAILSLOT\BROWSE"
  Data
    {
    OpCode        = 0x0B (BecomeBackupRequest)
    BrowserName   = <NetBIOS machine name of promoted node>
    }
  }
```

The message is an NBT multicast datagram sent to all Potential Browsers in the workgroup. The `BrowserName` field contains the name of the node that is being promoted (no suffix byte). That node will respond by sending a new `HostAnnouncement` frame and obtaining a fresh copy of the Browse List from the LMB. The newly promoted Backup Browser should refresh its Browse List copy every 15 minutes.

22.2.10 *The Undocumented Reset*

It is difficult to find documentation on this message — it's not written up in the Leach/Naik draft — but there is some information hiding around the web if you dig a little... and, of course, we're describing it here.

Big things come in small packages. Here's the `ResetBrowserState` frame:

```
struct
  {
  uchar OpCode;
  uchar Command;
  } ResetBrowserState;
```

Not much to it, but it can have an impact. This is how it's filled in:

```
NBT_Datagram
  {
  MsgType          = 0x11 (DIRECT_GROUP DATAGRAM)
  SourceName       = machine<00>
  DestinationName  = workgroup<1D>
  }
smb_Transaction_Request
  {
  TotalDataCount  = 2
  Name            = "\MAILSLOT\BROWSE"
  Data
    {
    OpCode        = 0x0E (ResetBrowserState)
    Command       = <Bitfield - see below>
    }
  }
```

The ResetBrowserState message can mess with a Local Master Browser's mind. There are three bits defined for the Command field, and here's what they do:

ResetBrowserState command bits

Bit	Name / Bitmask	Description
7–3	0xF8	<Reserved> (must be zero)
2	RESET_STATE_STOP 0x04	Tells the Local Master Browser not to be a browser any more. The LMB will de-register its <1D> and <1E> names and sulk in a corner. Many implementations ignore this command, even if they respect the others. DMBs should never accept this command.
1	RESET_STATE_CLEAR_ALL 0x02	Causes the LMB to clear its Browse List and start over.
0	RESET_STATE_STOP_MASTER 0x01	Causes the LMB to demote itself to a Backup Browser. This will, eventually, cause a new election (which may be won by the very same system).

22.2.11 *It's All in the Delivery*

Would a little more code be useful?

The code gets rather dull at this level because all we are really doing is packing and unpacking bytes. Unfortunately, that's what network protocols are all about. Not very glamorous, is it?

Listing 22.2 packs a `RequestElection` message into a byte block so that it can be handed to the `smb_TransRequest()` function via the `smb_Transaction_Request` structure. Sending election requests to a busy LAN can be kinda fun... and possibly a little disruptive.

Listing 22.2: SMBtrans messages

```
#define BROWSE_REQUEST_ELECTION 0x08

static smb_Transaction_Request TReqs[1];

static const ushort MailSlotSetup[3]
                  = { 0x0001, 0x0001, 0x0002 };
static const uchar *MailSlotName
                  = "\\MAILSLOT\\BROWSE";

int ElectionRequest( uchar *bufr,
                     int    bSize,
                     ulong  Criteria,
                     ulong  Uptime,
                     uchar *ServerName)
  /* -------------------------------------------------- **
   * Marshal an Election Request record.
   *
   * Returns the number of bytes used.
   * -------------------------------------------------- **
   */
  {
  size_t len;
  uchar  buildData[32];

  /* Initialize the TReqs block.
   */
  (void)memset( TReqs, 0, sizeof(smb_Transaction_Request) );
  TReqs->SetupCount = 3;
  TReqs->Setup      = MailSlotSetup;
  TReqs->Name       = MailSlotName;
```

```
/* Build the Browser message in 'buildData'. */
(void)memset( buildData, '\0', 32 );
buildData[0] = BROWSE_REQUEST_ELECTION;
len = 15;

/* If the ServerName is empty, assume that the
 * request is for a zero-filled election message.
 * Otherwise, fill in the rest of the message.
 */
if( NULL != ServerName && '\0' != *ServerName )
  {
  buildData[1] = 1;                          /* Version.  */
  smb_SetLong( buildData, 2, Criteria );   /* Criteria. */
  smb_SetLong( buildData, 6, Uptime );     /* Uptime.   */
                            /* Skip 4 reserved bytes. */

  /* Copy the ServerName, and make sure there's a nul.
   * Count the nul in the total.
   */
  (void)strncpy( &(buildbufr[15]), ServerName, 15 );
  bufr[31] = '\0';
  len += 1 + strlen( &(buildbufr[15]) );
  }

/* Finish filling in the transaction request structure.
 */
TReqs->TotalDataCount = (ushort)len;
TReqs->Data           = buildData;

/* Write the transaction into the buffer.
 * Return the transaction message size.
 */
len = smb_TransRequest( bufr, bSize, TReqs );
return( len );
} /* ElectionRequest */
```

22.3 RAPture

Understand this at the outset: Examining a function of the RAP protocol is like studying the runic carvings on the lid of Pandora's box. They might just be large friendly letters... or they could be the manufacturer's warning label.

We are *not* going to open the box.

The `NetServerEnum2` function can be implemented without having to fully understand the inner workings of RAP, so there really is no need. If you want to, you can rummage around in the RAP functions by reading through Appendix B of the X/Open book *Protocols for X/Open PC Interworking: SMB, Version 2*. After that, there is yet again another additional further Leach/Naik draft already. You can find the Leach/Naik *CIFS Remote Administration Protocol Preliminary Draft* under the filename `cifsrap2.txt` on Microsoft's FTP server. It is definitely a draft, but it provides a lot of good information if you read it carefully. One more resource a die-hard RAP-per will want to check is *Remoted Net API Format Strings*, which is an email message that was sent to Microsoft's CIFS mailing list by Paul Leach. It provides details on the formatting of RAP messages. All of these sources are, of course, listed in the References section.

One of the downsides of RAP, from our perspective, is that it defines *yet another layer* of parameters and data... and there's a heap, too.

Gotta love layers.

RAP provides a formula for marshalling its parameters, data, and heap, passing them over a network connection, and then passing the results back again. A complete RAP implementation would most likely automate the marshalling and unmarshalling process, and the human eye would never need to see it. That would be overkill in our case, so we're stuck doing things the easy way — by hand.

RAP functions are sent via a Named Pipe, not a Mailslot, so the whole communications process is different. Like the Mailslot-based functions, RAP functions are packed into an SMBtrans transaction, but that's just about all that's really the same. The steps which must be followed in order to execute a RAP call are:

- Open a TCP session.
  - NBT Session Request.
    - SMB Negotiate Protocol.
    - SMB Session Setup.
    - SMB Tree Connect (to **machine**\IPC$).
      - RAP call and reply.

- SMB Tree Disconnect (optional).
- SMB Logoff (optional).

- Close TCP session.

You can see all of this very clearly in a packet capture. Having a sniff handy as you read through this section is highly recommended, by the way. Don't forget to listen on 139/TCP instead of (or in addition to) 138/UDP.

22.3.1 `NetServerEnum2` *Request*

You can generate a `NetServerEnum2` exchange in a variety of ways. For example, you can refresh the server list in the Windows Network Neighborhood or use the jCIFS `List.java` utility with the URL "smb://**workgroup**/". The request, as displayed by the packet sniffer, should look something like this:

```
+ Transmission Control Protocol
+ NetBIOS Session Service
+ SMB (Server Message Block Protocol)
  SMB Pipe Protocol
- Microsoft Windows Lanman Remote API Protocol
    Function Code: NetServerEnum2 (104)
    Parameter Descriptor: WrLehDz
    Return Descriptor: B16BBDz
    Detail Level: 1
    Receive Buffer Length: 65535
    Server Type: 0xffffffff
    Enumeration Domain: WORKGROUP
```

The `Descriptor` fields are a distinctive feature of RAP requests. These are the cryptic runes of which we spoke earlier. They are format strings, used to define the structure of the parameters and data being sent as well as that expected in the reply. They can be used to automate the packing and unpacking of the packets, or they can be stuffed into the packet as constants with no regard to their meaning. The latter is the simpler course. With that in mind, here is the (simplified, but still correct) C-style format of a `NetServerEnum2` request:

```
struct
  {
  ushort RAPCode;
  uchar *ParamDesc;
  uchar *DataDesc;
  struct
    {
    ushort InfoLevel;
    ushort BufrSize;
    ulong  ServerType;
    uchar *Workgroup;
    } Params;
  } NetServerEnum2Req;
```

So, given the above structure, the NetServerEnum2 request is filled in as shown below. Note that, at the SMBtrans-level, there are no Setup[] words, the Data[] section is empty, and all of the above structure is bundled into the Parameter[] block.

```
smb_Transaction_Request
  {
  TotalParamCount    = 27 + strlen( Workgroup )
  MaxParameterCount = 8
  MaxDataCount       = <Size of the reply buffer>
  Name               = "\PIPE\LANMAN"
  Data
    {
    RAPCode          = 104 (0x0068)
    ParamDesc        = "WrLehDz"
    DataDesc         = "B16BBDz"
    RAP_Params
      {
      InfoLevel      = 1 <See below>
      BufrSize       = <Same as MaxDataCount>
      ServerType     = <See below>
      Workgroup      = <Name of the workgroup to list>
      }
    }
  }
```

A few of those fields need a little discussion.

TotalParamCount

The value 27 includes three short integers, one long integer, two constant strings (with lengths of 8 bytes each), and one nul byte to terminate the Workgroup field. That adds up to 27 bytes.

MaxDataCount and BufrSize

Samba allocates the largest size buffer it can (64 Kbytes minus one byte) to receive the response data. Other clients seem to have trouble with a 64K buffer, and will subtract a few bytes from the size. 64K minus 360 bytes has been seen, and jCIFS uses 64K minus 512 bytes.

 **Email**

From: Allen, Michael B
  To: jcifs@samba.org

I think I just made it up. I found 0xFFFF would result in errors. I never really investigated why.

InfoLevel

There are two `InfoLevels` available: 0 and 1. Level 0 is not very interesting. Note that if you want to try level 0, you will need to change the `DataDesc` string as well.

ServerType

There are two common values used in the request message. They are:

```
SV_TYPE_DOMAIN_ENUM == 0x80000000
SV_TYPE_ALL         == 0xFFFFFFFF
```

The first is used to query the browser for the list of all known workgroups. The second is used to query for a list of all known Providers in the specified (or default) workgroup.

Note that these are not the only allowed values. When we cover the reply message (next section) there will be a table of all known bit values. Queries for specific subsets of Providers can be generated using these bits.

Workgroup

In many cases, this will be an empty string (just a nul byte). An empty `Workgroup` field represents a request to list the Providers that are members of the browser's default workgroup. That means, of course, that the browser being queried *must have* a default workgroup.

This results in an interesting problem. Since the workgroup name is not always specified, a single system cannot (on a single IP address) be the LMB for more than one workgroup. If a node were to become the LMB for multiple workgroups, then it would not know which set of servers to report in response to a `NetServerEnum2` query with an empty workgroup name.

...and that is "all you need to know" about the `NetServerEnum2` request message.

22.3.2 `NetServerEnum2` *Reply*

The response message is a bit more involved, so you may want to take notes. A packet capture, once again, is a highly recommended visual aide.

Starting at the top... The `TotalParamCount` field in the SMBtrans reply message will have a value of 8, indicating the size of the SMBtrans-level `Parameter[]` block. Those bytes fall out as follows:

```
struct
  {
  ushort Status;      /* Error Code       */
  ushort Convert;     /* See below        */
  ushort EntryCount;  /* Entries returned */
  ushort AvailCount;  /* Entries available */
  }
```

Status

An error code. Available codes are listed in the Leach/Naik Browser draft.

Convert

More on this in a moment, when we get to the `Data[]` block.

EntryCount

The number of entries returned in the reply.

AvailCount

The number of available entries. This may be more than the number in `EntryCount`, in which case there are more entries than will fit in the data buffer length given in the request.

That's all there is to the `Parameter[]` block. It's nicely simple, but things get a little wilder as we move on. Do keep track of that `Convert` value...

The SMB-level `Data[]` block will start with a series of `ServerInfo_1` structures, as described below:

```
struct
  {
  uchar  Name[16];        /* Provider name    */
  uchar  OSMajorVers;     /* Provider OS Rev  */
  uchar  OSMinorVers;     /* Provider OS Point */
  ulong  ServerType;      /* See below        */
  uchar *Comment;         /* Pointer          */
  } ServerInfo_1;
```

There will be `<EntryCount>` such structures packed neatly together. It is fairly easy to parse them out, because the `Name` field is a fixed-length, nul-padded string and the `Comment` field *really is* a pointer. The Leach/Naik Browser draft suggests that the `Comment` strings themselves *may* follow each `ServerInfo_1` structure, but all examples seen on the wire show four bytes. Hang on to those four bytes... we'll explain in a moment.

Anywhich, the above structure has a fixed length — 26 bytes, to be precise. That makes it easy to parse `ServerInfo_1` structures from the `Data[]` block.

The values in the `ServerInfo_1` are the same ones announced by the Provider in its `HostAnnouncement` or `DomainAnnouncement` frames. They are stored in an internal database on the browser node. Some of these fields have been discussed before, but a detailed description of the `ServerType` field has been postponed at every opportunity. Similarly, the pointer value in the `Comment` field really needs some clarification.

Let's start with the `Comment` pointer...

The `Comment` pointer may just possibly be a relic of the long lost days of DOS. Those who know more about 16-bit DOS internals may judge. In any case, what you need to do is this:

- Read the `Comment` pointer from the `ServerInfo_1` structure.
- Remove the two higher-order bytes: `Comment & 0x0000FFFF`.
- Subtract the value of the `Convert` field: `offset = (Comment & 0x0000FFFF) - Convert`.
- Use the resulting offset to find the actual `Comment` string. The offset is relative to the start of the SMBtrans `Data[]` block.

Well *that* was easy. This stuff is so lovable you just want to give it a hug, don't you?

Some further notes:

- The `Comment` strings are stored in the RAP-level heap.
- The `ServerInfo_1` blocks are considered RAP-level "data."
- Both of those are collected into the SMBtrans-level `Data[]` block.
- Just to make things simple, the RAP-level parameters are gathered into the SMBtrans `Parameter[]` block.

Right... Having tilted that windmill, let's take a look at the (more sensible, but also much more verbose) `ServerType` field. We have delayed describing this field for quite a while. Here, finally, it is... well, mostly. The list below is based on Samba sources. It is close to Ethereal's list, and less close to the list given in the Leach/Naik draft. Let the buyer beware.

Browser Provider type bits

Bit	Name / Bitmask	Description
31	SV_TYPE_DOMAIN_ENUM 0x80000000	Enumerate Domains. This bit is used in the request to ask for a list of known workgroups instead of a list of Providers in a workgroup.
30	SV_TYPE_LOCAL_LIST_ONLY 0x40000000	This bit identifies entries for which the browser is *authoritative*. That is, it is set if the Provider (or workgroup) entry was received via an announcement message, and clear if the entry is the result of a sync with the DMB.
29	SV_TYPE_ALTERNATE_XPORT 0x20000000	No one seems to remember where this came from or what it means. Ethereal doesn't know about it.
28–24	0x1F000000	Unused.
23	SV_TYPE_DFS_SERVER 0x00800000	The Provider offers DFS shares. Possibly a DFS root.
22	SV_TYPE_WIN95_PLUS 0x00400000	Indicates a Provider that considers itself to be in the Windows 9x family.
21	SV_TYPE_SERVER_VMS 0x00200000	Indicates a VMS (Pathworks) server.

Browser Provider type bits

Bit	Name / Bitmask	Description
20	SV_TYPE_SERVER_OSF 0x00100000	Indicates an OSF Unix server.
19	SV_TYPE_DOMAIN_MASTER 0x00080000	Indicates a Domain Master Browser (DMB).
18	SV_TYPE_MASTER_BROWSER 0x00040000	Indicates a Local Master Browser (LMB).
17	SV_TYPE_BACKUP_BROWSER 0x00020000	Indicates a Backup Browser...
16	SV_TYPE_POTENTIAL_BROWSER 0x00010000	...and, of course, a Potential Browser.
15	SV_TYPE_SERVER_NT 0x00008000	Indicates a Windows NT Server.
14	SV_TYPE_SERVER_MFPN 0x00004000	Unknown. Ethereal ignores this one, and it's not listed in the Leach/Naik Browser draft.
13	SV_TYPE_WFW 0x00002000	Windows for Workgroups.
12	SV_TYPE_NT 0x00001000	A Windows NT client.
11	SV_TYPE_SERVER_UNIX 0x00000800	An SMB server running Xenix or Unix. Samba will set this bit when announcing its services.
10	SV_TYPE_DIALIN_SERVER 0x00000400	The Provider offers dial-up services (e.g. NT RAS).
9	SV_TYPE_PRINTQ_SERVER 0x00000200	The Provider has printer services available.
8	SV_TYPE_DOMAIN_MEMBER 0x00000100	The Provider is a member of an NT Domain. That means that the Provider itself has authenticated to the NT Domain.
7	SV_TYPE_NOVELL 0x00000080	The Provider is a Novell server offering SMB services. This is probably used with SMB over IPX/SPX, but may be set by Novell's SMB implementation as well.
6	SV_TYPE_AFP 0x00000040	The Provider is an Apple system. Thursby's Dave product and Apple's SMB implementation may set this bit.

Browser Provider type bits

Bit	Name / Bitmask	Description
5	SV_TYPE_TIME_SOURCE 0x00000020	The Provider offers SMB time services. (Yes, there is an SMB-based time sync service.)
4	SV_TYPE_DOMAIN_BAKCTRL 0x00000010	The Provider is a Backup Domain Controller (BDC).
3	SV_TYPE_DOMAIN_CTRL 0x00000008	The Provider is a Domain Controller.
2	SV_TYPE_SQLSERVER 0x00000004	The Provider offers SQL services.
1	SV_TYPE_SERVER 0x00000002	The Provider offers SMB file services.
0	SV_TYPE_WORKSTATION 0x00000001	This bit indicates that the system is a workstation. (Just about everything sets this bit.)

Just to polish this subject off, here's a little code that can parse a NetServerEnum2 response message and print the results:

Listing 22.3: Parsing NetServerEnum2 Replies

```
#define NERR_Success 0

#define SV_TYPE_ALL               0xFFFFFFFF
#define SV_TYPE_UNKNOWN           0x1F000000

#define SV_TYPE_DOMAIN_ENUM       0x80000000
#define SV_TYPE_LOCAL_LIST_ONLY   0x40000000
#define SV_TYPE_ALTERNATE_XPORT   0x20000000
#define SV_TYPE_DFS_SERVER        0x00800000
#define SV_TYPE_WIN95_PLUS        0x00400000
#define SV_TYPE_SERVER_VMS        0x00200000
#define SV_TYPE_SERVER_OSF        0x00100000
#define SV_TYPE_DOMAIN_MASTER     0x00080000
#define SV_TYPE_MASTER_BROWSER    0x00040000
#define SV_TYPE_BACKUP_BROWSER    0x00020000
#define SV_TYPE_POTENTIAL_BROWSER 0x00010000
#define SV_TYPE_SERVER_NT         0x00008000
#define SV_TYPE_SERVER_MFPN       0x00004000
#define SV_TYPE_WFW               0x00002000
#define SV_TYPE_NT                0x00001000
#define SV_TYPE_SERVER_UNIX       0x00000800
```

```
#define SV_TYPE_DIALIN_SERVER      0x00000400
#define SV_TYPE_PRINTQ_SERVER      0x00000200
#define SV_TYPE_DOMAIN_MEMBER      0x00000100
#define SV_TYPE_NOVELL             0x00000080
#define SV_TYPE_AFP                0x00000040
#define SV_TYPE_TIME_SOURCE        0x00000020
#define SV_TYPE_DOMAIN_BAKCTRL     0x00000010
#define SV_TYPE_DOMAIN_CTRL        0x00000008
#define SV_TYPE_SQLSERVER          0x00000004
#define SV_TYPE_SERVER             0x00000002
#define SV_TYPE_WORKSTATION        0x00000001

typedef struct
  {
  ushort Status;
  ushort Convert;
  ushort EntryCount;
  ushort AvailCount;
  } NSE2_ReplyParams;

void PrintBrowserBits( ulong ServerType )
  /* -------------------------------------------------- **
   * Itemize Browse Service Provider Type Bits.
   * This is boring, and could probably be done better
   * using an array and a for() loop.
   * -------------------------------------------------- **
   */
  {
  if( SV_TYPE_ALL == ServerType )
    {
    printf( "  All/Any Server types.\n" );
    return;
    }

  if( SV_TYPE_UNKNOWN & ServerType )
    printf( "  Warning: Undefined bits set.\n" );

  if( SV_TYPE_DOMAIN_ENUM & ServerType )
    printf( "  Enumerate Domains\n" );
  if( SV_TYPE_LOCAL_LIST_ONLY & ServerType )
    printf( "  Local List Only\n" );
  if( SV_TYPE_ALTERNATE_XPORT & ServerType )
    printf( "  Alternate Export (Unknown type)\n" );
  if( SV_TYPE_DFS_SERVER & ServerType )
    printf( "  DFS Support\n" );
  if( SV_TYPE_WIN95_PLUS & ServerType )
    printf( "  Windows 95+\n" );
```

```
if( SV_TYPE_SERVER_VMS & ServerType )
  printf( "   VMS (Pathworks) Server\n" );
if( SV_TYPE_SERVER_OSF & ServerType )
  printf( "   OSF Unix Server\n" );
if( SV_TYPE_DOMAIN_MASTER & ServerType )
  printf( "   Domain Master Browser\n" );
if( SV_TYPE_MASTER_BROWSER & ServerType )
  printf( "   Local Master Browser\n" );
if( SV_TYPE_BACKUP_BROWSER & ServerType )
  printf( "   Backup Browser\n" );
if( SV_TYPE_POTENTIAL_BROWSER & ServerType )
  printf( "   Potential Browser\n" );
if( SV_TYPE_SERVER_NT & ServerType )
  printf( "   Windows NT (or compatible) Server\n" );
if( SV_TYPE_SERVER_MFPN & ServerType )
  printf( "   MFPN (Unkown type)\n" );
if( SV_TYPE_WFW & ServerType )
  printf( "   Windows for Workgroups\n" );
if( SV_TYPE_NT & ServerType )
  printf( "   Windows NT Workstation\n" );
if( SV_TYPE_SERVER_UNIX & ServerType )
  printf( "   Unix/Xenix/Samba Server\n" );
if( SV_TYPE_DIALIN_SERVER & ServerType )
  printf( "   Dialin Server\n" );
if( SV_TYPE_PRINTQ_SERVER & ServerType )
  printf( "   Print Server\n" );
if( SV_TYPE_DOMAIN_MEMBER & ServerType )
  printf( "   NT Domain Member Server\n" );
if( SV_TYPE_NOVELL & ServerType )
  printf( "   Novell Server\n" );
if( SV_TYPE_AFP & ServerType )
  printf( "   Apple Server\n" );
if( SV_TYPE_TIME_SOURCE & ServerType )
  printf( "   Time Source\n" );
if( SV_TYPE_DOMAIN_BAKCTRL & ServerType )
  printf( "   Backup Domain Controller\n" );
if( SV_TYPE_DOMAIN_CTRL & ServerType )
  printf( "   Domain Controller\n" );
if( SV_TYPE_SQLSERVER & ServerType )
  printf( "   SQL Server\n" );
if( SV_TYPE_SERVER & ServerType )
  printf( "   SMB Server\n" );
if( SV_TYPE_WORKSTATION & ServerType )
  printf( "   Workstation\n" );
} /* PrintBrowserBits */
```

```
void PrintNetServerEnum2Reply( uchar *ParamBlock,
                               int    ParamLen,
                               uchar *DataBlock,
                               int    DataLen )
  /* --------------------------------------------------- **
   * Parse a NetServerEnum2 Reply and print the contents.
   * --------------------------------------------------- **
   */
  {
  NSE2_ReplyParams Rep;
  int              i;
  int              offset;
  uchar            *pos;

  /* Check for an obvious error.
   */
  if( ParamLen != 8 )
    Fail( "Error parsing NetServerEnum2 reply.\n" );

  /* Grab all of the parameter words.
   */
  Rep.Status     = smb_GetShort( ParamBlock, 0 );
  Rep.Convert    = smb_GetShort( ParamBlock, 2 );
  Rep.EntryCount = smb_GetShort( ParamBlock, 4 );
  Rep.AvailCount = smb_GetShort( ParamBlock, 6 );

  /* Check for problems (errors and warnings).
   */
  if( Rep.Status != NERR_Success )
    Fail( "NetServerEnum2 Error: %d.\n", Rep.Status );
  if( Rep.EntryCount < Rep.AvailCount )
    printf( "Warning: The list is incomplete.\n" );

  /* Dump the ServerInfo_1 records. */
  pos = DataBlock;
  for( i = 0; i < Rep.EntryCount; i++ )
    {
    printf( "%-15s V%d.%d\n", pos, pos[16], pos[17] );
    PrintBrowserBits( smb_GetLong( pos, 18 ) );
    offset  = 0x0000FFFF & smb_GetLong( pos, 22 );
    offset -= Rep.Convert;
    if( offset >= DataLen )
      Fail( "Packet offset error.\n" );
    printf( "  Comment: %s\n", (DataBlock + offset) );
    pos += 26;
    }
  } /* PrintNetServerEnum2Reply */
```

22.3.3 *On the Outskirts of Town*

There is another RAP call that you need to know about. It comes in handy at times. It doesn't really belong to the Browse Service, but you may have heard its name mentioned in that context. It lives on the edge, somewhere between browsing and filesharing, and it goes by the name NetShareEnum.

The NetShareEnum RAP call does the job of listing the shares offered by a server. The shares, as you already know, are the virtual roots of the directory trees made available via SMB.

The wire format of the request is as follows:

```
struct
  {
  ushort RAPCode;
  uchar *ParamDesc;
  uchar *DataDesc;
  struct
    {
    ushort InfoLevel;
    ushort BufrSize;
    } Params;
  } NetShareEnumReq;
```

and it is filled in like so:

```
NetShareEnumReq
  {
  RAPCode   = 0 (NetShareEnum)
  ParamDesc = "WrLeh"
  DataDesc  = "B13BWz"
  Params
    {
    InfoLevel = 1 (No other values defined)
    BufrSize  = <Same as smb_Transaction_Request.MaxDataCount>
    }
  }
```

Yes, the RAP code for NetShareEnum is zero (0).

There's not much to that call, particularly once you've gotten the NetServerEnum2 figured out. The response also contains some familiar concepts. In fact, the Parameter[] section is exactly the same.

The RAP-level data section is supposed to contain an array of ShareInfo_1 structures, which look like this:

```
struct
  {
  uchar   ShareName[13];
  uchar   pad;
  ushort ShareType;
  uchar *Comment;
  } ShareInfo_1;
```

Again, there are many similarities to what we have seen before. In this case, though, the `ShareType` field has a smaller set of possible values than the comparable `ServerType` field.

Share type values

Name	Value	Description
STYPE_DISKTREE	0	A disk share (root of a directory tree).
STYPE_PRINTQ	1	A print queue.
STYPE_DEVICE	2	A communications device (e.g. a modem).
STYPE_STYPE	3	An Inter-Process Communication (IPC) share.

...and that is "all you need to know" about the `NetShareEnum` call. Oh, wait... There is one more thing...

Can't Get It Out Of My Head Alert
There is one great big warning regarding the `NetShareEnum` response. Some Windows systems have been seen returning parameter blocks that are very large (e.g. 1024 bytes). The first eight bytes contain the correct values. The rest appear to be left-over cruft from the buffer on the server side. The server is returning the buffer size (and the whole buffer) rather than the `Parameter[]` block size.
Other transactions may exhibit similar behavior.

22.3.4 *Transaction Fragmentation*

A promise is a promise, and we did promise to cover fragmented transactions.[2]
  The idea is fairly simple. If you have twenty-five sacks of grain to bring to town, and a wagon that can hold only twelve sacks, then you will need to

---

2. Maybe we could cover them with leaves and fallen branches and just let them compost themselves quietly in an out-of-the-way place or something.

make a few trips. Likewise with transactions. Due to the limits of the negotiated buffer size, a transaction may attempt to transfer more data than can be carried in a single SMB. The solution is to split up the data and send it using multiple SMB messages.

The mechanism used is the same for SMBtrans, Trans2, and NTtrans. There are slight differences between the transaction request and transaction response, though, so pay attention.

Sending a fragmented transaction request works like this:

1. Fill in the transaction SMB, packing as many `Parameter[]` and `Data[]` bytes into the transaction as possible. `Parameter[]` bytes have precedence over `Data[]` bytes.

2. Send the initial message and wait for a reply (known as the "Interim Server Response"). This step is a shortcut. It gives the server a chance to reject the transaction before it has been completely transferred. Only the response header has any meaning. If there is no error, the transaction may proceed.

3. Send as many secondary transaction messages as necessary to transfer the remaining `Parameter[]` and `Data[]` bytes. Note that the SMB command and structure of secondary transactions is not the same as those of the initial message.

4. Wait for the server to execute the transaction and return the results.

Now go back and take a look at Listing 22.1. Note that the `smb_Transaction_Request` structure keeps track of the number of `Parameter[]` and `Data[]` bytes already packed for shipping. That makes it easy to build the secondary messages should they be needed.

Fragmenting a transaction response is a simpler process. The response SMBs all have the same structure (no special secondary messages) and they all have an SMB header, which may contain an error code if necessary. So, the server can just send as many transaction response SMBs as needed to transfer all of the results. That's it.

22.3.5 *RAP Annoyances*

RAP can be quite annoying — that's just its nature. There are two particular annoyances of which you should be aware:

Authentication

It is common for a server to deny a `NetShareEnum` request on an anonymous SMB connection. A valid username/password pair may be required. Some servers also require non-anonymous authentication for the `NetServerEnum2` request, though this is less common.

Limitations and Permutations

Grab a capture of a `NetShareEnum` request and take a look at the data descriptor string for the returned data (which should be "B13BWz", as described above). The number 13 in the string indicates the maximum length of the share names to be returned, and it includes the terminating nul byte.

"B13BWz" means that the `NetShareEnum` function will not return share names with a string length greater than 12 characters each. Of course, there are many systems that can offer shares with names longer than 12 characters. Thus, we have a problem.

One way to solve the problem would be to change the field size in the descriptor string to, for example, something like "B256BWz". That trick isn't likely to work against all servers, however, because the descriptor strings are constant enough that some implementations probably ignore them. Another option is to use short share names, but that only works if you have control over all of the SMB servers in the network.

The prescribed solution is to use a different function, called `NetrShareEnum`. Note that there's an extra letter 'r' hidden in there. Also note that the `NetrShareEnum` function is an MS-RPC call, not a RAP call, and thus is beyond the scope of this book. You can watch for it in packet captures, however, and possibly consider it as a starting point should you decide to explore the world of MS-RPC.

So, now you know.

23

The Better Browser Bureau

> There is a finite amount of clue
> in the Universe...
> and the Universe is expanding.
>
> — Unknown
> (thanks to John Ladwig
> and Marcus Ranum)

Hold on to your hoopskirts everyone, we're not there yet. We have a few more things to learn about the Network Neighborhood.

23.1 Running an Election

Elections may be called whenever a Consumer is unable to find a Local Master Browser, or when a jealous rival (known as a Preferred Master Browser) shows up. An election can also be forced by sending a zero-filled `RequestElection` frame.

When a `RequestElection` frame is received by a Potential Browser (including Backup Browsers, the LMB, and the DMB), the Potential Browser switches into election mode. The browser stays in election mode until a winner declares itself by sending a `LocalMasterAnnouncement` frame.

While in election mode, the browser sends and receives `RequestElection` frames. If another browser's credentials are better, then the browser knows that it has lost the election and will politely shut up, not participating further in the current election.

23.1.1 *Voting*

There is a bit of timing involved in the election process. If all Potential Browsers were to respond at once, things could get a little noisy.[1] So, as with the `AnnouncementRequest` frame, when a browser receives a `Request-Election` frame it will wait a random amount of time before sending its response. The amount of time to wait varies by the status of the node, however. A Potential Browser that is more likely to win the election will send its response to the `RequestElection` frame sooner than one that is less likely.

It's supposed to work like this:

Browser election timings

Response Delay	Node Credentials
0–100 ms	Local and Domain Master Browsers
200–600 ms	Backup Browsers
800–3000 ms	All others

The goal here is to cut down on network broadcast traffic. If the likely candidate votes first, the chances are good that the others won't have to vote at all.

After sending a `RequestElection` frame, a candidate should wait two or three seconds to be sure that all other candidates have voted. After that, if the candidate has won the round it can send another `RequestElection` frame. This marks the start of another round. The election runs four rounds, after which the browser still standing (there should be only one) declares itself the winner by sending a `LocalMasterAnnouncement` frame.

The timings above are provided in the Leach/Naik Browser draft. Whether existing implementations follow these guidelines or not is a question for further study.

---

1. It is possible that the reason behind this is that some older IP implementations would overflow their buffers if too many UDP packets all arrived at once. There is anecdotal evidence that such a problem did, at one time, exist.

23.1.2 *The Ballot*

The ballot is contained within the `RequestElection` frame which, just to review, looks like this:

```
struct
  {
  uchar  Opcode;
  uchar  Version;
  ulong  Criteria;
  ulong  UpTime;
  ulong  Reserved;
  uchar *ServerName;
  } RequestElection;
```

The `Opcode` and `Reserved` fields can be ignored. The rest comprise the election ballot. The winner of the election is determined by comparing the ballots using a somewhat arcane formula. Here, plain and simple, is how it works:

Test 1

> The higher `Version` wins. If they are the same, continue. The only values for `Version` seen on the wire are 0 and 1. Zero is only used when initiating an election by sending a zero-filled election request.

Test 2

> Compare the `Criteria`. The higher value wins. If they are equal, continue. The contents of the `Criteria` field still need to be analyzed.

Test 3

> The station that has the greatest `UpTime` wins. If they are equal, continue. The `UpTime` is measured in milliseconds,[2] so there is very little chance that two ballots will have the same value.

Test 4

> Compare the `ServerName` strings. The first, in comparison order, wins (e.g., "EARTH" would win over "OIL").

---

2. The maximum `UpTime` is a little less than 50 days, after which the 32-bit counter will wrap around to zero again.

There is one more test suggested in the Leach/Naik Browser draft. It might be "Test 0" in the list above. Test 0 says, essentially, that a browser that has recently lost an election is still a loser and should remain a loser until several seconds have passed.

Let's rip apart that `Criteria` field, shall we?

The `Criteria` field is handled like an unsigned long integer, but it can also be divided into four subfields, like so:

```
struct
  {
  uchar  OSlevel;
  uchar  BroMajorVers;
  uchar  BroMinorVers;
  uchar  Role;
  } Criteria;
```

The `OSlevel` is the highest order byte and, therefore, has the most impact when `Criteria` values are compared as unsigned longs. There are some known, predefined values, as shown:

> `0x01` = Windows for Workgroups and Windows 9x
> `0x10` = Windows NT Workstation
> `0x14` = Samba default
> `0x20` = Windows NT Server

The higher you crank the `OSlevel`, the better your chances of winning an election.

Moving along, the next subfields are the major and minor Browser Protocol Version numbers. In theory, they should have the values 15 and 1, respectively, but Windows 9x systems use 21 and 4 instead.

The final subfield is known as the `Role` field. It is a bitflag field. There seems to be some disagreement regarding the bits, though. Different sources provide different interpretations. The table below provides reasonable approximations.

Browser roles

Bit	Description
0x80	Set by the Primary Domain Controller (PDC).
0x20	The node is an NBNS client (a P, M, or H node).

Browser roles

Bit	Description
0x08	This is the "Preferred Master" bit. It can be enabled manually in Windows via a registry setting, and in Samba by using the PREFERRED MASTER option in the smb.conf file.
0x04	Set by the current Local Master Browser.
0x02	Set by a Backup Browser that was until recently the Local Master, but which has been downgraded after losing an election.[3]
0x01	Set by Backup Browsers.

It was stated earlier that the LMB election can be rigged so that a specific node always wins. For example, it is necessary that the DMB become the LMB for the LAN.

Higher OS level

In the Windows world, only an NT or W2K server can become a PDC and, therefore, only these can be DMBs. These systems will set the highest defined OS level which, as shown above, is 0x20. Thus, in a purely Windows environment, the only competition will be from other NT and W2K servers.

Preferred Master

To further bias the LMB election, the "Preferred Master" Role bit may be set. This provides an edge over otherwise identical servers. Preferred Master Browsers also force an election whenever they join a LAN.

NBNS Clients

The NBNS client bit is higher order than the Preferred Master bit. Setting this helps because only an NBNS client can contact a remote Domain Master browser to synchronize lists. Thus, an NBNS client is a better choice as an LMB than a B mode node (even a preferred master).

The DMB

The PDC bit is set to ensure that a PDC will win over any other NT or W2K server on the LAN. From a Windows perspective, the PDC must

---

3. Chances are good that this node is still bitter.

also be the DMB so setting this bit *should* ensure that the DMB will win the Local Master Browser election.

The thing is, there is no guarantee that a third-party browse server will obey the criteria conventions used in Windows. For example, a Samba server can be configured to have an OS level of 255 which would cause it to win the election over the Domain Master. Ouch.

23.2 Timing Is Everything

Several different Microsoft documents provide Browse Service timing information, much of which has already been presented. For the sake of clarity, the Browse Service timings are collected in the table below. These values may be verified against the Microsoft article *Browsing and Windows 95 Networking* as well as the Leach/Naik draft.

Browser Service timings

Period	Operation
15 minutes	**Backup Browser Sync.** The Backup Browser performs a `NetServerEnum2` operation with the Local Master Browser.
15 minutes	**Local Master Browser Sync.** The Domain Master Browser performs a `NetServerEnum2` operation with a Local Master Browser when it receives a `MasterAnnouncement` from the LMB, and then repeats the sync every 15 minutes.
15 minutes	**Domain Master Browser Sync.** Local Master Browsers will contact their Domain Master Browser and perform a `NetServerEnum2` operation to retrieve the merged Browse List.
1 minute, increasing to 12	**Host and Local Master Announcements.** These announcements are sent one minute apart at first. The period typically increases in the following sequence: 1, 2, 4, 8, 12, 12, 12...
1 minute, increasing to 15	**Domain Announcements.** Similar to the previous kind, except that they peg at 15 minutes instead of 12 and the series is reported to be: 1, 1, 1, 1, 1, 15, 15...
36 minutes	The timeout period for a Host entry to time out of the local Browse List. It should be 3 × the announcement period, but in testing, some Providers listed their `Periodicity` incorrectly.

Browser Service timings

Period	Operation
45 minutes	The timeout period for a Domain entry to time out of a foreign workgroup's Browse List.
15/2 minutes	The average amount of time required before a Backup Browser discovers that its Local Master is missing, and calls another election. Elections may also be called if a Preferred Master shows up on the LAN or if a Consumer gets no response to a `GetBackupListRequest`.

If you like playing with numbers (and really, who doesn't) you can spend some time going through the mental exercise of figuring out how long it takes for Host and Domain entries to time out across subnets.

...or you could take a nice quiet walk in the forest. The forest sounds good. Yep. Forest.

24

Samba Browse Service Enhancements

> If you want something done right
> you have to do it yourself.
>
> — Well-known axiom

Sit back and think about it for a minute... There are a lot of ways to fiddle with the Browse Service. That could be good, or it could be bad. (Now would be a good time to check your firewall configuration.)

Samba takes advantage of the fiddlability of the Browse Protocol to improve the workings of the Network Neighborhood. It may break a few rules, but it gets the job done... sort of like Chicago.[1]

Samba's Browse Service enhancements are worth a bit of study, because knowing how to gracefully break the rules can provide a better insight on the proper workings of the system.

24.1 Automatic LANMAN

There may still be systems out there that run the old LAN Manager style browsing. Things like that don't die, they fade away... but, just when you think they've finally faded entirely they reach a skeletal hand up through the damp

---

1. Don't argue. I used to live there.

earth and grab your ankle. It's best to be prepared for such events, and Samba offers a very simple clove of garlic.

Samba's `smb.conf` configuration file provides the `LM ANNOUNCE` parameter, which is used to enable or disable the transmission of LAN Manager Browse Service announcements. This parameter has three possible values: `TRUE`, `FALSE`, or `AUTO`. The third option is the interesting one.

In `LM ANNOUNCE = AUTO` mode, Samba will not send any LAN Manager-style announcements until (and unless) it hears a LAN Manager Browse Service message from another system. If it hears such a message, it knows that LAN Manager style browsing is being used on the local wire and will start participating. This mode is the default for Samba, and it means that System Administrators don't ever need to think about configuring LAN Manager style browsing. It's automagical!

24.2   UnBrowsable

The `BROWSABLE` parameter can be used to completely hide a share. Share names ending with a dollar sign ('$') are supposed to be hidden, but it is up to the client to decide whether or not to display these names. They are included in the reply to the `NetShareEnum` RAP call, so the client can do as it pleases with them.

Samba can be told not to include a share in the `NetShareEnum` reply message simply by setting `BROWSABLE = NO` in the share declaration. This moves control to the server side and allows a System Administrator to really truly hide a share.

24.3   NBNS Wildcard DMB Queries and Enhanced Browsing

Samba's implementation of the NBNS supports a non-standard wildcard Domain Master Browser query. You can send a query for the name "`*<1B>`" (that's an asterisk, followed by 14 bytes of *either* space or nul padding, with a suffix byte value of `0x1B`), and Samba's NBNS will return a list of all of the IP addresses of all Domain Master Browsers that have registered with it. In other words, all of the IP addresses for all of the `<1B>` names in its database.

If the ENHANCED BROWSING parameter is set to TRUE (the default), a Samba DMB will periodically send a query for "*<1B>" to the NBNS to get the list of DMB IPs. The Samba DMB will then go through the list of IPs and send a NODE STATUS REQUEST message to any IP address that it doesn't already recognize. The reply will contain the registered *workgroup*<1B> name of the "foreign" DMB.

This trick is used by Samba to short-cut the building of the workgroup list. The normal mechanism relies on Local Master Browsers to discover foreign workgroups on their own subnet and report them back to the DMB. That process is slow and, as shown in Figure 24.1, workgroups can be isolated on separate subnets where they will never see or be seen by foreigners. By querying the NBNS for the list of DMBs, Samba does a better job of ensuring that all of the workgroups within the NBT namespace know about one another.

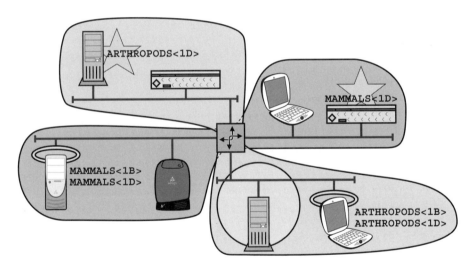

Figure 24.1: *Hidden workgroups*

The ARTHROPODS and MAMMALS workgroups are isolated because there is no subnet on which they both have a Local or Domain Master Browser. Workgroups normally find one another by broadcasting DomainAnnouncement messages on the local LAN. Samba can query the NBNS to find Domain Master Browsers on remote subnets, and synchronize with them to merge isolated Browse Lists.

...but it's not perfect. There might be workgroups out there that don't have a DMB, in which case querying the NBNS for DMB names won't help much. With Enhanced Browsing enabled, a Samba DMB will try to find lost workgroups by periodically querying other DMBs to see if they know about them. The Samba DMB then adds any missing workgroups to its internal list.

There is a downside to this second trick, which is that bogus or expired workgroup names, once added to the Browse List, may never disappear. Samba DMBs may wind up sending the bogus names back and forth like an urban legend. This is known as the "Dead Workgroup" problem. The comments under ENHANCED BROWSING in the smb.conf manual page suggest disabling this feature if empty workgroups won't go away.

Note that Windows also has a work-around for this problem. You can specify foreign DMBs in the LMHOSTS file on a known DMB, and the DMB will include the foreign names in its Browse List and try to synchronize with them.

24.4 Remote Announce

The Remote Announce feature allows a Samba server to announce itself to Local and Domain Master Browsers anywhere across the internetwork. The format of the REMOTE ANNOUNCE parameter is:

```
remote announce = [IP[/workgroup]{" "IP[/workgroup]}]
```

That is, a list of zero or more entries, separated by spaces, in which each entry consists of an IP address and an optional workgroup name. The IP and workgroup are separated by a slash. The Samba server will send HostAnnouncement Browser Frames to the specified IP address (which could be either a host or a broadcast address). If the workgroup name is specified, the Samba server will announce itself as a member of that workgroup, otherwise it will use the name specified by the smb.conf WORKGROUP parameter.

As a result of using this feature...

- An isolated server can send a directed broadcast to a subnet, where an LMB might pick it up.
- An isolated server can announce itself directly to the DMB.
- A single server can show up as a member of many workgroups.

Be careful, though, a misconfiguration can really mess things up.

24.5   Remote Browse Sync

Samba servers running as Local Master Browsers can be configured to synchronize with one another directly, without the need for a DMB. The notes in the `smb.conf` manual page explain that this is done in a Samba-specific way. The trick is fairly simple, though. Samba unicasts a `MasterAnnouncement Browser Frame` to the remote IP address.

You may recall that `MasterAnnouncement` messages are supposed to be sent to DMBs. An LMB sends them to let the DMB know that the LMB exists. The DMB then sends a `NetServerEnum2` request to the LMB to collect the Browse List and merge it with the master list... but you knew that.

Samba's extension is that a Samba LMB will also respond to a `MasterAnnouncement` message and synchronize with the sender.

It is suggested, in the `smb.conf` docs, that the destination addresses be specified as subnet broadcast addresses. Current network best practices recommend against allowing directed broadcasts, however, so on most networks you won't be able to send a broadcast message to a remote subnet. To really make this feature work, you will need to know the IP address of the Local Master Browser on the remote subnet. One way to do this is to ensure that a specific Samba server on that remote LAN always wins the LMB election.

You can fiddle the `PREFERRED MASTER` and `OS LEVEL` parameters in such a way that Samba will always win the election.

24.6   DMB != PDC

A Windows system cannot offer DMB services unless it is also the PDC.

Samba can.

Note that it doesn't work the other way 'round. If Samba is configured to be a PDC then, like Windows, it must also be the DMB for the NT Domain it serves.

25

It Can't Happen Here

> Debugging browsing
> problems is difficult
> to say the least...
>
> — Benjamin Carter
>   in an e'mail message
>   to the Samba-Technical
>   mailing list

Trouble in the Network Neighborhood? What could possibly happen to disrupt the peace and prosperity of such a stable, well run, and deliberately happy place?

Well, any society that puts presentation ahead of principle is bound to suffer. The Network Neighborhood is far from being an exception. Many things, most of them trivial, can throw a monkey-wrench into the works. To its credit, the Browse Service is fairly resilient and recovers quickly once the problem has been rectified. It also helps that it's a non-critical system. Still, fixing the problems generally requires intervention by a qualified expert. Unfortunatly, there aren't many of those around so trained professionals wind up with the job, poor dears. Let's see what we can do to help them...

25.1 Misconfigured Hosts

One of the most common and obvious problems, once you know what to look for, is a misconfigured host. Things that can go wrong include:

The wrong workgroup name in the configuration

Perhaps you entered "WROKGROPE" when you meant to type in "WEIMARANER".

425

Browser services disabled

There are Windows restistry settings and Samba configuration settings
that can prevent a node from beccomming a Potential Browser. If there
are no browser nodes on the LAN, then the Network Neighborhood will
fade away like Brigadoon.

Browser services over-enabled

A node with its OS level or other criteria set too high can win elections
over a node that is a better choice.

A misconfigured or missing NBNS server address

Local browsing will work fine without an NBNS, but cross-subnet
browsing will fail. Proper NBNS (WINS) configuration is required for
cross-subnet browsing.

P mode

In P mode, the Consumer *must* deal directly with the Domain Master
Browser. That only works if there is a DMB, and the NBNS is configured
correctly. In many cases, the Consumer node should really be running in
H or M mode.

User not authenticated

Some client systems require that the user be logged on before they start
SMB services. Also, some Browse Servers require authentication before
they permit access to the `NetServerEnum2` call.

Prolific protocol bindings

This is the biggie.

In the old IBM/Sytec days there were these things called LANAs
(**LAN A**dapters). We would call them NICs (**N**etwork **I**nterface **C**ards) today.
The original NetBIOS software spoke directly to the LANAs so, logically,
when you build an emulated NetBIOS LAN you also have virtual LANAs.

On some systems, such as Windows, you can "bind" the NetBIOS
layer to several different protocols. We have focused on NetBIOS over
TCP/UDP/IP, but Windows can also bind NetBIOS to NetBEUI and
to something called NWLink (which is Microsoft's implementation of
Novell's IPX/SPX). Each binding represents another virtual LANA. That
means that a Windows system with NetBIOS bound to multiple transport
protocols is a multi-homed host, as shown in Figure 25.1.

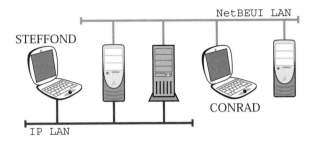

Figure 25.1:   *Multiple virtual networks*

A node with NetBIOS bound to two transport protocols is logically connected to two separate virtual NetBIOS LANs.

Consider what happens when node STEFFOND wins the Browser Election on the IP LAN, after which node CONRAD calls for an election on the NetBEUI LAN and wins. The two nodes are not on the same (virtual) LAN, so they do not know that they are competing.

One potential result of this configuration is an election storm, in which the RequestElection frames keep getting sent out (via both virtual LANAs, in some cases) but there is never any clear winner, so the elections have to start all over again. The Leach/Naik Browser draft addresses this issue by warning that a broswer node *must* be aware of the separate virtual LANs to which it is connected.[1]

25.2 Misconfigured Networks

Network configuration errors can also upset the teacart.

No DMB

If there's no Domain Master Browser, then cross-subnet browsing won't work (*unless* you set up Samba's extensions correctly).

Separated namespaces

Namespace manglement is a big deal in the CIFS world, in part because it is so easy to mess it up. The NBT namespace can be fractured if multi-

---

1. Do election storms really happen? I have heard reports of them, but never seen one first-hand.

ple, unsychronized NBNS servers are used or if P, B, and M/H nodes are mixed in the same environment.

The Browse Service relies heavily on the NBT Name Service, so it is important to make sure that the NBT namespace is consistent. Otherwise, the Browsers, Providers, and Consumers won't be able to find one another.

Isolated workgroups

Figure 24.1 showed what this problem looks like. Unless workgroups are physically mixed on the same LAN, the LMBs won't find one another and won't exchange `DomainAnnouncement` frames. That means that the workgroups will remain isolated.

25.3 Implementation Bugs

This is unverified,[2] but reliable sources report that Windows 9x systems running as Local Master Browsers do not bother to synchronize properly with the Domain Master Browser. If true, it would cause a bit of a problem with cross-subnet browsing. The common solution is to grab an old, outdated PC and load an Open Source OS on it. Then install Samba and configure it to win elections.

25.4 Troublemakers

Back several years, there was a bug in a release of Samba (somewhere in the 1.9.16 series) that would cause a Samba server to register the `<1B>` DMB name instead of the `<1D>` when it won a local election and became an LMB. This bug caused all sorts of trouble, particularly with regard to the Primary Domain Controller which, due to the rules of NetBIOS naming, was unable to register itself.

---

2. ...mostly because I don't have enough equipment to really test it.

25.5   Design Flaws

Now that you know how it works, you can decide for yourself.

26

At Home in the Network Neighborhood

Are we there yet?

— Kids in the back seat

The first time you visit a foreign country, things may seem strange and even a bit daunting. After a while, however, the scenery starts to become familiar, the customs seem less surprising, and even the rhythm of the language starts to feel comfortable.

The Browse Service is a complex system built on top of a complex set of protocols. It can also seem strange and daunting at first. Now that you have travelled through it and spent some time getting to know the inhabitants, you should feel much more at home.

By studying the Browse Service, we have also managed to provide an introduction to some of the more difficult sub-systems in the CIFS protocol suite — things like Named Pipes and SMB transactions. Understanding these is a prerequisite to dealing with the more advanced topics and sub-protocols that we have so carefully avoided.

Coverage of the Browse Service concludes our study of CIFS. Between the information presented here, the suggested references, and a good protocol analyzer there is more than enough information available to build a solid CIFS client implementation and probably a working server — but you won't really know until you try.

Welcome to the Network Neighborhood.

PART **IV**

Appendices

A

Making a Good Cup of Tea

I'm not a connoisseur.
I actually drink the stuff.

— Me

A.1 Basics of Making Tea

Most of the world knows how to make tea, but there is at least one major industrialized nation in which the preparation of a decent cup of tea is a lost art. These are very basic guidelines for the uninitiated, covering black tea in particular.

- Use loose tea; avoid teabags. Your best bet is to find a good tea shop with knowledgeable staff. If you live in the US, you may have to look online.
- Use a good teapot. A mostly-spherical ceramic pot is a good place to start. Make sure that the lid won't fall out when you pour.
- Warm the teapot by filling it with hot water.
- Bring fresh aerated water to a full boil. Just before it reaches boiling, empty your teapot and put in the tea.
- As soon as the water boils, pour it into the teapot. Cover the teapot with a towel or tea cozy.
- Let the pot sit quietly for about four minutes.
- Pour the tea from the pot through a strainer into your cup.

You will want to experiment with this a few times to find out how much tea to use, whether or not you like milk in your tea, and how much sugar (if any) you like. If you use milk, add it to the cup before you pour the tea. For a typical American mug, use approximately one glorp of milk, which is just a bit more than a full slosh. A glorp should more than cover the bottom of the mug and turn the tea a pleasant, warming, light brown color.

Never use cream in tea. Use whole milk, preferably at room temperature. The term "Cream Tea" refers to tea served with scones, jam, and whipped (or, preferably, Devonshire Clotted) cream. The cream and jam go onto the scones, not into the tea.

When putting tea into the teapot, forget everything you ever learned about coffee. The rule of thumb for tea is "one teaspoonful of tea for every cup plus one for the pot." Note, however, that the name "teaspoon" really does have meaning. If you use too much tea, the result will be heavy and bitter. Too little tea and you will have what Jonathan Swift described as "water bewitched."

 **Email**

From: Matthew Geddes, Xavier College, South Australia
  To: tng-technical@lists.dcerpc.org

I was just reading Appendix A and thought it might be worth
mentioning that tea should only be drunk from white cups. For some
reason, it don't taste right out of coffee cups (well, non-white
ones anyway). And china also appears to make the tea taste better.

A.2   About Tea

A neighbor of mine lived in India for a while, and told me that he had once toured a tea packing plant. He said that the best tea was sold to places like Australia, Russia, and the Middle East which have long had access to the very best quality tea. The middle quality tea was either kept for local consumption, or sold to Western Europe. The bottom quality tea was sent to the United States. This means that Americans need to do some looking if they want to find good tea.

Tea can be green, Oolong, or black, depending upon the degree of fermentation. A green tea is unfermented and will have the least caffeine, Oolong tea is partially fermented, and black tea is fully fermented.

The terms Assam, Ceylon, Darjeeling, and Yunnan all refer to the region in which the tea is grown. Each has its own characteristics. There are also special words describing which leaf of the tea shoot was picked and how the leaves were processed. Earl Grey tea is actually a blended black tea with a special flavoring added, and note that the term "Orange Pekoe" refers to the size of the processed tea leaves, not the variety of tea. A box labeled Orange Pekoe is typically a box of unspecified tea, probably packed into teabags.

 Email

From: Olaf Barthel
  To: Chris Hertel

```
...Incidentally, "pekoe" reportedly is chinese for "white down" and
refers to the young tender tea leaves. It doesn't have to be bad
tea, although it's often hard to tell what the heck "orange pekoe"
is supposed to be.
```

Tea is not really tea unless it is made from the leaves of a specific plant, *Camellia sinensis*. There are several products called "herbal tea" that are not tea at all, but fall instead into the category of "herbal infusion."

A.3   Nasty Habits

The teabags sold in UK supermarkets tend to make stronger tea than their rather frightening American counterparts. If you can get hold of some British teabags, you can make tea the way they do at London train stations. We call this British Rail tea.

When you order a cup of tea at a London train station they dump milk, sugar, teabag, and boiling water into the cup at the same time and then hand it to you. This makes for a uniquely generic flavor that is just right for an early morning zombie commute. You can achieve similar results on a larger scale by using a full-sized insulated carafe instead of a cup. This should last you all morning, and keep you "going" all afternoon.[1]

A.4   Decaffeinating Tea

You can decaffeinate tea at home by following these steps:

- Add a little extra tea to the pot. (This process will rob a little flavor from the tea. Adding more tea helps compensate.)
- When the water boils, pour it on and wait about twenty to thirty seconds.
- Pour the water out through a strainer, returning any captured leaves to the pot.
- Pour on freshly boiled water, and steep as usual.

This process will remove about eighty percent of the caffeine, which dissolves very quickly in water.

Author's note: I am not British. I live in Minnesota where hot drinks are required for winter survival. I did live in the UK for a year, many years ago. Being a foreigner I had to "try harder" in order to fit in — so I learned. Several years later someone accused me of being a "tea expert." I am no such thing. In fact, I know very little about tea. Unfortunately, the tiny amount of knowledge I do have seems to be more than most American restaurant and café employees can claim on the subject.

---

1. Caffeine is a diuretic. Tea generally has less caffeine than coffee, but if you drink an entire carafe's worth of either over the course of a morning you will need to visit the facilities.

B

Known NetBIOS Suffix Values

*...no warranty,
expressed or implied...*

— relevant disclaimer

B.1 NetBIOS Name Suffix Bytes

The table below classifies NetBIOS names according to their base names, the suffix byte, and their status as a unique or group name. The list was gathered from sources scattered around the Internet, old documentation, and hear-say. There are many references out there, and a good deal of variation among them. As usual, what is available is at times both contradictory and incomplete. As a result, the information presented below should be viewed with suspicion. If you have updates or comments which you can share freely, please send them to `ubiqx@ubiqx.org`.

Name Format	Suffix	Group/Unique	Service/Description
machine	<00>	unique	**Workstation Service** Known as the *NetBIOS Computer Name* or the Client Service Name because it is typically sent as the `CALLING NAME` (NBT source address) in NBT Session requests.

Name Format	Suffix	Group/Unique	Service/Description
			Some of the documentation indicates that the purpose of the Workstation Service is to receive mailslot messages directed at the node.
machine	<01>	unique	**Messenger Service** Under some versions of Windows, this name is registered by the Messenger Service and used as the CALLING NAME (NBT source address) when creating an NBT session with the Messenger Service on another node. Not all implementations use this name as the CALLING NAME when setting up a Messenger Service session. Samba uses the *machine*<00> name, and Windows 2000 uses the *machine*<03> name.
machine	<03>	unique	**Messenger Service** This name is registered by the Messenger Service, which is used to exchange "WinPopup" messages. Like the Server Service, the Messenger Service speaks SMB protocol, but it uses a different set of SMB messages and is a distinct service. When creating an NBT session, the Messenger Service client uses either the *username*<03> or *machine*<03> name as the CALLED NAME (NBT destination address) in the NBT SESSION REQUEST. The choice, of course, depends upon whether the message is being sent to a user or a node. Some, but not all, implementations of the Messenger Service client will also use the client's *machine*<03> name as the CALLING NAME in the NBT SESSION REQUEST. See also *machine*<01> and *username*<03>.

Name Format	Suffix	Group/Unique	Service/Description
machine	<06>	unique	**RAS Server Service**
machine	<1F>	unique	**NetDDE Service**
machine	<20>	unique	**File Server Service** This, of course, is the **Server Service**, which is the primary recipient of SMB connections. SMB services may be offered under any name, but this is the standard. Clients expect that the **Server Service** name will have a suffix value of 0x20.
machine	<21>	unique	**RAS Client Service**
machine	<22>	unique	**Microsoft Exchange**
machine	<23>	unique	**Microsoft Exchange**
machine	<24>	unique	**Microsoft Exchange**
machine	<2B>	group	**Lotus Notes Server Service**
machine	<30>	unique	**Modem Sharing Server Service**
machine	<31>	unique	**Modem Sharing Client Service**
machine	<42>	unique	**McAfee anit-virus** Several sites list this suffix as being used by McAfee (or, incorrectly, McCaffee) anti-virus software, but no further documentation was found to support the claim. The information may be out of date.
machine	<43>	unique	**SMS Client Remote Control**
machine	<44>	unique	**SMS Administration Remote Control Tool**
machine	<45>	unique	**SMS Client Chat**
machine	<46>	unique	**SMS Client Remote Transfer**
machine	<4C>	unique	**DEC Pathworks TCP/IP Service for Windows NT**
machine	<52>	unique	**DEC Pathworks TCP/IP Service for Windows NT**
machine	<6A>	unique	**Microsoft Exchange**
machine	<87>	unique	**Microsoft Exchange**

Name Format	Suffix	Group/Unique	Service/Description
machine	<BE>	unique	**Network Monitor Agent** Microsoft's Network Monitor (NetMon) is split into two pieces: the "Agent" and the "Client Application." The agent does the work of capturing packets, and the NetMon client provides the user interface. The advantage of this architecture is that agents and clients may run on separate machines. A single NetMon client can, therefore, have access to the capture services of multiple agents, scattered all around an intranet (or, in theory, the Internet). Putting aside the obvious security problems associated with having live capture agents on networks, this can be useful for testing and monitoring purposes. The *Network Monitor Agent* name is composed of the *machine* name padded with the value 0xBE (rather than the normal space padding) and ending with a suffix value of 0xBE. Microsoft's nbtstat utility has a strange habit of displaying this special padding character as a plus sign ('+').
machine	<BF>	unique	**Network Monitor Client Application** The Network Monitor Client Application is the GUI front-end that is used to control, filter, and display NetMon captures. The *Network Monitor Client* name is composed of the *machine* name padded with the value 0xBF (rather than the normal space padding or the 0xBE value used by the agent) and ending with a suffix value of 0xBF. Microsoft's nbtstat

Name Format	Suffix Group/Unique	Service/Description
		utility still has a strange habit of displaying this special padding character as a plus sign ('+'). The NetMon NetBIOS names may not be in use any longer. Newer versions of NetMon (starting with 2.0?) appear to use a different mechanism for communicating.
workgroup	\<00\> group	**LAN Manager Browse Service** This name is a remnant of an older Browse List distribution mechanism. There are still references to the older system in documents such as the Leach/Naik Internet Draft for Browsing (draft-leach-cifs-browser-spec-00.txt), copies of which can be found by searching the web.
workgroup or *nt_domain*	\<1B\> unique	**Domain Master Browser** This name identifies the Domain Master Browser (DMB). A Samba server can behave as a DMB without also being a Primary Domain Controller (PDC). The existence of a PDC promotes the Workgroup to the status of an NT Domain, in which case we write *nt_domain*\<1B\> instead of *workgroup*\<1B\>. If there is a PDC, it *must* provide the DMB service for the NT Domain. Domain Controllers (both Primary and Backup) register the *nt_domain*\<1C\> Internet Group name. Registration of the *nt_domain*\<1B\> name effectively distinguishes the PDC from all other DCs in the domain. The NBNS will ensure that the IP address of the (unique) \<1B\> name is the first in the list of IP addresses.

Name Format	Suffix	Group/Unique	Service/Description
nt_domain	<1C>	Internet Group	**Domain Controller** Every domain controller in the NT Domain will register this group name. The NBNS (WINS server) is expected to store all of the IP addresses associated with the name, though it will report at most 25 IP addresses in a NAME QUERY RESPONSE. The first entry in the list should be the IP address of the *Primary* Domain Controller (PDC). The rest of the IPs are ordered most recent first. This is atypical handling for group names under WINS. WINS (and, therefore, any NBNS which is WINS-compatible) will usually report only the limited broadcast address (255.255.255.255) when queried for a group name.
workgroup	<1D>	LAN unique	**Local Master Browser** This name identifies the Local Master Browser (LMB, sometimes called simply "Master Browser") for a subnet. A WINS server (and an NBNS which is WINS-compatible) will accept registration for <1D> unique names, but when queried, will always reply with a NEGATIVE NAME QUERY RESPONSE. As a result, the LMB name is unique within its local subnet only.
workgroup	<1E>	group	**Browser Election Service** Every node that is capable of acting as a browser registers this group name so that it can listen for election announcements.

Name Format	Suffix	Group/Unique	Service/Description
`\x01\x02__MSBROWSE__\x02`			**Local Master Browser**
	`<01>`	group	This group name is registered by all Local Master Browsers (LMBs). It allows LMBs on a local LAN to find one another in order to exchange Browse Lists. This is how Browse Lists for multiple Workgroups and/or NT Domains are combined.
username	`<03>`	unique	**Messenger Service**
			This name is used in the same way as *machine*`<03>` described above. A client opens an SMB connection to the Messenger Service (just as would be done with the Server Service) and uses SMB protocol to send the body of the message. The client that displays these messages is known as "WinPopup," and there are dozens of third-party implementations out there.
			Some Microsoft documentation lists this name as a group name, which would be nice. Unfortunately, in practice the name is a unique name which means that a single user logged on to multiple machines can only receive messages (sent to the *username*) on one of those machines.
			See also *machine*`<01>` and *machine*`<03>`.
internetgroup	`<20>`	Internet Group	**User Defined**
			This name type was probably introduced with Windows 2000. Group names with a suffix byte value of `0x20` can be defined as "Internet Group" names, which means that the NBNS must report up to 25 IP addresses per name when queried. The `0x20` Internet Group names are used to identify groups of systems for administrative purposes.

Name Format	Suffix	Group/Unique	Service/Description
*	<00>	unspecified	**Wildcard Name** The wildcard name is composed of an asterisk ('*') followed by fifteen nulls (the last of which is the suffix byte). This name is never registered, so it is neither a unique nor a group name. The wildcard name may be used when sending NBT NAME QUERY REQUEST and NODE STATUS REQUEST messages.
*SMBSERVER	<20>	unspecified	**File Server Service** This name is never registered (it begins with an asterisk and is, therefore, an illegal name under NBT). Many implementations, however, will accept it as a valid CALLED NAME in an NBT SESSION REQUEST message.
INet~Services	<1C>	[Internet] group	**Internet Information Server** This name is registered by IIS servers and handled as an Internet Group name. Note that the name is in mixed UPPER/lower case. It is, in fact, encoded that way, which is a little awkward.[1]
IS~*machine*	<00>	unique	**Internet Information Server** This name is formed by adding the prefix "IS~" to the machine name, padding with nuls, and using a suffix byte value of 0x00. The handling of NetBIOS names by IIS is a little... er... unusual. Nul bytes are not supposed to be used as padding except in the wildcard name. There is also a bug

---

1. As of this writing, Samba's nmblookup tool always uppercases NetBIOS names, so it cannot send a successful query for the INet~Services<1C> name. (Yes, when I get time I'll try to fix that. Maybe. Note that the libcifs nbtquery tool *can* handle mixed-case NetBIOS names; see http://ubiqx.org/libcifs/.)

Name Format	Suffix	Group/Unique	Service/Description
			(verified in testing against a set of Windows 2000 systems running IIS) which causes the suffix byte to be overwritten if the name is longer than 15 bytes. For example, adding "IS~" to the machine name "AHOSETHIULLMAN" (13 bytes) would give "IS~AHOSETHIULLMAN", which is 16 bytes long. The correct thing to do is to truncate the string and register the name "IS~AHOSETHIULLMA<00>". Instead, the trailing 'N' in the machine name overwrites the suffix byte, giving "IS~AHOSETHIULLMA<4E>" (the hex value of 'N' is 0x4E).[2]
IRISMULTICAST	<2F>	group	**Lotus Notes**
IRISNAMESERVER	<33>	group	**Lotus Notes**
Forte_$ND800ZA	<20>	group	**DCA IrmaLan Gateway Server Service**

B.2   Special Handling of NetBIOS Names in WINS

The Windows Internet Name Service (WINS) is Microsoft's implementation of the NetBIOS Name Server (NBNS) described in the RFCs. WINS does not match the RFC specifications, however, and its behavior is somewhat quirky. Known quirks are listed below.

---

2. I finally got to see this in the wild while trying to solve a browsing problem with Mike Langhus at the University of Minnesota. There were several IIS servers on the subnet, and roughly a third of them had names long enough to cause the suffix byte overwrite problem. I do not know which versions of IIS are affected, but it does not appear as though it causes any real trouble. It's more of a curiousity than a bug.

Unique names

Unique names are handled per the RFC specifications with two exceptions: multi-homed host names and the Domain Master Browser name. Read on...

Multi-homed host names

Multi-homed hosts register unique names by sending a special MULTI-HOMED NAME REGISTRATION REQUEST packet to the NBNS. The procedure is described in Section 4.3.1.4 on page 81 of this book. WINS servers (and WINS-compatible NBNS implementations) keep track of the list of IP addresses registered by a multi-homed host, and will report up to 25 IP addresses when queried for the multi-homed host name.

Group names

By default, in reply to a NAME QUERY REQUEST for a group name, WINS will send the limited broadcast address, 255.255.255.255. This is clearly not what the RFC authors had in mind.

Internet Group, Special Group, and Domain Group names

There are a few things to be said about these:

Thing I

The terms "Internet Group" and "Special Group" are used interchangeably in much of the available documentation.

Thing 2

Older references use the terms "Internet Group" and "Special Group" when referring to group names with the <1C> suffix. More recent sources add the term "Domain Group" specifically for the *nt_domain*<1C> names, and expand the use of the other terms to include groups defined by adding a special static entry, with a suffix value of <20>, to the WINS database.[3]

---

3. It was difficult to find more than superficial documentation regarding the <20> Internet Group names, which suggests that the feature is not widely used. If you want to dig deeper, search the web for information regarding the #SG and #DOM keywords used in the LMHOSTS file.

Thing 3

Internet (aka Special) and Domain Groups are defined by using the #SG and #DOM keywords in the LMHOSTS file, or via WINS configuration dialogs on Windows systems.

As with multi-homed host entries, the WINS server should keep track of as many IP addresses per name as it can handle. When queried, the POSITIVE NAME QUERY RESPONSE should list at most 25 IP addresses per Internet Group name.

Local Master Browser

The LMB registers the *workgroup*<1D> unique name. A WINS server will accept all such registrations, ignoring any conflicts, and will reply with a NEGATIVE NAME QUERY RESPONSE when queried for the name. This behavior forces M and H nodes to search for the LMB on the local IP subnet. If there is no LMB for the Workgroup on the local subnet, then the client that sent the request may call for a browser election. P nodes cannot talk to Local Master Browsers, so they communicate directly with the Domain Master Browser (if there is one).

Domain Master Browser

The DMB registers the unique *nt_domain*<1B> name. The WINS server will ensure that the IP address associated with the *nt_domain*<1B> name is always the first in the list of IPs associated with the *nt_domain*<1C> Domain Group name.

C

The SMB URL

There's a fly on the frog
On the bump on the log
In the hole in the middle of the sea.

— Traditional Folk Song

C.1   The Origins of the SMB URL

The idea of a URL scheme designed specifically for use with CIFS had been
kicked around before, but it was Richard Sharpe of the Samba Team who
finally pushed folks into digging a foundation and pouring concrete. Richard
proposed the idea to the readership of the Samba Technical mailing list, and
a lively discussion ensued. It took only a short while to work out the basic design
of the SMB URL, and most of those involved agreed that the rough-draft plans
were a good start. Richard then began work on a prototype implementation
to be included in Samba's `libsmbclient` library, and yours truly started
work on an Internet Draft for submission to the IETF.

In the broader CIFS community, however, the idea received mixed re-
views. Some thought that a URL scheme for use with SMB was a silly waste
of time. Others liked the idea so much that they started construction before
the foundation was complete, building their implementations on little more
than the nominal "specification" hammered out in the mailing list discussions.

So much for the standards process...

Fortunately, the early adopters were also CIFS-savvy folk, so as *de facto*
standards go, the SMB URL isn't all that bad. At the very least it can be said

451

that the known problems with the SMB URL are rooted firmly in the bedrock of the CIFS suite itself, and that the URL scheme doesn't do anything to make matters worse.

C.2   Of Round Pegs, Square Holes, and Big Mallets

The SMB URL might have turned out to be fairly simple and straight-forward, but this is CIFS we're talking about. CIFS is a complex protocol suite, and the requirements for the new URL scheme quickly became proportionally complex. Some of the things people wanted from the SMB URL included the ability to:

- specify SMB resources available via NBT *and* naked TCP transport,
- list all available NBT Workgroups,
- list the servers within an NBT Workgroup, and
- locate Active Directory servers and list the file servers within an Active Directory (W2K) domain.

In addition, there was a general hope that the SMB URL would look and feel a lot like the older UNC format used by Windows and OS/2, while still retaining all of the virtues of the more modern, user-friendly, and familiar URL format.

That's a lot to cram into a single URL scheme.

Although the basic design of the SMB URL took only a week or so to work out, some of the finer points required a lot more discussion. In fact, as of this writing the SMB URL Internet Draft is on its fourth revision and clearly needs to be overhauled at least one more time. The need for an update is due in part to the fact that the author didn't know much about writing IETF Internet Drafts when he started. It is also true, however, that a number of fiddly issues needed to be addressed — things like ensuring that the SMB URL scheme conformed to the general URI syntax, and annoying stuff like that.

The following discussion should, therefore, be considered unreliable. See the most current SMB URL Internet Draft or (some day, hopefully) SMB URL RFC.

C.3 Form Versus Function

The basic syntax of an absolute SMB URL looks something like this:

```
smb://[[[authdomain;]user@]host[:port][/share[/path][/name]]][?context]
```

The stuff in brackets is optional, of course, and there are a lot of brackets. That means that there's a lot of potential variety in the formation of SMB URLs. Note, too, that this is the format for the *absolute* form of the URL. An implementation should also support relative URLs.[1]

One of the fiddly bits that had to be handled when designing the SMB URL was whether the scheme identifier should be "SMB" or "CIFS". There wasn't a lot of argument over this. People just started using whichever they liked, so both were declared acceptable. In other words, "smb://" and "cifs://" both mean the same thing (and implementations should support both). We'll use "smb" here because it is more common (and because that's the one the author likes).

smb://

With no host specified, this form of the SMB URL indicates the local SMB filesharing network. In practical terms, it means the set of NBT Workgroups on the local subnet.

The way to handle this is to send an NBT broadcast query for the \x01\x02__MSBROWSE__\x02 name, thus locating any Local Master Browsers on the subnet. Query one or more of the LMBs for the list of known Workgroups, and report the results.

This form of the URL does not currently have a defined meaning in an Active Directory environment. The suggestion is that it might be used to find an Active Directory server, using the client's own fully qualified DNS domain name as a hint. If a server is found, then its W2K domain name would be returned.

---

1. This discussion assumes a basic knowledge of the workings of URLs and URIs (though it does not assume that you know the difference between a URL and a URI... I can't figure it out myself). For detailed information on URIs, URNs, and URLs see RFC 2396 and RFC 2732.

smb://netbios_name

If the host is specified using a NetBIOS name, then it *might* be the name of a Workgroup, or it *might* be the name of an SMB fileserver. The only way to know which is to send a few queries. Three queries, in fact — one for each of three different versions of the name:

- host<1B> (unicast),
- host<1D> (broadcast), and
- host<20>.

The <20> names, of course, are registered by SMB fileservers. The <1B> and <1D> names are registered by the Domain Master Browser and Local Master Browser, respectively.

Finding an SMB server is basic stuff; the browsers are a little bit trickier. LMBs can only be discovered using a broadcast query, but there may not be an LMB for the desired Workgroup on the local LAN. If the Workgroup has a DMB, it can be found by sending a query to the NBNS (assuming that the address of the NBNS is known). Not all Workgroups have a Domain Master Browser, however, so the <1B> query may also fail. Querying for both browser types simply increases the odds of finding something usable.

If, after all that, the netbios_name resolves to a Workgroup name, then the LMB or DMB should be asked for its list of member servers. If the URL resolves to an SMB fileserver, then the fileserver should be queried for the list of shares offered by the server.

There are rare cases in which the netbios_name may resolve to both a fileserver name and a Workgroup name. This is generally caused by a misconfigured NBT network. The recommended way to handle this situation is to issue a warning so that the user knows that there is a problem, but then go ahead and list both the servers in the Workgroup and the shares offered by the server. A tool with a graphical interface could, for example, provide different icons to distinguish the differnet object types as shown in Figure C.1.[2]

---

2. The network depicted in Figure C.1 is obviously poorly managed. Coffee. Pthah.

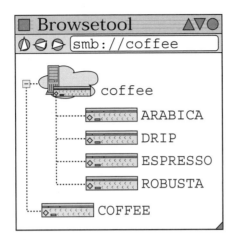

Figure C.1:   *Overloading in action*

It is rare, but possible in a misconfigured NBT network, that a Workgroup and an SMB file-server will share the same NetBIOS base name. The client application should probably make an effort to help the user sort things out.

`smb://dns_name`

If the `host` is specified as a DNS name or an IP address, then it can't represent an NBT Workgroup because Workgroups can only be identified by their NetBIOS names. It might, however, be an Active Directory server (a W2K Domain name).

Once again, the implementor is faced with having to go to the wire to discover the semantics of the URL. In this case, it may be necessary to send an LDAP query to the `host` in addition to attempting SMB connections. The `host` may be a W2K Domain Controller, an SMB server, or both.

Isn't overloading fun?

`smb://host/share`
`smb://host/share/path`
`smb://host/share/name`
`smb://host/share/path/name`

The share is the root of the shared directory tree, path is a subdirectory within the share, and name is a filename. That should all be fairly familiar stuff.

C.4 Additional Parts

Those are the basics, but there are a few more fields that need explaining.

user

> If given as part of the URL string, the username is separated from the host field using an "at" symbol ('@'). For example:
>
> ```
> smb://cue@cleden/corgi
> ```
>
> The user field is typically included in an SMB URL as an authentication shortcut, relieving the application from having to prompt for it. Note, though, that some SMB URL implementations support a further parsing of the user field into a username and password, e.g.:
>
> ```
> smb://cue:p%40ssw0rd@cleden/corgi
> ```
>
> This usage is considered bad practice, because it may encourage people to expose their passwords. Applications that handle SMB URLs should always prompt for a password, and should not support the use of the password field in the SMB URL.

authdomain

> This is a further refinement of the authentication shortcut offered by the user field. The authdomain is separated from the user name with a semicolon, as shown in the syntax expression above. As the name suggests, the authdomain represents the authentication domain in which the username is valid. The authentication domain may be either a W2K or an NT Domain name.

port

> This field, delimited by a colon, specifies the TCP port number to which to connect.

context

> The NBT layer presents some unique problems with regard to the design of a URL scheme. URLs, of course, are intended for use on the Internet, which is an IP-based network. Internet naming is handled by the DNS, and the addresses are all of the IPv4 or IPv6 variety. NBT adds a virtual NetBIOS layer, which brings with it a whole 'nother addressing system

plus a set of mechanisms to map the NetBIOS layer onto IP. The mapping requires a bit of context. In particular, the client needs to know:

- the IP address of the NBNS (WINS server), if there is one,
- the CALLING name (NetBIOS source address) to use, and
- the CALLED name (NetBIOS destination address) to use.

Clients typically gather this information from a configuration file, local host name, or destination name, but these values can be overridden using the context field of the SMB URL. The context field is set up as a URL query string. It must be at the end of the URL, separated from the rest of the string by a single question mark character. The context is given as a set of keyword/value pairs, separated by semicolons. For example:

```
smb://camarllyn/nell?called=nellie;calling=cue;nbns=10.9.7.3
```

The keywords defined in the fourth revision of the SMB URL IETF Internet Draft are:

- NBNS (alias WINS),
- CALLED,
- CALLING, and
- WORKGROUP (alias NTDOMAIN).

There is little reason to specify a Workgroup name in the context when it can be specified in the host field instead, so that one may be removed from the list. Others which may be added are:

- BROADCAST, to specify the broadcast address for B-mode operations,
- NODETYPE, to indicate B, P, M, or H mode behavior, and
- SCOPEID, to specify the Scope ID.

Putting the Scope ID into the context instead of including it as part of the NetBIOS name in the host field would greatly simplify the semantic interpretation of SMB URLs.

C.5   A Simple SMB URL Parser

Listing C.1 provides a simple, and not entirely robust, SMB URL parser. A better parser would consume a much larger portion of the time-space continuum than is available for example code. This one is a good place to start.

Listing C.1a: A simple SMB URL parser: `SMB_URL.h`

```
/* Typedefs.
 */

typedef struct
  {
  uchar *ntdomain;
  uchar *user;
  uchar *server;
  uchar *port;
  uchar *share;
  uchar *path;
  uchar *context;
  } smb_url;

/* Function prototypes.
 */

smb_url *smb_urlParse( char *src, smb_url *url );
  /* ------------------------------------------------- **
   * Parse an SMB URL string into an smb_url structure.
   * The function returns NULL on error.
   * ------------------------------------------------- **
   */

void smb_urlContent( smb_url *url );
  /* ------------------------------------------------- **
   * Dump the contents of an smb_url structure,
   * representing a parsed SMB URL string.
   * ------------------------------------------------- **
   */


/* ------------------------------------------------- */
```

Listing C.1b: A simple SMB URL parser: SMB_URL.c

```c
#include <stdio.h>
#include <string.h>

#include "smb_url.h"

smb_url *smb_urlParse( char *src, smb_url *url )
  /* ------------------------------------------------- **
   * Parse an SMB URL string into an smb_url structure.
   *
   * This is a very, very simplistic URL parser... just
   * enough for demonstration purposes.
   * It does not handle the full syntax of SMB URLs.
   * It only handles absolute URLs, and does not do
   * enough error checking.  You can certainly do better,
   * and superior examples can be found on on the web.
   *
   * The function returns NULL on error.
   * ------------------------------------------------- **
   */
  {
  int    pos;
  uchar *p;

  /* Clear the smb_url structure first. */
  (void)memset( url, 0, sizeof( smb_url ) );

  /* Check for a correct prefix. */
  pos = 0;
  if( 0 == strncasecmp( "smb://", src, 6 ) )
    pos = 6;
  else
    if( 0 == strncasecmp( "cifs://", src, 7 ) )
      pos = 7;
    else
      return( NULL );

  /* Check for an empty URL ("smb://"). */
  if( '\0' == src[pos] )
    return( url );

  /* Copy the original string so that we can carve it up. */
  src = strdup( &src[pos] );
```

```
/* Separate the server, share, path, and context
 * components.
 */
url->server = src;

/* Look for context. */
p = strrchr( src, '?' );
if( NULL != p )
  {
  *p = '\0';
  url->context = ++p;
  }

/* Share part next. */
p = strchr( src, '/' );
if( NULL != p )
  {
  *p = '\0';
  url->share = ++p;
  /* path part. */
  p = strchr( p, '/' );
  if( NULL != p )
    {
    *p = '\0';
    url->path = ++p;
    }
  }

/* Look for the ntdomain & username subfields
 * in the server string (the Authority field).
 */
p = strchr( url->server, '@' );
if( NULL != p )
  {
  *p = '\0';
  url->user = url->server;
  url->server = ++p;
  /* Split the user field into ntdomain;user */
  p = strchr( url->user, ';' );
  if( NULL != p )
    {
    *p = '\0';
    url->ntdomain = url->user;
    url->user    = ++p;
    }
  }
```

```
  /* Look for a port number in the server string. */
  p = strchr( url->server, ':' );
  if( NULL != p )
    {
    *p = '\0';
    url->port = ++p;
    }

  return( url );
  } /* smb_urlParse */

void smb_urlContent( smb_url *url )
  /* ---------------------------------------------------- **
   * Dump the contents of an smb_url structure,
   * representing a parsed SMB URL string.
   * ---------------------------------------------------- **
   */
  {
  if( url->ntdomain )
    (void)printf( "ntdomain: %s\n", url->ntdomain );
  if( url->user )
    (void)printf( "    user: %s\n", url->user );
  if( url->server )
    (void)printf( "  server: %s\n", url->server );
  if( url->port )
    (void)printf( "    port: %s\n", url->port );
  if( url->share )
    (void)printf( "   share: %s\n", url->share );
  if( url->path )
    (void)printf( "    path: %s\n", url->path );
  if( url->context )
    (void)printf( " context: %s\n", url->context );
  } /* smb_urlContent */


/* ---------------------------------------------------- */
```

D

CIFS Technical Reference

The only spec I trust
is written in C.

— Andrew Bartlett,
Samba Team

The SNIA CIFS Technical Reference is included by kind permission of the Storage Network Industry Association (SNIA). The author would like to thank the SNIA, particularly the members of the SNIA CIFS Technical Work Group, for making this document available. Please see page v of the CIFS Technical Reference for SNIA copyright information.

Please Note: The SNIA CIFS Technical Reference does not fall under the same copyright and licensing terms as the rest of the book. Special permission was obtained in order to include the CIFS Technical Reference in this book.

S N I A
Storage Networking Industry Association

Common Internet File System (CIFS)
Technical Reference
Revision: 1.0

SNIA Technical Proposal

USE OF THIS DOCUMENT IS GOVERNED BY THE TERMS AND CONDITIONS SPECIFIED ON PAGES iii-v

Release Date: 3/1/2002

Revision History

Date	By:	Comments
Feb 27, 2002	SNIA CIFS Technical Work Group	Version 1.0

Suggestion for changes or modifications to this document should be sent to the SNIA CIFS Technical Work Group at
snia-cifs@snia.org

Abstract

The Common Internet File System (CIFS) is a file sharing protocol. Client systems use this protocol to request file access services from server systems over a network. It is based on the Server Message Block protocol widely in use by personal computers and workstations running a wide variety of operating systems.   This document is a collaborative effort to produce more comprehensive documentation of the network protocol used by existing CIFS (Common Internet File System) implementations. Based on the widely used SMB (Server Message Block) network protocol, CIFS has become a key file sharing protocol due to its widespread distribution and its inclusion of enhancements that improve its suitability for internet authoring and file sharing. It is an integral part of workstation and server operating systems as well as embedded and appliance systems. In addition there has been a recent expansion of NAS (Network Attached Storage) and SAN-like (Storage Area Network) network storage server products based on CIFS. Although primarily a file sharing and authoring protocol, CIFS assumes even more importance due to the indirect use of CIFS as a transport protocol for various higher level NT and Windows9x communication protocols, as well as for network printing, resource location services, remote management/administration, network authentication (secure establishment services) and RPC (Remote Procedure Calls).

Intended Usage

The improved CIFS documentation, used as a development aid, will assist in decreased time-to-market for product developers and improved interoperability for products in the market place. It is the intent of the SNIA that this document reflect the best information available about the CIFS protocol. In certain places within the document indicated by MISSING, additional information is needed. The CIFS Technical Reference will be maintained by SNIA with the assistance of the collaborating organizations. This is not a standards document nor CIFS specification. It is a best effort at documenting the CIFS protocol as used by existing implementations. Inaccuracies or errors can be brought to the attention of the SNIA as well as new information on the existing protocol or new implementations. As new information or new implementations become available, it is the desire of the SNIA to collect and evaluate this information for possible incorporation into any future CIFS documentation that the SNIA CIFS documentation work group may choose to create.

While the authors did not intend to include any licensable material in the document, some licensable material may be present. If such material is brought to the attention of the SNIA, this material will be identified in future versions of this document, if any. The SNIA desires that any licensable material would be made available by the license owner in a reasonable and non-discriminatory fashion. If this material cannot be made available in a reasonable and non-discriminatory fashion, a best effort will be made to remove this material from any future versions of this document, if any. This intention does not reduce or diminish any rights reserved by the contributing companies with respect to their licensable material.

USE OF THIS DOCUMENT INDICATES THE USERS ASSENT TO THE DISCLAIMERS, LIMITATIONS, USAGE AGREEMENT AND OTHER TERMS AND CONDITIONS SPECIFIED ON PAGES iii-v.

DISCLAIMER OF WARRANTIES AND REPRESENTATIONS

This document is provided "as is", without any express or implied warranties or representations of any kind. Without limitation, there is no warranty of merchantability, no warranty of noninfringement, and no warranty of fitness for a particular purpose. All such warranties are expressly disclaimed.

The SNIA and the SNIA member organizations do not warrant or assume any responsibility for the accuracy or completeness of any information, text, graphics, links, cross-references, or other items contained herein.

No express or implied license to any intellectual property exists due to the presentation, publication, distribution, or other dissemination of this document, or due to any use or implementation based on the subject matter in this document.

This document is an informal Technical Reference and not a formal Standards Document or formal specification intended for adoption as a Standard. By releasing this document, the SNIA and the SNIA member organizations are neither guaranteeing nor implying that any CIFS implementation(s) distributed or sold by them, presently or in the future, are compliant or compatible with the implementation(s) described in this document. The release of this document does not prevent SNIA or any SNIA member organization from modifying and/or extending their CIFS implementation(s) at any time.

LIMITATION OF LIABILITY

The SNIA and the SNIA member organizations are not liable for any damages whatsoever arising out of the use of or inability to use this document, even if the SNIA or any SNIA member organization has been notified of the possibility of such damages.

INTELLECTUAL PROPERTY RIGHTS

The SNIA and the SNIA member organizations take no position regarding the validity or scope of any intellectual property or other rights that might be claimed to pertain to the implementation or use of the technology described in this document or the extent to which any license under such rights might or might not be available; neither do they represent that they have made any effort to identify any such rights.

COPYRIGHT AND USAGE AGREEMENT

Acknowledgements

The SNIA CIFS Documentation is a cooperative effort of the SNIA CIFS Documentation Work Group, bringing together the perspectives of system architects and developers from diverse backgrounds and perspectives in the storage industry. An effort of this scope could only be successful with support from each of the SNIA member organizations that sponsored the individuals contributing their time and knowledge to the creation and review of this document. The SNIA Board of Directors would like to extend its gratitude to this dedicated group of individuals and their sponsoring companies:

Work Group Chairman	Jim Norton, IBM
Co-Author	Bob Mastors, EMC
Co-Author	Byron Deadwiler, Hewlett-Packard
Co-Author	Bob Griswold & Jason Goodman, Microsoft
Co-Author	Christopher R. Hertel, Univ. of Minnesota
Co-Author	Dennis Chapman, Network Appliance
Co-Author	George Colley, Thursby Software Systems
Co-Author	Steve French, IBM
Co-Author	Tamir Ram, Veritas
The companies of the SNIA CIFS Documentation Work Group reflector:	ADIC, AMI, Cereva, CommVault, EMC, Eurologic, HP, IBM, KOM Networks, LSI Logic, Microsoft, Network Appliance, Novell, NSS, Quantum, Samba and Veritas

Table of Contents

Common Internet File System (CIFS)

1. Introduction

This document describes the file sharing protocol for a Common Internet File System (CIFS). CIFS is intended to provide an open cross-platform mechanism for client systems to request file services from server systems over a network. It is based on the standard Server Message Block (SMB) protocol widely in use by personal computers and workstations running a wide variety of operating systems. An earlier version of this protocol was documented as part of the X/OPEN (now Open Group) CAE series of standards [7]; this document updates the document to include the latest shipping versions, and is published to allow the creation of implementations that interoperate with those implementations.

The scope of this document is limited to describing requests and responses for file services. Separate documents exist for clients requesting services other than file services, e.g. print services.

Use of the Internet and the World Wide Web has been characterized by read-only access. Existing protocols such as FTP are good solutions for one-way file transfer. However, new read/write interfaces will become increasingly necessary as the Internet becomes more interactive and collaborative. Adoption of a common file sharing protocol having modern semantics such as shared files, byte-range locking, coherent caching, change notification, replicated storage, etc. would provide important benefits to the Internet community.

1.1. Summary of features

The protocol supports the following features:

- File access
- File and record locking
- Safe caching, read-ahead, and write-behind
- File change notification
- Protocol version negotiation
- Extended attributes
- Distributed replicated virtual volumes
- Server name resolution independence
- Batched requests
- Unicode file names

1.1.1. File access

The protocol supports the usual set of file operations: open, close, read, write, and seek.

1.1.2. File and record locking

The protocol supports file and record locking, as well as unlocked access to files. Applications that lock files cannot be improperly interfered with by applications that do not; once a file or record is locked, non-locking applications are denied access to the file.

1.1.3. Safe caching, read-ahead, and write-behind

The protocol supports caching, read-ahead, and write-behind, even for unlocked files, as long as they are safe. All these optimizations are safe as long as only one client is accessing a file; read-caching and read-ahead are safe with many clients accessing a file as long as all are just reading. If many clients are writing a file simultaneously, then none are safe, and all file operations have to go to the server. The protocol notifies all clients accessing a file of changes in the number and access mode of clients accessing the file, so that they can use the most optimized safe access method.

1.1.4. File change notification

Applications can register with a server to be notified if and when file or directory contents are modified. They can use this to (for example) know when a display needs to be refreshed, without having to constantly poll the server.

1.1.5. Protocol version negotiation

There are several different versions and sub-versions of this protocol; a particular version is referred to as a dialect. When two machines first come into network contact they negotiate the dialect to be used. Different dialects can include both new messages as well as changes to the fields and semantics of existing messages in other dialects.

1.1.6. Extended attributes

In addition to many built-in file attributes, such as creation and modification times, non-file system attributes can be added by applications, such as the author's name, content description, etc.

1.1.7. Distributed replicated virtual volumes

The protocol supports file system subtrees which look like to clients as if they are on a single volume and server, but which actually span multiple volumes and servers. The files and directories of such a subtree can be physically moved to different servers, and their names do not have to change, isolating clients from changes in the server configuration. These subtrees can also be transparently replicated for load sharing and fault tolerance. When a client requests a file, the protocol uses referrals to transparently direct a client to the server that stores it.

1.1.8. Server name resolution independence

The protocol allows clients to resolve server names using any name resolution mechanism. In particular, it allows using the DNS, permitting access to the file systems of other organizations over the Internet, or hierarchical organization of servers' names within an organization. Earlier versions of the protocol only supported a flat server name space.

1.1.9. Batched requests

The protocol supports the batching of multiple requests into a single message, in order to minimize round trip latencies, even when a later request depends on the results of an earlier one.

1.1.10.   Obsolescence

Throughout this document, references are made to obsolescent elements of the CIFS protocol. Note that these obsolescent elements are still observed in implementations. The "obsolescent" label only describes that these elements may be removed from implementations, in the future.

2. Protocol Operation Overview

In order to access a file on a server, a client has to:

- Parse the full file name to determine the server name, and the relative name within that server
- Resolve the server name to a transport address (this may be cached)
- Make a connection to the server (if no connection is already available)
- Exchange CIFS messages (see below for an example)

This process may be repeated as many times as desired. Once the connection has been idle for a while, it may be torn down.

2.1. Server Name Determination

How the client determines the name of the server and the relative name within the server is outside of the scope of this document. However, just for expository purposes, here are three examples.

In the URL "file://fs.megacorp.com/users/fred/stuff.txt", the client could take the part between the leading double slashes and the next slash as the server name and the remainder as the relative name – in this example "fs.megacorp.com" and "/users/fred/stuff.txt", respectively.

In the path name "\\corpserver\public\policy.doc" the client could take the part between the leading double backslashes and the next slash as the server name, and the remainder as the relative name -- in this example, "corpserver" and "\public\policy.doc" respectively.

In the path name "x:\policy.doc" the client could use "x" as an index into a table that contains a server name and a file name prefix. If the contents of such a table for "x" were "corpserver" and "\public", then the server name and relative name would be the same as in the previous example.

2.2. Server Name Resolution

Like server name determination, how the client resolves the name to the transport address of the server is outside the scope of this document. All that is required by CIFS is that a CIFS client MUST have some means to resolve the name of a CIFS server to a transport address, and that a CIFS server MUST register its name with a name resolution service known its clients.

Some examples of name resolution mechanisms include: using the Domain Name System (DNS) [1,2], and using NETBIOS name resolution (see RFC 1001 and RFC 1002 [3,4]). The server name might also be specified as the string form of an IPv4 address in the usual dotted decimal notation, e.g., "157.33.135.101"; in this case, "resolution" consists of converting to the 32 bit IPv4 address.

Which method is used is configuration dependent; the default SHOULD be DNS to encourage interoperability over the Internet.

Note: The name resolution mechanism used may place constraints on the form of the server name; for example, in the case of NETBIOS, the server name must be 15 characters or less, and MUST be upper case.

2.3. Sample Message Flow

The following illustrates a typical message exchange sequence for a client connecting to a user level server, opening a file, reading its data, closing the file, and disconnecting from the server. Note: using the CIFS request batching mechanism (called the "AndX" mechanism), the second to sixth messages in this sequence can be combined into one, so that there are really only three round trips in the sequence. The last trip can be handled asynchronously by the client.

Client Command	Server Response
SMB_COM_NEGOTIATE	Must be the first message sent by a client to the server. Includes a list of SMB dialects supported by the client. Server response indicates which SMB dialect should be used.
SMB_COM_SESSION_SETUP_ANDX	Transmits the user's name and credentials to the server for verification. Successful server response has Uid field set in SMB header used for subsequent SMBs on behalf of this user.
SMB_COM_TREE_CONNECT_ANDX	Transmits the name of the disk share (exported disk resource) the client wants to access. Printer device and interprocess communication devices are outside the scope of this document. Successful server response has Tid field set in SMB header used for subsequent SMBs referring to this resource.
SMB_COM_OPEN_ANDX	Transmits the name of the file, relative to Tid, the client wants to open. Successful server response includes a file id (Fid) the client should supply for subsequent operations on this file.
SMB_COM_READ	Client supplies Tid, Fid, file offset, and number of bytes to read. Successful server response includes the requested file data.
SMB_COM_CLOSE	Client closes the file represented by Tid and Fid. Server responds with success code.
SMB_COM_TREE_DISCONNECT	Client disconnects from resource represented by Tid.

2.4. CIFS Protocol Dialect Negotiation

The first message sent from a CIFS client to a CIFS server must be one whose Command field is SMB_COM_NEGOTIATE. The format of this client request includes an array of NULL terminated strings indicating the dialects of the CIFS protocol which the client supports. The server compares this list against the list of dialects the server supports and returns the index of the chosen dialect in the response message.

2.5. Message Transport

CIFS is transport independent. The CIFS protocol assumes:

- A reliable connection oriented message-stream transport, and makes no higher level attempts to ensure sequenced delivery of messages between the client and server.
- A well known endpoint for the CIFS service, such as a designated port number.
- Some mechanism to detect failures of either the client or server node, and to deliver such an indication to the client or server software so they can clean up state. When a reliable transport connection from a client terminates, all work in progress by that client is terminated by the server and all resources open by that client on the server are closed.

It can run over any transport that meets these requirements. Some transports do not natively meet all the requirements, and a standard encapsulation of CIFS for that transport may need to be defined. Appendix A defines how to run CIFS over NETBIOS over TCP; Appendix B defines how to run CIFS over TCP.

2.5.1. Connection Management

Once a connection is established, the rules for reliable transport connection dissolution are:

- If a server receives a transport establishment request from a client with which it is already conversing, the server may terminate all other transport connections to that client. This is to recover from the situation where the client was suddenly rebooted and was unable to cleanly terminate its resource sharing activities with the server.

- A server may drop the transport connection to a client at any time if the client is generating malformed or illogical requests. However, wherever possible the server should first return an error code to the client indicating the cause of the abort.

- If a server gets a unrecoverable error on the transport (such as a send failure) the transport connection to that client may be aborted.

- A server may terminate the transport connection when the client has no open resources on the server, however, we recommend that the termination be performed only after some time has passed or if resources are scarce on the server. This will help performance in that the transport connection will not need to be reestablished if activity soon begins anew. Client software is expected to be able to automatically reconnect to the server if this happens.

2.6. Opportunistic Locks

The CIFS protocol includes a mechanism called "opportunistic locks", or oplocks, that allows the client to lock a file in such a manner that the server can revoke the lock. The purpose of oplocks is to allow file data caching on the client to occur safely. It does this by defining the conditions under which an oplock is revoked.

When a client opens a file it may request an oplock on the file. If the oplock is given the client may safely perform caching. At some point in the future a second client may open the file. The following steps provide an overview of the actions taken in response to the open from the second client:

- The server holds off responding to the open from the second client.

- The server revokes the oplock of the first client.

- The first client flushes all cached data to the server.

- The first client acknowledges the revoke of the oplock.

- The server responds to the open from the second client.

As can be seen from the above steps, the first client has the opportunity to write back data and acquire record locks before the second client is allowed to examine the file. Because of this a client that holds an oplock can aggressively cache file data and state.

Anecdotal evidence suggests that oplocks provide a performance boost in many real-world applications running on existing CIFS client implementations while preserving data integrity.

2.6.1. Oplock Types

There are three types of oplocks:

- Exclusive
- Batch
- Level II

Versions of the CIFS file sharing protocol including and newer than the "LANMAN1.0" dialect support oplocks. Level II oplocks were introduced in NTLM 0.12.

2.6.1.1.   Exclusive and Batch Oplocks

When a client has an exclusive oplock on a file, it is the only client to have the file open. The exclusive oplock allows the client to safely perform file data read and write caching, metadata caching, and record lock caching. All other operations on the file cannot be safely cached.

The server may revoke the exclusive oplock at any time. The client is guaranteed that the server will revoke the exclusive oplock prior to another client successfully opening the file. This gives the client that holds the oplock the opportunity to write back cached information to the file.

The batch oplock was introduced to allow a client to defer closing a file that was opened and re-opened repetitively by an application. It has the same semantics as the exclusive oplock with the following additional guarantee. The client holding a batch oplock has the additional guarantee that the server will revoke the batch oplock prior to another client successfully making any change to the file.

When a client opens a file it can specify that it wants an exclusive oplock, a batch oplock, or no oplock. Exclusive and batch oplocks can only be obtained as a side effect of a file being opened. The protocol does not support other means to obtain exclusive and batch oplocks.

Oplocks can only be obtained on files. Oplocks are not supported on directories and named pipes. However it is not an error to request an oplock on directories and named pipes. In this case the server must return that no oplock was granted.

The server response to a successful open request includes information about what type of oplock was obtained. A server that does not support oplocks should always return that no oplock was granted.

A client that requests an exclusive oplock will get one of the following:

- An exclusive oplock
- A level II oplock
- No oplock

A client that requests a batch oplock will get one of the following:

- A batch oplock
- A level II oplock
- No oplock

A client that requests no oplock will always get no oplock.

The following diagrams the behavior of various clients and the server when an exclusive oplock is obtained on a file and subsequently revoked. The diagram also applies to a batch oplock.

Exclusive/Batch Protocol Oplock Example

Client A	Client B	< -- >	Server
Open file "foo"		- >	
		< -	Open response. Open succeeded. Exclusive oplock granted
Read data		- >	
		< -	Read response with data
Write data (cache)			
Read data (cache)			
	Open file "foo"	- >	
		< -	Oplock break to Client A
Write data		- >	
		< -	Write response
Discard cached data			
Release oplock		- >	
		< -	Open response to B. Open succeeded. No oplock granted.

The revoking of an exclusive or batch oplock involves the server sending an oplock break message to the client, followed by the client flushing file information to the server, followed by the client releasing the oplock. If the client does not respond by releasing the oplock within a period of time acceptable to the server, then the server may consider the oplock released and allow pending operations to proceed. The protocol does not define the duration of the time out period.

When a client opens a file that already has an exclusive oplock, the server first checks the share mode on the file. If the sharing allows the client open to succeed then the exclusive oplock is broken, after which the open is allowed to proceed.

When a client opens a file that already has a batch oplock, the server first revokes the batch oplock. Then the open is allowed to proceed. The reason for this server behavior is that it gives the holder of the oplock the opportunity to close the file. This in turn allows the open to obtain an exclusive or batch oplock.

When a client opens a file that has a security descriptor, the server first checks if the open for the desired access is allowed by the security descriptor. If access is not allowed, the open fails. Any exclusive or batch oplock on the file is not disturbed. Because of this behavior a client holding an exclusive or batch oplock cannot safely cache security descriptor information

2.6.1.2.   Level II Oplocks

When a client has a level II oplock on a file, it is an indication to the client that other clients may also have the file open. The level II oplock allows the client to safely perform file data read caching. All other operations on the file cannot be safely cached.

The server may revoke the level II oplock at any time. The client is guaranteed that the server will revoke the level II oplock prior to another client successfully writing the file. This gives the client that holds the level II oplock the opportunity to discard its cached data.

Note however that the level II oplock is revoked differently than an exclusive or batch oplock. A level II oplock break is sent to the client, but a response from the client is not expected. The server allows the write to proceed immediately after the level II oplock break is sent to the client.

A client cannot explicitly request that a level II oplock be granted. A level II oplock is granted either when a file is opened or when a server revokes an exclusive or batch oplock.

When a file is opened the client may request an exclusive or batch oplock. The server has the option of granting a level II oplock instead of the requested type of oplock. This is the only way to obtain a level II oplock when a file is opened.

When a server revokes an exclusive or batch oplock, it may indicate to the client that in conjunction with the revocation that the client is being granted a level II oplock.

The following diagrams the behavior of various clients and the server when a level II oplock is obtained on a file and subsequently revoked.

Level II Oplock Protocol Example

Client A	Client B	< -- >	Server
Open file "foo"		- >	
		< -	Open response. Open succeeded. Exclusive oplock granted
Read data		- >	
		< -	Read response with data
	Open file "foo"	- >	
		< -	Oplock break to Client A. Oplock downgraded to level II.
Release oplock to level II		- >	
		< -	Open response to B. Open succeeded. Oplock level II granted.

2.6.2. Comparison with Other File Locking Methods

The CIFS protocol has three mechanisms to enable a client to control how other clients access a file.

- Opportunistic locks
- Byte range locks
- Sharing locks

Of the three, the server may revoke only opportunistic locks. Byte range and sharing locks are held for as long as the client desires.

Historically on client systems, byte range and sharing locks are exposed to the application. This allows the application to have explicit control over the obtaining and releasing of these types of locks.

Typically however oplocks are not exposed to the application. They are implemented inside the client operating system. The client operating system decides when it is appropriate to obtain and release oplocks. It also handles all of the issues related to revoking of oplocks by the server.

2.6.3. Oplock SMBs

This section summarizes the SMB commands that affect oplocks.

2.6.3.1.   Obtaining an Oplock

The following SMB commands may be used to obtain an oplock:

- SMB_COM_OPEN
- SMB_COM_CREATE
- SMB_COM_CREATE_NEW
- SMB_COM_OPEN_ANDX
- SMB_COM_TRANSACTION2 (OPEN2)
- SMB_COM_NT_CREATE_ANDX
- SMB_COM_NT_TRANSACT (NT_CREATE)

The server may only grant a level II oplock to a client for a file when that file is opened using one of "SMB_COM_NT_CREATE_ANDX" or "SMB_COM_NT_TRANSACT (NT_CREATE)".

2.6.3.2.   Releasing an Oplock

A client releases an oplock with the SMB_COM_LOCKING_ANDX command. Alternatively the client may release the oplock by closing the file with the SMB_COM_CLOSE command. Any operation that would invalidate the file handle results in the oplock being released. This includes disconnecting the tree, logging off the user that opened the file, and any action that would disconnect the session.

A client should release its exclusive or batch oplock on a file in response to the server revoking the oplock. Failure to do so is a violation of the protocol.

A client does not need to release a level II oplock (i.e. respond to the server) on a file in response to the server revoking the oplock. However doing so is not an error.

2.6.3.3.   Revoking an Oplock

The server revokes a client's oplock by sending a SMB_COM_LOCKING_ANDX command to the client. The command is sent asynchronously sent from the server to the client. This message has the LOCKING_ANDX_OPLOCK_RELEASE flag set indicating to the client that the oplock is being broken. *OplockLevel* indicates the type of oplock the client now owns. If *OplockLevel* is 0, the client possesses no oplocks on the file at all. If *OplockLevel* is 1, the client possesses a Level II oplock. The client is expected to flush any dirty buffers to the server, submit any file locks, and respond to the server with either an SMB_LOCKING_ANDX SMB having the LOCKING_ANDX_OPLOCK_RELEASE flag set, or with a file close if the file is no longer in use by the client.

2.6.4. Other Issues

Since a close being sent to the server and break oplock notification from the server could cross on the wire, if the client gets an oplock notification on a file that it does not have open, that notification should be ignored. The client is guaranteed that an oplock break notification will not be issued before the server has sent the response to the file open.

Due to timing, the client could get an "oplock broken" notification in a user's data buffer as a result of this notification crossing on the wire with an SMB_COM_READ_RAW request. The client must detect this (use length of message, "FFSMB," MID of -1 and *Command* of SMB_COM_LOCKING_ANDX) and honor the "oplock broken" notification as usual. The server must also note on receipt of an SMB_COM_READ_RAW request that there is an outstanding (unanswered) "oplock broken" notification to the client; it must then return a zero length response denoting failure of the read raw request. The client should (after responding to the "oplock broken" notification) use a non-raw read request to redo the read. This allows a file to actually contain data matching an "oplock broken" notification and still be read correctly.

When an exclusive or batch oplock is being revoked, more than one client open request may be paused until the oplock is released. Once the oplock is released, the order that the paused open requests are processed is not defined.

The protocol allows a client to obtain an oplock and then issue an operation that causes the oplock to be revoked. An example of this is a client obtaining an exclusive oplock on a file and then opening the file a second time.

The protocol allows a client to have a file open multiple times, and each open could have a level II oplock associated with it. A server may choose not to support this situation by simply not handing out more than one level II oplock for a particular file to a particular client.

The protocol allows a server to grant on a single file a level II oplock for some opens and no oplock for other opens. A server may have heuristics that indicate some file opens would not benefit from a level II oplock.

A server that supports access to files via mechanisms other than this protocol must revoke oplocks as necessary to preserve the semantics expected by the clients owning the oplocks.

A client that has an exclusive or batch oplock on a file may cache file metadata. This includes the following information: create time, modify time, access time, change time, file size, file attributes, and extended attributes size. However a server is not required to break an oplock when a second client examines file metadata. Clients should be aware of this behavior when examining file metadata without having the file open.

When a server revokes an exclusive or batch oplock it may grant a level II oplock in its place. The client should consider the level II oplock in effect after the client has released the exclusive or batch oplock. The server may decide to revoke the level II oplock before the client has released the exclusive or batch oplock. In this situation the client should behave as if the revoke of the level II oplock arrived just after the exclusive or batch oplock was released.

2.7. Security Model

Each server makes a set of resources available to clients on the network. A resource being shared may be a directory tree, printer, etc. So far as clients are concerned, the server has no storage or service dependencies on any other servers; a client considers the server to be the sole provider of the file (or other resource) being accessed.

The CIFS protocol requires server authentication of users before file accesses are allowed, and each server authenticates its own users. A client system must send authentication information to the server before the server will allow access to its resources.

A server requires the client to provide a user name and some proof of identity (often something cryptographically derived from a password) to gain access. The granularity of authorization is up to the server. For example, it may use the account name to check access control lists on individual files, or may have one access control list that applies to all files in the directory tree.

When a server validates the account name and password presented by the client, an identifier representing that authenticated instance of the user is returned to the client in the Uid field of the response SMB. This Uid must be included in all further requests made on behalf of the user from that client.

2.8. Authentication

This section defines the CIFS user and message authentication protocols. User authentication allows the server to verify that the client knows a password for a user. Message authentication allows messages in a session to be verified by both the server and the client.

2.8.1. Overview

User authentication is based on the shared knowledge of the user's password. There are two styles of user authentication. The first involves the client sending passwords in plain text to the server. The second involves a challenge/response protocol.

Plain text password authentication exposes the user's password to programs that have access to the CIFS protocol data on the network. For this reason plain text password authentication is discouraged and by default should be disabled in CIFS protocol implementations.

With the challenge/response protocol the server sends a "challenge" to the client, which the client responds to in a way that proves it knows the user's password. A "response" is created from the challenge by encrypting it with a 168 bit "session key" computed from the user's password. The response is then returned to the server, which can validate the response by performing the same computation.

The user authentication protocol is described as if the CIFS server keeps a client's password. However an implementation might actually store the passwords on a key distribution server and have servers use a protocol outside the scope of this document to enable them to perform the steps required by this protocol.

Messages may be authenticated by computing a message authentication code (MAC) for each message and attaching it to the message. The MAC used is a keyed MD5 construction similar to that used in IPSec [RFC 1828], using a "MAC key" computed from the session key, and the response to the server's challenge. The MAC is over both the message text and an implicit sequence number, to prevent replay attacks.

2.8.2. Base Algorithms

Following are definitions of algorithms used by the authentication algorithms.

$E(K, D)$

denote the DES block mode encryption function [FIPS 81] , which accepts a seven byte key (K) and an eight byte data block (D) and produces an eight byte encrypted data block as its value.

Ex(K,D)

    denote the extension of DES to longer keys and data blocks. If the data to be encrypted is
longer than eight bytes, the encryption function is applied to each block of eight bytes in
sequence and the results are concatenated together. If the key is longer than seven bytes, each
8 byte block of data is first completely encrypted using the first seven bytes of the key, then
the second seven bytes, etc., appending the results each time. For example, to encrypt the 16
byte quantity D0D1 with the 14 byte key K0K1,

      Ex(K0K1,D0D1) = concat(E(K0,D0),E(K0,D1),E(K1,D0),E(K1,D1))

concat(A, B, ..., Z)

    is the result of concatenating the byte strings A, B, ... Z

head(S, N)

    denote the first N bytes of the byte string S.

swab(S)

    denote the byte string obtained by reversing the order of the bits in each byte of S, i.e., if S is
byte string of length one, with the value 0x37 then swab(S) is 0xEC.

zeros(N)

    denote a byte string of length N whose bytes all have value 0 (zero).

ones(N)

    denote a byte string of length N whose bytes all have value 255.

xor(A, B)

    denote a byte string formed by the bytewise logical "xor" of each of the bytes in A and B.

and(A, B)

    denote a byte string formed by the bytewise logical "and" of each of the bytes in A and B.

substr(S, A, B)

    denote a byte string of length N obtained by taking N bytes of S starting at byte A. The first
byte is numbered zero. I.e., if S is the string "NONCE" then substr(S, 0, 2) is "NO".

2.8.3. Authentication Algorithms

Following are definitions of the authentication algorithms.

2.8.3.1.   NT Session Key

The session key S21 and partial MAC key S16 are computed as

    S16 = MD4(PN)

    S21 = concat(S16, zeros(5))

where

- PN is a Unicode string containing the user's password in clear text, case sensitive, no maximum length

- MD4(x) of an byte string "x" is the 16 byte MD4 message digest [RFC 1320] of that string

2.8.3.2.   LM Session Key

The session key S21 and partial MAC key S16 are computed as

$$S16X = Ex(swab(P14), N8)$$
$$S21 = concat(S16X, zeros(5))$$
$$S16 = concat(head(S16X, 8), zeros(8))$$

Where

- P14 is a 14 byte ASCII string containing the user's password in clear text, upper cased, padded with nulls

- N8 is an 8 byte string whose value is {0x4b, 0x47, 0x53, 0x21, 0x40, 0x23, 0x24, 0x25}

2.8.3.3.   Response

The response to the challenge RN is computed as

$$RN = EX(S21, C8)$$

Where

- C8 is a 8 byte challenge selected by the server
- S21 is the LM session key or NT session key as determined above

2.8.3.4.   MAC key

The MAC key is computed as follows:

$$K = concat(S16, RN)$$

Where

- S16 is the partial MAC key computed with the LM session key or NT session key as determined above
- RN is the response to the challenge as determined above
- The result K is either 40 or 44 bytes long, depending on the length of RN. [ed: what determines length of RN?]

2.8.3.5.   Message Authentication Code

The MAC is the keyed MD5 construction:

$$MAC(K, text) = head(MD5(concat(K, text)), 8)$$

Where

- MD5 is the MD5 hash function; see RFC 1321
- K is the MAC key determined above
- text is the message whose MAC is being computed.

2.8.4. Session Authentication Protocol

2.8.4.1.   Plain Text Password

If plaintext password authentication was negotiated, clients send the plaintext password in `SMB_COM_TREE_CONNECT`, `SMB_COM_TREE_CONNECT_ANDX`, and/or `SMB_COM_SESSION_SETUP_ANDX`. The SMB field used to contain the response depends upon the request:

- *Password* in SMB_COM_TREE_CONNECT
- *Password* in SMB_COM_TREE_CONNECT_ANDX
- *AccountPassword* in SMB_COM_SESSION_SETUP_ANDX in dialects prior to "NTLM 0.12"
- *CaseInsensitivePassword* in SMB_COM_SESSION_SETUP_ANDX in the "NTLM 0.12" dialect
- *CaseSensitivePassword* in SMB_COM_SESSION_SETUP_ANDX in the "NTLM 0.12" dialect

2.8.4.2.   Challenge/Response

The challenge C8 from the server to the client is contained in the *EncryptionKey* field in the `SMB_COM_NEGPROT` response. Clients send the response to the challenge in `SMB_COM_TREE_CONNECT`, `SMB_COM_TREE_CONNECT_ANDX`, and/or `SMB_COM_SESSION_SETUP_ANDX`. The SMB field used to contain the response depends upon the request:

- *Password* in SMB_COM_TREE_CONNECT
- *Password* in SMB_COM_TREE_CONNECT_ANDX
- *AccountPassword* in SMB_COM_SESSION_SETUP_ANDX in dialects prior to "NTLM 0.12"
- *CaseInsensitivePassword* in SMB_COM_SESSION_SETUP_ANDX for a response computed using the "LM session key" in the "NTLM 0.12" dialect
- *CaseSensitivePassword* in SMB_COM_SESSION_SETUP_ANDX for a response computed using the "NT session key" in the "NTLM 0.12" dialect

The challenge/response authentication protocol has the following steps:

- The server chooses an 8 byte challenge C8 and sends it to the client.
- The client computes RN as described above
- The client sends the 24 byte response RN to the server
- The server computes RN as described above and compares the received response with its computed value for RN; if equal, the client has authenticated.

2.8.5. Message authentication code

Once a user logon has been authenticated, each message can be authenticated as well. This will prevent man in the middle attacks, replay attacks, and active message modification attacks.

To use message authentication, the client sets `SMB_FLAGS2_SMB_SECURITY_SIGNATURE` in SMB_COM_SESSION_SETUP_ANDX request to the server, and includes a MAC. If the resulting logon is non-null and non-guest, then the SMB_COM_SESSION_SETUP_ANDX response and all subsequent SMB requests and responses must include a MAC. The first non-null, non-guest logon determines the key to be used for the MAC for all subsequent sessions.

Message authentication may only be requested when the "NTLM 0.12" dialect has been negotiated. If message authentication is used, raw mode MUST not be used (because some raw mode messages have no headers in which to carry the MAC).

Let

- SN be a request sequence number, initially set to 0. Both client and server have one SN for each connection between them.
- RSN be the sequence number expected on the response to a request.
- req_msg be a request message
- rsp_msg be a response message

The SN is logically contained in each message and participates in the computation of the MAC.

For each message sent in the session, the following procedure is followed:

- Client computes MAC(req_msg) using SN, and sends it to the server in the request message. If there are multiple requests in the message (using the "AndX" facility), then the MAC is calculated as if it were a single large request.
- Client increments its SN and saves it as RSN
- Client increments its SN – this is the SN it will use in its next request
- Server receives each req_msg, validates MAC(req_msg) using SN, and responds ACCESS_DENIED if invalid
- Server increments its SN and saves it as RSN
- Server increments its SN – this is the SN it will expect in the next request
- Server computes MAC(rsp_msg) using RSN, and sends it to client in the response message. If there are multiple responses in the message (using the "AndX" facility) , then the MAC is calculated as if it were a single large response.
- Client receives each rsp_msg, validates MAC(rsp_msg) using RSN, and discards the response message if invalid

In each message that contains a MAC, the following bit is set in the flags2 field:

```
#define SMB_FLAGS2_SMB_SECURITY_SIGNATURES 0x0004
```

The sender of a message inserts the sequence number SSN into the message by putting it into the first 4 bytes of the SecuritySignature field and zeroing the last 4 bytes, computes the MAC over the entire message, then puts the MAC in the field. The receiver of a message validates the MAC by extracting the value of the SecuritySignature field, putting its ESN into the first 4 bytes of the SecuritySignature field and zeroing the last 4 bytes, computing the MAC, and comparing it to the extracted value.

Oplock break messages from the server to the client may not use message authentication, even if it has been negotiated.

2.8.6. Security Level

The SMB_COM_NEGPROT response from a server has the following bits in its *SecurityMode* field:

```
#define NEGOTIATE_SECURITY_USER_LEVEL            0x01
#define NEGOTIATE_SECURITY_CHALLENGE_RESPONSE    0x02
#define NEGOTIATE_SECURITY_SIGNATURES_ENABLED    0x04
#define NEGOTIATE_SECURITY_SIGNATURES_REQUIRED   0x08
```

If NEGOTIATE_SECURITY_USER_LEVEL is set, then "user level" security is in effect for all the shares on the server. This means that the client must establish a logon (with SMB_COM_SESSION_SETUP_ANDX) to authenticate the user before connecting to a share, and the password to use in the authentication protocol described above is the user's password. If NEGOTIATE_SECURITY_USER_LEVEL is clear, then "share level" security is in effect for all the shares in the server. In this case the authentication protocol is a password for the share.

If NEGOTIATE_SECURITY_CHALLENGE_RESPONSE is clear, then the server is requesting plaintext passwords.

If NEGOTIATE_SECURITY_CHALLENGE_RESPONSE is set, then the server supports the challenge/response session authentication protocol described above, and clients should use it. Servers may refuse connections that do not use it.

If the dialect is earlier than "NTLM 0.12" then the client computes the response using the "LM session key". If the dialect is "NTLM 0.12" then the client may compute the response either using the "LM session key", or the "NT session key", or both. The server may choose to refuse responses computed using the "LM session key".

If NEGOTIATE_SECURITY_SIGNATURES_ENABLED is set, then the server supports the message authentication protocol described above, and the client may use it. This bit may only be set if NEGOTIATE_SECURITY_CHALLENGE_RESPONSE is set.

If NEGOTIATE_SECURITY_SIGNATURES_REQUIRED is set, then the server requires the use of the message authentication protocol described above, and the client must use it. This bit may only be set if NEGOTIATE_SECURITY_SIGNATURES_ENABLED is set. This bit must not be set if NEGOTIATE_SECURITY_USER_LEVEL is clear (i.e., for servers using "share level" security).

2.9. Distributed File System (DFS) Support

Protocol dialects of NT LM 0.12 and later support distributed filesystem operations. The distributed filesystem gives a way for this protocol to use a single consistent file naming scheme which may span a collection of different servers and shares. The distributed filesystem model employed is a referral - based model. This protocol specifies the manner in which clients receive referrals.

The client can set a flag in the request SMB header indicating that the client wants the server to resolve this SMB's paths within the DFS known to the server. The server attempts to resolve the requested name to a file contained within the local directory tree indicated by the TID of the request and proceeds normally. If the request pathname resolves to a file on a different system, the server returns the following error:

STATUS_DFS_PATH_NOT_COVERED - the server does not support the part of the DFS namespace needed to resolve the pathname in the request. The client should request a referral from this server for further information.

A client asks for a referral with the TRANS2_DFS_GET_REFERRAL request containing the DFS pathname of interest. The response from the server indicates how the client should proceed.

The method by which the topological knowledge of the DFS is stored and maintained by the servers is not specified by this protocol.

3. SMB Message Formats and Data Types

Clients exchange messages with a server to access resources on that server. These messages are called Server Message Blocks (SMBs), and every SMB message has a common format.

This section describes the entire set of SMB commands and responses exchanged between CIFS clients and servers. It also details which SMBs are introduced into the protocol as higher dialect levels are negotiated.

3.1. Notation

This document makes use of "C"-like notation to describe the formats of messages. Unlike the "C" language, which allows for implementation flexibility in laying out structures, this document adopts the following rules. Multi-byte values are always transmitted least significant byte first. All fields, except "bit-fields", are aligned on the nearest byte boundary (even if longer than a byte), and there is no implicit padding. Fields using the "bit field" notation are defined to be laid out within the structure with the first-named field occupying the lowest order bits, the next named field the next lowest order bits, and so on. BOOLEAN is defined to be a single byte. The SHORT and LONG types are little endian.

3.2. SMB header

While each SMB command has specific encodings, there are some fields in the SMB header, which have meaning to all SMBs. These fields and considerations are described in the following sections.

```
typedef unsigned char UCHAR;        // 8 unsigned bits
typedef unsigned short USHORT;      // 16 unsigned bits
typedef unsigned long ULONG;        // 32 unsigned bits

typedef struct {
    ULONG LowPart;
    LONG HighPart;
} LARGE_INTEGER;                    // 64 bits of data

typedef struct {
    UCHAR Protocol[4];              // Contains 0xFF,'SMB'
    UCHAR Command;                  // Command code
    union {
        struct {
            UCHAR ErrorClass;       // Error class
            UCHAR Reserved;         // Reserved for future use
            USHORT Error;           // Error code
        } DosError;
        ULONG Status;               // 32-bit error code
    } Status;
    UCHAR Flags;                    // Flags
    USHORT Flags2;                  // More flags
    union {
        USHORT Pad[6];              // Ensure section is 12 bytes long
        struct {
            USHORT PidHigh;         // High Part of PID
            UCHAR SecuritySignature[8];   // reserved for MAC
        } Extra;
    };
```

```
        USHORT Tid;                              // Tree identifier
        USHORT Pid;                              // Caller's process ID, opaque for
    client use
        USHORT Uid;                              // User id
        USHORT Mid;                              // multiplex id
        UCHAR  WordCount;                        // Count of parameter words
        USHORT ParameterWords[WordCount];        // The parameter words
        USHORT ByteCount;                        // Count of bytes
        UCHAR  Buffer[ByteCount];                // The bytes
    } SMB_HEADER;
```

All SMBs in this document have an identical format up to the ParameterWords field. (However, this is not true for some obsolescent SMBs.) For the last fields in the header, different SMBs have a different number and interpretation of the ParameterWords and Buffer fields. All reserved fields in the SMB header must be zero.

3.2.1. Command field

The Command is the operation code that this SMB is requesting or responding to. See section 5.1 below for number values, and section 4 for a description of each operation.

3.2.2. Flags field

This field contains 8 individual flags, numbered from least significant bit to most significant bit, which are defined below. Flags that are not defined MUST be set to zero by clients and MUST be ignored by servers.

Bit	Meaning	Earliest Dialect
0	Reserved for obsolescent requests LOCK_AND_READ, WRITE_AND_CLOSE	LANMAN1.0
1	Reserved (must be zero).	
2	Reserved (must be zero).	
3	When on, all pathnames in this SMB must be treated as case-less. When off, the pathnames are case sensitive.	LANMAN1.0
4	Obsolescent – client case maps (canonicalizes) file and directory names; servers must ignore this flag.	
5	Reserved for obsolescent requests – oplocks supported for SMB_COM_OPEN, SMB_COM_CREATE and SMB_COM_CREATE_NEW. Servers must ignore when processing all other SMB commands.	LANMAN1.0
6	Reserved for obsolescent requests – notifications supported for SMB_COM_OPEN, SMB_COM_CREATE and SMB_COM_CREATE_NEW. Servers must ignore when processing all other SMB commands.	LANMAN1.0
7	SMB_FLAGS_SERVER_TO_REDIR - When on, this SMB is being sent from the server in response to a client request. The Command field usually contains the same value in a protocol request from the client to the server as in the matching response from the server to the client. This bit unambiguously distinguishes the command request from the command response.	PC NETWORK PROGRAM 1.0

3.2.3. Flags2 Field

This field contains nine individual flags, numbered from least significant bit to most significant bit, which are defined below. Flags that are not defined MUST be set to zero by clients and MUST be ignored by servers.

Bit	Name: SMB_FLAGS2_	Meaning	Earliest Dialect
0	KNOWS_LONG_NAMES	If set in a request, the server may return long components in path names in the response.	LM1.2X002
1	KNOWS_EAS	If set, the client is aware of extended attributes (EAs).	
2	SECURITY_SIGNATUR E	If set, the SMB is integrity checked.	
3	RESERVED1	Reserved for future use	
6	IS_LONG_NAME	If set, any path name in the request is a long name.	
11	EXT_SEC	If set, the client is aware of Extended Security negotiation.	NT LM 0.12
12	DFS	If set, any request pathnames in this SMB should be resolved in the Distributed File System.	NT LM 0.12
13	PAGING_IO	If set, indicates that a read will be permitted if the client does not have read permission but does have execute permission. This flag is only useful on a read request.	
14	ERR_STATUS	If set, specifies that the returned error code is a 32 bit error code in Status.Status. Otherwise the Status.DosError.ErrorClass and Status.DosError.Error fields contain the DOS-style error information. When passing NT status codes is negotiated, this flag should be set for every SMB.	NT LM 0.12
15	UNICODE	If set, any fields of datatype STRING in this SMB message are encoded as UNICODE. Otherwise, they are in ASCII. The character encoding for Unicode fields SHOULD be UTF-16 (little endian).	NT LM 0.12

3.2.4. Tid Field

Tid represents an instance of an authenticated connection to a server resource. The server returns Tid to the client when the client successfully connects to a resource, and the client uses Tid in subsequent requests referring to the resource.

In most SMB requests, Tid must contain a valid value. Exceptions are those used prior to getting a Tid established, including SMB_COM_NEGOTIATE, SMB_COM_TREE_CONNECT_ANDX, SMB_COM_ECHO, and SMB_COM_SESSION_SETUP_ANDX. 0xFFFF should be used for Tid for these situations. The server is always responsible for enforcing use of a valid Tid where appropriate.

On SMB_COM_TREE_DISCONNECT over a given transport connection, with a given Tid, the server will close any files opened with that Tid over that connection.

3.2.5. Pid Field

Pid is the caller's process id, and is generated by the client to uniquely identify a process within the client computer. Concurrency control is associated with Pid (and PidHigh)—sharing modes, and locks are arbitrated using the Pid. For example, if a file is successfully opened for exclusive access, subsequent opens from other clients or from the same client with a different Pid will be refused.

Clients inform servers of the creation of a new process by simply introducing a new Pid value into the dialogue for new processes. The client operating system must ensure that the appropriate close and cleanup SMBs will be sent when the last process referencing a file closes it. From the server's point of view, there is no concept of Fids "belonging to" processes. A Fid returned by the server to one process may be used by any other process using the same transport connection and Tid.

It is up to the client operating system to ensure that only authorized client processes gain access to Fids (and Tids). On SMB_COM_TREE_DISCONNECT (or when the client and server session is terminated) with a given Tid, the server will invalidate any files opened by any process on that client.tid Field

3.2.6. Uid Field

Uid is a reference number assigned by the server after a user authenticates to it, and that it will associate with that user until the client requests the association be broken. After authentication to the server, the client SHOULD make sure that the Uid is not used for a different user that the one that authenticated. (It is permitted for a single user to have more than one Uid.) Requests that do authorization, such as open requests, will perform access checks using the identity associated with the Uid.

3.2.7. Mid Field

The multiplex ID (Mid) is used along with the Pid to allow multiplexing the single client and server connection among the client's multiple processes, threads, and requests per thread. Clients may have many outstanding requests (up to the negotiated number, MaxMpxCount) at one time. Servers MAY respond to requests in any order, but a response message MUST always contain the same Mid and Pid values as the corresponding request message. The client MUST NOT have multiple outstanding requests to a server with the same Mid and Pid.

3.2.8. Status Field

An SMB returns error information to the client in the Status field. Protocol dialects prior to NT LM 0.12 return status to the client using the combination of Status.DosError.ErrorClass and Status.DosError.Error. Beginning with NT LM 0.12 CIFS servers can return 32 bit error information to clients using Status.Status if the incoming client SMB has bit 14 set in the Flags2 field of the SMB header. The contents of response parameters are not guaranteed in the case of an error return, and must be ignored. For write-behind activity, a subsequent write or close of the file may return the fact that a previous write failed. Normally write-behind failures are limited to hard disk errors and device out of space.

3.2.9. Timeouts

In general, SMBs are not expected to block at the server; they should return "immediately". There are however a series of operations which may block for a significant time. The most obvious of these is named-pipe operations, which may be dependent on another application completing a write before they can fully complete their read. (Most named-pipe operations are never expired unless cancelled). Similarly, with byte-range locking, the Timeout period is specified by the client, so the server is not responsible for blocking on this operation as long as the client has specified it may. A SMB server should put forth its best effort to handle operations as they arrive in an efficient manner, such that clients do not timeout operations believing the server to be unresponsive falsely. A client may timeout a pending operation by terminating the session. If a server implementation can not support timeouts, then an error can be returned just as if a timeout had occurred if the resource is not available immediately upon request.

3.2.10.   Data Buffer (BUFFER) and String Formats

The data portion of SMBs typically contains the data to be read or written, file paths, or directory paths. The format of the data portion depends on the message. All fields in the data portion have the same format. In every case it consists of an identifier byte followed by the data.

Identifier	Description	Value
Data Block	See below	1
Dialect	Null terminated string	2
Pathname	Null terminated string	3
ASCII	Null terminated string	4
Variable Block	See below	5

When the identifier indicates a data block or variable block then the format is a word indicating the length followed by the data.

In all dialects prior to NT LM 0.12, all strings are encoded in ASCII. If the agreed dialect is NT LM 0.12 or later, Unicode strings may be exchanged. Unicode strings include file names, resource names, and user names. This applies to null-terminated strings, length specified strings and the type-prefixed strings. In all cases where a string is passed in Unicode format, the Unicode string must be word-aligned with respect to the beginning of the SMB. Should the string not naturally fall on a two-byte boundary, a null byte of padding will be inserted, and the Unicode string will begin at the next address. In the description of the SMBs, items that may be encoded in Unicode or ASCII are labeled as STRING. If the encoding is ASCII, even if the negotiated string is Unicode, the quantity is labeled as UCHAR.

For type-prefixed Unicode strings, the padding byte is found after the type byte. The type byte is 4 (indicating SMB_FORMAT_ASCII) independent of whether the string is ASCII or Unicode. For strings whose start addresses are found using offsets within the fixed part of the SMB (as opposed to simply being found at the byte following the preceding field,) it is guaranteed that the offset will be properly aligned.

Strings that are never passed in Unicode are:

- The protocol strings in the Negotiate SMB request.
- The service name string in the Tree_Connect_AndX SMB.

When Unicode is negotiated, the SMB_FLAGS2_UNICODE bit should be set in the Flags2 field of every SMB header.

Despite the flexible encoding scheme, no field of a data portion may be omitted or included out of order. In addition, neither a WordCount nor ByteCount of value 0 at the end of a message may be omitted.

3.3. Name Restrictions

The following four reserved characters MUST not be used in share names (network names), user names, group names or domain names.

"\", "/", "?", "*"

The following ten characters SHOULD not be used in share names, user names, group names or domain names as they are considered reserved by multiple existing implementations:

"[", "]", ".", ";", "|", "=", ",", "+", "<", ">"

A share name or server or workstation name SHOULD not begin with a period (".") nor should it include two adjacent periods ("..").

The same naming considerations apply for RFC 1001 names for servers or workstations when using Netbios over TCP/IP name resolution mechanisms.

3.4. File Names

File names in the CIFS protocol consist of components separated by a backslash ('\'). Early clients of the CIFS protocol required that the name components adhere to an 8.3 format name. These names consist of two parts: a basename of no more than 8 characters, and an extension of no more than 3 characters. The basename and extension are separated by a '.'. All characters are legal in the basename and extension except the space character (0x20) and:

"""", ".", "/", "\", "[", "]", ":", "+", "|", "<", ">", "=", ",", ";", "*", "?"

If the client has indicated long name support by setting bit2 in the Flags2 field of the SMB header, this indicates that the client is not bound by the 8.3 convention. Specifically this indicates that any SMB which returns file names to the client may return names which do not adhere to the 8.3 convention, and have a total length of up to 255 characters. This capability was introduced with the LM1.2X002 protocol dialect.

The two special path components "." and ".." MUST be recognized. They indicate the current directory and the parent directory respectively. Although the use of ".." permits the specification of resources "above" the root of the tree connection, servers SHOULD prevent access to files or directories above the root of the exported share.

3.5. Wildcards

Some SMB requests allow wildcards to be given for the filename. The wildcard allows a number of files to be operated on as a unit without having to separately enumerate the files and individually operate on each one from the client. Two different sets of search semantics are supported. DOS search semantics are used for searching by 8.3 (or short names). Normal search semantics are used for searching by long names (those which support file names different from 8.3).

In the 8.3 naming scheme, each file name can contain up to 8 characters, a dot, and up to 3 trailing characters. Each part of the name (base (8) or extension (3)) is treated separately. The "*", the "?" and the "." can be used as wildcards. The "*" matches 0 or more characters until encountering and matching the "." in the name. The "?" matches any single character, or upon encountering a "." or end of name string, advances the expression to the end of the set of contiguous "?"s. So if the filename part commences with one or more "?"s then exactly that number of characters will be matched by the wildcards, e.g., "??x" equals "abx" but not "abcx" or "ax". When a filename part has trailing "?"s then it matches the specified number of characters or less, e.g., "x??" matches "xab", "xa" and "x", but not "xabc". If only "?"s are present in the filename part, then it is handled as for trailing "?"s. Finally, the "." Matches either a "." or an empty extension string.

In the normal naming scheme, the "." In the name is significant even though there is no longer a restriction on the size of each of the file name components. A file name may have none, one or more than one "."s within its name. Spaces " " are also allowed within file names and both follow normal wildcard searching rules. For example, if the files "foo bar none" and "foo.bar.none" exist, the pattern "foo*" equals both, "foo.*" equals "foo.bar.none" and "foo *" equals "foo bar none".

The ? character is a wildcard for a single character. If the match pattern commences with one or more "?"s then exactly that number of characters will be matched by the wildcards, e.g., "??x" equals "abx" but not "abcx" or "ax". When a match pattern has trailing "?"s then it matches the specified number of characters or less, e.g., "x??" matches "xab", "xa" and "x", but not "xabc". If only "?"s are present in the match pattern, then it is handled as for trailing "?"s.

The * character matches an entire name. For example, "*" matches all files in a directory.

If the negotiated dialect is "NT LM 0.12" or later, and the client requires MS-DOS wildcard matching semantics, UNICODE wildcards should be translated according to the following rules:

- Translate the "?" literal to ">"
- Translate the "." literal to """" if it is followed by a "?" or a "*"
- Translate the "*" literal to "<" if it is followed by a "."

The translation can be performed in-place.

3.6. DFS Pathnames

A DFS pathname adheres to the standard described in the FileNames section. A DFS enabled client accessing a DFS share should set the Flags2 bit 12 in all name based SMB requests indicating to the server that the enclosed pathname should be resolved in the Distributed File System namespace. The pathname should always have the full file name, including the server name and share name. If the server can resolve the DFS name to a piece of local storage, the local storage will be accessed. If the server determines that the DFS name actually maps to a different server share, the access to the name will fail with the 32-bit status STATUS_PATH_NOT_COVERED (0xC0000257), or DOS error ERRsrv/ERRbadpath.

On receiving this error, the DFS enabled client should ask the server for a referral (see TRANS2_GET_DFS_REFERRAL). The referral request should contain the full file name.

The response to the request will contain a list of server and share names to try, and the part of the request file name that junctions to the list of server shares. If the ServerType field of the referral is set to 1 (SMB server), then the client should resubmit the request with the original file name to one of the server shares in the list, once again setting the Flags2 bit 12 bit in the SMB. If the ServerType field is not 1, then the client should strip off the part of the file name that junctions to the server share before resubmitting the request to one of servers in the list.

A response to a referral request may elicit a response that does not have the StorageServers bit set. In that case, the client should resubmit the referral request to one of the servers in the list, until it finally obtains a referral response that has the StorageServers bit set, at which point the client can resubmit the request SMB to one of the listed server shares.

If, after getting a referral with the StorageServers bit set and resubmitting the request to one of the server shares in the list, the server fails the request with STATUS_PATH_NOT_COVERED, it must be the case that there is an inconsistency between the view of the DFS namespace held by the server granting the referral and the server listed in that referral. In this case, the client may

inform the server granting the referral of this inconsistency via the
TRANS2_REPORT_DFS_INCONSISTENCY SMB.

3.7. Time And Date Encoding

When SMB requests or responses encode time values, the following describes the various
encodings used.

```
struct {
        USHORT Day : 5;
        USHORT Month : 4;
        USHORT Year : 7;
} SMB_DATE;
```

The Year field has a range of 0-119, which represents years 1980 - 2099. The Month is encoded
as 1-12, and the day ranges from 1-31.

```
struct {
        USHORT TwoSeconds : 5;
        USHORT Minutes : 6;
        USHORT Hours : 5;
} SMB_TIME;
```

Hours ranges from 0-23, Minutes range from 0-59, and TwoSeconds ranges from 0-29
representing two second increments within the minute.

```
typedef struct {
    ULONG LowTime;
    LONG HighTime;
} TIME;
```

TIME indicates a signed 64-bit integer representing either an absolute time or a time interval.
Times are specified in units of 100ns.   A positive value expresses an absolute time. The time
base (the 64-bit integer with value 0) is the beginning of the year 1601 AD in the Gregorian
calendar UTC. However, file creation, modification and access times include an additional
correction factor as follows:

```
Tf = Tutc + Tdaf - Tdan
```

Where

```
Tf   time reported for file creation/modification/deletion
Tutc UTC time (secs since 1601 AD)
Tdaf Daylight savings adjustment (positive quantity) in effect at Tf
Tdan Current daylight savings adjustment (positive quantity)
```

For example, if a file is created in the summer - when daylight savings time is in effect - the
creation time will be reported as

```
Summer:  Tutc + 3600 - 3600 = Tutc
Winter:  Tutc + 3600 - 0    = Tutc + 3600
```

If a file is created during the winter - when daylight savings time not in effect - the creation time
will be reported as:

```
Summer:  Tutc + 0 - 3600 = Tutc - 3600
Winter:  Tutc + 0 - 0    = Tutc
```

A negative value expresses a time interval relative to some base time, usually the current time.

```
typedef unsigned long UTIME;
```

UTIME is the number of seconds since Jan 1, 1970, 00:00:00.0.

3.8. Access Mode Encoding

Various client requests and server responses, such as SMB_COM_OPEN, pass file access modes encoded into a USHORT. The encoding of these is as follows:

```
1111 11
5432 1098 7654 3210
rWrC rLLL rSSS rAAA
```

where:

```
W - Write through mode.  No read ahead or write behind allowed on
     this file or device.  When the response is returned, data is
     expected to be on the disk or device.
S - Sharing mode:
     0 - Compatibility mode
     1 - Deny read/write/execute (exclusive)
     2 - Deny write
     3 - Deny read/execute
     4 - Deny none
A - Access mode
     0 - Open for reading
     1 - Open for writing
     2 - Open for reading and writing
     3 - Open for execute

     rSSSrAAA = 11111111 (hex FF) indicates FCB open (???)

C - Cache mode
     0 - Normal file
     1 - Do not cache this file
L - Locality of reference
     0 - Locality of reference is unknown
     1 - Mainly sequential access
     2 - Mainly random access
     3 - Random access with some locality
     4 to 7 - Currently undefined
```

3.9. Access Mask Encoding

The ACCESS_MASK structure is one 32-bit value containing standard, specific, and generic rights. These rights are used in access-control entries (ACEs) and are the primary means of specifying the requested or granted access to an object.

The bits in this value are allocated as follows: Bits 0-15 contain the access mask specific to the object type associated with the mask. Bits 16-23 contain the object's standard access rights and can be a combination of the following predefined flags:

Flag	Value	Meaning
DELETE	0x00010000	Delete access
READ_CONTROL	0x00020000	Read access to the owner, group, and discretionary access-control list (ACL) of the security descriptor
WRITE_DAC	0x00040000	Write access to the discretionary access-control list (ACL)

WRITE_OWNER	0x00080000	Write access to owner
SYNCHRONIZE	0x00100000	Windows NT: Synchronize access
STANDARD_RIGHTS_REQUIRED	0x000F0000	
STANDARD_RIGHTS_READ	READ_CONTROL	
STANDARD_RIGHTS_WRITE	READ_CONTROL	
STANDARD_RIGHTS_EXECUTE	READ_CONTROL	
STANDARD_RIGHTS_ALL	0x001F0000	
SPECIFIC_RIGHTS_ALL	0x0000FFFF	
22		
23		
ACCESS_SYSTEM_SECURITY	0x01000000	This flag is not a typical access type. It is used to indicate access to a system ACL. This type of access requires the calling process to have a specific privilege.
MAXIMUM_ALLOWED	0x02000000	
26		Reserved
27		Reserved
GENERIC_ALL	0x10000000	
GENERIC_EXECUTE	0x20000000	
GENERIC_WRITE	0x40000000	
GENERIC_READ	0x80000000	

3.10. Open Function Encoding

OpenFunction specifies the action to be taken depending on whether or not the file exists. This word has the following format:

```
1111 11
5432 1098 7654 3210
rrrr rrrr rrrC rrOO
```

where:

```
C - Create (action to be taken if file does not exist)
    0 -- Fail
    1 -- Create file
r - reserved (must be zero)
O - Open (action to be taken if file exists)
    0 - Fail
    1 - Open file
    2 - Truncate file
```

3.11. Open Action Encoding

Action in the response to an open or create request describes the action taken as a result of the request. It has the following format:

```
1111 11
```

```
5432 1098 7654 3210
Lrrr rrrr rrrr rrOO
```

where:

```
L - Lock (single user total file lock status)
    0 -- file opened by another user (or mode not supported by server)
    1 -- file is opened only by this user at the present time
r - reserved (must be zero)
O - Open (action taken on Open)
    1 - The file existed and was opened
    2 - The file did not exist but was created
    3 - The file existed and was truncated
```

3.12. File Attribute Encoding

When SMB messages exchange file attribute information, it is encoded in 16 bits as:

Value	Description
0x01	Read only file
0x02	Hidden file
0x04	System file
0x08	Volume
0x10	Directory
0x20	Archive file
Others	Reserved – Must be 0

3.13. Extended File Attribute Encoding

The extended file attributes is a 32 bit value composed of attributes and flags.

Any combination of the following attributes is acceptable, except all other file attributes override FILE_ATTR_NORMAL:

Name	Value	Meaning
ATTR_ARCHIVE	0x020	The file has not been archived since it was last modified. Applications use this attribute to mark files for backup or removal.
ATTR_COMPRESSED	0x800	The file or directory is compressed. For a file, this means that all of the data in the file is compressed. For a directory, this means that compression is the default for newly created files and subdirectories. The state of the attribute ATTR_COMPRESSED does not affect how data is read or written to the file or directory using the SMB operations. The attribute only indicates how the server internally stores the data.
ATTR_NORMAL	0x080	The file has no other attributes set. This attribute is valid only if used alone.
ATTR_HIDDEN	0x002	The file is hidden. It is not to be included in an ordinary directory listing.
ATTR_READONLY	0x001	The file is read only. Applications can read the file but cannot write to it or delete it.
ATTR_TEMPORARY	0x100	The file is temporary.
ATTR_DIRECTORY	0x010	The file is a directory.
ATTR_SYSTEM	0x004	The file is part of or is used exclusively by the operating system.

Any combination of the following flags is acceptable:

Name	Value	Meaning
WRITE_THROUGH	0x80000000	Instructs the operating system to write through any intermediate cache and go directly to the file. The operating system can still cache write operations, but cannot lazily flush them.
NO_BUFFERING	0x20000000	Requests the server to open the file with no intermediate buffering or caching; the server is not obliged to honor the request. An application must meet certain requirements when working with files opened with FILE_FLAG_NO_BUFFERING. File access must begin at offsets within the file that are integer multiples of the volume's sector size; and must be for numbers of bytes that are integer multiples of the volume's sector size. For example, if the sector size is 512 bytes, an application can request reads and writes of 512, 1024, or 2048 bytes, but not of 335, 981, or 7171 bytes.
RANDOM_ACCESS	0x10000000	Indicates that the application intends to access the file randomly. The server MAY use this flag to optimize file caching.

Name	Value	Meaning
SEQUENTIAL_SCAN	0x08000000	Indicates that the file is to be accessed sequentially from beginning to end. Windows uses this flag to optimize file caching. If an application moves the file pointer for random access, optimum caching may not occur; however, correct operation is still guaranteed. Specifying this flag can increase performance for applications that read large files using sequential access. Performance gains can be even more noticeable for applications that read large files mostly sequentially, but occasionally skip over small ranges of bytes.
DELETE_ON_CLOSE	0x04000000	Requests that the server is delete the file immediately after all of its handles have been closed.
BACKUP_SEMANTICS	0x02000000	Indicates that the file is being opened or created for a backup or restore operation. The server SHOULD allow the client to override normal file security checks, provided it has the necessary permission to do so.
POSIX_SEMANTICS	0x01000000	Indicates that the file is to be accessed according to POSIX rules. This includes allowing multiple files with names differing only in case, for file systems that support such naming. (Use care when using this option because files created with this flag may not be accessible by applications written for MS-DOS, Windows 3.x, or Windows NT.)

3.14. Batching Requests ("AndX" Messages)

LANMAN1.0 and later dialects of the CIFS protocol allow multiple SMB requests to be sent in one message to the server. Messages of this type are called AndX SMBs, and they obey the following rules:

- The embedded command does not repeat the SMB header information. Rather the next SMB starts at the WordCount field.

- All multiple (chained) requests must fit within the negotiated transmit size. For example, if SMB_COM_TREE_CONNECT_ANDX included SMB_COM_OPEN_ANDX and SMB_COM_WRITE, they would all have to fit within the negotiated buffer size. This would limit the size of the write.

- There is one message sent containing the chained requests and there is one response message to the chained requests. The server may NOT elect to send separate responses to each of the chained requests.

- All chained responses must fit within the negotiated transmit size. This limits the maximum value on an embedded SMB_COM_READ for example. It is the client's responsibility to not request more bytes than will fit within the multiple response.

- The server will implicitly use the result of the first command in the "X" command. For example the Tid obtained via SMB_COM_TREE_CONNECT_ANDX would be used in the embedded SMB_COM_OPEN_ANDX, and the Fid obtained in the SMB_COM_OPEN_ANDX would be used in the embedded SMB_COM_READ.

- Each chained request can only reference the same Fid and Tid as the other commands in the combined request. The chained requests can be thought of as performing a single (multi-part) operation on the same resource.

- The first Command to encounter an error will stop all further processing of embedded commands. The server will not back out commands that succeeded. Thus if a chained request contained SMB_COM_OPEN_ANDX and SMB_COM_READ and the server was able to open the file successfully but the read encountered an error, the file would remain open. This is exactly the same as if the requests had been sent separately.

- If an error occurs while processing chained requests, the last response (of the chained responses in the buffer) will be the one which encountered the error. Other unprocessed chained requests will have been ignored when the server encountered the error and will not be represented in the chained response. Actually the last valid AndXCommand (if any) will represent the SMB on which the error occurred. If no valid AndXCommand is present, then the error occurred on the first request/response and Command contains the command which failed. In all cases the error information are returned in the SMB header at the start of the response buffer.

- Each chained request and response contains the offset (from the start of the SMB header) to the next chained request/response (in the AndXOffset field in the various "and X" protocols defined later e.g. SMB_COM_OPEN_ANDX). This allows building the requests unpacked. There may be space between the end of the previous request (as defined by WordCount and ByteCount) and the start of the next chained request. This simplifies the building of chained protocol requests. Note that because the client must know the size of the data being returned in order to post the correct number of receives (e.g. SMB_COM_TRANSACTION, SMB_COM_READ_MPX), the data in each response SMB is expected to be truncated to the maximum number of 512 byte blocks (sectors) which will fit (starting at a 32 bit boundary) in the negotiated buffer size with the odd bytes remaining (if any) in the final buffer.

3.15. "Transaction" Style Subprotocols

The "transaction" style subprotocols are used for commands that potentially need to transfer a large amount of data (greater than 64K bytes).

3.15.1.   SMB_COM_TRANSACTION2 Format

The following list describes the format of the TRANSACTION2 client request:

```
Primary Client Request          Description
========================        ============
Command                         SMB_COM_TRANSACTION2
UCHAR WordCount;                Count of parameter words; value =
                                         (14 + SetupCount)
USHORT TotalParameterCount;     Total parameter bytes being sent
USHORT TotalDataCount;          Total data bytes being sent
USHORT MaxParameterCount;       Max parameter bytes to return
USHORT MaxDataCount;            Max data bytes to return
UCHAR MaxSetupCount;            Max setup words to return
UCHAR Reserved;
USHORT Flags;                   Additional information:
                                   bit 0 - Disconnect TID
ULONG Timeout;
USHORT Reserved2;
USHORT ParameterCount;          Parameter bytes sent this buffer
USHORT ParameterOffset;         Offset (from header start) to
                                         Parameters
USHORT DataCount;               Data bytes sent this buffer
USHORT DataOffset;              Offset (from header start) to data
UCHAR SetupCount;               Count of setup words
UCHAR Reserved3;                Reserved (pad above to word boundary)
USHORT Setup[SetupCount];       Setup words (# = SetupWordCount)
```

```
USHORT ByteCount;               Count of data bytes
STRING Name[];                  Must be NULL
UCHAR Pad[];                    Pad to SHORT or LONG
UCHAR Parameters[              Parameter bytes (# = ParameterCount)
  ParameterCount];
UCHAR Pad1[];                   Pad to SHORT or LONG
UCHAR Data[DataCount];          Data bytes (# = DataCount)
```

The interim server response will consist of two fields:

```
UCHAR WordCount;                \\ Count of parameter words = 0
USHORT ByteCount;               \\ Count of data bytes = 0
```

The following list describes the format of the TRANSACTION2 secondary client request:

```
Secondary Client Request        Description
=========================       ============
Command                         SMB_COM_TRANSACTION_SECONDARY
UCHAR WordCount;                Count of parameter words = 8
USHORT TotalParameterCount;     Total parameter bytes being sent
USHORT TotalDataCount;          Total data bytes being sent
USHORT ParameterCount;          Parameter bytes sent this buffer
USHORT ParameterOffset;         Offset (from header start) to Parameters
USHORT ParameterDisplacement;   Displacement of these Parameter bytes
USHORT DataCount;               Data bytes sent this buffer
USHORT DataOffset;              Offset (from header start) to data
USHORT DataDisplacement;        Displacement of these data bytes
USHORT Fid;                         FID for handle based requests, else
                                    0xFFFF.  This field is present only
                                    if this is an SMB_COM_TRANSACTION2
                                    request.
USHORT ByteCount;               Count of data bytes
UCHAR Pad[];                    Pad to SHORT or LONG
UCHAR Parameters[              Parameter bytes (# = ParameterCount)
  ParameterCount];
UCHAR Pad1[];                   Pad to SHORT or LONG
UCHAR Data[DataCount];          Data bytes (# = DataCount)
```

And, the fields of the server response are described in the following list:

```
Server Response                 Description
=================               ============
UCHAR WordCount;                Count of data bytes; value = 10 +
                                    SetupCount
USHORT TotalParameterCount;     Total parameter bytes being sent
USHORT TotalDataCount;          Total data bytes being sent
USHORT Reserved;
USHORT ParameterCount;          Parameter bytes sent this buffer
USHORT ParameterOffset;         Offset (from header start) to Parameters
USHORT ParameterDisplacement;   Displacement of these Parameter
                                    bytes
USHORT DataCount;               Data bytes sent this buffer
USHORT DataOffset;              Offset (from header start) to data
USHORT DataDisplacement;        Displacement of these data bytes
UCHAR SetupCount;               Count of setup words
```

```
UCHAR Reserved2;                    Reserved (pad above to word boundary)
USHORT Setup[SetupWordCount];       Setup words (# = SetupWordCount)
USHORT ByteCount;                   Count of data bytes
UCHAR Pad[];                        Pad to SHORT or LONG
UCHAR Parameters[                   Parameter bytes (# = ParameterCount)
   ParameterCount];
UCHAR Pad1[];                       Pad to SHORT or LONG
UCHAR Data[DataCount];              Data bytes (# = DataCount)
```

3.15.2.   SMB_COM_NT_TRANSACTION Formats

The following list describes the format of the TRANSACTION primary client request:

```
Primary Client Request              Description
========================            ============
UCHAR WordCount;                    Count of parameter words; value =
                                              (19 + SetupCount)
UCHAR MaxSetupCount;                Max setup words to return
USHORT Reserved;
ULONG TotalParameterCount;          Total parameter bytes being sent
ULONG TotalDataCount;               Total data bytes being sent
ULONG MaxParameterCount;            Max parameter bytes to return
ULONG MaxDataCount;                 Max data bytes to return
ULONG ParameterCount;               Parameter bytes sent this buffer
ULONG ParameterOffset;              Offset (from header start) to Parameters
ULONG DataCount;                    Data bytes sent this buffer
ULONG DataOffset;                   Offset (from header start) to data
UCHAR SetupCount;                   Count of setup words
USHORT Function;                    The transaction function code
UCHAR Buffer[1];
USHORT Setup[SetupWordCount];       Setup words
USHORT ByteCount;                   Count of data bytes
UCHAR Pad1[];                       Pad to LONG
UCHAR Parameters[                   Parameter bytes
   ParameterCount];
UCHAR Pad2[];                       Pad to LONG
UCHAR Data[DataCount];               Data bytes
```

The interim server response will consist of two fields:

```
UCHAR WordCount;    \\ Count of parameter words = 0
USHORT ByteCount;   \\ Count of data bytes = 0
```

The following list describes the format of the TRANSACTION secondary client request:

```
Secondary Client Request            Description
==========================          ============
UCHAR WordCount;                    Count of parameter words = 18
UCHAR Reserved[3];                  MUST BE ZERO
ULONG TotalParameterCount;          Total parameter bytes being sent
ULONG TotalDataCount;               Total data bytes being sent
ULONG ParameterCount;               Parameter bytes sent this buffer
ULONG ParameterOffset;              Offset (from header start) to
                                      Parameters
```

```
ULONG ParameterDisplacement;        Specifies the offset from the start
                                    of the overall parameter block to
                                    the parameter bytes that are
                                    contained in this message
ULONG DataCount;                    Data bytes sent this buffer
ULONG DataOffset;                   Offset (from header start) to data
ULONG DataDisplacement;             Specifies the offset from the start
                                    of the overall data block to the
                                    data bytes that are contained in
                                    this message
UCHAR Reserved1;
USHORT ByteCount;                   Count of data bytes
UCHAR Pad1[];                       Pad to LONG
UCHAR Parameters[                   Parameter bytes
    ParameterCount];
UCHAR Pad2[];                       Pad to LONG
UCHAR Data[DataCount];              Data bytes
```

And, the fields of the server response are described in the following list:

```
Server Response                     Description
=================                   ===========
UCHAR WordCount;                    Count of data bytes; value = 18 +
                                    SetupCount
UCHAR Reserved[3];
ULONG TotalParameterCount;          Total parameter bytes being sent
ULONG TotalDataCount;               Total data bytes being sent
ULONG ParameterCount;               Parameter bytes sent this buffer
ULONG ParameterOffset;              Offset (from header start) to
                                    Parameters
ULONG ParameterDisplacement;        Specifies the offset from the start
                                    of the overall parameter block to
                                    the parameter bytes that are
                                    contained in this message
ULONG DataCount;                    Data bytes sent this buffer
ULONG DataOffset;                   Offset (from header start) to data
ULONG DataDisplacement;             Specifies the offset from the start
                                    of the overall data block to the
                                    data bytes that are contained in
                                    this message
UCHAR SetupCount;                   Count of setup words
USHORT Setup[SetupWordCount];       Setup words
USHORT ByteCount;                   Count of data bytes
UCHAR Pad1[];                       Pad to LONG
UCHAR Parameters[                   Parameter bytes
    ParameterCount];
UCHAR Pad2[];                       Pad to SHORT or LONG
UCHAR Data[DataCount];              Data bytes
```

3.15.3.   Functional Description

The transaction Setup information and/or Parameters define functions specific to a particular resource on a particular server. Therefore the functions supported are not defined by the transaction sub-protocol. The transaction protocol simply provides a means of delivering them and retrieving the results.

The number of bytes needed in order to perform the transaction request may be more than will fit in a single buffer.

At the time of the request, the client knows the number of parameter and data bytes expected to be sent and passes this information to the server via the primary request (TotalParameterCount and TotalDataCount). This may be reduced by lowering the total number of bytes expected (TotalParameterCount and TotalDataCount) in each (if any) secondary request.

When the amount of parameter bytes received (total of each ParameterCount) equals the total amount of parameter bytes expected (smallest TotalParameterCount) received, then the server has received all the parameter bytes.

Likewise, when the amount of data bytes received (total of each DataCount) equals the total amount of data bytes expected (smallest TotalDataCount) received, then the server has received all the data bytes.

The parameter bytes should normally be sent first followed by the data bytes. However, the server knows where each begins and ends in each buffer by the offset fields (ParameterOffset and DataOffset) and the length fields (ParameterCount and DataCount). The displacement of the bytes (relative to start of each) is also known (ParameterDisplacement and DataDisplacement). Thus the server is able to reassemble the parameter and data bytes should the individual requests be received out of sequence.

If all parameter bytes and data bytes fit into a single buffer, then no interim response is expected and no secondary request is sent.

The client knows the maximum amount of data bytes and parameter bytes which may be returned by the server (from MaxParameterCount and MaxDataCount of the request). Thus the client initializes its bytes expected variables to these values. The server then informs the client of the actual amounts being returned via each message of the server response (TotalParameterCount and TotalDataCount). The server may reduce the expected bytes by lowering the total number of bytes expected (TotalParameterCount and/or TotalDataCount) in each (any) response.

When the amount of parameter bytes received (total of each ParameterCount) equals the total amount of parameter bytes expected (smallest TotalParameterCount) received, then the client has received all the parameter bytes.

Likewise, when the amount of data bytes received (total of each DataCount) equals the total amount of data bytes expected (smallest TotalDataCount) received, then the client has received all the data bytes.

The parameter bytes should normally be returned first followed by the data bytes. However, the client knows where each begins and ends in each buffer by the offset fields (ParameterOffset and DataOffset) and the length fields (ParameterCount and DataCount). The displacement of the bytes (relative to start of each) is also known (ParameterDisplacement and DataDisplacement). The client is able to reassemble the parameter and data bytes should the server responses be received out of sequence.

The flow for these transactions over a connection oriented transport is:

1. The client sends the primary client request identifying the total bytes (both parameters and data) which are expected to be sent and contains the set up words and as many of the parameter and data bytes as will fit in a negotiated size buffer. This request also identifies the maximum number of bytes (setup, parameters and data) the server is to return on the transaction completion. If all the bytes fit in the single buffer, skip to step 4.

2. The server responds with a single interim response meaning "OK, send the remainder of the bytes" or (if error response) terminate the transaction.

3. The client then sends another buffer full of bytes to the server. This step is repeated until all of the bytes are sent and received.

4. The Server sets up and performs the transaction with the information provided.

5. Upon completion of the transaction, the server sends back (up to) the number of parameter and data bytes requested (or as many as will fit in the negotiated buffer size). This step is repeated until all result bytes have been returned.

The flow for the transaction protocol when the request parameters and data do not all fit in a single buffer is:

Client	< -- >	Server
Primary TRANSACTION request	- >	
	< -	Interim Server Response
Secondary TRANSACTION request 1	- >	
Secondary TRANSACTION request 2	- >	
Secondary TRANSACTION request n	- >	
	< -	Transaction response 1
	< -	Transaction response 2
	< -	Transaction response m

The flow for the transaction protocol when the request parameters and data do all fit in a single buffer is:

Client	< -- >	Server
Primary TRANSACTION request	- >	
	< -	Transaction response 1
	< -	Transaction response 2
	< -	Transaction response m

The primary transaction request through the final response make up the complete transaction exchange, thus the Tid, Pid, Uid and Mid must remain constant and can be used as appropriate by both the server and the client. Of course, other SMB requests may intervene as well.

There are (at least) three ways that actual server responses have been observed to differ from what might be expected. First, some servers will send Pad bytes to move the DataOffset to a 2- or 4-byte boundary even if there are no data bytes; the point here is that the ByteCount must be used instead of ParameterOffset plus ParameterCount to infer the actual message length. Second, some servers always return MaxParameterCount bytes even if the particular Transact2 has no parameter response. Finally, in case of an error, some servers send the "traditional WordCount==0/ByteCount==0" response while others generate a Transact response format.

3.15.4.   SMB_COM_TRANSACTION Operations

DCE/RPC documents were defined by the Open Group (TOG) used to be called the X/open group. CIFS uses DCE/RPC to process Server and User management information, like logon information, Local Security, Account management, Server/Workstation services and CIFS networking management functions (like browsing and domain controller management). DCE/RPC are implemented on top of SMB. SMB protocol is used as a transport for the DCE/RPC protocol. DCE/RPC uses Protocol Data Unit (PDU) fragments to communicate. The PDUs are totally independent of the SMB transmission size. So PDU can span over multiple SMB transmission boundaries and multiple PDUs can be transmitted in a single SMB transmission. Name Pipe are used as the transmission vehicle. Once and Named Pipe is opened all the DCE/RPC calls related to that Name Pipe will be written and read through SMB_COM_TRANSCATION operation. SMB_COM_TRANSACTION will communicate to the Name Pipe with as much PDU fragments it can contains, the rest of the fragments will follow with either SMBReadX or SMBWriteX. Some of the RPC calls are defined at Appendix E.

The "smb com transaction" style subprotocols are used mostly as MS RPC commands for managing the server and the client. Mail Slots are used for broadcasting and informing the other nodes on the networks. Named Pipes are mostly used for RPC. The details of the use of these RPCs are outside of the scope of this document. The following section describes the data format, but not the content of the content of the RPC. After the client or the server has open a Name Pipe the RPC are communicated using that pipe.

3.15.4.1. Mail Slot Transaction Protocol

The only transaction allowed to a mailslot is a mailslot write. The following table shows the interpretation of parameters for a mailslot transaction:

Name	Value	Description
Command	SMB_COM_TRANSACTION	
Name	\MAILSLOT\<name>	STRING Name of mail slot to write
SetupCount	3	
Setup[0]	1	Command code == write mailslot
Setup[1]		Ignored
Setup[2]		Ignored
TotalDataCount	n	Size of data to write to the mailslot
Data[n]		The data to write to the mailslot

3.15.4.2. Server Announcement Mailslot Transaction

A server announces its presence on the network by periodically transmitting an announcement mailslot message to a well known name. The server initially announces itself every minute, but as the server stays up for longer and longer periods, it should stretch out its announcement period to a maximum of once every 12 minutes. If a server has not been heard from for three announcements, it is considered unavailable. The announcements can be received by any entity on the network wishing to keep a reasonably up to date view of the available network servers.

Systems wishing to be visible on the network and compatible with LANMAN 1.0 periodically send the following announcement:

Name	Value	Description
Command	SMB_COM_TRANSACTION	
Name	\MAILSLOT\LANMAN	
SetupCount	3	
Setup[0]	1	Command code -- write mailslot
Setup[1]		Ignored
Setup[2]		Ignored
TotalDataCount	N	Size of following data to write to the mailslot

Data [n]	Description
USHORT Opcode;	Announcement (value == 1)
ULONG InstalledServices;	Bit mask describing the services running on the system
	0x1 SMB Workstation
	0x2 SMB Server
	0x4 SQL Server
	0x800 UNIX Operating System
	0x1000 NT Operating System
UCHAR MajorVersion;	Major version number of network software
UCHAR MinorVersion;	Minor version number of network software
USHORT Periodicity;	Announcement frequency in seconds
UCHAR ServerName[];	NULL terminated ASCII server name
UCHAR ServerComment[];	NULL terminated ASCII server comment (up to 43 bytes in length)

The NETBIOS address for this mailslot transaction is the domain name padded with blanks and having a zero as the sixteenth octet.

A client can cause LANMAN 1.0 severs to announce themselves to the client by sending the following mailslot transaction to the specific computer of interest or to the domain name as previously described:

Name	Value	Description
Command	SMB_COM_TRANSACTION	
Name	\MAILSLOT\LANMAN	
SetupCount	3	
Setup[0]	1	Command code -- write mailslot
Setup[1]		Ignored
Setup[2]		Ignored
TotalDataCount	N	Size of following data to write to the mailslot

Data [n]	Description
USHORT Opcode;	Request announcement (value == 2)
UCHAR ResponseComputerName[];	NULL terminated ASCII name to which the announcement response should be sent.

Nodes wishing to be visible on the network and compatible with systems using `Windows for Workgroups 3.1a` and later dialects periodically send the following directed mailslot message to a NETBIOS address consisting of the domain name padded with blanks and having a 0x1D in the sixteenth octet.

Name	Value	Description
Command	SMB_COM_TRANSACTION	
Name	\MAILSLOT\LANMAN	
SetupCount	3	
Setup[0]	1	Command code -- write mailslot
Setup[1]		Ignored
Setup[2]		Ignored
TotalDataCount	n	Size of following data to write to the mailslot

Data [n]	Description
UCHAR BrowseType;	Announcement (value == 1)
UCHAR Reserved;	value == 0
ULONG Periodicity;	Announcement frequency in milliseconds
UCHAR ServerName[16]	Name of this node doing the announcement. ServerName[16] == 0
UCHAR VersionMajor;	Major version number of network software
UCHAR VersionMinor;	Minor version number of network software
ULONG InstalledServices;	Bit mask describing the services running on the system
	0x1 SMB Workstation
	0x2 SMB Server
	0x4 SQL Server
	0x800 UNIX Operating System
	0x1000 NT Operating System
ULONG AStrangeValue;	== 0xAA55001F
UCHAR ServerComment[44];	NULL terminated ASCII server comment (up to 44 bytes in length)

3.15.4.3. Named Pipe Transaction Protocol

A named pipe `SMB_COM_TRANSACTION` is used to wait for the specified named pipe to become available (WaitNmPipe) or perform a logical "open -> write -> read -> close" of the pipe (CallNmPipe), along with other functions defined below.

The identifier "\PIPE\<name>" denotes a named pipe transaction, where the <name> is the pipe name to apply the transaction against.

Name	Value	Description
Command	SMB_COM_TRANSACTION	
Name	\PIPE\<name>	Name of pipe for operation
SetupCount	2	
Setup[0]	See Below	Subcommand code
Setup[1]	Fid of pipe	If required
TotalDataCount	n	Size of data
Data[n]		If required

The subcommand codes, placed in *SETUP[0]*, for named pipe operations are:

SubCommand Code	Value	Description
CallNamedPipe	0x54	open/write/read/close pipe
WaitNamedPipe	0x53	wait for pipe to be nonbusy
PeekNmPipe	0x23	read but don't remove data
QNmPHandState	0x21	query pipe handle modes
SetNmPHandState	0x01	set pipe handle modes
QNmPipeInfo	0x22	query pipe attributes
TransactNmPipe	0x26	write/read operation on pipe
RawReadNmPipe	0x11	read pipe in "raw" (non message mode)
RawWriteNmPipe	0x31	write pipe "raw" (non message mode) */

3.15.4.4. CallNamedPipe

This command is used to implement the Win32 CallNamedPipe() API remotely. The CallNamedPipe function connects to a message-type pipe (and waits if an instance of the pipe is not available), writes to and reads from the pipe, and then closes the pipe.

This form of the transaction protocol sends no parameter bytes, thus the bytes to be written to the pipe are sent as data bytes and the bytes read from the pipe are returned as data bytes.

The number of bytes being written is defined by *TOTALDATACOUNT* and the maximum number of bytes to return is defined by *MAXDATACOUNT*.

On the response *TOTALPARAMETERCOUNT* is 0 (no Parameter bytes to return), *TOTALDATACOUNT* indicates the amount of databytes being returned in total and *DATACOUNT* identifies the amount of data being returned in each buffer.

Note that the full form of the Transaction protocol can be used to write and read up to 65,535 bytes each utilizing the secondary requests and responses.

3.15.4.5. WaitNamedPipe

The command is used to implement the Win32 WaitNamedPipe() API remotely. The WaitNamedPipe function waits until either a time-out interval elapses or an instance of the specified named pipe is available to be connected to (that is, the pipe's server process has a pending ConnectNamedPipe operation on the pipe).

The server will wait up to *TIMEOUT* milliseconds for a pipe of the name given to become available. Note that although the timeout is specified in milliseconds, by the time that the timeout occurs and the client receives the timed out response much more time than specified may have occurred.

This form of the transaction protocol sends no data or parameter bytes. The response also contains no data or parameters. If the transaction response indicates success, the pipe may now be available. However, this request does not reserve the pipe, thus all waiting programs may race to get the pipe now available. The losers will get an error on the pipe open attempt.

3.15.4.6. PeekNamedPipe

This form of the pipe Transaction protocol is used to implement the Win32 PeekNamePipe() API remotely. The PeekNamedPipe function copies data from a named or anonymous pipe into a buffer without removing it from the pipe. It also returns information about data in the pipe.

TOTALPARAMETERCOUNT and *TOTALDATACOUNT* should be 0 for this request. The *FID* of the pipe to which this request should be applied is in Setup[1]. *MAXPARAMETERCOUNT* should be set to 6, requesting 3 words of information about the pipe, and *MAXDATACOUNT* should be set to the number of bytes to "peek".

The response contains the following *PARAMETER WORDS*:

Name	Description
Parameters[0, 1]	Total number of bytes available to be read from the pipe
Parameters[2,3]	Total number of bytes remaining in the message at the "head" of the pipe
Parameters[4,5]	Pipe status.
	1 Disconnected by server
	2 Listening
	3 Connection to server is OK
	4 Server end of pipe is closed

The *DATA* portion of the response is the data peeked from the named pipe.

3.15.4.7. GetNamedPipeHandleState

This form of the pipe transaction protocol is used to implement the Win32 GetNamedPipeHandleState() API. The GetNamedPipeHandleState function retrieves information about a specified named pipe. The information returned can vary during the lifetime of an instance of the named pipe.

This request sends no parameters and no data. The *FID* of the pipe to which this request should be applied is in Setup[1]. *MAXPARAMETERCOUNT* should be set to 2 (requesting the 1 word of information about the pipe) and *MAXDATACOUNT* should be 0 (not reading the pipe).

The response returns one parameter of pipe state information interpreted as:

```
Pipe Handle State Bits
       5 4 3 2 1 0 9 8 7 6 5 4 3 2 1 0
       B E * * T T R R |--- Icount --|
where:
   B - Blocking
       0 => reads/writes block if no data available
       1 => reads/writes return immediately if no data
   E - Endpoint
   0 => client end of pipe
       1 => server end of pipe
   TT - Type of pipe
       00 => pipe is a byte stream pipe
       01 => pipe is a message pipe
   RR - Read Mode
       00 => Read pipe as a byte stream
       01 => Read messages from pipe
   Icount - 8-bit count to control pipe instancing
```

The E (endpoint) bit is 0 because this handle is the client end of a pipe.

3.15.4.8. SetNamedPipeHandleState

This form of the pipe transaction protocol is used to implement the Win32 SetNamedPipeHandleState() API. The SetNamedPipeHandleState function sets the read mode and the blocking mode of the specified named pipe.

This request sends 1 parameter word (*TOTALPARAMETERCOUNT* = 2) which is the pipe state to be set. The *FID* of the pipe to which this request should be applied is in *SETUP[1].*

The response contains no data or parameters.

The interpretation of the input parameter word is:

```
Pipe Handle State Bits
       5 4 3 2 1 0 9 8 7 6 5 4 3 2 1 0
       B * * * * * R R 0 0 0 0 0 0 0 0
where:
   B - Blocking
       0 => reads/writes block if no data available
       1 => reads/writes return immediately if no data
   RR - Read Mode
       00 => Read pipe as a byte stream
       01 => Read messages from pipe
```

Note that only the read mode (byte or message) and blocking/nonblocking mode of a named pipe can be changed. Some combinations of parameters may be illegal and will be rejected as an error.

3.15.4.9. GetNamedPipeInfo

This form of the pipe transaction protocol is used to implement the Win32 GetNamedPipeInfo() API. The GetNamedPipeInfo function retrieves information about the specified named pipe.

The request sends 1 parameter word (*TOTALPARAMETERCOUNT* = 2) which is the information level requested and must be set to 1. The *FID* of the pipe to which this request should be applied is in *SETUP[1]*. *MAXDATACOUNT* should be set to the size of the buffer specified by the user in which to receive the pipe information.

Pipe information is returned in the data area of the response, up to the number of bytes specified. The information is returned in the following format:

Name	Size	Description
OutputBufferSize	USHORT	actual size of buffer for outgoing (server) I/O
InputBufferSize	USHORT	actual size of buffer for incoming (client) I/O
MaximumInstances	UCHAR	Maximum allowed number of instances
CurrentInstances	UCHAR	Current number of instances
PipeNameLength	UCHAR	Length of pipe name (including the null)
PipeName	STRING	Name of pipe (NOT including \\NodeName - \\NodeName is prepended to this string by the client before passing back to the user)

3.15.4.10. TransactNamedPipe

This form of the pipe transaction protocol is used to implement the Win32 TransactNamedPipe() API. The TransactNamedPipe function combines into a single network operation the functions that write a message to and read a message from the specified named pipe.

It provides an optimum way to implement transaction-oriented dialogs. TransactNamedPipe will fail if the pipe currently contains any unread data or is not in message read mode. Otherwise the call will write the entire request data bytes to the pipe and then read a response from the pipe and return it in the data bytes area of the response protocol. In the transaction request, *SETUP[1]* must contain the *FID* of the pipe.

If *NAME* is \PIPE\LANMAN, this is a server API request. The request encoding is:

Request Field	Description
Parameters[0->1]	API #
Parameters[2->N]	ASCIIZ RAP description of input structure
Parameters[N->X]	The input structure

The response is formatted as:

Response Field	Description
Parameters[0->1]	Result Status
Parameters[2->3]	Offset to result structure

The state of blocking/nonblocking has no effect on this protocol (TransactNamedPipe does not return until a message has been read into the response protocol). If *MAXDATACOUNT* is too small to contain the response message, an error is returned.

3.15.4.11. RawReadNamedPipe

RawReadNamedPipe reads bytes directly from a pipe, regardless of whether it is a message or byte pipe. For a byte pipe, this is exactly like SMB_COM_READ. For a message pipe, this is exactly like reading the pipe in byte read mode, except message headers will also be returned in the buffer (note that message headers will always be returned in toto--never split at a byte boundary).

This request sends no parameters or data to the server, and *SETUP[1]* must contain the *FID* of the pipe to read. *MAXDATACOUNT* should contain the number of bytes to read raw.

The response will return 0 parameters, and *DATACOUNT* will be set to the number of bytes read.

3.15.4.12. RawWriteNamedPipe

RawWriteNamedPipe puts bytes directly into a pipe, regardless of whether it is a message or byte pipe. The data will include message headers if it is a message pipe. This call ignores the blocking/nonblocking state and always acts in a blocking manner. It returns only after all bytes have been written.

The request sends no parameters. *SETUP[1]* must contain the *FID* of the pipe to write. *TOTALDATACOUNT* is the total amount of data to write to the pipe. Writing zero bytes to a pipe is an error unless the pipe is in message mode.

The response contains no data and one parameter word. If no error is returned, the one parameter word indicates the number of the requested bytes that have been "written raw" to the specified pipe.

3.16. Valid SMB Requests by Negotiated Dialect

CIFS clients and servers may exchange the following SMB messages if the "PC NETWORK PROGRAM 1.0" dialect is negotiated:

```
SMB_COM_CREATE_DIRECTORY        SMB_COM_DELETE_DIRECTORY
SMB_COM_OPEN                    SMB_COM_CREATE
SMB_COM_CLOSE                   SMB_COM_FLUSH
SMB_COM_DELETE                  SMB_COM_RENAME
SMB_COM_QUERY_INFORMATION       SMB_COM_SET_INFORMATION
SMB_COM_READ                    SMB_COM_WRITE
SMB_COM_LOCK_BYTE_RANGE         SMB_COM_UNLOCK_BYTE_RANGE
SMB_COM_CREATE_TEMPORARY        SMB_COM_CREATE_NEW
SMB_COM_CHECK_DIRECTORY         SMB_COM_PROCESS_EXIT
SMB_COM_SEEK                    SMB_COM_TREE_CONNECT
SMB_COM_TREE_DISCONNECT         SMB_COM_NEGOTIATE
SMB_COM_QUERY_INFORMATION_DISK  SMB_COM_SEARCH
SMB_COM_OPEN_PRINT_FILE         SMB_COM_WRITE_PRINT_FILE
SMB_COM_CLOSE_PRINT_FILE        SMB_COM_GET_PRINT_QUEUE
```

If the "LANMAN 1.0" dialect is negotiated, all of the messages in the previous list must be supported. Clients negotiating LANMAN 1.0 and higher dialects will probably no longer send SMB_COM_PROCESS_EXIT, and the response format for SMB_COM_NEGOTIATE is modified as well. New messages introduced with the LANMAN 1.0 dialect are:

```
SMB_COM_LOCK_AND_READ           SMB_COM_WRITE_AND_UNLOCK
SMB_COM_READ_RAW                SMB_COM_READ_MPX
SMB_COM_WRITE_MPX               SMB_COM_WRITE_RAW
SMB_COM_WRITE_COMPLETE          SMB_COM_WRITE_MPX_SECONDARY
SMB_COM_SET_INFORMATION2        SMB_COM_QUERY_INFORMATION2
SMB_COM_LOCKING_ANDX            SMB_COM_TRANSACTION
SMB_COM_TRANSACTION_SECONDARY   SMB_COM_IOCTL
SMB_COM_IOCTL_SECONDARY         SMB_COM_COPY
```

```
SMB_COM_MOVE                        SMB_COM_ECHO
SMB_COM_WRITE_AND_CLOSE             SMB_COM_OPEN_ANDX
SMB_COM_READ_ANDX                   SMB_COM_WRITE_ANDX
SMB_COM_SESSION_SETUP_ANDX          SMB_COM_TREE_CONNECT_ANDX
SMB_COM_FIND                        SMB_COM_FIND_UNIQUE
SMB_COM_FIND_CLOSE
```

The "LM1.2X002" dialect introduces these new SMBs:

```
SMB_COM_TRANSACTION2               SMB_COM_TRANSACTION2_SECONDARY
SMB_COM_FIND_CLOSE2                SMB_COM_LOGOFF_ANDX
```

"NT LM 0.12" dialect introduces:

```
SMB_COM_NT_TRANSACT               SMB_COM_NT_TRANSACT_SECONDARY
SMB_COM_NT_CREATE_ANDX            SMB_COM_NT_CANCEL
SMB_COM_NT_RENAME
```

Capabilities are used to determine which SMB requests a server supports. However, they do not directly map to which info levels associated with that particular request are supported. In the event that a client sends a request with an info-level that the server does not support or recognize (if it is legacy), it should return STATUS_UNSUPPORTED (or the non-NT equivalent). The extended functionality that was added later is then simply not available to client applications who would ask for it. (If a file system or SMB server does not support unique file ID's, then the query file information asking for it would return Unsupported, where as the query for other types of file information would return successfully.)

4. SMB Requests

This section lists the "best practice" SMB requests -- ones that would permit a client to exercise full CIFS functionality and optimum performance when interoperating with a server speaking the latest dialect as of this writing ("NT LM 0.12").

Note that, as of this writing, no existing client restricts itself to only these requests, so no useful server can be written that supports just them. The classification is provided so that future clients will be written to permit future servers to be simpler.

4.1. Session Requests

4.1.1. NEGOTIATE: Negotiate Protocol

The following list describes the format of the NEGOTIATE client request:

```
Client Request              Description
===============             ============
 UCHAR WordCount;           Count of parameter words = 0
 USHORT ByteCount;          Count of data bytes; min = 2
 struct {
   UCHAR BufferFormat;      0x02 -- Dialect
   UCHAR DialectName[];     ASCII null-terminated string
 } Dialects[];
```

The Client sends a list of dialects with which it can communicate. The response is a selection of one of those dialects (numbered 0 through n) or -1 (hex FFFF) indicating that none of the dialects were acceptable. The negotiate message is binding on the virtual circuit and must be sent. One and only one negotiate message may be sent, subsequent negotiate requests will be rejected with an error response and no action will be taken.

The protocol does not impose any particular structure to the dialect strings. Implementers of particular protocols may choose to include, for example, version numbers in the string.

If the server does not understand any of the dialect strings, or if PC NETWORK PROGRAM 1.0 is the chosen dialect, the response format is:

```
Server Response             Description
===============             ============
 UCHAR WordCount;           Count of parameter words = 1
 USHORT DialectIndex;       Index of selected dialect
 USHORT ByteCount;          Count of data bytes = 0
```

If the chosen dialect is greater than core up to and including LANMAN2.1, the protocol response format is:

```
Server Response             Description
===============             ============
 UCHAR WordCount;           Count of parameter words = 13
 USHORT DialectIndex;       Index of selected dialect
 USHORT SecurityMode;       Security mode:
                              bit 0: 0 = share, 1 = user
                              bit 1: 1 = use challenge/response
                              authentication
 USHORT MaxBufferSize;      Max transmit buffer size (>= 1024)
```

```
USHORT MaxMpxCount;              Max pending multiplexed requests
USHORT MaxNumberVcs;            Max VCs between client and server
USHORT RawMode;                 Raw modes supported:
                                  bit 0: 1 = Read Raw supported
                                  bit 1: 1 = Write Raw supported
ULONG SessionKey;               Unique token identifying this session
SMB_TIME ServerTime;            Current time at server
SMB_DATE ServerDate;            Current date at server
USHORT ServerTimeZone;          Current time zone at server
USHORT EncryptionKeyLength;     MUST BE ZERO if not LM2.1
                                  dialect
USHORT Reserved;                MUST BE ZERO
USHORT ByteCount;               Count of data bytes
UCHAR EncryptionKey[];          The challenge encryption key
STRING PrimaryDomain[];         The server's primary domain
```

MaxBufferSize is the size of the largest message which the client can legitimately send to the server.

If bit0 of the Flags field is set in the negotiate response, this indicates the server supports the obsolescent SMB_COM_LOCK_AND_READ and SMB_COM_WRITE_AND_UNLOCK client requests.

If the SecurityMode field indicates the server is running in user mode, the client must send appropriate SMB_COM_SESSION_SETUP_ANDX requests before the server will allow the client to access resources.   If the SecurityMode field indicates the client should use challenge/response authentication, the client should use the authentication mechanism specified in the Section 2.8.

Clients using the "MICROSOFT NETWORKS 1.03" dialect use a different form of raw reads than documented here, and servers are better off setting RawMode in this response to 0 for such sessions.

If the negotiated dialect is "DOS LANMAN2.1" or "LANMAN2.1", then PrimaryDomain string should be included in this response.

If the negotiated dialect is NT LM 0.12, the response format is:

```
Server Response                Description
================                ============
UCHAR WordCount;               Count of parameter words = 17
USHORT DialectIndex;           Index of selected dialect
UCHAR SecurityMode;            Security mode:
                                 bit 0: 0 = share, 1 = user
                                 bit 1: 1 = encrypt passwords
                                 bit 2: 1 = Security Signatures
                                   (SMB sequence numbers) enabled
                                 bit 3: 1 = Security Signatures
                                   (SMB sequence numbers) required
USHORT MaxMpxCount;            Max pending outstanding requests
USHORT MaxNumberVcs;          Max VCs between client and server
ULONG MaxBufferSize;          Max transmit buffer size
ULONG MaxRawSize;             Maximum raw buffer size
ULONG SessionKey;             Unique token identifying this session
ULONG Capabilities;           Server capabilities
```

```
ULONG SystemTimeLow;        System (UTC) time of the server (low)
ULONG SystemTimeHigh;       System (UTC) time of the server (high)
USHORT ServerTimeZone;      Time zone of server (minutes from UTC)
CHAR EncryptionKeyLength;   Length of encryption key
USHORT ByteCount;           Count of data bytes
UCHAR EncryptionKey[];      The challenge encryption key;
                            Present only for Non Extended Security i.e.,
                            CAP_EXTENDED_SECURITY is off in the Capabilities
                             field
UCHAR OemDomainName[];      The name of the domain (in OEM chars);
                            Present Only for Non Extended Security i.e.,
                             CAP_EXTENDED_SECURITY is off in the Capabilities
                             field
UCHAR GUID[16];             A globally unique identifier assigned to the
                             server; Present only when
                             CAP_EXTENDED_SECURITY is on in Capabilities field
UCHAR SecurityBlob[];       Opaque Security Blob associated with the
                             security package if CAP_EXTENDED_SECURITY
                             is on in the Capabilities field; else challenge
                             for CIFS challenge/response authentication
```

In addition to the definitions above, MaxBufferSize is the size of the largest message which the client can legitimately send to the server. If the client is using a connectionless protocol, MaxBufferSize must be set to the smaller of the server's internal buffer size and the amount of data which can be placed in a response packet.

MaxRawSize specifies the maximum message size the server can send or receive for the obsolescent SMB_COM_WRITE_RAW or SMB_COM_READ_RAW requests.

Connectionless clients must set Sid to 0 in the SMB request header.

The Capabilities field allows the server to tell the client what it supports. The client must not ignore any capabilities specified by the server. The bit definitions are:

Capability Name	Encoding	Meaning
CAP_RAW_MODE	0x0001	The server supports SMB_COM_READ_RAW and SMB_COM_WRITE_RAW (obsolescent)
CAP_MPX_MODE	0x0002	The server supports SMB_COM_READ_MPX and SMB_COM_WRITE_MPX (obsolescent)
CAP_UNICODE	0x0004	The server supports UNICODE strings
CAP_LARGE_FILES	0x0008	The server supports large files with 64 bit offsets
CAP_NT_SMBS	0x0010	The server supports the SMBs particular to the NT LM 0.12 dialect. Implies CAP_NT_FIND.
CAP_RPC_REMOTE_APIS	0x0020	The server supports remote admin API requests via DCE RPC
CAP_STATUS32	0x0040	The server can respond with 32 bit status codes in Status.Status
CAP_LEVEL_II_OPLOCKS	0x0080	The server supports level 2 oplocks

Capability Name	Encoding	Meaning
CAP_LOCK_AND_READ	0x0100	The server supports the SMB, SMB_COM_LOCK_AND_READ
CAP_NT_FIND	0x0200	Reserved
CAP_DFS	0x1000	The server is DFS aware
CAP_INFOLEVEL_PASSTHRU	0x2000	The server supports NT information level requests passing through
CAP_LARGE_READX	0x4000	The server supports large SMB_COM_READ_ANDX (up to 64k)
CAP_LARGE_WRITEX	0x8000	The server supports large SMB_COM_WRITE_ANDX (up to 64k)
CAP_UNIX	0x00800000	The server supports CIFS Extensions for UNIX. (See Appendix D for more detail)
CAP_RESERVED	0x02000000	Reserved for future use
CAP_BULK_TRANSFER	0x20000000	The server supports SMB_BULK_READ, SMB_BULK_WRITE (should be 0, no known implementations)
CAP_COMPRESSED_DATA	0x40000000	The server supports compressed data transfer (BULK_TRANSFER capability is required to support compressed data transfer).
CAP_EXTENDED_SECURITY	0x80000000	The server supports extended security exchanges

Undefined bit MUST be set to zero by servers, and MUST be ignored by clients.

Extended security exchanges provide a means of supporting arbitrary authentication protocols within CIFS. Security blobs are opaque to the CIFS protocol; they are messages in some authentication protocol that has been agreed upon by client and server by some out of band mechanism, for which CIFS merely functions as a transport. When CAP_EXTENDED_SECURITY is negotiated, the server includes a first security blob in its response; subsequent security blobs are exchanged in SMB_COM_SESSION_SETUP_ANDX requests and responses until the authentication protocol terminates.

If the negotiated dialect is NT LM 0.12, then the capabilities field of the Negotiate protocol response indicates whether the server supports Unicode. The server is not required to support Unicode. Unicode is supported in Win9x and NT clients. If Unicode is not supported by the server then some localized of these clients may experience unexpected behavior with filenames, resource names and user names.

ASCII defines the values of 128 characters (0x00 through 0x7F). The remaining 128 values (0x80 through 0xFF) are mapped into different DOS Code Pages (aka the OEM character set). Different localized clients may use different code pages. (For example, Code Page 437 is the default in English based systems). Clients can create file and folder names in their default code page that follows the file naming rules and may contain both ASCII and non-ASCII characters.

4.1.1.1.   Errors

```
SUCCESS/SUCCESS
ERRSRV/ERRerror
```

4.1.2. SESSION_SETUP_ANDX: Session Setup

This SMB is used to further "Set up" the session normally just established via the negotiate protocol.

One primary function is to perform a "user logon" in the case where the server is in user level security mode. The Uid in the SMB header is set by the client to be the userid desired for the AccountName and validated by the AccountPassword.

4.1.2.1.   Pre NT LM 0.12

If the negotiated protocol is prior to NT LM 0.12, the format of SMB_COM_SESSION_SETUP_ANDX is:

```
Client Request               Description
===============              ============
 UCHAR WordCount;            Count of parameter words = 10
 UCHAR AndXCommand;          Secondary (X) command; 0xFF = none
 UCHAR AndXReserved;         Reserved (must be 0)
 USHORT AndXOffset;          Offset to next command WordCount
 USHORT MaxBufferSize;       Client maximum buffer size
 USHORT MaxMpxCount;         Actual maximum multiplexed pending requests
 USHORT VcNumber;            0 = first (only), nonzero=additional
                                          VC number
 ULONG SessionKey;           Session key (valid iff VcNumber != 0)
 USHORT PasswordLength;      Account password size
 ULONG Reserved;             Must be 0
 USHORT ByteCount;           Count of data bytes; min = 0
 UCHAR AccountPassword[];    Account Password
 STRING AccountName[];       Account Name
 STRING PrimaryDomain[];     Client's primary domain
 STRING NativeOS[];          Client's native operating system
 STRING NativeLanMan[];      Client's native LAN Manager type
```

The server response is:

```
Server Response              Description
================             ============
 UCHAR WordCount;            Count of parameter words = 3
 UCHAR AndXCommand;          Secondary (X) command;  0xFF =
                              none
 UCHAR AndXReserved;         Reserved (must be 0)
 USHORT AndXOffset;          Offset to next command WordCount
 USHORT Action;              Request mode:
                              bit0 = logged in as GUEST
 USHORT ByteCount;           Count of data bytes
 STRING NativeOS[];          Server's native operating system
 STRING NativeLanMan[];      Server's native LAN Manager type
 STRING PrimaryDomain[];     Server's primary domain
```

If the server is in "share level security mode", the account name and password should be ignored by the server.

If challenge/response authentication is not being used, AccountPassword should be a null terminated ASCII string with PasswordLength set to the string size including the null; the password will be case insensitive. If challenge/response authentication is being used, then AccountPassword will be the response to the server's challenge, and PasswordLength should be set to its length.

The server validates the name and password supplied and if valid, it registers the user identifier on this session as representing the specified AccountName. The Uid field in the SMB header will then be used to validate access on subsequent SMB requests. The SMB requests where permission checks are required are those which refer to a symbolically named resource such as SMB_COM_OPEN, SMB_COM_RENAME, SMB_COM_DELETE, etc. The value of the Uid is relative to a specific client/server session so it is possible to have the same Uid value represent two different users on two different sessions at the server.

Multiple session setup commands may be sent to register additional users on this session. If the server receives an additional SMB_COM_SESSION_SETUP_ANDX, only the Uid, AccountName and AccountPassword fields need contain valid values (the server MUST ignore the other fields).

The client writes the name of its domain in PrimaryDomain if it knows what the domain name is. If the domain name is unknown, the client either encodes it as a NULL string, or as a question mark.

If bit0 of Action is set, this informs the client that although the server did not recognize the AccountName, it logged the user in as a guest. This is optional behavior by the server, and in any case one would ordinarily expect guest privileges to limited.

Another function of the Session Set Up protocol is to inform the server of the maximum values which will be utilized by this client. Here MaxBufferSize is the maximum message size which the client can receive. Thus although the server may support 16k buffers (as returned in the SMB_COM_NEGOTIATE response), if the client only has 4k buffers, the value of MaxBufferSize here would be 4096. The minimum allowable value for MaxBufferSize is 1024. The SMB_COM_NEGOTIATE response includes the server buffer size supported. Thus this is the maximum SMB message size which the client can send to the server. This size may be larger than the size returned to the server from the client via the SMB_COM_SESSION_SETUP_ANDX protocol which is the maximum SMB message size which the server may send to the client. Thus if the server's buffer size were 4k and the client's buffer size were only 2K, the client could send up to 4k (standard) write requests but must only request up to 2k for (standard) read requests.

The VcNumber field specifies whether the client wants this to be the first VC or an additional VC.

The values for MaxBufferSize, MaxMpxCount, and VcNumber must be less than or equal to the maximum values supported by the server as returned in the SMB_COM_NEGOTIATE response.

If the server gets a SMB_COM_SESSION_SETUP_ANDX request with VcNumber of 0 and other VCs are still connected to that client, they will be aborted thus freeing any resources held by the server. This condition could occur if the client was rebooted and reconnected to the server before the transport level had informed the server of the previous VC termination.

4.1.2.2.   NT LM 0.12

If the negotiated SMB dialect is "NT LM 0.12" and the server supports ExtendedSecurity i.e. the CAP_EXTENDED_SECURITY flag is set in the Capabilities field of the Negotiate Response SMB, the Extended Security SessionSetup SMB format is:

```
Client Request                    Description
================                  ============
```

```
UCHAR WordCount;              Count of parameter words = 12
UCHAR AndXCommand;            Secondary (X) command;  0xFF = none
UCHAR AndXReserved;           Reserved (must be 0)
USHORT AndXOffset;            Offset to next command WordCount
USHORT MaxBufferSize;         Client's maximum buffer size
USHORT MaxMpxCount;           Actual maximum multiplexed pending
                               requests
USHORT VcNumber;              0 = first (only), nonzero=additional
                               VC number
ULONG SessionKey;             Session key (valid iff VcNumber != 0)
USHORT SecurityBlobLength;    Length of opaque security blob
ULONG Reserved;               Must be 0
ULONG Capabilities;           Client capabilities
USHORT ByteCount;             Count of data bytes; min = 0
UCHAR SecurityBlob[];         The opaque security blob
STRING NativeOS[];            Client's native operating system,
                               Unicode
STRING NativeLanMan[];        Client's native LAN Manager type,
                               Unicode
```

And the server response is:

```
Server Response              Description
================             ============
UCHAR WordCount;             Count of parameter words = 4
UCHAR AndXCommand;           Secondary (X) command;  0xFF =
                              none
UCHAR AndXReserved;          Reserved (must be 0)
USHORT AndXOffset;           Offset to next command WordCount
USHORT Action;               Request mode:
                              bit0 = logged in as GUEST
USHORT SecurityBlobLength;   Length of Security Blob that
                              follows in a later field
USHORT ByteCount;            Count of data bytes
UCHAR SecurityBlob[];        SecurityBlob of length specified
                              by the field, SecurityBlobLength
STRING NativeOS[];           Server's native operating system
STRING NativeLanMan[];       Server's native LAN Manager type
STRING PrimaryDomain[];      Server's primary domain
```

There may be multiple round trips involved in the security blob exchange. In that case, the server may return an error STATUS_MORE_PROCESSING_REQUIRED (a value of 0xC0000016) in the SMB status. The client can then repeat the SessionSetupAndX SMB with the rest of the security blob.

If the negotiated SMB dialect is "NT LM 0.12" or later and the server does not support Extended Security (i.e. the CAP_EXTENDED_SECURITY flag in the Capabilities field of the Negotiate Response SMB is not set), the format of the response SMB is unchanged, but the request is:

```
Client Request               Description
================             ============
UCHAR WordCount;             Count of parameter words = 13
UCHAR AndXCommand;           Secondary (X) command;  0xFF = none
UCHAR AndXReserved;          Reserved (must be 0)
```

```
USHORT AndXOffset;                  Offset to next command WordCount
USHORT MaxBufferSize;               Client's maximum buffer size
USHORT MaxMpxCount;                 Actual maximum multiplexed pending
                                     requests
USHORT VcNumber;                    0 = first (only), nonzero=additional
                                     VC number
ULONG SessionKey;                   Session key (valid iff VcNumber != 0)
USHORT                              Account password size, ANSI
  CaseInsensitivePasswordLength;
USHORT                              Account password size, Unicode
  CaseSensitivePasswordLength;
ULONG Reserved;                     Must be 0
ULONG Capabilities;                 Client capabilities
USHORT ByteCount;                   Count of data bytes; min = 0
UCHAR                               Account Password, ANSI
  CaseInsensitivePassword[];
UCHAR                               Account Password, Unicode
  CaseSensitivePassword[];
UCHAR Reserved2                     Present if Unicode negotiated to even byte
                                     boundary
STRING AccountName[];               Account Name, Unicode
STRING PrimaryDomain[];             Client's primary domain, Unicode
STRING NativeOS[];                  Client's native operating system,
                                     Unicode
STRING NativeLanMan[];              Client's native LAN Manager type,
                                     Unicode
```

The client expresses its capabilities to the server encoded in the Capabilities field. The format of that field is:

Capability Name	Encoding	Meaning
CAP_UNICODE	0x0004	The client can use UNICODE strings
CAP_LARGE_FILES	0x0008	The client can deal with files having 64 bit offsets
CAP_NT_SMBS	0x0010	The client understands the SMBs introduced with the NT LM 0.12 dialect. Implies CAP_NT_FIND.
CAP_STATUS32	0x0040	The client can receive 32 bit errors encoded in Status.Status
CAP_LEVEL_II_OPLOCKS	0x0080	The client understands Level II oplocks
CAP_NT_FIND	0x0200	Reserved

The entire message sent and received including the optional ANDX SMB must fit in the negotiated maximum transfer size. The following are the only valid SMB commands for AndXCommand for SMB_COM_SESSION_SETUP_ANDX:

```
SMB_COM_TREE_CONNECT_ANDX        SMB_COM_OPEN
SMB_COM_OPEN_ANDX                SMB_COM_CREATE
SMB_COM_CREATE_NEW               SMB_COM_CREATE_DIRECTORY
SMB_COM_DELETE                   SMB_COM_DELETE_DIRECTORY
SMB_COM_FIND                     SMB_COM_FIND_UNIQUE
SMB_COM_COPY                     SMB_COM_RENAME
SMB_COM_NT_RENAME                SMB_COM_CHECK_DIRECTORY
SMB_COM_QUERY_INFORMATION        SMB_COM_SET_INFORMATION
SMB_COM_NO_ANDX_COMMAND          SMB_COM_OPEN_PRINT_FILE
```

```
SMB_COM_GET_PRINT_QUEUE          SMB_COM_TRANSACTION
```

4.1.2.3. Errors

```
ERRSRV/ERRerror - No NEG_PROT issued
ERRSRV/ERRbadpw - Password not correct for given username
ERRSRV/ERRtoomanyuids - Maximum number of users per session exceeded
ERRSRV/ERRnosupport - Chaining of this request to the previous is not
supported
```

4.1.3. LOGOFF_ANDX: User Logoff

This SMB is the inverse of SMB_COM_SESSION_SETUP_ANDX.

```
Client Request                   Description
===============                  ============
 UCHAR WordCount;                Count of parameter words = 2
 UCHAR AndXCommand;              Secondary (X) command;   0xFF =
                                 none
 UCHAR AndXReserved;             Reserved (must be 0)
 USHORT AndXOffset;              Offset to next command WordCount
 USHORT ByteCount;               Count of data bytes = 0
```

The server response is:

```
Server Response                  Description
=================                ============
 UCHAR WordCount;                Count of parameter words = 2
 UCHAR AndXCommand;              Secondary (X) command;   0xFF =
                                 none
 UCHAR AndXReserved;             Reserved (must be 0)
 USHORT AndXOffset;              Offset to next command WordCount
 USHORT ByteCount;               Count of data bytes = 0
```

The user represented by Uid in the SMB header is logged off. The server closes all files currently open by this user, and invalidates any outstanding requests with this Uid.

SMB_COM_SESSION_SETUP_ANDX is the only valid AndXCommand for this SMB.

4.1.3.1. Errors

```
ERRSRV/invnid - TID was invalid
ERRSRV/baduid - UID was invalid
```

4.1.4. TREE_CONNECT_ANDX: Tree Connect

The TREE_CONNECT_ANDX client request is defined below:

```
Client Request                   Description
===============                  ============
 UCHAR WordCount;                Count of parameter words = 4
 UCHAR AndXCommand;              Secondary (X) command; 0xFF = none
 UCHAR AndXReserved;             Reserved (must be 0)
 USHORT AndXOffset;              Offset to next command WordCount
 USHORT Flags;                   Additional information
                                 bit 0 set = Disconnect Tid
```

```
USHORT PasswordLength;              Length of Password[]
USHORT ByteCount;                   Count of data bytes; min = 3
UCHAR Password[];                   Password
STRING Path[];                      Server name and share name
STRING Service[];                   Service name
```

The serving machine verifies the combination and returns an error code or an identifier. The full name is included in this request message and the identifier identifying the connection is returned in the Tid field of the SMB header. The Tid field in the client request is ignored. The meaning of this identifier (Tid) is server specific; the client must not associate any standard meaning to it.

If the negotiated dialect is LANMAN1.0 or later, then it is a protocol violation for the client to send this message prior to a successful SMB_COM_SESSION_SETUP_ANDX, and the server ignores Password.

If the negotiated dialect is prior to LANMAN1.0 and the client has not sent a successful SMB_COM_SESSION_SETUP_ANDX request when the tree connect arrives, a user level security mode server must nevertheless validate the client's credentials as discussed earlier in this document.

Path follows UNC style syntax, that is to say it is encoded as \\server\share and it indicates the name of the resource to which the client wishes to connect.

Because Password may be an authentication response, it is a variable length field with the length specified by PasswordLength. If authentication is not being used, Password should be a null terminated ASCII string with PasswordLength set to the string size including the terminating null.

The server can enforce whatever policy it desires to govern share access. Typically, if the server is paused, administrative privilege is required to connect to any share; if the server is not paused, administrative privilege is required only for administrative shares (C$, etc.). Other such policies may include valid times of day, software usage license limits, number of simultaneous server users or share users, etc.

The Service component indicates the type of resource the client intends to access. Valid values are:

Service	Description	Earliest Dialect Allowed
A:	Disk share	PC NETWORK PROGRAM 1.0
LPT1:	Printer	PC NETWORK PROGRAM 1.0
IPC	Named pipe	MICROSOFT NETWORKS 3.0
COMM	Communications device	MICROSOFT NETWORKS 3.0
?????	Any type of device	MICROSOFT NETWORKS 3.0

If bit0 of Flags is set, the tree connection to Tid in the SMB header should be disconnected. If this tree disconnect fails, the error should be ignored.

If the negotiated dialect is earlier than DOS LANMAN2.1, the response to this SMB is:

```
Server Response                Description
===============                ===========
UCHAR WordCount;               Count of parameter words = 2
UCHAR AndXCommand;             Secondary (X) command;  0xFF = none
UCHAR AndXReserved;            Reserved (must be 0)
USHORT AndXOffset;             Offset to next command WordCount
```

```
    USHORT ByteCount;                    Count of data bytes; min = 3
```

If the negotiated is DOS LANMAN2.1 or later, the response to this SMB is:

```
    Server Response                      Description
    =================                    =============
    UCHAR WordCount;                     Count of parameter words = 3
    UCHAR AndXCommand;                   Secondary (X) command;  0xFF = none
    UCHAR AndXReserved;                  Reserved (must be 0)
    USHORT AndXOffset;                   Offset to next command WordCount
    USHORT OptionalSupport;              Optional support bits
                                           SMB_SUPPORT_SEARCH_BITS = 0x0001
                                         Exclusive search bits
                                           ("MUST HAVE BITS") supported
                                           SMB_SHARE_IS_IN_DFS = 0x0002
    USHORT ByteCount;                    Count of data bytes; min = 3
    UCHAR Service[];                     Service type connected (Always ANSII)
    STRING NativeFileSystem[];           Native file system for this tree
```

NativeFileSystem is the name of the filesystem. Expected values include FAT, NTFS, etc.

Some servers negotiate "DOS LANMAN2.1" dialect or later and still send the "downlevel" (i.e. wordcount==2) response. Valid AndX following commands are:

```
SMB_COM_OPEN              SMB_COM_OPEN_ANDX           SMB_COM_CREATE
SMB_COM_CREATE_NEW        SMB_COM_CREATE_DIRECTORY    SMB_COM_DELETE
SMB_COM_DELETE_DIRECTORY  SMB_COM_FIND                SMB_COM_COPY
SMB_COM_FIND_UNIQUE       SMB_COM_RENAME
SMB_COM_CHECK_DIRECTORY   SMB_COM_QUERY_INFORMATION
SMB_COM_GET_PRINT_QUEUE   SMB_COM_OPEN_PRINT_FILE
SMB_COM_TRANSACTION       SMB_COM_NO_ANDX_CMD
SMB_COM_SET_INFORMATION   SMB_COM_NT_RENAME
```

4.1.4.1. Errors

```
ERRDOS/ERRnomem
ERRDOS/ERRbadpath
ERRDOS/ERRinvdevice
ERRSRV/ERRaccess
ERRSRV/ERRbadpw
ERRSRV/ERRinvnetname
```

4.1.5. TREE_DISCONNECT: Tree Disconnect

This message informs the server that the client no longer wishes to access the resource connected via a prior SMB_COM_TREE_CONNECT or SMB_COM_TREE_CONNECT_ANDX.

```
    Client Request                       Description
    =================                    =============
    UCHAR WordCount;                     Count of parameter words = 0
    USHORT ByteCount;                    Count of data bytes = 0
```

The resource sharing connection identified by Tid in the SMB header is logically disconnected from the server. Tid is invalidated; it will not be recognized if used by the client for subsequent requests. All locks, open files, etc. created on behalf of Tid are released.

```
Server Response                   Description
================                  ============
  UCHAR WordCount;                Count of parameter words = 0
  USHORT ByteCount;               Count of data bytes = 0
```

4.1.5.1. Errors

```
ERRSRV/ERRinvnid
ERRSRV/ERRbaduid
```

4.1.6. TRANS2_QUERY_FS_INFORMATION: Get File System Information

This transaction requests information about a filesystem on the server. Its format is:

```
Client Request        Value
================      ======
WordCount             15
TotalParameterCount   2 or 4
MaxSetupCount         0
SetupCount            1 or 2
Setup[0]              TRANS2_QUERY_FS_INFORMATION
```

The request's parameter block encodes InformationLevel (a USHORT), describing the level of filesystem info that should be returned. Values for InformationLevel are specified in the table below.

The filesystem is identified by Tid in the SMB header.

MaxDataCount in the transaction request must be large enough to accommodate the response.

The encoding of the response parameter block depends on the InformationLevel requested. Information levels whose values are greater than 0x102 are mapped to corresponding operating system calls (NtQueryVolumeInformationFile calls) by the server. The two levels below 0x102 are described below. The requested information is placed in the Data portion of the transaction response.

Information Level	Value
SMB_INFO_ALLOCATION	1
SMB_INFO_VOLUME	2
SMB_QUERY_FS_VOLUME_INFO	0x102
SMB_QUERY_FS_SIZE_INFO	0x103
SMB_QUERY_FS_DEVICE_INFO	0x104
SMB_QUERY_FS_ATTRIBUTE_INFO	0x105
SMB_QUERY_CIFS_UNIX_INFO	0x200
SMB_QUERY_MAC_FS_INFO	0x301

The following sections describe the InformationLevel dependent encoding of the data part of the transaction response.

4.1.6.1. SMB_INFO_ALLOCATION

```
InformationLevel
```

```
Data Block Encoding       Description
=====================     ============
ULONG idFileSystem;       File system identifier (NT server always returns 0)
ULONG cSectorUnit;        Number of sectors per allocation unit
ULONG cUnit;              Total number of allocation units
ULONG cUnitAvail;         Total number of available allocation units
USHORT cbSector;          Number of bytes per sector
```

4.1.6.2. SMB_INFO_VOLUME

```
InformationLevel
Data Block Encoding       Description
=====================     ============
ULONG ulVsn;              Volume serial number
UCHAR cch;                Number of  characters in Label
STRING Label;             The volume label
```

4.1.6.3. SMB_QUERY_FS_VOLUME_INFO

```
InformationLevel
Data Block Encoding       Description
=====================     ============
SMB_TIME                  Volume Creation Time
ULONG                     Volume Serial Number
ULONG                     Length of Volume Label in bytes
BYTE                      Reserved
BYTE                      Reserved
STRING Label;             The volume label
```

4.1.6.4. SMB_QUERY_FS_SIZE_INFO

```
InformationLevel
Data Block Encoding       Description
=====================     ============
LARGE_INTEGER             Total Number of Allocation units on the Volume
LARGE_INTEGER             Number of free Allocation units on the Volume
ULONG                     Number of sectors in each Allocation unit
ULONG                     Number of bytes in each sector
```

4.1.6.5. SMB_QUERY_FS_DEVICE_INFO

```
InformationLevel
Data Block Encoding       Description
=====================     ======
ULONG                     DeviceType; Values as specified below
ULONG                     Characteristics of the device; Values as specified
below
```

For DeviceType, note that the values 0-32767 are reserved for the exclusive use of Microsoft Corporation. The following device types are currently defined:

```
FILE_DEVICE_BEEP                 0x00000001
FILE_DEVICE_CD_ROM               0x00000002
FILE_DEVICE_CD_ROM_FILE_SYSTEM   0x00000003
```

```
FILE_DEVICE_CONTROLLER                 0x00000004
FILE_DEVICE_DATALINK                   0x00000005
FILE_DEVICE_DFS                        0x00000006
FILE_DEVICE_DISK                       0x00000007
FILE_DEVICE_DISK_FILE_SYSTEM           0x00000008
FILE_DEVICE_FILE_SYSTEM                0x00000009
FILE_DEVICE_INPORT_PORT                0x0000000a
FILE_DEVICE_KEYBOARD                   0x0000000b
FILE_DEVICE_MAILSLOT                   0x0000000c
FILE_DEVICE_MIDI_IN                    0x0000000d
FILE_DEVICE_MIDI_OUT                   0x0000000e
FILE_DEVICE_MOUSE                      0x0000000f
FILE_DEVICE_MULTI_UNC_PROVIDER         0x00000010
FILE_DEVICE_NAMED_PIPE                 0x00000011
FILE_DEVICE_NETWORK                    0x00000012
FILE_DEVICE_NETWORK_BROWSER            0x00000013
FILE_DEVICE_NETWORK_FILE_SYSTEM        0x00000014
FILE_DEVICE_NULL                       0x00000015
FILE_DEVICE_PARALLEL_PORT              0x00000016
FILE_DEVICE_PHYSICAL_NETCARD           0x00000017
FILE_DEVICE_PRINTER                    0x00000018
FILE_DEVICE_SCANNER                    0x00000019
FILE_DEVICE_SERIAL_MOUSE_PORT          0x0000001a
FILE_DEVICE_SERIAL_PORT                0x0000001b
FILE_DEVICE_SCREEN                     0x0000001c
FILE_DEVICE_SOUND                      0x0000001d
FILE_DEVICE_STREAMS                    0x0000001e
FILE_DEVICE_TAPE                       0x0000001f
FILE_DEVICE_TAPE_FILE_SYSTEM           0x00000020
FILE_DEVICE_TRANSPORT                  0x00000021
FILE_DEVICE_UNKNOWN                    0x00000022
FILE_DEVICE_VIDEO                      0x00000023
FILE_DEVICE_VIRTUAL_DISK               0x00000024
FILE_DEVICE_WAVE_IN                    0x00000025
FILE_DEVICE_WAVE_OUT                   0x00000026
FILE_DEVICE_8042_PORT                  0x00000027
FILE_DEVICE_NETWORK_REDIRECTOR         0x00000028
FILE_DEVICE_BATTERY                    0x00000029
FILE_DEVICE_BUS_EXTENDER               0x0000002a
FILE_DEVICE_MODEM                      0x0000002b
FILE_DEVICE_VDM                        0x0000002c
```

Some of these device types are not currently accessible over the network, and may never be accessible on the network. Some may change to be accessible in the future. The values for device types that will never be accessible over the network may be redefined to be "reserved".

For the encoding of "Characteristics" in the protocol request, this field is the sum of any of the following:

```
FILE_REMOVABLE_MEDIA                   0x00000001
FILE_READ_ONLY_DEVICE                  0x00000002
FILE_FLOPPY_DISKETTE                   0x00000004
FILE_WRITE_ONE_MEDIA                   0x00000008
FILE_REMOTE_DEVICE                     0x00000010
```

```
FILE_DEVICE_IS_MOUNTED          0x00000020
FILE_VIRTUAL_VOLUME             0x00000040
```

4.1.6.6.   SMB_QUERY_FS_ATTRIBUTE_INFO

```
InformationLevel
Data Block Encoding         Description
====================        ============
ULONG                       File System Attributes;
                              possible values described below
LONG                        Maximum length of each file name component
                              in number of bytes
ULONG                       Length, in bytes, of the name of the file system
STRING                      Name of the file system
```

Where FileSystemAttributes are the sum of any of the following:

```
FILE_CASE_SENSITIVE_SEARCH   0x00000001
FILE_CASE_PRESERVED_NAMES    0x00000002
FILE_PERSISTENT_ACLS         0x00000004
FILE_FILE_COMPRESSION        0x00000008
FILE_VOLUME_QUOTAS           0x00000010
FILE_DEVICE_IS_MOUNTED       0x00000020
FILE_VOLUME_IS_COMPRESSED    0x00008000
```

4.1.6.7.   SMB_QUERY_CIFS_UNIX_INFO

```
InformationLevel
Data Block Encoding             Description
====================            ============
UNIT16 MajorVersionNumber;      Major version of CIFS UNIX supported by
                                  server
UNIT16 MinorVersionNumber;      Minor version of CIFS UNIX supported by
                                  server
LARGE_INTEGER Capability;       Capabilities of CIFS UNIX support by
                                  Server
```

Where Capability is the sum of the following:

CIFS_UNIX_FCNTL_CAP	0x1	Reserved. Should be zero
CIFS_UNIX_POSIX_ACL_CAP	0x2	Reserved. Should be zero

4.1.6.8.   SMB_QUERY_MAC_FS_INFO

```
InformationLevel
Data Block Encoding     Description
====================    ============
LARGE_INTEGER           CreationTime; Volume creation time - NT TIME.
LARGE_INTEGER           ModifyTime; Volume Modify time - NT TIME.
LARGE_INTEGER           BackUpTime; Volume was last Backup time - NT TIME.
                        Defaults to Create Time.
ULONG                   NmAlBlks; The number of allocation blocks in the
                        volume
ULONG                   AlBlkSiz; The allocation block size (in bytes) Must
                        be in multiple of 512 bytes
ULONG                   FreeBks; The number of unused allocations blocks on
                        the volume
UCHAR [32];             FndrInfo[32]; Information used by the finder that is
                        always in Big Endian.
                            Bytes 0-3 File Type
                                If a file default to 'TEXT' otherwise
                        default to zero
                            Bytes 4-7 File Creator
                                If a file default to 'dosa' otherwise
                        default to zero
                            Bytes 8-9 a UWORD flags field
                                If hidden item set this UWORD to 0x4000
                        else defaults to zero
                            All other bytes should default to zero and are
                        only changeable by the Macintosh
LONG                    NmFls; The number of files in the root directory;
                        Zero if not known
LONG                    NmRtDirs; The number of directories in the root
                        directory; Zero if not known
LONG                    FilCnt; The number of files on the volume; Zero if
                        not known
LONG                    DirCnt; The number of directories on the volume;
                        Zero if not known
LONG                    MacSupportFlags; Must be zero unless you support the
                        other Macintosh options
```

Where *MacSupportFlags* is the sum of any of the following:

SUPPORT_MAC_ACCESS_CNTRL	0x00000010	The server will return folder access control in the Trans2_Find_First2 and Trans2_Find_Next2 message described later in this document.
SUPPORT_MAC_GETSETCOMMENTS	0x00000020	Not currently supported.
SUPPORT_MAC_DESKTOPDB_CALLS	0x00000040	The Server supports setting and getting Macintosh desktop database information using the mechanism in this document.

| SUPPORT_MAC_UNIQUE_IDS | 0x00000080 | The server will return a unique id for files and directories in the Trans2_Find_First2 and Trans2_Find_Next2 message described later in this document. |
| NO_STREAMS_OR_MAC_SUPPORT | 0x00000100 | The server will return this flag telling the client that the server does not support streams or the Macintosh extensions. The client will ignore the rest of this message. |

4.1.6.9. Errors

```
ERRSRV/invnid - TID was invalid
ERRSRV/baduid - UID was invalid
ERRHRD/ERRnotready - The file system has been removed
ERRHRD/ERRdata - Disk I/O error
ERRSRV/ERRaccess - User does not have rights to perform this operation
ERRSRV/ERRinvdevice - Resource identified by TID is not a file system
```

4.1.7. ECHO: Ping the Server

This request is used to test the connection to the server, and to see if the server is still responding. The client request is defined as:

```
Client Request                Description
===============               ===========
UCHAR WordCount;              Count of parameter words = 1
USHORT EchoCount;             Number of times to echo data back
USHORT ByteCount;             Count of data bytes; min = 1
UCHAR Buffer[1];              Data to echo
```

And, the server response is:

```
Server Response               Description
===============               ===========
UCHAR WordCount;              Count of parameter words = 1
USHORT SequenceNumber;        Sequence number of this echo
USHORT ByteCount;             Count of data bytes; min = 4
UCHAR Buffer[1];              Echoed data
```

Each response echoes the data sent, though ByteCount may indicate "no data". If EchoCount is zero, no response is sent.

Tid in the SMB header is ignored, so this request may be sent to the server even if there are no valid tree connections to the server.

The flow for the ECHO protocol is:

Client Request	< -- >	Server Response
Echo request (EchoCount == n)	- >	
	< -	Echo response 1
	< -	Echo response 2
	< -	Echo response n

4.1.7.1. Errors

```
ERRSRV/ERRbaduid    - UID was invalid
ERRSRV/ERRnoaccess  - session has not been established
ERRSRV/ERRnosupport - ECHO function is not supported
```

4.1.8. NT_CANCEL: Cancel request

This SMB allows a client to cancel a request currently pending at the server. The client request is defined as:

```
Client Request                Description
===============               ===========
 UCHAR WordCount;             No words are sent (== 0)
 USHORT ByteCount;            No bytes (==0)
```

The Sid, Uid, Pid, Tid, and Mid fields of the SMB are used to locate an pending server request from this session. If a pending request is found, it is "hurried along" which may result in success or failure of the original request. No other response is generated for this SMB.

4.2. File Requests

4.2.1. NT_CREATE_ANDX: Create or Open File

This command is used to create or open a file or a directory. The client request is defined as:

```
Client Request                Description
===============               ===========
UCHAR WordCount;              Count of parameter words = 24
UCHAR AndXCommand;            Secondary command; 0xFF = None
UCHAR AndXReserved;           Reserved (must be 0)
USHORT AndXOffset;            Offset to next command WordCount
UCHAR Reserved;               Reserved (must be 0)
USHORT NameLength;            Length of Name[] in bytes
ULONG Flags;                  Create bit set:
                                   0x02 - Request an oplock
                                   0x04 - Request a batch oplock
                                   0x08 - Target of open must be directory
ULONG RootDirectoryFid;       If non-zero, open is relative to
                                   this directory
ACCESS_MASK DesiredAccess;    Access desired (See Section 3.8 for an
                                   explanation of this field)
LARGE_INTEGER AllocationSize; Initial allocation size
ULONG ExtFileAttributes;      File attributes
ULONG ShareAccess;            Type of share access
ULONG CreateDisposition;      Action if file does/does not exist
```

```
ULONG CreateOptions;              Options to use if creating a file
ULONG ImpersonationLevel;         Security QOS information
UCHAR SecurityFlags;              Security tracking mode flags:
                                     0x1 - SECURITY_CONTEXT_TRACKING
                                     0x2 - SECURITY_EFFECTIVE_ONLY
USHORT ByteCount;                 Length of byte parameters
STRING Name[];                    File to open or create
```

The Name parameter contains the full path from the tree connect point unless the RootDirectoryFid is used. To use the RootDirectoryFid perform a NT_CREATE_ANDX to open the directory and then use the returned Fid for subsequent NT_CREATE_ANDX calls to open/create files within that directory.

The DesiredAccess parameter is specified in section 3.8, Access Mask Encoding. If no value is specified, an application can still query attributes without actually accessing the file.

The ExtFileAttributes parameter specifies the file attributes and flags for the file. The parameter's value is the sum of allowed attributes and flags defined in section 3.12, Extended File Attribute Encoding.

The ShareAccess field specifies how the file can be shared. This parameter must be some combination of the following values:

Name	Value	Meaning
FILE_NO_SHARE	0x00000000	Prevents the file from being shared.
FILE_SHARE_READ	0x00000001	Other open operations can be performed on the file for read access.
FILE_SHARE_WRITE	0x00000002	Other open operations can be performed on the file for write access.
FILE_SHARE_DELETE	0x00000004	Other open operations can be performed on the file for delete access.

The CreateDisposition parameter can contain one of the following values:

Name	Value	Meaning
FILE_SUPERSEDE	0x00000000	*FILE_SUPERSEDE*- Indicates that if the file already exists then it should be superseded by the specified file. If it does not already exist then it should be created.
FILE_OPEN	0x00000001	*FILE_OPEN* - Indicates that if the file already exists it should be opened rather than creating a new file. If the file does not already exist then the operation should fail.
FILE_CREATE	0x00000002	*FILE_CREATE* - Indicates that if the file already exists then the operation should fail. If the file does not already exist then it should be created.
FILE_OPEN_IF	0x00000003	*FILE_OPEN_IF* - Indicates that if the file already exists, it should be opened. If the file does not already exist then it should be created.
FILE_OVERWRITE	0x00000004	*FILE_OVERWRITE* - Indicates that if the file already exists it should be opened and overwritten. If the file does not already exist then the operation should fail.
FILE_OVERWRITE_IF	0x00000005	*FILE_OVERWRITE_IF* - Indicates that if the file already exists it should be opened and overwritten. If the file does not already exist then it should be created.

Name	Value	Meaning
FILE_MAXIMUM_DIS POSITION	0x00000005	?

The ImpersonationLevel parameter can contain one or more of the following values:

Name	Value	Meaning
SECURITY_ANONYMOUS	0	Impersonation of the client at the Anonymous level
SECURITY_IDENTIFICATION	1	Impersonation of the client at the Identification level
SECURITY_IMPERSONATION	2	Impersonation of the client at the Impersonation level
SECURITY_DELEGATION	3	Impersonation of the client at the Delegation level

The SecurityFlags parameter can have either of the following two flags set:

Name	Value	Meaning
SECURITY_CONTEXT_TRACKING	0x00040000	Specifies that the security tracking mode is dynamic. If this flag is not specified, Security Tracking Mode is static.
SECURITY_EFFECTIVE_ONLY	0x00080000	Specifies that only the enabled aspects of the client's security context are available to the server. If this flag is not specified, all aspects of the client's security context are available. This flag allows the client to limit the groups and privileges that a server can use while impersonating the client.

The server response to the NT_CREATE_ANDX request is as follows:

```
Server Response                 Description
================                ===========
UCHAR WordCount;                Count of parameter words = 26
UCHAR AndXCommand;              0xFF = None
UCHAR AndXReserved;             MUST BE ZERO
USHORT AndXOffset;              Offset to next command WordCount
UCHAR OplockLevel;              The oplock level granted:
                                    0 - No oplock granted
                                    1 - Exclusive oplock granted
                                    2 - Batch oplock granted
                                    3 - Level II oplock granted
USHORT Fid;                     The file ID
ULONG CreateAction;             The action taken
TIME CreationTime;              The time the file was created
TIME LastAccessTime;            The time the file was accessed
TIME LastWriteTime;             The time the file was last written
TIME ChangeTime;                The time the file was last changed
ULONG ExtFileAttributes;        The file attributes
LARGE_INTEGER AllocationSize;   The number of byes allocated
LARGE_INTEGER EndOfFile;        The end of file offset
USHORT FileType;
USHORT DeviceState;             State of IPC device (e.g. pipe)
BOOLEAN Directory;              TRUE if this is a directory
USHORT ByteCount;               = 0
```

The following SMBs may follow SMB_COM_NT_CREATE_ANDX:
SMB_COM_READ   SMB_COM_READ_ANDX
SMB_COM_IOCTL

4.2.1.1.   Errors

```
ERRDOS codes
------------
ERRbadfile
ERRbadpath
ERRnofids
ERRnoaccess
ERRnomem
ERRbadaccess
ERRbadshare
ERRfileexists
ERRquota

ERRSRV codes
------------
ERRaccess
ERRinvdevice
ERRinvtid
ERRbaduid
```

4.2.2. NT_TRANSACT_CREATE: Create or Open File with EAs or SD

This command is used to create or open a file or a directory, when EAs or an SD must be applied to the file. The parameter and data blocks for the client's CREATE request include the following data:

Request Parameter Block Encoding	Description
`ULONG Flags;`	Creation flags (see below)
`ULONG RootDirectoryFid;`	Optional directory for relative open
`ACCESS_MASK DesiredAccess;`	Access desired (See Section 3.8 for an explanation of this field)
`LARGE_INTEGER AllocationSize;`	The initial allocation size in bytes, if file created
`ULONG ExtFileAttributes;`	The extended file attributes
`ULONG ShareAccess;`	The share access
`ULONG CreateDisposition;`	Action if file does/does not exist
`ULONG CreateOptions;`	Options for creating a new file
`ULONG SecurityDescriptorLength;`	Length of SD in bytes
`ULONG EaLength;`	Length of EA in bytes
`ULONG NameLength;`	Length of name in characters
`ULONG ImpersonationLevel;`	Security QOS information
`UCHAR SecurityFlags;`	Security QOS information
`STRING Name[NameLength];`	The name of the file (not NULL terminated)

```
Request Data Block Encoding          Description
============================         ============
  UCHAR SecurityDescriptor[
     SecurityDescriptorLength];
  UCHAR ExtendedAttributes[EaLength];
```

The Flags parameter can contain one of the following values:

Creation Flags Name	Value	Description
NT_CREATE_REQUEST_OPLOCK	0x02	Exclusive oplock requested
NT_CREATE_REQUEST_OPBATCH	0x04	Batch oplock requested
NT_CREATE_OPEN_TARGET_DIR	0x08	Target for open is a directory

The parameter block of the server response is defined as:

```
Response Parameter Block Encoding    Description
=================================    ============
  UCHAR OplockLevel;                 The oplock level granted
  UCHAR Reserved;
  USHORT Fid;                        The file ID
  ULONG CreateAction;                The action taken
  ULONG EaErrorOffset;               Offset of the EA error
  TIME CreationTime;                 The time the file was created
  TIME LastAccessTime;               The time the file was accessed
  TIME LastWriteTime;                The time the file was last written
  TIME ChangeTime;                   The time the file was last changed
  ULONG ExtFileAttributes;           The file attributes
  LARGE_INTEGER AllocationSize;      The number of byes allocated
  LARGE_INTEGER EndOfFile;           The end of file offset
  USHORT FileType;
  USHORT DeviceState;                State of IPC device (e.g. pipe)
  BOOLEAN Directory;                 TRUE if this is a directory
```

See the description of NT_CREATE_ANDX (section 4.2.1) for further definition of the CREATE request/response parameters.

4.2.2.1. Errors

```
ERRDOS codes
------------
ERRbadfile
ERRbadpath
ERRnofids
ERRnoaccess
ERRnomem
ERRbadaccess
ERRbadshare
ERRfileexists
ERRquota

ERRSRV codes
------------
ERRaccess
```

```
ERRinvdevice
ERRinvtid
ERRbaduid
```

4.2.3. CREATE_TEMPORARY: Create Temporary File

The server creates a data file in the specified Directory, relative to Tid in the SMB header, and assigns a unique name to it. The client request and server response for the command are:

```
Client Request                  Description
===============                 ============
UCHAR WordCount;                Count of parameter words = 3
USHORT reserved;                Ignored by the server
UTIME CreationTime;             New file's creation time stamp
USHORT ByteCount;               Count of data bytes; min = 2
UCHAR BufferFormat;             0x04
STRING DirectoryName[];         Directory name

Server Response                 Description
================                ============
UCHAR WordCount;                Count of parameter words = 1
USHORT Fid;                     File handle
USHORT ByteCount;               Count of data bytes; min = 2
UCHAR BufferFormat;             0x04
STRING Filename[];              File name
```

Fid is the returned handle for future file access. Filename is the name of the file that was created within the requested Directory. It is opened in compatibility mode with read/write access for the client.

Support of CreationTime by the server is optional.

4.2.3.1. Errors

```
ERRDOS codes
------------
ERRbadfile
ERRbadpath
ERRnofids
ERRnoaccess
ERRnomem
ERRbadaccess
ERRbadshare
ERRfileexists
ERRquota

ERRSRV codes
------------
ERRaccess
ERRinvdevice
ERRinvtid
ERRbaduid
```

4.2.4. READ_ANDX: Read Bytes

Client requests a file read, using the SMB fields specified below:

```
Client Request                 Description
===============                ============
UCHAR WordCount;               Count of parameter words = 10 or 12
UCHAR AndXCommand;             Secondary (X) command; 0xFF = none
UCHAR AndXReserved;            Reserved (must be 0)
USHORT AndXOffset;             Offset to next command WordCount
USHORT Fid;                    File handle
ULONG Offset;                  Offset in file to begin read
USHORT MaxCount;               Max number of bytes to return
USHORT MinCount;               Reserved for obsolescent requests
ULONG MaxCountHigh;            High 16 bits of MaxCount if
                                 CAP_LARGE_READX; else MUST BE ZERO
USHORT Remaining;              Reserved for obsolescent requests
ULONG OffsetHigh;              Upper 32 bits of offset (only if
                                 WordCount is 12)
USHORT ByteCount;              Count of data bytes = 0
```

And, the server response is:

```
Server Response                Description
===============                ============
UCHAR WordCount;               Count of parameter words = 12
UCHAR AndXCommand;             Secondary (X) command; 0xFF = none
UCHAR AndXReserved;            Reserved (must be 0)
USHORT AndXOffset;             Offset to next command WordCount
USHORT Remaining;              Reserved -- must be -1
USHORT DataCompactionMode;
USHORT Reserved;               Reserved (must be 0)
USHORT DataLength;             Number of data bytes (min = 0)
USHORT DataOffset;             Offset (from header start) to data
USHORT DataLengthHigh;         High 16 bits of number of data bytes if
                                 CAP_LARGE_READX; else MUST BE ZERO
USHORT Reserved[4];            Reserved (must be 0)
USHORT ByteCount;              Count of data bytes; ignored if
                                 CAP_LARGE_READX
UCHAR Pad[];
UCHAR Data[DataLength];        Data from resource
```

If the file specified by Fid has any portion of the range specified by Offset and MaxCount locked for exclusive use by a client with a different connection or Pid, the request will fail with ERRlock.

If the negotiated dialect is NT LM 0.12 or later, the client may use the 12 parameter word version of the request. This version allows specification of 64 bit file offsets.

If CAP_LARGE_READX was indicated by the server in the negotiate protocol response, the request's MaxCount field may exceed the negotiated buffer size if Fid refers to a disk file. The server may arbitrarily elect to return fewer than MaxCount bytes in response.

The SMB server MAY use the MinCount on named-pipe calls to determine if this is a blocking read or a non-blocking read. (Non blocking is determined by MinCount = 0). Note that for blocking reads, the length required to succeed is actually the ReadLength and not the MinCount. (So in some sense, MinCount has become more of an indicator of blocking vs. non-blocking rather than a true length)

The following SMBs may follow SMB_COM_READ_ANDX:

```
SMB_COM_CLOSE
```

4.2.4.1. Errors

```
ERRDOS/ERRnoaccess
ERRDOS/ERRbadfid
ERRDOS/ERRlock
ERRDOS/ERRbadaccess
ERRSRV/ERRinvid
ERRSRV/ERRbaduid
```

4.2.5. WRITE_ANDX: Write Bytes to file or resource

Client requests a file write, using the SMB fields specified below:

```
Client Request            Description
===============           ===========
UCHAR WordCount;          Count of parameter words = 12 or 14
UCHAR AndXCommand;        Secondary (X) command; 0xFF = none
UCHAR AndXReserved;       Reserved (must be 0)
USHORT AndXOffset;        Offset to next command WordCount
USHORT Fid;               File handle
ULONG Offset;             Offset in file to begin write
ULONG Reserved;           Must be 0
USHORT WriteMode;         Write mode bits:
                              0 - write through
USHORT Remaining;         Bytes remaining to satisfy request
USHORT DataLengthHigh;    High 16 bits of data length if
                              CAP_LARGE_WRITEX; else MUST BE ZERO
USHORT DataLength;        Number of data bytes in buffer (>=0)
USHORT DataOffset;        Offset to data bytes
ULONG OffsetHigh;         Upper 32 bits of offset (only present if
                              WordCount = 14)
USHORT ByteCount;         Count of data bytes; ignored if
                              CAP_LARGE_WRITEX
UCHAR Pad[];              Pad to SHORT or LONG
UCHAR Data[DataLength];   Data to write
```

And, the server response is:

```
Server Response           Description
===============           ===========
UCHAR WordCount;          Count of parameter words = 6
UCHAR AndXCommand;        Secondary (X) command; 0xFF = none
UCHAR AndXReserved;       Reserved (must be 0)
USHORT AndXOffset;        Offset to next command WordCount
USHORT Count;             Number of bytes written
USHORT Remaining;         Reserved
ULONG Reserved;
USHORT ByteCount;         Count of data bytes = 0
```

If the file specified by Fid has any portion of the range specified by Offset and MaxCount locked for shared or exclusive use by a client with a different connection or Pid, the request will fail with ERRlock.

A ByteCount of 0 does not truncate the file. Rather a zero length write merely transfers zero bytes of information to the file. A request such as SMB_COM_WRITE must be used to truncate the file.

If WriteMode has bit0 set in the request and Fid refers to a disk file, the response is not sent from the server until the data is on stable storage.

If the negotiated dialect is NT LM 0.12 or later, the 14 word format of this SMB may be used to access portions of files requiring offsets expressed as 64 bits. Otherwise, the OffsetHigh field must be omitted from the request.

If CAP_LARGE_WRITEX was indicated by the server in the negotiate protocol response, the request's DataLength field may exceed the negotiated buffer size if Fid refers to a disk file.

The following are the valid AndXCommand values for this SMB:

```
SMB_COM_READ                 SMB_COM_READ_ANDX
SMB_COM_LOCK_AND_READ        SMB_COM_WRITE_ANDX
SMB_COM_CLOSE
```

4.2.5.1. Errors

```
ERRDOS/ERRnoaccess
ERRDOS/ERRbadfid
ERRDOS/ERRlock
ERRDOS/ERRbadaccess
ERRSRV/ERRinvid
ERRSRV/ERRbaduid
```

4.2.6. LOCKING_ANDX: Lock or Unlock Byte Ranges

SMB_COM_LOCKING_ANDX allows both locking and/or unlocking of file range(s). A description of the fields of the client request, and explanations for several of the fields are provided below.

Client Request	Description
UCHAR WordCount;	Count of parameter words = 8
UCHAR AndXCommand;	Secondary (X) command; 0xFF = none
UCHAR AndXReserved;	Reserved (must be 0)
USHORT AndXOffset;	Offset to next command WordCount
USHORT Fid;	File handle
UCHAR LockType;	See LockType table below
UCHAR OplockLevel;	The new oplock level
ULONG Timeout;	Milliseconds to wait for unlock
USHORT NumberOfUnlocks;	Number of unlock range structures that follow
USHORT NumberOfLocks;	Number of lock range structures that follow
USHORT ByteCount;	Count of data bytes
LOCKING_ANDX_RANGE Unlocks[];	Unlock ranges
LOCKING_ANDX_RANGE Locks[];	Lock ranges

The LockType parameter can take on one of the values in the following table:

Flag Name	Value	Description
LOCKING_ANDX_SHARED_LOCK	0x01	Read-only lock
LOCKING_ANDX_OPLOCK_RELEASE	0x02	Oplock break notification
LOCKING_ANDX_CHANGE_LOCKTYPE	0x04	Change lock type
LOCKING_ANDX_CANCEL_LOCK	0x08	Cancel outstanding request
LOCKING_ANDX_LARGE_FILES	0x10	Large file locking format

The format for LOCKING_ANDX_RANGE is:

```
USHORT Pid;                    PID of process "owning" lock
ULONG Offset;                  Offset to bytes to [un]lock
ULONG Length;                  Number of bytes to [un]lock
```

And, for a large file, it is:

```
USHORT Pid;                    PID of process "owning" lock
USHORT Pad;                    Pad to DWORD align (Must be zero)
ULONG OffsetHigh;              Offset to bytes to [un]lock (high)
ULONG OffsetLow;               Offset to bytes to [un]lock (low)
ULONG LengthHigh;              Number of bytes to [un]lock
                                (high)
ULONG LengthLow;               Number of bytes to [un]lock (low)
```

The server response is:

```
Server Response                Description
===============                ===========
UCHAR WordCount;               Count of parameter words = 2
UCHAR AndXCommand;             Secondary (X) command; 0xFF = none
UCHAR AndXReserved;            Reserved (must be 0)
USHORT AndXOffset;             Offset to next command WordCount
USHORT ByteCount;              Count of data bytes = 0
```

Locking is a simple mechanism for excluding other processes read/write access to regions of a file. The locked regions can be anywhere in the logical file. Locking beyond end-of-file is permitted. Lock conflicts (overlapping lock-requests) should cause the server to refuse the lock to the latter requestor. Any process using the *Fid* specified in this request's *Fid* has access to the locked bytes; other processes will be denied the locking of the same bytes.

The proper method for using locks is not to rely on being denied read or write access on any of the read/write protocols but rather to attempt the locking protocol and proceed with the read/write only if the locks succeeded.

Locking a range of bytes will fail if any subranges or overlapping ranges are locked, if the PID/UID of the requestor is not the same, and the locks are not compatible. In other words, if any of the specified bytes are already locked, the lock will fail.

If NumberOfUnlocks is non-zero, the Unlocks vector contains NumberOfUnlocks elements. Each element requests that a lock at Offset of Length be released. If NumberOfLocks is nonzero, the

Locks vector contains NumberOfLocks elements. Each element requests the acquisition of a lock at Offset of Length.

Timeout is the maximum amount of time to wait for the byte range(s) specified to become unlocked. A timeout value of 0 indicates that the server should fail immediately if any lock range specified is locked. A timeout value of -1 indicates that the server should wait as long as it takes for each byte range specified to become unlocked so that it may be again locked by this protocol. Any other value of smb_timeout specifies the maximum number of milliseconds to wait for all lock range(s) specified to become available.

If any of the lock ranges timeout because of the area to be locked is already locked (or the lock fails), the other ranges in the protocol request which were successfully locked as a result of this protocol will be unlocked (either all requested ranges will be locked when this protocol returns to the client or none).

If LockType has the LOCKING_ANDX_SHARED_LOCK flag set, the lock is specified as a shared lock. Locks for both read and write (where LOCKING_ANDX_SHARED_LOCK is clear) should be prohibited, but other shared locks should be permitted. If shared locks can not be supported by a server, the server should map the lock to a lock for both read and write. Closing a file with locks still in force causes the locks to be released in no defined order.

If LockType has the LOCKING_ANDX_LARGE_FILES flag set and if the negotiated protocol is NT LM 0.12 or later, then the Locks and Unlocks vectors are in the Large File LOCKING_ANDX_RANGE format. This allows specification of 64 bit offsets for very large files.

If the one and only member of the Locks vector has the LOCKING_ANDX_CANCEL_LOCK flag set in the LockType field, the client is requesting the server to cancel a previously requested, but not yet responded to, lock.

If LockType has the LOCKING_ANDX_CHANGE_LOCKTYPE flag set, the client is requesting that the server atomically change the lock type from a shared lock to an exclusive lock or vice versa. If the server can not do this in an atomic fashion, the server must reject this request. (Note: Windows NT and Windows 95 servers do not support this capability.)

If the client sends an SMB_LOCKING_ANDX SMB with the LOCKING_ANDX_OPLOCK_RELEASE flag set and *NumberOfLocks* is zero, the server does not send a response. The entire message sent and received including the optional second protocol must fit in the negotiated maximum transfer size. The following are the only valid SMB commands for AndXCommand for SMB_COM_LOCKING_ANDX:

```
SMB_COM_READ          SMB_COM_READ_ANDX
SMB_COM_WRITE         SMB_COM_WRITE_ANDX
SMB_COM_FLUSH
```

4.2.6.1. Errors

```
ERRDOS/ERRbadfile
ERRDOS/ERRbadfid
ERRDOS/ERRlock
ERRDOS/ERRinvdevice
ERRSRV/ERRinvid
ERRSRV/ERRbaduid
```

4.2.7. SEEK: Seek in File

The seek message is sent to set the current file pointer for *Fid*.

```
Client Request                 Description
===============                =================================
UCHAR WordCount;               Count of parameter words = 4
  USHORT Fid;                  File handle
  USHORT Mode;                   Seek mode:
                                       0 = from start of file
                                       1 = from current position
                                       2 = from end of file
  LONG Offset;                   Relative offset
  USHORT ByteCount;            Count of data bytes = 0
```

The "current position" reflects the offset plus data length specified in the previous read, write, or seek request; and the pointer set by this command will be replaced by the offset specified in the next read, write, or seek command.

```
Server Response                Description
===============                ============
  UCHAR WordCount;             Count of parameter words = 2
  ULONG Offset;                        Offset from start of file
  USHORT ByteCount;            Count of data bytes = 0
```

The response returns the new file pointer in *Offset,* which is expressed as the offset from the start of the file, and may be beyond the current end of file. An attempt to seek to before the start of file sets the current file pointer to start of the file.

This request should generally be issued only by clients wishing to find the size of a file, because all read and write requests include the read or write file position as part of the SMB. This request is inappropriate for very large files, as the offsets specified are only 32 bits. A seek that results in an Offset that cannot be expressed in 32 bits returns the least significant.

4.2.7.1.   Errors

```
ERRDOS/ERRbadfid
ERRDOS/ERRnoaccess
ERRSRV/ERRinvdevice
ERRSRV/ERRinvid
ERRSRV/ERRbaduid
```

4.2.8. FLUSH: Flush File

The flush SMB is sent to ensure all data and allocation information for the corresponding file has been written to stable storage. When the Fid has a value -1 (hex FFFF), the server performs a flush for all file handles associated with the client and Pid. The response is not sent until the writes are complete.

```
Client Request                 Description
===============                =================================
  UCHAR WordCount;             Count of parameter words = 1
  USHORT Fid;                  File handle
  USHORT ByteCount;            Count of data bytes = 0
```

This client request is probably expensive to perform at the server, since the server's operating system is generally scheduling disk writes is a way which is optimal for the system's read and write activity integrated over the entire population of clients. This message from a client "interferes" with the server's ability to optimally schedule the disk activity; clients are discouraged from overuse of this SMB request.

```
Server Response                       Description
=================                     ============
 UCHAR WordCount;                     Count of parameter words = 0
 USHORT ByteCount;                    Count of data bytes = 0
```

4.2.8.1. Errors

```
ERRDOS/ERRbadfid
ERRSRV/ERRinvid
ERRSRV/ERRbaduid
```

4.2.9. CLOSE: Close File

The close message is sent to invalidate a file handle for the requesting process. All locks or other resources held by the requesting process on the file should be released by the server. The requesting process can no longer use Fid for further file access requests.

```
Client Request                        Description
=================                     ============
 UCHAR WordCount;                     Count of parameter words = 3
 USHORT Fid;                          File handle
 UTIME LastWriteTime;                 Time of last write
 USHORT ByteCount;                    Count of data bytes = 0
```

If LastWriteTime is 0, the server should allow its local operating system to set the file's times. Otherwise, the server should set the time to the values requested. Failure to set the times, even if requested by the client in the request message, should not result in an error response from the server.

If Fid refers to a print spool file, the file should be spooled to the printer at this time.

```
Server Response                       Description
=================                     ============
 UCHAR WordCount;                     Count of parameter words = 0
 USHORT ByteCount;                    Count of data bytes = 0
```

4.2.9.1. Errors

```
ERRDOS/ERRbadfid
ERRSRV/ERRinvdevice
ERRSRV/ERRinvid
ERRSRV/ERRbaduid
```

4.2.10.   CLOSE AND TREE DISCONNECT

Close the file and perform a tree disconnect.

The close and tree disconnect message is sent to close a file and perform a tree disconnect. All locks or other resources held by the requesting process on the file should be released by the server. The requesting process can no longer use Fid for further file access requests. The server will perform a TREE_DISCONNECT after completing the close operation. The requesting process can no longer use Tid for further access requests.

```
Client Request                     Description
===============                    ============
 UCHAR WordCount;                  Count of parameter words = 3
 USHORT Fid;                       File handle
 UTIME LastWriteTime;              Time of last write
 USHORT ByteCount;                 Count of data bytes = 0
```

If LastWriteTime is 0, the server should allow its local operating system to set the file's times. Otherwise, the server should set the time to the values requested. Failure to set the times, even if requested by the client in the request message, should not result in an error response from the server.

If Fid refers to a print spool file, the file should be spooled to the printer at this time.

```
Server Response                    Description
================                   ============
 UCHAR WordCount;                  Count of parameter words = 0
 USHORT ByteCount;                 Count of data bytes = 0
```

4.2.10.1. Errors

```
ERRDOS/ERRbadfid
ERRSRV/ERRinvdevice
ERRSRV/ERRinvid
ERRSRV/ERRbaduid
```

4.2.11.   DELETE: Delete File

The delete file message is sent to delete a data file. The appropriate Tid and additional pathname are passed. Read only files may not be deleted, the read-only attribute must be reset prior to file deletion.

```
Client Request                     Description
===============                    ============
 UCHAR WordCount;                  Count of parameter words = 1
 USHORT SearchAttributes;
 USHORT ByteCount;                 Count of data bytes; min = 2
 UCHAR BufferFormat;               0x04
 STRING FileName[];                File name
```

Multiple files may be deleted in response to a single request as SMB_COM_DELETE supports wildcards.

SearchAttributes indicates the attributes that the target file(s) must have. If the attribute is zero then only normal files are deleted. If the system file or hidden attributes are specified, then the delete is inclusive - both the specified type(s) of files and normal files are deleted. File attributes are described in the "Attribute Encoding" section (3.11) of this document.

If bit0 of the Flags2 field of the SMB header is set, a pattern is passed in, and the file has a long name, then the passed pattern must match the long file name for the delete to succeed. If bit0 is clear, a pattern is passed in, and the file has a long name, then the passed pattern must match the file's short name for the deletion to succeed.

```
Server Response                         Description
================                        ============
  UCHAR WordCount;                        Count of parameter words = 0
  USHORT ByteCount;                       Count of data bytes = 0
```

4.2.11.1. Errors

```
ERRDOS/ERRbadpath
ERRDOS/ERRbadfile
ERRDOS/ERRnoaccess
ERRHRD/ERRnowrite
ERRSRV/ERRaccess
ERRSRV/ERRinvdevice
ERRSRV/ERRinvid
ERRSRV/ERRbaduid
```

4.2.12.   RENAME: Rename File

The rename file message is sent to change the name of a file.

```
Client Request                          Description
================                        ============
  UCHAR WordCount;                        Count of parameter words = 1
  USHORT SearchAttributes;                Target file attributes
  USHORT ByteCount;                       Count of data bytes; min = 4
  UCHAR BufferFormat1;                    0x04
  STRING OldFileName[];                   Old file name
  UCHAR BufferFormat2;                    0x04
  STRING NewFileName[];                   New file name
```

The file, OldFileName, must exist and NewFileName must not. Both pathnames must be relative to the Tid specified in the request. Open files may be renamed.

Multiple files may be renamed in response to a single request as Rename File supports wildcards in the file name (last component of the pathname).

SearchAttributes indicates the attributes that the target file(s) must have. If SearchAttributes is zero then only normal files are renamed. If the system file or hidden attributes are specified then the rename is inclusive - both the specified type(s) of files and normal files are renamed. The encoding of SearchAttributes is described in section 3.11 - File Attribute Encoding.

```
Server Response                         Description
================                        ============
  UCHAR WordCount;                        Count of parameter words = 0
  USHORT ByteCount;                       Count of data bytes = 0
```

4.2.12.1. Errors

```
ERRDOS/ERRbadpath
ERRDOS/ERRbadfile
ERRDOS/ERRnoaccess
ERRDOS/ERRdiffdevice
ERRHRD/ERRnowrite
ERRSRV/ERRaccess
ERRSRV/ERRinvdevice
```

```
ERRSRV/ERRinvid
ERRSRV/ERRbaduid
```

4.2.13.   NT_RENAME:

The rename file message is sent to change the name of a file. This version of RENAME supports NT link tracking info.

```
Client Request                 Description
===============                ============
UCHAR WordCount;               Count of parameter words = 4
USHORT SearchAttributes;
USHORT Information Level;
ULONG ClusterCount;
USHORT ByteCount;              Count of data bytes; min = 4
UCHAR Buffer[1];                 Buffer containing:
                                 UCHAR BufferFormat1 0x04 -- ASCII
                                 UCHAR OldFileName[] Old file name
                                 UCHAR BufferFormat2 0x04 -- ASCII
                                 UCHAR NewFileName[] New file name

Server Response                Description
================               ============
UCHAR WordCount;               Count of parameter words = 0
USHORT ByteCount;              Count of data bytes = 0
UCHAR Buffer[1];                 empty
```

Non-NT machines can ignore the extra parameters (InfoLevel, SearchAttributes, ClusterCount) and just perform a normal rename.

4.2.13.1. Errors

```
ERRDOS codes
------------
ERRbadfile
ERRbadpath
ERRnofids
ERRnoaccess
ERRnomem
ERRfileexists

ERRSRV codes
------------
ERRaccess
ERRinvdevice
ERRinvtid
ERRbaduid
```

4.2.14.   MOVE: Rename File

The source file is copied to the destination and the source is subsequently deleted.

```
Client Request                 Description
===============                ============
UCHAR WordCount;               Count of parameter words = 3
```

```
USHORT Tid2;                            Second (target) file id
USHORT OpenFunction;                    What to do if target file exists
USHORT Flags;                           Flags to control move operations:
                                          0 - target must be a file
                                          1 - target must be a directory
                                          2 - reserved (must be 0)
                                          3 - reserved (must be 0)
                                          4 - verify all writes
USHORT ByteCount;                       Count of data bytes; min = 2
UCHAR Format1;                          0x04
STRING OldFileName[];                   Old file name
UCHAR FormatNew;                        0x04
STRING NewFileName[];                   New file name
```

OldFileName is copied to NewFileName, then OldFileName is deleted. Both OldFileName and NewFileName must refer to paths on the same server. NewFileName can refer to either a file or a directory. All file components except the last must exist; directories will not be created.

NewFileName can be required to be a file or a directory by the Flags field.

The Tid in the header is associated with the source while Tid2 is associated with the destination. These fields may contain the same or differing valid values. Tid2 can be set to -1 indicating that this is to be the same Tid as in the SMB header. This allows use of the move protocol with SMB_TREE_CONNECT_ANDX.

```
Server Response                         Description
=================                       ============
UCHAR WordCount;                        Count of parameter words = 1
USHORT Count;                           Number of files moved
USHORT ByteCount;                       Count of data bytes; min = 0
UCHAR ErrorFileFormat;                  0x04  (only if error)
STRING ErrorFileName[];                 Pathname of file where error
                                          Occurred
```

The source path must refer to an existing file or files. Wildcards are permitted. Source files specified by wildcards are processed until an error is encountered. If an error is encountered, the expanded name of the file is returned in ErrorFileName. Wildcards are not permitted in NewFileName.

OpenFunction controls what should happen if the destination file exists. If (OpenFunction & 0x30) == 0, the operation should fail if the destination exists. If (OpenFunction & 0x30) == 0x20, the destination file should be overwritten.

4.2.14.1. Errors

```
ERRDOS/ERRfilexists
ERRDOS/ERRbadfile
ERRDOS/ERRnoaccess
ERRDOS/ERRnofiles
ERRDOS/ERRbadshare
ERRHRD/ERRnowrite
ERRSRV/ERRnoaccess
ERRSRV/ERRinvdevice
ERRSRV/ERRinvid
```

```
ERRSRV/ERRbaduid
ERRSRV/ERRnosupport
ERRSRV/ERRaccess
```

4.2.15.   COPY: Copy File

The source file is copied to the target.

```
Client Request                     Description
===============                    ============
UCHAR WordCount;                   Count of parameter words = 3
USHORT Tid2;                       Second (target) path TID
USHORT OpenFunction;               What to do if target file exists
USHORT Flags;                      Flags to control copy operation:
                                     bit 0 - target must be a file
                                     bit 1 - target must be a dir.
                                     bit 2 - copy target mode:
                                       0 = binary, 1 = ASCII
                                     bit 3 - copy source mode:
                                       0 = binary, 1 = ASCII
                                     bit 4 - verify all writes
                                     bit 5 - tree copy
USHORT ByteCount;                  Count of data bytes; min = 2
UCHAR SourceFileNameFormat;        0x04
STRING SourceFileName;             Pathname of source file
UCHAR TargetFileNameFormat;        0x04
STRING TargetFileName;             Pathname of target file
```

The file at SourceName is copied to TargetFileName, both of which must refer to paths on the same server.

The Tid in the header is associated with the source while Tid2 is associated with the destination. These fields may contain the same or differing valid values. Tid2 can be set to -1 indicating that this is to be the same Tid as in the SMB header. This allows use of the move protocol with SMB_TREE_CONNECT_ANDX.

```
Server Response                    Description
===============                    ============
UCHAR WordCount;                   Count of parameter words = 1
USHORT Count;                      Number of files copied
USHORT ByteCount;                  Count of data bytes; min = 0
UCHAR ErrorFileFormat;             0x04 (only if error)
STRING ErrorFileName;
```

The source path must refer to an existing file or files. Wildcards are permitted. Source files specified by wildcards are processed until an error is encountered. If an error is encountered, the expanded name of the file is returned in ErrorFileName. Wildcards are not permitted in TargetFileName. TargetFileName can refer to either a file or a directory.

The destination can be required to be a file or a directory by the bits in Flags. If neither bit0 nor bit1 are set, the destination may be either a file or a directory. The Flags field also controls the copy mode. In a binary copy for the source, the copy stops the first time an EOF (control-Z) is encountered. In a binary copy for the target, the server must make sure that there is exactly one EOF in the target file and that it is the last character of the file.

If the destination is a file and the source contains wildcards, the destination file will either be truncated or appended to at the start of the operation depending on bits in OpenFunction (see section 3.7). Subsequent files will then be appended to the file.

If the negotiated dialect is LM1.2X002 or later, bit5 of Flags is used to specify a tree copy on the remote server. When this option is selected the destination must not be an existing file and the source mode must be binary. A request with bit5 set and either bit0 or bit3 set is therefore an error. When the tree copy mode is selected, the Count field in the server response is undefined.

4.2.15.1. Errors

```
ERRDOS/ERRfilexists
ERRDOS/ERRshare
ERRDOS/ERRnofids
ERRDOS/ERRbadfile
ERRDOS/ERRnoaccess
ERRDOS/ERRnofiles
ERRDOS/ERRbadshare
ERRSRV/ERRnoaccess
ERRSRV/ERRinvdevice
ERRSRV/ERRinvid
ERRSRV/ERRbaduid
ERRSRV/ERRaccess
```

4.2.16.   TRANS2_QUERY_PATH_INFORMATION: Get File Attributes Given Path

This request is used to get information about a specific file or subdirectory.

```
Client Request              Value
===============             ======
WordCount                   15
MaxSetupCount               0
SetupCount                  1
Setup[0]                    TRANS2_QUERY_PATH_INFORMATION
```

The request's parameter block uses the following format:

```
Parameter Block Encoding    Description
========================    ===========
 USHORT InformationLevel;   Level of information requested
 ULONG Reserved;            Must be zero
 STRING FileName;           File or directory name
```

InformationLevels are specified using these values:

InformationLevel	Value
SMB_INFO_STANDARD	1
SMB_INFO_QUERY_EA_SIZE	2
SMB_INFO_QUERY_EAS_FROM_LIST	3
SMB_INFO_QUERY_ALL_EAS	4
SMB_INFO_IS_NAME_VALID	6
SMB_QUERY_FILE_BASIC_INFO	0x101

InformationLevel	Value
SMB_QUERY_FILE_STANDARD_INFO	0x102
SMB_QUERY_FILE_EA_INFO	0x103
SMB_QUERY_FILE_NAME_INFO	0x104
SMB_QUERY_FILE_ALL_INFO	0x107
SMB_QUERY_FILE_ALT_NAME_INFO	0x108
SMB_QUERY_FILE_STREAM_INFO	0x109
SMB_QUERY_FILE_COMPRESSION_INFO	0x10B
SMB_QUERY_FILE_UNIX_BASIC	0x200
SMB_QUERY_FILE_UNIX_LINK	0x201

The requested information is placed in the Data portion of the transaction response. For the information levels greater than 0x100, the transaction response has 1 parameter word which should be ignored by the client.

The following sections describe the InformationLevel dependent encoding of the data part of the transaction response.

4.2.16.1. SMB_INFO_STANDARD & SMB_INFO_QUERY_EA_SIZE

```
Data Block Encoding           Description
===================           ============
  SMB_DATE CreationDate;       Date when file was created
  SMB_TIME CreationTime;       Time when file was created
  SMB_DATE LastAccessDate;     Date of last file access
  SMB_TIME LastAccessTime;     Time of last file access
  SMB_DATE LastWriteDate;      Date of last write to the file
  SMB_TIME LastWriteTime;      Time of last write to the file
  ULONG  DataSize;             File Size
  ULONG AllocationSize;        Size of filesystem allocation unit
  USHORT Attributes;           File Attributes
  ULONG EaSize;                Size of file's EA information
                                 (SMB_INFO_QUERY_EA_SIZE)
```

4.2.16.2. SMB_INFO_QUERY_EAS_FROM_LIST & SMB_INFO_QUERY_ALL_EAS

```
Response Field        Value
==============        ======
  MaxDataCount          Length of EAlist found (minimum value is 4)

Parameter Block
Encoding              Description
==============        ============
  USHORT EaErrorOffset;  Offset into EAList of EA error

Data Block Encoding   Description
===================   ============
  ULONG ListLength;    Length of the remaining data
  UCHAR EaList[];      The extended attributes list
```

4.2.16.3. SMB_INFO_IS_NAME_VALID

This requests checks to see if the name of the file contained in the request's Data field has a valid path syntax. No parameters or data are returned on this information request. An error is returned if the syntax of the name is incorrect. Success indicates the server accepts the path syntax, but it does not ensure the file or directory actually exists.

4.2.16.4. SMB_QUERY_FILE_BASIC_INFO

```
Data Block Encoding              Description
====================             ============
  TIME  CreationTime;          Time when file was created
  TIME  LastAccessTime;        Time of last file access
  TIME  LastWriteTime;         Time of last write to the file
  TIME  ChangeTime;            Time when file was last changed
  ULONG Attributes;              File Attributes
  ULONG Pad;                   Undefined
```

The valid file attributes are:

Attribute	Value	Description
FILE_ATTRIBUTE_READONLY	0x00000001	The file is read only. Applications can read the file but cannot write to it or delete it.
FILE_ATTRIBUTE_HIDDEN	0x00000002	The file is hidden. It is not to be included in an ordinary directory listing.
FILE_ATTRIBUTE_SYSTEM	0x00000004	The file is part of or is used exclusively by the operating system.
FILE_ATTRIBUTE_VOLUMEID	0x00000008	The corresponding object represents a label for a filesystem object (obsolete)
FILE_ATTRIBUTE_DIRECTORY	0x00000010	The file is a directory.
FILE_ATTRIBUTE_ARCHIVE	0x00000020	The file is an archive file. Applications use this attribute to mark files for backup or removal.
FILE_ATTRIBUTE_DEVICE	0x00000040	The file is mapped to a device e.g. a printer or serial device.
FILE_ATTRIBUTE_NORMAL	0x00000080	The file has no other attributes set. This attribute is valid only if used alone. All other attributes override this attribute.
FILE_ATTRIBUTE_TEMPORARY	0x00000100	The file is being used for temporary storage. Applications should write to the file only if absolutely necessary. Most of the file's data remains in memory without being flushed to the media because the file will soon be deleted.
FILE_ATTRIBUTE_SPARSE_FILE	0x00000200	The file is a sparse file.
FILE_ATTRIBUTE_REPARSE_POINT	0x00000400	The file has an associated reparse point.
FILE_ATTRIBUTE_COMPRESSED	0x00000800	The file or directory is compressed. For a file, this means that all of the data in the file is compressed. For a directory, this means that compression is the default for newly created files and subdirectories.

Attribute	Value	Description
FILE_ATTRIBUTE_OFFLINE	0x00001000	The data of the file is not immediately available. This attribute indicates that the file data has been physically moved to offline storage. This attribute is used by Remote Storage, the hierarchical storage management software in Windows 2000. Applications should not arbitrarily change this attribute.
FILE_ATTRIBUTE_NOT CONTENT INDEXED	0x00002000	The file will not be indexed by the content indexing service.
FILE_ATTRIBUTE_ENCRYPTED	0x00004000	The file or directory is encrypted. For a file, this means that all data streams in the file are encrypted. For a directory, this means that encryption is the default for newly created files and subdirectories.

4.2.16.5. SMB_QUERY_FILE_STANDARD_INFO

```
Data Block Encoding          Description
======================       =============
  LARGE_INTEGER AllocationSize;   Allocated size of the file in number
                                     of bytes
  LARGE_INTEGER EndOfFile;        Offset to the first free byte in the
                                     file
  ULONG NumberOfLinks;            Number of hard links to the file
  BOOLEAN DeletePending;          Indicates whether the file is marked
                                     for deletion
  BOOLEAN Directory;              Indicates whether the file is a
                                     Directory
```

4.2.16.6. SMB_QUERY_FILE_EA_INFO

```
Data Block Encoding          Description
======================       =============
  ULONG EASize;               Size of the file's extended
                                 attributes in number of bytes
```

4.2.16.7. SMB_QUERY_FILE_NAME_INFO

```
Data Block Encoding          Description
======================       =============
  ULONG FileNameLength;       Length of the file name in number of
                                 bytes
  STRING FileName;            Name of the file
```

NOTE: Do not include the path to the file.

4.2.16.8. SMB_QUERY_FILE_ALL_INFO

```
Data Block Encoding          Description
======================       =============
  TIME   CreationTime;        Time when file was created
  TIME   LastAccessTime;      Time of last file access
  TIME   LastWriteTime;       Time of last write to the file
  TIME   ChangeTime;          Time when file was last changed
```

```
USHORT Attributes;              File Attributes
LARGE_INTEGER AllocationSize;   Allocated size of the file in number
                                  of bytes
LARGE_INTEGER EndOfFile;        Offset to the first free byte in the
                                  file
ULONG NumberOfLinks;            Number of hard links to the file
BOOLEAN DeletePending;          Indicates whether the file is marked
                                  for deletion
BOOLEAN Directory;              Indicates whether the file is a
                                  directory
LARGE_INTEGER IndexNumber;      A file system unique identifier
ULONG EASize;                   Size of the file's extended
                                  attributes in number of bytes
ULONG AccessFlags;              Access that a caller has to the
                                  file; Possible values and meanings
                                  are specified below
LARGE_INTEGER IndexNumber1;     A file system unique identifier
LARGE_INTEGER                   Current byte offset within the file
    CurrentByteOffset;
ULONG Mode;                     Current Open mode of the file handle
                                  to the file; possible values and
                                  meanings are detailed below
ULONG AlignmentRequirement;     Buffer Alignment required by device;
                                  possible values detailed below
ULONG FileNameLength;           Length of the file name in number of
                                  bytes
STRING FileName;                Name of the file
```

The AccessFlags specifies the access permissions a caller has to the file. It can have any suitable combination of the following values:

AccessFlag Name	Value	Meaning
FILE_READ_DATA	0x00000001	Data can be read from the file
FILE_WRITE_DATA	0x00000002	Data can be written to the file
FILE_APPEND_DATA	0x00000004	Data can be appended to the file
FILE_READ_EA	0x00000008	Extended attributes associated with the file can be read
FILE_WRITE_EA	0x00000010	Extended attributes associated with the file can be written
FILE_EXECUTE	0x00000020	Data can be read into memory from the file using system paging I/O
FILE_READ_ATTRIBUTES	0x00000080	Attributes associated with the file can be read
FILE_WRITE_ATTRIBUTES	0x00000100	Attributes associated with the file can be written
DELETE	0x00010000	The file can be deleted
READ_CONTROL	0x00020000	The access control list and ownership associated with the file can be read
WRITE_DAC	0x00040000	The access control list and ownership associated with the file can be written
WRITE_OWNER	0x00080000	Ownership information associated with the file can be written

AccessFlag Name	Value	Meaning
SYNCHRONIZE	0x00100000	The file handle can waited on to synchronize with the completion of an input/output request

The Mode field specifies the mode in which the file is currently opened. The possible values may be a suitable and logical combination of the following:

Mode Name	Value	Meaning
FILE_WRITE_THROUGH	0x00000002	File is opened in a mode where data is written to the file before the driver completes a write request
FILE_SEQUENTIAL_ONLY	0x00000004	All access to the file is sequential
FILE_SYNCHRONOUS_IO_ALERT	0x00000010	All operations on the file are performed synchronously
FILE_SYNCHRONOUS_IO_NONALERT	0x00000020	All operations on the file are to be performed synchronously. Waits in the system to synchronize I/O queuing and completion are not subject to alerts.

The AlignmentRequirement field specifies buffer alignment required by the device and can have any one of the following values:

AlignmentRequirement Name	Value	Meaning
FILE_BYTE_ALIGNMENT	0x00000000	The buffer needs to be aligned on a byte boundary
FILE_WORD_ALIGNMENT	0x00000001	The buffer needs to be aligned on a word boundary
FILE_LONG_ALIGNMENT	0x00000003	The buffer needs to be aligned on a 4 byte boundary
FILE_QUAD_ALIGNMENT	0x00000007	The buffer needs to be aligned on an 8 byte boundary
FILE_OCTA_ALIGNMENT	0x0000000F	The buffer needs to be aligned on a 16 byte boundary
FILE_32_BYTE_ALIGNMENT	0x0000001F	The buffer needs to be aligned on a 32 byte boundary
FILE_64_BYTE_ALIGNMENT	0x0000003F	The buffer needs to be aligned on a 64 byte boundary
FILE_128_BYTE_ALIGNMENT	0x0000007F	The buffer needs to be aligned on a 128 byte boundary
FILE_256_BYTE_ALIGNMENT	0x000000FF	The buffer needs to be aligned on a 256 byte boundary
FILE_512_BYTE_ALIGNMENT	0x000001FF	The buffer needs to be aligned on a 512 byte boundary

Extended attributes are used primarily by OS/2 Network Clients since OS/2 1.2a, but are an optional feature (I.e., filesystems and network servers are not required to support it). Extended attributes provided alternate data streams that are most commonly used by OS/2 client programs for the following purposes:

1) Storing the compiled form of a batch file (the first time a REXX program is run it is compiled on the fly and stored in extended attributes, subsequent runs use the compiled form)

2) Storing desktop attributes for folders and desktop objects for the OS/2Workplace Shell.

Supporting extended attributes is not mandatory in order to support OS/2 clients or to support the vast majority of OS/2 programs. Note that Windows NT Workstations can generate extended attribute request when requested by older programs (such as OS/2) and Windows NT servers do support requests to get or set extended attributes. Windows NT programs with needs to store "extended" attribute information, now largely use the capability to associate data streams with files that was introduced in NT 4. In both cases, the general concept is similar to the data fork concept introduced by the Macintosh filesystem. Extended Attributes have been used for Macintosh compatibility in the past (to emulate data forks).

4.2.16.9. SMB_QUERY_FILE_ALT_NAME_INFO

Retrieves the 8.3 form of the file name, given the long name specified in the data block encoding.

```
Data Block Encoding                 Description
====================                ============
  ULONG FileNameLength;             Length of the file name in number
                                      of bytes
    STRING FileName;                Name of the file
```

4.2.16.10. SMB_QUERY_FILE_STREAM_INFO

```
Data Block Encoding                 Description
====================                ============
ULONG NextEntryOffset;              Offset to the next entry (in bytes)
ULONG StreamNameLength;             Length of the stream name in number
                                      of bytes
LARGE_INTEGER StreamSize;           Size of the stream in number of
                                      bytes
LARGE_INTEGER                       Allocated size of the stream in
 StreamAllocationSize;                number of bytes
STRING FileName;                    Name of the stream
```

NOTE: When more than one data block is returned, the NextEntryOffset is the offset to the next entry and is 0 for the last entry. STATUS_INVALID_PARAMETER is returned if file streams are not supported.

4.2.16.11. SMB_QUERY_FILE_COMPRESSION_INFO

```
Data Block Encoding                 Description
====================                ============
  LARGE_INTEGER                     Size of the compressed file in
   CompressedFileSize;                number of bytes
   USHORT CompressionFormat;        A constant signifying the
                                      compression algorithm used. Possible
                                      values are:
                                      0 - There is no compression
                                      2- Compression Format is LZNT
  UCHAR CompressionUnitShift;
  UCHAR ChunkShift;                 Stored in log2 format (1 << ChunkShift =
                                      ChunkSizeInBytes)
  UCHAR ClusterShift;               Indicates how much space must be
                                      saved to successfully compress a
                                      compression unit
  UCHAR Reserved[3];
```

4.2.16.12. SMB_QUERY_FILE_UNIX_BASIC

Used to retrieve UNIX specific file information

```
Data Block Encoding             Description
=====================           ============
 LARGE_INTEGER EndOfFile;       File size
 LARGE_INTEGER NumOfBytes       Number of file system bytes used to store file
 TIME LastStatusChange;         Last time the status of the file was changed.
                                  This is in DCE time.
 TIME LastAccessTime;           Time of last file access.  This is DCE time.
 TIME LastModificationTime;     Last modification time.  This is DCE time.
 LARGE_INTEGER Uid;             Numeric user id for the owner
 LARGE_INTEGER Gid;             Numeric group id of owner
 ULONG Type;                    Enumeration specifying the file type.
                                   0 -- File
                                   1 -- Directory
                                   2 -- Symbolic Link
                                   3 -- Character device
                                   4 -- Block device
                                   5 -- FIFO
                                   6 -- Socket
 LARGE_INTEGER DevMajor;        Major device number if file type is device.
 LARGE_INTEGER DevMinor;        Minor device number if file type is device.
 LARGE_INTEGER UniqueId;        This is a server-assigned unique id for the
                                  file. The client will typically map this onto
                                  an inode number.  The scope of uniqueness is
                                  the share.
 LARGE_INTEGER Permissions;     Standard UNIX file permissions
 LARGE_INTEGER Nlinks;          The number of directory entries that map to
                                  this entry or number of hard links.
```

4.2.16.13. SMB_QUERY_FILE_UNIX_LINK

Used to retrieve destination file of a symbolic link

```
Data Block Encoding             Description
=====================           ============
 STRING LinkDest;                Destination for symbolic link
```

4.2.16.14. SMB_MAC_DT_GET_APPL

The Macintosh needs to be able to get an application name and its creator from a database. The Client sends a Trans2_Query_Path_Information call in which the name field is just ignored. The Client will send an info level that represents getting an application name with a structure that contains the File Creator and index. Where index has the following meaning.

- Index = 0; Get the application path from the database with the most current date.

- Index > 0; Use the index to find the application path from the database. e.g. index of 5 means get the fifth entries of this application name in the database.

- If no more entry return an error. The Server returns with a structure that contains the full path to the application and it's creator's data.

- Supporting the Desktop Database calls requires having a way to store information in a database. There are two kinds of information store in the database. Applications path that is associated with an application signature. Icons are stored based on size, icon type, file creator, and file type.

Data Block Encoding	Description
ULONG FileCreator;	The application's signature. Always in big endian.
WORD Index;	

Response Field	Description
LARGE_INTEGER CreationTime;	The application's creation time NT date type
LONG FullPathLength;	Length field for Unicode
STRING FullPath;	If Unicode supported then Unicode string otherwise a ASCII string

4.2.16.15. SMB_MAC_DT_GET_ICON

The Macintosh needs to be able to get an icon from a database. The Client sends a Trans2_Query_Path_Information call in which the path name is ignored. The Client will send an info level that represents getting an icon with a structure that contains the Requested size of the icon, the Icon type, File Creator, and File Type. The Server returns with a structure that contains the actual size of the icon (must be less than requested length) and the icon bit map.

Data Block Encoding	Description
ULONG ReqCount;	Size of the icon being requested
ULONG FileCreator;	The application's signature. Always in big endian.
ULONG FileType;	The application's type. Always in Big Endian
WORD IconType;	The icon type. Always in Big Endian

Response Field	Description
UCHAR IconData[];	Icon data. Always in Big Endian

4.2.16.16. SMB_MAC_DT_GET_ICON_INFO

The Macintosh needs to be able to get an icon from a database. The Client sends a Trans2_Query_Path_Information call in which the path name is ignored. The Client will send an info level that represents getting an icon with a structure that contains File Creator. The index allows the client to make repeated calls to the server gathering all icon stored by this file creator. The Server returns with a structure that contains the actual size of the icon (must be less than requested length) and the icon bit map, File Type, and Icon Type.

Data Block Encoding	Description
ULONG FileCreator;	The application's signature. Always in big endian.
ULONG Index;	

Response Field	Description
ULONG ActCount;	Size of the icon being requested
ULONG FileType;	The application's type. Always in Big Endian
WORD IconType;	The icon type. Always in Big Endian

4.2.16.17. Errors

```
ERRDOS codes
------------
ERRbadfile
ERRbadpath
ERRnoaccess
ERRnomem

ERRSRV codes
------------
ERRaccess
ERRinvdevice
ERRinvtid
ERRbaduid
```

4.2.17.   TRANS2_QUERY_FILE_INFORMATION: Get File Attributes Given FID

This request is used to get information about a specific file or subdirectory given a handle to it.

```
Client Request          Value
===============         ======
WordCount               15
MaxSetupCount           0
SetupCount              1
Setup[0]                TRANS2_QUERY_FILE_INFORMATION

Parameter Block Encoding   Description
========================   ============
USHORT Fid;                Handle of file for request
USHORT InformationLevel;   Level of information requested
```

The available information levels, as well as the format of the response are identical to TRANS2_QUERY_PATH_INFORMATION.

4.2.18.   TRANS2_SET_PATH_INFORMATION: Set File Attributes given Path

This request is used to set information about a specific file or subdirectory.

```
Client Request          Value
===============         ======
WordCount               15
MaxSetupCount           0
SetupCount              1
Setup[0]                TRANS2_SET_PATH_INFORMATION
```

```
Parameter Block Encoding     Description
=========================     ============
  USHORT InformationLevel;    Level of information to set
  ULONG Reserved;             Must be zero
  STRING FileName;            File or directory name
```

The following Information Levels may be set:

InformationLevel Name	Value	Meaning
SMB_INFO_STANDARD	1	
SMB_INFO_QUERY_EA_SIZE	2	
SMB_INFO_QUERY_ALL_EAS	4	
SMB_SET_FILE_UNIX_BASIC	0x200	
SMB_SET_FILE_UNIX_LINK	0x201	
SMB_SET_FILE_UNIX_HLINK	0x203	

The response formats are:

4.2.18.1. SMB_INFO_STANDARD & SMB_INFO_QUERY_EA_SIZE

```
Parameter Block Encoding              Description
=========================             ============
  USHORT Reserved                       0

Data Block Encoding                   Description
====================                  ============
  SMB_DATE CreationDate;                Date when file was created
  SMB_TIME CreationTime;                Time when file was created
  SMB_DATE LastAccessDate;              Date of last file access
  SMB_TIME LastAccessTime;              Time of last file access
  SMB_DATE LastWriteDate;               Date of last write to the file
  SMB_TIME LastWriteTime;               Time of last write to the file
  ULONG  DataSize;                      File Size
  ULONG AllocationSize;                 Size of filesystem allocation
                                         unit
  USHORT Attributes;                    File Attributes
  ULONG EaSize;                         Size of file's EA information
                                         (SMB_INFO_QUERY_EA_SIZE)
```

4.2.18.2. SMB_INFO_QUERY_ALL_EAS

```
Response Field            Value
==============            ======
  MaxDataCount              Length of FEAlist found (minimum value is 4)

Parameter Block
Encoding                  Description
===============           ============
  USHORT EaErrorOffset;     Offset into EAList of EA error
```

Data Block Encoding	Description
====================	============
ULONG ListLength;	Length of the remaining data
UCHAR EaList[];	The extended attributes list

4.2.18.3. SMB_SET_FILE_UNIX_BASIC

Used to set UNIX specific file attributes and create files

Data Block Encoding	Description
====================	============
LARGE_INTEGER EndOfFile;	File size
LARGE_INTEGER NumOfBytes;	Number of file system bytes used to store file
TIME LastStatusChange;	Last time the status of the file was changed. This is in DCE time.
TIME LastAccessTime;	Time of last file access. This is DCE time.
TIME LastModificationTime;	Last modification time. This is DCE time.
LARGE_INTEGER Uid;	Numeric user id for the owner
LARGE_INTEGER Gid;	Numeric group id of owner
ULONG Type;	Enumeration specifying the file type.
	0 -- File
	1 -- Directory
	2 -- Symbolic Link
	3 -- Character device
	4 -- Block device
	5 -- FIFO
	6 -- Socket
LARGE_INTEGER DevMajor;	Major device number if file type is device
LARGE_INTEGER DevMinor;	Minor device number if file type is device
LARGE_INTEGER UniqueId;	This is a server-assigned unique id for the file. The client will typically map this onto an inode number. The scop of uniqueness is the share
LARGE_INTEGER Permissions;	Standard UNIX file permissions
LARGE_INTEGER Nlinks;	The number of directory entries that map to this entry or number of hard links

4.2.18.4. SMB_SET_FILE_UNIX_LINK

Used to create symbolic link file.

Data Block Encoding	Description
====================	============
STRING LinkDest;	Destination for symbolic link

4.2.18.5. SMB_SET_FILE_UNIX_HLINK

Used to create hard link file.

```
Data Block Encoding                     Description
====================                    ===========
  STRING LinkDest;                      Destination for hard link
```

4.2.18.6. SMB_MAC_SET_FINDER_INFO

Parameter Block Encoding	Description
USHORT Reserved	0

Data Block Encoding	Description
WORD Type;	Type of action to take, described below
UCHAR FLAttrib;	Macintosh SetFLock if a 1 then the file is Macintosh locked
UCHAR Pad;	
LARGE_INTEGER CreationTime;	Time of file creation
LARGE_INTEGER LastWriteTime;	Time of file last modify
LARGE_INTEGER ChangeTime;	Time of file last change
ULONG ExtFileAttributes;	Extended file attributes
UCHAR FndrInfo1[16];	Information set by the finder. Described above in MacFindBothInfo structure
UCHAR FndrInfo2[16];	Information set by the finder. Described above in MacFindBothInfo structure

Listed below are the types of actions that the client may request with this Information Level:

SetCreateDate	0x0001	If this is set then set the create date of the file/folder
SetModDate	0x0002	If this is set then set the modify date of the file/folder
SetFLAttrib	0x0004	If this is set then set the Macintosh lock bit of the file/folder
FndrInfo1	0x0008	If this is set then set the first 16 bytes of finder info
FndrInfo2	0x0010	If this is set then set the second 16 bytes of finder info
SetHidden	0x0020	The Client is either setting or unsetting the hidden bit

4.2.18.7. SMB_MAC_DT_ADD_APPL

The Macintosh needs to be able to store an application name and its creator in a database. The Client sends a Trans2_Set_Path_Information call with the full path of the application in the path field. The Client sends an info level that represents adding an application name and creator to the database. The Client will pass the File Creator in the data message. The Server should just respond with no error if it was successful or an error if the operation failed

.

Parameter Block Encoding	Description
USHORT Reserved	0

Data Block Encoding	Description
ULONG FileCreator;	The application's signature. Always in big endian. The path name passed in this calls needs to be stored with this signature.

4.2.18.8. SMB_MAC_DT_REMOVE_APPL

The Macintosh needs to be able to remove an application name and its creator from a database. The Client sends a Trans2_Set_Path_Information call with the full path of the application in the path field. The Client will send an info level that represents removing an application name and creator from the database. The Client will pass the File Creator in the data message. The Server should just respond with no error if it was successful or an error it the operation failed.

Parameter Block Encoding	Description
USHORT Reserved	0

Data Block Encoding	Description
ULONG FileCreator;	The application's signature. Always in big endian. The path name passed in this calls needs to be removed with this signature.

4.2.18.9. SMB_MAC_DT_ADD_ICON

The Macintosh needs to be able to add an icon to a database. The Client sends a Trans2_Set_Path_Information call in which the path name is ignored. The Client will send an info level that represents setting an icon with a structure that contains the icon data, icon size, icon type, the file type, and file creator. The Server returns only if the call was successful or not.

Parameter Block Encoding	Description
USHORT Reserved	0

Data Block Encoding	Description
ULONG IconSize;	Size of the icon in bytes.
ULONG FileCreator;	The application's signature. Always in big endian.
ULONG FileType;	The application's type. Always in big endian.
WORD IconType;	The icon type. Always in big endian.
UCHAR IconData[];	Icon data,

4.2.18.10. Errors

```
ERRDOS codes
------------
ERRbadfile
ERRbadpath
ERRnoaccess
ERRnomem
ERRbadaccess
ERRbadshare
```

```
ERRSRV codes
------------
ERRaccess
ERRinvdevice
ERRinvtid
ERRbaduid
```

4.2.19.   TRANS2_SET_FILE_INFORMATION: Set File Attributes Given FID

This request is used to set information about a specific file or subdirectory given a handle to the
file or subdirectory.

```
Client Request               Value
================             ======
 WordCount                    15
 MaxSetupCount                0
 SetupCount                   1
 Setup[0]                     TRANS2_SET_FILE_INFORMATION

Parameter Block Encoding     Description
========================     ============
 USHORT Fid;                  Handle of file for request
 USHORT InformationLevel;     Level of information requested
 USHORT Reserved;             Ignored by the server
```

The following InformationLevels may be set:

InformationLevel Name	Value	Meaning
SMB_INFO_STANDARD	1	
SMB_INFO_QUERY_EA_SIZE	2	
SMB_SET_FILE_BASIC_INFO	0x101	
SMB_SET_FILE_DISPOSITION_INFO	0x102	
SMB_SET_FILE_ALLOCATION_INFO	0x103	
SMB_SET_FILE_END_OF_FILE_INFO	0x104	
SMB_SET_FILE_UNIX_BASIC	0x200	
SMB_SET_FILE_UNIX_LINK	0x201	
SMB_SET_FILE_UNIX_HLINK	0x203	

The two levels below 0x101 and the three levels 0x200, 0x201, and 0x202 are as described in the
NT_SET_PATH_INFORMATION transaction. The requested information is placed in the Data
portion of the transaction response. For the information levels greater than 0x100 and below
0x200, the transaction response has 1 parameter word, which should be ignored by the client.

4.2.19.1. SMB_FILE_BASIC_INFO

```
Data Block Encoding          Description
===================          ============
 TIME CreationTime;           Time when file was created
 TIME LastAccessTime;         Time of last file access
 TIME LastWriteTime;          Time of last write to the file
 TIME ChangeTime;             Time when file was last changed
 ULONG Attributes;            File Attributes
```

The valid file attributes are listed in section 4.2.15.4 SMB_QUERY_FILE_BASIC_INFO:

4.2.19.2. SMB_FILE_DISPOSITION_INFO

```
Response Field          Value
===============         ======
  BOOLEAN               A boolean which is TRUE if the file is marked
   FileIsDeleted;         for deletion
```

4.2.19.3. SMB_FILE_ALLOCATION_INFO

```
Response Field          Value
===============         ======
  LARGE_INTEGER         File Allocation size in number of bytes
```

4.2.19.4. SMB_FILE_END_OF_FILE_INFO

```
Response Field          Value
===============         ======
  LARGE_INTEGER         The total number of bytes that need to be
                          traversed from the beginning of the file in
                          order to locate the end of the file
```

4.2.19.5. Errors

```
ERRDOS codes
------------
ERRbadfile
ERRbadpath
ERRnoaccess
ERRnomem
ERRbadaccess
ERRbadshare

ERRSRV codes
------------
ERRaccess
ERRinvdevice
ERRinvtid
ERRbaduid
```

4.3.   Directory Requests

4.3.1. TRANS2_CREATE_DIRECTORY: Create Directory (with optional EAs)

This requests the server to create a directory relative to Tid in the SMB header, optionally
assigning extended attributes to it.

```
Client Request          Value
===============         ======
WordCount               15
MaxSetupCount           0
SetupCount              1
Setup[0]                TRANS2_CREATE_DIRECTORY
```

```
Parameter Block Encoding    Description
=========================   ============
 ULONG Reserved;             Reserved--must be zero
 STRING Name[];              Directory name to create
 UCHAR Data[];               Optional FEAList for the new directory

Response Parameter Block    Description
=========================   ============
 USHORT EaErrorOffset        Offset into FEAList of first error which
                             occurred while setting Eas
```

4.3.1.1. Errors

```
ERRDOS codes
------------
ERRbadfile
ERRbadpath
ERRnoaccess
ERRnomem
ERRbadaccess
ERRfileexists
ERRquota

ERRSRV codes
------------
ERRaccess
ERRinvdevice
ERRinvtid
ERRbaduid
```

4.3.2. <u>DELETE_DIRECTORY: Delete Directory</u>

The delete directory message is sent to delete an empty directory. The appropriate Tid and additional pathname are passed. The directory must be empty for it to be deleted.

```
Client Request             Description
===============            ============
 UCHAR WordCount;           Count of parameter words = 0
 USHORT ByteCount;          Count of data bytes; min = 2
 UCHAR BufferFormat;        0x04
 STRING DirectoryName[];    Directory name
```

The directory to be deleted cannot be the root of the share specified by Tid.

```
Server Response            Description
===============            ============
 UCHAR WordCount;           Count of parameter words = 0
 USHORT ByteCount;          Count of data bytes = 0
```

4.3.2.1. Errors

```
ERRDOS codes
------------
ERRbadfile
ERRbadpath
ERRnoaccess
```

```
ERRnomem
ERRbadaccess
ERRfileexists

ERRSRV codes
------------
ERRaccess
ERRinvdevice
ERRinvtid
ERRbaduid
```

4.3.3. <u>CHECK_DIRECTORY</u>: Check Directory

This SMB is used to verify that a path exists and is a directory. No error is returned if the given path exists and the client has read access to it. When the path turns out to specify a file (non-directory) then STATUS_NOT_A_DIRECTORY is returned. Client machines which maintain a concept of a "working directory" will find this useful to verify the validity of a "change working directory" command. Note that the servers do NOT have a concept of working directory for a particular client. The client must always supply full pathnames relative to the Tid in the SMB header.

```
Client Request              Description
===============             ============
 UCHAR WordCount;            Count of parameter words = 0
 USHORT ByteCount;           Count of data bytes; min = 2
 UCHAR BufferFormat;         0x04
 STRING DirectoryPath[];     Directory path

Server Response             Description
===============             ============
 UCHAR WordCount;            Count of parameter words = 0
 USHORT ByteCount;           Count of data bytes = 0
```

DOS clients, in particular, depend on the SMB_ERR_BAD_PATH return code if the directory is not found.

4.3.3.1. Errors

```
ERRDOS/ERRbadfile
ERRDOS/ERRbadpath
ERRDOS/ERRnoaccess
ERRHRD/ERRdata
ERRSRV/ERRinvid
ERRSRV/ERRbaduid
ERRSRV/ERRaccess
```

4.3.4. <u>TRANS2_FIND_FIRST2</u>: Search Directory using Wildcards

```
Client Request              Value
===============             ======
 WordCount                   15
 TotalDataCount              Total size of extended attribute list
 SetupCount                  1
 Setup[0]                    TRANS2_FIND_FIRST2
```

```
Parameter Block Encoding      Description
==========================    ============
USHORT SearchAttributes;
USHORT SearchCount;           Maximum number of entries to return
USHORT Flags;                 Additional information:
                                Bit 0 - close search after this request
                                Bit 1 - close search if end of search
                                  reached
                                Bit 2 - return resume keys for each
                                  entry found
                                Bit 3 - continue search from previous
                                  ending place
                                Bit 4 - find with backup intent
USHORT InformationLevel;      See below
ULONG SearchStorageType;
STRING FileName;              Pattern for the search
UCHAR Data[TotalDataCount];   FEAList if InformationLevel is
                                QUERY_EAS_FROM_LIST

Response Parameter Block      Description
==========================    ============
USHORT Sid;                   Search handle
USHORT SearchCount;           Number of entries returned
USHORT EndOfSearch;           Was last entry returned?
USHORT EaErrorOffset;         Offset into EA list if EA error
USHORT LastNameOffset;        Offset into Data[] holding the file name of
                                the last entry, if server needs it to resume
                                search; else 0
UCHAR Data[TotalDataCount];   Level dependent info about the matches
                                found in the search
```

This request allows the client to search for the file(s) which match the file specification. The search can be continued if necessary with TRANS2_FIND_NEXT2. There are numerous levels of information which may be obtained for the returned files, the desired level is specified in the InformationLevel field of the request. The following values can be specified for InformationLevel:

InformationLevel Name	Value	Meaning
SMB_INFO_STANDARD	1	
SMB_INFO_QUERY_EA_SIZE	2	
SMB_INFO_QUERY_EAS_FROM_LIST	3	
SMB_FIND_FILE_DIRECTORY_INFO	0x101	
SMB_FIND_FILE_FULL_DIRECTORY_INFO	0x102	
SMB_FIND_FILE_NAMES_INFO	0x103	
SMB_FIND_FILE_BOTH_DIRECTORY_INFO	0x104	
SMB_FIND_FILE_UNIX	0x202	

The following sections detail the data returned for each InformationLevel. The requested information is placed in the Data portion of the transaction response. Note: a client which does not support long names can only request SMB_INFO_STANDARD.

The search Id is the Search Handle returned back from the server on the FindFirst response which can be used on the FindNext request so that the full path can be avoided. Search Handle is session wide. The server doesn't care what process uses it on the client.

A four-byte resume key precedes each data item (described below). The return of resume keys is dependent upon setting the flag SMB_FIND_RETURN_RESUME_KEYS in the FLAGS of the REQ_FIND_NEXT2 packet. The resume key tells the server where to resume the operation on the FindNext request in order to avoid duplicate entries. The contents of the resume key are opaque to the client.

If the search doesn't find any names, the server should return either STATUS_NO_SUCH_FILE or the corresponding error code ERROR_FILE_NOT_FOUND.

4.3.4.1.   SMB_INFO_STANDARD

```
Response Field                   Description
================                 ============
  SMB_DATE CreationDate;         Date when file was created
  SMB_TIME CreationTime;         Time when file was created
  SMB_DATE LastAccessDate;       Date of last file access
  SMB_TIME LastAccessTime;       Time of last file access
  SMB_DATE LastWriteDate;        Date of last write to the file
  SMB_TIME LastWriteTime;        Time of last write to the file
  ULONG  DataSize;               File Size
  ULONG AllocationSize;          Size of filesystem allocation unit
  USHORT Attributes;             File Attributes
  UCHAR FileNameLength;          Length of filename in bytes
  STRING FileName;               Name of found file
```

4.3.4.2.   SMB_INFO_QUERY_EA_SIZE

```
Response Field                   Description
================                 ============
  SMB_DATE CreationDate;         Date when file was created
  SMB_TIME CreationTime;         Time when file was created
  SMB_DATE LastAccessDate;       Date of last file access
  SMB_TIME LastAccessTime;       Time of last file access
  SMB_DATE LastWriteDate;        Date of last write to the file
  SMB_TIME LastWriteTime;        Time of last write to the file
  ULONG DataSize;                File Size
  ULONG AllocationSize;          Size of filesystem allocation unit
  USHORT Attributes;             File Attributes
  ULONG EaSize;                  Size of file's EA information
  UCHAR FileNameLength;          Length of filename in bytes
  STRING FileName;               Name of found file
```

4.3.4.3.   SMB_INFO_QUERY_EAS_FROM_LIST

This request returns the same information as SMB_INFO_QUERY_EA_SIZE, but only for files which have an EA list which match the EA information in the Data part of the request.

4.3.4.4.   SMB_FIND_FILE_DIRECTORY_INFO

```
Response Field                   Description
================                 ====================================
  ULONG NextEntryOffset;         Offset from this structure to
```

```
                                          the beginning of the next one
     ULONG FileIndex;
     TIME  CreationTime;         File creation time
     TIME  LastAccessTime;       Last access time for the file
     TIME  LastWriteTime;        Last write time for the file
     TIME  ChangeTime;           Last attribute change time for the file
     LARGE_INTEGER EndOfFile;      File size
     LARGE_INTEGER AllocationSize;  Size of filesystem allocation
                                    information
     ULONG ExtFileAttributes;      Extended file attributes (see
                                    Section 3.12)
     ULONG FileNameLength;         Length of filename in bytes
     STRING FileName;              Name of the file
```

4.3.4.5.   SMB_FIND_FILE_FULL_DIRECTORY_INFO

```
     Response Field              Description
     ===============             ===========
     ULONG NextEntryOffset;      Offset from this structure to
                                  the beginning of the next one
     ULONG FileIndex;
     TIME  CreationTime;         File creation time
     TIME  LastAccessTime;       Last access time for the file
     TIME  LastWriteTime;        Last write time for the file
     TIME  ChangeTime;           Last attribute change time for the file
     LARGE_INTEGER EndOfFile;      File size
     LARGE_INTEGER AllocationSize;  Size of filesystem allocation
                                    information
     ULONG ExtFileAttributes;      Extended file attributes (see
                                    Section 3.12)
     ULONG FileNameLength;         Length of filename in bytes
     ULONG EaSize;                 Size of file's extended attributes
     STRING FileName;              Name of the file
```

4.3.4.6.   SMB_FIND_FILE_BOTH_DIRECTORY_INFO

```
     Response Field              Description
     ===============             ===========
     ULONG NextEntryOffset;      Offset from this structure to
                                  the beginning of the next one
     ULONG FileIndex;
     TIME  CreationTime;         File creation time
     TIME  LastAccessTime;       Last access time for the file
     TIME  LastWriteTime;        Last write time for the file
     TIME  ChangeTime;           Last attribute change time for the file
     LARGE_INTEGER EndOfFile;      File size
     LARGE_INTEGER AllocationSize;  Size of filesystem allocation
                                    information
     ULONG ExtFileAttributes;      Extended file attributes (see
                                    Section 3.12)
     ULONG FileNameLength;         Length of FileName in bytes
     ULONG EaSize;                 Size of file's extended attributes
     UCHAR ShortNameLength;        Length of file's short name in
                                    bytes
     UCHAR Reserved;
```

```
     WCHAR ShortName[12];            File's 8.3 conformant name in Unicode

     STRING FileName;                File's full length name
```

4.3.4.7.   SMB_FIND_FILE_NAMES_INFO

```
Response Field                  Description
===============                 ===========
  ULONG NextEntryOffset;            Offset from this structure to
                                     the beginning of the next one
  ULONG FileIndex;
  ULONG FileNameLength;           Length of FileName in bytes
  STRING FileName;                File's full length name
```

4.3.4.8.   SMB_FIND_FILE_UNIX

Used to return UNIX attribute information in a file search response

```
Data Block Encoding             Description
===================             ===========
  ULONG NextEntryOffset;            Offset from this structure to the beginning
                                     of the next one
  ULONG ResumeKey;                Used for continuing search
  LARGE_INTEGER EndOfFile;        File size
  LARGE_INTEGER NumOfBytes        Number of file system bytes used to store
                                     file
  TIME LastStatusChange;          Last time the status of the file was changed.
                                     This is in DCE time.
  TIME LastAccessTime;            Time of last file access.  This is DCE time.
  TIME LastModificationTime;      Last modification time.  This is DCE time.
  LARGE_INTEGER Uid;              Numeric user id for the owner
  LARGE_INTEGER Gid;              Numeric group id of owner
  ULONG Type;                     Enumeration specifying the file type.
                                          0 -- File
                                          1 -- Directory
                                          2 -- Symbolic Link
                                          3 -- Character device
                                          4 -- Block device
                                          5 -- FIFO
                                          6 -- Socket
  LARGE_INTEGER DevMajor;         Major device number if file type is device
  LARGE_INTEGER DevMinor;         Minor device number if file type is device
  LARGE_INTEGER UniqueId;         This is a server-assigned unique id for the
                                     file. The client will typically map this onto
                                     an inode number.  The scop of uniqueness is
                                     the share
  LARGE_INTEGER Permissions;      Standard UNIX file permissions
  LARGE_INTEGER Nlinks;           The number of directory entries that map to
                                     this entry or number of hard links
  STRING Name;                    Case-preserved alternative filename
```

4.3.4.9.   SMB_ FINDBOTH_ MAC_HFS_INFO

Response Field	Description
ULONG NextEntryOffset;	Offset from this structure to beginning of next one
ULONG FileIndex;	
LARGE_INTEGER CreationTime;	file creation time
LARGE_INTEGER LastWriteTime;	last write time
LARGE_INTEGER ChangeTime;	last attribute change time
LARGE_INTEGER EndOfFile;	Data stream file size
LARGE_INTEGER EndOfFile_R;	Resource stream file size
LARGE_INTEGER AllocationSize;	Data stream size of file system allocation information
LARGE_INTEGER AllocationSize_R;	Resource stream size of file system allocation information
ULONG ExtFileAttributes;	Extended file attributes
UCHAR FLAttrib;	Macintosh SetFLock if a 1 then the file is locked.
UCHAR Pad;	
UWORD DrNmFls;	If a directory the number of items in that directory otherwise ignored.
ULONG AccessCntrl;	Ignored unless SUPPORT_MAC_ACCESS_CNTRL is set.
UCHAR FndrInfo[32];	FndrInfo[32]; Information used by the finder that is always in Big Endian.
	Bytes 0-3 File Type
	If a file default to 'TEXT' otherwise default to zero
	Bytes 4-7 File Creator
	If a file default to 'dosa' otherwise default to zero
	Bytes 8-9 a UWORD flags field
	If hidden item set this UWORD to 0x4000 else defaults to zero
	All other bytes should default to zero and are only changeable by the Macintosh
ULONG FileNameLength;	Length of Filename in bytes
UCHAR ShortNameLength;	Length of file's short name in bytes
UCHAR Reserved	
WCHAR ShortName[12];	File's 8.3 conformant name in Unicode
STRING Filename;	Files full length name
LONG UniqueFileID;	Unique file or directory identifier - only supported if the SUPPORT_MAC_UNIQUE_IDS bit is set in the MacSupportFlags.

4.3.4.10. Errors

```
ERRDOS codes
------------
ERRbadpath
ERRnoaccess
ERRnomem

ERRSRV codes
------------
ERRaccess
ERRinvdevice
ERRinvtid
ERRbaduid
```

4.3.5. TRANS2_FIND_NEXT2: Resume Directory Search Using Wildcards

This request resumes a search which was begun with a previous TRANS2_FIND_FIRST2 request.

```
Client Request              Value
===============             ======
WordCount                   15
SetupCount                  1
Setup[0]                    TRANS2_FIND_NEXT2

Parameter Block Encoding    Description
========================    ============
USHORT Sid;                 Search handle
USHORT SearchCount;         Maximum number of entries to return
USHORT InformationLevel;    Levels described in
                              TRANS2_FIND_FIRST2 request
ULONG ResumeKey;            Value returned by previous find2 call
USHORT Flags;               Additional information: bit set-
                    0 - close search after this request
                    1 - close search if end of search reached
                    2 - return resume keys for each entry found
                    3 - resume/continue from previous ending place
                    4 - find with backup intent
STRING FileName;            Resume file name
```

Sid is the value returned by a previous successful TRANS2_FIND_FIRST2 call. If Bit3 of Flags is set, then FileName may be the NULL string, since the search is continued from the previous TRANS2_FIND request. Otherwise, FileName must not be more than 256 characters long.

```
Response Field              Description
===============             ============
USHORT SearchCount;         Number of entries returned
USHORT EndOfSearch;         Was last entry returned?
USHORT EaErrorOffset;       Offset into EA list if EA error
USHORT LastNameOffset;      Offset into Data[] holding the file name
                              of the last entry, if server needs it
                              to resume search; else 0
UCHAR Data[TotalDataCount]; Level dependent info about the
                              matches found in the search
```

4.3.5.1. Errors

```
ERRDOS codes
------------
ERRnomem

ERRSRV codes
------------
ERRinvtid
ERRbaduid
```

4.3.6. FIND_CLOSE2: Close Directory Search

This SMB closes a search started by the TRANS2_FIND_FIRST2 transaction request.

```
Client Request                    Description
================                  ============
 UCHAR WordCount;                 Count of parameter words = 1
 USHORT Sid;                      Find handle
 USHORT ByteCount;                Count of data bytes = 0

Server Response                   Description
================                  ============
 UCHAR WordCount;                 Count of parameter words = 0
 USHORT ByteCount;                Count of data bytes = 0
```

4.3.6.1. Errors

```
ERRDOS/ERRbadfid
ERRSRV/ERRinvid
ERRSRV/ERRaccess
```

4.3.7. NT_TRANSACT_NOTIFY_CHANGE: Request Change Notification

```
Client Setup Words                Description
==================                ============
 ULONG CompletionFilter;          Specifies operation to monitor
 USHORT Fid;                      Fid of directory to monitor
 BOOLEAN WatchTree;               TRUE = Watch all subdirectories too
UCHAR Reserved;                   MUST BE ZERO
```

This command notifies the client when the directory specified by Fid is modified. It also returns the name(s) of the file(s) that changed. The command completes once the directory has been modified based on the supplied CompletionFilter. The command is a "single shot" and therefore needs to be reissued to watch for more directory changes.

A directory file must be opened before this command may be used. Once the directory is open, this command may be used to begin watching files and subdirectories in the specified directory for changes. The first time the command is issued, the MaxParameterCount field in the transact header determines the size of the buffer that will be used at the server to buffer directory change information between issuances of the notify change commands.

When a change that is in the CompletionFilter is made to the directory, the command completes. The names of the files that have changed since the last time the command was issued are returned to the client. The ParameterCount field of the response indicates the number of bytes that are being returned. If too many files have changed since the last time the command was issued, then zero bytes are returned and the NTSTATUS code STATUS_NOTIFY_ENUM_DIR (0x0000010C) is returned in the Status field of the response.

The CompletionFilter is a mask created as the sum of any of the following flags:

```
FILE_NOTIFY_CHANGE_FILE_NAME       0x00000001
FILE_NOTIFY_CHANGE_DIR_NAME        0x00000002
FILE_NOTIFY_CHANGE_NAME            0x00000003
FILE_NOTIFY_CHANGE_ATTRIBUTES      0x00000004
FILE_NOTIFY_CHANGE_SIZE            0x00000008
FILE_NOTIFY_CHANGE_LAST_WRITE      0x00000010
FILE_NOTIFY_CHANGE_LAST_ACCESS     0x00000020
FILE_NOTIFY_CHANGE_CREATION        0x00000040
FILE_NOTIFY_CHANGE_EA              0x00000080
FILE_NOTIFY_CHANGE_SECURITY        0x00000100
FILE_NOTIFY_CHANGE_STREAM_NAME     0x00000200
FILE_NOTIFY_CHANGE_STREAM_SIZE     0x00000400
FILE_NOTIFY_CHANGE_STREAM_WRITE    0x00000800
```

```
Server Response                   Description
================                   ============
 ParameterCount                   # of bytes of change data
 Parameters[ParameterCount ]      FILE_NOTIFY_INFORMATION
                                   Structures
```

The response contains FILE_NOTIFY_INFORMATION structures, as defined below. The NextEntryOffset field of the structure specifies the offset, in bytes, from the start of the current entry to the next entry in the list. If this is the last entry in the list, this field is zero. Each entry in the list must be longword aligned, so NextEntryOffset must be a multiple of four.

```
typedef struct {
    ULONG NextEntryOffset;
    ULONG Action;
    ULONG FileNameLength;
    WCHAR FileName[1];
} FILE_NOTIFY_INFORMATION;
```

Where Action describes what happened to the file named FileName:

```
FILE_ACTION_ADDED             0x00000001
FILE_ACTION_REMOVED           0x00000002
FILE_ACTION_MODIFIED          0x00000003
FILE_ACTION_RENAMED_OLD_NAME  0x00000004
FILE_ACTION_RENAMED_NEW_NAME  0x00000005
FILE_ACTION_ADDED_STREAM      0x00000006
FILE_ACTION_REMOVED_STREAM    0x00000007
FILE_ACTION_MODIFIED_STREAM   0x00000008
```

The client waits on the response after it sends the notify change request. If the client wants to discard the request, it can send NT_CANCEL to the server which should return STATUS_CANCELED. The server can reject the request with STATUS_NOT_IMPLEMENTED.

4.3.7.1. Errors

```
ERRDOS codes
------------
ERRbadpath
ERRnoaccess
ERRnomem

ERRSRV codes
------------
ERRaccess
ERRinvdevice
ERRinvtid
ERRbaduid
ERRSRV/ERROR_NOTIFY_ENUM_DIR
```

4.4. DFS Operations

4.4.1. TRANS2_GET_DFS_REFERRAL: Retrieve Distributed Filesystem Referral

The client sends this request to ask the server to convert RequestFilename into an alternate
name for this file. This request can be sent to the server if the server response to the
NEGOTIATE SMB included the CAP_DFS capability. The TID of the request must be IPC$. Bit15
of Flags2 in the SMB header must be set, indicating this is a UNICODE request.

```
Client Request               Description
===============              ============
WordCount                    15
TotalDataCount               0
SetupCount                   1
Setup[0]                     TRANS2_GET_DFS_REFERRAL


Parameter Block Encoding     Description
========================     ============
USHORT MaxReferralLevel;     Latest referral version number understood
WCHAR RequestFileName[];     DFS name of file for which referral is
                               sought


Response Data Block          Description
===================          ============
USHORT PathConsumed;         Number of RequestFilename bytes consumed
                                 by the server
USHORT NumberOfReferrals;    Number of referrals contained in this
                               response
USHORT Flags;                Bit0 - The servers in Referrals are
                               capable of fielding
                               TRANS2_GET_DFS_REFERRAL.
                               Bit1 - The servers in Referrals should
                               hold the storage for the requested file
REFERRAL_LIST Referrals[];   Set of referrals for this file
UNICODESTRING Strings;       Used to hold the strings pointed to by
                               Version 2 Referrals in REFERRALS
```

The server response is a list of Referrals which inform the client where it should resubmit the request to obtain access to the file. PathConsumed in the response indicates to the client how many characters of RequestFilename have been consumed by the server. When the client chooses one of the referrals to use for file access, the client may need to strip the leading PathConsumed characters from the front of RequestFileName before submitting the name to the target server. Whether or not the pathname should be trimmed is indicated by the individual referral as detailed below.

Flags indicates how this referral should be treated. If bit0 is clear, any entity in the Referrals list holds the storage for RequestFileName. If bit0 is set, any entity in the Referrals list has further referral information for RequestFileName - a TRANS2_GET_DFS_REFERRAL request should be sent to an entity in the Referrals list for further resolution.

The format of an individual referral contains version and length information allowing the client to skip referrals it does not understand. MaxReferralLevel indicates to the server the latest version of referral which the client can digest. Since each referral has a uniform element, MaxReferralLevel is advisory only. Each element in Referrals has this envelope:

```
REFERRAL_LIST Element
=====================
  USHORT VersionNumber;       Version of this referral element
  USHORT ReferralSize;        Size of this referral element
```

The following referral element versions are defined:

```
Version 1 Referral Element Format
=================================
  USHORT ServerType;          Type of Node handling referral:
                              0 - Don't know
                              1 - SMB Server
                              2 - Netware Server
                              3 - Domain
  USHORT ReferralFlags;       Flags which describe this referral:
                              01 - Strip off PathConsumed characters
                                 before submitting RequestFileName to Node
  UNICODESTRING Node;         Name of entity to visit next

Version 2 Referral Element Format
=================================
  USHORT ServerType;          Type of Node handling referral:
                              0 - Don't know
                              1 - SMB Server
                              2 - Netware Server
                              3 - Domain
  USHORT ReferralFlags;       Flags which describe this referral:
                              01 - Strip off PathConsumed characters
                                 before submitting RequestFileName to Node
  ULONG Proximity;            A hint describing the proximity of this
                              server to the client. 0 indicates the
                              closest, higher numbers indicate
                              increasingly "distant" servers. The
                              number is only relevant within the
                              context of the servers listed in this
                              particular SMB.
  ULONG TimeToLive;           Number of seconds for which the client
                              can cache this referral.
```

```
USHORT DfsPathOffset;            Offset, in bytes from the beginning of
                                 this referral, of the DFS Path that
                                 matched PathConsumed bytes of the
                                 RequestFileName.
USHORT                           Offset, in bytes from the beginning of
   DfsAlternatePathOffset;       this referral, of an alternate name
                                 (8.3 format) of the DFS Path that
                                 matched PathConsumed bytes of the
                                 RequestFileName.
USHORT NetworkAddressOffset;     Offset, in bytes from the beginning of
                                 this referral, of the entity to visit next.
```

The CIFS protocol imposes no referral selection policy.

4.4.1.1.   Errors

```
ERRDOS codes
------------
ERRnoaccess
ERRnomem

ERRSRV codes
------------
ERRaccess
ERRinvdevice
ERRinvtid
ERRbaduid
```

4.4.2. TRANS2_REPORT_DFS_INCONSISTENCY: Inform a server about DFS Error

As part of the Distributed Name Resolution algorithm, a DFS client may discover a knowledge inconsistency between the referral server (i.e., the server that handed out a referral), and the storage server (i.e., the server to which the client was redirected by the referral server). When such an inconsistency is discovered, the DFS client optionally sends this SMB to the referral server, allowing the referral server to take corrective action.

```
Client Request                  Description
===============                 ============
WordCount                       15
MaxParameterCount               0
SetupCount                      1
Setup[0]                        TRANS2_REPORT_DFS_INCONSISTENCY

Parameter Block Encoding        Description
========================        ============
UNICODESTRING RequestFileName;  DFS Name of file for which
                                   referral is sought
```

The data part of this request contains the referral element (Version 1 format only) believed to be in error. These are encoded as described in the TRANS2_GET_DFS_REFERRAL response. If the server returns success, the client can resubmit the TRANS2_GET_DFS_REFERRAL request to this server to get a new referral. It is not mandatory for the DFS knowledge to be automatically repaired - the client must be prepared to receive further errant referrals and must not wind up looping between this request and the TRANS2_GET_DFS_REFERRAL request.

Bit15 of Flags2 in the SMB header must be set, indicating this is a UNICODE request.

4.4.2.1.   Errors

```
ERRDOS codes
------------
ERRnoaccess
ERRnomem

ERRSRV codes
------------
ERRaccess
ERRinvdevice
ERRinvtid
ERRbaduid
```

4.5.   Miscellaneous Operations

4.5.1.   NT_TRANSACT_IOCTL

This command allows device and file system control functions to be transferred transparently from client to server.

```
Setup Words Encoding       Description
=====================      ============
ULONG FunctionCode;        NT device or file system control code
USHORT Fid;                Handle for i/o or file system control,
                                unless BIT0 of ISFLAGS is set
BOOLEAN IsFsctl;           Indicates whether the command is for device
                             (FALSE) or a file system control (TRUE)
UCHAR IsFlags;             BIT0 - command is to be applied to share
                             root handle.  Share must be a DFS share.

Data Block Encoding        Description
=====================      ============
UCHAR Data[                Passed to the Fsctl or Ioctl
    TotalDataCount];

Server Response            Description
===============            ============
SetupCount                 1
Setup[0]                   Length of information returned by
                             i/o or file system control
DataCount                  Length of information returned by
                             i/o or file system control
Data[DataCount]            The results of the i/o or file system
                             control
```

4.5.1.1.   Errors

```
ERRDOS codes
------------
ERRnoaccess
ERRnomem
```

```
ERRSRV codes
------------
ERRaccess
ERRinvdevice
ERRinvtid
ERRbaduid
```

4.5.2. NT_TRANSACT_QUERY_SECURITY_DESC

This command allows the client to retrieve the security descriptor on a file.

```
Client Parameter Block       Description
========================     ============
 USHORT Fid;                  FID of target
 USHORT Reserved;             MUST BE ZERO
 ULONG SecurityInformation;   Fields of descriptor to get
```

NtQuerySecurityObject() is called, requesting SecurityInformation. The result of the call is returned to the client in the Data part of the transaction response.

4.5.2.1. Errors

```
ERRDOS codes
------------
ERRnoaccess
ERRnomem
ERRbadaccess

ERRSRV codes
------------
ERRaccess
ERRinvdevice
ERRinvtid
ERRbaduid
```

4.5.3. NT_TRANSACT_SET_SECURITY_DESC

This command allows the client to change the security descriptor on a file.

```
Client Parameter Block Encoding   Description
===============================   ============
 USHORT Fid;                       FID of target
 USHORT Reserved;                  MUST BE ZERO
 ULONG SecurityInformation;        Fields of Security Descriptor to set

Data Block Encoding               Description
====================              ============
 Data[TotalDataCount]              Security Descriptor information
```

Data is passed directly to NtSetSecurityObject(), with SecurityInformation describing which information to set. The transaction response contains no parameters or data.

4.5.3.1. Errors

```
ERRDOS codes
------------
ERRnoaccess
ERRnomem
ERRbadaccess
ERRbadshare

ERRSRV codes
------------
ERRaccess
ERRinvdevice
ERRinvtid
ERRbaduid
```

5. SMB Symbolic Constants

5.1. SMB Command Codes

The following values have been assigned for the SMB Commands.

```
SMB_COM_CREATE_DIRECTORY            0x00
SMB_COM_DELETE_DIRECTORY            0x01
SMB_COM_OPEN                        0x02
SMB_COM_CREATE                      0x03
SMB_COM_CLOSE                       0x04
SMB_COM_FLUSH                       0x05
SMB_COM_DELETE                      0x06
SMB_COM_RENAME                      0x07
SMB_COM_QUERY_INFORMATION           0x08
SMB_COM_SET_INFORMATION             0x09
SMB_COM_READ                        0x0A
SMB_COM_WRITE                       0x0B
SMB_COM_LOCK_BYTE_RANGE             0x0C
SMB_COM_UNLOCK_BYTE_RANGE           0x0D
SMB_COM_CREATE_TEMPORARY            0x0E
SMB_COM_CREATE_NEW                  0x0F
SMB_COM_CHECK_DIRECTORY             0x10
SMB_COM_PROCESS_EXIT                0x11
SMB_COM_SEEK                        0x12
SMB_COM_LOCK_AND_READ               0x13
SMB_COM_WRITE_AND_UNLOCK            0x14
SMB_COM_READ_RAW                    0x1A
SMB_COM_READ_MPX                    0x1B
SMB_COM_READ_MPX_SECONDARY          0x1C
SMB_COM_WRITE_RAW                   0x1D
SMB_COM_WRITE_MPX                   0x1E
SMB_COM_WRITE_MPX_SECONDARY         0x1F
SMB_COM_WRITE_COMPLETE              0x20
SMB_COM_QUERY_SERVER                0x21
SMB_COM_SET_INFORMATION2            0x22
SMB_COM_QUERY_INFORMATION2          0x23
SMB_COM_LOCKING_ANDX                0x24
SMB_COM_TRANSACTION                 0x25
SMB_COM_TRANSACTION_SECONDARY       0x26
SMB_COM_IOCTL                       0x27
SMB_COM_IOCTL_SECONDARY             0x28
SMB_COM_COPY                        0x29
SMB_COM_MOVE                        0x2A
SMB_COM_ECHO                        0x2B
SMB_COM_WRITE_AND_CLOSE             0x2C
SMB_COM_OPEN_ANDX                   0x2D
SMB_COM_READ_ANDX                   0x2E
SMB_COM_WRITE_ANDX                  0x2F
SMB_COM_NEW_FILE_SIZE               0x30
SMB_COM_CLOSE_AND_TREE_DISC         0x31
SMB_COM_TRANSACTION2                0x32
SMB_COM_TRANSACTION2_SECONDARY      0x33
SMB_COM_FIND_CLOSE2                 0x34
```

```
SMB_COM_FIND_NOTIFY_CLOSE        0x35
/* Used by Xenix/Unix 0x60 - 0x6E */
SMB_COM_TREE_CONNECT             0x70
SMB_COM_TREE_DISCONNECT          0x71
SMB_COM_NEGOTIATE                0x72
SMB_COM_SESSION_SETUP_ANDX       0x73
SMB_COM_LOGOFF_ANDX              0x74
SMB_COM_TREE_CONNECT_ANDX        0x75
SMB_COM_QUERY_INFORMATION_DISK   0x80
SMB_COM_SEARCH                   0x81
SMB_COM_FIND                     0x82
SMB_COM_FIND_UNIQUE              0x83
SMB_COM_FIND_CLOSE               0x84
SMB_COM_NT_TRANSACT              0xA0
SMB_COM_NT_TRANSACT_SECONDARY    0xA1
SMB_COM_NT_CREATE_ANDX           0xA2
SMB_COM_NT_CANCEL                0xA4
SMB_COM_NT_RENAME                0xA5
SMB_COM_OPEN_PRINT_FILE          0xC0
SMB_COM_WRITE_PRINT_FILE         0xC1
SMB_COM_CLOSE_PRINT_FILE         0xC2
SMB_COM_GET_PRINT_QUEUE          0xC3
SMB_COM_READ_BULK                0xD8
SMB_COM_WRITE_BULK               0xD9
SMB_COM_WRITE_BULK_DATA          0xDA
```

5.2. SMB_COM_TRANSACTION2 Subcommand codes

The subcommand code for SMB_COM_TRANSACTION2 request is placed in Setup[0]. The parameters associated with any particular request are placed in the Parameters vector of the request. The defined subcommand codes are:

Setup[0] Transaction2 Subcommand Code	Value	Meaning
TRANS2_OPEN2	0x00	Create file with extended attributes
TRANS2_FIND_FIRST2	0x01	Begin search for files
TRANS2_FIND_NEXT2	0x02	Resume search for files
TRANS2_QUERY_FS_INFORMATION	0x03	Get file system information
	0x04	Reserved (TRANS_SET_FS_INFORMATION?)
TRANS2_QUERY_PATH_INFORMATION	0x05	Get information about a named file or directory
TRANS2_SET_PATH_INFORMATION	0x06	Set information about a named file or directory
TRANS2_QUERY_FILE_INFORMATION	0x07	Get information about a handle
TRANS2_SET_FILE_INFORMATION	0x08	Set information by handle
TRANS2_FSCTL	0x09	Not implemented by NT server
TRANS2_IOCTL2	0x0A	Not implemented by NT server
TRANS2_FIND_NOTIFY_FIRST	0x0B	Not implemented by NT server
TRANS2_FIND_NOTIFY_NEXT	0x0C	Not implemented by NT server
TRANS2_CREATE_DIRECTORY	0x0D	Create directory with extended attributes
TRANS2_SESSION_SETUP	0x0E	Session setup with extended security information

Setup[0] Transaction2 Subcommand Code	Value	Meaning
TRANS2_GET_DFS_REFERRAL	0x10	Get a DFS referral
TRANS2_REPORT_DFS_INCONSISTENCY	0x11	Report a DFS knowledge inconsistency

5.3. SMB_COM_NT_TRANSACTION Subcommand Codes

For these transactions, Function in the primary client request indicates the operation to be performed. It may assume one of the following values:

Transaction Subcommand Code	Value	Meaning
NT_TRANSACT_CREATE	1	File open/create
NT_TRANSACT_IOCTL	2	Device IOCTL
NT_TRANSACT_SET_SECURITY_DESC	3	Set security descriptor
NT_TRANSACT_NOTIFY_CHANGE	4	Start directory watch
NT_TRANSACT_RENAME	5	Reserved (Handle-based rename)
NT_TRANSACT_QUERY_SECURITY_DESC	6	Retrieve security descriptor info

5.4. SMB Protocol Dialect Constants

This is the list of CIFS protocol dialects, ordered from least functional (earliest) version to most functional (most recent) version:

Dialect Name	Comment
PC NETWORK PROGRAM 1.0	The original MSNET SMB protocol (otherwise known as the "core protocol")
PCLAN1.0	Some versions of the original MSNET defined this as an alternate to the core protocol name
MICROSOFT NETWORKS 1.03	This is used for the MS-NET 1.03 product. It defines Lock&Read,Write&Unlock, and a special version of raw read and raw write.
MICROSOFT NETWORKS 3.0	This is the DOS LANMAN 1.0 specific protocol. It is equivalent to the LANMAN 1.0 protocol, except the server is required to map errors from the OS/2 error to an appropriate DOS error.
LANMAN1.0	This is the first version of the full LANMAN 1.0 protocol
Windows for Workgroups 3.1a	Windows for Workgroups Version 1.0 (similar to LANMAN1.0 dialect)
LM1.2X002	This is the first version of the full LANMAN 2.0 protocol
DOS LM1.2X002	This is the DOS equivalent of the LM1.2X002 protocol. It is identical to the LM1.2X002 protocol, but the server will perform error mapping to appropriate DOS errors. See section 6.0
DOS LANMAN2.1	DOS LANMAN2.1
LANMAN2.1	OS/2 LANMAN2.1
NT LM 0.12	The SMB protocol designed for NT networking. This has special SMBs which duplicate the NT semantics.

CIFS servers select the most recent version of the protocol known to both client and server. Any CIFS server, which supports dialects newer than the original core dialect, must support all the messages and semantics of the dialects between the core dialect and the newer one. This is to say that a server, which supports the NT LM 0.12 dialect, must also support all of the messages of the previous 10 dialects. It is the client's responsibility to ensure it only sends SMBs, which are appropriate to the dialect negotiated. Clients must be prepared to receive an SMB response from an earlier protocol dialect -- even if the client used the most recent form of the request.

6. Error Codes and Classes

This section lists all of the valid values for Status.DosError.ErrorClass, and most of the error codes for Status.DosError.Error. Additionally, a mapping between STATUS codes and DOS errors are provided.

The following error classes may be returned by the server to the client.

```
Class     Code    Comment
=======   =====   ========
SUCCESS   0       The request was successful.
ERRDOS    0x01    Error is from the core DOS operating system set.
ERRSRV    0x02    Error is generated by the server network file
                  manager.
ERRHRD    0x03    Error is a hardware error.
ERRCMD    0xFF    Command was not in the "SMB" format.
```

The following error codes may be generated with the SUCCESS error class.

```
Class     Code    Comment
=======   =====   ========
SUCCESS   0       The request was successful.
```

The following error codes may be generated with the ERRDOS error class.

```
Error         Code    Description
======        =====   ============
ERRbadfunc    1       Invalid function.  The server did not
                      recognize or could not perform a system call
                      generated by the server, e.g., set the
                      DIRECTORY attribute on a data file, invalid
                      seek mode.
ERRbadfile    2       File not found.  The last component of a
                      file's pathname could not be found.
ERRbadpath    3       Directory invalid.  A directory component in
                      a pathname could not be found.
ERRnofids     4       Too many open files.  The server has no file
                      handles available.
ERRnoaccess   5       Access denied, the client's context does not
                      permit the requested function.  This includes
                      the following conditions: invalid rename command,
                      write to Fid open for read only, read on Fid
                         open for write only, attempt to delete a
                      non-empty directory
ERRbadfid     6       Invalid file handle.  The file handle
                      specified was not recognized by the server.
ERRbadmcb     7       Memory control blocks destroyed.
ERRnomem      8       Insufficient server memory to perform the
                      requested function.
ERRbadmem     9       Invalid memory block address.
ERRbadenv     10      Invalid environment.
ERRbadformat  11      Invalid format.
ERRbadaccess  12      Invalid open mode.
ERRbaddata    13      Invalid data (generated only by IOCTL calls
```

		within the server).
ERRbaddrive	15	Invalid drive specified.
ERRremcd	16	A Delete Directory request attempted to remove the server's current directory.
ERRdiffdevice	17	Not same device (e.g., a cross volume rename was attempted)
ERRnofiles	18	A File Search command can find no more files matching the specified criteria.
ERRbadshare	32	The sharing mode specified for an Open conflicts with existing FIDs on the file.
ERRlock	33	A Lock request conflicted with an existing lock or specified an invalid mode, or an Unlock requested attempted to remove a lock held by another process.
ERRfilexists	80	The file named in the request already exists.
ErrQuota	512	The operation would cause a quota limit to be exceeded.
ErrNotALink	513	A link operation was performed on a pathname that was not a link.

The following error codes may be generated with the ERRSRV error class.

Error	Code	Description
======	=====	============
ERRerror	1	Non-specific error code. It is returned under the following conditions: resource other than disk space exhausted (e.g. TIDs), first SMB command was not negotiate, multiple negotiates attempted, and internal server error.
ERRbadpw	2	Bad password - name/password pair in a Tree Connect or Session Setup are invalid.
ERRaccess	4	The client does not have the necessary access rights within the specified context for the requested function.
ERRinvtid	5	The Tid specified in a command was invalid.
ERRinvnetname	6	Invalid network name in tree connect.
ERRinvdevice	7	Invalid device - printer request made to non-printer connection or non-printer request made to printer connection.
ERRqfull	49	Print queue full (files) -- returned by open print file.
ERRqtoobig	50	Print queue full -- no space.
ERRqeof	51	EOF on print queue dump.
ERRinvpfid	52	Invalid print file FID.
ERRsmbcmd	64	The server did not recognize the command received.
ERRsrverror	65	The server encountered an internal error, e.g., system file unavailable.
ERRbadBID	66	(obsolete)
ERRfilespecs	67	The Fid and pathname parameters contained an invalid combination of values.
ERRbadLink	68	(obsolete)
ERRbadpermits	69	The access permissions specified for a file or directory are not a valid combination. The server cannot set the requested attribute.
ERRbadPID	70	

```
ERRsetattrmode       71    The attribute mode in the Set File Attribute
                              request is invalid.
ERRpaused            81    Server is paused. (Reserved for messaging)
ERRmsgoff            82    Not receiving messages. (Reserved for messaging)
ERRnoroom            83    No room to buffer message.(Reserved for messaging)
ERRrmuns             87    Too many remote user names.(Reserved for messaging)
ERRtimeout           88    Operation timed out.
ERRnoresource        89    No resources currently available for request.
ERRtoomanyuids       90    Too many Uids active on this session.
ERRbaduid            91    The Uid is not known as a valid user
                              identifier on this session.
ERRusempx            250   Temporarily unable to support Raw, use MPX mode.
ERRusestd            251   Temporarily unable to support Raw,
                              use standard read/write.
ERRcontmpx           252   Continue in MPX mode.
ERRbadPassword       254   (obsolete)
ERR_NOTIFY_ENUM_DIR 1024   Too many files have changed since the last time a
                              NT_TRANSACT_NOTIFY_CHANGE was issued
ERRaccountExpired    2239
ERRbadClient         2240  Cannot access the server from this workstation.
ERRbadLogonTime      2241  Cannot access the server at this time.
ERRpasswordExpired   2242
ERRnosupport         65535 Function not supported.
```

The following error codes may be generated with the ERRHRD error class.

```
Error           Code    Description
======          =====   ============
ERRnowrite      19      Attempt to write on write-protected media
ERRbadunit      20      Unknown unit.
ERRnotready     21      Drive not ready.
ERRbadcmd       22      Unknown command.
ERRdata         23      Data error (CRC).
ERRbadreq       24      Bad request structure length.
ERRseek         25      Seek error.
ERRbadmedia     26      Unknown media type.
ERRbadsector    27      Sector not found.
ERRnopaper      28      Printer out of paper.
ERRwrite        29      Write fault.
ERRread         30      Read fault.
ERRgeneral      31      General failure.
ERRbadshare     32      A open conflicts with an existing open.
ERRlock         33      A Lock request conflicted with an existing
                          lock or specified an invalid mode, or an
                          Unlock requested attempted to remove a lock
                          held by another process.
ERRwrongdisk    34      The wrong disk was found in a drive.
ERRFCBUnavail   35      No FCBs are available to process request.
ERRsharebufexc  36      A sharing buffer has been exceeded.
```

These are the mappings of the listed STATUS_codes to the DOS errors.

DOS Error	Status Code
========	=========
ERROR_INVALID_FUNCTION	STATUS_NOT_IMPLEMENTED
ERROR_FILE_NOT_FOUND	STATUS_NO_SUCH_FILE_
ERROR_PATH_NOT_FOUND	STATUS_OBJECT_PATH_NOT_FOUND
ERROR_TOO_MANY_OPEN_FILES	STATUS_TOO_MANY_OPENED_FILES
ERROR_ACCESS_DENIED	STATUS_ACCESS_DENIED
ERROR_INVALID_HANDLE	STATUS_INVALID_HANDLE
ERROR_NOT_ENOUGH_MEMORY	STATUS_INSUFFICIENT_RESOURCES
ERROR_INVALID_ACCESS	STATUS_ACCESS_DENIED
ERROR_INVALID_DATA	STATUS_DATA_ERROR
ERROR_CURRENT_DIRECTORY	STATUS_DIRECTORY_NOT_EMPTY
ERROR_NOT_SAME_DEVICE	STATUS_NOT_SAME_DEVICE
ERROR_NO_MORE_FILES	STATUS_NO_MORE_FILES
ERROR_WRITE_PROTECT	STATUS_MEDIA_WRITE_PROTECTED
ERROR_NOT_READY	STATUS_DEVICE_NOT_READY
ERROR_CRC	STATUS_CRC_ERROR
ERROR_BAD_LENGTH	STATUS_DATA_ERROR
ERROR_NOT_DOS_DISK	STATUS_DISK_CORRUPT_ERROR
ERROR_SECTOR_NOT_FOUND	STATUS_NONEXISTENT_SECTOR
ERROR_OUT_OF_PAPER	STATUS_DEVICE_PAPER_EMPTY
ERROR_SHARING_VIOLATION	STATUS_SHARING_VIOLATION
ERROR_LOCK_VIOLATION	STATUS_FILE_LOCK_CONFLICT
ERROR_WRONG_DISK	STATUS_WRONG_VOLUME
ERROR_NOT_SUPPORTED	STATUS_NOT_SUPPORTED
ERROR_REM_NOT_LIST	STATUS_REMOTE_NOT_LISTENING
ERROR_DUP_NAME	STATUS_DUPLICATE_NAME
ERROR_BAD_NETPATH	STATUS_BAD_NETWORK_PATH
ERROR_NETWORK_BUSY	STATUS_NETWORK_BUSY
ERROR_DEV_NOT_EXIST	STATUS_DEVICE_DOES_NOT_EXIST
ERROR_TOO_MANY_CMDS	STATUS_TOO_MANY_COMMANDS
ERROR_ADAP_HDW_ERR	STATUS_ADAPTER_HARDWARE_ERROR
ERROR_BAD_NET_RESP	STATUS_INVALID_NETWORK_RESPONSE
ERROR_UNEXP_NET_ERR	STATUS_UNEXPECTED_NETWORK_ERROR
ERROR_BAD_REM_ADAP	STATUS_BAD_REMOTE_ADAPTER
ERROR_PRINTQ_FULL	STATUS_PRINT_QUEUE_FULL
ERROR_NO_SPOOL_SPACE	STATUS_NO_SPOOL_SPACE
ERROR_PRINT_CANCELLED	STATUS_PRINT_CANCELLED
ERROR_NETNAME_DELETED	STATUS_NETWORK_NAME_DELETED
ERROR_NETWORK_ACCESS_DENIED	STATUS_NETWORK_ACCESS_DENIED
ERROR_BAD_DEV_TYPE	STATUS_BAD_DEVICE_TYPE
ERROR_BAD_NET_NAME	STATUS_BAD_NETWORK_NAME
ERROR_TOO_MANY_NAMES	STATUS_TOO_MANY_NAMES
ERROR_TOO_MANY_SESS	STATUS_TOO_MANY_SESSIONS
ERROR_SHARING_PAUSED	STATUS_SHARING_PAUSED
ERROR_REQ_NOT_ACCEP	STATUS_REQUEST_NOT_ACCEPTED
ERROR_REDIR_PAUSED	STATUS_REDIRECTOR_PAUSED
ERROR_FILE_EXISTS	STATUS_OBJECT_NAME_COLLISION
ERROR_INVALID_PASSWORD	STATUS_WRONG_PASSWORD
ERROR_INVALID_PARAMETER	STATUS_INVALID_PARAMETER
ERROR_NET_WRITE_FAULT	STATUS_NET_WRITE_FAULT
ERROR_BROKEN_PIPE	STATUS_PIPE_BROKEN
ERROR_OPEN_FAILED	STATUS_OPEN_FAILED
ERROR_BUFFER_OVERFLOW	STATUS_BUFFER_OVERFLOW
ERROR_DISK_FULL	STATUS_DISK_FULL
ERROR_SEM_TIMEOUT	STATUS_IO_TIMEOUT
ERROR_INSUFFICIENT_BUFFER	STATUS_BUFFER_TOO_SMALL
ERROR_INVALID_NAME	STATUS_OBJECT_NAME_INVALID

ERROR_INVALID_LEVEL	STATUS_INVALID_LEVEL
ERROR_BAD_PATHNAME	STATUS_OBJECT_PATH_INVALID
ERROR_BAD_PIPE	STATUS_INVALID_PARAMETER
ERROR_PIPE_BUSY	STATUS_PIPE_NOT_AVAILABLE
ERROR_NO_DATA	STATUS_PIPE_EMPTY
ERROR_PIPE_NOT_CONNECTED	STATUS_PIPE_DISCONNECTED
ERROR_MORE_DATA	STATUS_BUFFER_OVERFLOW
ERROR_VC_DISCONNECTED	STATUS_VIRTUAL_CIRCUIT_CLOSED
ERROR_INVALID_EA_NAME	STATUS_INVALID_EA_NAME
ERROR_EA_LIST_INCONSISTENT	STATUS_EA_LIST_INCONSISTENT
ERROR_EAS_DIDNT_FIT	STATUS_EA_TOO_LARGE
ERROR_EA_FILE_CORRUPT	STATUS_EA_CORRUPT_ERROR
ERROR_EA_TABLE_FULL	STATUS_EA_CORRUPT_ERROR
ERROR_INVALID_EA_HANDLE	STATUS_EA_CORRUPT_ERROR

7. Security Considerations

MISSING

Suggested content for this section:

Define share security level. What dialects support it?

1. Define user security level.

2. How is it supported in PDC/BDC environment (NT4)

3. How it supported in Active directory environment. Define the different security considerations in different Active Directory modes.

4. How Kerberos security is used?

5. What are the protocols (or DCE/RPC) needed for each of the User level security models

6. Some discussion on how file access is authenticated, or how the SID is retrieved in each of the user level environments mentioned above for ACL

7. Include the security protocol, or reference to it

8. References

[1] P. Mockapetris, "Domain Names - Concepts And Facilities", RFC 1034, November 1987

[2] P. Mockapetris, "Domain Names - Implementation And Specification", RFC 1035, November 1987

[3] Karl Auerbach, "Protocol Standard For A Netbios Service On A TCP/UDP Transport: Concepts And Methods", RFC 1001, March 1987

[4] Karl Auerbach, "Protocol Standard For A Netbios Service On A TCP/UDP Transport: Detailed Specifications", RFC 1002, March 1987

[5] US National Bureau of Standards, "Data Encryption Standard", Federal Information Processing Standard (FIPS) Publication 46-1, January 1988

[6] Rivest, R. - MIT and RSA Data Security, Inc., "The MD4 Message Digest Algorithm", RFC 1320, April 1992

[7] Rivest, R. – MIT and RSA Data Security, Inc., "The MD5 Message-Digest Algorithm", RFC 1321, April 1992

[8] Metzger, P. Piermont, Simpson, W. Daydreamer, "IP Authentication using Keyed MD5", RFC 1828, August 1995

[9] Leach, P. – Microsoft, "CIFS Authentication Protocols Specification, Author's Draft 4

[10] B. Kaliski, M.Robshaw, "Message Authentication with MD5", CryptoBytes, Spring 1995, RSA Inc, (ftp://ftp.rsasecurity.com/pub/cryptobytes/crypto1n1.pdf)

[11] X/Open Company Ltd., "X/Open CAE Specification - Protocols for X/Open PC Interworking: SMB, Version 2", X/Open Document Number: CAE 209, September 1992.

9. Appendix A -- NETBIOS transport over TCP

With respect to the 7-layer OSI reference model, NetBIOS is a session layer (layer 5) Application Programmer's Interface (API). The NetBIOS API has been implemented on top of a variety of transports (layer 4), including TCP/IP. NetBIOS over TCP/IP transport is specified in RFC 1001 and RFC 1002 (IETF Standard #19).

NetBIOS is the traditional session layer interface for SMB/CIFS. For backward compatibility with older systems, CIFS implementations SHOULD provide support for RFC 1001/1002 transport.

9.1. Connection Establishment

Connections are established and messages transferred via the NetBIOS session service (see section 5.3 of RFC 1001 and section 4.3 of RFC 1002). The system that originates the connection is the "calling" node; the target node is the "called" node. In order to establish an SMB session, a TCP connection must be established between the calling and called nodes. If a TCP connection already exists, the SMB session may make use of the existing connection.

9.2. Connecting to a server using the NetBIOS name

Before a NetBIOS session can be established, the node initiating the session (the "calling" node) must discover the IP address of the target node (the "called" node). This is done using the NetBIOS name service (see section 5.2 of RFC 1001 and section 4.2 of RFC 1002). NetBIOS names are always 16 bytes, padded with spaces (0x20) if necessary, as specified in the RFCs. The 16th byte has been reserved, however, for use as a service indicator. This field is known as the "suffix byte".

The NetBIOS session service requires that the client provide the NetBIOS names of both the calling and called nodes. The calling name is the default NetBIOS name of the client, space padded as described, with a suffix byte value of 0x00. The called name is the NetBIOS name of the server with a suffix byte value of 0x20. Server implementations which support SMB via NetBIOS over TCP/IP MUST support the registration and use of the server NetBIOS name.

The calling name is not significant in CIFS, except that an identical name from the same transport address is assumed to represent the same client. SMB session establishment is initiated using a "Session Request" packet sent to port 139 (see section 4.3.2 of RFC 1002).

9.3. Connecting to a server using a DNS name or IP address

Implementations MAY support the use of DNS names or IP addresses in addition to NetBIOS names when initiating SMB connections via NetBIOS over TCP/IP transport. This functionality is an extension to the NetBIOS over TCP/IP behavior specified in RFC 1001 and RFC 1002, and is not part of that standard.

As stated above, the Session Request packet requires a called and a calling name, both of which are NetBIOS names. In order to create a Session Request packet, the DNS name or IP address of the server must be reverse-mapped to the server's NetBIOS name. Mechanisms for doing so are as follows:

9.3.1. NetBIOS Adapter Status

A NetBIOS Adapter Status Query is sent to the target IP address. If a response is received and the target is offering SMB services via NetBIOS over TCP, then the response will include a NetBIOS name with a suffix byte value of 0x20. This NetBIOS name may be used as the called name in a Session Request packet.

9.3.2. Generic Server Name

Servers offering SMB services via NetBIOS over TCP/IP MAY accept the generic SMB server name "*SMBSERVER". A client can simply use the name "*SMBSERVER" as the called name in a Session Request packet. As with all SMB server NetBIOS names, the "*SMBSERVER" name must be space padded and terminated with a suffix byte value of 0x20.

The "*SMBSERVER" name MUST NOT be registered with the NetBIOS name service, as it is an illegal NetBIOS name (see section 5.2 of RFC 1001).

The target may return a CALLED NAME NOT PRESENT error. This may simply indicate that the server does not support the "*SMBSERVER" generic name.

9.3.3. - Parsing the DNS Name (guessing)

Systems which support NetBIOS transport over TCP/IP will often use the same base name within the DNS and NetBIOS name spaces. Thus, the first label of the DNS name represents a good guess at the NetBIOS name of the server.

The first label of the DNS name consists of the initial portion of the DNS name string, up to but not including the first dot character ('.'). If the label is greater than 15 bytes in length, it must be truncated to 15 bytes. The result is then space padded to a total of 15 bytes, and a suffix value 0x20 is used. This forms a valid NetBIOS name that may be used as a called name in a Session Request packet.

If the target returns a CALLED NAME NOT PRESENT error, then the DNS name guess is incorrect. If the original user input was an IP address, the DNS name can be determined using a reverse lookup against the DNS. Any or all of the above MAY be tried in any order.

9.4. NetBIOS Name character set

There is no standard character set for NetBIOS names. NetBIOS names are simply strings of octets, with the following restrictions:

- Names which are to be registered with the NetBIOS Name Service must not begin with an asterisk (0x2A). (The *SMBSERVER name is never registered.)

- Names should not contain a NUL (0x00) octet. Common implementation languages may interpret the NUL octet value as a string terminator.

10.   Appendix B -- TCP transport

When operating CIFS over TCP, connections are established to TCP port 445, and each message is framed as follows:

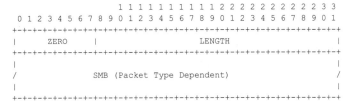

```
                               1 1 1 1 1 1 1 1 1 1 2 2 2 2 2 2 2 2 2 2 3 3
           0 1 2 3 4 5 6 7 8 9 0 1 2 3 4 5 6 7 8 9 0 1 2 3 4 5 6 7 8 9 0 1
          +-+-+-+-+-+-+-+-+-+-+-+-+-+-+-+-+-+-+-+-+-+-+-+-+-+-+-+-+-+-+-+-+
          |    ZERO     |                     LENGTH                       |
          +-+-+-+-+-+-+-+-+-+-+-+-+-+-+-+-+-+-+-+-+-+-+-+-+-+-+-+-+-+-+-+-+
          |                                                               |
          /                SMB (Packet Type Dependent)                    /
          |                                                               |
          +-+-+-+-+-+-+-+-+-+-+-+-+-+-+-+-+-+-+-+-+-+-+-+-+-+-+-+-+-+-+-+-+
```

Each CIFS request starts with a 4 byte field encoded as above: a byte of zero, followed by three bytes of length; after that follows the body of the request.

11. Appendix C – Share Level Server Security

Each server makes a set of resources available to clients on the network. A resource being shared may be a directory tree, named pipe, printer, etc. As far as clients are concerned, the server has no storage or service dependencies on any other servers; a client considers the server to be the sole provider of the file (or other resource) being accessed.

The CIFS protocol requires server authentication of users before file accesses are allowed, and each server authenticates its own users. A client system must send authentication information to the server before the server will allow access to its resources.

The CIFS protocol used to define two methods that can be selected by the server for security: *share level* and *user level*. User level security is the only non-obsolescent method.

A *share level* server makes some directory on a disk device (or other resource) available. An optional password may be required to gain access. Thus, any user on the network who knows the name of the server, the name of the resource, and the password has access to the resource. Share level security servers may use different passwords for the same shared resource with different passwords, allowing different levels of access.

Share-level-only clients do not send SESSION_SETUP_ANDX requests. Instead, they send TREE_CONNECT_ANDX requests that include a password or use challenge/response authentication to prove that they know a password.

When a *user level* server validates the account name and password presented by the client, an identifier representing that authenticated instance of the user is returned to the client in the *Uid* field of the response SMB. In contrast, a *share level* server returns no useful information in the *Uid* field.

If the server is executing in share level security mode, *Tid* is the only thing used to allow access to the shared resource. Thus, if the user is able to perform a successful connection to the server specifying the appropriate netname and passwd (if any), the resource may be accessed according to the access rights associated with the shared resource (same for all who gained access this way).

The user level security model was added after the original dialect of the CIFS protocol was issued, and subsequently some clients may not be capable of sending account name and passwords to the server. A server in user level security mode communicating with one of these clients *may* allow a client to connect to resources even if the client has not sent account name information:

1) If the client's computer name is identical to an account name known on the server, and if the password supplied or authenticated via challenge/response to connect to the shared resource matches that account's password, an implicit "user logon" will be performed using those values. If the above fails, the server may fail the request or assign a default account name of its choice.

2) The value of *Uid* in subsequent requests by the client will be ignored, and all access will be validated assuming the account name selected above.

12.   Appendix D – CIFS UNIX Extension

12.1. Introduction

The purpose of these extensions is to allow UNIX based CIFS clients and servers to exchange information used by UNIX systems, but not present in Windows based CIFS servers or clients. These extensions may not be implemented by all UNIX systems. Two simple examples are symbolic links and UNIX special files (e.g. UNIX named pipes).

The CIFS UNIX Extension are intended for use by all UNIX and UNIX-like systems the implement the CIFS protocol.

12.2. Principles

These are a set of principles that the extensions meet.

Minimal changes	To make the extensions easier to implement, the number of changes and additions were minimized.
Can be implemented on non-UNIX systems	While being useful for UNIX, the extension allow one end of the connection to be a non-UNIX system. This is so that other CIFS servers and clients can better integrate with a UNIX CIFS client or server.
Use current commands	The changes only affect current commands. There was no need for UNIX CIFS clients to use CIFS commands marked as obsolete, nor should there be any changes to obsolete requests.
Retain existing CIFS semantics	The existing semantics of CIFS are retained. Perhaps the most notable is that file names are case insensitive, but case should be preserved.
Use CIFS security model	The standard CIFS security model is still used. This requires each distinct user to be logged into the server.
Addition to dialect	This specification is an addition to the CIFS dialect, currently NT LM 0.12. It is selected by the capability bit in the server's Negotiate protocol response.
Future resilient	Future enhancements MUST not modify or change the meaning of previous implementations of the specification.

12.3. CIFS Protocol Modifications

This section details the require changes to the CIFS protocol that are needed to support CIFS UNIX Extensions. A summary of the changes is listed below.

In the Negotiate Protocol SMB reserve a capabilities bit, CAP_UNIX with the value of 0x00800000, in the Server capabilities field to indicate support of CIFS Extension for UNIX.

Reserve information levels numbers 0x200-0x2FF

TRANS2_QUERY_FS_INFORMATION, TRANS2_QUERY_PATH_INFO, TRANS2_QUERY_FILE_INFO, TRANS2_SET_PATH_INFO, TRANS2_SET_FILE_INFO, TRANS2_FINDFIRST, and TRANS2_FINDNEXT SMBs for CIFS Extensions for UNIX.

12.4. Modified SMBs

SMB	Modification
NEGOTIATE	Added CAP_UNIX (0x00800000) to the server capabilities field. See 4.2
TRANS2_QUERY_FS_INFORMATION	Added Following Information Levels: SMB_QUERY_CIFS_UNIX_INFO (0x200) See 4.1.6.7
TRANS2_QUERY_PATH_INFORMATION	Added Following Information Levels: SMB_QUERY_FILE_UNIX_BASIC (0x200) See 4.2.15.12 SMB_QUERY_FILE_UNIX_LINK (0x201) See 4.2.15.13
TRANS2_QUERY_FILE_INFORMATION	Same modification as done in TRANS2_QUERY_PATH_INFORMATION
TRANS2_SET_PATH_INFORMATION	Added Following Information Levels: SMB_SET_FILE_UNIX_BASIC (0x200) See 4.2.17.3 SMB_SET_FILE_UNIX_LINK (0x201) See 4.2.17.4 SMB_SET_FILE_UNIX_HLINK (0X203) See 4.2.17.5
TRANS2_SET_FILE_INFORMATION	Same modification as done in TRANS2_SET_PATH_INFORMATION
TRANS2_FINDFIRST	Added following Information Levels: SMB_FIND_FILE_UNIX (0X202) See 4.3.4.8
TRANS2_FINDNEXT	Same modification as done in TRANS2_FINDFIRST

12.5. Guidelines for implementers

- Once the Client determines that the server supports the CIFS UNIX Extension it should first send SMB_QUERY_CIFS_UNIX_INFO before sending any other CIFS UNIX Extension SMBs to determine the version and capabilities that are supported by the server.

- Clients or servers using this extension should have no specific reserved filenames (e.g. CON, AUX, PRN), and should not need to take specific action to protect the other end of the connection from them. If they have any such requirements, they must do them internally. This also applies to reserved characters in filenames (e.g. : \ |).

- Inodes can be transferred in the uniqueid field of SMB_QUERY_FILE_UNIX_BASIC (0x200).

- Clients should operate in UNICODE if at all possible. A useful bridging step is to implement UTF-8

- Symbolic links are created by calling TRANS2_SET_PATH_INFO with the SMB_QUERY_FILE_UNIX_LINK infolevel data structure provided.

- Device file (and other special UNIX files) are created by calling TRANS2_SET_PATH_INFO with the SMB_QUERY_FILE_UNIX_BASIC infolevel data structure appropriately filled in for a device node.

- Servers should return their timezone as UTC. This will then require no timezone mapping by the client or server. The NetRemoteTimeOfDay IPC should still return the real local time.

- Creates with particular permissions can be achieved by sending a CREATE_AND_X and a TRANS2_SET_PATH_INFO SMBs.

13.   Appendix E – CIFS Macintosh Extension

13.1. Introduction

The purpose of these extensions is to allow the Macintosh to better interoperate in a CIFS network. With these extensions Macintosh Clients will be able to reduce network traffic generated by the Macintosh, which in turn would speed up file access by the Client. These extensions will allow non-Macintosh Clients access to Macintosh files and also allow for the server to decide how to store Macintosh files and folders.

The CIFS Macintosh Extension is intended for use by all systems that implement the CIFS protocol.

13.2. Principles

These are a set of principles that the extensions meet.

Minimal changes	To make the extensions easier to implement, the number of changes and additions were minimized.
Can be implemented on non-Macintosh systems	While being useful for Macintosh, the extension allows one end of the connection to be a non-Macintosh system. This is so that other CIFS servers and clients can better integrate with a Macintosh CIFS client or server.
Use current commands	The changes only affect current commands. There is no need for CIFS clients to use CIFS commands marked as obsolete, nor should there be any changes to obsolete requests.
Retain existing CIFS semantics	The existing semantics of CIFS are retained.
Use CIFS security model	The standard CIFS security model is still used. This requires each distinct user to be logged into the server.
Addition to dialect	These items are an addition to the CIFS dialect, currently NT LM 0.12. These extensions are turn on by the server responding with out an error to the TRANS2_QUERY_FS_INFORMATION call with an info level of Trans2_GetSMB_MAC_QUERY_FS_INFO.
Future resilient	Future enhancements MUST not modify or change the meaning of previous implementations of the specification.

13.3. CIFS Protocol Modifications

This section details the require changes to the CIFS protocol that are needed to support CIFS Macintosh Extensions. These extensions require support of the NT LM 0.12 dialect with some minor additions. The Server must support the NT stream format for the opening of the resource, comments, and data streams of a file. A summary of the changes is listed below.

Reserve information levels numbers 0x300-0x3FF in the TRANS2_QUERY_FS_INFORMATION, TRANS2_QUERY_PATH_INFO, TRANS2_SET_PATH_INFO, TRANS2_FINDFIRST, and TRANS2_FINDNEXT SMBs for CIFS Extensions for Macintosh.

13.4. Modified SMBs

SMB	Modification
TRANS2_QUERY_FS_INFORMATION	Added Following Information Levels: SMB_QUERY_MAC_FS_INFO (0x301) See 4.1.6.7
TRANS2_FINDFIRST	Added following Information Levels: SMB_FINDBOTH_MAC_HFS_INFO (0X302) See 4.3.4.9
TRANS2_FINDNEXT	Same modification as done in TRANS2_FINDFIRST
TRANS2_SET_PATH_INFORMATION	Added Following Information Levels: SMB_MAC_SET_FINDER_INFO (0x303) See 4.2.18.6 SMB_MAC_DT_ADD_APPL (0x304) See 4.2.18.7 SMB_MAC_DT_REMOVE_APPL (0x305) See 4.2.18.8 SMB_MAC_DT_ADD_ICON (0x309) See 4.2.18.9
TRANS2_QUERY_PATH_INFORMATION	Added Following Information Levels: SMB_MAC_DT_GET_APPL (0x306) See 4.2.16.14 SMB_MAC_DT_GET_ICON (0x307) See 4.2.16.15 SMB_MAC_DT_GET_ICON_INFO (0x308) See 4.2.16.16

13.5. Guidelines for implementers

- These extensions will be processed on share-by-share bases. This means that the Client will have to confirm that each share supports these extensions not just that the Server supports these extensions. This will allow a server to have some shares that are Macintosh aware and others that are not.

- When a file or folder is deleted then all streams and information stored on the sever associated with that file or folder should be removed. When a file or folder is Copied/Renamed/Moved then all streams and information stored on the sever associated with that file or folder should be Copied/Renamed/Moved.

- Clients or servers using this extension should have no specific reserved filenames (e.g. CON, AUX, PRN), and should not need to take specific action to protect the other end of the connection from them. If they have any such requirements, they must do them internally. This also applies to reserved characters in filenames (e.g. : \ |).

- Clients should operate in UNICODE if at all possible.

- Supporting the Desktop Database calls requires having a way to store information in a database. There are two kinds of information store in the database. Applications path that is associated with an application signature. Icons are stored based on size, icon type, file creator, and file type.

14.   Appendix F – API Numbers for Transact based RAP calls

API_WshareEnum	0
API_WshareGetInfo	1
API_WshareSetInfo	2
API_WshareAdd	3
API_WshareDel	4
API_NetShareCheck	5
API_WsessionEnum	6
API_WsessionGetInfo	7
API_WsessionDel	8
API_WconnectionEnum	9
API_WfileEnum	10
API_WfileGetInfo	11
API_WfileClose	12
API_WserverGetInfo	13
API_WserverSetInfo	14
API_WserverDiskEnum	15
API_WserverAdminCommand	16
API_NetAuditOpen	17
API_WauditClear	18
API_NetErrorLogOpen	19
API_WerrorLogClear	20
API_NetCharDevEnum	21
API_NetCharDevGetInfo	22
API_WCharDevControl	23
API_NetCharDevQEnum	24
API_NetCharDevQGetInfo	25
API_WCharDevQSetInfo	26
API_WCharDevQPurge	27
API_WCharDevQPurgeSelf	28
API_WMessageNameEnum	29
API_WMessageNameGetInfo	30
API_WMessageNameAdd	31
API_WMessageNameDel	32
API_WMessageNameFwd	33
API_WMessageNameUnFwd	34
API_WMessageBufferSend	35
API_WMessageFileSend	36
API_WMessageLogFileSet	37
API_WMessageLogFileGet	38
API_WServiceEnum	39
API_WServiceInstall	40
API_WServiceControl	41
API_WAccessEnum	42
API_WAccessGetInfo	43
API_WAccessSetInfo	44
API_WAccessAdd	45
API_WAccessDel	46
API_WGroupEnum	47
API_WGroupAdd	48
API_WGroupDel	49
API_WGroupAddUser	50
API_WGroupDelUser	51
API_WGroupGetUsers	52
API_WUserEnum	53
API_WUserAdd	54
API_WUserDel	55
API_WUserGetInfo	56
API_WUserSetInfo	57

```
API_WUserPasswordSet          58
API_WUserGetGroups            59
API_DeadTableEntry            60
/*This line and number replaced a Dead Entry */
API_WWkstaSetUID              62
API_WWkstaGetInfo             63
API_WWkstaSetInfo             64
API_WUseEnum                  65
API_WUseAdd                   66
API_WUseDel                   67
API_WUseGetInfo               68
API_WPrintQEnum               69
API_WPrintQGetInfo            70
API_WPrintQSetInfo            71
API_WPrintQAdd                72
API_WPrintQDel                73
API_WPrintQPause              74
API_WPrintQContinue           75
API_WPrintJobEnum             76
API_WPrintJobGetInfo          77
API_WPrintJobSetInfo_OLD      78
/* This line and number replaced a Dead Entry */
/* This line and number replaced a Dead Entry */
API_WPrintJobDel              81
API_WPrintJobPause            82
API_WPrintJobContinue         83
API_WPrintDestEnum            84
API_WPrintDestGetInfo         85
API_WPrintDestControl         86
API_WProfileSave              87
API_WProfileLoad              88
API_WStatisticsGet            89
API_WStatisticsClear          90
API_NetRemoteTOD              91
API_WNetBiosEnum              92
API_WNetBiosGetInfo           93
API_NetServerEnum             94
API_I_NetServerEnum           95
API_WServiceGetInfo           96
/* This line and number replaced a Dead Entry */
/* This line and number replaced a Dead Entry */
/* This line and number replaced a Dead Entry */
/* This line and number replaced a Dead Entry */
/* This line and number replaced a Dead Entry */
/* This line and number replaced a Dead Entry */
API_WPrintQPurge              103
API_NetServerEnum2            104
API_WAccessGetUserPerms       105
API_WGroupGetInfo             106
API_WGroupSetInfo             107
API_WGroupSetUsers            108
API_WUserSetGroups            109
API_WUserModalsGet            110
API_WUserModalsSet            111
API_WFileEnum2                112
API_WUserAdd2                           113
API_WUserSetInfo2             114
API_WUserPasswordSet2         115
API_I_NetServerEnum2          116
API_WConfigGet2               117
```

Glossary

It's a *thingy!*

— Prairie Barnes

Abstract Syntax Notation One (ASN.1)

A language used to define the structure and content of objects such as data records and protocol messages, along the lines of a super-duper version of the `typedef` in C, only a lot more powerful. ASN.1 was developed as part of the Open Systems Interconnection (OSI) environment, and was originally used for writing specifications. More recently, though, tools have been developed that will generate software from ASN.1.

See also: Distinguished Encoding Rules

Web reference: The ASN.1 Consortium
(`http://www.asn1.org/`)

Astoundium

The element of suprise.

Attacker

In this context, one who attacks a computer system either to gain access or, as in a "Denial of Service attack," to cause a failure in the system or data loss.

See also: Cracker

Backup Browser

A Browser node which is not elected to be the Local Master Browser, but which stores a backup copy of the Browse List and will respond to client requests for the Browse List. A Potential Browser may decide on its own to become a Backup Browser, or it may be appointed by the Local Master Browser.

See also: Local Master Browser, Potential Browser

Backup Domain Controller (BDC)

A Windows NT Domain Controller (DC) which keeps a backup copy of the user/group authentication database in an NT Domain. The master copy is maintained by the Primary Domain Controller (PDC). A Backup Domain Controller can be promoted to the role of PDC in a pinch. Only one PDC is permitted per NT Domain, but there may be any number of BDCs.

See also: Domain Controller, Primary Domain Controller

BAF Protocol

The very first name for the protocol formerly known as SMB. The SMB protocol was originally developed by Dr. Barry A. Feigenbaum at IBM and, according to legend, was originally given his initials. It was later renamed SMB and, more recently, CIFS.

See also: CIFS, SMB

Bran

Pronounced *Brahhn.* The name of my dog.

Browser Node

See: Potential Browser

Browser Election

The process by which a browser node on a NetBIOS LAN is chosen to be the primary repository of service information for that LAN (that is, the Local Master Browser). Under NBT, the election process takes place within the confines of the local IP subnet.

CIFS

Common Internet File System. The protocol formerly known as Server Message Block (SMB) and, before that, as the BAF protocol (after its original creator, Dr. Barry Feigenbaum). CIFS is a protocol for file and device sharing across a network.

See also: SMB

Cracker

One who attacks a system in an effort to break security, probably to gain unauthorized access.

Goodguy[1] crackers (sometimes called "White Hat" crackers) used to provide the very beneficial service of exposing weaknesses so that they could be fixed, but then the US Congress enacted the Digital Millennium Copyright Act (DMCA) which made talking about such things illegal in the US and potentially dangerous elsewhere.

See also: Attacker

Do not see also: Hacker

Distinguished Encoding Rules (DER)

A set of rules for encoding and decoding ASN.1 data for network transport. DER provides a standard format for transport of data over a network so that the receiving end can convert the data back into their correct ASN.1 format. DER is a specialized form of a more general encoding known as BER (**B**asic **E**ncoding **R**ules). DER is designed to work well with security protocols, and is used for encoding Kerberos and LDAP exchanges.

See also: ASN.1, Kerberos, LDAP

Domain Controller (DC)

An authentication server in a Windows NT or Windows 2000 Domain. A Domain Controller maintains a database of user, group, and machine accounts and other security information, and provides authentication services to the NT or W2K Domain.

In an NT Domain, one of the DCs will be designated the *Primary* Domain Controller (PDC). All security database administration is handled via the PDC, and copies of the database are then distributed to any available *Backup* Domain Controllers (BDCs). NT Domain controllers register the Group Special NetBIOS name *nt_domain*<1C> to identify themselves.

---

1. The use of the term "good*guy*" is in no way intended to imply gender.

In Windows 2000 Domains the security database is stored in the Active Directory, and there is no distinction between primary and secondary controllers.

See also: Backup Domain Controller, Primary Domain Controller

Domain Name System (DNS)

The Domain Name System is a distributed database system that provides mappings between Internet names and Internet Protocol (IP) addresses. The DNS name space is hierarchical in structure.

Web reference: the DNS Resources Directory
(`http://www.dns.net/dnsrd/`)

Domain Master Browser (DMB)

A host system that is designated to coordinate Browse Lists for matching workgroups across multiple subnets. The DMB receives subnet Browse List updates from Local Master Browsers, combines those lists, and distributes the combined list back to the Local Masters for the workgroup.

See also: Local Master Browser

Doveryay, no proveryay

Trust, but verify.

Encoded NBT Name

The term used in this book for the fully qualified Second Level Encoded form of the NetBIOS Name and Scope ID. For example, the string

```
"\x20EGEFCACACACACACACACACACACACACACA\x2FI\x2FO\x3FUM\0"
```

is the fully encoded form of the NetBIOS name *FE*<20> and the scope ID "`FI.FO.FUM`".

See also: NBT Name, First Level Encoding, Scope ID, Second Level Encoding

First Level Encoding

The conversion of a NetBIOS name to a format complying with DNS "best practices."

NetBIOS names may contain characters which are not considered valid for use in DNS names, yet RFC 1001 and RFC 1002 attempted to map the NetBIOS name space into the DNS name space. To work around this conflict, NetBIOS names are encoded by splitting each byte of the name into two nibbles and then adding the value of 'A' (0x41). Thus, the '&' character (0x26) would be encoded as "CG". NetBIOS names are usually padded with spaces before being encoded.

In this book, the term "NBT Name" is used to indicate the fully qualified form of the First Level Encoded name. The NBT Name includes the Scope ID.

See also: NBT Name, Scope ID, Second Level Encoding

GSS-API

Generic **S**ecurity **S**ervice **A**pplication **P**rogram **I**nterface. A generic interface to a set of security services. It makes it possible to write software that does not care what the underlying security mechanisms actually are.

See: RFC 2078

(http://www.faqs.org/rfcs/rfc2078.html)

See also: SPNEGO

Hacker

One who fiddles with an existing system to see if it can be improved. Hacking is generally the fine art of [creating and] recursively revising software or a software-based system.

Do not see also: Cracker

Kerberos

A network authentication service developed at MIT and later adopted by Microsoft for use with Windows 2000 and SMB over naked TCP/IP transport.

See: RFC 1510

(http://www.faqs.org/rfcs/rfc1510.html)

LANA

NetBIOS **LAN A**dapter card.

For the original PC Network System, IBM sold both Broadband and Baseband network interface cards, which they called LAN Adapters. The NBT system supports the concept of a "virtual LANA."

See also: NBT

LDAP

The **L**ightweight **D**irectory **A**ccess **P**rotocol. A standard protocol used to access directory services based on the X.500 directory service model (e.g., Novell Directory Services and Microsoft Active Directory).

See: RFC 2251
(`http://www.faqs.org/rfcs/rfc2251.html`)

Local Master Browser (LMB)

A host system that is "elected" to manage the Browse List for the local IP LAN. The LMB collects service announcements from servers on the local LAN, distributes the Browse List to any Backup Browsers on the LAN, and exchanges service lists with the Domain Master Browser (if there is one).

See also: Domain Master Browser, Backup Browser

Machine Name

Host name. A name which is typically assigned in the system configuration and used as the base name creating the NetBIOS names of several important services. The service names are composed by appending a service-specific suffix to the machine name.

Master Browser

A common shorthand for "Local Master Browser."

See: Local Master Browser

MIDL

Microsoft **I**nterface **D**efinition **L**anguage, Microsoft's version of the **I**nterface **D**efinition **L**anguage (IDL). MIDL is used to specify the parameters to MS-RPC function calls. MIDL is also used to define the interfaces to Microsoft's **D**ynamically **L**inked **L**ibrary (DLL) functions.

See also: MS-RPC

Moore's Law

The observation (by Gordon Moore) that the transistor density on computer chips doubles roughly every 1.5 years. This is generally taken to mean that processing speeds also double every 1.5 years. Software developers compensate by writing bad code and adding unnecessary features to maintain status quo.

MS-RPC

Microsoft **R**emote **P**rocedure **C**all. RPC in general is a system that allows a process on one system to make function calls against libraries on another system. MS-RPC is Microsoft's implementation of RPC.

See also: MIDL

NBDD

Net**B**IOS **D**atagram **D**istribution Server. This server relays broadcast and multicast (group) datagrams to all intended recipients.

When a P, M, or H node wishes to send a broadcast or multicast datagram, it will send the datagram to the NBDD. The NBDD will obtain the list of destination IPs from the NBNS and then unicast the datagram to each of those nodes.

Most implementations do not provide NBDD support.

See also: NBNS

NBNS

Net**B**IOS **N**ame **S**erver. A server providing NetBIOS name to IP address mapping. The NBNS is part of the NBT mechanism and does not need to participate directly in the NetBIOS LAN.

See also: WINS

NBT

Net**B**IOS over **T**CP/IP; also known as NetBT and, less commonly, as TCPBEUI. NBT is an implementation of the NetBIOS API on top of a TCP/IP transport layer.

NBT Name

The term used in this book for the fully qualified First Level Encoded form of the NetBIOS Name and Scope ID. For example, the NBT name

```
EGEFCACACACACACACACACACACACACACA.FI.FO.FUM
```

is composed of the NetBIOS name *FE*<20> and the scope ID "FI.FO.FUM".

See also: Scope ID, First Level Encoding

Network Data Representation (NDR)

The on-the-wire encoding for parameters passed via MS-RPC. MS-RPC input parameters are marshalled into NDR format for transmission over the network, and then unmarshalled on the server side. The process is then reversed to return the results.

See also: MS-RPC

NetBEUI

NetBIOS **E**xtended **U**ser **I**nterface. Also known as **NetB**IOS **F**rame Protocol (NBF). NetBEUI provides a simple mapping of NetBIOS API parameters and data to a transport suitable for passing messages on Ethernet and Token Ring networks.

Web reference: NetBIOS NetBEUI NBF Networking, by Timothy D. Evans (http://ourworld.compuserve.com/homepages/timothydevans/contents.htm)

NetBIOS

Network **B**asic **I**nput **O**utput **S**ystem. NetBIOS is the **A**pplication **P**rogramming **I**nterface (API) to a proprietary LAN system that was developed by IBM and Sytec. The NetBIOS API has been implemented on top of several different network transports including TCP/IP, DECnet, IPX/SPX, and others.

See also: NBT, NetBT

NetBT

NetBIOS over TCP/IP. Better known as NBT.

See: NBT

NT Domain

A Workgroup with a Domain Controller.

See also: Domain Controller, Workgroup

Phrep

An expletive, roughly equivalent to "dang," "drat," or "bother," but without connotation.

Primary Domain Controller (PDC)

A Windows NT Domain Controller (DC) which keeps the master copy of the user/group authentication database in an NT Domain. Only one PDC is permitted per NT Domain. In addition to registering the *nt_domain*<1C> Group Special name, the PDC also registers the unique *nt_domain*<1B> NetBIOS name (where *nt_domain* is the name of the NT Domain). Microsoft's WINS server ensures that the IP address registered to the *nt_domain*<1B> name is always at the top of the list of IPs associated with the *nt_domain*<1C> Group Special name.

See also: Backup Domain Controller, Domain Controller

Potential Browser

Any node on a local IP LAN that is willing and able to participate in browser elections and take on the role of Local Master Browser or Backup Browser.

See also: Local Master Browser, Backup Browser

Scope ID

A string of dot-separated labels, formatted per DNS naming rules. The Scope ID defines a virtual NBT LAN by dividing the NetBIOS namespace.

See also: NBT Name, DNS, First Level Encoding, Second Level Encoding

Second Level Encoding

The on-the-wire format of an NBT name. The encoding scheme replaces the familiar dot characters used in DNS names with a byte containing the length of the next label. The Second Level Encoded form of the NBT Name

```
EGEFCACACACACACACACACACACACACACA.FI.FO.FUM
```

would be

```
"\x20EGEFCACACACACACACACACACACACACACA\x02FI\x02FO\x03FUM\0"
```

See also: NBT Name, DNS, First Level Encoding

Server Message Block (SMB)

A file- and print-sharing protocol developed by IBM, Intel, 3Com, and Microsoft for use with PC-DOS and MS-DOS. It has since been renamed CIFS.

Also a name for the messages exchanged via the SMB or CIFS protocol. An SMB message is often referred to simply as "an SMB."

See also: CIFS

Server Service

An SMB filesharing service provider. The Server Service registers a NetBIOS name consisting of the machine name with a suffix value of

`0x20`. On many platforms, the Server Service will also accept NBT connection requests with a `CALLING NAME` of `*SMBSERVER<20>`.

Simple Protected Negotiation (SPNEGO)

The "Simple and Protected GSS-API Negotiation Mechanism" is a protocol used with GSS-API to negotiate authentication mechanisms between a client and server.

See: RFC 2478

(`http://www.faqs.org/rfcs/rfc2478.html`)

See also: GSS-API

Suffix Byte

The sixteenth byte of a NetBIOS name. This byte is used to indicate the type of service that has registered the name.

TCPBEUI

Yet another name for NBT. The name TCPBEUI is primarily used by folks from IBM.

See: NBT

Thermomostat

The internal sensor that causes your mother to tell you to put on a sweater when she is cold.

WINS

Windows **I**nternet **N**ame **S**ervice. Microsoft's name for their NBNS implementation.

See: NBNS

Workgroup

An NT Domain without a Domain Controller. The distinction between an NT Domain and a Workgroup is blurry. The two are basically the same thing, except that an NT Domain has a Domain Controller, which provides authentication services. The Primary Domain Controller also always runs the Domain Master Browser (DMB) service, which coordinates the workgroup Browse Lists across subnets.

See also: Domain Master Browser, Domain Controller, Primary Domain Controller

References

Freedom of information is
a fundamental human right and is
the touchstone of all the freedoms.

— United Nations General Assembly
Resolution 59(i), adopted 1946

Books

Applied Cryptography, Second Edition: Protocols, Algorithms, and Source Code in C
Bruce Schneier. ISBN 0–471–11709–9, John Wiley & Sons, Inc., 1996.

C Programmer's Guide to NetBIOS, IPX, and SPX
W. David Schwaderer. ISBN 0–672–30050–8, Sam's Publishing, 1992.

Corgiville Fair
Tasha Tudor. ISBN 0316853127, Little, Brown & Company, April 1998.

A Decent Cup of Tea
Malachi McCormick. ISBN 0–517–58462–X, Clarkson N. Potter Publishers, 1991.

DCE/RPC over SMB: Samba and Windows NT Domain Internals
Luke Kenneth Casson Leighton. ISBN 1–57870–150–3, Macmillan Technical Publishing, December 1999.

Fog on the Tyne: The Official History of Lindisfarne
> Dave Ian Hill. ISBN 1–900711–07–9, Northdown Publishing, November 1998.

IPC Mechanisms for SMB
> ISBN 1–872630–28–6, The Open Group, February 1992. (Now available online at: `http://www.opengroup.org/products/publications/catalog/c195.htm`)

The Lindisfarne Gospels
> Janet Backhouse. ISBN 0–7148–2461–5, Phaidon, April 1993.

Network Programming in C
> Barry Nance. ISBN 0–88022–569–6, Que Corporation, 1990.

NT Network Plumbing: Routers, Proxies, and Web Services
> Anthony Northrup. ISBN 076453209X, IDG Books, July 1998.

Protocols for X/Open PC Interworking: SMB, Version 2
> ISBN 1–872630–45–6, The Open Group, October 1992. (Now available online at: `http://www.opengroup.org/products/publications/catalog/c209.htm`)

Samba: Integrating Unix and Windows
> John D. Blair. ISBN 1–57831–006–7, Specialized Systems Consultants, 1998.

SAMS Teach Yourself Samba in 24 Hours
> Gerald Carter and Richard Sharpe. ISBN 0–67231–609–9, MacMillan Publishing, April 1999.

The Unix System Today
> ISBN 1–85912–296–5, The Open Group in association with VA Linux Systems, April 2000.

Using Samba
> Robert Eckstein, David Collier-Brown, and Peter Kelly. ISBN 1–56592–449–5, O'Reilly, November 1999. (This book has been officially adopted by the Samba Team. It is available online under an open content license.)

Windows NT TCP/IP

Dr. Karanjit Siyan. ISBN 1–56205–887–8, New Riders, August 1998.

See Also:

The Samba Team maintains a list of books about Samba and SMB/CIFS networking in general. See any of the Samba mirror sites, and select "books" from the menu at the top of each page.

Web

Note that the Web is a dynamic medium. Things tend to move around a bit, and the URLs listed below may change without notice, rhyme, or reason.

Browsing and Windows 95 Networking

Microsoft TechNet, December, 1996.
```
http://www.microsoft.com/technet/archive/
default.asp?url=/TechNet/Archive/win95/w95brows.asp
```

CIFS: A Common Internet File System

Paul Leach and Dan Perry. Microsoft Interactive Developer magazine, November, 1996.
```
http://www.microsoft.com/mind/1196/cifs.asp
```

CIFS Authentication and Security [TR3020]

Bridget Allison. Network Appliance, Inc., 199?.
```
http://www.netapp.com/tech_library/3020.html
```

Draft-leach-cifs-browser-spec-00: CIFS/E Browser Protocol Preliminary Draft

Paul J. Leach and Dilip C. Naik. Expired Internet Draft. IETF, January 10, 1997.
```
ftp://ftp.microsoft.com/developr/drg/CIFS/
cifsbrow.txt
```

Draft-leach-cifs-rap-spec-00: CIFS Remote Administration Protocol, Preliminary Draft

Paul J. Leach and Dilip C. Naik. Expired Internet Draft. IETF, February 26, 1997.
```
ftp://ftp.microsoft.com/developr/drg/cifs/
cifsrap2.txt
```

Draft-leach-cifs-v1-spec-02: A Common Internet File System (CIFS/1.0) Protocol
Paul J. Leach and Dilip C. Naik. Expired Internet Draft. IETF, March 13, 1997.
`http://www.ubiqx.org/cifs/rfc-draft/`
`draft-leach-cifs-v1-spec-02.html`

How to Disable LM Authentication on Windows NT
Microsoft Knowledge Base Article #147706.
`http://support.microsoft.com/`
`default.aspx?scid=KB;en-us;147706`

How to Enable NTLM 2 Authentication for Windows 95/98/2000 and NT
Microsoft Knowledge Base Article #239869.
`http://support.microsoft.com/`
`default.aspx?scid=KB;en-us;239869`

IETF RFC 883: Domain Names — Implementation and Specification
Paul Mockapetris. IETF, November 1983.
`http://www.faqs.org/rfcs/rfc883.html`

IETF RFC 1001: Protocol Standard for a NetBIOS Service on a TCP/UDP Transport: Concepts and Methods
Karl Auerbach, Avnish Aggarwal, et al. IETF, March, 1987.
`http://www.ubiqx.org/cifs/rfc-draft/rfc1001.html`

IETF RFC 1002: Protocol Standard for a NetBIOS Service on a TCP/UDP Transport: Detailed Specifications
Karl Auerbach, Avnish Aggarwal, et al. IETF, March, 1987.
`http://www.ubiqx.org/cifs/rfc-draft/rfc1002.html`

IETF RFC 1034: Domain Names — Concepts and Facilities
Paul Mockapetris. IETF, November, 1987.
`http://www.faqs.org/rfcs/rfc1034.html`

IETF RFC 1035: Domain Names — Implementation and Specification
Paul Mockapetris. IETF, November, 1987.
`http://www.faqs.org/rfcs/rfc1035.html`

IETF RFC 1149: A Standard for the Transmission of IP Datagrams on Avian Carriers
David Waitzman. IETF, April, 1990.
`http://www.faqs.org/rfcs/rfc1149.html`

IETF RFC 1320: The MD4 Message-Digest Algorithm
Ron Rivest. IETF, April, 1992.
`http://www.faqs.org/rfcs/rfc1320.html`

IETF RFC 1321: The MD5 Message-Digest Algorithm
Ron Rivest. IETF, April, 1992.
`http://www.faqs.org/rfcs/rfc1321.html`

IETF RFC 1510: The Kerberos Network Authentication Service (V5)
J. Kohl and C. Neuman. IETF, September, 1993.
`http://www.faqs.org/rfcs/rfc1510.html`

IETF RFC 1964: The Kerberos Version 5 GSS-API Mechanism
J. Linn. IETF, June, 1996.
`http://www.faqs.org/rfcs/rfc1964.html`

IETF RFC 2078: Generic Security Service Application Program Interface, Version 2
J. Linn. IETF, January, 1997.
`http://www.faqs.org/rfcs/rfc2078.html`

IETF RFC 2104: HMAC: Keyed-Hashing for Message Authentication
H. Krawczyk, M. Bellare, and R. Canetti. IETF, February, 1997.
`http://www.faqs.org/rfcs/rfc2104.html`

IETF RFC 2181: Clarifications to the DNS Specification
Randy Bush and Robert Elz. IETF, July, 1997.
`http://www.faqs.org/rfcs/rfc2181.html`

IETF RFC 2251: Lightweight Directory Access Protocol (v3)
M. Wahl, T. Howes, and S. Kille. IETF, December, 1997.
`http://www.faqs.org/rfcs/rfc2251.html`

IETF RFC 2396: Uniform Resource Identifiers (URI): Generic Syntax
Tim Berners-Lee, Roy Fielding, and Larry Masinter. IETF, August, 1998.
`http://www.faqs.org/rfcs/rfc2396.html`

IETF RFC 2478: The Simple and Protected GSS-API Negotiation Mechanism
E. Baize and D. Pinkas. IETF, December, 1998.
`http://www.faqs.org/rfcs/rfc2478.html`

IETF RFC 2732: Format for Literal IPv6 Addresses in URL's
R. Hinden, B. Carpenter, and L. Masinter. IETF, December, 1999.
`http://www.faqs.org/rfcs/rfc2732.html`

IETF RFC 3244: Microsoft Windows 2000 Kerberos Change Password and Set Password Protocols
M. Swift, J. Trostle, and J. Brezak. IETF, February, 2002.
`http://www.faqs.org/rfcs/rfc3244.html`

Information on Browser Operation
Microsoft Knowledge Base Article #102878.
`http://support.microsoft.com/`
`default.aspx?scid=KB;en-us;102878`

Inside SP4 NTLMv2 Security Enhancements
Randy Franklin Smith. Windows & .Net Magazine, September, 1999.
`http://www.winnetmag.com/Articles/`
`Index.cfm?ArticleID=7072`

Jargon File
Edited by Eric S. Raymond. V4.3.3, September, 2002.
`http://catb.org/esr/jargon/`

jCIFS Project
CIFS in Java.
`http://jcifs.samba.org/`

Just What is SMB?
Richard Sharpe. V1.2, October, 2002.
`http://www.samba.org/cifs/docs/what-is-smb.html`

LAN Technical Reference: 802.2 and NetBIOS APIs
IBM Corp., 1986, 1996.
`http://publibz.boulder.ibm.com/cgi-bin/`
`bookmgr_OS390/BOOKS/BK8P7001/COVER`

More Than You Ever Wanted to Know about NT Login Authentication
> Philip C. Cox and Paul B. Hill. SystemExperts Corporation, 2001.
> [PDF file] `http://www.systemexperts.com/tutors/`
> `NT_Login_3.0.pdf`

Microsoft's CIFS FTP site
> `ftp://ftp.microsoft.com/developr/drg/cifs/`

Microsoft's CIFS mailing list archives
> `http://discuss.microsoft.com/archives/`
> `cifs.html`

Microsoft Networks/OpenNet Filesharing Protocol, Version 2.0
> Microsoft Corporation/Intel Corporation, November 7, 1988.
> `ftp://ftp.microsoft.com/developr/drg/cifs/`
> `smb-core.ps`

Microsoft Networks/SMB File Sharing Protocol Extensions, Version 2.0, Document Version 3.3
> Microsoft Corporation, November 7, 1988.
> `ftp://ftp.microsoft.com/developr/drg/cifs/`
> `SMB-LM1X.PS`

Microsoft Networks/SMB File Sharing Protocol Extensions, Version 3.0, Document Version 1.11
> Microsoft Corporation, June 19, 1990.
> `ftp://ftp.microsoft.com/developr/drg/cifs/`
> `SMB-LM20.PS`

Microsoft Networks/SMB File Sharing Protocol Extensions, Document Version 3.4
> Microsoft Corporation, February 29, 1992.
> `ftp://ftp.microsoft.com/developr/drg/cifs/`
> `SMB-LM21.DOC`
>
> *Note:* The ".DOC" format is proprietary and may be unreadable on many platforms without the use of special software. Fortunately, the Google service can convert the ".DOC" format to HTML. Try searching for "SMB-LM21.DOC" and look for results that offer an option to "View as HTML."

NetBIOS NetBEUI NBF Networking
Timothy D. Evans. February, 2002.
`http://ourworld.compuserve.com/homepages/`
`timothydevans/contents.htm`

NetBIOS Specification
Gavin Winston.
`http://members.tripod.com/~Gavin_Winston/`
`NETBIOS.HTM`
(Warning! Frames, pop-ups, advertisements...)

NT Cryptographic Password Attacks & Defences
Alan Ramsbottom. July, 1997.
`http://www.ntbugtraq.com/`
`default.asp?sid=1&pid=47&aid=17`

The NTLM Authentication Protocol
Eric Glass, 2003
`http://davenport.sourceforge.net/ntlm.html`

NTLM Authentication Scheme for HTTP
Ronald Tschalär. March, 2001.
`http://www.innovation.ch/java/ntlm.html`

Remoted Net API Format Strings
Archived Email from Paul Leach. Microsoft, September 27, 1996.
`http://discuss.microsoft.com/SCRIPTS/`
`WA-MSD.EXE?A2=ind9609d&L=cifs&T=0&F=&S=&P=1674`

Russian Tea HowTo
Dániel Nagy. April, 2002.
`http://www.fazekas.hu/~nagydani/rth/`
`Russian-tea-HOWTO-v2.html`

Samba web sites
`http://www.samba.org/`

SNIA Common Internet Filesystem Technical Reference
Storage Network Industry Association, CIFS Workging Group.
`http://www.snia.org/tech_activities/CIFS`

Tea Health Homepage
   The Tea Council.
   `http://www.teahealth.co.uk/`

Unicode in the Unix Environment
   Roman Czyborra.
   `http://czyborra.com/`

Unicode, Inc.
   `http://www.unicode.org/`

User Authentication with Windows NT
   Microsoft Knowledge Base Article #102716.
   `http://support.microsoft.com/`
   `default.aspx?scid=KB;en-us;102716`

Using jCIFS to Connect to Win32 Named Pipes
   Michael B. Allen.
   `http://jcifs.samba.org/src/docs/pipes.html`

Who Will Own Your Next Good Idea?
   Charles C. Mann. The Atlantic Online, September, 1998.
   `http://www.theatlantic.com/issues/98sep/copy.htm`

Windows 2000 Authorization Data in Kerberos Tickets
   Microsoft Corporation, 2002.
   `http://msdn.microsoft.com/library/en-us/dnkerb/`
   `protocol/windows_2000_authorization_data_`
   `in_kerberos_tickets.asp`

Index

Upon reading these words,
flames suddenly burst from his neck,
a horn grew on his knee,
fangs and claws tore at the backs
of his shins,
and he sneezed violently.

— Me